D0959099

Rock Garden Plants of North America

Rock Garden Plants
of
North America

An Anthology from the
Bulletin of the North American Rock Garden Society

EDITED BY JANE MCGARY

Timber Press
in association with the North American Rock Garden Society

Text copyright © 1996 by The North American Rock Garden Society, Inc. All rights reserved.

ISBN 0-88192-343-5

Printed in Hong Kong

Published by Timber Press, Inc.
The Haseltine Building
133 S.W. Second Avenue, Suite 450
Portland, Oregon 97204, U.S.A.

Library of Congress Cataloging-in-Publication Data

Rock garden plants of North America : an anthology from the Bulletin of the
     North American Rock Garden Society / edited by Jane McGary.
          p.   cm.
     Includes index.
     ISBN 0-88192-343-5
     1. Rock plants—United States. 2. Rock gardens—United States. 3.
McGary, Mary Jane. I. North American Rock Garden Society. II. Bulletin
(North American Rock Garden Society)
QK115.R63   1996
635.9′6727′0973—dc20   95-23104
                                                                    CIP

Contents

Color plates follow pages 48 and 224

Foreword

This is an appropriate occasion for a note on the origin of the *Bulletin* of the North American Rock Garden Society (formerly the ARGS), which has now concluded a half-century of publication. It is coincident that I have been active in the affairs of this Society for even longer. It was in early 1942 that the struggling ARGS was informed of the suspension of the periodical *Gardeners' Chronicle*, which had included a section devoted to the affairs of the Society. There were no other horticultural publications that could be substituted. Discussions then revolved about a possible journal devoted to our affairs and subject matter. There was little encouragement because of a lack of finances and of an editor. I offered to edit, solicit advertising, and print Volume 1. Within a few months the first issue, dated January–February 1943, was circulated; this encouraged Dr. Edgar T. Wherry, a botanist at the University of Pennsylvania, to take on the job of editor. He continued for eight years.

The greater part of that first volume was devoted to the flora of the woodland, prairie, and alpine areas of North America. Throughout the following years there were many other subjects, but the dominant theme has always been the tremendous variety of our native wildflowers. Consequently it is appropriate that a 50-year retrospective focus on this. Readers will note an emphasis on articles of more recent vintage, and this is frankly due to the rising quality brought about by the efforts of the current editor, Gwen Kelaidis.

Harold Epstein
President Emeritus
North American Rock Garden Society

Preface and Acknowledgments

This volume is a collection of articles that appeared in the quarterly *Bulletin* of the American Rock Garden Society during its first 50 years of publication. (The organization has been renamed the North American Rock Garden Society [NARGS], and its journal, as of 1995, the *Rock Garden Quarterly*.) Many of the most noted American horticulturists and botanists contributed to the *Bulletin* over the years, as they continue to do today. It is fitting that the first anthology drawn from its pages takes as its organizing principle the native plants of North America and their cultivation.

In the first stage of preparing this anthology, all issues of the *Bulletin* from 1942 through 1991 were read by a large group of volunteer NARGS members throughout North America. The readers filled out evaluation sheets, rating each article for audience appropriateness, quality of writing, level of information, and overall appeal. Next, the articles were separated into subject categories, and each resulting group was sent to a reviewer with expertise in that area. The results of these two review processes were tabulated, and about 200 of the more highly rated articles were sent to the volume editor, who suggested the final selection for approval by a committee appointed by the Society's president. The criteria for selection included not only those used in the initial evaluation, but also considerations of broad representation and uniqueness. Some good articles were omitted because the information they contained was readily available elsewhere, and other articles were included essentially because they were the only available sources on a given subject.

When all the *Bulletin* articles had been categorized, it became apparent that, predictably, the largest group dealt with plants native to North America. Committee members also felt that this was the topic most likely to appeal to a readership beyond North America and the subject area in which the NARGS was able to make a unique contribution to knowledge. (The significant group of articles on design, construction, and cultivation techniques would form another excellent anthology.)

This collection is arranged according to larger geographic areas of the United States: Far West, Great Basin and Rocky Mountains, Plains States, Northeast, and Southeast. Each section includes both articles describing natural areas and vegetation communities and articles dealing with specific plants native to the region. Discussions of genera occurring throughout North America are grouped at the end of the volume.

This is by no means an encyclopedic account of North American rock plants. Many wonderful areas have never been described in the *Bulletin*; in particular, there is next to nothing on the plants of Canada, and only a brief note on Alaska. It is to be hoped that the yawning gaps in this anthology will inspire future contributions on the less accessible parts of the continent.

It was not a primary purpose of this collection to reflect the history of the NARGS, hence the omission of works by some revered early members of the society. Rather, the needs of contemporary readers for useful information guided the choice of contents. A note is in order, however, on the limited appearance of H. Lincoln Foster, that mainstay of the *Bulletin* over so many years. Foster's shorter works have already been collected in book form as *Cuttings from a Rock Garden* (1990). His "The Elusive Shortia" in this volume is a good example of his humanistic approach to the study of American plants.

All the articles have been edited for this volume. An old-fashioned style characterizes some of the older articles, lending historical depth and nostalgic grace. Metric measurements have been supplied to make the work accessible to readers outside the United States.

A less than gracious element that recurs in some early articles is the unquestioning acceptance of the practice of digging plants in the wild, both for the garden and for resale. The consciousness that this practice was not quite proper sometimes emerges, but early issues of the *Bulletin* are full of accounts of wholesale collecting trips and tired but happy plant enthusiasts returning to the garden with the trunk of the Hudson stuffed with rarities. I do not espouse the viewpoint of the opposite extreme—that the taking of any plant material whatsoever from the wild is a deadly sin—but to spare the sensibilities of today's readers, I have deleted descriptions of collecting activities when they did not seem to contribute any useful information. It is good to know, for example, that a certain cultivar was found at a certain place and time; but there is no value in reading that some magnificent plant dug by the author promptly perished in his garden. In a related vein, I have occasionally condensed an argument on behalf of conservation, in the assumption that this now constitutes preaching to the converted.

The criterion of contemporary interest has not precluded the selection of certain articles with a view to historical interest. This is particularly so in the inclusion of two works on a single area, the New Jersey Pine Barrens. The 1953 article by G. G. Nearing exemplifies the culture from which North American rock gardening arose among intelligent amateurs who learned their subject over years of immersion in a natural landscape, often motivated initially by a simple love of wildflowers. By contrast, Rick Darke's article, which appeared in 1989, is informed by an academic perspective that relates the plant community under discussion to its larger ecological setting and the social and economic issues affecting them. Taken together, the two discussions present an impression of the Pine Barrens that is both intellectually and emotionally satisfying. There is room in rock gardening for both points of view and for much mutual respect between them.

Readers planning field trips based on these articles are advised to consult current maps and tourist information. The status of public lands may change, and roads, especially in national forests, may be altered. Some of the plant communities described may have disappeared owing to fires, agriculture, or development.

One of the most challenging editorial problems has been the treatment of a large number of changes in botanical nomenclature. Paul Jones, who reviewed the nomenclature in all the articles, used John T. Kartesz's *A Synonymized Checklist of the Vascular Flora of the United States, Canada, and Greenland* (2d ed., 1994) as the authority for current names; Jones's revisions were incorporated in the text by the editor. In general, the following conventions were observed. (1) When a plant was renamed after the publication of the article, and the current name has since become generally known to amateur botanists and gardeners, the current name has been substituted without comment. (2) When the renamed plant is not generally known, or when the change is recent but apparently uncontroversial, the current name is given followed by the previous name in parentheses; thus "*Aspidotis densa* (formerly *Pellaea densa*)." (3) When a species has been revised to a subspecies or variety retaining the same epithet (or vice versa), the current name is usually substituted without comment; thus *Penstemon crandallii* subsp. *procumbens*, formerly *P. procumbens*, appears without comment. (4) A few changes that are not yet fully accepted but that are cited as authoritative in Kartesz (1994) are noted in the form, "*Lewisia tweedyi* (recently renamed *Cistanthe tweedyi*)"; this strategy has also been used with regard to the revision of *Potentilla*. (5) When the form of the discussion makes it necessary, changes are noted as editorial interpolations in brackets. The last convention is used particularly when an author has written at some length about a plant that is no longer a recognized taxon; it is useful to preserve such discussions because the form described may still be grown under the obsolete name.

Many gardeners and wildflower-lovers react irritably to changes in nomenclature, just as some speakers of a language are infuriated by neologisms in general. Botany is not static; it is constantly enriched by new techniques in microbiology, biochemistry, and statistical analysis, as well

13

as by new theoretical approaches. Taxonomic revisions should not be interpreted as insults to the memory of deceased botanists or attempts to raise the blood pressure of gardeners. There will inevitably be readers who consider their specialties to have been mistreated in this volume; I encourage them to present their points of view to the botanists and the readers of plant journals. Not a few taxonomic revisions are owed to the observations of amateurs, as pointed out in Edith Dusek's article in this volume.

Thomas Stuart, with the assistance of Anne Spiegel and Jacques Mommens, coordinated this project from its inception, devoting many hours to masterminding the review process and supervising the preparation of copy and other volunteer activities. Paul Jones, horticulturist of the Asiatic Arboretum, Duke University, reviewed botanical nomenclature in all the articles. Shan Cunningham gathered and selected the illustrations. More than 100 volunteers evaluated articles and typed copy in preparation for editing; both reviewers and typists contributed many useful comments and corrections.

Authors who updated their articles for this publication include LeRoy Davidson, Edith Dusek, John Gyer, and Jay Lunn. Gwen Kelaidis, present editor of the *Bulletin*, provided electronic copy from the most recent volumes and assisted with needed information at various stages.

Jane McGary

PART ONE: FAR WEST

Wildflower Haunts of California

WAYNE RODERICK

In California there is so much diversity in climate and topography that it takes nearly a lifetime to see all our interesting plants. July is too late in the year to visit the deserts, to see the fields of annual wildflowers, or to find flowers on most of the bulbous plants. It is the higher areas of the state that may be seen in full flower by the visitor at midsummer.

Rock gardeners are fortunate that there are still many of California's alpine plants left in the wild. We never had a Carl Purdy digging these plants by the millions, as he did the bulbous plants of lower-elevation California. There are, however, millions of humans building houses, roads, and highways and bringing ever more acreage under cultivation. Our list of rare and endangered plants is more than 160 pages long. If this is not enough to discourage the collection of plants from nature in California, consider that we have a long dry summer. This means that plants must produce a long taproot to survive the dry period, and this, in turn, means nearly certain death to any plant dug. Many of the places I describe here are in plant preserves or wilderness areas. I have personally fought to have some of these areas set aside, and I will personally hate you, too, if you use this information to exploit them by digging plants.

Highway 395 south from Reno is a scenic drive in itself, and every road that turns off it into the mountains leads up to natural rock gardens. A short way up Monitor Pass on Highway 89 one can find masses of *Eriogonum wrightii*. This white-leaved mat does not bloom until fall, but what a plant to see! The flowers are not the main attraction; the foliage is wonderful. Farther south along Highway 395 into Bridgeport Valley there are sheets of *Iris missouriensis* (Plate 4) in the meadows, and the high, snow-covered mountains above can be spectacular in June. From Bridgeport south, all the little roads lead to campgrounds, good fishing, and good plant-hunting. Just south of Lee Vining, the Tioga road takes off to Yosemite National Park and all its wonders. Just east of Tioga Pass is the road to Saddlebag Lake at 10,000 feet/3100 meters elevation, where it is a short hike to the alpine zone. About 200 yards/meters beyond the parking area are masses of *Phyllodoce breweri* with some good color forms, then a glorious meadow of *Aquilegia pubescens* and its hybrids. These are so beautiful that they alone provide enough reason for coming. *Aquilegia pubescens* is white, and the other species involved in this swarm is *A. formosa*, with red-and-yellow flowers. In this population the flowers are lovely shades of pink and yellow, with an occasional pure white. On up the trail are more little lakes—some with golden trout—and then Mount Conness and its glacier. Fine plants abound all the way up.

Still farther south on Highway 395 is Bishop, whence many interesting roads depart. Before you explore these, load up with gas and water and head south to Big Pine; there, turn east on Highway 168 into the White Mountains and up to Westgard Pass, then up to the Ancient Bristlecone Pines Preserve. From the desert floor to White Mountain Road at 7000 feet/2100 meters, until you turn around at perhaps 12,000 feet/3700 meters, there are thousands of pictures to take, so make sure you have plenty of film. There are choice rock plants everywhere, with mat plants at every turn. Eriogonums are perhaps the most common. In Grand View Campground you must park and camp on *Phlox covillei*, eriogonums, and drabas. The road is paved to the Schulman Grove, but above this and on to the Patriarch Grove are the most fantastic plants and scenic areas. There is so much to see, plan to spend two days or more. Most important, remember to spend the mornings up at high elevations, in areas like the Patriarch Grove, because bad thunderstorms are frequent in the afternoons. Of all the areas to look at dwarf plants, I think the best is a little pass about 0.5 mile/800 meters past the turnoff to the Patriarch Grove. At the road summit at 12,000 feet/3700 meters on Sheep Mountain you will find the greatest variety of species. This is a nearly flat area, and plant-hunting is fine in nearly every direction, but the best is the area west and slightly north of the pass. Here are *Castilleja nana*, *Eriogonum gracilipes*, a few specimens of *E. ovalifolium* (Plate 6), townsendias, phloxes, drabas, and potentillas, among others.

We return to the desert proper (it is really desert all the way to the top in these mountains). From the campground on down there are four penstemons, interesting eriogonums, *Argemone munita* (prickly poppy), and *Mentzelia laevicaulis* (blazing star), all in bloom in July. Growing in shady cracks in the narrows is a heuchera similar to *Heuchera rubescens*. In hot, rocky areas down to the valley are three species of cactus, *Stanleya elata* (prince's plume), and *Encelia farinosa* (brittle-bush). From Big Pine south on Highway 395 the desert gets very hot this time of year, but to climb Mount Whitney you must go south to Lone Pine and drive up to Whitney Portal. Ascending from here, you can find *Primula suffrutescens* (Plate 10). At the end of the road are campgrounds that can be full in midsummer. At these elevations there can be frost every night, so be sure to bring warm clothing. About 2.5 miles/4 km out of Lone Pine toward Mount Whitney is a turnoff up to the right; it goes into the Alabama Hills, where many Wild-West movies are filmed. Just south of Lone Pine is the turnoff to Death Valley, 100 miles/160 km away. It can be hellish getting there in July, and once in the valley you *are* in hell. On 4 July 1989, the temperature at Furnace Creek was 122°F/50°C. The National Park Service asks visitors to stay out of the Valley at this season.

If you have time and want respite from the heat, I suggest a trip from Lake Tahoe to Carson City and Reno, then north on Highway 395. Go on to Susanville and then west on Highway 36 and north on Highway 89 to the entrance to Lassen National Park. From here north all the roads are scenic. In moist areas are carpets of phyllodoce and *Kalmia polifolia* (Plate 12). Nearly every parking area along this stretch of road has interesting plants. Farther north, the only questions are how much time the traveler has and which direction to choose: up Mount Shasta or Mount Eddy, to Castle Lake or Cedar Lake, or on to other fabulous spots.

In the middle of the town of Mount Shasta is the road that leads up onto the mountain. There are only a few good rock garden plants here, but those few are not just good but great. The road ends at an old ski area, and just before that is a parking area to the right. Park here and walk over the little rise at the end; veer to your left into the swale. Here are carpets of *Penstemon davidsonii* (Plate 28) by the acre, as well as phloxes, anemones, and ferns.

West and over the freeway, on the road to Lake Siskiyou (with a good campground), take the road to picturesque Castle Lake (with a tiny campground of the finest class, but without water). From the parking lot to the top of the mountain you will find one interesting plant after another. Several species are rare elsewhere but common here, and there are at least three species listed as rare and endangered. At the lake, walk around to the left and watch for the trail up the hill. When you leave the pavement, you will see *Calyptridium umbellatum* (formerly *Spraguea* and recently placed in *Cistanthe*), and then at the stream, dodecatheons. Your first steps up will lead to *Fritillaria affinis* (formerly *F. lanceolata*; Plate 3), delphiniums, hackelias, and more. Near the top of the climb, out in the open areas, explore the rock outcrops off to the right. Between the outcrops are the best color forms of *Lewisia leana* (Plate 31) I have ever seen, plus masses of the rare and endangered *Erythronium klamathense*. In the rocks are penstemons and small ferns, and on the far side is *Triteleia crocea* var. *modesta* (formerly *Brodiaea modesta*), another endangered plant. Veer a little to the right of the straight ascent and look carefully, and you may find the rare *Dicentra pauciflora*. The extremely rare and highly en-

19

dangered *Campanula shetleri* is found in a few granite outcrops along the crest of the hill above a faint trail. It blooms in late July, but even without flowers the lacework of the leaves in the crevices of the rocks is nice to see. The trail continues behind a small hill to a tarn with masses of *Phyllodoce empetriformis* and *Leucothoe davisiae* near it. On the north side of this little hill, where the snow persists until midsummer, there may be many erythroniums in bloom. Take a long look at the magnificent view of Mount Shasta, then return to the trail and back down to Castle Lake. This walk is little more than 2 miles/3 km, but the day is nearly gone, and so back to camp and a nice glass of wine before dinner while we contemplate all the wonderful plants of the day. Going down the road from the lake the next day, you will have to stop to look at *Xerophyllum tenax* (beargrass), *Linnaea borealis*, irises, lilies, phantom orchids, and much more.

At the bottom of the hill, turn left up the south fork of the Sacramento River. After 3 or 4 miles/5 or 6 km, the road crosses the river. Watch for moist areas with mats of *Mimulus primuloides* var. *linearifolius*. This is a very free-flowering plant that does well in gardens, and there are usually a few ripe seedpods. Ten or twelve miles/16 to 19 km farther along this road, watch for the sign to Cedar Lake. The turnoff to this lake is about a mile/1600 meters before Gumboot Lake, but it is much faster to walk the short mile than to take the car over this "road," along which you can see 10 species of conifers. At the lake, turn left. There are seven genera of ericaceous plants along the shore, as well as *Gentiana newberryi* (Plate 2), a few *Darlingtonia californica*, and *Drosera rotundifolia* making red patches. If there is time and you are a good hiker, follow the "road" to Cliff Lake and try to find the trail up (and I mean up) to Upper Cliff Lake. Here grow more species of ericaceous plants, as well as thousands of *Lewisia leana* (Plate 31) making masses of brightly-colored lace. This little lake is privately owned, but the owners are very kind to plantpersons as long as they do not dig. After you return to your car, there is time to go on west and up over the crest into Mumbo Basin. This is one area where the fragrant white *Lilium washingtonianum* still grows on the dry hillsides. This species is nearly impossible to grow outside its native range and has become rare because of people digging plants and taking them home to die. Down in Mumbo Basin, along streams, are still more interesting plants, but nothing so spectacular as at Castle Lake.

Returning to the freeway and driving north past the town of Weed, watch for the exit to Gazelle and Stewart Springs. Take the road to Stewart Springs, but do not go through the gates; instead, turn and keep going up. By early July the snow should be gone from the road, so it is passable over the summit. Along this road there are many places to stop and spend time, so plan on no less than a full day. Every moist area and stream has some interesting plants, such as *Darlingtonia*, *Potentilla fruticosa* (syn. *Pentaphylloides floribunda*), dodecatheons, *Adiantum aleuticum* (formerly *A. pedatum* var. *aleuticum*), *Polystichum lemmonii*, lilies, orchids, and many more. The best plants are at the summit where the Pacific Crest Trail crosses the road; many choice plants had to be bulldozed to make the road and parking lot. Regardless of where you leave the car, ten steps will have you walking on plants you would love to grow at home. There are brilliant blobs of *Castilleja*, two or three species of *Penstemon*, and three of *Eriogonum*, including the tight rosettes of the rare *E. siskiyouense*. *Anemone multifida* (Plate 7) is here, along with *Allium siskiyouense*, *Fritillaria atropurpurea* (Plate 9), sedums, and much more—until you run out of film.

The next day, come back and continue on down the hill to a switchback with a parking lot. From here make the all-day hike up Mount Eddy. Going up through the wet meadows, you will see masses of gentians, *Darlingtonia*, and dodecatheons. At Deadfall Lakes there are not so many plants of interest, but this changes as soon as the trail starts up the south side of the old crater. Here is *Campanula scabrella* in the rock screes, at the southern limit of its range. At the top of this scree is an unusual community of eriogonums, *Gentiana calycosa*, and some fine specimens of *Pinus balfouriana*. Near the summit of Mount Eddy is *Hulsea nana* (Plate 1), a lovely short golden daisy. The eriogonums are mats with flower heads of white, pink to nearly red, and occasionally yellow, growing among other low plants and grasses on a stable scree. *Hulsea nana* grows in gravel with hardly any other plants. *Gentiana calycosa* grows in moist places and forms mounds up to 2 feet/60 cm across, covered with dozens of light blue trumpets.

After returning to the car, continue down the Trinity River to Highway 3. Along the road there has been too much mining on the river and too much logging on the hillsides, so not many undisturbed areas remain. At Highway 3 turn south to Coffee Creek and go up into the Trinity Alps Wilderness, or turn north up to Scott Mountain Summit. In the northwest section of the summit is the rare endemic *Phacelia dalesiana*, a tiny plant with white flowers and black anthers, discovered and named only about 20 years ago. In the wet meadows on each side of the campground are many nice plants, including *Calochortus nudus* in shades of pink.

From here the road drops down to Scott River and Scott Valley. There, turn right and go to Kangaroo Lake, where there are many interesting plants, or continue on Highway 3 through the old mining towns of Callahan and Etna to the edge of Fort Jones. Here, turn left and go down the Scott River to the Klamath River. From Mount Eddy to the Klamath River you have driven over or around many different ranges, grouped as the Klamath Mountains.

Now turn left to Seiad Valley, where the store is the last chance for supplies and gasoline before taking off to Cook and Green Pass in the middle of the Siskiyou Mountains. Just west of the store, cross a bridge and at once find the road up to Cook and Green. This road is paved for about 5 miles/8 km and goes straight ahead. There is a wide side road turning off to the right and crossing the creek: do not take this. The road you want becomes a rather narrow mountain dirt road which most cars can travel with no trouble. Perhaps three-quarters of the way up is Horsetail Falls, where we find the rare *Lilium wigginsii* in all its golden splendor.

Drive on to the summit, where three roads meet. The Pacific Crest Trail crosses Cook and Green Pass. In the area where you can park your car, you may find tall plants of *Lilium washingtonianum* with as many as 15 large trumpets. The trail east from the pass to Copper Butte leads up to one of the best stands of *Lewisia cotyledon* that I know, growing by the thousands. About 0.25 mile/400 meters up, this trail emerges among rock outcrops splattered with lewisias ranging in color from white to nearly red. Climb up the slope to the large open area ahead; here are lewisias so thick it is difficult not to step on them. This hillside generally is at its best late in June, but in July there will still be a few flowers. Before the plants are finished blooming, the seed is ripe, and by growing a few plants from seed you may keep your memories of a magnificent sight. On your way back down to the pass, note the Brewer's weeping spruce (*Picea breweriana*), two dwarf oaks (*Quercus* spp.), eriogonums, penstemons, and *Eriophyllum lanatum*, the odd dodecatheon, calochortus, or fritillaria, three species of sedums, dwarf ferns, and *Lewisia leana*. I estimate that there are more than 500 species of noteworthy plants to be seen in and around Cook and Green Pass.

Once back at the car, walk 0.25 mile/400 meters along the road toward Oregon to see even more desirable plants. The most noteworthy is *Phlox adsurgens*, here displaying all its variability, with no two plants alike. Other good plants include more penstemons, *Linnaea borealis* in carpets, and a tiny *Rubus* that looks like a strawberry.

At the parking area there is a level trail to the northwest, leading to a spring (once the best drinking water in all California, but now, unfortunately, it may no longer be safe to drink). Along this woodland trail you will not find lewisias, but what a mass of other exciting plants— lilies, anemones, pyrolas, *Arnica, Vancouveria, Mahonia, Chimaphila, Phlox,* lupines, orchids, and dogwoods.

West of the pass the road very shortly turns into a poor four-wheel-drive trail that ends in about 3 miles/5 km, with Lily Pad Lake on one side and Hello Canyon on the other. Wonderful plants can be found both along the road and at its end. The road follows a ridge of serpentine for perhaps 1.5 miles/2 km and then enters an area of volcanic soils. Here in the good soil are masses of *Lilium washingtonianum* var. *purpurascens* and *Xerophyllum tenax*. In rock outcrops here the lewisias tend to yellow shades. A short way farther on there should be a big snowbank, and around any snowbank you will find *Erythronium grandiflorum*. At the end of the "good" road, look down into Hello Canyon to see what was once a road that now ends at a large limestone outcrop. There are seven genera of ferns here, including four species of *Polystichum*. At the very end of the road, among the large rocks, grow mats of *Epilobium siskiyouense* (formerly *E. obcordatum* var. *siskiyouense*) and *Veronica copelandii*. If these two plants are at their peak, it is well worth the long hike to see them.

After returning to the car, should you still have energy and time, follow the Pacific Crest Trail to the west. Along this trail there was once a fine clump of *Cypripedium montanum* (Plate 8), the lady's-slipper orchid; but after I showed it to a group, the plants were dug, so now I tell no one where to see any of these orchids. There is a carpet of pipsissewa (*Chimaphila* sp.) under the trees near the parking area, and various interesting conifers and the rare dwarf Sadler oak (*Quercus sadleriana*), but we must keep moving to see more.

After going back down to Seiad Valley and farther down the Klamath River to Happy Camp, turn north up over the Siskiyou Mountains to O'Brien, Oregon. Just over the summit are the finest mats of *Phlox adsurgens* I have ever seen. There is so much to see, plan on 3 hours for this short drive of about 30 miles/48 km. On arriving at Highway 199 at O'Brien, cross over and take the road alongside the store, which will become the Patrick's Creek Road back into California. When the pavement ends, slow down; soon many interesting plants will appear. Along this 25-mile/40-km stretch of road, each month from early spring until fall brings new combinations of good plants into bloom. By mid-June the erythroniums, *Trillium rivale* (Plate 5), *Phlox speciosa*, *Darlingtonia*, *Dicentra formosa* subsp. *oregana*, and *Vancouveria chrysantha* have finished blooming, but there remain many beautiful species. Three species of lilies can be found where the bridge crosses Whisky Creek. An odd lily resembling *Lilium pardalinum*, as well as *Narthecium californicum*—which should be in full bloom in July—are both here. At the summit, which is also the state line, keep left because the right fork becomes nearly impassable. But first, stop and spend some time at the summit, where several good plants are found in the serpentine scree areas, including *Lewisia oppositifolia*, *Epilobium rigidum*, erigerons, and sedums. On down the road, *Lilium bolanderi* flowers bright red; occasionally one can also see a plant or two of *L. kelloggii*. About three-quarters of the way down, the main road turns left, but keep to the right for about half a mile/800 meters. This is the Old Gasquet Toll Road. After crossing the bridge, go on to a small stream and stop at a large parking area, which is never used except by crazy plant people. A few paces up this stream, look for *Lilium pardalinum* subsp. *vollmeri*. From here the road becomes rather poor, so it is best to turn around, return to the left fork, and continue down to Highway 199. About 10 to 15 miles/16 to 24 km down Highway 199, you come to the redwood forest.

Farther on is Highway 101 (the Redwood Highway), and the road turns south. South of Klamath River is Prairie Creek Redwoods State

Park; here, ask how to find Davison Road to see Fern Canyon. This is not much of a canyon, but what a sight to see! The 30- to 50-foot/9- to 15-meter walls are covered with five-finger ferns, *Adiantum pedatum* rather than its cousin *A. aleuticum*. There is no place like this in all the world.

There are many other interesting places to see in California at other times of the year. Visit Death Valley in late March or early April, along with Joshua Tree National Monument or Anzo-Borrego Park. All the desert can be a carpet of color at this time of year if the rains have been good. The Mother Lode area, where gold was mined in the nineteenth century, is great earlier in the spring; you might explore from Grass Valley to Mariposa.

From mid-May to about mid-June *Calochortus kennedyi* is in bloom in the Mount Pinos area, where its color is the wildest flame-red. You will have to brave the heat of the San Joaquin Valley to drive down Interstate 5 to the small town of Gorman, and there turn west through Frazier Park and on to Lake of the Woods. Beyond Lake of the Woods the road climbs up a side valley, and where it forks, keep left to drive up onto Mount Pinos. Watch closely for spots of the bright red of *C. kennedyi* and the white of *C. venustus*. At the end of the pavement at the ski area there is a bad dirt road onto the top of the mountain, where you can find natural rock gardens filled with many wonderful rock plants.

I have left out so many good places that some people will think there is something wrong with me, but most visitors will have less than a month's time, and exploring all the places mentioned here will keep them going much longer. If you have years to play, there are the Mount Hamilton Range, the San Benito Range, the Warner Mountains, the high North Coast Ranges, and on south to San Diego County, all filled with wonderful and intriguing plants.

Originally published in the Bulletin of the American Rock Garden Society, *vol. 48, no. 1, pp. 3–12 (1990).*

Some Plants of the Sierra Nevada

MARGARET WILLIAMS

How would one describe a typical day in the Sierra Nevada? From my home in Reno, a great many day trips can be taken, all interesting. We have explored many spots but have spent the most time in the mountains above the Feather River and in a series of small valleys leading to Blue Lakes near Kit Carson Pass. The scenery is superb, the flowers are abundant—and the fishing is good, which pleases other members of the family. Elevations in these areas range from 6000 to 8000 feet/1800 to 2400 meters.

One July day, as we drove slowly along the last 10 miles/16 km to Blue Lakes, from the car window we counted 58 species of plants in bloom. Not only does this area have more plant species than any comparable area I have visited, it also has an abundance of most of them. The Feather River country we explore has many of the same plants, as well as a few not found in the Blue Lakes area.

Each succeeding trip to these favorite spots brings new surprises. It would be impossible to discuss every plant, so I will limit myself to the groups here that fascinate me most: plants of the heath family (Ericaceae), their former allies now grouped in the Pyrolaceae, and a primula. These groups typify the Sierras to me; they include not only some of the commonest and most abundant species, but also some of the rarest and most strikingly beautiful.

On any trip to the eastern slopes of the Sierras you will find *Arctostaphylos patula*, the green manzanita. Many hillsides are covered by it, and, because of its uniformity of growth, from a distance it looks like a grassy carpet. It also occurs in combination with other plants and in varied situations. One of the handsomest manzanitas, this is a diffusely branching evergreen shrub, 3 feet/1 meter tall and as broad. The smooth, bright green leaves are rounded and about 1.5 inches/4 cm long. Most of the leaves stand vertically on the stems. The bark is a reddish-chocolate color, smooth and polished. The pink flowers appear in a dense terminal panicle about 2 inches/5 cm long and can be found (depending on altitude and season) from April to June. The corolla is urn-shaped and less than 0.25 inch/6 mm long. The flowers are followed by green berries which darken with age.

Less common is pine-mat manzanita (*Arctostaphylos nevadensis*), found only at higher elevations. Its flowers are white, a bit smaller, and fewer in the panicle. The plants form a rough mat on the forest floor, the main stems creeping or trailing, with branches sticking up 3 to 9 inches/8 to 23 cm. Often the plants creep across rocks and mold to them.

The snow plant (*Sarcodes sanguinea*) is the delight of all who chance upon it. Probably the most spectacular plant among the peculiar, chlorophyll-lacking forest saprophytes, it is common under pine trees; it may also grow out of fallen logs. It has a thick, fleshy, scaly stem rising from 6 to 12 inches/15 to 30 cm. The entire plant is brilliant crimson and catches the eye of the most casual passerby. The individual flowers face outward on short pedicels and are packed tightly together, filling most of the stem. The campanulate corolla is five-lobed and about 0.75 inch/2 cm long and 0.5 inch/13 mm across. Each plant produces only one stem, but often several plants grow in a clump. Snow plants can be found from May to early July, depending on elevation.

Pine drops (*Pterospora andromedea*) is not so dramatic, but nonetheless interesting. It can be found in more limited areas, sometimes growing near snow plants in dense shade. It emerges from the ground a few weeks to a month later than snow plants, usually at middle elevations, and dies after flowering. Pine drops are very unusual in all stages of development. The reddish-brown dried stems of this saprophytic herb are often 2 to 3 feet/60 to 90 cm tall and are sought after by flower arrangers. The many showy, bell-like seedpods hang gracefully along the long stem. As the stem emerges from the ground it is quite fleshy and thick; it becomes more slender as it elongates. The beige stem is quite sticky and fuzzy and is beautifully marked with rose-pink vertical streaks. The urn-shaped white corolla is inconspicuous.

A carpet of *Pyrola picta* (formerly *P. dentata* var. *integra*) can be found nestling at the bases of pine trees in many places. The cream-colored flowers appear in August in a terminal raceme on a leafless stem rising about 6 inches/15 cm above ovate, evergreen leaves. The globular corolla is less than 0.5 inch/13 mm across and faces downward. It has five distinct petals which curve inward. The thickish, elongated style curves abruptly and hangs out conspicuously.

In contrast, *Pyrola asarifolia* subsp. *asarifolia* (formerly variety *incarnata*) can be found growing in a swamp. It has thinner, round leaves and a less conspicuous style, but the same growth habit otherwise. It is distinguished by the color of its graceful, delicate flowers, which are waxy white, suffused with pink which deepens at the edge of the petals. Reginald Farrer describes it as "the loveliest thing in the race."

Chimaphila umbellata and *C. menziesii* can be found growing together in a few shady spots. They are dwarfs, rarely over 4 inches/10 cm tall, woody at the base, with large, oval, toothed evergreen leaves about three times as long as wide. Farrer calls these "very lovely woodland fairies." The pink flowers of *C. umbellata* are shaped like those of a pyrola but are more charming and graceful because the stigma is round and flattened and is on an inconspicuous style. The real darling is *C. menziesii*, with its five reflexed, waxy white petals and 10 sturdy stamens standing around the stigma like golden points of a tiny crown. Both species are few-flowered, and the flowers are large in proportion to the size of the plants. They flower in late summer, usually with last season's seedpod persisting. The flat, round brown capsule is five-celled, opening from above. Pyrolas have a similarly shaped pod, but it opens from the bottom upward.

One of the most beautiful small shrubs in our mountains is red heather (*Phyllodoce breweri*). It grows about 12 inches/30 cm tall; the linear leaves are evergreen and crowded on the stem. The showy corolla is bowl-shaped, about 0.5 inch/13 mm across, and five-parted with recurving lobes. Each flower has 8 to 10 long, conspicuous stamens. The flower clusters are poised at the ends of the branches like bright rose-red froth. An enchanting sight as we rounded a bend in the road was a tiny lake amid trees, bordered with red heather in bloom. In another spot we found it growing in a large area of moist ground.

That same mid-July day, in a moist meadow, *Kalmia polifolia* (Plate 12) was in bloom. It is an erect shrub about 9 inches/23 cm tall, with leathery evergreen leaves. The delicate pink flowers are delightful, but the plants are few-flowered and thus not showy. The corolla is about 0.75 inch/2 cm across, saucer-shaped and five-lobed, with two pouches below each lobe; each pouch holds an anther.

Blooming near the kalmia were plants of *Vaccinium uliginosum* (formerly *V. occidentale*), the western blueberry, a deciduous shrub about 18 inches/45 cm tall. The pendulous white flowers are urn-shaped and very small, usually solitary and inconspicuous; I have never seen the fruit.

Rhododendron occidentale blooms at middle elevations in early June. It is common on the western slopes of the Sierras, but not common in the sites we visited. It makes an elegant, widely branching shrub about 5 feet/1.5 m tall here. The thin leaves are about 3 inches/8 cm long and 1 inch/2.5 cm across, crowded on the stems. The creamy white corolla is funnelform and slightly irregular, about 1.5 inches/4 cm long. The upper lobe of the five lobes in the corolla has a large yellow spot on it. The five long stamens curve gracefully upward. A dozen or so flowers make a showy umbel on the tip of each branch. It is as beautiful a rhododendron as any cultivated variety.

Ledum glandulosum or Labrador tea is a less spectacular shrub. The olive-green leaves are about 1 inch/2.5 cm long and half as wide, and they smell like shoe polish when crushed. It is a neat, rounded plant growing about 3 feet/1 meter tall. The creamy white flowers are about 0.5 inch/13 mm across and are borne in flat heads, 1 to 2 inches/2.5 to 5 cm across, on the tips of the branches. The flowers have five distinct petals which spread flat; the 10 stamens stand rather erect, producing a fuzzy effect. The plant grows in moist places and blooms in late July.

The view from a Jeep road on a divide at about 8000 feet/2400 meters is breathtaking. Far below to the left are three crystal-clear lakes: one a meadow lake, one surrounded by conifers, and the third rockbound. To the right, amid rock formations, are twin lakes that appear tiny from so far above but are actually quite large. One day in mid-July we were startled to see a crimson streak on the edge of a nearby snowbank. Closer inspection revealed plants of *Primula suffrutescens* (Plate 10). The glossy green leaves on woody, ground-hugging stems were in many places just emerging through the snow. Within a foot/30 cm of the snowbank the plants were coming into full bloom.

Primula suffrutescens bears several typical primrose blooms in an umbel on a naked stem about 6 inches/15 cm long, well above the leaves. The flowers are a glistening rose-red with a yellow eye and measure about 0.75 inch/2 cm across. These primrose plants grew in a large colony on a steep, rocky hillside; although the plants grew among rocks here, they did not come out of crevices as the botanist W. L. Jepson observed them growing. A return trip several weeks later found these plants gone to seed, but others had emerged from the snow and were blooming.

The same day, farther along the road, *Leucothoe davisiae* was blooming along the bank of a tumbling stream and again in a mass on the shore of a lake. It is an erect shrub, at least 3 feet/1 meter tall, with evergreen, leathery leaves about 2 inches/5 cm long and 1 inch/2.5 cm wide. The small, bell-shaped flowers are nearly closed. They hang on short pedicels in an erect terminal raceme about 3 inches/8 cm long. A white calyx fits like a little cap over each flower. The contrast between the satiny white flowers and the glossy green leaves is striking.

The most elusive member of the Ericaceae here is *Cassiope mertensiana* (Plate 11). It should grow in the places I have been, but so far I have not found it. It is reported to grow in many areas of the high Sierras. This year I intend to explore Desolation Valley west of Lake Tahoe, where this white heather is said to grow on a lakeshore. Jepson reports it growing in granite rocks and clefts at 8000 to 10,000 feet/2400 to 3100 meters, in the Sierras west and south of Reno. It is a diminutive tufted shrub whose stems are crowded with short, thick evergreen leaves. The small white bell-like flowers are borne on 1-inch/2.5-cm stems in the axils of the leaves.

Except for the Sierra primrose, all these plants grow in springy, humusy soil in either deep shade or meadows. Several grow in almost boggy sites. In most cases, however, the moisture is supplied by seepage from melting snow, and when that is gone, the areas dry out. There is very little summer rain, and snow does not fall again until after their growing season is over. I have not tried growing any of these plants because I did not feel that I could duplicate their growing conditions; instead, I do my collecting with a camera.

Although none of the plants mentioned—except pine-mat manzanita and Sierra primrose—was found growing in rocks, the chimaphilas, pyrolas, kalmia, and phyllodoce would be handsome additions to any rock garden. Farrer says *Primula suffrutescens* "is easy in cultivation ... in warm sandy, stony, and well drained peat." Pyrolas and chimaphilas are hard to move and establish, he says, because of their "frail wandering root habit." Even *Sarcodes sanguinea* might be attempted from its dustlike seed. With luck, you might suddenly see it emerging in the garden four or five springs after the seed had been scattered and forgotten.

Originally published in the Bulletin of the American Rock Garden Society, *vol. 17, no. 4, pp. 117–120 (1959).*

Plant Gems of the Golden State

JOHN ANDREWS

Among rock gardeners, California is probably best known for its monocots, yet its flora contains many other choice subjects for the rock garden that will appeal to the beginner and experienced grower alike. Several discussed here will be familiar, but others may be new to most rock gardeners. Many of these plants are from the arid environment of the Great Basin, and others from the highest mountain ranges of the state.

One delightful species of the genus *Astragalus* ranges along the eastern edge of California and into the Great Basin. Within the large range of *A. purshii* var. *tinctus* there are many forms, but the best have short stems and form silvery-silken mounds. Near the base appear large pink and violet flowers, followed by silky pods like a rabbit's foot, with beaks as sharp as the rabbit's toenail. These plants inhabit rocky, semibarren sagebrush plains and put on an April display that will bring passing plant-hunters to a screeching halt.

Continuing the theme of silky silver foliage and fuzzy pods, but with flowers as crimson as those of any zauschneria, is *Astragalus coccineus* (Plate 15) of the Inyo-White Mountains. I have not seen it anywhere in large numbers, so it remains a cherished experience to stumble on it. Its habit of growing in low-rainfall, exposed, sunny positions on the edge of the Mohave Desert might suggest that this plant would be ungrowable in more hospitable climates; try it in the bulb frame, however, or plant it out in a well-drained sunny position late in the spring where it has protection from late frosts. Some plants actually grow very near desert springs, where the roots must reach some moisture. They may tolerate considerably more water than nature offers them in their native habitat.

Few alpine campanulas can rival the extreme expressions of the genus in California. *Campanula scabrella* usually grows on exposed rocky slopes or fellfields from Mount Eddy northward into the Cascades. It has canescent gray tufts of leaves on the ends of buried stems that reach up through shifting rocks, forming small mats in more stable situations. These mats are topped in season with gemlike gray-blue flowers on minute stems. This is the perfect alpine if grown hard in full sun, but it becomes a little lanky in sheltered spots.

On the shady sides of cliffs and cracks in the Mount Shasta area grows another species, *Campanula shetleri*. Gray-blue bells sit on short stems over mounds of puberulent green, dentate leaves, often packed tightly into rock crevices. Some plants try to mimic dionysias by growing upside-down under rock ledges. This is a plant for moister conditions. The best-looking, denser individuals are on the edges of exposure to the sun, peeking out from under a ledge or around a rock, still in the shade but where they get a lot of indirect light.

Two potentially frustrating pan plants for the alpine house are *Dicentra uniflora* and *D. pauciflora*. These plants disappear in summer, when the rocky, gravelly, vernally wet areas where they grow become dry. *Dicentra uniflora* looks like a longhorn steer's head, with its long outer petal tips; the petals of *D. pauciflora* are shorter. The flowers of both are pale pink with darker outer petals. The leaves of *D. uniflora* are a little more substantial, and their dissected lobes are rounded. *Dicentra pauciflora* grows in areas with slightly more humus and has beautiful pink or near-white flowers over extremely dissected, pointed foliage. It may be the easier of the two in cultivation, having a cluster of pale, tuberous roots that is easier to keep under observation.

The California species of *Epilobium* are well known but deserve to be mentioned. *Epilobium rigidum* and *E. siskiyouense* (formerly considered a subspecies of *E. obcordatum*) both have glaucous foliage and large, soft to bright pink flowers, displayed beautifully against the gray-blue serpentine rocks of their native homes. *Epilobium siskiyouense* prefers an alpine, exposed rocky field, while *E. rigidum* occurs at lower elevations in dry runoff channels. Good seed is difficult to get owing to the vagaries of the Californian dry season in which it blooms. Plants are easy to grow and look best around the bases of rocks. *Epilobium siskiyouense* is difficult in pots, but small plants are possible. *Epilobium obcordatum* wants to make mats, while *E. siskiyouense* is supposed to be more clumping; however, it too seems to run to some extent.

The name *Hesperochiron* can occasionally be seen on seed lists, but this genus is little known. These flowers occur in large displays, usually growing with *Viola beckwithii*, an association that should have made them a little better known. These perennials of the Hydrophyllaceae, or waterleaf family, are summer-dormant. A slightly larger plant than *Hesperochiron pumilus*, *H. californicus* has crystalline white to pinkish, funnelform flowers on rosettes of canescent leaves; it grows in slightly wetter, sandier situations. *Hesperochiron pumilus* is more a clay-lover, with pink to purple veins pencilling the flattened, cup-shaped flowers of the smaller plants. Both are inhabitants of sagebrush plains and ridges, vernally very moist and always in full sun, except for the shelter of an occasional artemisia. These should be very good bulb-frame items.

To come up with clumps of foliage covered with spider webs and topped by regal sunflowers that battle the ridgetop winds, take up the challenge of the genus *Hulsea*. *Hulsea nana* (Plate 1) is the shortest at less than 6 inches/15 cm high, and like *Campanula scabrella* it grows on Mount Eddy and to the north. The rosettes are fantastic in themselves—glandular and usually white-woolly, densely packed on the branching caudex. *Hulsea algida* is a slightly larger plant found on screes from Mount Rose northward through the arid ranges on the eastern side of the Sierra Nevada and into eastern Oregon and Idaho.

Ivesias are not quite perfect alpines, usually with a few ferny, potentilla-like leaves and small yellow flowers. An exception is my recent find *Ivesia lycopodioides*. It makes clumps of finely dissected, glandular leaves no more than 3 inches/8 cm tall, topped by an equally short stem bearing a few yellow flowers, the largest of the genus. Without flowers this plant looks something like a large clubmoss. It comes from the windswept ridges of the central Sierra Nevada.

Growing throughout much of the Sierra Nevada is *Lupinus breweri*, making mats of silken-leaved, silver plants with heads of blue-and-white flowers. These bloom over a long period if given occasional water. Jim Archibald has said that if others have suggested that the West is continuously carpeted with *Phlox hoodii*, then he may claim that Mount Rose is woven together by mats of *Lupinus breweri*.

Growing in barren areas of the Sierra is the beautiful *Oenothera xylocarpa*. From its minutely pubescent, lyre-shaped, spotted leaves to its huge soft yellow flowers that open in the evening and age to salmon, it is stunning. Recently separated from this genus is *Camissonia tanacetifolia*, with finely dissected foliage and cup-shaped flowers, which grows on vernally moist plains. It can sometimes be found in communities with *Hesperochiron californicus*.

Growing close to *Polemonium pulcherrimum* you may find *Ranunculus eschscholtzii* var. *oxynotus* (Plate 14), forming large clumps of foliage topped with bright, waxy yellow buttercups. The flowering follows the snowmelt along the ridge tops. Fresh seed is the best means of propagating this plant.

California also has some spectacular penstemons. *Penstemon newberryi* subsp. *sonomensis* grows on a few rocky ridge tops in a few counties of the Coast Ranges, making mats of small, dark green leaves topped with stems of intense dark red bloom, punctuated with the fuzzy white dots of the anthers. These plants are usually in somewhat north-facing crevices. The typical *P. newberryi* (Plate 13) is a more moderate shade of red and forms a taller clump up to 2 feet/60 cm high. It comes from the northern and central Sierra. *Penstemon purpusii* grows on more exposed serpentine ridges, with a prostrate rosette or two of leaves and many large blue and violet flowers. The leaves are an attractive feature in themselves, being slightly folded, pubescent, and glaucous. A species that I have never seen in flower, which must be stunning, is *P. tracyi* of the Trinity Alps area. It makes mounds of bright green leaves, leathery and red on the reverse, topped with a large ball of small, long-tubed white or pinkish flowers. It sits on hot volcanic rocks, in crevices, usually with an eastern exposure to escape the worst of the summer heat. Finally, for masses of floral display, few penstemons can match *P. speciosus* and the form representing the extreme of its dwarf development, formerly known as subspecies *kennedyi* but now not considered distinct. It grows in a wide area of the West in barren or disturbed sites such as road cuts. It has huge blue flowers.

Silene hookeri is a stunning plant, usually found in barren, rocky areas. It sends up stems from a buried crown, and these increase in number with age. They have grayish leaves topped with white, pink, or violet flowers. The flowers approach 1 inch/2.5 cm in diameter in *S. hookeri* subsp. *bolanderi*. This subspecies grows in heavy, rocky serpentine clays and is usually dwarfest in full sun.

California has only one native primula, *Primula suffrutescens* (Plate 10). It makes large mats of rooting stems with green leaves, dentate on the tips, topped with glandular stems bearing many glowing magenta flowers. These have an exotic oriental fragrance. The mats usually occur along drainages below peaks with north to northeast exposures. The smaller plants of the Trinity Alps actually grow in glacial meltwater. The Sierran plants get meltwater under the boulder rubble on which they grow. I have never been successful with this plant, but I still try, and others have grown fine plants.

Finally, the violets are classic plants and should be tried whenever possible. *Viola beckwithii* from the sagebrush plains of eastern California, growing in wet areas that dry out in the summer, has bluish lower petals with purple petals above, and finely palmately dissected, glaucous foliage. In the northwest corner of the state, extending into Oregon, is *V. hallii*. I prefer the latter, which has lower petals white or cream and upper petals reddish-purple. The leaves have a few palmate dissections. Both plants can be quite sizable and floriferous in nature, inhabiting similar areas of rocky, vernally moist, summer-dry ridges and flats. They are a challenge for the most dedicated grower, requiring a period of summer dormancy during which they must not get wet and yet must not dry out completely.

This in no way exhausts the worthy plants that may be encountered in California and brought into cultivation. Here I suggest only a few possibilities and offer them up as challenges to the alpine grower.

Originally published in the Bulletin of the American Rock Garden Society, *vol. 48, no. 1, pp. 35–46 (1990).*

California Rock Ferns

MARGERY EDGREN

When hiking through the coastal areas, foothills, and mountain slopes of California, one encounters many small, attractive ferns. They occur in an abundance of shapes, sizes, colors, and textures that make them stimulating objects of contemplation. The backs of the fronds are particularly interesting and sometimes quite beautiful. The spore cases are formed in a great variety of distinctive patterns in dark brown or black, standing out sharply against the smooth green of the fronds.

Pentagramma triangularis (formerly *Pityrogramma triangularis*) has soft golden powder covering the reverse of the leaves, in delightful contrast to the dark green of the upper surface. This striking feature has earned it the common name "goldback fern." *Pentagramma triangularis* subsp. *viscosa*, the silverback fern, has sparkling white powder that is equally attractive. In nature, the fronds of this genus curl up and die back during the dry summer season, but with water in the garden they remain green throughout the year.

Another little fern, widespread from areas near the coast to the Sierras, grows in thick tufts, with new growth a rich green and fronds deeply cut in lacy patterns. Later, near the end of the dry summer, its color changes to gray-green. It has several common names, including "Indian's dream" and "Oregon cliff brake." It seems to have puzzled the taxonomists, who over the years have assigned it to several different genera and changed the species epithet as well. It is currently known as *Aspidotis densa*. Quite similar in appearance is *A. californica*. The two may easily be confused without close inspection of key characteristics involving distribution of the sporangia and the shape of the false indusium. Both species can be used for similar garden effects.

My first glimpse of *Cheilanthes gracillima* (Plate 16) was on a hike near Cook and Green Pass in the Siskiyou Mountains. As we settled ourselves among the rocks for a picnic lunch, we glanced up at the cliff above us, and there, filling the crevices that crisscrossed the rock face, were masses of little ferns spilling out in sprays of soft green. The beadlike segments of their deeply dissected pinnules produce richly textured fronds, making the plant ideal for distinctive accents in the garden.

One can see *Cryptogramma acrostichoides* while hiking at Squaw Valley, California, where it springs in clumps from pockets of soil between the rocks. The sterile fronds have crenate, rounded pinnules producing shapes resembling parsley—hence its common name "parsley fern." It has completely separate fronds for the production of spores, in pleasing contrast to its vegetative foliage, and is particularly appealing when these fertile fronds are present.

Pellaea bridgesii is a small mountain fern of exposed cliffs and rocky slopes, occurring from 6000 to 10,000 feet/1800 to 3100 meters elevation in the Sierra Nevada. It has handsome fronds with short, linear blades and broadly oval pinnae of a gorgeous blue-green hue. Their smooth edges are curled under, forming false indusia that cover the spore cases. Tufted in habit and difficult in cultivation, it is a particularly choice fern for narrow crevices and a true gem for the rock garden.

The fronds of *Polypodium californicum* are relatively small in size and are once-pinnately divided with smooth edges. The resulting broadly scalloped outline provides a bold contrast for dainty shade plants. The new growth is bright green and darkens with age. The plant is most attractive in confined areas such as chinks or niches, where the elongating rhizome is crowded to mass the fronds in clumps, or in a crevice where it must run along a distinct line. In the wild it is summer-deciduous, but in the garden it can be encouraged to extend its growing season somewhat with occasional irrigation. The new fronds appear quite early in the fall.

Athyrium americanum (formerly called *A. alpestre* var. *americanum* and *A. distentifolium* var. *americanum*) has much the same upright, feathery fronds in delicate shades of light green as the more widely known lady fern, but its small size and less invasive nature make it a charming companion for many rock garden plants. Its lacy, oblong blades are often less than 12 inches/30 cm long, with a maximum range to about 23 inches/58 cm. It grows in moist habitats from 6000 to 10,000 feet/1800 to 3100 meters elevation throughout the Sierra Nevada, frequently among granite rocks.

The range of *Asplenium trichomanes* (Plate 105) barely dips into northern California at its southern limit along the coast. Reliably small and clumping in nature, this fern is perfect for an accent in a shady trough or terrarium, where it thrives in the moist atmosphere. Distinctive spore patterns on the backs of the fronds add to its overall appeal.

Dainty *Adiantum jordanii*, the California maidenhair, with its delicate, low-growing fronds, is another fine plant for the shade garden. Found in moist canyons at low altitudes, it is common in Marin County on shaded, rocky slopes and in open woods. Its gracefully arching leaves are similar to taller maidenhairs, but they have shorter leafstalks; its well-spaced, rounded pinnules give an airy, casual appearance compared to the refined and elegant *A. pedatum* or the full, lush fronds of *A. capillus-veneris*. It is particularly useful on shady banks and walls. Summer-deciduous in its native habitat, it has proved somewhat difficult in cultivation but is a worthy challenge to dedicated gardeners.

Surely these ferns would grace many a rock garden if only they were available to us. They are not unobtainable: you can grow them from spores more easily than you may suppose. Watch for the spores in seed exchange lists, where they do appear occasionally; as the demand increases, so will the supply. Spores are easily collected at the proper time. Collectors need to be alert to the likelihood that gardeners are willing to grow them, and here is an easy method.

Forget about sterilizing pans and spores and media. At the local garden center, find some plastic saucers made to set under potted plants. Slip one into a plastic bag with a zip closure, and you have an individual greenhouse to take your fern from spore to sporophyte. A saucer 5 inches/13 cm in diameter and a sandwich bag fit well together. Next, fill the saucer halfway to the rim with a mixture of 4 or 5 parts perlite to 1 part milled sphagnum. (This moss is a finely chopped, dried product of fresh sphagnum sold in small bags, not to be confused with the sphagnum peat products used for soil amendment.) Moisten this mixture with a solution of hydroponic fertilizer specially formulated for raising plants in liquid solution without soil. Bare roots are bathed in such a solution without danger of burning, and it has proved equally safe for fern spore pans. The dry chemicals for this solution may be mixed with ordinary tap water. Hydroponic fertilizer is not always available in garden centers, but several brands can be obtained through mail-order catalogs. Drain the sphagnum mixture on clean newspaper before filling the saucer. Press the medium firmly into the bottom so that it forms a smooth, tightly knit base on which to spread the layer of spores. It is essential to leave the medium damp but not wet. Excess moisture may be drained off as you press the medium into the saucer.

Again, forget about trying to sow powdery spores evenly. Instead, put a heaping teaspoonful of very fine vermiculite into a small plastic cup and moisten it with hydroponic fertilizer. Then add the fern spores and mix thoroughly. Next, spread the vermiculite evenly over the medium in the saucer, and a good distribution of spores will result. Press firmly to make good contact with the medium below. The tiny spores will not be crushed.

Subdued, reliable light from fluorescent tubes is an excellent source of illumination for spore pans. Either place the pans around the edges of other plants that require more intense light, or keep them about 12 to 18 inches/30 to 45 cm away from the tubes. Filtered natural light can also be used.

The spores germinate in a few days to a couple of weeks, although this can only be seen through a dissecting microscope or lens. They develop rapidly at around 70°F/21°C with continuous fluorescent light. (Combining a warm white with a cool white tube gives an excellent spectrum of light without investment in expensive plant growth tubes. Even cool white alone is entirely satisfactory.) The single most important factor in producing good healthy spore pans is moisture control. Using too much moisture is far worse than letting the pan become slightly dry. Overwhelming contamination with algae, fungi, and mosses results from keeping the pan too wet. To reduce moisture, it is far safer to open the bag frequently and wipe off the moisture condensed on the plastic than to leave the pan open to the air to dry off. How easy it is to forget and allow it to dry up completely! When necessary, a little more moisture can be added by gently misting the medium with a spray bottle of tap water.

Prothallia resembling little liverworts grow first. When mature they produce gametes. At this stage a thin film of water on the prothallia is necessary for fertilization to take place; a light misting of the pan should suffice. Tiny sporophytes start appearing on the prothallia after 2 or 3 months, depending on growing conditions and species. They soon stick up above the mat of prothallia and will grow into the ferns you want for the garden. They may be pricked out while tiny, or you may move them out in clumps later if you prefer working with reasonably large plantlets that require less attention after transplanting. A mixture of sphagnum peat, vermiculite, and sand or pea gravel makes a good potting medium for the young sporophytes. Perlite may be added for species needing fast drainage. Continue to use the hydroponic nutrients or a dilute solution of liquid fertilizer. Continuous light will promote fast growth, and a plastic cover keeps humidity high without excessive misting. Open the cover occasionally or provide for some circulation of air.

Attractive young plants can be produced in 12 to 18 months. Propagators wait longer than that for many choice alpines! When the time comes to plant these young ferns in the garden, you can fill many niches, thus multiplying your chances of success many times over what you get by buying a single plant.

Originally published in the Bulletin of the American Rock Garden Society, *vol. 48, no. 1, pp. 31–34 (1990).*

Liliaceous Bulbs

WAYNE RODERICK

My subject is liliaceous bulbs in the broadest sense—true bulbs, tubers, corms, or thickened rootstocks. My work has always been with California plants, so I will restrict this article to those native to California. I will describe methods of culture I have developed for some of our more temperamental species, including information on soil amendments we have worked out at the University of California at Berkeley Botanic Garden.

For instance, many *Calochortus* species are very challenging to grow. Over the years, we have found the best compost to be one part leafmold, one part good garden loam (a light soil if you can get it), and one part coarse sand. Although we have had very good results using this mix for many of the plants, some species have become invasive in it, and some have died.

To grow our bulbs, we use special boxes approximately 2 feet/60 cm square and 1 foot/30 cm deep. The soil is generally about 8 inches/20 cm deep—deeper if specific bulbs require it. We have wire screen on the bottom and over the top to keep out obnoxious pests such as field mice, as well as birds, which love to eat foliage and buds. These boxes are not watered at all in summer (with a few exceptions, all of them shade-dwelling plants, such as *Trillium rivale*, most of the lilies, and a couple of the erythroniums). *Trillium chloropetalum* and *T. ovatum* are given two or three waterings in summer. All the other species are given full sun and are never watered.

Brodiaea, _Triteleia_, and _Dichelostemma_

In considering individual species, let us look first at the group once lumped under _Brodiaea_; some of these have now been segregated into _Dichelostemma_ and _Triteleia_. _Dichelostemma congestum_ (formerly _Brodiaea pulchella_) shows great variation in color, number of flowers in the cluster, and height. A fine large, light-colored form from Santa Cruz Island off the coast of Santa Barbara has multiplied slowly. The little scrubby forms manage to spread, even though we try to cut off every old flower head before it goes to seed. We dig them, too; we even eat them—this is one of the main plants of the Indians' traditional summer diet.

Triteleia hyacinthina has been quite amenable. In the wild it generally grows rather deep in heavy clay, but in our loose soil it stays shallower. We have had these plants in irrigated sites and in bone-dry sites, and they do about as well either way. The only thing they seem to require in the garden is the hottest spot with the least watering. Another good garden subject is _T. ixioides_, again with much color variation from pale cream to bright yellow. Where there are summer rains, give them the driest spot available.

One of the most spectacular is _Triteleia laxa_. It has quite a range of color variation, from the normal light blue to deep purple along the coast. How this dark form has spread around! I never brought it home, but I have it in three places—one in near-bog conditions, where it is doing well. It might do quite well in areas with summer rains but would probably have to be sheltered in cold climates. There were masses of the dark form this past spring; they seem to have enjoyed the dry winter.

My favorite plant of this group is little _Brodiaea terrestris_, probably our best rock garden species. It has gone under some unwieldy names, the worst being nearly as long as the plant is high: _B. coronaria_ var. _macropoda_. It grows about 2 inches/5 cm tall and up to 3 inches/8 cm across, and multiplies slowly into nice clumps. Field mice love it; occasionally it is eaten very badly, but it slowly builds up to nice clumps again. The bulbs planted in dry areas do not do as well as those given water. This one should prosper in areas with summer rains. The only trouble is trying to collect seeds: one pod opens at a time, and one has to part all the old flowers to hunt for the open pods and pick them individually.

Dichelostemma ida-maia has grown under various conditions for us at the University of California. We have it in complete drought, in hot, dry loose soil, in hard clay soil, in dry part shade, in wet part shade, and in deep shade. It does well in all but the last. The light, loose, dry soil and the light shade with moist soil have produced the finest heads of flowers on good 2-foot/60-cm stems. The plants multiply rapidly, and seed is easy to collect. As the pods form, they turn upward. The corolla holds its color until after the seed is ripe. If the pods are split, they are ready to pick.

The plant once known as *Brodiaea venusta*, and now as *Dichelostemma* × *venustum*, is probably the rarest of all our bulbous plants. There may be only around 10 individuals in the wild. Our collection at the botanic garden came from the type locality. I went there with a man who was writing his thesis on this species, and we found a bulldozer straightening the road; we dug the last seven bulbs to save them from destruction. We now have nearly a hundred bulbs and will start planting some back in the wild, farther away from the road. It has been suggested that this is a hybrid between *D. ida-maia* and *D. congestum*, but when this cross was attempted in cultivation, it took about 500 attempts to set three pods. It has multiplied rapidly in cultivation and probably will be as easy to grow as *D. ida-maia*. The botanic garden has only a few planted out for the public to see; we are building up a supply before experimenting to see how much moisture and shade and which soil types this species will take.

Another unusual species is *Dichelostemma volubile* ("twining"). It is a lovely thing with large heads of pink flowers at the tips of long stems that spiral up through shrubs. It grows mostly in the foothills in the northern half of the Central Valley and is almost impossible to collect because it often grows amid poison oak (*Rhus diversiloba*). It has proven easy to grow in clay as well as in our bulb mix. The few bulbs I have planted where they were given summer water soon died out, so I think this species has to be kept in pots and given a good summer baking.

Triteleia peduncularis has done well in wet conditions and light shade to full sun at the botanic garden, in my garden, and elsewhere. It has big umbels—up to 10 inches/25 cm in diameter—which have a glistening white, lacy effect. A clump of these at their prime is quite nice in the garden. Unfortunately, they hold the old flowers and look unhappy and withered after flowering. I believe they will grow under most conditions, though probably they will not take much cold.

Fritillaria

There is a wonderful group of fritillarias on the West Coast. *Fritillaria liliacea* grows in clay in nature, and in cultivation it must have clay. The petite bells are cream to pale green, sometimes with a few brown spots. They have done poorly for us, even when we bring in the soil. This species is one that I love very dearly, so I go out to enjoy it in the wild.

Fritillaria biflora, from the southern half of the state, grows rather close to the coast. Again a clay-dweller, it has done fairly well for us. Those I have kept in boxes have done poorly, but others planted out in the open ground have done much better; maybe the clay stays a bit damp. I think there is a chance of good results in summer-rain areas if the bulbs are kept in pots.

Fritillaria agrestis is a stinker in more ways than one: it is a stinker to grow, a stinker to dig, and worst of all, when you get your nose close to the flowers, you will know why they are commonly called "stink bells." It grows in stiff clay, mostly in the Sacramento and San Joaquin valleys. It intergrades into *F. biflora*, and I found one plant close to *F. liliacea*.

One of the most delightful fritillarias, and the rarest of the clay-dwellers, is *Fritillaria striata*, found in only two or three places. It blooms in late February and early March. It has multiplied slowly for us, making a nice small colony. On a warm, dry day you can smell its exquisite fragrance half a block downwind. The flowers are white, streaked with pink. I have a white form of this species which I selected and grew on from seed. I sent three bulblets to E. B. Anderson; one turned out to be white with about twice as many bells as any I have ever grown.

Fritillaria pluriflora is commonly called "pink adobe lily." Adobe is a black clay that early Hispanic settlers used to make building bricks. When wet, it is gooey; when dry, it is hell. The bulbs lie about 10 inches/25 cm deep in this clay. When I go to collect seed at the end of May, the temperature is just 2 degrees less than purgatory. By this time, the ground has wide cracks, and if I look down in the cracks, I may see a bulb here and there. By the first of June the temperature may be over 100°F/38°C, and the field brown where in March it had been pink with fritillarias. The species is poor to fair in cultivation. I have had most success in a soil made by taking about 5 percent humus and 5 percent grit to 90 percent clay, mixing this with my bare feet as the early settlers had their Indian slaves do to make bricks.

Fritillaria falcata grows about 75 miles/120 km southeast of San Francisco on steep serpentine talus slopes. It is impossible to walk across the steep slopes without sliding down to the bottom. You run like the devil across and hope that when you do see a plant, you can stop without sliding clear off. You could run your hand under the plant and pick it up, but what's the use? Nobody can grow it. *Fritillaria falcata* is one of our rare and endangered species, so I have never taken more than a bulb or two to try to grow. I have brought in soil, I have tried seed, I have tried flowering-sized bulbs and seedling bulbs, and so far all have come to nothing. This jewel has greenish petals with reddish-brown markings and bright red anthers.

Fritillaria purdyi grows with its bulbs wedged in between rocks, so that it is almost impossible to pry them out without crushing them. If you can get seeds, they are quite easy to grow. I have grown this species with good results both in the soil they were found in and in a soil-and-rock mixture. One plant lived for 10 years in another garden in ordinary soil, producing 8 to 10 bells every year until suddenly it disappeared. This amenable plant has much color variation; the best forms are those with white flowers heavily suffused with reddish-brown splotches. The white gradually fades to pink.

Fritillaria glauca grows close to *F. purdyi* in some areas, but generally in a screelike soil where the bedrock is deep. In one place they come together, with plants only inches apart; we have hunted for years for hybrids between these two and have yet to find one. The bulbs of *F. glauca* are 3 to 4 inches/8 to 10 cm down in a soil composed of lots of rock and fine, humusy, rich, sandy loam, topped with a rock mulch which gives coolness in summer. There are a few summer rains to keep the soil from becoming completely baked and dry. *Fritillaria glauca* is usually yellow-flowered, but brown forms can be found. It is a temperamental plant to grow and does not last long.

Probably the most sought-after fritillary is *Fritillaria recurva*. This species has been difficult to grow and seems to want gritty, humusy red clay with a thick humus topping. I have spent a couple of weekends bringing in the soil layer by layer; now I will bring in a few bulbs and see if they will grow well in their own soil. They have persisted only a very short time for me, and few others have had good results. One thing to remember, if you try these, is that the bulbs do like baking, but not the full hot baking tolerated by some other species. I have noted that in areas heavily browsed by deer, *F. recurva* is found growing up through brush, while in areas with few deer, plants will be seen in open woodland. It is rare to find seeds in deer areas, as the seeds of liliaceous plants are much favored by deer.

About 50 miles/80 km north of San Francisco grows a form of *Fritillaria recurva* formerly called variety *coccinea* but not now formally distinguished. I used to live within 20 miles/32 km of its type locality; I have gone over acres and acres and have never found one absolutely true form. I believe the type specimen was a chance variation without recurved tepals and with more brilliant color. All the plants I have seen have recurved tepals.

Fritillaria affinis (formerly *F. lanceolata*; Plate 3) is a delightful plant in all its many forms. If gardeners in summer-rain areas wish to grow this plant, they should try to get seed collected in parts of Oregon or Washington where summer rains sometimes occur; these should be much easier to grow. There is tremendous variation, from small, heavily spotted flowers, to some that are all chocolate, to others that are almost green. Some grow 5 to 6 inches/13 to 15 cm tall; others grow waist-high—even up to 3 feet/1 meter, with as many as 68 bells, each bell more than 1 inch/2.5 cm in diameter. I have also seen plants with bells as small as 0.5 inch/13 mm in diameter.

Calochortus

Now we move on to the calochortuses, beginning with *Calochortus uniflorus*, one of the easier ones to cultivate. In fact, it can get around quite a bit on its own, and delightfully so. At the Botanic Garden, where we give it the full summer baking, it has done better and is a bit more compact. In my garden it has bloomed for a longer period and has not multiplied so fast. It shows some variation, from pale lavender or mauve to quite a nice pink form seen along some ocean bluffs. The parts I like most are the anthers, which are a lively blue to turquoise to green. *Calochortus uniflorus* produces many bulblets on the stems and quite a bit of seed, so one can get a nice colony in a short time.

Calochortus nudus, which grows at higher elevations in wet meadows with snow cover in winter, has done practically nothing at the Botanic Garden, probably from lack of cold as well as lack of special attention. I have sent seed of this species and a few bulbs to friends in England, where they did very well. *Calochortus nudus* shows a little color variation, mostly in shadings of pink. I believe this should do well in any northern climate with cold winters and summer rains.

Calochortus albus has been an excellent doer for us. We have found that where it gets a little water once a month, it has done better than where it is completely unirrigated. It generally grows in light shade in humus-rich soil on well-drained slopes. It has done especially well in our lily mix. It has lovely, delicate flowers that range from snow-white to pink to the nearly blood-red flowers of the plant formerly called variety *rubellus*. This species and the following three are known as "lantern" types because of the shape of their flowers.

Calochortus amabilis (Plate 21) is found north of San Francisco. It has been erroneously known, in cultivation, as *C. pulchellus*, another species entirely. The petals of *C. amabilis* are fringed, and the inner surface is without hairs and of a darker shade of yellow. Often there is a brown ring around the gland area. *Calochortus pulchellus* is a lighter yellow and has hairs on the inner surface of the petals. It is very restricted in distribution and is listed as rare and endangered. These two species, like all the other lantern types, prefer humus-rich soil in light shade.

The fourth species of the lantern type is *Calochortus amoenus* (Plate 19), found only in the southern part of the foothills of the Sierra Nevada. It grows on north-facing slopes, generally under deciduous oaks and digger pines (*Pinus sabiniana*), which are very open trees. All the surrounding countryside will be dried up except where one finds this species in bloom. *Calochortus amoenus* has been fairly adaptable but has done better for us in pots. It seems to want more summer baking than the other lantern types.

Calochortus coeruleus grows from the ocean bluffs to elevations of 6000 or 7000 feet/1800 or 2100 meters. It intergrades into *C. tolmiei*; in a large patch one can find these growing together. The surfaces of the petals are covered with hairs, which are white in *C. coeruleus* and purple in *C. tolmiei*. Along the ocean bluffs one finds that nearly all the calochortuses there are *C. tolmiei*, and at higher elevations, they are mostly *C. coeruleus*. The coastal form has been rather amenable to cultivation but will not take any nonsense about summer watering; yet it does not want to be too dried out. Collected bulbs of the high-elevation forms have never come up in the garden.

Without doubt the most delightful little fellow is *Calochortus monophyllus*, a bright yellow, furry-petaled species which has been quite difficult to grow. It is found in the foothills of the Sierra Nevada where the yellow pines (*Pinus ponderosa*) start and where deciduous oaks (*Quercus kelloggii*) are mixed in with the pines. It blooms in early spring. I am having quite good results growing this species in my garden, where there is little summer fog. Grown under pines at the Botanic Garden, where there is summer fog, the plants died. There I have tried them in light shade, and in sun; I have tried everything, and said to hell with them.

Now to the large-flowered types we call "mariposas." (This group was once split away as genus *Mariposa* by Robert Hoover.) *Calochortus luteus* was rather a common plant on my father's farm, so when I think of mariposas, I immediately think of this species. Without doubt the most exquisite form of this widespread, variable species occurs north of San Francisco, where I grew up. It has a delicate green cast over the bright yellow, and brown speckles around the gland. In other areas one can find flowers from near-white to pale yellow to clear yellow, with or without brown. In the Sierra Nevada foothills this species intergrades with *C. venustus* and *C. superbus* until it is hard to distinguish among them.

Calochortus vestae is found in the northern inner Coast Range in hot, dry valleys; it is, I believe, a variation of *C. venustus*. The flowers are white with dark red markings near the bases of the petals. The same colors and markings are found in *C. venustus* and *C. superbus*, with only variations of the glands to distinguish them from one another. *Calochortus venustus* varies greatly: it can have double spots, and its color ranges from white through pink to shades of red. All have similar requirements in cultivation, enjoying our lily soil mix and a summer baking.

From southern California to about the middle of the state we find *Calochortus clavatus*. The northern form is clear yellow with red anthers, while the southern form has brown markings on the lower parts of the petals. The southern form has proven a good doer, lasting about 20 years with us. The latter form blooms well each year on low, many-branched plants.

Also from southern California is *Calochortus catalinae*. It has come up and bloomed in a wet spot in my garden. I do not know how much summer wetness it will take, but it has proven quite adaptable for us.

The most difficult of all the mariposas is *Calochortus kennedyi*. I have never seen it in bloom in the wild, though I have grown it to flowering a couple of times in the Botanic Garden. I have collected bulbs several times from various parts of the California deserts, but invariably they die before blooming. I have never tried the species in pots put up against the glass in our cactus house; that might be just the trick it wants. The southwestern Mojave Desert is where the flame-and-black forms are found.

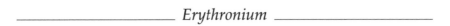

Erythronium

I shall mention here only those few erythroniums with which I have had experience. *Erythronium klamathense* is a high-elevation species that absolutely despises the mild temperature of the San Francisco Bay area. No plants have ever come up after being collected as dormant bulbs. I believe our mild, wet winters are what they loathe. I think this species would be adaptable in summer-rain areas given cold winters. I have also tried *E. grandiflorum* subsp. *grandiflorum* (the form previously known as variety *pallidum*) and *E. purpurascens* with the same results.

Erythronium californicum and *E. multiscapoideum* have done well in the light shade of trees. They have been planted both where they get some summer watering and where they get none. All have done well, but those planted where they were dry did best.

The very restricted *Erythronium helenae* grows on serpentine; it is distinguished from *E. californicum* by its brilliant yellow anthers. I have grown this species only in dry places, where it has done well.

Erythronium tuolumnense often grows in large clumps with as many as 20 flowering stems. It is found on north slopes in rich soil with a thick layer of humus from the oaks and pines overhead, where it is completely dry all summer. If we bring these plants into cultivation, however, we must give them water, or they will dry up and die.

Originally published in Alpines of the Americas: Report of the First Interim International Conference *(1976), now out of print. This article is reprinted here for its excellent coverage of information not otherwise available in* Bulletin *articles.*

Calochortus: Why Not Try Them?

BOYD C. KLINE

Why not grow calochortuses as well as tulips or daffodils? In dry country you won't have to worry about watering in the summer, as you would with some other bulbs. Common garden bulbs appear in early spring, but calochortuses bloom later, giving you marvelous color for months after other bulbs are gone. Here in Medford, Oregon, they start to bloom in late April or May, and different species continue to August. If you have a collection, you will have bloom all summer long.

I grow calochortuses in the open ground of my garden, 150 miles/ 240 km inland from the Pacific Ocean. Here we have no summer rains, or at most scattered showers which pass quickly and never saturate the ground. I grow many species from seed, leaving the seedlings in the seed pot for two summers. The pots of newly germinated seed are sunk to the rim in sand and kept thoroughly shaded their first summer, so that they do not get completely baked. Calochortuses send up only one thin leaf the first year. As summer goes on, the tiny plants go dormant. Don't worry; just give the pots complete drainage, shade them well, and don't water them much. I water seedlings slightly all year so they do not dry out completely.

Calochortuses do not like pots, so after the plants have gone dormant late in their second season I plant them out in the garden. Alternatively, right after the new leaves appear in March or April, I line them out in a row in a nursery bed, where they remain until they bloom. When the first flowers appear, I place a marker next to each plant to mark the spot. After they go dormant, I transplant them to their permanent position in the garden.

Perhaps the most common reason given for not growing calochortuses is the length of time from seed to flowering plant. Most species take 5 to 7 years to reach blooming size, although a few bloom in 3 years. In my experience, few of these plants increase much vegetatively in cultivation. *Calochortus luteus* and *C. venustus* are the most vigorous in this respect, while most other species remain as solitary bulbs.

Fully mature plants do not require any shade. We have hot summers and grow them in full sun. During the growing season calochortuses can take about as much water as you can give them, but as soon as the flower buds begin to show color, it is very important not to water any more. Let the plants dry out completely. I used to grow calochortuses in pure sand with good success, but then we had several summers with long periods of 100°F/38°C weather, and they seemed to suffer. Now I grow them in a mixture of sand and loam with a lot of red serpentine soil added. (Serpentine is a metamorphic rock, very common in the coastal ranges of Oregon and California, which has a high concentration of magnesium and other metals. Many plants find serpentine quite toxic, but almost all calochortuses love it.)

I ensure perfect drainage by layering a mixture of 4 to 5 inches/10 to 13 cm of soil mix over 6 inches/15 cm of pure sand. The bulbs are usually planted about 3 inches/8 cm deep in the soil. I like to mulch the bed with conifer needles to keep the soil somewhat cooler and retain a little moisture in the summer months. I have a number of deodar cedar trees nearby, which shed a lot of needles.

Where do calochortuses grow in nature? Many species grow on serpentine ridges, and many in grasslands or sagebrush, with few other flowering plants in evidence.

I grow about 30 kinds of calochortus. Here are some of the species with which I have had success. Each seems to have an internal clock that specifies a different period of bloom.

Cat's-ears

In this group of species the inner surface of the petal is covered with a coat of fine hairs, and so they are commonly referred to as "cat's-ears." These species are relatively easy to grow and would be good for beginners to try.

Calochortus tolmiei is one of the first to bloom. The flower is usually pale lavender, although in different areas there are many different shades; on the coast it is deep purple. This species is closely related to *C. coeruleus*, with which I have not been so successful. In the mountains *C. coeruleus* is usually pale lavender and very hairy. Both species grow in rocky areas among grasses.

Calochortus elegans (Plate 20) is a tiny species that grows at 6000 to 7000 feet/1800 to 2100 meters in well-drained but heavy soil. The flowers vary from mountaintop to mountaintop: in the Siskiyou Mountains they tend to be pale lavender, and in the Cascades I have found deep purple forms with the flowers on 2-inch/5-cm stems and the leaves 8 inches/20 cm long.

Calochortus monophyllus, the "little yellow cat's-ear," is one of the first to bloom. I have found populations where the plants were only 3 inches/8 cm tall, but I have also found plants as tall as 8 or 9 inches/20 or 23 cm. This species usually occurs in shady places under pine and fir trees. It is found in California as far north as Mount Lassen. The soil of its native habitat is rather heavy but drains well. This species blooms in Medford the second week in May.

Calochortus subalpinus is a nice high-altitude species I have seen at McKenzie Pass near Bend, Oregon, at about 5000 feet/1500 meters. It grows in forest duff and very loamy soils. It is rather low, reaching only 8 inches/20 cm or so. The flower is a soft, creamy white with a few markings inside. It is supposed to bloom in August, but I went over to collect seed in September this year and found it still in flower.

Calochortus coxii is a very short species, 6 to 10 inches/15 to 25 cm tall, sometimes called the "upright cat's-ear." The blossom is creamy white with very beautiful purplish markings in the throat. A Mr. Cox from Canyonville first found it and thought it an unusual form of *C. tolmiei,* blooming very late. The botanists he consulted thought that it was unremarkable, but later it was studied and published as a new species by Frank Callahan, an Oregon seedsman.

Globe Tulips and Fairy Lanterns

This group of only five calochortuses is utterly different from the cat's-ears. The pendulous flowers hang down like Chinese lanterns, while the cat's-ears have flowers held upright like tulips. The entire group blooms early in the calochortus season, starting in May most years. I grow all of these in the open, and they all seem to like serpentine. This group does most of its growing in the wet winter season of the Mediterranean climate, and perhaps for that reason these species seem to be more difficult to grow in areas where winters are severe; some may also be cold-tender.

Calochortus amabilis (Plate 21) is one of the Chinese lanterns, with round yellow balls of bloom. It is usually found on yellow clay soils in deep grass along the back roads of California. It can be from 8 to 14 inches/20 to 35 cm tall. *Calochortus amoenus* (Plate 19) is similar, but usually creamy white, although there is also a red form. *Calochortus albus* has a pure white flower distinguished by the shape of the gland. *Calochortus pulchellus* has much larger flowers, twice the size of *C. amabilis,* of a beautiful greenish-yellow.

PLATE 1. *Hulsea nana* (John Andrews)

PLATE 2. *Gentiana newberryi*
(Panayoti Kelaidis)

PLATE 3. *Fritillaria affinis*
(William Jennings, NARGS Archives)

PLATE 4.
Iris missouriensis
(Shan Cunningham)

PLATE 5. *Trillium rivale*
(Jay Lunn)

PLATE 6. *Eriogonum ovalifolium*
(Margaret Williams)

PLATE 7. *Anemone multifida*
(Shan Cunningham)

PLATE 8. *Cypripedium montanum*
(NARGS Archives)

PLATE 9. *Fritillaria atropurpurea*
(Shan Cunningham)

PLATE 10. *Primula suffrutescens* (Jay Lunn)

PLATE 11. *Cassiope mertensiana* (Ronald Taylor)

PLATE 12. *Kalmia polifolia* (Lawrence Mellichamp)

PLATE 13.
Penstemon newberryi
(NARGS Archives)

PLATE 14. *Ranunculus eschscholtzii*
(John Andrews)

PLATE 15. *Astragalus coccineus* (Boyd Kline)

PLATE 16. *Cheilanthes gracillima*
(Bonnie Brunkow)

PLATE 17. *Erythronium montanum*
(David Dobak)

PLATE 18. *Erythronium oregonum*
(David Dobak)

PLATE 19. *Calochortus amoenus*
(John Erwin)

PLATE 20. *Calochortus elegans* (John Erwin)

PLATE 21. *Calochortus amabilis* (John Erwin)   PLATE 22. *Calochortus greenei* (John Erwin)

PLATE 23. *Iris innominata* (Lewis Lawyer)

PLATE 24. *Lewisia rediviva* (Joel Spingarn)

PLATE 25. *Lewisia stebbinsii* (Sean Hogan)

PLATE 26. *Lewisia pygmaea*
(Shan Cunningham)

PLATE 27. *Lewisia tweedyi*
(Phil Pearson)

PLATE 28. *Penstemon davidsonii*
(NARGS Archives)

PLATE 29. *Dodecatheon alpinum*
(Jay Lunn)

PLATE 30. *Kalmiopsis leachiana* (Jay Lunn)

PLATE 31. *Lewisia leana* (John Erwin)

PLATE 32. *Penstemon rupicola* (Phil Pearson)

PLATE 33. *Eriogonum lobbii* (Ted Kipping)

PLATE 34. *Silene acaulis* (Ronald Taylor)

PLATE 35. *Kalmia microphylla* (Frederick Case, Jr.)

PLATE 36.
Penstemon fruticosus var. *serratus*
(Todd Boland)

PLATE 37. *Clematis columbiana*
(Phil Pearson)

PLATE 38. *Saxifraga bronchialis* (Todd Boland)

PLATE 39. *Oenothera caespitosa* (Shan Cunningham)

PLATE 40. *Lloydia serotina* (H. Lincoln Foster)

PLATE 41. *Eriogonum douglasii* (Phil Pearson)

PLATE 42. *Eriogonum thymoides* (Phil Pearson)

PLATE 43. *Viola trinervata* (Phil Pearson)

PLATE 44. *Fritillaria pudica* (Jay Lunn)

PLATE 45. *Claytonia megarhiza* (Coleman Leuthy)

PLATE 46. *Douglasia nivalis* (Phil Pearson)

PLATE 47. *Ranunculus glaberrimus* (Phil Pearson)

PLATE 48. *Pediocactus simpsonii* (Panayoti Kelaidis)

PLATE 49. *Campanula piperi* (Margaret Mulligan)

PLATE 50. *Anemone drummondii* (Ronald Taylor)

PLATE 51. *Castilleja rupicola* (Ronald Taylor)

PLATE 52. *Lupinus lepidus* var. *lobbii*
(Jay Lunn)

PLATE 53. *Draba paysonii*
(Phil Pearson)

PLATE 54. *Synthyris reniformis*
(Bonnie Brunkow)

PLATE 55. *Synthyris stellata*
(Bonnie Brunkow)

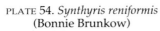

PLATE 56. *Parrya nudicaulis* (Jay Lunn)

PLATE 57. *Anemone narcissiflora* (Jay Lunn)

PLATE 58. *Eritrichium aretioides* (Crawford, NARGS Archives)

PLATE 59. *Campanula lasiocarpa* (Jay Lunn)

_____ Other Calochortuses _____

Calochortus clavatus is a very late blooming species, often flowering in August. It has upright, cup-shaped, deep yellow flowers with purple outer shading, and clavate, or club-shaped, hairs. Some have quite deep purple shading. I have never seen this species in the wild, but I have grown it from seed.

Calochortus bruneaunis superficially resembles *C. nuttallii* from farther east, but it has a number of consistent, minor differences in structure, and a consistently different chromosome count.

Calochortus eurycarpus is from Montana and Idaho south to Nevada. It grows 12 to 18 inches/30 to 45 cm tall. Its native habitat is heavy soil in meadows. It usually has pointed petals and blossoms a pale, silver white with dark markings at the base of the petals. It is a rather late bloomer, lasting into late July.

Calochortus greenei (Plate 22) grows on the tops of the Siskiyou Mountains and on the other side of the Klamath Basin, over an area of about 20 square miles/50 square km. The flowers are a beautiful reddish-lavender or sometimes purple, and the plants are from 10 to 16 inches/25 to 40 cm tall. It grows in a peculiar black adobe clay, in which the bulb can be 12 inches/30 cm or more deep, but I grow it in ordinary soil. It has a wide leaf and is a rather late bloomer, especially in the wild, beginning to flower in mid-July.

Calochortus gunnisonii grows and blooms nicely but does not increase much. I have never seen it in the wild, but it grows well in cultivation if you let it dry out. My form is a greenish-white, not particularly colorful. It blooms in July and August.

Calochortus howellii grows at lower elevations than do many other species—1300 to 2000 feet/400 to 600 meters—in various heavy soils, usually yellowish-brown clays. The bulb is not very deep. In the areas where it grows, the ground often cracks during the dry summers. The flower is silvery white with a black center. It blooms in late June or early July in the garden.

Calochortus kennedyi is regarded by many as the most beautiful "mariposa tulip." It grows primarily in the desert areas of Arizona and southern California. I used to think that the bright yellow form once distinguished as variety *munzii* grew in geographically distinct populations until I saw a large population where yellow flowers were mixed with vermilion-orange ones. Until 1989 I assumed that *C. kennedyi* was quite tender, but a pot full of seedlings came through last winter's 5°F/−15°C temperatures unscathed. This calochortus blooms from late April to June, depending on altitude.

Calochortus leichtlinii is another high-altitude species, growing from 8 to 12 inches/20 to 30 cm tall. It occurs at 5000 to 6000 feet/1500 to 1800 meters on high plateaus from Modoc County, California, south to Lake

Tahoe. It tends to grow in rocky meadows where the soil is a pumice sand that dries out quickly. In nature it blooms as late as August, and seed ripens in September, but in the garden it blooms the second week of July. It responds to the same cultural treatment as the other species.

Calochortus luteus is one of the elite species, an upright, golden yellow mariposa that grows 1 foot/30 cm or so tall, however deep the grass is. I know it from the California ranges around Clear Lake. It is relatively early in the garden, blooming around the first of June; in the wild it blooms around the first of May.

Calochortus macrocarpus is the giant of the genus. It needs to be staked in the garden, because it has a huge flower that makes the long stem flop over. The beautiful lavender to purple flowers, appearing in July, have a prominent green stripe down the center of the outside of each petal. The very narrow sepals stand out straight from the base of the flower like a clown's collar.

Calochortus nudus grows on flat sites where there is plenty of moisture. In the high mountains it can be found in valleys, often near bogs. Its entirely hairless flowers are brilliant lavender on stems from 3 to 9 inches/8 to 23 cm tall. The species is found from near Mount Shasta south to El Dorado County, California.

I have never seen *Calochortus nuttallii* in the wild. It usually flowers creamy white and has pointed petals. It is one of the most widespread species, occurring from California to Nebraska and from Canada practically to Mexico. *Calochortus aureus* is a closely related species from southern Utah and northern Arizona, once considered a variety of *C. nuttallii*. It has flowers of a pure, deep golden yellow.

Calochortus persistens is a rarity that only grows near Yreka, California. The flower is a gorgeous pink. I have to admit that it looks better in the wild than it does in captivity. In the wild it is only 6 to 8 inches/15 to 20 cm tall, but in the garden it can be 1 foot/30 cm tall, and the mid-July flowers are paler.

Calochortus plummerae is a late-blooming lavender-flowered species and is rather tall. It grows in the mountains of southern California.

I grew *Calochortus tiburonensis* from seed and it bloomed one year, but it hasn't bloomed in the 4 or 5 years since. It is the only species that does not bloom every year for me. I think it may not like the cold winters of Medford, so I cover my beds now to protect this and other tender species. The small, yellow-green flowers have many fine hairs. The species comes from the Tiburon Peninsula in San Francisco Bay and flowers in June.

Calochortus umpquaensis is found near Roseburg, Oregon. Botanists with the U.S. Forest Service consider it a form of *C. howellii*, but the latter has upright seedpods, and the former has pendant ones. The flower resembles that of *C. howellii* but is much larger. Its color is silvery white with a very black center. Frank Callahan has found three locations now in addition to the original site, so the species is not quite as rare as was once supposed. It is found on serpentine ridges on the east side of the Coast Range.

Calochortus uniflorus grows at 1500 feet/500 meters and is very much like *C. nudus*, although the plant grows only 3 to 4 inches/8 to 10 cm tall, and the leaf to 8 inches/20 cm long.

Calochortus venustus blooms a week or two before *C. vestae*. It seems most common in sandy grassland at elevations between 3000 and 5000 feet/900 and 1500 meters in both the Sierra Nevada and the Coast Range. This is unquestionably the most variable mariposa. It has a tremendous variety of colors that attract everybody, especially the crushed-strawberry reds and purple-reds. There are yellowish forms and creamy whites as well, with individual markings that vary tremendously.

Calochortus vestae is much like a late-blooming *C. venustus*, although its flowers are a more uniform white, with beautiful deep reddish-purple markings. It begins to flower in June but can start as late as July, and I've even seen it in bloom in August.

Growing lilies has long been my main horticultural hobby. I am also very interested in fritillaries, and from these two groups I have learned patience, so I no longer mind waiting years for bloom. I have always admired the calochortuses, and as I tried them over the years I have found that they are not as difficult as their reputation might make you think. I just kept trying them and found I could succeed. Perhaps you will, too. They are certainly a beautiful part of the western flora and very worthy plants to grow in the garden.

Originally published in the Bulletin of the American Rock Garden Society, *vol. 48, no. 1, pp. 25–29 (1990).*

Irises of the Pacific Coast

B. LEROY DAVIDSON

In articles in the *Bulletin of the American Rock Garden Society*, Henry Fuller (Fall 1963) and Mrs. Raleigh Harold (Winter 1964) praised the white forms of West Coast irises. I submit that good white forms are extremely lovely, but then, I nurse a fondness for all white flowers. I only wish it were possible for me to tell how to grow them, white and colored alike, in climates unlike that of their homeland, the Pacific slope of Washington, Oregon, and California. I might give some clues, however, by reviewing first the irises, and then the climate in which they have evolved. I will preface these remarks with the observation that the climates of England, Scotland, and at least parts of New Zealand and Australia are to their liking, to the extent that in these places self-sown seedlings may occur in gardens.

It seems that cold-tenderness limits the distribution of *Iris douglasiana* to the central coastal area of Oregon and southward. In the southern portion of its range along the Pacific shore, the species apparently is denied success below the general vicinity of Monterey Bay, California, by the extreme drought of the summers. It may grow throughout a mild winter with repeated warm and cold cycles but is severely injured by hard freezes. In areas where it usually survives winter in a dormant condition, it is less subject to injury. Thus it appears to be a plant for moderate climates with winter conditions that do not induce it to break dormancy prematurely. White forms are not unknown; I have four in my garden, two of my own collecting.

Of the other Pacific Coast species, only *Iris munzii*, which comes from a very small warm area at the base of the Sierra Nevada in south-central California, is limited for garden use by its tenderness. It is well known in cultivation for yielding remarkable true blue colors in its hybrids.

This leaves us about 10 species or subspecies, some more beautiful and useful than others. *Iris tenax* may be the most worthy of trial in really cold climates; it is the northernmost in natural distribution of this closely related group, and it loses its leaves in complete winter dormancy—the only fully deciduous species of this section. (There are two western species placed in other sections, considered later in this article—*I. missouriensis* and *I. tenuis*.)

Iris tenax comes in both purple and yellow color forms; the latter was once known as *I. gormanii*. Although the yellow color is not as deep as it is in *I. innominata*, its best forms are just as lovely. Where both color forms of *I. tenax* interbreed, in nature or in gardens, a pleasing array of "art shades" results. In Washington County, Oregon, just west of Portland, we find every color form from white through yellow to pale blue, lavender, orchid, lilac-pink, raspberry, and fuchsia-purple, with or without contrasting deeper markings, besides the yellow median lines usual to these species. In general, *I. tenax* becomes deeper in its purple tones the farther south it is found; in the southern Willamette Valley and in the Umpqua drainage, both in Oregon, there are fewer orchid shades and more deep purples—even some pansy-black. It is perhaps significant that white irises are not unusual in the northern part of the species' range in Washington but are quite rare in the southern part.

Iris chrysophylla, rather widespread in western Oregon, is somewhat more of a mountain plant. It has evergreen leaves, ordinarily protected from winter cold by heavy snow. This species is limited in color to near-white and pale yellow; in the southern populations the falls are heavily marked with deeper yellow or brown. The ranges of *I. chrysophylla* and *I. tenax* merge in many areas, and lovely hybrids have been found, some exceeding either species in beauty. Some have color patterns not usual in either parent, such as bicolors and white with orchid standards and heavy butterfly-wing patterns on the falls.

Probably *Iris innominata* (Plate 23) has elicited more interest than all the other Pacific Coast irises combined since its official "discovery" in about 1930, and its immediate adoption as the darling of its kind. Until the construction of highways through the mountains of southwestern Oregon, this part of the state was accessible mainly by boat along the coastline. It is in the previously unfrequented high, inland areas that *I. innominata* is found, away from the fog belt in areas with cold winters and hot summers. It comes in both yellow and purple shades, with a great array of intermediate and blended colors. Its yellows vary from lemon and pale primrose to deep egg-yolk orange. Some wild populations are very mixed and do not have the charm of either the pure purple or the yellow colonies; calico coloring does not become them at all. This species enters into all the hybrid strains generally known, usually in combination with *I. douglasiana*. The glowing color of *I. innominata*, the width of its flower parts, and its indefinable charm endear it to all iris-lovers. There is at least one white form known, as well as several near-whites with large yellow spots.

Very similar to the yellow form of *Iris innominata* is *I. bracteata*, found even farther inland in southwestern Oregon, nearly confined to Josephine County in an area of extremely hot summers and cold winters. This comes only in yellow, with the falls veined, ordinarily in brown, as are most yellow forms of *I. innominata*. However, *I. bracteata* is about twice the size and height, with coarser evergreen foliage. Its tousled clumps are no garden asset.

Farther south on the dry side of the redwood belt of northern California's coastal mountains, *Iris purdyi* makes its home. Its long-tubed, rather flat flowers occur in both orchid and pale yellow forms. Nearby, but in more extreme conditions of heat and cold, *I. tenuissima*, a taller look-alike of *I. chrysophylla*, populates the mountains and canyons of inland northern California, west of the Cascade-Sierra axis. It has a narrow-petaled, spidery flower, but a clump in blossom is very graceful.

Another California species is the variable *Iris macrosiphon*, which can exist in nature in the hardest adobe soil in the baking sun of summer. It comes in a pale yellow form, but its best forms are the purples and rich deep blues. The areas where yellow and blue grow together produce another of those art colonies where smoked salmon, peach, and pearl-gray forms have been discovered. The finest are the intense deep blue and violet forms from Sonoma County. This species has handsome, grassy, tough, gray-blue foliage. It is not successful when moved to a cool, moist climate, even though it is evergreen. It tolerates a few degrees of frost.

Iris fernaldii is a pale yellow species from a similar area, although it prefers to grow in the light shade of bracken and deciduous oaks rather than in the open sun. Since most of its growth is in a period when neither of these companions is casting much shade, the oak not leafing out until late spring, the shade acts more as protection from the extreme drought and heat of summer during the resting stage of the plant, and may not be necessary to the plant's cultivation elsewhere.

The charming pale yellow *Iris hartwegii* is found on the lower slopes of the Sierras and in the foothills; good forms are among the loveliest of the irises. It should be winter-hardy and drought-resistant. A form found only farther south in the general area of the San Bernardino Mountains at 6000 feet/1800 meters and above is now known as *I. hartwegii* subsp. *australis*, and has in the past been called *I. tenax australis* and *I. parishii*. It is in general appearance like *I. tenax*, but not as pretty. It might take to cultivation in an area where *I. tenax* would not succeed. This completes the list of the major species of the group botanically termed the Californicae Apogon (nonbearded, rhizomatous) irises.

Iris missouriensis (Plate 4) and the plant once distinguished as *I. longipetala* belong to another group, series Longipetalae. The former is a deciduous meadow plant of the arid, intermountain western United

States. The latter, now considered the same species, is its stocky coastal form, which grows on hillsides and in meadows, wet in winter and spring and parched in summer. It has reversed the dormancy period of inland *I. missouriensis*, growing all winter in its frost-free climate and going completely dormant as soon as flowers and seed are past. Both forms are veined heavily with blue-violet on creamy-white ground, and albinos are known in both.

To the north, in Alaska and the Yukon Territory, the tall, soft-leaved purple *Iris setosa* is frequent in wet places that dry in summer. The unmistakable flower has three large falls and three standards so small they may seem absent altogether. This is the only *Iris* species found in both the Old and New worlds, occurring in Japan, Kamchatka, coastal Siberia, and Alaska, with a disjunct occurrence in easternmost Canada. Although from subarctic regions, it is quite suited to most temperate gardens if the soil does not bake. The smaller forms of the Laurentian variety *canadensis* (syn. *I. hookeri*) can be particularly appealing in the rock garden.

The last to be discussed is the most misunderstood of western irises, *Iris tenuis*. It is puzzling that this species was for a long time considered a member of the section Californicae; it is not at all similar and has recently been grouped with the eastern American *I. cristata* and *I. gracilipes* in section Lophiris. It is intermediate in appearance between these and the related Japanese species *I. tectorum*. The flower is white, with some lines of purple or brown. It runs by stolons, making large colonies in cool humus in the northern Cascades of Oregon, where it is endemic to only two river drainages. Although often seen in the shade of Douglas firs, it flowers better in more open sites such as clearcuts and roadsides.

The best way to understand how to grow these plants is to study their home environment. Where they have evolved to become among the most common wildflowers, there are two marked seasons: a wet, cold season, and a dry, hot one. A distribution map of their occurrence coincides with a similar map for the natural distribution of the coniferous forests of the same area. They enjoy the same soil and moisture conditions as firs (*Abies*), Douglas fir (*Pseudotsuga menziesii*), western cedar (*Thuja plicata*), and Port Orford cedar (*Chamaecyparis lawsoniana*). The coastal species will also be found with the beach pine (*Pinus contorta*, a moisture-loving species), redwood (*Sequoia sempervirens*), and Sitka spruce (*Picea sitchensis*). The dry, inland species of irises may be found in the pine belt with such species as digger pine (*Pinus sabiniana*) and the two yellow pines (*P. ponderosa* and *P. jeffreyi*). Like almost all irises, they like plenty of light and flourish best in the forest openings. In general, they grow in disintegrated mineral soils, often with a high percentage of coarse debris, gravelly and well-drained but high in humus, and slightly acid to neutral—never alkaline. Such soils are retentive of moisture, but the 3-month drought of summer makes it necessary for any plant to root deeply to survive.

Excess moisture is quickly drained away, usually very rapidly, because of the steepness of the terrain. Only the maritime *Iris douglasiana* and *I. missouriensis* will tolerate much standing water, and then only in the growing period; wetness during summer dormancy is as fatal to them as to the rest. These irises tolerate cold below 0°F/−18°C and heat above 110°F/43°C. *Iris bracteata* may survive the greatest extremes of any of the group. In general, the humidity is moderate to high in the growing season, except in the coldest part of the winter, and very low in summer. The fog belt along the coast is an exception to this, with constantly high humidity and cool temperatures.

I hope this will help make these charming plants easier to grow in gardens. Perhaps the prospect of their becoming good general plants for most climates lies with the plant breeders, who are hybridizing all the species and growing the resultant hybrids in a variety of climates, in the hope that tolerant strains may be developed. Toward this end many amateurs, as well as some professional breeders, are at work with them, both here and abroad. To the purist who would grow only nature's species, I would say that here at least is one case where there is a perfect excuse for tampering with nature's products.

I would now like to discuss my experience with some of the named forms or clones. Although these irises are easy from seed, perpetuation of selected superior clones is assured only by division, and this is certainly worth the time and trouble.

Do not divide to single "fingers" the tiny rhizomes of such species as *Iris tenax* and *I. innominata*; the husky-rhizomed *I. munzii* and *I. douglasiana* may be more safely broken down to single shoots. Food stored in the gnarled and knotted back portions of the older rhizome is necessary for the quick growth of the sturdy new roots essential to the successful establishment of divisions. Leave as much of the foliage as possible to manufacture food. I have learned, through the bitter experience of losing my choicest plants, never to lift an entire clump, but to take divisions from the perimeter, leaving the clump essentially undisturbed until the divisions have been established for a year.

Division of irises in the fall should not even be contemplated before a finger-examination around the clump shows that the white thong-roots are beginning to push out of the growing ends of the thickened, swollen rhizomes. These will be mainly at the very edge of the clump. The true dormant period of this group of irises, as with most irises, is in the summer, when the roots lose their plumpness, all top growth ceases, and the rhizomes become fat with promise. Transplanting must be done only during the period of active root growth, which may commence at the end of summer with the first fall rains, or under certain conditions not until mid-autumn, even early November. Success with growing divisions depends on conditions of moisture and temperature for several weeks following the dividing. Unless the new plant can make the necessary amount of root growth before winter, chances of its survival in the open are slim. If division must be delayed until mid-October, the plants may come through a mild winter, but the odds are against it, at least in the north. California gardeners, who have grown these irises far longer than most of us, advise fall division, but there they enjoy growing weather almost all winter.

In the Puget Sound climate of my own garden I prefer early spring. Root growth, slowed by winter, recommences as the top growth begins to lengthen. With proper care, division can be successful until the seed capsules are forming. As these ripen, the dormant period sets in, although leaves persist in their green, functional form and the plant does not appear dormant. One exception to this pattern of dormancy is *Iris tenax*, which is deciduous in winter and has a more complete dormant rest during its leafless period, but it can be divided in early fall or early spring as can the others.

To set a calendar date for spring division would be presumptuous: are any two springs ever the same? Certainly mid-April, in this area, would be safe, but if one could be positive in March that two or three weeks of warm days and frost-free nights would follow, then earlier division is to be preferred, though this would sacrifice the season's blossoming. Californians lose spring divisions because their hot, arid summer follows too soon. Whether in fall or spring, protect divisions from wind and heavy rain; excess moisture or soil drought, or desiccation of the foliage, can all lessen the plant's chances of survival. Of course, it is ideal to pot the divisions and carry them on in a lath house, frame, or cold house, with the well-rooted new individuals put in the garden later or shared with others.

Possibly the most favored of the many Pacific Coast iris clones in my garden, year after year, is Ruth Hardy's 'Valley Banner', a form of *Iris tenax* to all appearances, white with a sharp pattern of electric violet-blue over the falls in a butterfly-wing design; the standards are white with a few lines and shadings of the same violet in the midrib and to the base, and the style arms are brilliant red-purple. It is vigorous, floriferous, and quite surprisingly can duplicate itself (approximately) from self-pollinated seed. There are several superior albino *I. tenax* here; the finest for size of blossom, vigor, floriferousness, and substance has been named 'Bella Blanca'. Collected in Washington County, Oregon, this has produced offspring with well-branched flower stems when crossed with 'Agnes James', the well-known wild-collected albino *I. douglasiana*. A dainty white *I. tenax*, quite different in aspect, has been named 'Monday's Child', and it is indeed "fair of face." Zelne Quigley found and named it.

Among forms of *Iris innominata*, 'Rogue', selected by Marvin Black, is a warm white with a bright golden spot on the falls. Lee Lenz's innominata-like 'Santa Paula' is similar, but in two tints of yellow. Another innominata-like treasure is the reddest of several "red" irises in the garden, 'Hinges of Hades', displaying the blended fiery reds of molten metal.

Another favorite is a child of the bitoned *Iris douglasiana* that Eric Nies named 'Amiguita'. The fledgling, called 'Ami-Royale', is about half the size of the parent, but done in sharper contrasts of sky-blue and pansy-violet. It came here from the California garden of Helen and Dick Luhrson and is derived from 'Santa Paula' on the other side of the family. From another California garden, that of Marion Walker, came the douglasiana-like 'Ojai', a subtle, silky blend of ecru and palest lilac with a few accent lines of deep violet toward the midsection. This is for the larger garden, its douglasiana foliage being a bit coarse in a small place, but the flowers are elegant. Bob Nourse has sent for all to enjoy a fascinating novelty that he named 'Greenbriar Contrast', which appears to be a smaller or refined form of *I. douglasiana*. It is a rich jersey cream with the trinity of styles in the center a clear amethyst-lilac—a most beguiling flower.

These have been assembled with all the other Western irises, collected and garden-grown, as a focal point for study, propagation, and breeding in hopes of deriving a hybrid strain—perhaps a series of color strains—that will be easier to grow in a greater range of climates and conditions than are their wildflower ancestors. The first seed is to be offered through the Seed Exchange as the 'Rosedown strain of Pacifica irises'. Rosedown is the name of the garden; "Pacifica" is an allusion to the popular horticultural name for the section Californicae of the Apogon irises.

Seed sown in autumn germinates the following spring and flowers 2 years later. The soil should be a friable, well-drained mixture high in humus; the exposure should be open to the sun but protected from extremes of wind and temperature in cold climates. It is to be hoped that from these and similar efforts will come an easily grown strain so that everyone may enjoy these daintiest of irises.

Originally published in the Bulletin of the American Rock Garden Society, *vol. 22, no. 2, pp. 83–86 (1964). The final section, on propagation, appeared as a separate article under the title "Pacific Irises in Gardens" in vol. 23, no. 3, pp. 90–92 (1965). Comments on the first article by correspondents appeared in vol. 23, no. 1 (Winter 1965). Some material has been incorporated from another article by the same author, "Western American Irises" (vol. 40, no. 4, pp. 163–166, 1982).*

Lewisias of the Sierra Nevada

B. LEROY DAVIDSON

Roy Elliott, in his horticultural monograph (1966) of the genus *Lewisia*, complimented California and the Sierra Nevada by referring to Yosemite National Park as "the home of the *Lewisia*," because of the perhaps twenty-five taxa in the genus, no fewer than six are found within the park's boundaries, with a seventh just outside. Although this is numerically accurate, not one of these seven is among the great beauties of the clan, and some are only of botanical interest; in mass in the wild, however, each has its own individual if wan charm.

About a dozen taxa of the genus *Lewisia* are found within the Sierran Floristic Province, which includes the foothills as well as the towering peaks of the great mountain chain east of the Central Valley Floristic Province, from Plumas County south to Kern County—that is, from Mount Lassen south to where the Sierra Nevada diminishes into the east-west Tehachapi Range at the northern margin of southern California.

Included in the Sierran flora are lewisias of all sections of the genus, as classified by Brian Mathew (1989), except for the section Strophiolum (consisting of *Lewisia tweedyi*, recently placed in the genus *Cistanthe*). The sole member of Section Erocallis, the little carpeter *Lewisia triphylla*, occurs widely in vernally wet woodland in various exposures and elevations, particularly in the snowbed habitat, where it often disappears for the season within a few brief weeks of its emergence. A tiny thing, white or faintly blush and pretty enough en masse, it is easily overlooked, being both precocious and diminutive.

The vast uptilted block of the Sierra Nevada is some 400 miles/640 km in length and from 50 to 80 miles/80 to 129 km in width. It is principally a granitic mass but has certain other components, such as basalt and serpentine, and the northern segment is overlain by a dark metamorphic mantle that often resembles pudding stone. During the five major periods of the Ice Age, the greater part of the Sierra was at one time or another deeply buried; only the highest of its spires escaped as nunataks projecting out of the ice, thus preserving at least a portion of the plant life.

These valley glaciers were not as cold as their polar counterparts. Some were as enormous as the one that gouged out Lake Chelan trench in Washington to the north, well over a mile/1600 meters in depth. The largest Sierran glacier appears to have occupied the gorge of the present Tuolumne River, at least 60 miles/96 km in length. Throughout the West, most of the precipitation comes in the cooler months, and summers may be very parched, although both precipitation and temperature vary a great deal from place to place. Snowdrifts may persist for most or all of the summer, and there are also a number of small valley glaciers remaining. The weather gods are whimsical: following several recent drought years and consequent water rationing, more than 12 inches/30 cm of rain fell on one coastal point within a 32-hour period; in the mountains, snowfall was proportionately heavy.

Section Rediviva is represented, of course, by the bitterroot, *Lewisia rediviva* (Plate 24), particularly in the smaller, depauperate phase known as variety *minor* (apparently more an environmental than a genetic phase). This looks much like the typical Montana bitterroot except for being paler—white or ivory to pale pink. In the Sierra it dwells in the foothills. *Lewisia disepala* is smaller by far, and distinct in its fewer petals and its pair of enormously exaggerated, winglike sepals cupping the exquisite white, lilac, or mauve flowers. It is seen on granite screes in the vicinity of Yosemite Valley, but only by hikers who come early while the snow still lies in patches on the slopes; it somehow reminds one of a carpet of crocuses.

Sierran lewisias of the section Pygmaea number about half a dozen, some obviously quite distinct and others not at all so. Among Californian botanists it has been traditional to consider *Lewisia pygmaea* (Plate 26) and *L. nevadensis* a pair of similar species, although outside the state, particularly to the north, they are not so easily separable. The former is supposedly marked by sepals that are rounded and glandular-serrulate, while sepals in the other tend to be more sharply acute and quite entire. Margaret Williams (1971) has also noted that blossoms of the latter are subregular or out-of-round, quite oval in outline. The botanist William Weber (1987) maintained that in western Colorado these two are recognizable both morphologically and ecologically, with *L. pygmaea* growing in open, stony alpine meadowlands, and *L. nevadensis* less frequent and lower, on the plateaus. He felt, as did P. A. Rydberg, that the bitterroot is the only proper *Lewisia*, and referred other taxa to the genus *Oreobroma*, which was merged by other botanists into the genus *Lewisia* as long ago as 1897.

Within the high cirques and adjacent nunatak plateaus of the Sierra, the tundra supports the tiny, bright pink, candy-striped *Lewisia sierrae*, with sepals almost but not quite entire. Adjacent to this, particularly on unglaciated plateaus, *L. pygmaea* var. *glandulosa* is an equally tiny plant, with flowers rose-red, veined, or white; the purple-stalked glands on the sepals are particularly noticeable. Similar developments in some other high places in *Lewisia*-land have been described and given specific or varietal status in the past, but later submerged.

Lewisia longipetala has oblong pink petals and purple-stalked glands that make it one of the most distinct of section Pygmaea. It occurs in the north-central Sierra at considerable heights, often with two or three other members of this moisture-loving group; such communities can present some problems of identity. The cytotaxonomist G. L. Stebbins (1968), however, has maintained that they all remain constant, with no interbreeding. Of the Sierran *L. pygmaea* relatives, *L. kelloggii* is most distinct: a compact plant with lanceolate or spatulate leaves, at least as neat as *L. brachycalyx* (which does occur in California, but only south of the Sierra). *Lewisia kelloggii* is known also in Idaho in occasional disjunct colonies; both it and *L. brachycalyx* are white or occasionally pink.

Then, of course, there are the species of section Cotyledon, usually spoken of as evergreen lewisias. *Lewisia cotyledon* itself does not occur in the Sierra, although it does come near in the form of variety *howellii* (found between Mount Shasta and Mount Lassen in the McCloud and Pitt River canyons). Within a high and remote basin in Fresno County in the central Sierra exists an oddly disjunct colony of the quill-shaped rosettes that typify *L. leana* (Plate 31), otherwise restricted to the Klamath Floristic Province; its flowers are reminiscent of the more northern *L. columbiana*. Rather nearby from a mapper's viewpoint, Elliott's seventh species, *L. congdonii*, forms infrequent but extensive colonies at high elevations just outside Yosemite National Park. This species has flowers very similar to those of *L. leana* and is curiously deciduous by flowering time: the large fleshy leaves on distinct petioles turn a bright chamois yellow as they collapse—the oddball in this otherwise evergreen company. Farther north still in the Sierra, in a few remote canyons, are found *L. cantelovii* and the similar *L. serrata*, both with flowers remarkably like those of *L. columbiana* and rosettes of plane foliage, rather leathery and intricately cut and toothed to form plants of great attractiveness. In *L. serrata* the leaves are even toothier, frequently compoundly so.

Though brief, these notes may prove an aid to quick identification of any lewisia encountered within the Sierra Nevada. A hand glass will be a great aid to enjoying their intricacies and delicacies, as well as to noting how nearly alike they are, aside from some obvious distinctions.

Bibliography

Elliott, Roy C. 1966. "The Genus *Lewisia*." *Bulletin of the Alpine Garden Society* 34, 1–76.

Mathew, Brian. 1989. *The Genus Lewisia*. Kew: Royal Botanic Gardens.

Stebbins, G. Ledyard. 1968. "A Lost Species Rediscovered." *Journal of the California Native Plant Society* 4.5, 1–3.

Weber, William A. 1987. *A Colorado Flora*. Boulder: Colorado Associated University Press.

Williams, Margaret. 1971. "Rock Garden Plants from Western North America." In *The World of Rock Plants*. Woking, England: Alpine Garden Society.

Originally published in the Bulletin of the American Rock Garden Society, *vol. 48, no. 1, pp. 13–16 (1990).*

Lewisias in Cultivation

SEAN HOGAN

The first modern record of lewisia cultivation is of *Lewisia rediviva* (Plate 24). The plant was collected in Montana on the return trip of the Lewis and Clark Expedition of 1804–1806. Several years later, the Philadelphia botanist Frederick Pursh removed the dried plant from the press as he prepared to describe it and noticed life remaining in the succulent root. A few days after it was planted, rice-grainlike leaves appeared. The cultural requirements were not known and the plant soon died, but the brief reappearance of leaves resulted in the specific epithet *rediviva*, meaning "coming back to life." Because Meriwether Lewis was the first to collect specimens of the genus, it was named for him.

The beautiful rosettes of *Lewisia cotyledon* were first introduced to cultivation from the remote regions of the Siskiyou Mountains nearly a century later. Other species also made brief appearances in pots, but it was not until the late 1920s that catalogs began to offer enough lewisias to make the most easily propagated species—and unfortunately also the most easily collected—relatively readily available in the United States and Britain. The few species to be widely distributed became instant favorites among rock gardeners and collectors of succulents.

Even now some of the choicest species are rare in cultivation. This is not due merely to another of Murphy's laws, which states that the most beautiful members of a genus are the most frustrating to grow. Successful cultivation of lewisias can be rather complex because of the great variation in climate and substrate of the natural habitats in which they grow; however, with a basic feel for the native ecology and a few reliable horticultural techniques, a gardener can grow any of the species to perfection.

Little literature on the cultivation of the genus appeared even after its horticultural popularization in the 1920s and 1930s. The catalogs of early nurserymen and collectors in southwestern Oregon and northern California offered some tips but were often vague. More writing has appeared subsequently, beginning with Roy Elliott's monograph in 1966. Brian Mathew's monograph, *The Genus Lewisia*, clarifies the taxonomic problems of the genus, so I will concentrate here on a few observations concerning the dos, don'ts and whys of lewisia culture.

Lewisias fall loosely into three groups, the sections Cotyledon, Pygmaea, and Rediviva, each named for a typical member of that section. All have in common a need for winter and spring moisture with immediate drying afterward to facilitate summer dormancy. They vary, however, in the timing of dormancy, in tolerance for exposure to drying wind and sun, and in preferred soil type. Let's look first at the conditions under which these plants grow in nature.

The Cotyledon group is the largest and is confined to the areas most affected by Pacific moisture. Although the need for a dry summer cannot be overlooked, the growth period can be extended to span most of the summer if temperatures are cool (below 78°F/25°C) and the plants are not allowed to become completely dry. *Lewisia columbiana* and its varieties *rupicola* and *wallowensis* are possibly the most adaptable to moister conditions, because they grow from the coastal mountains of British Columbia to Oregon, and east to the Montana-Idaho divide. *Lewisia cotyledon* of northwestern California and southwestern Oregon is one of the parents of most horticultural crosses. Its varieties *fimbriata*, *howellii*, and *purdyi* are the easiest to grow, while varieties *heckneri* and *cotyledon* are more susceptible to rot. All grow on very rocky ridge tops that often catch the fog, or on steep cliffs near flowing water. *Lewisia cotyledon* var. *heckneri*, for example, often grows in horizontal cracks in metamorphosed shale and folds its leaves out and down over its crown, shading the easily baked center and guiding water away with the help of upward-pointing teeth. Even with these adaptations, a single summer rain can kill the plants in the wild. *Lewisia leana* (Plate 31) is another ridgetop plant; it often grows and hybridizes with *L. cotyledon*.

Lewisia cantelovii and the similar *L. serrata*, as well as *L. congdonii*, are Sierran foothills plants. They are most often found growing on steep north-facing cliffs dripping with water from October through April. *Lewisia congdonii* is the only deciduous member of the Cotyledon group. Until recently, many botanists assumed it was evergreen and were frustrated by their inability to find it during the summer months. It can hold its leaves most of the summer if given cool moist conditions, but it never does so in nature. As with most of its kin, a fine line exists between the well-pampered plant and the compost pile.

Lewisia tweedyi (recently renamed *Cistanthe tweedyi*; Plate 27), distributed from central Washington to extreme southern British Columbia, has long been considered the most temperamental species. The first instinct of growers, when the plant seems to be in trouble, is to decrease water. A closer look at the conditions of central Washington dictates different treatment. Although the summers are dry, the various soils derived from sandstone, granite, basalt, or volcanic ash are deep and well drained, but often hold moisture just under the surface. The plants' crowns usually face downhill, avoiding stagnant water, but the constant availability of some moisture ensures healthy roots on these fast-growing, naturally short-lived beauties. Damp but not saturated conditions in winter are preferred, with as little fluctuation in soil moisture as possible. Early dry spells send the plants into premature dormancy, promoting the chance of rot upon subsequent application of water.

The Pygmaea group occupies the high country, often growing above timberline. Frozen below a deep layer of snow for up to 10 months a year, they are the true alpines of the genus. *Lewisia pygmaea* (Plate 26) is the most widespread of all lewisias, extending from the McKinley Range in southern Alaska to northern Mexico. The entire Pygmaea group is summer-deciduous and summer-dormant and inhabits areas that are vernally wet. Plants such as *L. kelloggii, L. triphylla, L. sierrae, L. pygmaea* and its varieties, and to a lesser extent *L. nevadensis* and *L. stebbinsii* (Plate 25), often emerge downhill from snowbanks and sit in running water for most of their growth period. At the highest elevations this might not be until the end of August, when frost has already begun. At lower elevations the plants may emerge as early as April or May and become dormant at spring's end, remaining so until moisture returns in the fall. Careful attention should be given to the timing of dormancy in cultivation. Plants from different areas in the wild—even plants of the same species—can begin dormancy weeks apart.

Lewisia oppositifolia is a low-elevation exception to this group of mostly alpine plants, growing in the Illinois Valley just north of the California-Oregon border. It grows as low as 975 feet/300 meters in eroded serpentine. It emerges about the beginning of November, after the first rains and cool weather. *Lewisia brachycalyx*, although a high-elevation plant from the Southwest, also emerges in the late fall and grows through the entire winter whenever the temperature is above freezing. Watering can generally begin early in the fall, with the first green shoot being the "go" sign.

The final group consists of *Lewisia rediviva* (Plate 24) and two obscure plants that are barely known. *Lewisia rediviva* inhabits a vast area from southern British Columbia to southern California and east to the Rockies; it is variable in flower color and form. The plants in the rain shadow of the Sierra Nevada and Cascade Mountains exist in areas that may receive less than 6 inches/15 cm of precipitation annually. In contrast, some of the higher Californian serpentine-substrate populations are soaked by more than 40 inches/100 cm of rain. All are adapted to areas where the first frost, or the first diurnal temperatures averaging below

50°F/10°C, coincide with the first rains. Even in its native habitat, hot weather after the beginning of cool-season growth can rot the plants.

The other two members of this group, *Lewisia disepala* and *L. maguirei*, adhere to a similar regime. They are montane and adapted to thundershowers. *Lewisia maguirei* is a limestone endemic of central Nevada. It looks much like *L. rediviva* but has as many as three flowers per stem, rather than one. It hangs onto gently sloping scree at 6335 to 7800 feet/ 1930 to 2400 meters. *Lewisia disepala* turns the tops of several granitic domes in the southern Sierra Nevada pink in April and May as the snow recedes. At one low-elevation site at about 3900 feet/1200 meters, these little jewels are the first of the spring flowers in early March. They blossom happily, sitting soaked with water in shallow pans in the granite. By May this colony must be found by feeling for the dormant crowns under the fine gravel. In cultivation they can remain nearly evergreen. Because they are shallow-rooted, they should be kept in the shade when they are allowed to go dry, to avoid loss of soil humidity.

There are as many philosophies on how to grow alpines in containers as there are people who grow them. Lewisias, like so many other tricky plants, respond to certain methods of treatment that at first may seem complicated but are actually rather simple. Each revelation results from the loss of many plants, and with each new disaster even the most hard-won theories of cultivation are subject to change.

Constant fall-to-spring moisture is essential for proper growth, as all lewisias are cool-season growers. Moisture may be given beginning in midwinter to members of the Pygmaea group that are frozen under snow in nature and therefore remain dry most of the cold season, as well as to other species that grow in areas where temperatures regularly drop below 5°F/−14°C. Most species of *Lewisia* prefer to be wet almost the entire season of active growth. Although succulent, they need not dry out between waterings. As the warmth of late spring induces dormancy, the water must be turned off for all but the most vigorous members of the Cotyledon group. The soil should dry but should not bake. Adequate soil humidity can be maintained by keeping direct sun off the pots and giving the general area an ever-so-slight splash of moisture every few days.

Cool temperatures combined with bright light are perfect for lewisias, but few growers can achieve this in cultivation. Plants grown with too much shade will lose compactness and red tones in the leaves; flowering will be reduced as well. On the Pacific slope, where winter sun is never strong, lewisias benefit from full exposure between the fall and spring equinoxes, and they prefer a cover of 40-percent shade cloth during the summer months. As most species are not in growth at that time, even more shade does not hurt. In the open rock garden, where the mass of the soil keeps temperature and moisture levels more constant than can be achieved in a pot, even the more sun-sensitive plants such as

Lewisia cantelovii can take a lot of light. Placement on an open north exposure or on the north side of a rock is best.

For most lewisias, too much water during the winter growth period is scarcely possible. Any combination of ample moisture, too much shade, and too heavy feeding can produce either robust, overly plump plants that some term "cabbages," or leggy, spindly plants. These both rot easily because of their bloated leaves and stems, and dormancy is often fatal to them. Especially in summer heat, full sun can overheat the center of the rosette. If any moisture is present, the plant becomes more susceptible to the invasion of soil-borne fungi. In general, lack of water simply reduces the size of the leaves and slows growth. Only in spring can drought cause the loss of the season's flowers or seriously damage the plant.

Soil mix and potting are always subjects for friendly argument. It is important to provide a situation where excess water is drained away but some moisture is held. Lewisias do need good drainage, but every time they dry out when they shouldn't, the roots die back. Then the plants have to be brought back out of dormancy, expending energy on new roots and setting back growth. The second principle is the use of almost entirely mineral soil, with no more than 10 to 15 percent well-rotted organics. Most commercial organic mixes use raw wood products, which are often dyed to appear rotted. These might be fine for begonias, but the toxins released by fungi and other factors are often more than lewisias can handle. Any root dieback is a perfect place for rot to enter. The best potting mixes for lewisias consist of about 40 percent coarse grit (such as quarter-inch/6-mm crushed stone, pumice, or expanded shale), 25 percent builder's sand, 25 percent lava fines or decomposed granite, and the rest a well-rotted compost. The soil should be very gritty on the surface, becoming denser toward the bottom of the pot. The addition of some clay aggregates or a couple of crystals of soil polymer can help with moisture retention. The object is to have the constant moisture necessary for vigorous growth but to keep that moisture away from the plant's crown. Narrow, deep pots are preferred, as they drain more rapidly than shallow, wide pots but retain moisture near the bottom, remaining cooler. Several light feedings in the cool season are also beneficial.

Finally, when a flourishing assortment of these plants once thought so difficult to grow has been achieved, the instinct to share with a friend will arise. Better yet, increasing the number of these plants in cultivation will lead to a reduction of pressure on wild populations. Cuttings are easy once the plants are large enough. Most members of the Cotyledon group form offsets, and these can be removed and rooted easily. Spring is the most logical time for this propagation technique, as the warmer soil induces quick root formation, and lower humidity allows both surfaces of the cut to dry quickly. A little sulfur or fungicide is good insurance against rot. Root cuttings can work, too, especially with the Rediviva group. If you sever a large root near the caudex and lift the cut end above the soil, new rosettes will often form in time at the cut end.

For plants that remain single rosettes, seed is the obvious solution. Cold stratification of at least 30 days is preferred, but seeds in nature can germinate their first autumn. Storage in the refrigerator may lengthen the viability of lewisia seed. Seeds sown in the fall have the longest growth period and therefore the best success. The seed should be placed on the soil surface with a light covering, and the soil should then be soaked and chilled. My method involves putting the flat of freshly sown seed on the roof of the car outside on chilly November evenings and allowing the soil to freeze. This does have a few dangers, such as forgetting the seed when leaving for work the next morning! Any cold area outside will do. If no November frost occurs in your area, lewisias sprout very well in the refrigerator at a couple of degrees above freezing. It is best to remove the seed within a week or so of germination to a cool, light spot. With most species it is possible to have flowering plants in one season with a little pampering. Even growing from seed can be a tricky method of propagation in some species of the Pygmaea group, such as *Lewisia kelloggii*; germination is sparse and may take two or three seasons.

Lewisias have had a fairly short history of cultivation, and there is a lot to learn. They may not become the next supermarket primroses, but they will be seen in a lot more nurseries and gardens in the future.

Originally published in the Bulletin of the American Rock Garden Society, *vol. 48, no. 1, pp. 47–52 (1990).*

Trilliums of the West

EDITH L. DUSEK

Casual spring visitors to western woodlands are apt to call one of the showiest plants there the "Easter lily"; to botanists, it is *Trillium ovatum*. Similar but not identical to the eastern *T. grandiflorum*, it has equally wide distribution. Found from California to Canada and eastward into Montana and Colorado, it is so polymorphic that some botanists have separated it into several species; others retain the single species.

Familiarity with *Trillium ovatum* over much of its range leads me to believe that despite great variation, most of these plants belong to one species. An exception is the extremely dwarf plant known as *T. hibbersonii*, which has been variously regarded as a separate species or simply a form of *T. ovatum*. My extensive study of trilliums both in the field and in the garden makes me feel that these little plants differ in too many ways, both in morphology and in their inability to cope with environmental variations, for them to be classed as *T. ovatum*. Unlike its robust cousin, *T. hibbersonii* has a very restricted range and time of growth, flowering, and fruiting. Morphologically, the production of the pigment anthocyanin occurs at a different time, and the fruit resembles none of the variants seen in *T. ovatum*.

In marked contrast, *Trillium ovatum* can put up with a wide variety of conditions, and it can remain above ground for as much as 8 months. If it does not thrive, it can at least endure for years until conditions are favorable once more. No one knows how long individual plants can live, but by counting the annual rings on the rhizome one can gain some idea of a plant's age. Ages of 40 years are not uncommon; I have examined plants whose ring count exceeded 75, and that with generous portions of the older end of the rhizome obviously lost to time.

After studying *Trillium ovatum* in the field over a considerable part of its range, I have found that plants in one stand may be markedly uniform, while a nearby stand in similar conditions may display a great range of forms. Many compare favorably with the best forms of eastern *T. grandiflorum*. The appearance of an individual plant results from the interaction of growing conditions and its genetic inheritance. Within limits determined by the latter, improved conditions will result in marked improvement in appearance.

Of all western *Trillium* species, *T. ovatum* displays the widest tolerance of varied growing conditions. Its distribution within its range reflects the amount of available soil moisture: too little, and the plants remain small and may not bloom. They may even remain below ground for a year or more. The other limiting factor is shade; the plants do not thrive in dense shade under conifers, where the soil is excessively dry. The vast majority of wild plants have only one stem. That this reflects a battle for survival becomes obvious when plants removed to the bounty of a garden form large clumps which can be divided with no trouble.

When the weather is warm and sunny, the flowers of *Trillium ovatum* are fragrant. Individual plants are as variable in this as in other features, ranging from pleasantly sweet to rather acrid. At close quarters, the scent give some people a headache.

The restricted botanical description of *Trillium ovatum* as white, turning to pink or dark red, scarcely does the plants justice. A few flowers appear to be true albinos, never turning color with age. The rest contain anthocyanin, which develops as the blossom ages. Some show color sooner than others, and there is said to be a "permanent" pink form (a phenomenon also found in *T. grandiflorum*). Individuals vary from good clear pinks to a rather dirty old rose, or red shades. Flowers that turn deep red tend to be smaller than others; only once have I found a large-flowered red. Some flowers develop a central stripe of color; in others color may be confined to one or both ends of the petals. Perhaps the most remarkable form I have found is a double that opens noticeably yellow at the center, an effect that fades as the flowers change from white through pink to beet-red.

In addition to the variable distribution of the red pigment anthocyanin, occasional plants show green markings on the petals. This is usually a seasonal variation which has no relation to the green striping found in *Trillium grandiflorum* and attributed to a contagious disease. The green markings on the petals seem always to be random. They are usually accompanied by constriction of the petal margin beyond the green portion, suggesting that the phenomenon represents the misplacement of sepal tissue. It is extremely rare to find a flower in which all the petals are so marked. Transfer of white petal tissue to all or a portion of a sepal is also a rare occurrence; such aberrant white portions are always considerably larger than their normal green counterparts. I have never found a plant in which all sepals were marked. Even rarer are flowers that display both forms of displacement. Misplaced color occurs most often as an adjunct to unstable polymerism (the production of a surplus number of parts, but not to the extent of full doubling); as such, the phenomenon lasts only one season in most individuals.

It is a common error to refer to "the double form" of a *Trillium* species. For better or worse, this is a rare occurrence in most of the 50 or so species distributed through much of the United States and in parts of eastern Asia. Doubling has been observed numerous times in both *T. ovatum* and *T. grandiflorum,* and the various clones differ markedly among themselves. Named double clones of *T. ovatum* include 'Kenmore', 'Tillicum', and 'Edith'; I know of about a dozen others of varying merit, including one with green flowers. Fully double flowers are sterile, but an incomplete double in my garden has produced a few seeds.

There is no mistaking *Trillium rivale* (Plate 5) for a form of *T. ovatum.* Generally, it is smaller than even the smallest forms of the latter. Its petals, although variable, are always rather square and somewhat reflexed. This shape, combined with a decided tendency to freckling, makes the plants unmistakable. This species occurs in a restricted range in northern California and southern Oregon.

Initially the pedicel of *Trillium rivale* is of moderate length, but it soon begins to lengthen and twist oddly. If fertilization has taken place, the pedicel then arches downward to place the fruit against the soil. The seeds are embedded in a rather dry, mealy substance (as in *T. hibbersonii*) instead of the sticky goo found in *T. ovatum.* Despite its dwarf stature, if mischance buries the plants deeply, the tiny rhizomes can produce extraordinarily long stems to attain the surface.

Little *Trillium rivale,* again like *T. hibbersonii,* reverses the usual habit of pedicellate trilliums in aging: not infrequently its buds are pink, and the flowers blush for a few days before turning white. (This pattern is more prevalent in sessile-flowered species.) Its flowers vary in depth of color, some opening darker and holding color to the end. The occasional plant may have pure white or pink flowers, but most have tiny dots and dashes of deep maroon on the petals—usually more toward the center, but sometimes extending to the outer edge. This freckling seems unique in the genus, but *T. rivale* shares with most other trilliums the habit of producing rare yellow-flowered specimens.

Curiously, I found that plants from northern California flowered somewhat later than those found in Oregon. California plants found in a rather dense, damp woodland were larger than the Oregon plants in all respects, with more tendency toward colored and heavily mottled flowers. In contrast, Oregon plants were in dry, open woodland, and the plants were tiny, with their white flowers more or less freckled.

In the wild, *Trillium rivale* usually occurs as a single stem, but it loves garden life: a single plant may readily expand to produce a dozen or

71

more flowers a year. These plants should be as easy to divide as their larger cousins.

Of all the *Trillium* species, *T. petiolatum* is the most improbable. Its development begins demurely enough. Young plants look not too unlike those of *T. ovatum*, with which it sometimes grows. With the advent of the bud, things get completely out of hand. Instead of a stem of respectable length, round leaves shoot aloft on exaggerated petioles, leaving the often nondescript, malodorous flower at a considerable distance below.

The flower is usually seen in muddled shades of green and brown; the petals are narrow and not very long. Rarely, they are large, broad, and vibrantly colored in red or clear yellow. The botanical description would have them stemless, but in actual fact, immature plants seem always to have a rather long stem and short petioles. In mature plants there may be several inches of stem, or those unbelievable petioles may arise from below ground level.

Trillium petiolatum ranges over portions of Washington, Oregon, and Idaho, confined to mountainous areas where it finds some moisture amid more general dryness. It can be very hard to find, or locally common. We have found it in scrub under pines, in short grass and brushy pastures, and in a meadow kept very wet by a braided stream. In the first two cases it was frequently associated with snowberry (*Symphoricarpos*), and in the last with a gentian (probably *Gentiana calycosa*). In the wet site some of the juvenile plants had modestly mottled leaves, a feature not noted in the botanical description.

Distinguishing the other sessile trilliums of the West Coast is not such a simple task. When they were first investigated more than a century ago, these plants were swept into the same hopper as eastern *Trillium sessile*, despite numerous differences. The lumping of the western sessile trilliums under the name *T. chloropetalum* was the next step. Later still, John D. Freeman (1975) separated these plants into four species, retaining the name *T. chloropetalum* for certain plants found only in California, and assigning other exclusively Californian plants to *T. angustipetalum*. At the other end of the range of sessile trilliums with colored flowers, *T. kurabayashii* is restricted to a small area in northwestern California and adjacent Oregon. The fourth species, which Freeman named *T. albidum*, extends from central California to central Washington. It was in the last group of mostly white-flowered plants that there arose a problem in getting all of them to fit the given description.

My field studies suggested that there was no way to accommodate a significant portion of these plants under the description of *Trillium albidum*. In an attempt at clarification, I contacted numerous people familiar with the plants in their areas, only to wind up feeling like one of the blind men who examined the elephant. In recourse I studied as many natural stands as I could find with the help of my contacts. Having the use of my eyes, I soon discovered why I had been getting such confusing reports.

Dr. Victor G. Soukup of the University of Cincinnati had also been working with the genus, although not in northwestern Washington. It was only natural that we would finally combine our efforts. Familiar with *Trillium albidum* in California, he took one look at the modest sessile trilliums that are so hard to find in Washington, and he shook his head, saying, "You're right, they can't possibly be the same thing."

Dr. Soukup drove along miles of back roads while I stuck my head out the window in the rain, acting as spotter. We examined one stand after another, from just south of Seattle to northern California, sometimes wading through rain-soaked brush or being pelted with snow. Occasionally we made uncomfortable landings on steep slopes or barked our shins, but we got answers.

When Dr. Soukup returned home to do some sophisticated testing, I continued field studies on various aspects of trilliums. One of the results was the addition of a new species, which Dr. Soukup published under the name *Trillium parviflorum*.

Trillium parviflorum is found in a few widely separated and very small stands in Washington, and even less commonly in northernmost Oregon. It has a very narrow range of tolerance in regard to the moisture content of the soil, so that stands are frequently no larger than a city lot, and some much smaller. Within these restricted bounds it may be a prolific seeder, with specimens of all ages intermingling. It grows in association with native oaks.

It is neither as large nor as showy as any of the California sessile trilliums. The plants are small, with petals about 1 inch/2.5 cm in length; only rarely is one found surpassing the minimum petal size described by Freeman for *Trillium albidum*. The petals appear rather straight-sided and blunt-tipped. They are white, with about 10 percent having a faint flush of purple at the base. In all plants the latter color is confined to the reverse of the stigmatic branches. The base of the stamens is often similarly colored. The flowers have a light bitter or rank odor.

The leaves are lightly mottled, the markings tending to become obscure with age. Occasionally one finds a plant with immaculate leaves, or an attractive form in which the mottling appears black. Prettiest are those with strong markings in which chartreuse is added to the mix. Leaves on immature plants have (or give the impression of having) petioles. Mature leaves are broadly overlapping and sessile.

Attractive maroon fruits are prominently displayed amid the widely spreading sepals. Evidence of stigmatic remains in the form of ridging is minimal and limited to the top of the fruit; rarely it can be seen in the form of small, plump "fingers" atop the fruit. The skin has a patent-leather shine and is so thin that the bulges of the seeds can be seen.

Plants in the wild are almost invariably single-stemmed, but in the garden they may form small clumps. Wild plants favor gravelly soils enriched with leafmold. They are often mingled with *Trillium ovatum*; immature plants of both have well-separated leaves, and those of *T. parviflorum* lack mottling. Polymerism and other aberrant forms appear to be very rare in this species.

Plants of *Trillium albidum* from southern Oregon and California are very different. They are much larger and more robust, and they form clumps as freely in the wild as they do in the garden. Specimens with many flowering stems are not uncommon, and the flowers average 3 inches/8 cm in petal length. The petals are widest in the middle, half or more as wide as long, curving gracefully from tip to constricted base. Generally they are white. Their rose scent can be very strong. The leaves may be unmottled or obscurely mottled with silver on green.

The dull, greenish fruits of *Trillium albidum* bear tattered remains of the stigma as strong ridges which often extend to the base. The fruit is bluntly triangular in outline, and these ridges give it the appearance of being constructed of a series of planes. This rather unattractive fruit is partially concealed by sturdy sepals, which are held stiffly erect.

In Oregon I found a cline—a situation in which plants of two extremes gradually intergrade—involving little *Trillium parviflorum* in the north and robust *T. albidum* in the south. Plants to the north have more characteristics of *T. parviflorum*, while those to the south more closely resemble *T. albidum*. The evidences of intergradation are such that those familiar with them throughout their range can generally tell where photos were taken, or where garden plants originated. Similar phenomena can be observed involving eastern *Trillium* species.

Because they do not accommodate to the description of either species, I proposed the name *Trillium* × *oregonum* for these populations. Moving south from the Columbia River, one first notices the much larger size of plant and flower, as well as the fact that they are often multistemmed. The incidence and size of the purple blotch at petal bases also increase. Pink-flowered forms were found at one site. In other respects, these plants in northern Oregon adhere to the characteristics of *T. parviflorum*, although leaf size, shape, and markings vary enormously.

As one travels south, plant and flower size increase, and there is a change in petal shape. Clumps are more frequent and larger. As if to compensate for the added vigor, the incidence of seedlings and juveniles decreases. Although these plants are not severely restricted by their habitat, ring counts we made indicate that they had been growing for decades with few or no juvenile replacements.

Next the fruit lost its high gloss and changed from a smooth globe to a ridged triangular shape. Last to alter was the fruit color. The northern plants had fruits resembling those of *Trillium parviflorum*, then the fruits became a dull green blotched with purple. In the Salem-Eugene area the variation seemed greatest; some plants here had rose-scented flowers, while others retained the rank odor. Here, too, I encountered a number of strange plants whose sepals displayed misplaced petal color.

In southwestern Oregon, just north of the California line, I found plants that seemed to march to an entirely different drummer. They were subalpine, their flowering delayed by lingering snow until May or early June. The flowers were pale yellow or creamy (not white), with no purple pigment anywhere. The petals, 1.25 to 4 inches/3 to 10 cm long and 0.25 to 1.25 inches/6 mm to 3 cm wide, were on average slightly smaller than those of typical *Trillium albidum*. The scent was intensely floral-soapy. The anthers dehisced introrsely. Stamen length was about twice that of the stigmas. The latter were carried stiffly upright, with the receptive surfaces usually touching for a considerable distance.

The leaves were immaculate, or rarely chartreuse with irregular mottling of the normal green. The latter pattern may be extended to the sepals, which at flowering were generally stiffly upright to slightly spreading.

The fruits were small, round, and creamy, with pale green markings along the stigmatic sutures and no evidence of ridging. The stigmatic remains at the apex were reduced to a small dark crumb. The skin of the fruit was so thin and transparent that the brown seeds could be seen within. The flimsy sepals curled away so that the fruit was prominently displayed.

Most plants were in clumps of 2 to 20 stems (occasionally 50 or more). Juvenile plants were conspicuous by their rarity. Rhizome ring-counts for smaller plants gave approximate ages from 17 to 40 or more years. It was impossible to guess how old the big ones might be. The plants were catholic in their choice of habitat, occurring under or near scattered trees on open wet meadows, in moist to dry woodland, or under small stands of oaks in dry terrain. Polymerism and misplaced color occurred at about the same rate as in *Trillium ovatum*.

Trillium chloropetalum might well be called the prima donna of western trilliums; it has by far the greatest number of color forms. Freeman assigned to variety *chloropetalum* those with flowers containing yellow pigment, whether this is readily visible or not. Such flowers range from brown to bronze and yellow. Those without yellow pigment he placed in variety *giganteum*, including white, pinks, and clear deep reds. The flowers of either variety may be self-colored or may have beautifully contrasting colors in various patterns. One of my favorites has deeply colored veins on a pale background. Regardless of petal color, the sexual parts of *T. chloropetalum* are always purple. These trilliums have the potential to develop as wide a variety of color forms as any common garden plant.

Although the similar *Trillium kurabayashii* has been known for a long time, only recently has it been regarded as a separate botanical entity. Flowers with petals 5.5 inches/14 cm long have been recorded, making this the largest-flowered of all sessile trilliums. Although it is described only as red-flowered, I have found its color to vary from deep glowing red through brownish tones, grading to butterscotch tan with greater or lesser suffusion of red toward the tips. The most uncommon color was a clear, rich yellow, but probably a yellow factor is present in all plants. The leaves can be immaculate to heavily mottled, with leaf color bearing no relationship to flower color. The fruits are equally variable in shape and the amount of stigmatic remains displayed, but they seem always to ripen to a dark mahogany. Generally wild plants were single-stemmed; I found no massive clumps. The only aberrant form seen was a rare quadramerous (four-parted) plant.

At the southern edge of the range of western sessile trilliums, *Trillium angustipetalum* (sometimes considered a variety of *T. chloropetalum*) indeed has very narrow petals, which twist like those of most sessile trilliums. Described only as red, the color may be rich and luminous or dulled by the yellow factor. A yellow-flowered plant has been reported, and there are also dull bronzes. The immaculate or faintly mottled leaves are notable for a sudden constriction at the base, in imitation of a pedicel. Like the other western colored forms of sessile trilliums, it can make fairly large clumps under garden conditions, where it may self-sow.

In the 15 years since my field studies were made, some of the stands I examined have disappeared under the heels of progress. It is to be hoped that species of a genus that has been so poorly understood have not been lost in the process. The ability to survive for many decades (if undisturbed) has stood trilliums in good stead. However, in the face of humanity's King-Midas determination to turn everything into gold, the inability of some species to replace their populations regularly by means of seedlings is a decided drawback.

Originally published in the Bulletin of the American Rock Garden Society, *vol. 38, no. 4, pp. 157–167 (1980), and extensively revised by the author in October 1994.*

A Plant Hunt in Northern California

MARGARET WILLIAMS

The casual question, "Have you seen *Cassiope mertensia* subsp. *ciliolata* in the wild?" asked by Miss W. M. Muirhead at the Edinburgh Botanic Garden in Scotland triggered a pleasant series of events that led us to new friends, new plants, and new mountains to climb. Pursuing *C. mertensia* (Plate 11) in the Sierra Nevada and Cascade Mountains of California had been a continuing diversion for our small group of plant enthusiasts for several previous summers. We had found it in many sites and felt well acquainted with it. Plants from different areas exhibited the expected variation in size, flower form, and growth habit, but we had assumed there were no botanical differences among them. Thus it was surprising to be asked about a "hairy" cassiope that we hadn't realized existed.

A search of the literature revealed that Piper (1907) recognized two subspecies in California, describing them as follows:

1. *Cassiope mertensiana ciliolata*. Leaves ciliolate with delicate white fugacious hairs. Calyx lobes entire. Apparently confined to Siskiyou County, California. Specimens examined from: Cliffs at Castle Lake, 1882; north of Mount Shasta, 1897; Mount Eddy, Copeland, 1903, elevation 2550 meters [8200 feet], type location.

2. *Cassiope mertensiana californica*. Leaves rather large, very minutely glandular-ciliate; calyx lobes and corolla lobes more or less erose-denticulate. Many specimens examined from Lassen Peak southward through the Sierra Nevada. Type location, Mount Lyall, 3300 meters [10,725 feet], 1902.

The modern botanical authors Munz and Keck (1959) no longer distinguish these, treating both under *C. mertensiana*.

Our curiosity was piqued. We wondered how long the white hairs persisted and whether they changed the appearance of the plant. The locations cited were interesting ones, and so the search was on. Surely, with three chances we couldn't miss. The three locations mark out an isosceles triangle around the town of Mount Shasta in Siskiyou County of northern California. It is about 18 miles/29 km by air from Mount Shasta (the mountain) to Mount Eddy, and from Mount Shasta to Castle Lake. Mount Eddy and Castle Lake are about 9 miles/14 km apart. The statement "north of Mount Shasta" is vague, and none of us liked the idea of climbing the cliffs at Castle Lake, so we settled on Mount Eddy (the type location) for our first attempt.

As we drove north on a hot day in late July and approached the town of Mount Shasta, the snow-covered slopes of Mount Shasta looked infinitely more appealing than bald Mount Eddy to the west across the valley, so we couldn't resist a brief detour to Panther Meadow on Mount Shasta. There were ideal places in the meadow for a cassiope to grow, and we couldn't believe it wasn't under the next rock. The search was delightful; the meadow was carpeted with *Phyllodoce empetriformis* in rosy bloom, while *Kalmia microphylla* (Plate 35) and a *Vaccinium* species had finished. Phlox, violets, and mimulus added their bits of color to the intricate, undulating tapestry. On the slopes above the meadow, *Luetkea pectinata* and *Penstemon davidsonii* (Plate 28) grew in tight mats, hugging the rocks. Shrubby but prostrate, *Polygonum shastense* blended into the hillside. Cushions of eriogonums and an anemone with woolly seedheads completed the picture.

We thought briefly about climbing higher, but the snow-covered peak looming above was an unlikely habitat for cassiope, and "north of Mount Shasta" could be anywhere. As we looked across the valley at Mount Eddy, we began to feel doubtful. Its slopes did not look very arctic-alpine, but we could see a few patches of snow, so perhaps our "hairy" cassiope was below one of them.

It had taken only a few minutes to drive up the paved road to Panther Meadow—even allowing time to look at *Lilium washingtonianum* and a particularly bright red *Penstemon newberryi* (Plate 13)—but it took the rest of the day to grind up a tortuous road to Morgan Meadow on the southeastern side of Mount Eddy. We spotted *Xerophyllum tenax*, but it was impossible to focus on smaller plants as we inched joltingly upward. A forest ranger we had consulted had no idea what a cassiope was, but he assured us that Morgan Meadow was a flower garden. He was right, but it was quite a different sort of garden than we were looking for. It was almost a bog, with lilies taller than our heads, *Veratrum californicum*, *Darlingtonia californica*, *Frasera albicaulis* and associated plants—interesting, but hardly bedfellows for a cassiope. Nonetheless, here at an elevation of about 5600 feet/1700 meters we were within striking distance of the cited 8200 feet/2550 meters on Mount Eddy.

Early the next morning we were on the trail leading to a mine on the southeast side of Mount Eddy. Most of the plants were dried up, and even their seed was gone. The anemones, astragalus, and phloxes must have been a sight earlier. The scattered flowers of lupines, *Monardella*, and *Eriophyllum* scarcely rated a cursory glance as we passed upward, but we did pause to examine all the seepage spots under the trees. *Linnaea borealis* and *Adiantum aleuticum* were the choicest things we found.

Finally we were above the trees on an open scree slope. Our excitement mounted. Here the plants were at their prime, and many were new to us. A tiny blue campanula threaded its spaghetti-like roots under the rocks and poked gray-green leaves above: *Campanula scabrella* would be a treasure for any rock garden. Furry *Veronica copelandii* with a short spike of dark blue flowers was appealing, too, and suggested that Copeland must at least have been here. Were we on the right track? The precious violet matted under the rocks surprisingly was just a diminutive form of the widespread *Viola adunca*, but it has remained compact in the garden. A grayed mat of leaves called our attention to an *Epilobium* (perhaps *E. clavatum*), still not in bloom. Gaudiest of all were the clumps of *Hulsea nana* (Plate 1). Although this is a low-growing plant, its boldness is best suited for a rock garden on a grand scale. Some of the boulders had green petticoats made by the fronds of *Polystichum lemmonii*. We coveted the cushions of eriogonums with interesting leaf forms and subtle grayed colors, but there was not a bit of ripe seed.

Rounding a corner, we came upon a small cirque with a snowbank on the edge of a fairy pool. We were reminded of our objective; our senses quickened. Would the cassiope be here? A few early buttercups were charming, but not what we were searching for. Now the day was spent, and we were almost at the right elevation—but were we on the wrong side of this big mountain? The barren-looking peak of Mount Eddy was still above us, but it was just more scree.

We still had Castle Lake. This was a fisherman's paradise, with each campsite in its own leafy bower. Deer daintily picked their way through patches of *Rhododendron occidentale* and tall lilies. These lilies of the northern California mountains are difficult to sort out but are of the *Lilium pardalinum* complex.

Castle Lake is enclosed on two sides by huge, rounded boulders and rugged, steep cliffs. One of the other sides is thickly wooded. On the remaining side, a trail upward to Little Castle Lake had been carved through the dense brush for the convenience of fishermen. Would the cassiope be at the top of the majestic cliffs? We could approach them from the top of the trail, so up we headed.

When the trail leveled off, the shrubs became more scattered and we were in the open, high above Castle Lake. Under the manzanitas and

79

ceanothus grew *Erythronium klamathense*, its yellow-and-white flowers replaced by seed. A few furry cat's-ears, softly lined with blue, sat on the ground. There was even a pinkish one. If they weren't *Calochortus elegans* (Plate 20), at least they were elegant! The ivory-and-pink flowers of *Dicentra pauciflora* reminded us of ghostly versions of *D. uniflora* on long stems. Ferns, mosses, and sedums filled the chinks in a rocky outcrop. Hybrid Dasanthera penstemons liked the rocks, too. At first we weren't aware of the many plants of *Lewisia leana* (Plate 31); their myriads of tiny rosy flowers on wiry stems were almost hidden by the grass.

Farther on, it was exciting to find a tiny campanula growing out of crevices in a huge rock outcrop. It was very much like *Campanula piperi* of the Olympic mountains of Washington, but we were far south of its range. Since then it has been described by Heckard (1969) and named *C. shetleri*.

Good plants appeared at every turn. In shady places, *Luetkea pectinata* grew with abandon. Brodiaeas were coming up thickly in a drying meadow that earlier had been full of ranunculus. Again the cassiope had eluded us. Had the climate had been different in 1882, and was the environment wrong now for cassiope? Or should we have been more daring and climbed the precipitous cliffs?

Though specifically this trip was a failure, floristically it had been fantastically successful. Even though we went home somewhat daunted, we were determined to have another go at it.

The following year we approached Mount Eddy from the northwest. It was early in September, and we were surprised to find that the lower meadows still had flowers. We were excited by *Mimulus primuloides* var. *pilosellus* in the streambeds. But the queen of the day was *Gentiana newberryi* (Plate 2), its emerald-green mats studded with stunning blue trumpets. The usual Sierra form of this gentian has greenish-white flowers and is one of our favorites, but there is something special about gentian-blue. Untidy clumps of *G. calycosa* sprawled in the lush meadow and on the slopes above; although its flowers too were rich blue, they were not so choice. Annual *G. amarella*, though covered with lavender-blue flowers, seemed pallid in comparison. Again we had a glorious day; there were wet places, dry slopes, scree slopes, many of the same plants we had seen on the opposite face, and the same final result.

Now it seemed that we had exhausted our original objectives. Finally, we consulted the herbarium of the California Academy of Sciences. We should have done this much earlier, for here was an actual specimen of our elusive heather, collected in Caribou Basin in the Trinity Alps of Siskiyou County about 30 years earlier. By now our imaginations had clothed the cassiope leaves with ermine, so we were quite surprised: to the casual eye, the pressed plant could have been any ordinary *Cassiope mertensiana*. Satisfying as it was to see the "hairy" cassiope, it was disappointing, because the hairs are not visible without a hand lens. Nonetheless, our desire to see the "hairy" cassiope in the wild had not diminished, and Caribou Basin became our next objective.

Caribou Basin lies within the rugged Trinity Alps, about 50 miles/80 km west of Mount Shasta. This is isolated, wild country; its icy lakes are favorites of fishermen, and the mules of the pack stations on Coffee Creek make the trip up and over Caribou Mountain easier. At the time we made the trip, the trail ascended and descended very steeply, but now a longer but more gradual trail can be traversed more quickly. The eastern part of the trail led through a deep forest where occasionally we caught glimpses of Mount Shasta.

The trail became exceedingly steep near the rocky summit, and here each mule had its own style of forging upward. It was torture: some scrambled groaning over the rocks, others progressed with jerking plunges. It was hardest to cling to a "hopper," which would teeter indecisively on the rocks before each leap, and the rider, even though braced, somehow was never really prepared. Over the summit the trail became a chute of granitic sand, and the mules simply sat back on their haunches and slid down the first steep part. The animals were amazingly sure-footed; what they lacked in grace, they made up for in experience and instinct.

Again the trail wound through a thick stand of pines and firs, now with an occasional stately *Picea breweriana*. Then the trees thinned, we were on level ground, and the trail led through a patch of *Leucothoe davisiae* and across a meadow. The packer deposited our gear in a small grove of trees near Lower Caribou Lake, and then with the promise to be back to pick us up four days later, he and the mule train clattered off.

Our camp was primitive indeed, but rock ledges were conveniently located to serve as furniture. A great granite slab was our terrace overlooking our private lake. Other slabs paved the way down to the lake on our side, but trees hugged the shore on the two sides adjacent to us and swept up the slope in a green wave. On the far side the trees melted into the horizon, and the sinking sun streaked the sky with rose and gold. Except for the well-trodden trail and the pile of firewood by the blackened stones of the campfire, we almost had the feeling that no one had ever been in this idyllic spot before.

Our lake seemed too hemmed-in for cassiope, but there was plenty of territory for exploring. The jagged Sawtooth Range was silhouetted starkly against the sky, and deep shadows still darkened the precipitous slope above Snowslide Lake, as we followed the trail to it next morning. The jumbled rocks seemed too barren and perilous for cassiope. We didn't linger but pressed on up the steep trail toward Upper Caribou Lake.

Abruptly, there at our feet, in the granite sand alongside the trail, was cassiope. The search was over. A hand lens confirmed that the leaves indeed had a few hairs on their margins, though not fur; otherwise, they were indistinguishable from any other California cassiope. It was now mid-August and there were no remnants of flowers left, so we had no idea if they might look unique in flower, or if they might have been hairier earlier. We felt inclined to agree with the botanist who lumped the California cassiopes, even though a cassiope buff might not have.

This area seemed quite dry now—hardly the spot we might have picked for ericaceous plants, but growing with the cassiope were *Phyllodoce empetriformis*, *Kalmia polifolia* (Plate 12), *Gaultheria ovatifolia*, and *Vaccinium uliginosum*. These plants grew in rather isolated colonies on a shelf carved in the granite wall. Their roots must have dug in deeply, watered by seepage from high above.

Exploring the basin was intriguing, and although we kept our eyes open, we didn't see a cassiope anywhere else. It was dry everywhere; even *Gentiana newberryi* and *G. calycosa* were blooming sparsely in grassy areas, reserving their strength for a better year. Both *Parnassia fimbriata* and *P. californica* managed a few flowers, and there were straggling blooms on asters, erigerons, and castillejas. There was evidence that earlier, several kinds of mimulus and penstemon had flowered well. *Luetkea pectinata*, *Pyrola secunda* and *P. occidentale* had sought out shady spots. Many lewisias were in the rock crevices; although their leaves had been well nibbled, we identified both *Lewisia cotyledon* and *L. leana*. Sedums and ferns also decked the rocks. It was challenging to try to identify the plants so late in such a dry season.

The spectacular scenery more than made up for the lack of flowers. Whenever we climbed to the top of a ridge, other ridges marched ahead of us in endless tempting succession. Over one ridge lay another basin with its own jewel-like lakes. With each hour the scene changed. Each bend in the trail opened a new vista; marvelous pictures appeared in every direction. The charm of this tranquil wilderness lingers in our memories, and I hope someday we can return and see the cassiope in flower.

Bibliography

Heckard, Lawrence R. 1969. *Madroño* 20.4, 231–235.
Munz, Philip A., and David D. Keck. 1959. *A California Flora*. Berkeley: University of California Press.
Piper, Charles V. 1907. *Smithsonian Miscellaneous Collections* 50.4, 195–202.

Originally published in the Bulletin of the American Rock Garden Society, *vol. 28, no. 4, pp. 149–153 (1970).*

A Visit to the Siskiyous

JAMES MACPHAIL AND ROBERT WOODWARD

We visit the Siskiyou Mountains in southern Oregon and northern California more frequently than any other mountains. Not only is the flora remarkably distinct and appealing, but there are also a great many sites to investigate and two seasons of interest. The lower Siskiyous, which paradoxically have the better plants, begin to burgeon toward the end of March, become supreme in April, and are fascinating up to the middle of May in a normal season. The higher Siskiyous lose their snow cover in early July and are at their zenith about midmonth, seeding by mid-August. Few of the Siskiyou plants gain points for their habit alone, but they more than compensate in the flamboyance of their flowers.

The Siskiyou Mountains, which straddle the Oregon-California border, connecting the Cascade and Coast ranges, are the most northerly of the Klamath Ranges. The Siskiyous are probably older than the Cascades and very high. The sharp ridges are poorly covered with soil; the predominant rocks are variously granite, limestone, serpentine, and other sedimentaries. These mountains are the northern limit of many California plants and also possess a distinct flora of their own. One never knows what will turn up in the Siskiyous.

To begin with the best, almost on the California border, in late April we visit O'Brien Bog, as it is known among *aficionados*. For sheer concentration of good plants this area of about 2 square miles/5 square km cannot be surpassed.

The most ubiquitous plants of the area are two prostrate ceanothus. They are difficult to tell apart, although superficially *Ceanothus prostratus* is somewhat larger and more robust, with more toothed foliage that is almost glistening; *C. prostratus* subsp. *pumilus* (formerly *C. pumilus*) has smaller leaves that are round and blunt, with no teeth. Both send up sprays of phosphorescent blue flowers in umbels no higher than about 6 inches/15 cm in flower. This blue has been impossible for us to capture on film—it positively glows. The plants achieve a picturesque old age, gnarled, twisted, and contorted, the perfect bonsai. One is tempted to transplant these seniors, but despite the fact that both species root as they go, neither is a willing transplant. Both need to be treated as cuttings until they reestablish. Even then they are appallingly miffy; both may die off readily at any moment, mostly because of improper watering. But if they do persist (as one plant of rooted pieces from a tiny-leafed, intricately congested form has for us), give them sun and cold, and they will bloom. Our most generous bloomer was confined in a pot in the alpine house. We once found the rare white form of subspecies *pumilus*, a startling contrast to the phosphorescent blues.

Our first love at O'Brien Bog is the violets. There are four beautiful ones here. The best is minute, cut-leafed, shaggy *Viola hallii* with its pert flower-faces in all colors of the rainbow and all in proportion. *Viola cuneata* is entire-leafed, with almost equally joyful flowers in shades of white and blue. *Viola lobata* has strongly lobed, substantial foliage with more ordinary yellow flowers. Least interesting of all, but still good, is yellow-flowered *V. praemorsa*. All are plants for the rock garden—best in scree—requiring perfect drainage, full sun, and as they aestivate, very little water from May to March.

Difficult in the open garden but quite easy in the alpine house or covered scree, these violets are too little known. The problem is the slowness of the seed to germinate; indeed, seed is rarely available because of the notorious difficulty of timing the capture of violet seed. However, the two great plantsmen of the Siskiyous, Lawrence Crocker and Boyd Kline, often collected and distributed seeds of these precious plants.

Not found in O'Brien Bog but definitely Siskiyou plants are more treasures of this genus. *Viola douglasii* has very large flowers, yellow-marked and brown-backed, and cut foliage even lacier than that of *V. hallii*; it is one of the best but one of the trickiest violets to grow. We grow *V. douglasii* best in a bulb frame where it is bone-dry all summer and winter. Even better, but nearly impossible, is *V. beckwithii*, with hues of pink and purple, magically large flowers, and finely dissected foliage. Why it should be more recalcitrant than the others is a mystery. We suspect it is definitely a serpentine plant with the choosiness notorious in this breed. Occasionally one also comes across *V. sheltonii*, which has the usual cut foliage, but whose flowers are smaller and a so-so yellow. This is a wide-ranging rock violet that reaches its northernmost station in the Wenatchees near the town of Cle Elum.

There is even one good wet-growing violet in O'Brien Bog, where many of the plants are well watered by underground seepage and do not dry up even at the height of summer. (And what a height! We have collected seed in 110°F/43°C in July here.) This is *Viola lanceolata* subsp. *occidentalis*, a bit reminiscent of *V. cuneata*, but neither so bold nor so haunting.

The most spectacular of the actual bog plants is, of course, *Darlingtonia californica*, the cobra plant. Although many may consider it a plant of unmitigated ugliness, at least before flowering, it exerts a fascination on us. Those jade hoods—death traps, as this is an insectivorous plant— have an uncommon beauty, much enhanced when the large, fritillary- colored flowers appear, drooping in stately fashion. Grown in a care- fully constructed sphagnum bog, *Darlingtonia* can be tamed, although it does not always flower profusely.

Its companions may include the small white-pouched orchid *Cypripedium californicum*, one of the most amenable of a distinctly testy genus. In a sphagnum bog or even a peat bed, it will multiply and almost al- ways bloom. In summer here, one of the few flowering plants is fat-bu- gled *Gentian setigera* (formerly *G. bisetaea*), not great but definitely at- tractive and garden-worthy.

On the adjacent dry flats many fine plants abound. Lewisias flourish in the Siskiyous, although at O'Brien the dominant species is the some- times maligned *Lewisia oppositifolia*. True, it is frail in appearance, even wispy, but such a splendid—if evanescent—white flower! When the sun shines, it opens its virginal flowers with a heartwarming dignity. It is a deciduous species, blooming in surprisingly wet soil but baked hard and dry in summer. Especially prized is a selected dwarf form about 4 inches/10 cm tall, with rather larger flowers than usual. There are other lewisias with minute flowers and, except that they belong to a noble genus, readily dismissed: *L. nevadensis*, definitely dingy; forked *L. triphylla*, difficult and hardly worth it; and *L. pygmaea* (Plate 26), another winsome nothing. Higher up is succulent-foliaged *L. leana* (Plate 31), such a compact plant it is definitely garden-worthy. Its small but abun- dant flowers are rosy-magenta.

In May the O'Brien flats are aglow with one of the greatest of North American plants, *Silene hookeri*: huge, fringed flowers on a squat plant, in shades of pink to apricot, really superb and quite variable. One would be unwise to try to collect a specimen because of its formidable taproot, but it comes readily from seed, often blooming in its first season. If carefully tended—and marked, since it is soon dormant—it will be persistent. We have always loved and grown *S. hookeri*, preferring the soft pink or peach forms. The form previously distinguished as variety *ingramii* grows more to the north near the town of Roseburg; it is easier to tame, but it is a rather screaming magenta. It has, nonetheless, the same huge, fringed flowers on a frail bit of plant, so it is not to be overlooked.

Often one sneaks up on a suspected *Silene hookeri* in the O'Brien area only to discover that it is actually the similarly colored *Phlox speciosa*. This is a very good phlox with needle foliage and large pink-purple flow-

Silene hookeri
(Drawing by Laura Louise Foster. Courtesy of Hunt Institute for
Botanical Documentation, Carnegie Mellon University,
Pittsburgh, Pennsylvania.)

ers, often beautifully notched. It is also quite variable, but with care and
aridity it can be grown, at least for a while. The secret is to keep it dry in
summer. Of all the versions of *P. speciosa* we have seen, this is our favorite. We once found a white form of this, too.

Irises of the section Californicae are some of the most useful Siskiyou
plants. Here is one of the most garden-worthy: with stiff, swordlike foliage, about 1 foot/30 cm tall, and beautifully pencilled yellow flowers,
Iris bracteata is a plant every gardener should grow. These irises are easy
to tame but take some time to adjust to new surroundings. They are easy
from seed and can be divided in early spring. There are other species in
the Siskiyous, including the widespread and variable *I. tenax*. The best
forms are found on Monument Peak. Sometimes this iris can be positively inspiring, in clear shades of sky-blue, but usually the colors are
muddied and purplish. Other Siskiyou irises include *I. chrysophylla*,
which is about 8 inches/20 cm tall, with pale-yellow or whitish flowers
and slender foliage; *I. tenax* in the phase once distinguished as *I. gormanii*,
whose bloom can be anything from soft yellow to cream to blue-white
with an orange blotch; and *I. purdyi*, with large creamy flowers. *Iris
macrosiphon* has fragrant purple flowers banded with white and darkly
veined. *Iris thompsonii* is not always given specific rank; it is rather like *I.
tenax* but much more spectacularly colored and veined.

Blooming at the same time as the irises is one of our favorite bleeding-
hearts, *Dicentra formosa* subsp. *oregana*. This is one of the gray-leafed
dicentras (similar to *D. nevadensis*), bearing fat, pouchy flowers in white or

pale pink. It is a tricky plant, but one should try it. We have found it needs scree conditions but some shade, a habitat not always easily provided.

In the shaded shelter of the various shrubs—especially *Arctostaphylos manzanita* with its beautiful peeling bark—one often finds the best of the vancouverias, *Vancouveria chrysantha*. These are epimedium relatives in the family Berberidaceae; almost all have impressive foliage, but only this species has flowers of good size and substance, yellow and cheery. And wouldn't you know it, it is the most difficult to grow; we manage it in peat beds in less shade than its wild relatives.

On an island in Rough and Ready Creek near O'Brien we find the delightfully hairy, cushion-forming *Arabis oregona* (formerly *A. purpurascens*), with ethereal claret-colored flowers, a little long of stem but certainly lovely. Like many crucifers, it is not so long-lived as the gardener would like, but the cushion alone is a continuous attraction.

There are also deep blue *Delphinium decorum* and *D. menziesii*; common spraguea (*Cistanthe [Calyptridium] umbellata*) with its pink pussy-paws; the small yellow-flowered *Lithospermum californicum*; various species of *Mahonia*; *Hesperochiron pumilus*; and many *Castilleja* species.

The most notable family of the bog is the Liliaceae. From the fringed onion, *Allium falcifolium*, which is purple and everywhere, to the equally common and much more fringed little *Calochortus tolmiei*, liliaceous plants hold pride of place. None is more notable than the most aristocratic of lilies, *Lilium bolanderi*, with its thick whorl of textured leaves and reddish fritillary-like flowers, all on a plant 1 foot/30 cm high. It is a great plant, and alas, now rare. But you can grow it from seed, and if you have patience it will be sturdy and garden-adaptable.

Late in summer the much taller tiger-lily *Lilium pardalinum* (or one of its close relatives, *L. kelloggii*, *L. occidentale*, or *L. parvum*) will bloom. This is such an easy plant that it should not be overlooked for the woodland garden. Would one could say the same for late-blooming *Calochortus howellii*, with its chartreuse centers, muted and mysterious. We have never kept it more than a season, but each time it blooms we are converts anew.

Even less amenable is the last great plant of O'Brien Bog, the August-September fireweed, *Epilobium rigidum*. It is a striking plant with strange, stiff, glaucous foliage and oversized, flat purple flowers. It grows in very specialized localities, and we know of none in cultivation.

The lower Siskiyous have a wealth of other plants, some found very near the bog. What could be more enticing than the minute *Trillium rivale* (Plate 5)? It has flowers that are usually spotted and dull white, on stems about 6 inches/15 cm tall, and is one of the most charming of its genus— and such an asset in the early spring garden. It can bloom in February, and it actually multiplies. Everyone looks for the special forms, especially the pinks. The best we have was an inadvertent find, collected out of flower, and the following spring blooming a rich pink.

Although this trillium can grow in full sun, one usually finds it nestled among other low-growing plants, such as either of the magnificent *Erythronium* species—lemon-yellow, prolific *Erythronium citrinum*, or rich-violet, black-banded *E. hendersonii*. The latter is our favorite erythronium, and for once this accolade applies to a plant which, given rich humus soil, thrives beyond expectations. These are the best of the Siskiyou erythroniums, but there are others, including the ever-present *E. grandiflorum*, *E. oregonum* (Plate 18), and *E. revolutum*. *Erythronium howellii*, to the untrained eye, is very similar to *E. citrinum*, and *E. klamathense* is slight and pale-yellow in flower, with mottled foliage.

The lowland dodecatheons are confusing taxonomically and not particularly distinguished. *Dodecatheon hendersonii* is here in multitudes. Higher up grows *D. alpinum* (Plate 29), a useful adjunct in the rock garden and very easily grown, but not so alpine-looking as one would hope.

A rather startling Siskiyou plant, although too tall for the rock garden, is the stalwart borage *Cynoglossum grande*. Often over 1 foot/30 cm tall and very leafy, it is admissible only in the woodland, but if you can grow it (and this is only possible from seed, as it is monstrously taprooted), you will appreciate it for the startling clarity of the blue flowers and for their texture, the element that surprised us when we first saw it. We discovered it in lightly wooded areas, often accompanied by the flaming-red parasite *Pedicularis densiflora* or Indian warrior.

With the Siskiyou ginger, *Asarum hartwegii*, we are back to subtleties. If you are a cyclamen-leaf nut, you had better acquire this asarum. Variously mottled and silvered, with the usual clandestine mousy flowers, it is a plant for year-round effect. Once established it will self-sow in the peat bed or woodland border, but never weed out the seedlings: wait to see if you have a special form. Trundle your spares to the local plant sale, where they are always a hit. This is a plant for the tasteful, and it is very plentiful in the low areas of the Siskiyous, even in campgrounds.

The Siskiyou Range is noted for the genus *Fritillaria*. Either you're a "frit-freak" or you're not, and we most avidly are. Indeed, almost everyone is when it comes to *F. recurva*, a scarlet wonder. It is the most immediately impressive species of the genus, but in the end others inspire more affection. The shape of its petals (recurved, upward-turning) is its unique feature in addition to the color, and this distinguishes it from the rare and protected *F. gentneri*, which is usually taller, unrecurved, and less flamboyantly scarlet. These fritillaries are by no means easy garden subjects, but in sand, gritty (preferably red sand) mixes, with a sloping bank, they can be grown and will persist if they receive a long and hard summer dormancy. Otherwise they will split into myriad minute bulblets or "rice grains" and take forever to rebuild to flowering size.

The smaller fritillaries of the Siskiyous include a dwarf, distinctive form of *Fritillaria affinis* (formerly *F. lanceolata*; Plate 3), which a splitter would saddle with specific rank. It stays small and has an altogether different appearance from the usual *F. affinis*, if the term "usual" is possible in such a variable species.

Best of all, and found in only a few remote stations, is the stunted *Fritillaria glauca*, with grayish foliage and huge, wide bells ranging from pure soft yellow to checkered yellows, greens, browns, or blues. One of our favorite haunts of this stirring little plant is an island in the middle of a creek. The fritillary does not wander to the shores, where the drainage is unsuitable. Only in the accumulated silt of the island, mostly rocky and sandy, does *F. glauca* survive. When we first found it, one of us was severely admonished by the photographing other for touching the leaves before the picture was snapped, so farinose is the surface. *Fritillaria glauca* is considered difficult to grow, but one spring at the University of British Columbia Botanical Garden a beautiful patch bloomed in an open, very sharply drained scree.

Kalmiopsis leachiana (Plate 30) deserves a section all its own. Many know of its late discovery, first by a postman on his rural rounds, and later by Lilla Leach, who gave the genus its name after some waffling by botanists, who fancied first *Rhododendron*, then more nearly accurately *Rhodothamnus* before assigning it to a new monotypic genus. Today most colonies of this rigorously specialized plant are isolated in mountain fastnesses and require arduous climbs. A few, however, abut civilization and can be reached by the shortest of climbs. In late April they may be seen draping the rocks, cascading over cliffs, and even inhabiting dim caves, flourishing their beautiful pink-purple flowers. It is an amazing sight, yet somehow *Kalmiopsis*, which has all the traditional attributes of the true alpine but is by no means always found in alpine situations, misses true glory. The color is a little too strident, the proportions not exact. When seen in the wild or on the show bench, and even rather often in the garden, it is a plant that stirs many hearts—but not the purest.

There are of course many forms, with several color variations—the truest pinks, closest to high-mountain forms of the genus *Kalmia*, are to our minds the best—and differing habits; some root as they creep along, while others are upright. The plant is definitely growable, although a bit daphnesque in its occasionally suicidal bent. We have always grown it in peat beds, but in nature, although it thrives in duff, it is most often found in rocky outcrops, often in blazing sun. We often treat pot or trough plants this way and are amazed at their floriferousness.

Although *Kalmiopsis* is the rarest and most legendary plant here, there are other very special plants found in only a few stations in the Siskiyous. There is a special form of *Silene hookeri*, sometimes called subspecies *bolanderi*, found in the northern California part of the Siskiyous, which is surely one of the greatest American alpines. The flowers are huge and snow-white, with fringed petals like a parasol. We have had it several times; we no longer do. Either we overwater it, or we do not permit enough leg room for it to wander. Carroll MacDonald of Salem, Oregon, who has a superb miniature garden called Wee Plant Haven, grows this plant (of which he was party to the discovery) to perfection in open scree with only a cloche for winter protection.

There is a special polemonium, *Polemonium chartaceum,* so far known from only one mountain. It is reputedly similar to *P. elegans* but more delicate, more compact, and less sticky. Also very rare is *Phacelia dalesiana,* with white un-Phacelia-like flowers, large and substantial, and even more effective than *P. sericea.*

There are many calochortuses, but mostly this is a California genus, although pink and frightfully rare *Calochortus persistens* grows on serpentine in very localized situations in the Siskiyous. *Calochortus greenei* (Plate 22) is not so good (a bit too lavender, and hairless) nor so rare. Both are large-flowered mariposas.

The phloxes are very special and difficult to separate. The Siskiyous have *Phlox diffusa* as a common plant, but the best of all is the very rare *P. hirsuta,* a shrublet with huge, dark-centered pink flowers. None of these plants has much of a hold in cultivation.

The penstemons of the Siskiyous are not a particularly distinguished lot. Most of them are plants of the high mountains. The exceptions are lowland *Penstemon rattanii,* about 1 foot/30 cm tall, with lavender flowers in panicles, and shrubby *P. lemmonii* (recently renamed *Keckiella lemmonii*).

The most sought-after plant of the highlands is *Lewisia cotyledon* in its various color forms. Somehow in the wild, especially when one is looking for true pink forms or even cream-bordering-on-yellow forms, they are much more exciting than in the garden. Once a true yellow was found and named 'Carol Watson'. Somehow, however, the interbreeding that has occurred among garden plants has produced colors of singular garishness—hot roses, simmering purples, and apricots. These are exciting at first, but once you have seen the simple wild plant with its purity of tone and proportion of flower, you much prefer its artlessness to the obviously human-influenced strains. We have never found any rare forms in the wild, not even the white one, which is a magnificent garden plant. We keep ours potted as, like most albinos, it lacks vigor.

Other plants of the high Siskiyou screes include various eriogonums, notably the silver buns of *Eriogonum ovalifolium* (Plate 6), symmetrical and white with sprays often rose-red, yellow, or sulphur. Usually the eriogonums are in the same areas as the wonderful *Orthocarpus cuspidatus,* with flowering spikes like miniature blue-purple candles dotting the hillsides. Like the castillejas which are close relatives, *Orthocarpus* is tainted with the curse of parasitism and not for gardens.

The finest phlox, very common even in some lowland stations, is the legendary *Phlox adsurgens,* which usually inhabits shady ground under subalpine shrubs or trees. It is also quite variable, with pinks, soft or hard, petals more or less notched (a form discovered by Crocker and

Kline, dubbed 'Wagon Wheel', is one of the most vigorous in the garden), deep or dark centers, and so on. The ordinary plant itself is good enough, and growable, but not for long. We have tried it in peat beds, in screes with some shade, and in ordinary rock garden conditions. It almost always survived for awhile and bloomed and thrilled us in April, but then it almost always petered out. Fortunately *P. adsurgens* is one of the easiest plants to strike from cuttings (in about May), and so we have always had it.

The high-alpine lupine in the Siskiyous is *Lupinus breweri*, very similar in its silkiness to *L. lyallii* but more compact, with usually bluer flower spikes. But it is just as temperamental.

An epilobium not quite so sensational as *Epilobium rigidum* is *E. obcordatum*, praised by Farrer, with shiny, almost glistening, compact foliage and good-sized purple fireweed blooms, which must have the sun to open up. I confess I have only once—at the height of a bright sunny day—seen our scree-frame plant look like anything.

The other plants are either a bit nondescript or found elsewhere: *Dicentra pauciflora, Eriogonum sphaerocephalum*, and *Astragalus whitneyi* var. *siskiyouensis*. There are also interesting lewisia hybrids, chiefly between *Lewisia leana* and *L. cotyledon*.

We could not leave the Siskiyous without mention of the alpine ferns, so useful in garden settings, and one not-so-alpine fern which is nevertheless quite handsome: the chain-fern, *Woodwardia radicans*, which seems to erupt from rocky outcrops where there is constant seepage. We planted it in a similar poolside setting in the garden, where it was an architectural delight for many years until the cold finally got it.

The true alpine ferns are, for the most part, much more cold-resistant. *Cheilanthes intertexta* is the local lacefern, for non-botanists indistinguishable from *C. gracillima* (Plate 16). *Pentagramma triangularis* (formerly *Pityrogramma triangularis*), the goldback fern, is found here in a more growable form just as attractive as that from the Cascades. The pellaeas are all choice, with *Pellaea mucronata*, the bird's-nest fern, much more growable than the more beautiful (because more intractable?) *P. breweri*. Look also for *Botrychium multifidum*, the best of the grape ferns; *Adiantum jordanii*, a dwarf maidenhair; *Pellaea brachyptera*, a truly first-class dwarf fern; and the taller coffee fern, *P. andromedaefolia*.

We leave the Siskiyous reluctantly, but not for long. Of all the alpine areas we have explored it is the one to which we return most readily, in the expectation of finding something new and beautiful. We have not been disappointed yet.

Originally published in the Bulletin of the American Rock Garden Society, *vol. 35, no. 4, pp. 167–174 (1977).*

The Red Buttes

BOYD KLINE

For the past 10 years I have been fortunate to have as a friend a great plantsman, Marcel LePiniec. We met at his nursery, where I had gone to inquire about the native lilies of our area in southern Oregon.

We have since been on many trips, exploring the vast, wonderful area surrounding our homes. One of the most memorable is the trip we made to a new site for *Kalmiopsis leachiana* (Plate 30) that he had discovered before I met him. Other explorations have taken us through the most interesting sites of the Siskiyou Mountains, the peaks of the Coast Range, Oregon Mountain, Pearsoll Peak, Vatican Peak, Snow Camp, and many other places.

Once we were lunching in a majestic grove of weeping spruce (*Picea breweriana*) on Pearsoll Peak when Marcel began to reminisce about a pack trip he and some friends had made a few years earlier, scouting along the crest of the Applegate River watershed, starting from Grayback Mountain in the northwest and traveling southeast to end at the base of Red Buttes. My only acquaintance with this place, at that time, was a cross on a map labeled "Red Buttes, alt. 6731 feet" (2053 meters). By the time Marcel's account ended, I imagined that this split monolith might be the original point of dispersion for all the Siskiyou endemics.

One reason we had not made the trip before was that the southern approach, a rough mountain road, had been blocked by slides for several years, and the foot trails on the northern slope were 4 miles/6 km of arduous climbing, often obstructed by snowdrifts. In mid-June of 1959 we decided to go up the trail. It had been a mild winter and a rather warm spring. We started before dawn, hoping the snow had melted enough to permit our ascent. Lawrence Crocker, another enthusiastic plantsman, came along.

Our first find, near the beginning of the trail, was a young weeping spruce, out of place at this low elevation; it is a subalpine species rarely found below 6000 feet/1800 meters. Farther along we found good specimens of *Phlox adsurgens* and marked several outstanding plants with large flowers—some deep rose and some good white forms—to be collected on the way back. Familiar plants began to appear along the trail: *Dodecatheon hendersonii, Triteleia crocea, Lilium columbianum, L. washingtonianum, Trillium ovatum, T. chloropetalum* var. *giganteum, Fritillaria recurva,* and *F. affinis* (Plate 3). About 1 mile/1600 meters along, where the trail passed through tall pines and firs, we came upon one of my favorite groundcovers, the glossy trailing blackberry or snow bramble, *Rubus nivalis*. We were at about 4000 feet/1200 meters altitude, and the rare evergreen deer oak (*Quercus sadleriana*) was beginning to appear. This is an intriguing shrub, growing to some 5 feet/1.5 meters in height by 6 to 8 feet/2 to 2.4 meters wide, with long slender branches, rather large leaves, and the usual catkins and acorns.

From this point on the trail passed through deep forest with occasional open areas, where we found *Iris chrysophylla, Erythronium klamathense, Disporum hookeri,* and *Calochortus tolmiei*. The season regressed as we climbed, and soon we were finding *Synthyris reniformis, Calypso bulbosa,* and the snow plant (*Sarcodes sanguinea*). On the edges of occasional patches of snow appeared the colorful blossoms of *Erythronium grandiflorum*.

At last we came to the long scree meadow at the base of the awe-inspiring crags of the Red Buttes. Snow lay deep in protected areas and melted to form torrents rushing down the hillsides. On their banks we found *Mertensia longiflora* and *Dodecatheon jeffreyi* intermingled in a nice combination of blue and pink. Dwarf buttercups and ferns further enhanced the scene. Leading back from the creek's edge into the massive boulders at the foot of the crags was a profusion of ferns, including maidenhair (*Adiantum pedatum*), fragile fern (*Cystopteris fragilis*), holly fern (*Polystichum lonchitis*), the rare *P. lemmonii,* and *P. scopulinum*. Among the ferns appeared the nodding heads of *Lilium wigginsii*.

In some places slabs of very hard limestone protruded, and on these grew a variety of plants, including *Phlox diffusa* in many shades of white, blue, and pink, *Penstemon rupicola* (Plate 32), and several heucheras and arabises. Good rock ferns were flourishing here: *Aspidotis densa,* which has light-green fronds 6 inches/15 cm tall; *Cheilanthes gracillima* (Plate 16), graceful as the name implies, with 4-inch/10-cm, dark green lacy fronds; and the aptly named *Cryptogramma acrostichoides* or parsley fern. The most interesting was the rare Brewer's cliffbrake (*Pellaea breweri*), a small plant about 4 inches/10 cm tall with straight, delicate fronds 0.5 inch/13 mm wide; it is difficult to keep in captivity.

On our left as we faced upstream was a large rounded ledge covered with plants of *Lewisia cotyledon* with flowers of an unusual apricot with pink stripes. At the base of this ledge we found a real gem: *Dicentra pauciflora*, a delicate little plant of exquisite beauty. Spreading in mats of gray-green, finely cut foliage, topped with flesh-colored "steer's head" blossoms, the whole plant was about 3 to 4 inches/8 to 10 cm tall. It is rather similar to *D. uniflora* but has a larger flower.

On the steep slope leading to the ridge of the mountain grew *Lewisia leana* (Plate 31), *Phlox diffusa*, and numerous species of *Penstemon*, *Erigeron*, and *Eriogonum*, along with colonies of the pine-mat manzanita (*Arctostaphylos nevadensis*) and the green manzanita (*A. patula*). Very few plants grow on the hard rock of the Butte itself, but an exceptional one is a tiny cushion, *Draba howellii*, a gray-green tuft wedged into clefts of the rock. It has loose racemes of deep-yellow flowers on stems about 3 inches/8 cm tall.

As we worked our way from the ridge down onto the southeast slope, we spotted a grove of Brewer's spruce (*Picea breweriana*) and one lone Baker's cypress (*Cupressus bakeri*). Another sharp ridge pointed directly south, and on it grew a very curious plant, *Eriogonum lobbii* (Plate 33), which in bloom appears much like a huge spraguea (*Calyptridium* [or *Cistanthe*] *umbellatum*). Farther down the slope a steep fall of large boulders was afroth with the blossoms of *Lewisia cotyledon*, and below this alpine rock garden was a gently sloping, sandy scree with masses of *L. leana* in bloom. We were soon searching for natural hybrids of these two species, which Marcel had first found on his previous trip here. The hybrid plants have foliage and flowers intermediate between the two; we collected only a few, as they were quite scarce.

By now it was late afternoon and our interest was sated for the time being, although we could see many exciting-looking peaks and ridges in every direction. Our weary return to the car took only half the time of the ascent. We were exhausted from our day's effort, but we had the pleasant feeling that the Red Buttes were balm for the plant-hunter's fever.

Originally published in the Bulletin of the American Rock Garden Society, *vol. 22, no. 4, pp. 97–99 (1964).*

The Wallowa Mountains:
Ice Lake and the Matterhorn

MARVIN E. BLACK AND DENNIS THOMPSON

Joseph, Oregon, lies in an oasis of irrigated pastureland; the water is supplied by the melting snows of the Wallowa Mountains, which form a north-pointing horseshoe with Joseph between the two ends. The main road from the west—Interstate 84, leading to Pendleton and Portland—crosses dusty, dry land with basalt cliffs deeply cut by little rivers, and rolling plateaus cultivated for wheat. East beyond Joseph, things get hotter and drier. Twenty-five miles/40 km down that road, at Imnaha, *Opuntia polyacantha* and *Oenothera caespitosa* (Plate 39) dot the roadbank.

Joseph is the jumping-off point (last grocery, motel, and liquor store) for the high Wallowas. Close by are some of the finest Pacific Northwest alpine areas. Ice Lake is one of our great favorites, situated right at the 8000-foot/2400-meter timberline. Less than 2 miles/3 km beyond it, the Matterhorn (at 9845 feet/3000 meters, the highest Wallowa peak) looks down.

Unlike the Rockies and other more civilized ranges where high-speed roads disgorge camera-laden travelers directly onto the roadside eritrichiums, Northwest mountain roads tend to follow river courses and low ridges. Thus one must earn one's way up to timberline. This somewhat insulates the alpine plants from casual plunderers; it also challenges the less active. Arriving at these cliffs across talus slopes requires strenuous effort. The 8-mile/13-km trail up to Ice Lake is measured in backache, blisters, and sweat.

A drive out of Joseph and beyond the 5-mile/8-km length of Wallowa Lake south of town leads to a large campground, resorts, a stable with pack-horse rental, and the trailhead for major routes into the mountains. The heart of the Wallowas is directly ahead in the Eagle Cap Wilderness Area.

At first the West Fork Trail is rocky and cool, deep in the canyon of the West Fork of the Wallowa River. We climb steadily, in and out of the woods. Rare pteridophytes grow here, including *Botrychium virginianum*; there are five species of *Pyrola*, *Disporum trachycarpum*, and *Calypso bulbosa*, which blooms early in the season. The 5-foot/1.5-meter towers of purple *Delphinium occidentale* and pink *Mimulus lewisii* flourish near seeps and springs. *Linnaea borealis* keeps company with *Aquilegia formosa* in moist woodland, recalling hillsides 200 miles/320 km nearer the Pacific Ocean. The clamoring river enlivens the hike, roaring and tumbling over the rocks.

After 3 miles/5 km, the Ice Lake Trail takes off to the right, crossing the river westward on a wooden bridge. Beyond that it begins to zigzag, climbing lazily through a baked, rock-strewn meadow of *Calochortus macrocarpus* with 3-inch/8-cm wide, luminous orchid and white flowers, and 5-foot/1.5-meter tall sprays of *Senecio serra* bearing masses of yellow daisies. The trail meanders in and out of the cool woods, reversing itself at the foot of rock walls, venturing into rockslides, and making switchbacks. In hotter places, *Artemisia michauxiana* offers gray-green foliage and thin spikes of moonlight yellow, surprising us with its sweet chamomile scent in place of the usual bitter wormwood.

Clematis columbiana (Plate 37) drapes an occasional trailside shrub, offering demure lavender pendant blooms; flaming *Castilleja* brightens the dry meadows. These mountains are home to about a dozen species of *Castilleja*, and these paintbrushes will accompany us all the way to the high scree slopes. The fragrant western mock-orange (*Philadelphus lewisii*) loads its branches with exquisite white flowers along this lower hillside at 5500 feet/1700 meters. An array of small fruiting shrubs greets us, with species of *Ribes*, *Rubus*, *Rosa*, *Lonicera*, *Sambucus*, *Symphoricarpos*, and *Vaccinium*.

The trail steepens and our legs ache a little; there are no level places to rest as we scramble up the rockslides. In these glaring dry basalt outcrops grow mats of *Penstemon fruticosus* var. *serratus* (Plate 36), happy 2-inch/5-cm evergreens with holly-like foliage and airy rose-orchid blooms. Their constant companion, *Heuchera cylindrica* var. *alpina*, has dark, tufted rosettes of rich green with 6- to 10-inch/15- to 25-cm greenish-white flower spikes.

Another pair of penstemons is prominent along the trail. *Penstemon venustus* thrusts up husky spikes of strangely luminous lavender on sturdy plants that suggest good possibilities for the garden border; it is found on well-drained sites, usually in sun but tolerating some shade. Similarly versatile but even more shade-tolerant is the equally tall but thinner-spiked *P. wilcoxii*, usually purple-flowered but occasionally a vivid gentian-blue.

The bold-leaved plant with bright apple-green flower spikes in damp shade here is *Veratrum viride*. It is coveted by outsiders who are not long accustomed to its handsome pleated foliage and tall flower spike.

At the 5-mile/8-km mark (5800 feet/1770 meters elevation), the rocky meadows have given way to a grim landscape of rock outcrops and boulders tumbled down the mountain face. We have had no glimpse of the Matterhorn yet, but its aura reaches here. The trail encounters Adam Creek, the outlet stream plunging down in leaping falls from Ice Lake. Creek and trail approach each other as we proceed up the mountain in 24 switchbacks.

Anything growing in this landscape deserves to be called a rock plant; there are no alternatives. Here is a golden daisy, *Eriophyllum lanatum*; a brilliant green-sulfur species of *Eriogonum*, a genus richly represented in the Wallowa flora; and knee-high plants of pale-pink-flowered *Ageratina occidentalis* (formerly *Eupatorium occidentalis*), in its best form achieving some merit with heads of little tube-flowers, looking quite unlike a composite.

Elegant groups of dwarf ferns decorate the sunny cliffs, with *Cheilanthes gracillima* (Plate 16), a species of *Cryptogramma*, and *Polystichum lonchitis* along the trail above 6500 feet/2000 meters elevation. All are excellent in the open rock garden if not kept overly wet. The ferns are sometimes accompanied by mats of *Juniperus communis* var. *montana*. Another fern, *Adiantum aleuticum*, the delicate western maidenhair, grows by wet seeps where the trail passes into the trees, its lacy froth joined by filmy little orchids—habenarias and *Listera cordata*—and the bold orbicular leaves of *Saxifraga mertensiana*.

Legs and feet plead for relief as the trail levels deceptively near the 7-mile/11-km mark, but the mosquitoes from lingering snowdrifts drive us on. Waist-high stems of the rayless western coneflower *Rudbeckia occidentalis* are a diversion.

The last long mile/1600 meters into Ice Lake is an ordeal of steep switchbacks, a challenge demanding total concentration; yet we are still distracted by the trailside flowers. A most unlikely onion is *Allium validum*, the swamp onion, which raises a noble stem to sometimes 3 feet/1 meter, topped by a bright rose-orchid head the size of an egg. It is a striking bloom on a plant that grows sometimes in dry rocks, but more often in standing water. The showiest of the death camas group, *Zigadenus elegans*, regularly mingles with the swamp onion here. It makes a bold spike-foliage accent crowned with ivory wands of starry blooms tattooed lime and orange.

Aster alpigenus var. *haydenii* appears at 7800 feet/2400 meters to announce our impending arrival at Ice Lake. The plant is only an inch or two high, with lax, narrow-lanceolate leaves and few lively violet, narrow-rayed daisies. The penstemon that accompanies it with 6-inch/15-cm spikes of tubular blue-purple flowers is probably *Penstemon spatula-*

tus; it chooses dry slopes rather than rocks. The leveling trail swings 90 degrees westward, and a delightful phlox look-alike appears beside it: *Linanthus nuttallii* smothers its 6-inch/15-cm mounds under fragrant, starry blossoms in varied pastel shades. This beauty compares favorably with the best phloxes.

At the 7900-foot/2410-meter level, the light woodland of lodgepole and whitebark pines (*Pinus contorta* and *P. albicaulis*) parts suddenly, and we are at the shore of Ice Lake. Its half-mile/800-meter extent of shimmering surface is cradled against the mountain by a textbook lava dike. Here, reflected in the mirror, is the first view of the Matterhorn straight ahead, looking not at all like its European namesake. It is not the neatly pointed cinnamon summit that occupies the foreground—that is a subsidiary peak—but the hulking silver-gray dome peering over its shoulder.

Dazzling clear and blue-green, the lake is a point where several geological events converge. It lies behind its volcanic dike below the west-facing summits of the Matterhorn and Sacajawea (to the northwest, the second highest peak in the Wallowas at 9833 feet/2994 meters), both gray limestone uplifts from the floor of an ancient sea. Along the shores and, incongruously, along high-ridge talus slopes we can find fractured rock bearing shells and obvious marine fossils. Farther up on the alpine slopes toward either peak, the land is striped vertically with seams alternating among acid-volcanic basalts, granular white, iron-free granitic grits (which we descriptively call "sugar-rock"), and alkaline silver-gray, sculpted limestone. Each of these geological elements has its own dramatic plant community.

The campground areas at the east end of Ice Lake have a flora worthy of their own brochure: sky-blue dwarf *Penstemon tolmiei*, ivory *Zigadenus* species with magenta *Allium* species, mats of dwarf phlox, *Polemonium pulcherrimum*, *Heuchera cylindrica*, *Linanthus*, *Erigeron compositus*, *E. poliospermus*, *E. bloomeri*, arenarias, eriogonums, and castillejas. The tall lupine nearby with spectacular, bold, white-hairy foliage (and disappointing small lilac flowers) is *Lupinus leucophyllus*.

The main trail toward the Matterhorn follows Ice Lake's north shore, notched into the talus slopes that spill into the lake. *Hypericum scouleri* subsp. *nortoniae* is here, a fine rock garden candidate. Fire-engine red buds are the glory of this mat-former, which grows in the rocks here. It is perhaps drought-tolerant but seems to prefer subsoil moisture. Nearby, *Monardella odoratissima* bears above its peppermint-scented leaves feathery flower heads of bright orchid—a much livelier color at Ice Lake than elsewhere. Choosing the hottest, driest rock banks, it makes compact, pillow-shaped plants wider than their 4-inch/10-cm height, with neat paired ovate leaves of gray-green. *Hedysarum occidentale* presents a flamboyant rose-fuchsia show on nearby talus; it is one of the best in an underrated genus.

A flat meadow at the end of the lake is the habitat of willows and such ericaceous plants as *Kalmia microphylla* (Plate 35), *Ledum glandulo-sum*, and species of *Phyllodoce*. In wet talus near the little streams grows peach-and-gold *Aquilegia flavescens*; there are showy ivory sprays of bloom on 1-foot/30-cm *Polygonum phytolaccaefolium*, pretty enough that someone should try it in a garden; and *Epilobium latifolium*, the large-flowered dwarf fireweed, runs in the gravel.

One is apt to miss these flatlanders, however, for the lure of mountains is overwhelming. There are unbroken open slopes to the ridge tops and summit from this point. Although trails cease, there is no danger of getting lost; the lake below is in view at all times, and there are many obvious courses up through the rocks.

First come gardens in the vertical seams of rocks mentioned earlier. The flashiest and most diminutive yellow American erigeron, *Erigeron chrysopsidis*, complete with 20 gold daisies, is no larger than a silver dollar. This midget variety is a high Wallowa endemic first collected by William Cusick in 1900. Tight miniatures of *Eriogonum ovalifolium* (Plate 6), the desire and despair of European gardeners, grow in this garden. *Anemone multifida* var. *globosa* (Plate 7) occurs here in both a sulfur-ivory color form and a glowing rose form; the latter gives the lie to authors who have belittled this plant for its often disappointing color.

To crawl about this natural rock garden is to experience paradise. Species grow more reduced and compact here than elsewhere. These have given varied results when the dwarf forms were tried at sea level. One encounters, as did Morton E. Peck, a reduced, tiny-belled campanula, which he christened *Campanula sacajaweana*; it has now been reduced to a mere form of *C. rotundifolia*, leaving no flower to commemorate the guide of the Lewis and Clark Expedition, which passed near these mountains. Its campanulate blooms with shorter, less starry lobes than *C. piperi* are sometimes upfacing, but more often pendant or outfacing. Stem length varies from 1 to 4 inches/2.5 to 10 cm, the stems arising from thin underground rhizomes that either emerge from rock cracks or venture a few inches into the fine white granite grit. Grown hard, like *C. piperi*, this rare form is a promising trough or pot plant.

Plants of *Potentilla fruticosa* (now *Pentaphylloides floribunda*) that grow in this acid rock are ground-huggers, mostly under 2 inches/5 cm tall. The same species colonizes more exposed limestone rocks 100 yards/meters away at ten times this stature. The reduction may relate at least in part to the different mineral content of these apparently starved rocks and may offer an insight into the plant's cultivation.

A legume from these rocks sends "belly-planters" into rhapsodies. *Astragalus kentrophyta* var. *tegetarius* makes a doll's carpet; it would have to stand on tiptoe to be 0.5 inch/13 mm tall, although the little furry pads might reach teacup width in old age. It is a quiet plant. Its little mauve-purple pea flowers, smaller than matchheads, are tucked singly or in twos and threes among the narrowly cut leaves. Quite ungrowable, it is a pleasant diversion while you catch your breath during the scramble up the rocks.

In rock crevices above, *Pellaea breweri* makes ladderlike bands of light green, refreshing among so much gray, hairy foliage. On the same limestone outcrops *Dryas octopetala* spreads its dark mats catlike in the sun, with golden *D. drummondii* growing nearby, rarely opening fully the petals of its lovely rose-like buds. We have found no hybrids of the two here.

In warmer screes nearby grows an interesting trio, including a fine lavender-blue flax, *Linum lewisii*, large-flowered and 9 inches/23 cm tall. Stubby spikes of large-flowered *Penstemon speciosus* mingle with them, sometimes approaching gentian-blue in this patch growing 2000 feet/600 meters higher than the usual range of the species. Then, like a demure bride, *Pedicularis racemosa* subsp. *alba* displays spiky racemes of lovely ivory bonnets. This plant, first described by David Douglas from the "summit of the high mountains of the Grand Rapids of the Columbia," has not been championed as it deserves. Perhaps it would succeed if the seed were broadcast in a gritty or scree part of the rock garden so the semiparasitic seedlings could find hosts, as some growers are now succeeding with *Castilleja* species. The louseworts deserve better than Reginald Farrer's tirade: "Also their ephemeral air of effectiveness makes them seem rather like vicious fungoid emanations that will soon collapse into rottenness and disappear in half an hour." Farrer's digestion must have been terrible.

Clinging to granitic rock here are pastel draperies of *Phlox pulvinata* (Plate 104), one of the best western rock-carpeters. According to C. Leo Hitchcock, our most respected northwestern botanist, this is the species usually encountered in the trade as *P. caespitosa*, which itself is a compact form of the taxon formerly called *P. douglasii*. Hitchcock allies *P. pulvinata* with the Rocky Mountain *P. condensata*, which is still more reduced but similar. Growing out of the phlox mats we often find *Ivesia gordonii*, with neat rosettes of carrot-like foliage above a taproot and numerous 5-inch/13-cm stems with inch-wide balls of tiny yellow flowers.

The most natural course, when one has looked at these hanging gardens, is to follow for a while a stream that slices a little canyon through the rocks. Above the small gorge it forms a miniature cirque populated by mats of dwarf willows, mostly *Salix reticulata* subsp. *nivalis*, but some *S. arctica* and occasionally other, mostly prostrate, larger-leafed willows.

Climb up to the south and you will see, clinging to the sides and tops of these rocks, great plants of *Silene acaulis* (Plate 34) up to a yard/meter across, with uniformly brilliant rose flowers, much brighter than those of the central Rockies. Little bunlike *Saxifraga caespitosa* and *S. bronchialis* var. *austromontana* (Plate 38) with white or ivory blossoms are common. As we climb, they are joined by hard-mat forms of *S. oppositifolia*, its rose-purple blooms long spent by early August, when we made this trip.

We look back toward Ice Lake 400 feet/120 meters below; the Matterhorn is steadily in sight and perhaps 3 hours away. The easiest approach is to bear toward the left of the mountain. A direct route would bring us up against the several-hundred-foot precipitous headwall that faces us. The cinnamon-colored, unnamed peak in the left foreground (elevation about 9000 feet/2740 meters) is easy to steer by. Across the scree slopes ahead, aiming somewhat to the right of the peak, are new treasures, such as the upright, succulent, 4-inch/10-inch-high stems of *Sedum rosea* topped by maroon flowerheads.

The wetter rocky seep drainages here hold a series of prizes. One is the alpine form of *Viola adunca*, formerly distinguished as variety *bellidifolia*. It forms rotund clumps 2 inches/5 cm high, studded with twilight-blue flowers. *Dodecatheon alpinum* (Plate 29), never a tall plant, has elfin stature here, bearing its blooms on stems a scant inch/2.5 cm high— never more than 3 inches/8 cm—sharing turf with the violets. So does *Pedicularis groenlandica*, commonly called "elephant-head" for the trunk-like appendages on the fuchsia-pink blooms. This species sometimes attains 24 inches/60 cm on Mount Rainier; here one sees dwarf pink elephants only 4 inches/10 cm tall. *Polemonium pulcherrimum* grows here, and a superior form of *Cassiope mertensiana* var. *gracilis* with outsized snowy bells highlighted by the red sepals that mount each bloom like a fine jewel. Rose-pink *Phyllodoce empetriformis* and moonlight-yellow *P. glanduliflora* grow in nearby colonies, and here and there is the pale pink hybrid so dependably present that Hitchcock calls it *Phyllodoce × intermedia*. Another plant of these rocky wet-seep minimeadows is the littlest lily, *Lloydia serotina* (Plate 40), with small, fragile, upfacing pearly flowers. These usually solitary flowers are borne on thin 4-inch/10-cm stems above grassy leaves. Nearby, *Ranunculus eschscholtzii* (Plate 14) shuns companionship, preferring wet, open, granite grit sites to display its lemony flowers, 1 inch/2.5 cm wide on 3-inch/8-cm-high stems.

In open screes at 8700 feet/2600 meters, the eritrichiums begin. There is an electricity present when we view these cushions of incredible blue. Perhaps the reason for this emotional response lies in the inaccessibility of these populations. One's heart is in one's mouth even before the plants appear, from the intensity of the climb. Perhaps it is the size of these clumps, sometimes larger than one's hand, or the intensity of the blues, from delphinium to the lighter color of *Gentiana sino-ornata*. Maybe it is because these alpine forget-me-nots grow in open grit scree without companions, like great blue drops left when someone painted the sky. The one here is *Eritrichium nanum*; Hitchcock says it is very close to European forms.

Steve Doonan made an interesting discovery in 1984. Tiny *Eritrichium* cuttings brought down in August failed to root then, but some held refrigerated in a plastic bag were trying to make roots in the refrigerator by spring and formed new roots readily when placed in rooting medium. The best of the cuttings achieved good spread and bloomed that summer at his nursery near Seattle.

A fine rose-pink *Lewisia pygmaea* (Plate 26), similar to the superbly colored Colorado plants, grows on the Matterhorn in scree. The woolly buns of drabas dot this open scree, either *Draba paysonii* (Plate 53) or *D. oligosperma*; both these pale-yellow-flowered species grow here. Flashy alpine daisies make intermittent appearances—*Townsendia alpigena*, *T. parryi*, *Aster sibiricus* var. *meritus*, and other alpine asters and erigerons. Few of these are white; most are strong blues, pinks, or purples, difficult to match with botanical descriptions of plants reported from here. With them on the slopes grow *Eriogonum ovalifolium* (Plate 6), species of *Castilleja*, and *Calyptridium umbellata* var. *caudicifera* (formerly *Spraguea*, and recently placed in *Cistanthe*), while nearby rocks boast *Silene acaulis* and *Saxifraga oppositifolia* by the hundreds.

Those who have stood on the Matterhorn's summit (we always finish our trek in the eritrichium field) speak of a knifelike ridge with a 1000-foot/300-meter vertical wall dropping to the west. Photos show a landscape of dozens of peaks still snow-covered in August, looking like the Rockies in July.

On summer afternoons, thunderstorms often sweep the slopes. Hidden by the bulk of the Matterhorn until 15 minutes before the rains come, they streak in from the west on powerful winds. Travelers to these high slopes must have appropriate protection in their packs and a dry tent pitched at Ice Lake. When a thunderstorm hits, that tent in view below, even if it is an hour away, is reassuring.

Almost certainly there are still undiscovered species or subspecies here. There are also many plants that grow especially dwarf here, which will be useful for troughs or small rock gardens. Several plants collected here only once, about 80 years ago, have never been rediscovered. Whether one discovers something new or old, or nothing at all, there is the exhilarating feeling of tramping one of the best remaining botanical frontiers in this country. The flowers alone are reward enough.

Originally published in the Bulletin of the American Rock Garden Society, *vol. 43, no. 1, pp. 1–10 (1985).*

Growing Wenatchee Wildflowers

STEPHEN DOONAN

One and a half hours by freeway east of Seattle, Washington, lies a floristically varied range of mountains, the Wenatchees. The climate in this range is predominantly continental, that is, warm in summer and cold in winter. The vegetation is entirely different from the Puget Sound flora only 90 miles/144 km away. Rainfall here on the lee side of the Cascade Mountains is considerably lower. Low moisture and relative humidity greatly affect the density and stature of plants: unlike the coastal rain forests, the woods of the Wenatchees are open, and one can easily walk through them. Because of the distinctive climate, many of the unique and desirable plants of these mountains are a challenge to grow for alpine enthusiasts both in the Pacific Northwest and elsewhere.

The dry, treeless eastern hills near the Columbia River are extensions of the greater Wenatchee Mountains. They are made up mostly of lava flows, and evidence of prehistoric flora remains as petrified wood and leaf fossils. Such well-known trees as the ginkgo and metasequoia were found here as fossils before the discovery of their living relicts in China.

On one hill in this rain-shadow area, Whiskey Dick Mountain, grows the barrel cactus *Pediocactus simpsonii* (Plate 48), which is less than 6 inches/15 cm tall and 3 inches/8 cm wide. Its ball-shaped stems occur singly or as clumps, and its intense cerise flowers have bright yellow stamens. *Eriogonum thymoides* (Plate 42) is a picturesque, shrubby little plant of this area, its tiny leaves curled under at the edges in an adaptation to conserve moisture. The short flower stems bear clusters of small, bright red to yellow flowers. The apparent age of the plants is a testament to their hardiness: this area is not only dry but extremely hot in the summer and may have winter temperatures of −25°F/−32°C, with strong winds at times. *Eriogonum thymoides* has survived in my nursery for many years in a pot with sharp drainage, but it never equals the wild specimens. Another eriogonum of intense beauty is *E. douglasii* (Plate 41), which in early spring develops red flower buds that open to bright yellow. The contrast between the developing buds and the open flowers on the small shrub makes this one of the showiest members of its genus.

In the same area, large sagebrush (*Artemisia tridentata*) forms a continuous low cover, intermixed with *Phlox longifolia*, *Fritillaria pudica* (Plate 44), the lovely desert violet *Viola trinervata* (Plate 43), many showy composites, and bunchgrasses. This community of plants continues from the Columbia River westward toward the high peaks of the Wenatchees. *Fritillaria pudica* occurs nearly to timberline in open fields. It grows 2 to 3 inches/5 to 8 cm tall, with two leaves at the ground and one on the flowering stem. As tempting as this plant is to the gardener, it is best left to the bulb specialist, for its culture is complex. A large bulb is necessary to produce flowers, but the bulb tends to break down into many smaller bulblets and then does not bloom. The flower is a golden, nodding bell that turns deep orange-red as it ages. The large maturing seedpod stands erect long after all traces of the leaves have disappeared.

During the short spring interlude another bulb makes its colorful appearance. *Calochortus lyallii* has an odd three-petaled flower with hairs on both the inner and outer surfaces of the petals. It is quite successful in what appears to be barren terrain. Also found in these dry places is *Penstemon gairdneri*, a rather weak-growing plant whose large pink flowers with hairs in the throat make it quite showy. Surprisingly, it is a promising garden plant, although some other dryland penstemons resent our moist coastal climate.

From these earliest plants of low elevations, the flowering season extends with the receding winter snows to the plants of higher elevations as summer progresses. Growing on exposed rocky spines of the low foothills where there is a small accumulation of loess soil, *Ranunculus glaberrimus* (Plate 47) is one of the first to show color. This tiny buttercup will capture your fancy; its intense, bright yellow flowers are of exceptional size relative to the entire plant, but successful garden or pot culture is difficult. *Ranunculus glaberrimus* produces lots of seed, but chipmunks are very efficient collectors, and few can be found. The plants wither away completely after flowering, leaving no trace of their existence. The shallow soil in which they grow becomes quite dry, and only infrequent summer thunderstorms temporarily moisten the dormant crowns. These environmental conditions are hard to imitate in pot culture or in rock gardens with different climatic cycles.

The terrain of the foothills breaks into deep canyons, often with clear running streams, steep hillsides with varying amounts of soil, and rocky outcrops. On sites with better soil, the dominant conifer at lower elevations is *Pinus ponderosa*, a stately tree with patterned yellow-brown bark, which may reach more than 100 feet/30 meters. The cones of previous years litter the ground along with fallen needles and form a carpet of unique design. The resinous aroma of this dry forest sets an adventurous mood for a flower hunt.

One of the most beautiful flowers, found only in the geographically small area of the Wenatchees, is the famous *Lewisia tweedyi* (recently renamed *Cistanthe tweedyi*; Plate 27). We have made many observations of this plant over the years. It first flowers at lower-elevation sites, along with *Ranunculus glaberrimus*. On rocky outcrops with a scattering of ponderosa pines and Douglas firs, bloom commences in early May. Large plants of *Lewisia tweedyi* with dozens of flowers grow on the road cuts, with passing motorists apparently oblivious to the roadside floral display. Along Highway 97 as it follows the canyons of Tronsen and Peshastin creeks into the mountains, many large plants annually produce their colorful show. The rock here consists of uplifted strata bearing gold, which has attracted miners for more than a century. The lower canyons on the east side warm up early, and *L. tweedyi* will have gone to seed and withered to a less handsome appearance here when at its highest stations it is just beginning to flower. *Lewisia tweedyi* is basically an evergreen species, but in drier years the leaves can disappear, leaving only dormant buds that reemerge with the fall rains.

The culture of *Lewisia tweedyi* has tested the skill of the best alpine gardeners. How can a plant that can stand −25°F/−32°C in winter, and above 100°F/30°C in summer, be so temperamental in captivity? In nature the plant is attacked by a rust that disfigures the leaves but seldom does serious damage. In rare years when the weather pattern in the Wenatchees is a reverse flow, with clouds approaching the mountains from the east, bringing spring rain for an extended period, wild plants may suffer rot in the leaves and crown. For garden culture, use a well-aerated soil mixture. Keep the main stem under the whorl of leaves free of soil for more than 1 inch/2.5 cm, and water moderately. The plant must not be allowed to dry out completely, since this will weaken it and make basal rot more likely. A raised bed facing east, preferably under a canopy of evergreens to shed excess rain, is ideal. In pot culture, place the plants under cover and protect them from cold below 20°F/−7°C for best results.

There are three other lewisias in the Wenatchees. *Lewisia triphylla* is a small, insignificant species found in heavier soils that are wet in early spring and considerably drier in the summer. *Lewisia columbiana* occurs along ridge tops in decaying rock soils among dwarfed trees; the flowers are white with a pink stripe through the middle. *Lewisia columbiana* is completely resistant to rot if the soil is well drained and is a useful hybrid parent because of this characteristic. Its small size and longevity make it a good prospect for troughs. The last species, *L. rediviva* (Plate 24), is wide-ranging in the western United States. It occurs in the Wenatchees from rocky outcrops near the Columbia River to above 5000 feet/1500 meters on Entiat Ridge. Distinct color races occur in scattered colonies; the flowers may be very pale pink in one colony and an intense fuchsia 50 miles/80 km away. Seed grown from these different sources comes true. On Entiat Ridge a large colony of broad-petaled white *L. rediviva* grew in a sunny, open space, while nearby under the dappled shade of ponderosa pine and Douglas fir, *L. tweedyi* covered the ground in a nearly solid mat. Unfortunately, a firebreak bulldozed to stop a large fire destroyed this colony, at least temporarily.

Lewisia rediviva flowers 2 months later at higher elevations than it does by the Columbia River at Vantage. It revives from its summer dormancy with the first fall rains. The foliage consists of tufts of fleshy leaves that photosynthesize throughout the cold winter months. By the time the large rose-pink flowers open in spring, the foliage has nearly disappeared. Garden culture requires a soil with sharp drainage and protection from all summer rain or irrigation while the thick, fleshy root is dormant. If we mimic nature's weather pattern, this lewisia will indeed revive come autumn. If the growing medium is properly drained, winter moisture will not cause decay.

A sprawling, tangled vine clambering over rocks, *Clematis columbiana* (Plate 37) makes colorful displays. It has nodding, bell-like flowers ranging in color from pale lavender and blue to very nice pinks. The plant has a wide altitudinal range. Attempts to cultivate it have so far not been successful. Cuttings are slow and weak to root, and slugs find the foliage appetizing. Near the clematis, a perennial violet makes its appearance for 4 months each year, its lobed leaves flat to the ground. The slight purple undercoloring of the leaves gives *Viola purpurea* its name; the flower is yellow and typical in form. When collecting seed from this plant, remember that violet seed is "either green or gone." I pick the ripest pods and keep the cut stems moist in a closed container until the ripening pod explodes with a force that could send the seeds several feet.

The intense color of *Dodecatheon meadia* subsp. *meadia* (formerly *D. pauciflorum*) stands out in the Wenatchee landscape. In early spring it can be found at lower elevations persisting in seasonally wet seeps, where it makes its yearly display and then disappears, leaving only maturing seed capsules as the seeps dry up through summer and fall. On higher, rocky open spaces that have a thin layer of wind-blown soil, dodecatheons produce spectacular displays, with hundreds of plants from the time the last snow melts until summer drought brings complete dormancy. In garden culture, excess summer moisture causes most dodecatheons with this type of growth cycle to rot, so protection against excess watering in the hot months is important. Plants have succeeded with very open, loose soil around the crown and heavier soil below for the extensive root system.

Dodecatheon hendersonii can usually be found growing along cold, fast-moving streams in the moist accumulation of peatlike soil among mosses and sedges. In the same environment *Mimulus lewisii* forms colonies with dozens of bright rose-pink flowers in mid-spring and early summer. Both these plants are better enjoyed in their native haunts, as they will never equal their wild charm or vigor away from these natural gardens. One orchid, *Platanthera dilatata* (formerly *Habenaria dilatata*) occasionally grows in these wet areas, its tall spires of miniature flowers with their sweet fragrance a pleasure to find. We know one colony that has persisted for more than 20 years and is increasing slowly.

Another orchid, *Calypso bulbosa*, is found in the humus-rich soil under *Abies amabilis*, nestled among mosses with *Viola sempervirens*, *Linnaea borealis*, and *Chimaphila umbellata*. *Calypso* is difficult to grow away from its native haunts, as fungus attacks the leaves and prevents formation of the large, bulbous storage stem. While the plants rest through the summer, slugs, mice, and birds find them tasty treats in the garden. To enjoy *Calypso* properly, get down on your knees so you can see it and enjoy its delicate scent. This is the proper homage to pay this plant; then return another time to enjoy it. Often in the same location *Corallorhiza maculata*, the spotted coral-root orchid, makes small clumps of flowering stems. Coral-root does not make any of its own food from photosynthesis but subsists on decaying humus as a saprophyte. Again, to your knees with a hand lens to see its floral design.

The showy *Cypripedium montanum* (Plate 8) makes a many-stemmed clump in open spaces of the forest but generally produces only a single stem in the deeper shade of trees. One particular plant that I know has continued to increase in size since I discovered it and now boasts more than 60 blooms. The sepals are brown, the white pouch lip is veined with purple, and the central column that contains the reproductive parts is golden-yellow with red spots. These flowers are also fragrant. The plants have large, vigorous root systems extending through heavy soils that never dry completely during the summer. *Cypripedium montanum* has been grown successfully here in a container. Success in the open garden in the Pacific Northwest is problematic because slugs consistently destroy new buds. Collection from the wild is now prohibited by law in the hope of protecting wild populations from extinction. Progress in growing seedlings of temperate orchids in laboratory situations may make these plants commercially available to gardeners.

At higher elevations, in open fields and in groves of *Abies amabilis*, great patches of *Erythronium grandiflorum* make known their presence with myriads of swaying yellow flowers. The stamens and pistil of the flower point downward, and the petals reflex upward. Plants grown from seed collected in lower-elevation colonies succeed in cultivation.

The spring flower show of *Penstemon fruticosus* (Plate 36) turns the hillsides and ridges of the Wenatchees blue for a month. Out of flower, this penstemon is rather inconspicuous. Some plants are more than 3 feet/1 meter across and completely cover themselves in June with snapdragon-like flowers. *Penstemon fruticosus* is rather large for most rock gardens, but once established on dry walls or in poor stony soils it can be just as nice as in the wild. In areas of high rainfall, fungus attack can disfigure the foliage. Selections more amenable to garden culture have been found, and these proven cultivars should be sought out.

Penstemon rupicola (Plate 32) is not so ubiquitous, but its intense cerise flowers contrasting with the rounded blue-gray foliage make it an eye-catcher. As you drive along, someone is sure to yell out, "Stop!" when this plant appears. It roots readily from cuttings, but sadly, it rarely makes the same show in the garden as it does in the wild. *Penstemon rupicola* grows naturally in cracks on southeast-facing rock cliffs. It requires a well-drained soil mix. The difficulty is that in areas with cool, wet springs, the developing foliage is seriously attacked by foliar fungus. One year there was a perfectly dry spring in our area, and *P. rupicola* was disease-free and made a spectacular show.

As we climb to higher elevations, taller eriogonums make their appearance, occurring with *Penstemon fruticosus*. The eriogonums have large heads of intense yellow or soft cream. These plants grow among large rocks, and in the grand spaciousness of this vast wilderness, they are completely in scale. On sunny days *Eriogonum umbellatum* makes unbelievable floral shows, each plant vigorous and about 1 foot/30 cm tall.

Along the road on north-facing slopes at intermediate elevations, we occasionally see *Rhododendron albiflorum* with its bell-like, white clusters of flowers. This species is so distinct in the genus *Rhododendron* that it has been assigned to its own section. The Cascade azalea, as it is commonly known, has been successfully grown by few people; it seems to require a cool, moist habitat.

On some of the highest roads, built for access to now-dismantled fire lookouts, we reach an environment that favors extensive colonies of *Douglasia nivalis* (Plate 46). The plants form rounded mounds of glaucous, needlelike foliage, and the intense rose-violet flowers resemble those of the genus *Androsace*. Again, this is a difficult plant to grow in a maritime climate. What a shame! If we could succeed with them, the cushion phloxes would have real competition.

The plants mentioned so far can be seen by botanizing from the car window, but to see the gems of the highest elevations we need to don our hiking boots. The peaks are home to many special plants worth the arduous climb. Growing in magnesium-rich soil is the lovely alpine *Claytonia megarhiza* var. *nivalis* (Plate 45). The spoon-shaped leaves arranged in compact rosettes with large, pink flowers make this a plant worth any effort to grow it. The large black seeds germinate in a heavy soil, or side shoots can readily be rooted in sand. Transfer small seedlings to a better-drained soil when they are about 1 inch/2.5 cm across. To prevent rot in the congested crown, continually make cuttings and keep excess moisture from the crown.

On north-facing rock chimneys *Saxifraga oppositifolia* forms mounded cushions. Its sessile rose-purple flowers appear long before the trails are free of winter snowpack. Snowshoes help us get to the ridge tops to see this spectacular plant in bloom. Most North American forms of *S. oppositifolia* are not amenable to cultivation; they resent our hot summers and can literally die overnight.

Along Beverly Ridge, southwest of Mount Stewart, *Erigeron aureus* forms a large colony. The large, golden yellow daisies with short stems on rather small rosettes of leaves are worth the hike. The erigeron is also found in other high places, but generally as small, scattered plants, so that the effect of masses of bloom is lost. This is a good garden plant, grown from seed or divisions, providing sunny flowers on short stems in the scree. A loose, gritty soil or a deep sand bed suits its needs. Routinely bait for slugs, since they like this plant, too.

Phlox diffusa, a colorful cushion plant, grows in rocky screes and out on shallow soils. The color range varies in the extensive population, as do size, shape, and overall habit. Each specimen is unique, and it is difficult to make selections because of the variety from which to choose. Cuttings made from wild plants can be difficult to root; take larger cuttings and place them in a north exposure until rooted; once *P. diffusa* is established, it is a long-lived plant and flowers profusely every spring. Cuttings taken from garden-grown plants root more readily.

One of the showiest plants in the Wenatchees is *Phacelia sericea*, a spire of blue flowers with gray-blue, pubescent foliage. The species is found in many Western mountains, but the particular form found here is shorter and more colorful. It has grown and flowered well in a scree bed, but excess winter wet combined with cold has caused loss in the open ground. Gardeners in more arid locations could succeed with it.

These are only a few of the worthy plants found in this mountain range. A lifetime would be needed to find, study, and enjoy them all, not to mention the challenge of growing them.

Originally published in the Bulletin of the American Rock Garden Society, *vol. 49, no. 4, pp. 193–206 (1991).*

Mount Townsend

DENNIS THOMPSON

Mount Townsend is one of the lesser-known peaks of the Olympic Range of Washington. Unlike the major tourist attractions of Hurricane Ridge and Deer Park to the north in Olympic National Park, and the Hoh rainforest to the west, Mount Townsend is on the dry side of the mountain range. The western slope is claimed to receive as much as 200 inches/500 cm of precipitation annually, but the lower eastern side may experience as little as 5 inches/13 cm.

Although in the rain shadow, the lower Mount Townsend forest receives enough moisture to support the water-loving *Abies grandis* and *Tsuga heterophylla*. Mount Townsend, now included in the Buckthorn Wilderness Area, is not noticeably marked on maps or by road signs; even in the small town of Quilcene at the base of the mountain, few people seem aware of the trail's existence.

To reach the trail, head out of Quilcene past the fish hatchery 1.4 miles/2 km. Turn left on Forest Service Road 2812 and drive 13.5 miles/ 22 km. Avoid turning onto any of the more important-appearing side roads until the junction with F.S. Road 2764. Turn left and wind on about 1.5 miles/2 km to the parking lot at the end of the road. The trail begins here at an elevation of 3600 feet/1100 meters and rises almost 3000 feet/ 900 meters in just over 3.5 miles/5.6 km to the summit saddle.

The summit of the trail is the highest rise on a rolling meadow and scree ridge about 100 to 300 feet/30 to 90 meters above timberline. Below this ridge are the last *krummholz* (wind-dwarfed) forms of *Pinus contorta*, *Abies lasiocarpa*, and *Tsuga mertensiana*. This summit is due west of Quilcene about 8 miles/13 km. The Big Quilcene and Little Quilcene rivers arise on its slopes. About 5 miles/8 km southwest of Townsend toward the interior is well-known Marmot Pass, which is about 3 miles/5 km north of Mount Constance.

Some visitors who do not want to make this stiff climb choose to spend more time in the lower areas, often exploring Windy Camp or some of the lower meadows. We usually climb to Windy Camp for lunch and explore the alpine areas later. Even though this is on the dry side of the Olympics, there are often sudden fogs and sprinkles in the afternoon, even in July, so it is best to pack some light rain gear. If there is no breeze around Windy Camp, we also have a chance to meet some of Washington's voracious wildlife, the Olympic mosquito. The streams, though beautiful and cold, should not be used as a water source because of the presence of *Giardia*, which can cause severe illness.

Why would anyone want to find a mountain that not even the natives know about, walk 3 miles/5 km climbing 3000 feet/900 meters, possibly to be rained on or attacked by mosquitoes, where it is not even safe to drink the water? The answer is that Mount Townsend holds one of the greatest varieties of common, rare, and endemic mountain plants of any area in the Pacific Northwest.

This article was compiled from worksheets prepared by Marvin Black, Dan Douglas, and myself between 1975 and 1985. In general, the best floral displays have been in mid-July, although the trail is usually accessible between the first of June and the end of September. We have collected seeds on the saddle as late as the first weekend in October.

The trailhead is in typical high woodland. The forest includes *Pseudotsuga menziesii*, *Tsuga heterophylla*, *Thuja plicata*, and *Abies grandis*, with occasional *Acer macrophyllum*, *Alnus rubra*, *Prunus emarginata* and *P. virginiana* var. *demissa*. This is one of the few areas I have found where populations of *Acer glabrum* var. *douglasii* and *A. circinatum* often grow interspersed. A number of the plants appear to exhibit intermediate characteristics.

Under the trees in sunnier areas grows *Gaultheria shallon*, and at the upper reaches of the zone we find *G. ovatifolia*, *Rhododendron macrophyllum*, *Rubus parvifolius*, *Mahonia nervosa*, *Sambucus racemosa*, *Ribes lacustre*, and *Rosa gymnocarpa*. Some of the *Rubus parviflorus* have fringed petals. Two huckleberries, *Vaccinium parvifolium* with red berries and *V. membranaceum* with blue-black berries, are present.

The woodland floor for about the first 1.5 miles/2 km is thickly carpeted with herbaceous shade-dwellers, including *Achlys triphylla*, *Actaea rubra*, *Oxalis oregana*, *Cornus canadensis*, and *Linnaea borealis*. In the upper areas of the woodland zone these are replaced by *Rubus lasiococcus*, *Asarum caudatum*, *Mitella trifida*, and *Parnassia fimbriata*. Above these low groundcovers are gracefully arching *Smilacina racemosa*, *S. stellata* (recently renamed *Maianthemum racemosum* and *M. stellatum*), *Aruncus dioicus* var. *vulgaris* (formerly *A. sylvester*), and the rarely seen liliaceous *Stenanthium occidentale*. Its small, waxy mahogany bells are easily missed by

111

the unobservant but possess a delightful shy elegance. *Clintonia uniflora* is common in more open areas. In deeper shade grow a number of small semiparasitic or saprophytic plants, including *Chimaphila umbellata*, *Pyrola asarifolia*, *P. minor*, *P. secunda* (now *Orthilia secunda*), *Pterospora andromedea*, and *Monotropa hypopitys*. The pyrolas I find intriguing, although *Pyrola asarifolia* is the only one with sufficient allure to tempt me to the inevitable garden failure. *Pyrola asarifolia* has a fragile, rich green, oily-appearing leaf that is striking in dark shade against soft green moss. The pinedrop (*Pterospora*) and pinecap (*Monotropa*) seem like objects left over from "Fantasia": *Pterospora andromedea* rises like clumps of yard-tall cinnamon-colored wands; *Monotropa hypopitys* ranges from cream to florescent pink in all its parts—stem, leaves, and nodding flower clusters.

In sunny forest breaks on well-drained soil are the small *Lonicera utahensis*, *Paxistima myrsinites*, and *Heuchera micrantha*. Some forms of *Heuchera* from this area are especially floriferous, looking a great deal like a dwarf baby's-breath. The honeysuckle is refined in its native habitat but took on an awkward lankiness in the garden. The false boxwood (*Paxistima*) has always fascinated me, but while cuttings rooted readily, I could not get it established until Frances Roberson explained that the plant hated root disturbance and that lifting the cutting could be enough to kill it. Rooting it in well-drained soil mix and planting the entire root ball seemed to solve the problem.

Anywhere there is a bit of sun there will be fireweed (*Epilobium angustifolium*). In the sun in moist areas grow *Mimulus guttatus* and *M. dentatus*, as well as the tall, pale *Delphinium glaucum*. Where the site is not both dry and sunny, swordfern (*Polystichum munitum*) makes itself at home. *Notochelone nemorosa* (formerly *Penstemon nemorosus*) rises in the light shade like some wild snapdragon—only a few in any place. Where the shade is deepest and only mosses and the occasional pyrola survive, *Goodyera oblongifolia* is as happily at home as it is 50 miles/80 km away on exposed rocks just above the ocean spray.

Many of the plants that first appear in this woodland continue into upper areas. Both *Viola sempervirens* and *V. glabella* fall into this category. Since *V. sempervirens* is native through the woodlands around Seattle, it is a safe plant for neglected garden nooks. I truly love its companion, *V. glabella*, which I first learned about from the garden of taxonomist Helen Gilkey in Corvallis, Oregon. I was told she did not garden, but her entire yard was carpeted with this 8-inch-/20-cm yellow johnny-jump-up. It is intriguing how our memories emotionally color plants even when we see them in the wild.

About 2 miles/3 km up the trail, the woodland opens dramatically onto less stable slopes. Trees still form isolated groves, but the views are now of spectacular ridges up scree slopes and meadows. Many of the plants that first make their appearance here continue into the alpine zone. The larger ones include *Pinus contorta*, *Chamaecyparis nootkatensis*, and *Abies lasiocarpa*. The creeping *Juniperus communis* var. *montanus* tangles with *Arctostaphylos uva-ursi* (kinnikinnick). Threaded in among the kinnikinnick are two particularly good garden plants, *Symphoricarpos hesperius* (snowberry) and the Olympic form of *Potentilla fruticosa* (syn. *Pentaphylloides floribunda*). The snowberry is absolutely prostrate. It shows fresh green leaves early in the spring and a rather strong red fall color. The flowers are usually hidden in the foliage so that I miss them in the garden when so many flowers are in spring bloom, and I have never noticed them in the mountains. About the first of July they develop clusters of small, flattened white berries that last late into autumn. The white berries with the red of the kinnikinnick, and then the bright evergreen leaves of the latter covering the departure of the red snowberry foliage, form a composition to thrill a florist. The snowberry grows in Seattle rockeries with no summer care. The potentilla, a cultivar of which was selected by Bob Putnam from Mount Townsend, grows in very mobile screes. I have not seen any but the prostrate form on Mount Townsend. The flowers are light yellow, and the plant is a strong grower in a pot or well-drained soil.

In the scree and meadow slopes, herbaceous perennials become common. The plants from the lower sunny areas are joined by *Aquilegia formosa*, *Anaphalis margaritacea*, *Minuartia [Arenaria] obtusiloba*, *Aster foliaceus*, *Cerastium berringianum*, *Phacelia sericea*, *Sedum divergens*, and the weedy *Hieracium gracile* and *Agoseris aurantica*. The large, carroty *Heracleum lanatum* (now *H. maximum*) and various lomatiums tangle with the daisies of *Leucanthemum vulgare* (field daisy).

Bulbs appear, too, including *Lilium columbianum*, *Fritillaria affinis* (Plate 3), *Allium amplectens*, *A. acuminatum*, and *Zigadenus venenosus* in the rocks. The lily is a dwarfer form than is usually seen, under 1 foot/30 cm tall with full-sized flowers. Considering the vigor of most of the plants here, it seems unlikely that this is simply a starvation reaction. Brian Halliwell took bulbs back to Kew, but I have not heard how they performed there, and I do not know of anyone else who has tried them in the garden. The fritillary seems happy both here and in the higher elevations. The small-flowered *Z. venenosus* grows well but is a bit dowdy. The onions are interesting and quite growable: *Allium acuminatum* has a small cluster of intense rose-purple flowers; *A. amplectens* is a narrow-leafed onion with papery pink flowers that seems confined to this middle elevation.

The family Scrophulariaceae is especially well represented. In sunny breaks in the woods *Penstemon rupicola* (Plate 32) grows in isolated crevices. In the middle and alpine zones *P. davidsonii* var. *menziesii* (Plate 28) and *P. procerus* var. *tolmiei* are frequently seen. *Penstemon davidsonii* var. *menziesii* forms tight mats of rather dense, oval, serrate leaves, often tinged purple, topped by clusters of violet-blue flowers. *Penstemon procerus* var. *tolmiei* is lankier with larger, more extended flower clusters of

113

slate-blue. Because of its more refined character, *P. davidsonii* tends to attract more attention despite its smaller size. *Penstemon rupicola* puts in a brief appearance near the trailhead on rock outcrops, but its red flowers are duller here than in many of its better forms. Several species of *Castilleja* make an appearance, ranging from golden to fuchsia, red, and orange. The closely allied *Orthocarpus imbricatus* joins in with straw-colored inflorescences. A dwarf yellow *Mimulus* peeks out in wet locations in the lower zones. The soft pink-lavender heads of *Pedicularis racemosa* also put in an occasional appearance beside conifers.

We have found two colonies of *Lewisia columbiana* var. *rupicola* on this route. Unlike the elegant form named by Carl English from Saddle Mountain in Oregon, the Olympic plants have spatulate leaves of pale green; they remain "trunkless" (without an extended caudex), but the flowers are blush-pink rather than white with pink stripes. There is no intense cerise as in the Saddle Mountain plants.

The rock-clingers are common through the cliffs of this area. There are two mat-forming silenes, *Silene douglasii* and *S. parryi*. Both are rather pallid, greenish-white to mauve, although *S. douglasii* may attain some brilliant color on occasion. I am more attracted by some of the smaller crevice-dwellers. *Solidago multiradiata* var. *scopulorum* is a tiny goldenrod; the form on Mount Townsend is often under 4 inches / 10 cm tall, with vivid green leaves and sunflower-yellow-rayed flowers. Another daisy, *Senecio flettii*, grows to about 8 inches / 20 cm, with a compact cluster of globose yellow heads. *Erigeron flettii*, an endemic, forms clumps of large white flowers held 2 to 5 inches / 5 to 13 cm above the ground. *Erigeron compositus* (the plant was formerly distinguished as variety *glabratus*) may have either button flowers or rayed daisies; the leaves are attractive in all individuals, and the 1-inch / 2.5-cm dwarf forms are spectacular. *Viola adunca* here is compact and showy, the purple flowers usually found huddling in the shelter of a rock in almost full sun.

This area has a number of good forms of rock garden shrubs, including *Artemisia suksdorfii*, *Cassiope mertensiana* (Plate 11), *Luina hypoleuca*, and *Phyllodoce empetriformis*, as well as the arctostaphylos, potentilla, and vacciniums mentioned above. *Luina hypoleuca* is reminiscent of a miniature *Senecio* 'Sunshine' (*S. greyi*) with lemon-colored rayless daisy flowers. It is growable in a scree situation in Seattle gardens but is rarely seen. The cassiope and phyllodoce are grown by specialists in the Ericaceae.

There are several ferns among the loose rocks. Moving from the shade of the lower zone into the rocks of the middle elevation is *Polystichum munitum*. In the loose scree is a colony we have tentatively identified as *P. lonchitis*. *Cryptogramma sitchensis* fringes the loose stones. In the shade of the lower zone are lycopodiums and selaginellas. *Selaginella oregana* will even occasionally venture into the scree. *Athyrium filix-femina* and *Blechnum spicant* are common at low elevations.

The lunch stop, Windy Camp, is at the lower edge of the alpine zone. There is a small lake surrounded by subalpine conifers. In the lee of the trees are patches of subirrigated soil populated by *Parnassia fimbriata*, *Trollius laxus* var. *albiflorus*, *Salix arctica*, and *Sorbus sitchensis* var. *grayi*. From this point up there are frequent breezes and occasional fog and showers.

Assuming that people have made it this far and consumed their meal before the mosquitoes consumed them, the most exciting plants are now at hand. The trail steepens, the rocks are looser, and the trees quickly disappear.

Just above the lake is the pale pink *Pedicularis racemosa*. *Penstemon procerus* var. *tolmiei* occurs in a very good form here, and *P. davidsonii* (Plate 28) is compact and seems to become better and better as the saddle is approached. In the loose talus slopes are *Delphinium glareosum*, a blue larkspur, and budded mats of the Olympic aster, *Aster paucicapitatus*. *Abies amabilis* and *A. lasiocarpa* have great skirts of *krummholz*, usually edged with masses of alliums, *Zigadenus elegans*, *Douglasia laevigata*, and *Campanula piperi* (Plate 49). The rarely seen *Oxytropis campestris* and *Smelowskia calycina* put in an appearance near the saddle.

The cracks in large rocks become an important habitat. All plants seem to lessen in size and to mingle, making small gardens. *Douglasia laevigata* var. *ciliolata* sports pale purple flowers, and *Epilobium glaberrimum* produces a shocking display of fuchsia-colored bloom over short trailing stems with glaucous leaves. The magenta *Hedysarum occidentale* is mixed with the orange of *Castilleja miniata* and the gold of *Eriophyllum lanatum*. Near the saddle, silver-leafed *Phacelia sericea* adds its purple flowers to the mixture, and large-flowered *Zigadenus elegans* appears. The miniature *Viola adunca* (a form once called variety *bellidifolia*) adds more purple, and *Erysimum arenicola* contrasts with brilliant yellow. Flowering stems of *Saxifraga bronchialis* var. *vespertina* (Plate 38) and *S. caespitosa* dangle from crevices, and *Campanula piperi* (Plate 49) marks the stony fractures with evergreen leaves and staunch blue-purple flowers. Occasionally one finds the felty white *Synthyris pinnatifida* var. *lanuginosa*; long past bloom, the silver tufts imitate a miniature, snowy parsley.

Above the saddle to the right about 200 to 250 yards/meters are larger populations of the *Synthyris* and a marvelously compact, dark green *Arctostaphylos uva-ursi*. There are also very good dwarf forms of two daisies, *Erigeron flettii* and *E. compositus*. My favorite was always the dissected-leaf *E. compositus*, which has flowers varying from rayless buttons to graceful white daisies much like *Bellis perennis*. Marvin Black preferred *E. flettii*, with entire leaves and larger white flowers. The form of *Potentilla fruticosa* (*Pentaphylloides floribunda*) that has been distributed as the 'Olympic Mountain Form' is common in the lower elevations, but in the talus fields ascending to the rock outcrops, the plants are ancient, contorted, and dwarf. In less stable areas near the outcrops there are mar-

115

velous patches of *Elmera racemosa*, which looks like an elegantly fringed heuchera. In the course of a good slide you can observe three or four distinctive forms before skidding to a stop on the rocky brink.

Back to the saddle and farther east about 1 mile/1600 meters, you come to cliffs of deteriorating rock studded with *Petrophyton hendersonii*, *Silene acaulis* (Plate 34), and a dwarf willow, *Salix arctica*, about 7 feet/2 meters in diameter and 1 inch/2.5 cm in height. *Saxifraga oppositifolia* clings to the vertical walls. Swales of *Lupinus lepidus* var. *lobbii* (Plate 52) carpet the more level areas, and the dusty-rose blooms of *Geum triflorum* var. *campanulatum* overhang them. At this point you have to remember that it is about an hour down to the parking lot—though I must admit that sunset on the ridge with a bottle of wine is well worth a trek in the dark.

Originally published in the Bulletin of the American Rock Garden Society, *vol. 46, no. 4, pp. 169–176 (1988).*

Chowder Ridge:
An Alpine Showcase

RONALD J. TAYLOR

The North Cascade Mountains are one of nature's masterpieces, with many panoramic vistas. Although beauty is subjective, no one can fail to be impressed by the grandeur of the lofty mountains and the striking contrast between the green of the forests, the many-colored wildflowers of the alpine and subalpine slopes, the brilliant white of the snow, and the pale blue of the ice fields. To this setting are added many lakes and sparkling streams that cascade down to form the rivers below.

The crown jewel of the North Cascades is the Mount Baker Wilderness of Washington State. Chowder Ridge, a major part of this wilderness, contains the largest area of continuous alpine vegetation. The ridge crest is approximately 3.2 miles/5 km long and is oriented from northwest to southeast, abutting the west slope of Mount Baker. The elevation varies from approximately 6500 to 7500 feet/2000 to 2300 meters, the highest point being Hadley Peak. Near the center of Chowder Ridge and perpendicular to it, extending northward, is Cougar Divide. Expansive subalpine meadows and scattered groves of trees occur in the area of the T formed by these joining ridges. These meadows are lush with colorful wildflowers.

Wild animals move between forest and meadow or feed on the lush meadow vegetation. Blue grouse are often heard but seldom seen as they emit their low calls from the shelter of trees. The shrill whistles of marmots pierce the thin mountain air as sentinels warn of approaching danger. The burrows of marmots characteristically mark the meadows, especially in dense vegetation below snowfields. Pikas are common inhabitants of coarse talus slopes and rock outcrops. Deer frequent the region, grazing on the meadow vegetation or browsing on shrubs but never wandering far from the safety of the continuous forest. Mountain goats range from the upper limits of the forest zone to the alpine slopes of Chowder. Bears forage through the area, especially in autumn when the huckleberries are ripe. Finally, everywhere there is evidence of small rodents, such as the heather vole, which burrows beneath the snow leaving long dirt mounds, nests of dried plants, and latrine piles.

The north slope of Chowder Ridge is steep and covered in its higher parts by permanent or late-melting snowfields toward the west, and by the Mazama Glacier adjacent to Mount Baker. Vegetation is sparse on this expansive slope except toward the base and where the scree, talus, and rock outcrops are interrupted by benches; the latter appear as islands of dwarf shrubs and stunted mountain hemlocks and subalpine firs (*krummholz*). From a distance, the north slope is spectacular with its contrasting colors and rugged topography. The foothills immediately above Cougar Divide are blanketed by Cascade huckleberries (*Vaccinium deliciosum*), which take on brilliant fall colors of red, orange, and yellow. The purple fruits of these 6-inch/15-cm shrubs are as delectable as the botanical name suggests. A prominent, mat-forming associate of the huckleberry is partridge-foot (*Luetkea pectinata*). This low herb has attractive small flowers in dense, terminal clusters, and divided leaves that give it its common name.

The scattered dwarf shrub communities at middle elevations on the north slope are dominated by the heaths *Phyllodoce empetriformis* and *Cassiope mertensiana* (Plate 11), associated with a mixture of subalpine and alpine plant species. Among the former are the conspicuous subalpine daisy *Erigeron peregrinus* and *Lupinus latifolius*. On moist scree slopes the unusual and attractive *Saxifraga tolmiei* is frequent. Along streams formed from melting snow, the beautiful alpine monkeyflower *Mimulus tilingii* can occasionally be seen.

An unusual attraction of the north slope is the fossil fauna, primarily clamshells, for which Chowder Ridge was named. The ridge is largely of sedimentary origin but has andesitic deposits associated with volcanic eruptions of Mount Baker. Alpine glaciers of the Pleistocene period were also involved in forming and shaping the ridge.

The crest of Chowder Ridge narrows progressively from the northwest toward the southeast, developing into a series of spirelike pinnacles around Hadley Peak and toward Mount Baker. Along this southeast section of the ridge, the south slope is uniformly very steep and covered mostly by loose talus. Here the vegetation is sparse and floristically depauperate, but still interesting. The predominant species is *Potentilla fruticosa* (or *Pentaphylloides floribunda*) which spreads to form broad and often spectacular mats. Other attractive mat-forming plants of this area are *Anemone drummondii* (Plate 50), *Smelowskia ovalis*, *Saxifraga bronchialis*

(Plate 38), and *Penstemon davidsonii* (Plate 28). The purple *Saxifraga oppositifolia*, a species uncommon in the North Cascades, occurs in abundance here, growing as if painted on vertical rock walls and cliffs.

While the eastern half of Chowder has spectacular topography with Mount Baker in the background, the western half is an alpine showcase. The ridge crest consists of a series of rounded prominences and shallow depressions. The south slope remains steep but is largely covered with vegetation. The various erosional phenomena that shape and characterize alpine areas are conspicuously evident: solifluction with mass sloughing of soil occurs along some of the steeper drainages on the south slope; near the crest, wind scars and blow-outs are frequent. Here the dominant plants are dwarf shrubs, including *Salix cascadensis* and the crowberry, *Empetrum nigrum*. These shrubs spread along the ground, rooting at the nodes, so they tolerate the high winds and resist uprooting. On scree and gravelly slopes, the small rocks have been sorted by percolating water and gravity. Here the vegetation is arranged in long strips 9 to 18 inches/23 to 45 cm wide, the strip being separated by about 3 feet/1 meter of scree material. Cushion plants dominate these vegetation strip communities; some of the most common are *Silene acaulis* (Plate 34), *Phlox diffusa*, the paintbrush *Castilleja rupicola* (Plate 51), and a variety of grasses and sedges. Frost-heaving is evident where the soil is rather well developed on shallow slopes, supporting herb-field communities.

The most widespread community types on the western half of Chowder are herb-fields, fellfields (cushion-plant communities), and dwarf shrub communities. Fellfields occur along or near the ridge crests and are characterized by cushion plants scattered on a rocky substrate; these are the rock gardens of the alpine zone. The stereotypic cushion plant of tundra areas in North America, *Silene acaulis* (Plate 34), achieves its greatest abundance in these fellfields. Its flowers are tubular, restricting the nectar rewards to long-tongued insects; individual plants may be pistillate, staminate, or perfect (hermaphroditic). Perhaps the most common cushion plant of Chowder is *Phlox diffusa*, another species with tubular flowers. *Saxifraga bronchialis* is also abundant, forming large mats that become senescent in the center and along the trailing edge, leading to fragmented cushions. An alpine form of the prairie lupine, *Lupinus lepidus* var. *lobbii* (recently renamed *L. sellulus* var. *lobbii*; Plate 52), is common here and reflects the volcanic influence that helped shape the ridge.

Other conspicuous species of the fellfields include an alpine ecotype of the field chickweed *Cerastium arvense*, and two species of stonecrop—*Sedum divergens* and *S. lanceolatum*. There is *Oxytropis campestris*, the favorite forage species of bumblebees, and *Potentilla diversifolia*, one of the favorite food sources of syrphid flies. *Phacelia sericea* is an extremely attractive plant, with dense clusters of bright blue flowers and exserted purple anthers contrasting with the gray-green, silky pinnate leaves. Two yellow composites are *Solidago multiradiata* and *Tonestus lyallii* (formerly *Haplopappus lyallii*). The brilliantly spotted petals of *Saxifraga bronchialis* are apparent only under close examination. Two uncommon fellfield species, rare south of Canada and Alaska, are *Gentiana glauca* and *Aster sibiricus*.

Herb-field communities are characterized by having more or less continuous vegetation comprised of a rich assemblage of plants with a cushion or matted habit. These communities occur along the ridge top and gentle south slopes where the soil is relatively stable. The most conspicuous species here include *Phlox diffusa, Potentilla diversifolia, Oxytropis campestris, Solidago multiradiata,* an alpine form of *Achillea millefolium,* the small-flowered but beautiful *Penstemon procerus,* an unusually large-flowered form of *Campanula rotundifolia,* and a variety of sedges and grasses. Within these communities can be found *Androsace septentrionalis,* the only annual plant known to occur on Chowder Ridge; although it is small and inconspicuous, it deserves an honorable mention.

Dwarf shrub communities of the alpine zone have close floristic affinities with the subalpine heath communities but differ in the dominant presence of yellow-flowered *Phyllodoce glanduliflora.* This species frequently hybridizes with the red *P. empetriformis* in mixed communities, producing a pale pink intermediate. Other dwarf shrubs include *Salix cascadensis, S. reticulata* subsp. *nivalis, Vaccinium deliciosum, Cassiope mertensiana,* and *Empetrum nigrum.*

Other habitat types on Chowder Ridge include rock outcrops and rock crevices. The former are marked by a colorful combination of crustose lichens and a few specialized flowering plants, such as *Draba paysonii* (Plate 53), a dense cushion plant with a brilliant display of bright yellow flowers. In rock crevices, *Oxyria digyna* is a regular inhabitant.

There are also small pockets of subalpine vegetation in protected sites along the ridge top. A conspicuous representative of these sites is *Veronica cusickii,* an unusually attractive member of the genus. Another beautiful plant found in these refugia is the rare yellow-flowered form of spring beauty, *Claytonia lanceolata* var. *chrysantha.*

Although many animals spend part of their lives in the alpine zone, few live there the year round. The animals most often associated with the high treeless slopes of Chowder Ridge are mountain goat and ptarmigan, the latter as fearless as the former is wary. The ptarmigan is a master of camouflage, with white plumage in winter and gray in summer. Even during the molt, its white and gray patches match those of its world of boulders. Nevertheless, ptarmigan can frequently be seen, often with a family of chicks.

In spite of its awesome beauty, the alpine area of Chowder Ridge, like the alpine zone everywhere, is a hostile environment. Unlike the animals, the plants cannot seek shelter during adverse conditions. They must have special morphological and physiological adaptations to survive. They must be generalists, in the sense that they tolerate the extreme and variable climate and adverse soil conditions. Many have a cushion habit, providing protection from wind and desiccation while concentrating solar energy at ground level and warming the roots. Most plants are covered with silky hairs, which form an insulating layer against rapid temperature change and water loss during hot, windy summer days. Finally, all must be metabolically in tune with the unpredictable, non-rhythmic climatic conditions.

Chowder Ridge is not easily accessible. It can be reached from Skyline Divide, a 6-mile/10-km hike terminated by a scramble up the rocky western end of Chowder; or from Cougar Divide, a 5-mile/8-km hike terminated by traversing a very steep north slope covered by a snow-field. Both routes have their ups and downs—mostly ups. Neither should be attempted before July. Skyline and Cougar divides are accessible from the Mount Baker Highway, east of Bellingham, Washington. Visitors should check in at the Glacier Ranger Station en route.

Originally published in the Bulletin of the American Rock Garden Society, *vol. 49, no. 4, pp. 285–289 (1991).*

Some Elegant Eriogonums

B. LEROY DAVIDSON

Not all the eriogonums or false buckwheats can be said to be of equal attractiveness; indeed, some are gawky, dowdy weeds. Nonetheless, the more refined among them are elegant indeed, constituting such gorgeous foliage plants that their flowers can be a mere distraction. Accordingly, nature, with the subtlety of a great artist, has given the flowers a subordinate role.

Few American genera suited to rock gardens are so rich in first-rate cushion plants, and few are so perplexing. As to selecting which to attempt in the garden, Ira N. Gabrielson wrote in *Western American Alpines*, "To dive into the tremendous welter at random expecting to find anything satisfactory would be hopeless." He added that while there were plenty of worthwhile subjects among them, the trick was as much in adapting them to garden life as in determining which to try.

From observation in nature it is easily divined that eriogonums are best suited to conditions that are arid, even harshly so. This applies even to the alpine species, which are typically found in immediate proximity to exceptionally xeric conditions. The soils they grow in are commonly dry and stony, highly mineral but frequently with a top stratum of fine humus composed in part of the eriogonums' own decaying foliage. The majority possess some degree of protective hirsuteness, variable as to its distribution on the plant parts; this adds considerably to their attractiveness. Their roots are deeply penetrating and ordinarily as brittle as kindling, with little fiber to them. Almost without exception, eriogonums insist on blazing sunshine, so they will thrive only in the hottest and driest parts of the garden; possibly they are best suited to troughs or alpine houses, where conditions can be controlled. Certainly it is safest to allow them water only sparingly. In the wild they receive moisture only in the melt season, and this diminishes to the merest trace by summer.

Perhaps because William Robinson had been attracted to some western American eriogonums, Reginald Farrer was prepared to be unimpressed by them; he called them "an interesting rather than brilliant race, suggesting clustered everlastings." Quite true, but a bit understated for one who wrote so glowingly of the castillejas "flaming out of the bushes," a wonderful contrast with eriogonum foliage.

There are between 150 and 200 species, distributed mainly in western North America. They are confusing to identify in the wild. They seem to intergrade chaotically, but this is actually the mark of an unusual degree of natural plasticity that allows survival under variable conditions. Unless one can select a particular wild form to perpetuate from seed (the only really satisfactory way of obtaining them), gardeners should be wary of what they plant, lest they end up with collections of merely "interesting" things. For example, a tiny seedling of *Eriogonum umbellatum* found in the Columbia Gorge—felted beige-and-brown, heart-shaped leaves an inch/2.5 cm long—was so irresistible that I pried it out and put it in a suitable place on the rockwork. In a year it had to be hauled away in barrow-loads; it was too happy, and rather than remaining compact, provocatively downy, and softly tinted, it became a lush shrub with leaves to 6 inches/15 cm long.

Those who seek out the good, better, and best would certainly want the following species from the Pacific Northwest. *Eriogonum ovalifolium* (Plate 6) is one of the most variable and also has a great range of distribution: into the Great Basin and to California, almost throughout the West, but not on the moist Pacific Slope. Although it always has a white lanose covering, those plants from higher sites are more compact, forming close rosettes like "vegetable sheep," above which leafless stalks rise a few inches bearing pompons of pale cream to soft yellow, usually flushed with pale rose. At Craters of the Moon in southeastern Idaho, *E. ovalifolium* is probably at its best, and every effort ought to be made to obtain a form as good as that. Two recognized compact varieties—*nivale* and *depressum*—should be sought for in seed lists. The leaves are quite marcescent, remaining fresh in appearance for several seasons and then blackening in decay, by which time a series above them has taken over life-support functions; the youngest, centermost leaves are the pale, luscious green of a honeydew melon. This is one of the easier species, and certainly one of the loveliest of the genus.

From a similar range, yet only infrequently co-occurring, and more commonly found outside the Northwest, is the almost equally variable *Eriogonum caespitosum*. It forms cushions of densely hairy (silky, never woolly) leaves, also marcescent but purplish-brown. The mat thus has a distinct appearance; the individual leaves are more oblanceolate, giving a looser look to the plant. The flowers on leafless stalks are yellow, some-

times tinged with rust or rose, and in the finest forms from high elevations they are adpressed right into the cushion, as stemless as the best *E.
ovalifolium*. In intense light the plants may be as burnished as the flowers,
creating a glowing autumnal effect that is unforgettable. Alpine forms of
E. caespitosum have been called *E. andinum* (or variety *andinum*), and seed
lists may use that name. Although this species sounds similar to *E. ovalifolium*, the two create a beautiful contrast when found together, as in the
White Clouds peaks of Idaho, and they cannot then be confused.

In the highest places in the northern Rocky Mountains the searcher
will find *Eriogonum androsaceum*, also a congested bun, forming a domed,
rosy-tinted mound with brown marcescent leaves below; the fresh leaves
are pallid green and cobwebbed with hairs, turning prettily pinkish and
then to a soft brown-rose. Above this the flowers are a strong mustard-
yellow, also with a rosy glow, topping short stalks with small leafy bracts
midway. This species may be found listed as a taxonomic ally of *E.
flavum*, from which it is said to differ markedly in its compact habit (and
consequent greater appeal to the gardener); certainly it is a rich reward in
itself.

Eriogonum pyrolaefolium extends from the northern Cascades south to
Mount Lassen and Mount Shasta in California, and east to the Bitterroot
Mountains of Idaho, always on high ridges or on talus. It forms loose,
shrubby mats of glabrous foliage in rosetted clusters, bearing short-
stalked little umbels of whitish flowers with bluish or violet anthers. The
handsome variety *coryphaeum* has leaves white-felted on the reverse and
a somewhat lanose inflorescence.

The complex species *Eriogonum umbellatum* displays about as much
variation as is allowable to a single species. It is found in a variety of
habitats, ranging from foothill-sagebrush to the summits of the western
ranges, on cliffs and in crevices. Its leaves may be glabrous to medially,
marginally, or wholly felted. Consequently, the list of names that have
been given it is a long one. The connoisseur will seek out the one called
variety *hausknechtii*, from the northern Cascades; it sprawls freely,
branches frequently, and clothes itself in glossy green, 1-inch/2.5-cm,
somewhat oblong leaves, woolly-white beneath, bearing little ball-
shaped inflorescences of white to cream. Others varieties are larger and
looser, with not so much contrast in leaf.

Quite as desirable, yet not at all a congested cushion, is the fascinating *Eriogonum thymoides* (Plate 42), found on the Columbia Basin's basalt
plains and ridges, in shallow-soiled sagebrush communities with *Viola
trinervata* (Plate 43), *Penstemon gairdneri*, and other such treasures, all difficult to please away from their natural scene. This eriogonum forms
beautiful little bonsai bushlets, with manzanita-brown papery bark and
tiny rolled leaves that turn to fantastic, glowing metallic tints in summer,
as the sulfur-yellow flowers become red-tarnished from the intense sun;
this effect persists until the first snows. The leaves appear slim and

needlelike, but they are actually inrolled at both margins and finely and densely tomentose. The species is sometimes confused with the rather similar but coarser *Eriogonum douglasii* (Plate 41), but the two are sometimes found growing together, in which case their differences are apparent. Roots of the former reach deeply into cool subterranean crevices, but in cultivation the plant must not be given a trace of irrigation in summer. This might prove true with the other eriogonums, too; an excess of water at any time past the first day of spring seals their death. *Eriogonum thymoides* may be transplanted in spring, with great care; at any other time there is no use making the effort. It is possible in the winter to pry out a chunk of its frozen desert, using a crowbar and first extracting the surface stones; the roots will come out unhurt, but the task is considerable!

Still another view of what is "good" among the false buckwheats relates to those few actually grown for their flowers, especially the good old-rose forms of *Eriogonum niveum*, which are found in a variety of waste places throughout the Columbia Basin. From an attractive, loosely packed gray mound arises, in late summer up to mid-autumn, a branched and rebranched woolly stalk with conspicuous bracts at each node, which bursts into a profusion of whitish, papery flowers fading to blush; occasionally they open pinkish, turning to the lovely faded color once called "ashes of roses." The effect persists until the fall rains or the first snows. This species may be found listed as *E. decumbens*, in which case it is to be avoided, as it will flop; a yellow form has been called *E. strictum*, but it could hardly be as lovely as the rose forms.

Although this selection by no means covers anything near the total of the best species of this wondrous xeric genus of clustered everlastings, those discussed would never be a disappointment, even though in cultivation they might not form such hard and beautifully colorful domes and stemless masses of flowers. There are equally attractive species from farther south, among them the stunning *Eriogonum kennedyi*, whitelanose and rose-to-raspberry red in flower, and the densely tomentose, oval-leaved *E. lobbii* (Plate 33). By all means, if seed of Wyoming's *E. acaule* is offered, take it and marvel at one of the most fantastic of all western American rock plants.

Originally published in the Bulletin of the American Rock Garden Society, *vol. 34, no. 4, pp. 168–171 (1976).*

Penstemons of Value

B. LEROY DAVIDSON

The American genus *Penstemon* (Scrophulariaceae) includes a tremendous variety of plants: some are showy, and not a few weedy; some are bold, some shy; many are easy, and a few challenging. There are plants for the border and wild garden among them, as well as many of a scale suitable for use in the rock garden (even the most fastidious alpine garden), with certain species at the extreme of tiny plants with comparatively huge flowers. Of greatest use in the rock garden are the evergreen shrubs that constitute several important groups within the genus.

Penstemons are logically divided into subgeneric groups, or sections, according to similarities that undoubtedly represent genetic relationships. Most species are somewhat woody at the base, making a spreading crown that produces the annual growth. Some are of woodier development, and a few of these groups include true shrubs, whose growth is persistent and woody, with only the inflorescence being of annual duration. Of these groups, the southwestern subgenus *Ericopsis*, from Colorado, New Mexico, Nevada, southern California, and Baja California, is generally characterized by fine, linear leaves, hence the name, meaning to resemble *Erica* (heath). These plants may be erect or procumbent, with green or grayish foliage, mostly turning burnished bronze hues in winter. Included here are *Penstemon crandallii*, *P. linarioides*, and *P. linarioides* subsp. *coloradoensis*. Their flowers are usually some shade of lilac-blue, but occasionally pink or white. There are a few caespitose "tuft" or "bun" plants among them, for the collector's alpine crevice garden or scree.

Related in habit, if not in phylogeny, are the little needle-leaved "firecracker" species, *Penstemon pinifolius*, from Arizona and northern Mexico, and *P. gairdneri* from the semideserts of the inland Northwest in Washington and Oregon, with orchid- or rose-colored flowers of surprising size on glaucous-leaved mounded bushlets. These profit from a maximum of sun, almost a minimum of moisture in the soil, and certainly a minimum of moisture in the atmosphere, although *P. pinifolius* is much more adaptable than the others. There are also some easy dwarf forms of species normally more suited to the border. *Penstemon laetus* var. *roezlii* (not the plant misnamed *P. roezlii* in the British horticultural trade, which is actually a selection of *P. rupicola*) is an alpine development of the species from the Klamath-Siskiyou area of Oregon and California; it is a low subshrub with rich blue flowers, rather adaptable in cultivation and valuable for its depth of color.

The northwestern United States and adjacent Canada is the habitat of two of the most important races of the true shrubby penstemons. The first, the woolly-anthered subgenus *Dasanthera*, extends from the Rocky Mountains in Alberta and British Columbia south to Wyoming, west to the seacoast, and south down the spine of the Cascade and Sierra Nevada ranges and Coast Ranges into California. The other is a group of subgenus *Procerus*, growing from the Great Plains to subalpine altitudes, variable according to elevation, and found mainly in interior regions from the Yukon south to Colorado, Oregon, and northern California.

The finest forms now subsumed within *Penstemon procerus* are undoubtedly the alpine ones, such as *P. procerus* var. *tolmiei* from the Olympic and Cascade mountains of British Columbia and Washington, extending somewhat into Oregon. These form loose mats of rather ovate leaves, pointed or blunt, tapering abruptly to a long spade-shaped petiole, from which stalks of blossoms arise, each small but dense, like a large head of clover. In color they are blue or lavender, occasionally orchid or pink, or rarely white. Although taxonomists have allied variety *tolmiei* with *P. procerus*, ecologically it is distinct, and it is quite tolerant of the humid conditions from which its close relatives literally shrink.

Penstemon procerus var. *brachyanthus*, growing farther south into the Oregon Cascades and to northern California, as well as in the Wallowa Mountains of northeastern Oregon, has a similarly well-developed basal foliage mat, but the leaves tend to be longer and lance- or lance-ovate-shaped, giving a distinctly different look to the plant, which is not as neat in habit. It flowers in lilac to blue, rarely white.

The darling of the group is *Penstemon procerus* var. *formosus*, distributed from the Wallowa and Strawberry peaks (around 9000 feet/2700 meters) of Oregon into northern California and Nevada. It has leaves 0.25 inch/6 mm long, rather trowel-shaped, forming remarkably prostrate little condensed mats. It bears relatively huge ball-shaped inflorescences, sometimes nearly stemless and always more condensed than the similar inflorescence of variety *tolmiei*.

Penstemon procerus var. *procerus* in its typical form is a more eastern plant found from plains to considerable altitudes in the Rocky Mountains, from the Yukon south to Colorado. Typically the foliage is not dense enough to give this variety the attractive aspect of the varieties mentioned above; the leaves are sparsely produced, and so the plant has less garden value, although some alpine forms are well worth garden space.

Another good plant of the Procerus alliance is *Penstemon peckii*, especially in its dainty gray-leaved, pink-flowered form, from the cinder area of the central Oregon Cascades—also the home of the very blue, gray-leaved *P. cinicola*. Selections of these should be made for larger flowers; the foliage is not of value in itself, being narrow and sparse. *Penstemon spatulatus*, endemic to the high Wallowas, is quite a nice plant, with lilac to blue flowers and attractive foliage. *Penstemon washingtonensis*, another member of the Procerus alliance, has good foliage of a crisp, bright green; its flowers are blue-purple, or rarely yellow. It comes from the east side of the Cascades of northern Washington.

There are some exclusively yellow-flowered species in the Procerus alliance, but the form of *Penstemon confertus* called 'Kittitas', from the southern Wenatchee Range in Washington, is the neatest, making an attractive olive mat with sulfur-yellow flowers in an appropriately arid situation. 'Kittitas' is quite easily propagated from cuttings, and fresh stock should be kept coming along, because older, woody plants have a way of disappearing almost overnight, leaving their blackened corpses in moist gardens.

As nice as these species are, the most useful of the shrubby penstemons are those of subgenus *Dasanthera*, which includes about a dozen taxa, with forms varying from minute matted plants to striking bushes 1 foot / 30 cm or more high, spreading to 3 feet / 90 cm, or occasionally to as much as 6 feet / 180 cm. Thus there is a variety for any garden, large or small. In flower color these penstemons fall into two main groups, commonly characterized as red and blue. *Penstemon newberryi* (Plate 13) and *P. rupicola* (Plate 32) are the reds (with some blue in the color), and the remaining taxa are more or less blue, although the blue never has the clarity or intensity of some of those in the Procerus alliance. The qualities of the foliage, however, make the subgenus *Dasanthera* outstanding as garden material. The leaves range from 0.25 to 5 inches / 6 mm to 13 cm; they are linear to spatulate to ovate, with margins thickened and entire or finely serrate to coarsely dentate. This leads to great variety in the way light is reflected from the gleaming leaf surfaces. Leaf colors include powdery gray-blue to metallic silver-blue, felty gray, olive-green with a crystalline finish, and deep moss-green with the texture of leather. Many leaves have a contrasting color in the petiole and leaf margin—for instance, raisin-purple on pallid yellow-green. In addition, they assume lovely, subtle winter tints of olive, burnished copper, bronze, or livid purple. Then there is the infinite variety of plant habit—tiny carpets, cascading trailers, or decumbent, procumbent, or completely erect mounds. A few may be useful for their architectural qualities, and all have value for color and texture of foliage; the silky blossoms are to be enjoyed as a bonus.

Of the red Dasantheras, *Penstemon rupicola*, from the Cascades of Washington and Oregon and the Klamath-Siskiyou ranges at high altitudes, is typically a glaucous, matted plant with serrate leaf margins; the plant may be neatly condensed or loosely trailing. The silky flowers have a color range in cerise and fuchsia-purples, paling to lovely pinks; a white form is known. *Penstemon newberryi* is perhaps more variable in habit and foliage, forming low mounds or small bushes to 1 foot/30 cm and spreading equally, or else decumbent in mats to 3 feet/90 cm or more across. (The cultivar 'Newberryi' once widely distributed in commerce is actually a form of *P. cardwellii*.) The leaves are bright olive-green or bronze with sharp serration and a crystalline texture; the flower is narrowly tubular, rose-cerise to crimson with the cream-white anthers protruding from the constricted mouth. A variation is *P. berryi*, sometimes considered as a subspecies; it occurs within the distribution pattern somewhat between *P. rupicola* and *P. newberryi*, and is morphologically intermediate between the two. Its flower color may be more purple than red; the plant is intermediate in size, and the foliage subglaucous if at all so. A stable purple-flowered, gray-leaved population from the border of Del Norte and western Siskiyou counties is under investigation as a possible new species; it is mat-forming, and the leaves are more spatulate than ovate.

Of the blue-flowered Dasantheras, mostly lilac- and lavender-flowered, *Penstemon davidsonii* (Plate 28) has tiny oval-spatulate foliage with thick, entire margins arranged on tidy, twiggy, matted plants. Subspecies *praeteritus* is found at the highest elevations from northernmost Washington, south through the Cascades and the Sierra Nevada, and in an outlying station on Steens Mountain in southeastern Oregon and southward into Nevada. It is reminiscent of a diminutive *P. fruticosus*. It is not free-flowering for most gardeners; it seems to miss the long cold dormancy or the cool summer dew of its mountaintop home.

Penstemon davidsonii var. *menziesii* has leaves finely toothed to refract light. In nature it is often found at or just below the elevations where *P. davidsonii* subsp. *davidsonii* occurs, only in Washington and somewhat into Oregon in the Columbia Gorge; it occurs in the absence of subspecies *davidsonii* in the Olympic Mountains and on Vancouver Island, where it comes down to near sea level on the west coast.

A tiny variant, once called *Penstemon serpyllifolius* but not now taxonomically distinguished, is probably one of the smallest penstemons: a dense, woody little mound with intricately toothed leaves only 0.25 inch/6 mm long or smaller. The 1-inch/2.5-cm flowering stems have one to three oversized lavender trumpets.

129

A distinctive erect form of *Penstemon davidsonii* occurs in the cinders of Modoc and Siskiyou counties in northern California; it may prove easier to flower in gardens. The entity named *P. thompsoniae*, from the Wenatchee Mountains, has proven on examination to be a hybrid swarm between *P. davidsonii* and *P. fruticosus*, with many individuals menziesii-like. Similar hybrids are to be noted where other dentate-leaved species interbreed with *P. davidsonii*; among the other parents recorded are *P. rupicola*, *P. cardwellii*, and *P. newberryi*, in addition to further encounters with *P. fruticosus*. [*P. thompsoniae* is now recognized as a valid species, with several varieties.—Ed.]

Two larger blue Dasantheras, somewhat similar to each other, are *Penstemon cardwellii* and *P. fruticosus*. Both are semi-erect to sprawling, typically with toothed leaves. The former is from the moist western side of the Cascades, from the northern drainage of Mount St. Helens south to the Siskiyou Range. Both species are of stout growth, with evenly dentate and ovate, leathery foliage, and rich, blue-purple flowers in cut-flower-quality racemes. There is an especially fine strong white form, known as 'John Bacher' for the Portland nurseryman who found and perpetuated it. Some good pink and rose hybrids with *P. rupicola* have been found; a good one is called 'Cardinal'.

On the eastern, arid side of the same area, *Penstemon cardwellii* is replaced by *P. fruticosus*, with a leaf less ovate and more lanceolate, sharply serrate and gray-olive. It extends north into the Okanogan Highlands, where it assumes many variations, notably in a form that has been called "crassifolius" (not taxonomically recognized), with entire leaf margins, often with blunted apex. Although it is a wanderer, there is not much variation in floral coloration; in the Wenatchee Mountains, however, a good number of pinkish individuals are to be found.

Two recognized variants of *Penstemon fruticosus* are both superior garden subjects. To the north in the range, generally north of the Columbia River and into British Columbia, and east into northernmost Idaho, variety *scouleri* prevails, with perhaps slightly smaller overall size and a more decumbent habit; its linear leaves are olive and glitter with light reflected from many prominent, sharp teeth. The typical *P. fruticosus* is usually too large and sprawling for most gardens, but variety *scouleri* is far neater. In addition, its colors tend to pleasing orchid tints, and two good pink clones have been designated 'Charming' and 'Mrs. Rutherford'; several albinos have also been selected. William Lohbrunner's *P. fruticosus* var. *scouleri* 'Alba' is of good garden constitution as well as exceptional beauty.

The finest form of *Penstemon fruticosus* for gardens, however, is variety *serratus* (Plate 36) from the highest elevations surrounding Hell's Canyon of the Snake River in Washington, Idaho, and Oregon, and grading at lower elevations to nondescript or typical *P. fruticosus*. This seems to be an alpine development: the entire plant is condensed, the leaves being short and ovate to lanceolate with exceedingly serrate margins. The flowers are the usual lilac to lavender, but a good pink form and a white form have been noted. There is one form designated 'Zaza' with leaves variegated olive-green and yellow, and one with sharply toothed and reflexed leaves called 'Holly'. The winter aspect of variety *serratus* is noteworthy, the foliage becoming variously burnished. Another compact plant, but with foliage similar to the form known as "crassifolius," is unique to the Wallowa peaks.

The northern Rocky Mountains, from British Columbia and Alberta, Montana, and Idaho to Wyoming and Utah, harbor several species of the Dasanthera alliance that are lovely in blossom but, because they are less shrubby or not fully evergreen, are of less value in the garden. Included in this group is *Penstemon lyallii*, a herbaceous member of little value for the rock garden. *Penstemon ellipticus*, from the range just noted, is rather like a thin-leaved *P. davidsonii* var. *menziesii*, with lovely large, silky lilac-blue flowers, though an untidy plant. Some hybrids of it with *P. lyallii* have proven attractive subjects, not unlike a good *P. fruticosus* in general appearance and culture. In the southern part of this range is found *P. montanus*, a similar plant with toothed, succulent, crystalline leaves; it is a subshrub or herb that trails down through talus and crevices, bearing lilac flowers. It may have curiosity value for its foliage texture in a collector's assemblage.

A most distinct and lovely penstemon from the Sawtooth Range of south-central Idaho, *Penstemon idahoensis*, is sometimes regarded as a variety or subspecies of *P. montanus* but is quite distinct in appearance. Its untoothed, ovate foliage is gray and velvety, and the large flowers are lilac-satin above the casually formed low mounds. Though deciduous, the species may be forgiven because of its quiet beauty.

The last of the Dasantheras to be mentioned may be the most spectacular; certainly it is of great interest to the student of plants, because it is quite unlike any of its kin in several ways and is curiously disposed in only three known colonies at low elevations in the Columbia Gorge and nearby Klickitat Canyon. This is *Penstemon barrettiae*. Its leaves are 3 to 5 inches / 8 to 13 cm long, thickly succulent, glazed as if varnished, and both glaucous and shiny, in color olive-green turning to purple-bronze in cold weather. The plant may be 1.5 feet / 45 cm tall and as much as 4 feet / 120 cm in diameter, with the stem a couple of inches thick at the base—a giant of its kind. In flowering time it is lovely; the flowers on strong, tall racemes are of an iridescent tint between pink and blue, above foliage that is a soft lavender-gray, with the new leaf growth simultaneously pale lettuce-green. This plant is for large gardens, although a single plant in a collection of other kinds offers a stunning contrast and a conversation piece of changeable aspect the year round. Hybrids of this species with *P. rupicola* (the deliberate one known as *P. × edithiae* was made by Carl English) have much the same character, though they are smaller in all parts except the flower, which is the largest of the Dasanthera alliance. The clone 'Manito' is a particularly happy combination of the best points of the two species.

Some of the most prized penstemons of the Dasanthera alliance are the white forms of *Penstemon rupicola*, *P. scouleri*, *P. cardwellii*, and *P. davidsonii* var. *menziesii*. In general, albino forms are not of hearty constitution; however, this is not true of *P. cardwellii* 'John Bacher', robust and floriferous, nor of Lohbrunner's selection of *P. scouleri* 'Alba'. An even better form was found by Dave Every on Mount St. Helens before its eruption. Most white forms may require a little more protection from burning summer sun.

Penstemons are not the easiest subjects in many gardens. In nature they are almost always found in close relation to rocks, and those here discussed fare perfectly well in a scree formation built up for drainage, filled with humus and a high percentage of gravel; they demand good aeration and soil drainage. Probably the greatest difficulty in gardens comes from overwatering; when correctly placed, the plants cannot be underwatered. They are sometimes, even in nature, subject to attacks of scale, which is a menace to be guarded against. The only other trouble to plague penstemons is a wilt disease which results when humidity and soil moisture are too great. A gardener should not be afraid to prune, and just after flowering is the best time to remove the spent stalks and to tidy the planting, for they do grow, often becoming too large for their area. The new growth stimulated by pruning is more likely to resist disease and produce good flowers. Cuttings may be taken during pruning, or (perhaps more successfully) in early fall when new root growth becomes apparent.

In any low-rainfall area, a great mass planting of penstemons adorning lichen-encrusted rocks would be an enviable display; gardens with plenty of moisture can still have them, but not so easily. There they require good planning and hard work, and they are worth it.

Originally published in the Bulletin of the American Rock Garden Society, *vol. 27, no. 3, pp. 141–146 (1969).*

Synthyris *Today*

B. LEROY DAVIDSON

Among the many good western American plants for gardens, the members of the genus *Synthyris* have been entirely neglected or only slightly regarded. This group of precocious flowerers is of value not only for the blossom, often produced in a balmy midwinter break in the weather, but also for the foliage, which adorns shaded, mossy woodlands or, in a few species, sun-drenched alpine screes. They are of a quality comparable to the western lewisias and phloxes, though perhaps not quite so splendid in flower.

Synthyris species should be in every good collection of rock plants, and their cultivation presents no problems. The shade-lovers, with handsome, rather large leaves, want a cool place in some good light, but they must have ample drainage. A soil rich in humus and filled with grit suits them all. None seems to be sensitive to soil acidity, although a strongly alkaline soil would doubtless be toxic to them. The sun-lovers have smaller, more laciniate leaves and flourish in the open, with their roots well-sheltered from baking by buried stones, or in a trough, where the thick walls provide cooling. Although constant moisture is necessary, no excess should accumulate. They must never suffer parching, however, for permanent damage will result—not immediately apparent, perhaps, but even well-established colonies may dwindle following such an experience.

Propagation is by seed, easy but quite slow, or by division of the crown, the only way to increase choice forms. The species of *Synthyris* are among the finest winter and early spring flowers of North America, or anywhere else.

Synthyris and Related Genera

The genus _Synthyris_ is one of several closely allied members of the Veronicae tribe of the Scrophulariaceae, particularly close to the Himalayan _Picrorhiza_, the Eurasian _Wulfenia_, and _Lagotis_ of Asia, Alaska, and the Yukon. Depending on which interpretation is accepted, there are as few as eight or nine species in _Synthyris_, or as many as a couple of dozen. Pennell (1933) accepted 14 (with four subspecies), of which no fewer than 10 were new, and 3 more were revised concepts of prior taxa. (One additional species was to follow: _S. platycarpa_ Gail and Pennell 1937). In this treatment, nine others were taken as constituting _Besseya_, erected as a separate genus by Rydberg (1903).

Cronquist (1959) was not so confident that the species should be thus segregated. Kruckeberg and Hedglin (1963) were inclined to agree, following their study of a natural hybrid population involving _Synthyris missurica_ and _Besseya rubra,_ and their laboratory hybridization of both those two species and the hybrids _Synthyris missurica_ × _S. reniformis_ and _S. missurica_ × _S. platycarpa_. Behavioristic patterns suggested to them that certain species of _Besseya_ were more nearly allied to certain _Synthyris_ species, while at least one of the latter was rather poorly related to all others of its genus. Thus a more realistic representation might result from considering all these plants within a single genus, perhaps with subgeneric separation; lopping such an alliance at any given point presents an illogical discontinuity. Most members of the genus _Besseya_, however, are not very attractive as garden plants, though they may have some curiosity value; their "kitten-tail" inflorescences are oddly furry.

Both _Synthyris_ and _Besseya_ consist of low, fibrous-rooted, perennial herbs with subterranean, rhizomatous rootstocks and basal, long-petioled leaves with rather broad blades. (The leaves of many species are often described as "reniform," but actually they are only remotely or inconsistently so, and this term is qualified or avoided here.) The inflorescence is a scapose, terminal raceme of few to many small-bracted, complete flowers, with a calyx of four partly united sepals, and a corolla of four usually quite unequal petals, united basally (or only rudimentary to totally absent in most _Besseya_ species), blue to violet-purple, or infrequently orchid, lilac, pink, or white (yellow in some _Besseya_ species).

Subgenus _Plagiocarpus_

Pennell (1933) bisected his genus _Synthyris_ into two subgenera, based on morphological and ecological factors. The first, subgenus _Plagiocarpus_, consisted of the single species _Synthyris reniformis_ (Plate 54), characterized by widely spreading carpels, each of the pair with two dull brown seeds. It occurs only in the relatively mild and humid Pacific

Slope, from just north of the mouth of the Columbia River south to San Francisco Bay. The remaining species were put into subgenus *Eusynthyris*, with many small yellowish-brown seeds, the capsule a flattened oval. They are found mainly in montane situations and away from the moderating influence of the Pacific Ocean.

Synthyris reniformis occurs in cool shade with ample moisture, usually in close association with coniferous forests. Floral color is ordinarily lilac-blue, pale to deeper, or sometimes pink or white; the southern form, from the Siskiyou area southward, tends toward a pallid grayish or whitish hue, and has leaves two to three times as long as broad, rather than the more oval-reniform leaf of the type. This southern form has been designated *S. reniformis* var. *cordata*, and has also been called *S. rotundifolia* var. *sweetseri* (the latter is described as having deep blue flowers). The corolla of this species in both forms is unique in that the four segments are of almost equal size, all other species being distinctly zygomorphic. The entire plant may be quite pilose, even on the upper leaf surfaces, and the undersides are commonly colored a rather bright purple. The flowers of some forms are rather few and are borne on weak, slender scapes which become quite lax on maturity; other forms are densely flowered on strongly and persistently erect scapes. The local name "spring queen" refers to its heralding the vernal season. A clonal selection was named 'Regina' by Carl English.

Subgenus *Eusynthyris*

The remaining species, comprising Pennell's subgenus *Eusynthyris*, are found in harsher climates, from the Alaska-Yukon ranges to the Rocky Mountains (though not in the Canadian Rockies), extending as far south as southern Nevada and west to Washington's Olympic Mountains. They are plants exclusively of high valleys and slopes to the topmost talus screes, where the laciniate-leaved species grow in the most severe arctic-alpine conditions.

As the first species discovered, *Synthyris missurica* might be considered the most important in this subgenus; certainly its high ornamental quality makes it so for gardeners. It was named from a specimen Lewis and Clark collected in 1806 along the Nez Perce Indians' Lolo Trail in the Clearwater drainage of present-day Idaho. It is the one species that has a really wide range—north to the northern margin of the Selkirk range in northeastern Washington, south of the Clearwater drainage somewhat into the Salmon, Sawtooth, and Seven Devils ranges, and west into the Wallowa and Blue mountains of Oregon and Washington, with a disjunct southern population in inland northwestern California and adjacent Oregon. As might be expected, the species displays much variation, but it is essentially glabrous, with rather oval and cordate leaves, thick,

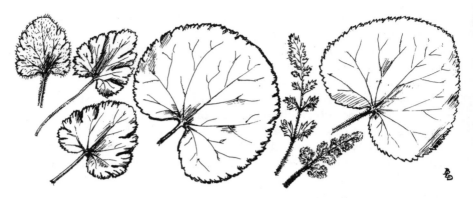

Most *Synthyris* species may be recognized from their distinctive leaves. From left to right, *S. borealis*, *S. canbyi*, *S. laciniata*, *S. missurica*, *S. pinnatifida* and its var. *lanuginosa*, and *S. platycarpa*. (Drawing by B. LeRoy Davidson)

shiny, and turgid, rich green with a coppery tint when young and often vinous or bronzed in decline. The margins are shallowly lobed, with each of the 15 to 20 lobes incised into several usually blunt teeth, like a dull saw. Such details would seem to be of minor importance, but most *Synthyris* species can be readily identified from the foliage alone. Certainly from the standpoint of beauty, the leaves of *S. missurica* are second to none, well worth garden space the year round, and rather reminiscent of a waxed *Galax*.

Many forms of *Synthyris missurica* are lush growers, with leaves as much as 6 inches / 15 cm in diameter, sometimes with a white pubescence (except on the upper surface). These have sometimes been designated variety *major*, and they remain in character when brought into the garden. Cronquist (1959) noted that they "probably warrant recognition"; Pennell (1933) ranked this as a subspecies, followed by Abrams (1951), but Davis (1952) gave it only varietal status. Subsequent cytological study has revealed that both diploid and tetraploid forms of *S. missurica* exist, which may explain the observed variation in size. In view of the other extremes—concise dwarf forms and nearly glabrous forms—that also occur, it would seem to represent the inherent variation of the species. The so-called alpine forms from the altitudinal extremes at around 4000 to 5000 feet / 1200 to 1500 meters, often growing in crevices, remain dwarf in cultivation, slow in growth and grudging in flower.

The usual flower color of *Synthyris missurica* is a strong blue, from a steely tone to electric intensity, tending to violet; albinos have been recorded, and St. John's forma *rosea* was found by Marion Ownbey and established in cultivation, the original collection having been enshrined in the herbarium case. A local common name for this species is "grape hyacinth," which gives a good impression of its effect in flower.

Synthyris missurica subsp. *hirsuta* was named from a single collec-

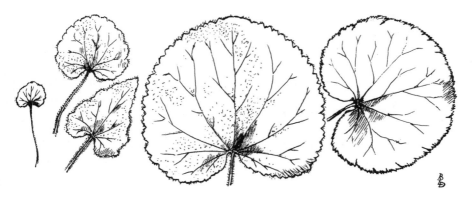

All leaves are approximately 1/2 natural size except *Synthyris stellata,* which is 1/4. From left to right, *S. ranunculina, S. reniformis* and its var. *cordata, S. schizantha,* and *S. stellata.* (Drawing by B. LeRoy Davidson)

tion made 50 years earlier by Howell. Since the subspecies has never been found again, and no other member of its alliance occurs in the reported region, the name should not be perpetuated. It is, of course, quite possible that the subspecies may have perished owing to the devastation of logging and other activities. Moreover, errors in recording of collections have been perpetuated before. The single specimen was uniquely brown-pubescent on immature growth, if it had not altered while reposing in dried oblivion.

There is some difference of opinion over acceptance of *Synthyris stellata* (Plate 55) as a good and distinct species, separate from *S. missurica.* Following Pennell's original publication of 1933, it was accepted by Abrams (1951), but Cronquist (1959) noted (under *S. missurica*) that *S. stellata* might constitute a "rather weak variety" of that species. Peck (1961) followed Pennell, but not many other writers have done so. Whatever its proper place in phylogeny, the name *S. stellata* has found wide acceptance in horticulture; indeed, it must be treated as a synonym in part of *S. missurica* of horticulture, which in cultivation has often been called *S. stellata*—innocently enough, since there is little to distinguish the two. *Synthyris stellata* occurs in the wet lower areas of the Columbia River Gorge. It appears as a more compact version of *S. missurica,* with leaves more sharply dentate. The floral color is the heavenly blue of spring skies, and a very fine white form is in cultivation. A telltale pair of leaflike bracts below the inflorescence sets it apart to the taxonomic worker.

_____ Fringed *Synthyris* Species _____

Obviously related, though geographically separated, are the two species with fringed flowers. *Synthyris schizantha,* from moist, shaded cliffs on the Pacific side of Washington's Olympic Peninsula, was recognized first by Piper in 1902; it is so distinct in several respects as not to be confused with any other. It may be the largest of its genus, with leaves well over 6 inches / 15 cm broad recorded. These leaves are unique in being thin and deciduous. Thus the startling purple flowers emerge from bare earth, with the four unequal petals deeply slashed into soldanella-like fringes. There is a pair of large leafy bracts beneath the inflorescence, giving the effect of green foliage, but the true leaves emerge only later.

The very similar *Synthyris platycarpa* is endemic to some unglaciated areas (nunataks) of central Idaho, far from its sister, where it is surrounded by populations of *S. missurica*, though occurring at higher altitudes, apparently isolated by conditions of moisture and temperature. Except for being smaller in flower as well as in all other parts, it is much like the Olympic plant, but the leaves are firm and persistent through the winter. Although this leaf is reminiscent of that of *S. missurica*, it lacks the rich waxy luster of the latter, and *S. platycarpa* is a rather dull garden subject by comparison. The undersides of its leaves are rather hairy, especially on the nerves; the leaf outline may be oval to remotely reniform, strongly cordate, lobed and dentate, the teeth not decidedly sharp. Certainly its present range suggests that it is one of the ancestral species of *Synthyris* that has survived glaciation *in situ*.

Northern and Southern Extremes

There is one species from Alaska and the adjacent Yukon Territory, shown by Pennell as found only north of the ice sheet of the Wisconsin glaciation, whereas all other *Synthyris* species are found entirely south of that line. It is absorbing to wonder how many must once have grown in the great expanse that is now western Canada. None survive there now, apparently, nor have others replaced them in the 20,000 years since the ice last receded. The little-known *S. borealis* Pennell 1933 was described from the type plant photographed before its collection near the base of Mount Denali. The photo showed a hairy huddle, profuse with flower stems. Another illustration in Hultén (1968) depicted a subject of considerable appeal: very floriferous, flowers the rich blue typical of the genus, and a habit of obvious charm to gardeners. The leaf is oval in outline but lobed rather deeply, and the marginal teeth blunt. The flower is reminiscent of that of some *Besseya* species in being trilobed on the lowermost segment, with toothy bracts conspicuously adorning the lower scape.

The charming little *Synthyris ranunculina* appears to be confined today to cool seepages in the northwest-facing canyon walls of the Spring (or Charleston) Mountains of Nevada, surviving in the light shade of pines. In ancient times it must have found favorable habitat on the many ranges intervening, before the upthrust of the Sierra Nevada and Cascade ranges converted the Great Basin to desert. (Today the perimeter of this basin is rimmed with populations of no less than four species: *S. missurica, S. pinnatifida, S. laciniata,* and *S. ranunculina*). It is a plant to delight those who are mesmerized by the miniature, for its diminutive stature clearly shows the evidence of struggle for survival. The plant is quite glabrous; the long slender pedicels present leaf blades about 0.5 inch / 13 mm broad, roughly oval to more or less reniform, and distinctly though shallowly palmate-lobed into five or seven parts, each with about three small sharp teeth. It is thus much like a tiny *S. missurica,* and in fact it much resembles some of the "alpine forms" of that species. It was said by Heller (who first collected it in 1913) to be "a new species," but it was not to be so recognized until 20 years later.

Alpine Laciniate Species

The remaining three *Synthyris* species occur mostly on the highest summits of the Rocky Mountains, usually above timberline, where they are among the few flowering plants of those extreme elevations. The one exception is from Washington's Olympic Mountains—still at the summits. All have leaves reduced to being deeply cleft or lobed into "skeletons." They are attractive to those who enjoy observing the effects of the most severe alpine conditions; in the garden they are suited to the crevice or scree, or to the trough where their delicacy is perhaps best appreciated, huddled among lichened stones. They do not flower readily in cultivation and do not make much of a show when coaxed into performing, yet they appeal to alpine gardeners as do other plants from such heights. Arthur Kruckeberg calls attention to their ability to blossom beneath the snow, a curious characteristic occasionally noted among denizens of the highest peaks.

Synthyris canbyi is endemic to the Mission Range of Montana, the barrier that prevented farther southern advancement of the glacier that gouged out the Flathead Basin west of Glacier National Park. It is undoubtedly correct to regard it as a relict endemic left marooned by postglacial warmth, unable to migrate farther. It was first recognized by Pennell (1933), having been regarded by Rydberg (1922) as conspecific with the similar *S. laciniata.* Its leaf is broadly ovate and cordate, cut to about half its depth into toothed lobes; the entire plant is glabrous except in the inflorescence, which is densely compact and blue-flowered.

Cronquist (1959) said that the closely related, pale violet *Synthyris laciniata* differs in a more distinctly and shallowly cleft leaf; it is from the Wasatch Range of central Utah. Pennell segregated a few individual collections from the disjunct Deep Creek Mountains of western Utah as subspecies *ibapahensis,* with foliage more sharply toothed and thicker and with flowers of deeper blue—certainly minor distinctions.

The best known of the laciniate, high montane species of *Synthyris* is the wide-ranging and somewhat variable *S. pinnatifida* Watson 1871, with leaves, as the name would indicate, cut deeply in a pinnate manner. Cronquist (1959) condensed seven of Pennell's taxa into three varieties of Watson's *S. pinnatifida*; the type specimen was collected by Watson in 1869 from a 9000-foot/2700-meter summit at the head of American Fork Canyon in the Wasatch Range of northern Utah, whence it ranges to cliffs, crags, and screes in all directions, varying as Pennell's splitting treatment suggests. The variety (or subspecies, if one prefers) *pinnatifida* ("the typical phase," as interpreted by Cronquist) includes those individuals that are only slightly villous, if at all, with bracts of the inflorescence more rounded, to obovate, and the capsule glabrous. To this description conform plants from the northern Wasatch and Bear River mountains of Utah, those from adjacent Wyoming, and probably those from the Bitterroot Range on the Idaho-Montana border. Two additional varieties (or subspecies) would be separated from each other only with some difficulty were they ever to occur together; both differ from the type in having more acute and angular bracts and in being more hairy (sometimes densely so), the petioles no more hairy at the base than they are above.

Synthyris pinnatifida var. *canescens* may be subglabrous to villous to tomentulose, becoming glabrate with age, with capsules either hirsute or glabrous. Pennell's *S. cymopteroides* subsp. *canescens* was taken by Cronquist as the type for this phase of the species, as it is found in the headwaters of the Salmon River in central Idaho, whence it ranges northward into southwestern Montana. Variety *lanuginosa* might at some stages of growth resemble variety *canescens*. Variety *lanuginosa* is densely and permanently white-tomentulose throughout, even to the capsules; it is based on Piper's *S. lanuginosa*, from the high Olympic Mountains of Washington. Its disjunct and restricted range, so far west of others of its ilk, is a mystery, but surely it too must represent a survivor of glaciation. It is a real treasure in the garden and might be likened to a pygmy dusty miller; its very bright blue, though infrequent flowers belong to the skies and the alpine lakes reflecting them. These alpine species of *Synthyris* slowly spread to colonize a suitable place in the garden, to be prized indeed.

Sorting Out the Nomenclature

Identities of *Synthyris* species have been rather muddled, owing in part to what amounts to "false synonymy," and to what on the surface would appear to be intergradation of species. Pennell's (1933) specific nomenclature gave a false impression, too. In reality the species are remarkably distinct, and some misconceptions as to significant variation can be ascribed to earlier taxonomic errors. As within any genus, however, there are greater similarities among some species than others, and again, there are great gaps in continuity elsewhere. Confusion in the nomenclature must be laid to a series of events that led to the lumping of two very distinct members as conspecific. The muddling of names has long ago been set to rights, but it often takes some time for such wisdom to trickle down to garden-label level.

The genus *Synthyris* was founded by George Bentham in 1846 to include four species, three of which were later removed to *Besseya*; it was based on *Synthyris reniformis* as the type of the genus. Here, however, lurks a bit of uncertainty, for Bentham's description was based (as was Hooker's prior text and illustration of 1840) on two distinct individuals—one in flower, the other in fruit. The former was after the specimen collected by David Douglas in March 1827 in the "mountains of the Grand Rapids of the Columbia River," described in 1835 by Bentham as *Wulfenia reniformis*, and later interpreted by Asa Gray in 1878 as *Synthyris rotundifolia*. The fruiting portion of the specimen on Hooker's plate was based on a different Douglas collection from the Blue Mountains, this one interpreted by Gray as the "true" *S. reniformis*—but actually the plant we now know as *S. missurica*! Pennell (1933) pointed out that either of these two could be taken as the type of the genus (or both might be rejected). Although this detail has little bearing on their horticultural merit, which is our main concern here, retelling this chain of events does recall the clay feet of even the most astute botanists, and helps us understand how error crept into interpretation; corrections come more easily with a full, clear picture.

Further complications arose when another specimen, taken by Lewis and Clark in June 1806 on Hungry Creek (a minor tributary of the Lochsa River, part of the Clearwater drainage), was described by Pursh in 1814 as *Veronica reniformis*, and credited in error to the "banks of the Missouri." This was described by Rafinesque in 1818 as *V. missurica*, and once again by Don in 1838 as *V. purshii*. It is readily understandable how it came to be confused both with *V. reniformis* of Rafinesque 1808 (an entirely distinct plant) and with *Synthyris reniformis* of Bentham (the Douglas plant from the Columbia, originally called *Wulfenia reniformis*). This was the state of the nomenclature until the publication of Pennell's 1933 revision, in which he separated several species as *Besseya* and also liberated the Lewis and Clark plant as *Synthyris missurica*, although the specific epithet still credits the plant to the wrong river system. (It could conceivably have been named "*S. kooskooskiensis*," for the name of its native river was Kooskoosky!)

It was a request for clarification of yet another Columbia River species, *Synthyris stellata*, that led Pennell to discover this appalling confusion and to the study that was to bring order to the genus. But the weed seeds of error had been sown, and they continued to produce their annual crop of doubt. The splitting interpretation Pennell published has been considerably reduced by lumping in later interpretations of the genus. The plants themselves, however, remain as beautiful as ever, both in nature and in the garden.

Finding List of Taxa within the Genus *Synthyris*
(Valid names are given in italic type, invalid names in roman type.)

borealis Pennell 1933

canbyi Pennell 1933

cymopteroides = *pinnatifida* var. *canescens*

cymopteroides canescens = *pinnatifida* var. *canescens*

dissecta = *pinnatifida* var. *canescens*

hendersonii = *pinnatifida* var. *canescens*

ibapahensis (possibly a "weak form" of *laciniata*) Pennell 1933

laciniata (Gray) Rydberg 1900

lanuginosa = *pinnatifida* var. *lanuginosa*

major = *missurica* var. *major*

missurica (Rafinesque) Pennell 1933

missurica hirsuta (uncertain) Pennell 1933

missurica var. *major* (Hooker) Pennell 1933

missurica var. stellata = *stellata*

paysoni = *pinnatifida* var. *pinnatifida*

pinnatifida var. *canescens* (Pennell) Cronquist 1959

pinnatifida var. *lanuginosa* (Piper) Cronquist 1959

pinnatifida var. *pinnatifida* Watson 1871

pinnatifida laciniata = *laciniata*

platycarpa Gail and Pennell 1937

ranunculina Pennell 1933

reniformis (Douglas) Bentham 1846

reniformis var. *cordata* A. Gray 1876

reniformis major = *missurica* var. *major*

rotundifolia = *reniformis*

rotundifolia var. sweetseri = *reniformis* var. *cordata*

schizantha Piper 1902

stellata Pennell 1933

Excluded Species
The following nine taxa are generally (but not universally) considered within the allied genus *Besseya*:

alpina (very strongly resembles a *Synthyris* species)

arizonica

bullii (also called *Wulfenia bullii*)

cinerea = *wyomingensis*

flavescens = *ritteriana*

goodingii

gymnocarpa = *wyomingensis*

houghtoniana = *bullii*
oblongifolia
plantaginea
reflexa = *ritteriana*
ritteriana
rubra (close to *Synthyris*; also called *S. rubra*)
wyomingensis

Bibliography

Abrams, Leroy. 1951. *Illustrated Flora of the Pacific States*. Palo Alto, California: Stanford University Press.

Britton, N. L., and Addison Brown. 1913. *Illustrated Flora of the Northern States and Canada*.

Clements, Frederic E., and Edith G. Clements. 1914. *Rocky Mountain Flowers*. Denver: W. B. Conkey.

Clokey, I. W. 1951. *Flora of the Charleston Mountains*. Berkeley: University of California Press.

Cronquist, Arthur. 1959. "*Synthyris*." In C. Leo Hitchcock, Arthur Cronquist, Marion Ownbey, and J. W. Thompson, *Vascular Plants of the Pacific Northwest*, vol. 4. Seattle: University of Washington Press.

Davis, Ray J. 1952. *Flora of Idaho*. Provo, Utah: Brigham Young University Press.

Gabrielson, Ira. 1932. *Western American Alpines*. New York: Macmillan.

Haskins, Leslie. 1934. *Wild Flowers of the Pacific Coast*. Portland, Oregon: Binfords and Mort.

Howell, Thomas. 1903. *Flora of Northwest America*. Portland, Oregon: Privately printed.

Hultén, Eric. 1968. *Flora of Alaska and Neighboring Territories*. Stanford, California: Stanford University Press.

Jepson, W. D. 1925. *A Manual of the Flowering Plants of California*. Berkeley: University of California Press.

Kruckeberg, Arthur, and A. Hedglin. 1963. "Natural and Artificial Hybrids of *Besseya* and *Synthyris*." *Madroño* 17.4.

Munz, Philip A., and David D. Keck. 1959. *A California Flora*. Berkeley: University of California Press.

Peck, Morton E. 1961. *Higher Plants of Oregon*. 2d ed. Portland, Oregon: Binfords and Mort.

Pennell, F. W. 1933. "Review of *Synthyris* and *Besseya*." Proc. Acad. Phila.

Piper, Charles V., and A. Beattie. 1915. *Flora of the Northwest Coast*. Corvallis: Oregon State Cooperative Association.

Rydberg, P. A. 1922. *Flora of the Rocky Mountains and Adjacent Plains*. New York: Privately printed.

St. John, Harold. 1956. *Flora of Southeastern Washington and Adjacent Idaho*. 2d ed. Pullman, Washington: Student Book Corporation.

Originally published in the Bulletin of the American Rock Garden Society, *vol. 30, (1972).*

Eagle Summit, Alaska

HELEN A. WHITE

On the Steese Highway, 108 miles / 173 km out of Fairbanks, Alaska, is one of the best botanizing areas in Alaska. It ranks with Attu Island in the Aleutians, Point Hope in northwestern Alaska, and the Teller Road out of Nome. The good thing about Eagle Summit is that it is readily accessible by a well-maintained road. Even better, because the timberline is so low at this far northern latitude, you can view alpine plants at elevations so low you will never feel short of breath. If you are traveling in a camper or motorhome, just come on up and camp for a few days and browse among nature's gems.

Many local people camp at Eagle Summit on the nights of June 20, 21, or 22 to watch and photograph the midnight sun, a phenomenon not visible from Fairbanks itself. The plant enthusiast will want to visit a week or two later, both to encounter peak flowering and to avoid the crowds. The nearest settlements are Circle City (54 miles / 86 km farther), Circle Hot Springs (27 miles / 43 km farther, with resort accommodations), and Central (only 19 miles / 30 km from the summit). Circle City is on the bank of the mighty Yukon River.

The botanizing feast really begins at Twelvemile Summit back at milepost 89.6, where the Pennell Mountain Trail takes off up the slope across the road from a parking turnout. From here to Eagle Summit and beyond, the surrounding mountainsides host a fabulous array of alpine plants. One could easily spend a week in this general area without seeing all that is to be seen. Eagle Summit, at an elevation of 3624 feet / 1105 meters, probably will not seem like a very high mountain to people from the "Lower 48"; however, at this latitude that elevation is floristically equivalent to at least 10,000 feet / 3100 meters in the Colorado Rockies. Many of the plants here will be familiar to those who have botanized the Rockies.

Eagle Summit is a place of extremes. I have seldom been more uncomfortable from the heat than here. On another day I saw it raining harder than I have ever seen it rain before or since in Alaska. I could not see at all through the summer downpour and had to stop driving for half an hour until the torrent lessened somewhat. At times the afternoon thunderstorms turn to violent hail, punctuated by terrifying lightning bolts, so make the 2-hour drive from Fairbanks as early as possible. Moreover, I have seen more vicious mosquitoes per square inch on Eagle Summit than anywhere else, yet as long as a slight breeze is blowing, the mosquitoes are unable to take wing and attack.

One summer I arrived at Eagle Summit to find virtually no plants showing. It had been an exceedingly dry season and everything seemed to be dead. The next summer, however, the swarms of plants grew and blossomed as usual.

There is a rough Jeep road to the summit itself. It makes a good trail for the walker, and many interesting plants can be seen taking advantage of the disturbed soil, notably *Campanula lasiocarpa* (Plate 59), which flowers late in the season. You will never see finer specimens of *Silene acaulis* (Plate 34) than those here. Among the jumbled rocks are two unshowy but charming plants—*Melandrium apetalum*, with huge inflated calyces, and *Crepis nana*, a minute tufted composite.

The craggy summit is dry and windswept, hosting a plant community different from that anywhere else on the mountain. Two characteristic plants of such crags are *Saxifraga tricuspidata* and *Potentilla hyparctica*. After looking around here, you can leave the trail and wander down the moist tundra slope, finding wonderful things wherever you turn. Keep alert for families of ptarmigan and the various upland shorebirds that summer here.

The lowly saxifrages are said to be our basic rock garden plants, and there are several species of *Saxifraga* in the neighborhood. The most noticeable are *S. bronchialis* (Plate 38), growing in the lee of rocks; *S. tricuspidata*, on the dry summit; and *S. punctata*, in wetter places. This is the first place I saw *Rhododendron lapponicum*. If it is not in flower, you may have difficulty finding it: it is there, but the plants are so dwarf that their flowering stems barely rise above the mat of sphagnum and prostrate willows. There are perhaps 10 species of the intriguing little dwarf willows (*Salix* spp.).

Lloydia serotina (Plate 40) is not an imposing plant, but there are many of these little lilies. *Polygonum bistorta* stands out with its elegant plumes of pink. There are a couple of claytonias and stellarias, too. *Oxyria digyna* with its oddly shaped leaves is abundant. *Anemone richardsonii, A. drummondii* (Plate 50), *A. parviflora*, and *A. narcissiflora* (Plate 57) can all be seen. In the wettest spots two bright yellow-flowered, taller plants grow, *Geum rossii* and the nodding *Arnica lessingii*.

145

Many species of caryophyllaceous plants—*Minuartia, Arenaria,* and *Melandrium*—are also found in this area, growing in very rocky sites. The strange little blue flowers of *Corydalis pauciflora* are in evidence in seasonal drainages early in the season, and we cannot overlook *Papaver macounii* with its gay yellow flowers dancing in the mountain breeze. *Parrya nudicaulis* (Plate 56) is a very showy crucifer, its large round inflorescences varying here from white to deep lavender. There are several cardamines as well, including the appealing little *Cardamine purpurea*. You will see *Sedum rosea*, often in company with the tiny *Gentiana glauca* with its closed flower of peculiar metallic blue-green. There are about a dozen species of drabas. *Cornus canadensis* (now *Chamaepericlymenum canadense*) is present, of course, as it is over so much of Alaska. The legumes are certainly well represented in the region: six species of *Oxytropis*, *Lupinus arcticus*, six species of *Astragalus*, and two species of *Hedysarum*.

In peaty pockets or along the few streams you may come across *Viola epipsila*, and *V. biflora* can be found on some of the slopes. Several nice potentillas make their home in these mountains and some species of *Rubus* and *Vaccinium* do well in the surrounding area. *Dryas octopetala* is interspersed here with *D. integrifolia*, forming hybrid swarms. Alaska's state flower, *Myosotis asiatica* (formerly *M. alpestris*), is present, usually in sheltered depressions.

A related plant, *Eritrichium nanum* var. *aretioides* (Plate 58), is the jewel of the natural flower garden on Eagle Summit, and a real jewel it is. Those who know *Eritrichium* elsewhere will be startled to find it flowering here with meltwater running around the furry rosettes. *Androsace chamaejasme* is another gem, a sarmentose plant with sweetly fragrant flowers, and it is here in great abundance.

The northwest slope of Eagle Summit should be visited, especially if you are there late in the season. On this cooler exposure the plants bloom a little later. Some of the larger, more moisture-loving plants favor this site, among them *Dodecatheon pulchellum* and the peculiar blue-spiked *Lagotis glauca*. Much the same assemblage grows on the middle portion of the slope at Twelvemile Summit.

I have heard that both *Cypripedium guttatum* and *C. passerinum* are in the area but I have not seen them. A species of *Platanthera*, however, is easily recognizable on the lower side of the road. The remarkable, tiny cushion plant *Douglasia gormanii* is supposed to be up here, too, but I have not seen it either.

As you drive back toward Fairbanks, stop between Eagle Summit and Twelvemile Summit and scramble up the steep cutbank in a dry area. On a nearly level tableland "Dryas barrens" extend for acres, where almost the only plants present are *Dryas* species, *Diapensia lapponica*, and *Minuartia grandiflora*, growing in a concretelike mixture of small broken rock and windblown loess soil. They are all minute forms, perhaps dwarfed by the nearly constant wind.

A walk for a mile or two / 1600 meters to 3 km up the Pennell Mountain trail will disclose many of the same plants seen on Eagle Summit, but here there is a wider array of dwarf shrubs—willows, cassiopes, *Andromeda polifolia*, and the ubiquitous dwarf birches. Hard buns of *Diapensia lapponica* perch on rocks just above the moist layer, and many interesting plants can be found in the damp hollows. This slope is wetter than almost any part of Eagle Summit; in fact, a plank trail has been built across the wettest portion to help preserve the fragile vegetation.

Originally published in the Bulletin of the American Rock Garden Society, *vol. 37, no. 3, pp. 142–143 (1979). The present version includes additional sections written by Jane McGary.*

PART TWO: GREAT BASIN AND ROCKY MOUNTAINS

The Great Basin Phenomenon

B. LEROY DAVIDSON

The western United States beyond the Continental Divide consists geographically of the Pacific Slope and the drainages of two great river systems—the Columbia to the northwest and the Colorado to the southwest—and a vast midsection known as the Great Basin. One of the Earth's great deserts, 570 miles/910 km broad and 880 miles/1400 km long, the Great Basin is a physiographic province of some 210,000 square miles/540,000 square km; it comprises around 90 separate valleys, each an individual drainage basin with no outlet. The whole encompasses most of Nevada, half of Utah, the eastern edge of California (reaching nearly into Mexico), a large "bowl" in southeastern Oregon, bits and pieces of Idaho, and a sliver of Wyoming.

The present northern boundaries may not have been constant over time; probably more of Oregon and Idaho were part the Great Basin at one period or another as a result of damming by basalt flows and subsequent channel-cutting by the Snake River, fed by overflow from the Great Basin during frequent wet periods in ancient times. The physiography of these ancient portions remains similar, and their floras are closely related. An example is the Klamath Basin, which is partially drained in modern times.

The Great Basin lies within a cordilleric syncline, having alternately been submerged beneath the seas and uplifted (much limestone is evident). Fault-block mountain ranges comparable to the Alps and Andes once caught the atmospheric moisture, gathering it into floods and glaciers. The combined forces of water and ice have eroded these ancient heights down to low ranges separated by broad plains, deep in detritus and sometimes containing a playa lake, a marsh, or a lake basin. All these

151

wetlands are shrinking in our time. The Great Salt Lake is the largest, over 1 million acres/400,000 hectares in extent; others are much smaller, such as Pyramid Lake (120,000 acres/48,000 hectares).

The Sierra Nevada forms the main portion of the western rim, while the Wasatch Range is its eastern counterpart in Utah. Lying between them is a series of eroded parallel fault-block ranges separating the Great Basin into its many components, each with its own identity, elevation, and microclimate. Included is a broad spectrum of life zones, from the Sonoran to the Canadian, and one can rather quickly experience several of them within a short climb in these "included ranges."

Oddly, the eastern reaches of the Great Basin do not border on the Continental Divide; there is a broad separation—the headwaters drainages of the Snake River (flowing to the Columbia) and the Green River (to the Colorado)—in southwestern Wyoming, in what is essentially a high desert adjacent to a small arid basin situated astraddle the Continental Divide. These areas are part of the Great Basin in character, but not geographically.

John C. Fremont was the first explorer to realize the existence of such an inward-draining area when, in 1844, in search of the mythological San Buenaventura River (claimed to be the mightiest of western drainages), he realized not only that there was no such river, but that the vast area presumed to be its drainage was in reality "a great inland basin." He found it an area of wondrous grandeur and simple beauty, with pure air and great distances, clear skies, intense sunshine, and fresh, invigorating fragrances, as it remains today. Most of it is also as inhospitable to the inroads of civilization now as ever.

Here the Desert Culture of the Native Americans developed, whose precarious existence depended largely on the exhaustive harvest of shoots, leaves, seeds, fruits, roots, and bulbs. Every possible resource had to be fully exploited to sustain life. It is engrossing to travel through this land today and marvel that humans could have existed there; and it is sad to realize that this unique culture was still vigorous a century ago, only to dissipate with the coming of the wagon trains.

The people of the Desert Culture were symbiotes with the deserts; they practiced only traces of agriculture. The drought conditions that had reduced their domain from one of forest and savanna to one of desert and marsh had extinguished the once-plentiful large game, leaving the pronghorn antelope and the ubiquitous jackrabbit as the primary game animals, in addition to migratory waterfowl. The Desert Culture thus came to be based on vegetation. Water both limited and directed their lives, not so much by its presence as by its absence. This will always be true here.

While I was plotting *Synthyris* distributions on the range map, it became obvious to me that only cataclysmic changes in the environment could be responsible for the perimeter pattern; no fewer than four of the taxa I was studying were distributed around the basin, but none within it (with one exception on Mount Ibapaha in western Utah). A field study has borne this out and also revealed a great wealth of other plants, many of them well worth cultivation. From the southern valley floors (mostly 1 mile/1600 meters or more in altitude) to the mountaintops (as high as 12,000 feet/3700 meters), we found startling diversity.

The Western Perimeter

In summer 1973 several friends and I made an expedition we termed "the Great Basin swing." We left the state of Washington on the last day of June and in a period of only 18 days covered almost 5000 miles/8000 km, circumscribing the Basin's entire perimeter except for the Mojave extension into southern California and southernmost Nevada. It is advisable to attempt the latter portion only in spring because of the intense heat. Traveling southward into Oregon on the Pacific Slope, we crossed the Cascade Range over Santiam Pass, passing through cinderfields and great snakes of relatively recent lava flows rich with a variety of interesting growth. We emerged on the high desert of the eastern Cascades, into a northward-flowing drainage to the Columbia, whose sources included springs of phenomenal volume. We were soon to see evidence that similar fountainheads had existed within the deserts, their sources completely or nearly dried up today.

Proceeding southward, we were soon within the Klamath Basin drainage, in an arid, stony landscape thinly set with lodgepole and ponderosa pines over porous basalt bedrock. This pattern was repeated day after day; the species might differ, but the basic picture was much the same. We passed Klamath Lake and the channeled outflow of its river to the Pacific, between the Trinity and Siskiyou ranges of the Klamath mountain system, the only major mountains of the West that extend on an east-west axis.

Our first plant stations were in the vicinity of Mount Shasta and Lassen Peak, where the Cascades end and the Sierra Nevada begins. From here on we were within the Great Basin proper, though nearly on its borders, and the flora was by and large Sierran. Many short, swift rivers flow from this vicinity out into the desert, to be entrapped and doomed. A few terminate in rocky basins as lakes, grown brackish with time and shrinking in size, while others simply disappear into the stony valley floors. In a wet season they may push farther, only to expose more vulnerable surface and be soaked up just as quickly by both soil and atmosphere.

We followed the eastern Sierra southward from Lake Almanor, a diked impoundment resulting from volcanic activity in the Lassen area, to Donner Lake. From there we climbed up into the Sierra, to find at

153

around 8000 feet/2400 meters a great many interesting plants, among them *Eriogonum lobbii* (Plate 33), *Artemisia arbuscula*, and *Calochortus leichtlinii*. In a rubble-plain of granitic derivation which must have been thoroughly soaked in the melt season, we saw the rather infrequent *Lewisia kelloggii* with the diminutive *Allium tribracteatum*; here the timber was scattered pine. A few plant species of this western rim of the Great Basin are endemic there, while others extend to some degree into the Basin itself, or are represented there by closely related species. Although in the main the flora of the Great Basin floor seems to be unique, the widespread species are distributed above it at various levels depending on their tolerance of local conditions. We were to find phloxes, penstemons, drabas, astragalus, and eriogonums particularly adaptable and widespread, with a few other genera widely represented but not so diverse.

Thirsty Deserts

Our party was hosted in Nevada by Margaret and Loring Williams and their son, Steve, a geologist, who served as our guides to the next part of our exploration. Probably the most adventuresome single day of the expedition was the first of several spent on the desert floor. We traveled east from Reno about 240 miles/380 km, covering the ups and downs of the tilted fault-block ranges and the valleys between them. Some of the depressions held streams; others glistened with an eerie purple tone in the intense sunlight. Each held its characteristic plants—even the saline playa and stony, baked slopes.

On the mountainsides were the predictable phloxes, astragalus, and eriogonums, quite a few bearing ripe seed here at elevations between 6000 and 7500 feet/1800 and 2300 meters. *Stenotis acaulis* (formerly *Haplopappus acaulis*; Plate 62), which we were to follow north to Idaho, caught our attention as an attractive little silver-leafed golden-flowered daisy. On Austin Summit (7484 feet/2283 meters) we came upon a most curious association of soft-leaved plants, including such shrubs as a rose and a species of *Symphoricarpos*, with herbs such as *Mertensia* and *Agastache*; this was unique only in being found here, where the usual rule is hard, waxen, gray, or spiny, or all of the above! This community grew in a north-facing swale reminiscent of the Palouse Prairies of Washington and reappeared in the Wasatch of Utah a few days later.

Opuntias and other cacti, with many spined, prickly companions, seemed much more appropriate to the parched landscape. *Pediocactus simpsonii* (Plate 48) was familiar; this barrel cactus extends to eastern Washington, British Columbia, and Idaho. Here, however, it seemed congested or compact, even for a squat cactus, so that a maximum of its spines were evident and little of its skin showed through.

The goal of the day was a worthy one: an enormous, doughnut-shaped tufa formation standing moundlike about 40 feet/12 meters above the desert floor and covering an acre or more, with a deep water basin in its crown. This formation must have resulted from a vast lime-water spring submerged in a now-vanished prehistoric lakebed. The water flow is today reduced to a trickle, which seeps out of the lowest side about 20 feet/6 meters below the colossal rim to water a thin field of alfalfa. The surface of the tufa dome, worn by frosts and mellowed by lichen growth, supports an unusual group of cushion plants—an artemisia, *Phlox griseola* subsp. *tumulosa*, *Ionactis alpina* (formerly *Aster scopulorum*), *Ipomopsis congesta* (formerly in *Gilia*, then *Leptodactylon*), and a *Tetradymia* species growing above as a loose bushlet. The sensational mats of *Lepidium nanum* (Plate 63) were nearly overwhelming—or was it the heat and intensity of the sun?

Though only one of many springs we saw, this was surely the most spectacular. This portion of the Great Basin holds an abundance of water in its underground cisterns, but it only seeps or springs when forced to flow over shallow or exposed bedrock. *Argemone munita*, the lovely prickly poppy, was everywhere, especially along the shoulders of the roadways where runoff from the pavement encourages it.

The following day was one of comparative rest, and much appreciated. On Mount Peavine (7800 feet/2400 meters), very near Reno, we gathered seed of the few plants already ripened: several eriogonums, including the endemic *Eriogonum rosense*; *Lewisia rediviva* var. *minor*, with overlapping ivory petals on a very compact plant; *Fritillaria atropurpurea* (Plate 9), and a few hard-earned bulbs; and no fewer than three phloxes—*Phlox austromontana* subsp. *prostrata*, *P. hoodii*, and *P. stansburyi*. The last-named, a lovely warm pink, was to become familiar as we moved farther out into the desert ranges.

Mount Peavine is the subject of an interesting study in ecology in which Margaret is participating. Now bare of its trees, it was once a densely forested mountain, denuded for shoring-timbers and rails in the mines of the area. Just as an overgrazed pasture cannot rejuvenate itself, so the overharvested mountain was unable to regrow its trees, and the original cover of conifers is now being replaced with an entirely new sort of flora. Many species never before recorded there are now reported.

In the cool of the evening we drove north to Pyramid Lake for a cookout and to watch the desert sunset and afterglow play mauve and apricot on a sere, stony landscape. At this time of day the desert is quite at its best—or is it at dawn? One of the larger of the Great Basin waters, Pyramid Lake terminates the Truckee River, which rises only a short distance above in the spectacular jewel of Lake Tahoe, at the crest of the Sierra Nevada. Pyramid Lake is about 32 miles/51 km long and 12 miles/19 km at its broadest, covering about 120,000 acres/48,000 hectares, but as the thirsty desert and urban and agricultural uses continue to deplete the river, the lake is receding at an alarming rate. Anahoe Island, its breeding ground of the white pelican, is threatened with becoming a peninsula, endangering the waterfowl. On the north shore stands the curious white, pyramid-shaped limestone formation, some 475 feet/145 meters high, that gives the lake its name. Much tufa is visible along both the present shoreline and the ancient shorelines are evident on the barren mountainsides above. Several interesting small plants grow in the present shorelands, including a tiny *Oenothera* species.

Moving south next day against the sheer east face of the Sierra Nevada, we found the desert almond, *Prunus andersonii*, in ripe fruit, making a most attractive dense shrub or small tree. Two other notables were *Iris missouriensis* (Plate 4), still flowering in damp meadows at 8000 feet/2400 meters, and *Penstemon rostriflorus* (formerly *P. bridgesii*), the first of several scarlet, hummingbird-pollinated species frequent in the Great Basin and south into Mexico. A neat *Holodiscus* embellished its small, tidy bushes with the typical creamy froth of blossom. The plant found here (the genus ranges from British Columbia to Peru) was once known as *H. microphyllus* var. *boursieri* but is now included in the widespread *H. discolor*; this form extends eastward into the desert ranges. In cultivation this has given tremendous satisfaction, being very tidy and floriferous.

The heat of the desert was oppressive, and we soon climbed up to near 10,000 feet/3100 meters in the Saddlebag Lake basin, just east of Yosemite, at the foot of glaciers coming off Mount Conness (12,556 feet/3830 meters). There is great contrast on the Sierra rim of the Great Basin: we found *Kalmia polifolia* (Plate 12), *Salix reticulata* subsp. *nivalis*, species of *Phyllodoce* and *Cassiope*, *Gentiana newberryi* (Plate 2), good pink forms of *Lewisia pygmaea* (Plate 26), and two *Penstemon* species of the subgenus *Dasanthera*—*P. davidsonii* (Plate 28) and *P. newberryi* (Plate 13), as well as hybrids between them. These and many more good plants adorned the green meadowland between icy streams. (Mount Conness is the type station for *P. davidsonii*.) This is all within one of the southernmost and largest arctic-alpine tundra areas of the Sierra, chilled by glaciers, so of course when we descended again, the heat was all the more unbearable.

In a pleasant, cool area of the June Lakes resort settlement, we came onto a lovely stand of one of the California leopard-spotted lilies, *Lilium kelleyanum* (syn. *L. shastense*) in a grove of aspen; these are becoming all too rare. We had passed over a series of ridges and depressions overlying vast ancient glacial deposits. As we crested the last, the stark majesty of the well-named White Mountains loomed dead ahead against the eastern sky at what seemed incredible heights, so close at hand were they. Then we plunged into the furnace of the Owens Valley to restock fuel, water, and food for their ascent. This valley, a very long, narrow, and deep fault-trench at the eastern base of the Sierra, once contained a vast lake, long ago receded to mere puddles; now even those have been drained off to water arid southern California, to the devastation of the valley.

The White Mountains, one of the Great Basin's highest and driest ranges, are a formation of forbidding yet fascinating grandeur, much of it dolomitic limestone and quite unlike anything else nearby. The range is the home of the Earth's oldest living trees, a good enough reason for going there, and we found others. Our dry camp was beneath a venerable, ice-blasted *Juniperus osteosperma*, and a surprising number of flowers surrounded us—a swertia, penstemons, and *Phlox stansburyi* among them. Here the last was especially appealing, with its huge, long-tubed pink flowers, reminiscent of rhodohypoxis, topping inch-wide tufts of needlelike foliage.

The Schulman Grove of Bristlecone Pines at 10,000 feet/3100 meters contains the first of these trees to be dated as more than 40 centuries in age, designated "Pine Alpha." It is sobering to stand in its quiet presence and realize that it "had been growing on this slope for 500 years when man invented the spoked wheel; it was nearly 1500 years old when Moses led the people out of Egypt, and 2800 years old when Rome fell," according to the Forest Service interpretive sign. The Methuselah Grove has the very oldest trees—one dated at 4600 years—and is a 4-hour loop hike from this point to the east in a calcareous region of less than 10 inches/25 cm annual rainfall. These oldest trees (along with all others lacking resin glands in the needles) have now been segregated as distinct from *Pinus aristata* and given the name *P. longaeva* Bailey. The area has a small cover population of lesser plants, among which *Salvia dorrii* was prominent in blue and silver.

Climbing farther, we reached a saddle on the spine of the White Mountains which bore cushions of the tiniest form of *Lupinus breweri*; it appears the rule that all plants of this range are smallest, the woolly ones woolliest, the colors the most intense. Bright blue cloverheads of lupine flowers were appressed right into the silver-downy mounds—a total delight, and with seed capsules paling in promise. At 11,000 feet/3400 meters, we reached the Patriarch Grove of trees, including the largest known bristlecone pine, 37 feet/11 meters in girth near its multitrunked base, but only a youngster of 1500 years! In spite of the combined forces of extreme aridity and extreme desiccation, it had been able to grow far faster than most of its kind. This area was carpeted with an astragalus so tiny one had to belly-flop to see it—a slender, thready little one with silver-gray leaves and lilac flowers; we took this for *Astragalus kentrophyta* var. *tegetarius*.

The blinding glare of white and colored flowers on silver cushions in the high screes of white dolomitic limestone was like the brilliance of a noonday midsummer beach, yet it was set 2 miles/3 km in the sky! Two phloxes, two drabas, a small red castilleja, *Linanthus nuttallii*, *Hymenoxys*

cooperi, Lesquerella kingii, Eriogonum caespitosum (some a brilliant raspberry), and other miniatures contributed to the jewel-box community
here. A few were past flowering, and some seed was ready for harvest.
From this vantage point the Sierra Nevada was in splendid view, 35
miles / 56 km to the southwest; it traps most of the moisture coming from
the Pacific, resulting in the drought responsible for the tiny flora about
us. We were looking directly at the 14,000-foot / 4300-meter Mount Whitney cluster of peaks, the highest in the contiguous United States.

Farther east, we continued for several days of travel over the high
valley floors, at elevations well over a mile / 1600 meters. We passed
through large stands of the Joshua tree (*Yucca brevifolia*) and through the
deserted ghost towns of the mining booms, some now only beautifully
laid, weathered stone foundations which would make lovely planted
dry walls. On dry roadsides grew the curious *Eriogonum inflatum* with its
odd stems like living green clay pipes.

The ascent of 11,260-foot / 3430-meter Troy Peak for elusive primulas
and columbines was another memorable day. From a waterless camp
east of Tonopah, we set out in the pale dawn, turning off highways onto
roads, then onto mere tracks, and finally into a trough of clattering talus
(a seasonal streambed) and up a steep, dry gulch. Troy Canyon is an
open forest, mainly aspen and pine; as in the White Mountains, both
Pinus longaeva and *P. flexilis* were present, as well as pinyon, juniper, and
a fir, making a total of five needle conifers, plus the related ephedra, a curious leafless stick plant. We saw as many interesting shrubs as in any
one place: *Grayia spinosa, Purshia tridentata* (antelope bush), *Philadelphus
microphyllus,* the solanaceous *Lycium andersonii* (a food plant of native
people, with tiny hard gray leaves and quantities of tiny, bland chili-like
capsules), a rather pretty apricot-colored ribes, *Mahonia fremontii* (glaucous, graceful, and very spiny), and *Rhus trilobata* (from whose gummy
red fruits can be made a refreshing "pink lemonade"). Rosaceous shrubs
were numerous, including the cosmopolitan *Potentilla fruticosa* (syn. *Pentaphylloides floribunda*), and *Holodiscus,* as in the Sierra; *Amelanchier pallida,*
a food plant; a rose; *Purshia mexicana* (formerly *Cowania mexicana*), and
Fallugia paradoxa, both with long, silky, glistening tails to their seeds, a
ghostly luminescence in desert moonlight; *Chamaebatiaria millefolium*;
and the remarkable *Petrophyton caespitosum,* cloaking one cool limestone
crumble. An additional rosaceous subject, though usually a mere shrub,
growing slowly to a small tree on stony ledges, is *Cercocarpus ledifolius,*
widespread in dry western ranges.

From the end of the track at an abandoned mine shaft, it was a 4-
hour walk up an easy incline, but over loose detritus that never would
stay put underfoot, until we arrived at the broad band of limestone cliff
that crowned the mountain. Here in cool clefts grew the charming little
Primula nevadensis (Plate 81); but we never saw a sign of the aquilegia,
said to be found in all colors, and thus allied to the varicolored *Aquilegia*

scopulorum (sometimes called var. *perplexans*) of the Charleston Mountains near Las Vegas, or identical to it. We spied one of the fern treasures of the cool limestone, *Pellaea breweri*, as well as the ever-present (at high elevations) *Oxyria digyna*, and refreshed ourselves by chewing the latter; the mild acetic acid is quite pleasant to a parched mouth. Delightfully tiny forms of *Heuchera rubescens* are found on this limestone rim, one of which has been brought into cultivation under the name 'Troy Boy'.

Returning to the valley, we were further refreshed at being able to soak our aching feet in the good cold stream at one of many shallow fords. Penstemons of many species brightened somber hillsides and copses with scarlet, purple, lilac, and blue. Then we traveled across a stretch of dusty desert and a spine of the Quinn Canyon range via a low divide to one of our most delightful campsites, beside a broad rush of cold water passing through red sandstone cliffs. *Echinocereus triglochidiatus* var. *mojavensis* (Plate 60) grew nearby, and there were deep green groves of chokecherry (*Prunus virginiana*), yet another member of the Rosaceae; its nearness always promised songbirds. This part of the Great Basin has just such a stream in every side canyon, yet none last long once exposed to the open desert.

We were successful the next day in finding a few seeds of the unusual *Lewisia maguirei* adjacent to *Fritillaria atropurpurea, Calochortus bruneaunis, Physaria eastwoodiae* with its gray felt "penwiper" rosette, a neat blue scutellaria only a few inches high yet broad in colonies from thickened underground stolons, and *Frasera albomarginata* (formerly *Swertia albomarginata*), a neat gentian relative with fritillary-marked, purple-brown and yellow-green flowers. Below on the edge of the roadway, the attractive small *Yucca harrimaniae* (formerly *Y. gilbertiana*) is endangered by road-grader blades about once a year.

A midday search of certain calcareous desert outfans failed to turn up one of the species we most wished to see: *Polygala subspinosa* would not reveal itself to us, but perhaps our hearts were not really in it, at high noon. After lunch in another stream-washed campsite, and a swim in the cool water, we found still another of the Basin's rosaceous inhabitants, *Peraphyllum ramosissimum*, an aboriginal food shrub with fruits like tiny apples, not unlike those of *Amelanchier*.

Quite a number of oenotheras had attracted our attention, though we probably missed most of them because of their nocturnal flowering. However, near Ely we did come onto a scissor-cut, flannelly one we presumed to be that which Dr. Worth had reported as infrequent thereabout. We rushed on to cross a great stretch of desert by night. Camped on a roadside in ghostly moonlight reflected off the glazed marshes adjacent to Sevier Lake, another of the Great Basin's terminal cases, we dreamed of the Wasatch Rim the next day.

Basin Echoes

Meadowlarks, crowing farmyard cocks, and a chatter of sparrows announced the end of a short night all too soon, and we headed directly into the sunrise to breakfast en route. Snow near the top of Mount Nebo (11,877 feet/3622 meters) promised that we had come at the right time. As we topped a low summit and drove into the charming little Mormon village of Fountain Green, our goal lay in sight, with an enticing snow-covered cliffside breaking away from the summit plateau. We gained that summit via Ephraim Canyon in the Manti-LaSal National Forest. Perhaps we had been anticipating too much; a profusion of wildflowers such as lupines was only commencing, while the more precocious flowers, including *Erythronium grandiflorum*, had gone by. In one snowbank we did locate *Ranunculus adoneus* (or *eschscholtzii?*), and nearby on open, newly bare, stony ground, already in flower, were broad carpets of a stemless white *Townsendia*. In another opening in the snow a *Caltha* was lighting the cold, barren landscape, but in all, there was not much to promise arctic-alpine treasures.

This station, on the drainage east to the Green River, the northernmost tributary of the Colorado River system, consists of a nearly level and only slightly tilted plateau of great size and beauty, with colonies of conifers below. Beyond and all about lay acres of green pastures which had for years been grazed by sheep. Could the constant browsing have depleted the flora that once must have been there? Here at 10,200 feet/ 3110 meters we certainly should have found much more interesting plants. Although we felt somewhat deflated, the area did have its lesson. We had come from below through a new and very different plant association, at first with cover of low *Quercus utahensis* scrub and an occasional specimen of *Acer grandidentatum*, the western counterpart of the sugar maple and a handsome small tree that should find more use in cultivation. We were also interested by the educational roadside exhibits of the Great Basin Experimental Station of the U.S. Department of Agriculture, established in 1912 with the primary purpose of studying how to maintain, improve, and rehabilitate the forest and rangeland ecosystems. Of greatest import here is the control of devastating erosion resulting from the violent summer storms famous in the Wasatch Range. Overgrazing, of course, was soon blamed as well.

The terrain from the basin floor to Skyline Drive at more than 10,000 feet/3100 meters includes five life zones, from Upper Sonoran to Alpine, each with its own characteristic growth. We noted an *Aquilegia* about midway, in more than one zone. We made a quick visit to project headquarters in a big aspen-clothed cirque, finding a well-labeled natural planting of native subjects.

A nursery lower down grows a thousand exotic species in trials aimed at introducing cover to reduce erosion and slow runoff. The purist would condemn this, and the tall bearded garden irises looked mighty strange on the steep roadbanks, yet they have proven to be invaluable soil-binders. Ponderosa pine, introduced as early as 1913, seemed quite at home though considerably stunted by the dry conditions; it was deemed unsuccessful, however, because it was not able to reproduce by seed. At several elevations, enclosures had for years excluded any grazing or browsing, and these clearly showed the contrast and effect of depletion of the natural cover outside their bounds. A great marsh near the summit was abloom with dodecatheons, and the hillsides of penstemon had given the area the name "Bluebell Flat."

Again, as at the base of the Sierra Nevada, we suffered intensely from the heat when we drove down to the basin floor, and we stopped frequently to cool ourselves with rootbeer floats and wading in flooded street drains along with village children. We were proceeding south toward the second of the three planned Wasatch stations—this one west of Marysvale on the flanks of Mount Belknap in the Tushar Range, a spur of the Wasatch, draining north to two branches of the Sevier River.

From a base camp on another of these sparkling snow-fed streams, we left early the next morning but were soon stopped by snowdrifts blocking the road. We hiked onward and upward, confident of finding good things. A towering cliff-face rose some 200 feet / 60 meters, all its crevices crammed with heucheras. This we felt to be one of several favorite places to which we could return again and again. *Aquilegia scopulorum* was beginning to flower; at one place on the lower side of the road-bank a huge old plant bore what must have been a hundred buds. *Silene acaulis* was here, as was the sky-pilot, *Polemonium viscosum*, a lovely thing but "skunky"; other plants included *Cerastium berringianum*, a species of *Arenaria*, *Stellaria*, or *Minuartia*, and a white violet.

A great cirque of weathered sandstone (we were nearing the "canyon country") held an overflow of *Synthyris laciniata*, which I found surprisingly similar to alpine forms of *S. missurica* in the southern Wallowas of Oregon. In the saddle leading over to the western fork of the Sevier River, we took to the talus to climb to about 11,000 feet / 3400 meters, not finding much that was not also growing below, until we were driven back by a threatening black cloud, remembering the lessons taught us by the Wasatch storms.

The storm was short-lived but violent, and it caught us near the limited shelter of a few small *Abies lasiocarpa*; then we descended the snow-blocked roadway to find our camp quite dry! Two penstemons (scarlet *Penstemon eatonii* with long hummingbird tubes, and a brilliant blue one) embellished the upper roadbanks. A quieter combination was afforded by a curious milkweed growing with rosettes of *Physaria newberryi* (Plate 66), another felty "penwiper"; *Asclepias asperula* (syn. *Asclepiodora decumbens*) bore 3-inch / 8-cm, ball-shaped inflorescences of a lime-green color with the hoods of the stamens colored pure violet.

161

Thus began our encounter with the Wasatch storms of summer; we broke camp under threat of a downpour, and it poured off and on for the following two days. We took a motel room that night, swimming into it and darting out periodically to salvage things. Here our dried specimens began their slow deterioration, so that many of their identities remain obscure.

A bright dawn the next morning was deceptive, though it allowed us to enjoy some good plant stations out on the Markagunt Plateau, southwest of the Wasatch. There were several penstemons, all blue-flowered. Some were cinereous gray in leaf; others, belonging to the section Ericopsis, we took to be *Penstemon caespitosus* and *P. crandallii*—attractive, shining, matted plants. There was a small and very appealing white-flowered *Oenothera* species, still good in the early morning; *Antennaria parviflora*, a tidy little carpeter of the *A. rosea* persuasion; and another carpeter, a delicate pink daisy composite with pink buds, as well as small pale yellow-flowered lupine. All these were among grasses, interspersed with *Pinus ponderosa*, the presence of which, along with large flows of basalt, reminded us of the Colockum area east of Washington's Cascades. Farther along, spotting *P. aristata* returned us to a proper perspective. The basalt flows afforded a cool place for *Aquilegia caerulea* var. *ochroleuca*, apparently the western (Utah-Idaho) counterpart of the Colorado columbine. On the ascent up to Cedar Breaks, we found the pretty tall "pink dandelion" *Lygodesmia grandiflora*, the bewitching, notch-petaled, golden-orange, gaillardia-like *Thelyspermum subnudum*, and a brilliant roadside show of salmon-pink gilia directly across from a cobalt-blue penstemon. How often we find such spectacles on disturbed places —which ought to suggest possible uses in cultivation.

The Rim Road around Cedar Breaks amphitheater (its lower elevation is more than 8000 feet/2400 meters) skirts the awesome canyon and then leads off toward Brianhead Peak (11,335 feet/3457 meters), from which point all the colorful sandstone canyons of the southwest break away. This is a low, mounded terminus, not at all a peak, and we were alone on it in a stupendous roll of thunder-drums with occasional far-off lightning. The brewing storm kept saner people in safer places, and we wandered alone over the vast silvery tapestry of phloxes and eriogonums. In a large cirque to the north we found huge plants of the spectacular *Primula parryi* (Plate 61) in full glory (another skunky-smelling plant), accompanied by *Synthyris laciniata*. The rain had not yet come, but the din continued unabated, reechoing from every direction. It was a little cooler.

On the descent we searched successfully for the glaucous blue form of *Petrophyton caespitosum* on the puddingstone topping of red sandstone cliffs. As we came to the valley floor, the heavens opened totally and we experienced again the full force of a Wasatch rainstorm. The roadside ditches were soon full; we were grateful for the new freeway and headed directly north, taking rooms in Salt Lake City, where it was still unbearably hot, and without rain.

By seven the next morning it had cooled down to a bearable 70°F/21°C, and we prepared to drive over the north rim of the Great Basin via the low gap through which overflow waters from ancient Lake Bonneville had once emptied north into the Snake River drainage. The old lakeshore was plainly evident on the mountainsides, as at Pyramid Lake. The high plateau of the Upper Snake River in southern Idaho is a desert plain similar to that through which we had been traveling, and many of the same species grow there, such as *Chamaebatiaria millefolium, Stanleya*, and *Penstemon palmeri*. The seed of many was ready for gathering, and so we set about harvesting it.

Anyone traveling in this vicinity should visit the Craters of the Moon. It is a unique experience for the perceptive, though it might be a big bore to many—so big, so empty, and so "useless." The national monument grounds are laid out with campsites and surfaced roads to some of the main features, including volcanic spatter cones and ice-caves just below the ground surface. The black cinder and pumice fields are tufted with the flannelly *Eriogonum ovalifolium* (Plate 6) and the white-flowered form of *Lewisia rediviva* (Plate 24); the little bright purple annual *Mimulus nanus* was everywhere. We could not remain for long, however, and so we moved on.

The Lost River Range, climaxing in Idaho's highest peak, Mount Borah (12,662 feet/3862 meters), is a rugged limestone formation. It seemed strangely familiar after our weeks in similar ranges to the south. We camped in the traditional spot to convene the official get-together of "Kelsey-moss Admirers, Universal," devotees of *Kelseya uniflora* (Plate 64)—another of western America's unusual rosaceous shrubs, a dense mat-forming plant that intrigues rock gardeners. It is found throughout this precipitous limestone range at considerable heights. It may be able to find a foothold in this, its lowest station, because there is a constant cooling downdraft passing through the narrow canyon, which hosts one of the very few permanent streams in the range. At the time of our trip, *Kelseya* was known from only two other places, one in Montana and the other in Wyoming, but since then it has been found in many other Wyoming stations. Another interesting plant here was *Petrophyton caespitosum*, its adpressed mats sometimes mingling with the similar ones of *Kelseya*; when not immediately adjacent they are likely to be confused, except for their slightly different foliage color. *Draba oreibata* did a credible job of mimicry, though on a smaller scale; and in pockets of cool soil, the annual *Androsace septentrionalis* made an attractive design, threadlike and precise. Spiny, phlox-like *Leptodactylon pungens* with pale apricot flowers was attractive enough unless one got too close, and a wispy little shrub, a pink-flowered *Polygonum* species, straggled in clefts beneath gnarled old *Cercocarpus ledifolius*, with silvery mats of gold-flowered *Haplopappus* [*Stenotis*] *acaulis*. *Cheilanthes feei* studded the limestone occasionally, once in the overhang to a cave mouth, and *Iris missouriensis* was lush in the narrow meadow along the streamside. We had a big ceremonial bonfire, and when it died down and the moon had climbed high enough to peer into this narrow slit of canyon, its brilliance was not to be believed.

Rivers hereabout sink into the deserts as they do in Nevada. We followed the Big Lost River up to its source in enormous meadows near the base of Mount Borah, passing a fine colony of *Sphaeralcea munroana*, colored pale carrot to rusty brick. All the close-carpet species of this high dry area are tiny and silver, gray, and/or spiny; among them were a phlox and a tiny eriogonum (probably *Eriogonum ovalifolium*); the rest were too unfamiliar to be guessed at out of flower. The effect is a close carpet, blended, tufted, and newly brushed. Our friend *Pediocactus* was here too, making little accents in what we refer to as the "Doublesprings Flora." On limestone crevices near the old town of Mackay, we came upon the tiny form of *Penstemon humilis* we are calling "Mackay form," an ashen tuft with 2-inch/5-cm stems of turquoise-blue flowers.

Passing north over Willow Creek Summit brought us into the drainage of the Salmon River and out of the Basin extension, though still in the Snake-Columbia drainage. We were to reemerge on the old north rim in several places in the Salmon River ranges, the first station being in the White Cloud Peaks. Arriving in the late afternoon, we immediately saw that we would need plenty of time. We descended to a base camp, although another time we might consider camping at the top; in spite of deserted mine buildings and rusting machinery, the majesty of the place remains quite undiminished.

Not really unusual is the great cirque at the top, a wet meadow garden filling it to the brim. A spectacular fragment of a mountain shell (ca. 11,000 feet/3400 meters) props up the sky beyond, marked with a series of color-bands breaking off skyward in a great upthrust that only hints at its former grandeur. Another road led up to near its base, whence we hiked out onto the perimeter of the cirque, amid a throng of flowering eriogonums. There were three species, with no two individuals identical; flower color ranged from ivory and blush to baby-ribbon pink (*Eriogonum ovalifolium*, Plate 6), and from melon and salmon to tangerine and rust or raspberry-red (*E. caespitosum*). The blossoms were nearly all stemless, with some flowers even pressed into buns of gray leafage; the rusty-haired mounds of *E. androsaceum* were unmistakably distinct by contrast.

We hiked for some time on this vast scree, marveling at distant views into the Salmon River country to the north; at the steepness of the nearby canyon walls through which we glimpsed little lakes below; at the profusion of an exquisitely fragrant, blue-flowered and silver-leafed 8-inch/20-cm lupine; and at the bold beauty of *Hymenoxys* (*Rydbergia*) *grandiflora* (Plate 70), the "old man of the mountain." This is one of the known sites for *Primula broadheadiae*, which has now been submerged in *P. cu-sickiana* (Plate 83), although some botanists believe them to be distinct; as we were not so fortunate as to find it, we cannot venture an opinion, other than to remark that ecologically, the two were certainly far apart, whatever their resemblances. On a steeply eroding cliffside we came on a "motherland" of synthyris in the type area for the former *Synthyris cymopteroides*, now considered to be *S. pinnatifida* var. *canescens*. A larger form of *Penstemon humilis* and the rather similar *P. rydbergii* were painting the scree with blue, the grayish tint of the former possibly giving it an edge in appeal.

As we began the descent, we interrupted the browsing of a big buck mule deer; lower down we found he had had the good taste to eat an especially fine clump of penstemons we had wanted to photograph! A large colony of a white-flowered, 6-inch/15-cm silene (or perhaps a lychnis) eluded identification, although its dark purplish eye seemed very individual. In the seepages in the cirque were the heaths *Cassiope mertensiana* var. *gracilis* and *Phyllodoce empetriformis*, as well as *Salix nivalis*; and the ever-fascinating elephant's head, *Pedicularis groenlandica*, with light blue *Veronica wormskjoldii* and *Swertia perennis*, a graceful little plant. There was also a small tangerine-disked, golden-rayed composite in the wet meadow, which we could never find again, much less identify. An endemic of the region that extends east to the Bitterroot Range is the 7-inch/18-cm plant once known as *Penstemon* (or *Penstemonopsis*) *tweedyi* and now allied to a Colorado species in the genus *Chionophila*. This has pale powder-blue flowers, flattened as if sat upon, dangling up the short stem and facing out at the same angle and direction; it grows in open stony glades associated with, but not crowded by, phyllodoce. Nearby the blue cups of *Gentiana calycosa* were beginning to pop open; *Phacelia sericea* was pluming a dry bank with amethyst; and *Gilia spicata* var. *orchioides* hovered between them, a pretty little white-flowered alpine form being endemic here. Another apricot-colored phlox relative, *Linanthus douglasii*, sat on stony banks.

Farther below the roadside was emblazoned with huge cups of *Oenothera caespitosa* (Plate 39), rosy in decline. A sliding talus both above and below the roadway was haven to the rather uncommon *Penstemon montanus*, spreading widely in the cool root-run beneath the stones. It is related to *P. fruticosus*, of which a weak colony was seen not too far distant; but in this knifelike canyon, only a goat could seek a mergence zone where they might be expected to be interbreeding.

And so we reluctantly broke camp and began our way homeward. At Galena Summit we paused at the overlook for the breathtaking view of the Sawtooth Range and Stanley Basin, but we could find not even the foliage of *Beckwithia* (*Ranunculus*) *andersonii*, a "pink buttercup" of repute. We wondered if it too had not been browsed.

From Stanley Basin one end of a great meadow gives rise to the main

165

fork of the Salmon River, and the other to a fork of the west-flowing Payette River; we followed the latter. The short, soft-yellow *Castilleja glandulifera* was lighting the broad roadside meadows in profusion, particularly attractive in the low light of evening against somber pines. This appeared to be the same as the species in the high meandering meadows atop the Wallowa range in northeast Oregon—not unexpectedly, as the Wallowa flora contains a number of these plants of the northern Rockies and Salmon River ranges, representing their westernmost extensions. Together these mountains must have represented the old northern rim of the Great Basin. North of this the original cover must have been much altered, decimated, or destroyed in the Ice Age, with the old rim acting as a refugium for those we now find there.

We climbed again up onto the northern rim, where we camped for the night in an expanse of wet meadow that was alive with all the wildflowers of the region, plus mosquitoes! This night we kept a campfire going, and at breakfast the temperature read 34°F/1°C.

Two additional days were required to return to Seattle, with an occasional stop for a plant or a cool drink. We found extensive colonies of *Petrophyton* growing happily on granite rather than limestone in several stations in the Salmon River ranges. On the west end of the range we stopped to see the gray-felt-leafed penstemon that has been allied with *Penstemon montanus* as variety *idahoensis*. It is quite distinct both morphologically and ecologically and would seem to be a perfectly good species in its own right. Apparently at some station someone observed the two in proximity and interbreeding; thus they were allied. (The same situation can, however, exist wherever any two of the woolly-anthered *Dasanthera* penstemons come together.)

We arrived in Lewiston, Idaho in the late afternoon with the thermometer reading 103°F/39°C and not much shade available. The following day was a traverse of the state of Washington, with a special stop to visit *Pediocactus simpsonii* (Plate 48) in the Columbia basalt. And so our journey ended.

The little we may have contributed to the total knowledge of the plants of the Great Basin is dedicated to those who went before and so willingly helped in our efforts. We have not disclosed here explicit stations for some of the scarce or endemic species we saw; however, we do invite inquiries from those who would go to see them, to study or photograph them, or to seek seed. We owe a great deal to Rupert Barneby and the late Dwight Ripley, to Carl Worth, Carl English, Margaret Williams and Charley Thurman, and we have been truly pleased to have been asked to share our experiences through these pages.

Originally published in the Bulletin of the American Rock Garden Society, *vol. 32, pp. 15–25 (1974); vol. 33, pp. 64–71 (1975).*

The Sandstone Barrens of Uncompahgre Plateau

PANAYOTI KELAIDIS

The Uncompahgre Plateau is not for everyone. This remote table-land in western Colorado is difficult of access, rugged, and extensive. Winding up its many canyons are numerous roads that are quagmires when cloudbursts pass and powder factories when dry, made torturous by rocks and potholes. Because the plateau has no permanent streams or lakes, fishermen avoid it; only during hunting season does it have many visitors other than ranchers, loggers, and naturalists. Although the many canyons carved into its sides are as dramatic as more famous canyonlands, and the top displays melting vistas and dramatic outcrops, there are virtually no conveniences along the 70-mile / 112-km length of the plateau, except for a few primitive campgrounds.

This lack of visitors is part of the Uncompahgre's charm. Although the top of this long, broad mountain is almost flat, there is a great variety of rock types and vegetation on its slopes. Granite can be found along the western base of the Uncompahgre, along the Dolores River. A number of sandstone formations comprise the bulk of the mountain. The summit is not high enough for true alpines, but there are patches of subalpine forest there, as well as dense spruce and fir forest in the higher reaches of most canyons descending from the rim. The Hudsonian forest here is unusually floriferous once the snows begin to melt in early May. The mesic forest floor is a thickly woven carpet of *Claytonia lanceolata* (Plate 69), *Thlaspi montanum*, many *Ranunculus* species, *Erythronium grandiflorum*, and the endemic *Mertensia fusiformis*.

Mertensia fusiformis, a furry-leaved "bluebell," is one of the finest plants on the mountain. Although it occurs over much of the higher reaches of the Navajoan desert, it is especially common on the Uncompahgre. Here it is found in practically every ecotone above the desert— in running freshets, in the densest Gambel oak copses, under aspens, among spruce, with cacti on barren rock, and in mountain meadows. Its large cluster of semituberous roots, furry stems, and bluish leaves are unmistakable. This is one of the loveliest western *Mertensia* species and also one of the most amenable to cultivation, needing only a scree soil in full sun.

However lovely the subalpine woods, the real appeal of the Uncompahgre lies elsewhere. For the rock gardener, the dry tableland that stretches over most of the top must be one of the grandest natural rock gardens in North America. Most of the top is composed of exposed sandstone bedrock, sometimes gouged into deep ravines and curious outcrops. In the southern, more hilly portions of the plateau there are greater accumulations of soil, and forests of ponderosa pine (*Pinus ponderosa*) and aspen (*Populus tremuloides*) predominate. On more exposed sites the Uncompahgre is an uninterrupted series of outcrops and bedrock basins. Little snow accumulates on these exposed slopes, despite the 10,000-foot/3150-meter altitude, and the barrens burst into bloom with the first warm spells of late May. By mid-July the top is dry and sere, except where a little seepage animates the grasses. In the brief 2 months of verdure, the barrens are covered with a profusion of montane and low-country rock plants in flower.

In wet years *Delphinium nuttallianum* (formerly *D. nelsonii*) is very common, covering the barrens with bright pools of deep cobalt larkspurs. The color is intensified by the proximity of dwarf crimson paintbrushes (*Castilleja* sp.), which are nearly as abundant. *Lithophragma parviflorum* adds a patriotic note of white to the red and blue; it is prevalent on drier soils, while *Lithophragma glabrum* (formerly *L. bulbiferum*) occurs in moister spots with its smaller, pinker flowers.

More than 40 other species bloom at the same time on these barrens. *Townsendia glabella* (Plate 68) is one of the loveliest, resembling the common prairie Easter daisy (*T. exscapa*) except that its lax rosette is greener, and the flowers somewhat larger and more clearly purple. It inhabits shallow soils on the Uncompahgre but responds well in cultivation to ordinary scree conditions in a warm exposure. In Denver it is much longer-lived than its equivalent from the eastern slope of the Rockies.

Townsendia incana (Plate 67) can be found on almost any dry exposure from the desert up, but it generally blooms much later over its tiny, gray rosettes. *Mertensia fusiformis* is everywhere, often growing with *Fritillaria atropurpurea* (Plate 9), which grows only where not grazed by cattle. In the aspen and oak woods this fritillary can grow 2 feet/60 cm tall, bearing five or more dark bells. On the barrens it is minute, with flowers of a brighter, brassier color. Little colonies are not rare, but they are quite inconspicuous until you are practically stepping on them.

The mountain ball cactus *Pediocactus simpsonii* (Plate 48) is especially abundant here, so thick on the rocks that it is hard to walk without crushing plants underfoot. The form on the Uncompahgre is less brightly colored than the eastern slope subspecies. The flowers are smaller and generally white or dirty pink, but the stems grow to considerable size: even at this high elevation, plants 10 inches/25 cm across may be found. Nearby you are sure to find *Penstemon crandallii* subsp. *procumbens* forming extensive mats and resembling a dusty heather; by late June these are studded with many gentian-blue, tubular flowers. *Phlox longifolia* is the dominant phlox of the mesa, as it is over much of this region. *Zigadenus elegans* nods in bud here and there; species of *Arenaria*, *Cerastium*, *Astragalus*, and *Oxytropis* are scattered throughout.

It is hard to describe the quiet ecstasy one experiences here after a walk of a few minutes, but every rock gardener has experienced something comparable. There is always a gentle wind up on the plateau, and the sun is usually intense. Members of the party drift off in different directions, but pretty soon someone calls, "Come here, quick, what in the heck is this?" You gingerly dance over the lichened, selaginella-studded bedrock, trying to crush as little as possible and spotting at least five new flowers on your way. A dozen different composites are already coming into bloom, eriogonums in dense mats, large colonies of *Allium acuminatum* showing the first magenta tint, and the bright purple leaves of *Sedum lanceolatum* have yet to take on their summer green. (This sedum is so abundant over the entire mesa that the ground takes on a purple color.) Down in a moister hollow you can see the lush foliage of *Aquilegia caerulea* and lupines developing. *Clematis hirsutissima* is opening its first blooms. But you constantly find yourself returning to the bedrock gardens. After a while, you find a place to sit down and just look.

To the east the Grand Mesa looms some 50 miles/80 km away across the arid Gunnison Valley. In June the lakes are still thawing all over its flat top, dark with forests. Even then it must be full of fishermen and flowers. Hill after hill extends northward toward the distant White River Plateau and its volcanic cliffs. The Manti-La Sal Mountains in Utah to the west are always evident, blue and deceptively near. Only occasionally do you catch glimpses of the San Juan Mountains, usually masked by hillier portions of the plateau. Mount Sneffels is the nearest crag, standing at the head of the long valley to the south.

Most of the time you are looking down, though, however wonderful the view. Wandering off the bedrock into a copse of oak and scattered pines, you may encounter one of the easternmost colonies of manzanita (*Arctostaphylos*). Manzanitas led me to discover this area. Paul Maslin had collected a small layer of Green's manzanita (*A. patula*) many years before, which had become a giant mound clambering over the rocks in his front yard. The plant was getting old and rangy, and Paul decided to return and look for other interesting clones that might be worthy of introduction. The manzanitas of the Uncompahgre are remarkable for several reasons. At over 9000 feet / 2700 meters, these are some of the hardiest clones of this typically mild-climate genus. The thickest colonies occur in an area where giant ponderosa pines are being logged, so there is special urgency to find desirable clones. Perhaps because this station is rather remote from the center of distribution of manzanitas, the plants are especially variable, ranging from prostrate kinnikinick (*A. uva-ursi*) to 1-foot / 30-cm high mats of *A. nevadensis* var. *coloradensis* (*A.* × *coloradensis* of Rollins), to 3-foot / 90-cm high mounds of *A. patula*.

After the disastrously dry winter of 1976–1977, almost three-fourths of the mesa's plants showed severe damage, and most appeared to have been killed outright. Paul Maslin wanted to see what plants had survived undamaged, since these would best promise to endure the sunny, dry winters of the Colorado Front Range. We found a number of plants in exposed sites that showed no damage; these were marked and rocks placed on stems to make layers. We returned several times to compare the plants we had marked for bloom and berry color. Four clones were selected for superior qualities on all counts; numerous cuttings were made and established as plants in a number of local gardens for testing.

What struck us in 1981, three summers following the drought, was the total absence of dead plants. Although every bit of growth on most manzanitas on the Uncompahgre had appeared dead, there are as many plants as ever, and they are uniformly green and healthy. Only the relative lack of flowers and fruits on many plants suggests the catastrophe.

As you wander through the high chaparral with its dozens of distinctive manzanitas, through dense mats of bearberry and flowery meadows, another aspect of this mercurial plateau begins to appear. Suddenly the slope steepens, the undergrowth thickens, and aspens appear. You are on the verge of a miniature canyon. As you scramble down through vacciniums and manzanita, spruce and fir suddenly close around you, and a dark north slope appears opposite. Pyrolas, pipsissewa (*Chimaphila* sp.) and twinflower (*Linnaea borealis*) show deep-green foliage near a still extensive snowbank. Arnicas are starting into growth, and a few specimens of *Calypso bulbosa* are blooming. *Aquilegia elegantula* is quite common on this slope, where this dainty cousin of *A. formosa* and *A. canadensis* tends to have a tinge of green on the attenuated red sepals. The woods are surprisingly lush, considering the harshness of the sandstone barrens and chaparral over the brink of the hill.

As you wander back onto the top, you notice a herd of cattle, the commonest visitors here. When camping on this lonely plateau, be aware that the cows are lonely too. If you like to sleep in the open (and the stars up here are worth it), don't be surprised to awaken surrounded by their giant silhouettes. At least one rock gardener is reported to have been seen leaping and screaming across the top of the Uncompahgre on a moonlit night.

As you come down off the mountain, you have many more surprises in store. The roads westward are steep and less varied in vegetation, but to the east the roads slope gently, neatly transecting all the major ecological zones of western Colorado. As you descend from the Hudsonian forest in the upper canyons you begin to see more aspen, Douglas fir, and ponderosa pine, trees typical of the montane zone throughout the Rocky Mountains. Gradually, Gambel's oak begins to predominate along the southern slopes, along with a thick growth of shrubs: *Purshia*, Utah serviceberry (*Amelanchier utahensis*), artemisias, and mountain mahogany (*Cercocarpus* sp.). On steep cliffs *Cowania*, *Philadelphus*, *Holodiscus*, and evergreen mountain mahogany form gnarled forests. Gigantic rosettes of *Yucca baccata*, sometimes 5 feet/1.5 meters across, occur on the granite cliffs.

This chaparral predominates for many miles, until a number of junipers creep in. Pinyon pines (*Pinus cembroides*) are suddenly everywhere, and the typical southwestern "pygmy forest" of dwarfed, gnarled conifers prevails over most of the lower reaches of the mountain. Meadows of scant blue grama grass (*Bouteloua gracilis*) are filled with a hundred kinds of composites, *Astragalus*, and *Penstemon* species. *Calochortus nuttallii* opens its creamy chalices in late June. Here as everywhere in the arid west, *Sphaeralcea coccinea* specializes in brightening the road cuts.

The road gradually levels out, and the woods grow thinner. This is the prime territory for cacti on the mountain: rocky outcrops are studded with claret cups (*Echinocereus triglochidiatus*, Plate 60), sometimes in mats 5 feet/1.5 meters across. Coloradoa (*Sclerocactus mesae-verdae*) is encountered, though rarely, in a few canyons. Strange euphorbias and eriogonums abound, together with singleleaf ash (*Fraxinus anomala*), broad mounds of perennial four-o'clock (*Mirabilis multiflora*), a wealth of oenotheras and bewilderingly varied dwarf yuccas. A special feature of the Navajoan desert sometimes occurs in this level, where a cliff collapses to form a broad "concave" where constant seepage gives rise to rich hanging gardens. These are festooned with the tiny but giant-flowered *Mimulus eastwoodiae* with scarlet blooms in late summer. Below there is a thick growth of *Aquilegia micrantha* with its glossy, sticky, deep-green leaves and tiny, multicolored flowers. *Epipactis gigantea* usually forms the next layer, with strange "chatterbox" flowers. *Parnassia parviflora* and a dozen other delicate flowers can be found in the wet, alkaline screes. A few canyons have some of the highest known stations of *Adiantum capillus-veneris* in North America.

As you leave a hanging canyon, the heat and sunlight are oppressive. It is easy to ignore the desolate landscape around you as you descend toward the Gunnison Valley. Yet although these flats resemble a furnace floor in summer, they contain a tremendous variety of flowers in spring. Wet years bring out large numbers of sego lily (*Calochortus nuttallii*). *Psilostrophe newberryi*, with frosted leaves and everlasting flowers, forms frequent colonies. Lush mounds of *Gaillardia pinnatifida* are common. The tiny *Allium* relative *Androstephium coeruleum* grows in dense populations on many bluffs, and *Phlox hoodii* subsp. *muscoides* (formerly *P. bryoides*) is not rare. Occasionally you can find the endangered barrel cactus, *Sclerocactus whipplei*, on these flats. More often, *Echinocereus triglochidiatus* crowns a rocky outcrop. There are countless varieties of daisies and strange legumes. By June these flowers are usually drying up, and even at the height of bloom, many visitors pass these meadows unnoticing.

Rock gardeners seem to insist on racing straight to the heights, neglecting an important fact. The areas in the southern Rockies over 10,000 feet/3100 meters in elevation are largely secure from development, but it is in the lowlands—quickly being razed by booming cities, irrigation, strip-mining, and overgrazing—that the overwhelming bulk of native species occur. The lower you go in the Rockies, the greater the floristic diversity and number of indigenous, rare, and unusual taxa. It is imperative that these areas be studied and preserved wherever possible. Rock gardeners can serve a valuable purpose in supporting the preservation of threatened habitats.

As I look over this description of a single western mountain, I am a little intimidated: hundreds of similarly rich habitats can be found throughout America, with more than 300 mountain groups between the Great Plains and the Sierra Nevada. Even more intimidating is the number of plants I have seen on this one vast plateau but omitted mentioning here. Nonetheless, I hope I have managed to convey at least some sense of the magic with which Uncompahgre Plateau has enchanted me.

Originally published in the Bulletin of the American Rock Garden Society, *vol. 40, no. 1, pp. 27–32 (1982).*

Dryland Bunneries:
Persian Carpets of the West

PANAYOTI KELAIDIS

By June in most years, the hot summer sun turns the prairies and grasslands of the West into a symphony of subtle neutral colors: silver and gray, brown and beige, straw-white and dusky green. Even native westerners may be a little apologetic about this state of affairs; they will assure you that it's been unusually dry this year, and the weather has been abominably hot. Don't be fooled: it's like that every summer.

It is hardly surprising, then, that most visitors from cities and maritime climates waste no time in escaping the drylands to ascend the mountains, where snow lingers all summer and thunderstorms keep the vegetation green and flowery. Even sophisticated rock gardeners may curse the sagelands for their heat, emptiness, and vastness.

Much of the West consists of relatively flat terrain, covered (depending on precipitation) by various short grasses and tiny shrubs. Among these grow, in their season, a tremendous variety of wildflowers. Where this native landscape has not been overgrazed, bulldozed, or built over, it glows with herbaceous and subshrubby plants. For a brief period in mid-spring, and often again in the fall, the western drylands are one of the loveliest of wildflower gardens.

So great are the extremes of hot and cold, cloudburst and drought, that it is difficult to predict from year to year when the flatlands will bloom. In many years flowering is uneven. Some plants may fail to set seed several years in succession, but then one year the snow accumulates and spring comes gently. The landscape unfolds hundreds of jewel-like wildflowers as far as the eye can see, as intricate and rich as a Persian carpet.

It is not easy to generalize about the dryland West. It stretches from Mexico almost to the Arctic Circle in Canada, intricately compartmentalized by hundreds of separate mountain ranges and by a network of rivers. Now farms, cities, mines, and millions of miles of barbed wire further partition it.

What can be said with a degree of certainty is that almost any piece of undisturbed dryland from the east face of the Rocky Mountains to the Sierra Nevada and Cascade Mountains is sure to have at least one species of cushion phlox, two species of penstemons, present, and two or more eriogonums, which can vary from a few inches to several feet in height. Composites are especially well represented, from *Townsendia* and *Erigeron* in spring to *Aster* and *Gutierrezia* in autumn. Virtually every self-respecting bunnery is sure to have one of the many permutations of *Hymenoxys acaulis* (syn. *Tetraneuris acaulis*) or *Haplopappus acaulis* (syn. *Stenotis acaulis*; Plate 62). And this is only the beginning.

It is useless to generalize about the plants of this region, for just as each island or mountain in the Mediterranean region has evolved its own special flora, so too have the basins and ranges throughout the West isolated plants and provided a multitude of microhabitats for plant speciation.

So rich is the West in wildflowers that in a good year something of interest may be found at nearly any stop. Nonetheless, every botanical explorer in the West soon notices that certain places harbor special concentrations of unusual plants. Frequently these are low ridges at the bases of mountains, colloquially referred to as "hogbacks," where strata are somewhat tilted. Often several different rock substrates can be found in close proximity. Here the soil is shallowest, and the wind and sun are fiercest. Grasses no longer outcompete the little forbs, and a cushion flora dominates the scene. In his monograph on the genus *Astragalus* in America, Rupert Barneby described one such habitat as "pseudo-alpine."

Although often 5000 feet/1500 meters or more below the tree line, this sagebrush tundra frequently contains a few of the same species of cushion plants as the tops of nearby mountains. Thus, on the plains of Montana, *Douglasia montana* and *Eriogonum ovalifolium* (Plate 6) are found on both the eastern escarpment of the Rockies and the sagelands far below. In Wyoming, *Astragalus kentrophyta* subsp. *tegetarius* can occur on dry plains below 5000 feet/1500 meters and on alpine summits at 10,000 feet/3100 meters. The same is true of *Hymenoxys acaulis* and *Eriogonum flavum*, which have both desert and alpine subspecies. *Haplopappus acaulis* forms spiny mats on the exposed tundra of the Sierra Nevada in California; very similar forms are found throughout the Great Basin on various exposed hills all the way to the Rockies.

Because the climate of the high steppe in the West is so unpredictable, it is no surprise that this landscape is vulnerable as well. Just as on the tundra, the dryland cushions must struggle with the elements to survive in these bunneries, and like the plants of the tundra, they are very vulnerable to abuse. Range managers have traditionally concentrated only on maximizing forage, so large tracts were seeded to competitive exotic grasses. One or two years of overgrazing can eliminate many palatable wildflowers over whole regions. During the long dry season, few people notice the dry and dusty ancient cushions, and regard the landscape as desolate. Motorcyclists find driving through such places irresistible, and off-road vehicles leave especially unsightly devastation. Mining creates wastelands that only centuries will heal in this extreme climate. The drylands of the West are a treasure trove for knowledgeable rock gardeners, and I can think of no area more deserving of our attention and protection.

The Laramie Plains

Practically all the unforested portions of Albany County in Wyoming constitute a giant bunnery. It is ironic that the little university town of Laramie struggles to plant trees and lawns when the native prairie there contains more desirable cushion plants and wildflowers than many of us manage to maintain in our gardens.

At least three species of *Astragalus* of section *Orophaca* (the most dramatic and pulvinate of native peas) can be found in this broad valley. At spots along Highway 287 ancient specimens of *A. tridactylicus* form silvery mats up to 3 feet / 1 meter across, which must be decades old. For a few weeks in early spring these are smothered by vivid pink blossoms. Farther west, the smaller-leaved *A. sericoleucus* does the same thing a few weeks later. Much easier to grow than these is *A. spatulatus* (Plate 71), which belongs to section *Drabelliformis*. This is frequently a much smaller plant that forms cushions usually smaller than a dinner plate and as tight and silvery as *Raoulia australis*. In June the plants, hidden under pink, purple, or pure white pea blossoms, are as floriferous as cushion phlox.

Almost any stop in this valley is sure to produce one of several phloxes. *Phlox hoodii* subsp. *muscoides*, with its minuscule leaves forming mosslike cushions, is especially common. It seems rarely to bloom prolifically and often sends out long underground rhizomes that pop up here and there, many feet from the parent plant.

The form of *Phlox hoodii* formerly distinguished as *P. bryoides* is a larger plant, but still fairly congested and desirable. It has silvery, overlapping leaves that resemble a little clubmoss much more than any *Bryum* species, to my eyes. These are so tightly packed that when they are in bloom hardly a leaf can be discerned. The flowers are perhaps half the size of typical eastern creeping phloxes, but lovely nonetheless. As with most western phloxes, they are intensely fragrant. Fifty miles / 80 km south of the Laramie area, in Colorado, the plant is restricted to steep

175

limestone cliffs—for all the world like a dionysia—but in Wyoming it grows practically anywhere: in pastures, on hilltops, even colonizing in ditches and old roads.

One particular hilltop in this valley has not only all the plants mentioned thus far, but several dozen additional cushion plants and miniatures. *Eriogonum ovalifolium* occurs in a white-flowered phase (this is practically its southeastern limit), and *E. flavum* var. *flavum* is everywhere. The latter is a surprisingly adaptable buckwheat producing vivid yellow flowers on 5-inch/13 cm stems over a very long period in the summer. The gem of the genus is undeniably *E. acaule*, the tiniest of all the buckwheats, forming cushions up to 1 foot/30 cm across composed of literally hundreds of minuscule rosettes of greenish gray-green leaves barely 0.06 inch/1.5 mm long. The flowers vary from yellow to reddish shades. They are tiny things, half buried in the cushion for a few weeks in June, turning these low mounds into platters of color. This delightful plant, largely restricted to Wyoming, is by no means common, but farther north and west there are hogbacks where thousands of individuals occur—some of the choicest bunneries of the West.

Sphaeromeria capitata (formerly *Tanacetum capitatum*) was first found by Thomas Nuttall not far north of here. This minute, mat-forming tansy is white-tomentose, resembling an especially desirable artemisia. In early summer the clumps are covered with egg-yolk yellow lollipops of blossom. It has proven surprisingly adaptable to cultivation over the past few years. Its cousin *Sphaeromeria argentea* (formerly *S. nuttallii*) grows in choice bunneries much farther west and is even tinier.

Penstemons occur in variety. The specialty of this region is *Penstemon laricifolius* var. *exilifolius*, around half the size of variety *laricifolius*, with ivory-white bells. It is a perfect size for trough gardens, where it is far more likely to prosper than in the open garden. It is fiercely resentful of excess water. The plant is universal in meadows throughout the Laramie Plains and in the foothills beyond. *Penstemon eriantherus* (Plate 78) has an especially dwarf form here, and *P. virens* and *P. secundiflorus* are common along the margins of the plains. More than a dozen species of *Erigeron* and *Townsendia* occur here, most of them quite dwarf and floriferous.

The list of cushions never seems to end: *Paronychia sessiliflora* forming tight wads on the roadside, the starfish rosettes of several species of *Physaria* and *Lesquerella* that are almost as decorative in seed as in flower, several silvery-leaved *Senecio* species, and the dark green, congested mounds of *Arenaria hookeri*. This valley is a cornucopia of desirable cushion plants and alpines, and virtually none of it is protected.

Arenaria hookeri
(Drawing by Bianca Iano Davis)

Eureka County, Nevada

Most cross-country travelers find the Great Basin the least inspiring part of the nation: so few towns, such arid gray landscapes! This should be a signal to plantspeople that there are riches to be found here. Indeed, there are perhaps more cushion plants in this vast series of basins and ranges than on all the alpine tundra of North America.

On one rapid trip in the 1980s, we stopped along a major highway in Eureka County. The tremendous variety of cushion plants on a blazing white substrate suggested that this would be an interesting place to explore. The rock was a very sharp and pitted limestone that resembled tufa but was whiter than any tufa we had seen.

The first plant to attract our notice was a huge cushion of *Astragalus calycosus* var. *calycosus*. Almost as tight as the *Orophaca* astragali from farther east, this form had furry, overlapping, pinnate foliage of a deep blue-green color. The flowers were tiny, but their two-toned lilac-purple was irresistible to photograph. Nearby, a much tighter cushion began to appear. At first the cruciferous seed pods reminded us of a tiny draba, but after a moment's reflection, it dawned on us: *Lepidium nanum* (Plate 63)! Obviously it requires great heat and drought to retain its tight habit.

Astragalus kentrophyta occurs in a laxer, intensely spiny form nearby that can spread up to 3 feet / 1 meter across. What would it take to grow such a fine specimen in the garden? Suddenly, I noticed that it was growing not on the white limestone, but on an abandoned roadbed—in pure asphalt!

Haplopappus acaulis occurs here in the tiniest form we have ever seen, rosettes barely 0.25 inch / 6 mm across, flowering on stems only an inch or two high—a perfect trough plant. There were *Erigeron*, *Lesquerella*, and tiny, bonsai-like *Artemisia* species, mostly resembling *A. arbuscula*. An-

177

other glory of this locality was *Penstemon janishiae*, now segregated from the widespread *P. miser*, producing huge, gaping amethyst flowers on stems a few inches tall.

After gathering seed for an hour or two, trying to key out the several species of phlox here from vegetative characters, and puzzling over fascinating mounds of this or that, we realized that we were dangerously near sunstroke. The bank thermometer in the nearest town, about 100 miles / 160 km away, read 104°F / 40°C. The cushion form apparently protects from heat as well as from cold.

Over the years it is possible to find hundreds of places as rich as these throughout the dry tablelands of the West. Let us hope the plants will endure and adapt to the region's increasing urbanization and development as well as they have to the relentless natural elements.

Originally published in the Bulletin of the American Rock Garden Society, *vol. 44, no. 2, pp. 70–76 (1986).*

Flowers of the Friendly Mountains

JOHN F. GYER

The prairie was hot and sun-drenched as I searched the cliffs and dry runnels near Cuny Table in western Souh Dakota for the lacy pattern of Fairburn agate or a scrap of fossil oreodont bone. I found nothing of significance, but the gravel tracks I traveled were lined with dense masses of orange *Sphaeralcea coccinea* and the prairie coneflower *Ratibida columnifera*. One sandhill was a veritable forest of *Yucca glauca*, and the gumbo muds of the deltas beneath the table escarpment erupted with blooming rosettes of *Oenothera caespitosa* (Plate 39). That night the prairie treated me to a sky full of lightning and luminous thunderheads that drifted slowly eastward to the horizon.

In 1959 the West seemed open, welcoming discovery. Then the Powder River Basin of Wyoming was best known for its namesake river, running "an inch deep and a mile wide" north to the Yellowstone. Gillette was a small town at the edge of an open-pit coal mine. By the mid-1970s the mines were churning the shortgrass prairie into vast spoil piles that were laid aside to cover the mined-out strip with dirt that can be reseeded with grass. Revegetation will probably be successful, but it is uncertain when or if the native plants will reclaim the land. Plants such as *Lewisia rediviva* (Plate 24), *Phlox hoodii, Liatris punctata, Oxytropis sericea, Astragalus spatulatus* (Plate 71), and *Arenaria hookerii* are being pushed into the hills at the basin edges, where some seek pockets in the spongy red rock called scoria, a natural clinker formed when an ancient coal seam burned.

The basin's coal was once live plants growing in vast swamps and delta lands. Now there are great fossilized trees 6 feet/2 meters in diameter under the prairie hills, standing where they were buried by volcanic ash that came from the west to suffocate and fossilize grazing herds in what is now Nebraska. New trees and swamps, in turn, were buried and turned to coal as the Big Horn mountains to their west rose 2 miles/ 3 km high. From the Powder River Basin, the traveler now first sees these mountains as a rime of white on the horizon, exciting and mysterious, and a welcome change from the parched summer of the basin.

In the Big Horn Mountains, the story woven into the slopes began about 3 billion years ago when granite rocks formed the first mountains there. These wore away; a shallow sea spread across their space and laid down mud where trilobites could swarm. Coral reefs eventually overgrew the mud and have now become the massive cliffs of dolomite and lime that characterize the northern Big Horns. New mountains rose beneath the coral; the aging sea drained, and new seas formed; mountain rivers carried stone and soil into these to start the cycle once again.

About 10,000 years ago, the cycle phase was one of waning ice and wetter weather. In the basins near the Big Horns the mammoth and the giant bison were hunted by the first Americans. Perhaps it was these people who built the ceremonial wheels of stone in the northern Big Horns, the most elaborate to be seen on Medicine Wheel Mountain.

As I wandered through the mountains, I began to marvel how the rocks and animals and people were bound together by the plants that grew upon their slopes. These plants must survive a constant struggle against cold, drought, and wind, and the adaptations they have evolved are both functional and beautiful. The plants fascinated me, but if I wanted to watch some grow in my New Jersey garden, I would have to learn their needs and change the garden to suit them. They were not going to change to suit my garden.

In the Big Horns, as elsewhere, plants grow in habitats that depend on the interplay of geology, exposure, temperature, and moisture. To my mind, geology dominates the other factors, because it determines elevations, drainage, and the mineral nutrition available in the soil. Geologically the northern Big Horns are like a layer cake of dolomite and limestone set atop a granite cake-stand. A slice through this layer cake suggests seven habitat types that help to classify the needs of the mountain plants: the summit plateau; meadow areas of varying degrees of dryness; scree and talus slopes; sheer cliff faces; snow pockets; solifluction terraces; and springs and seepage areas. Although each of these habitats has its typical plant community, there are broad overlaps. Plants are opportunists: if they find a favorable place, they will grow there.

Summit Plateau

The summits of the northern Big Horns are open, windswept, rolling areas, creased by the remains of collapsed caves that formed as limestone slowly dissolved along lines of weakness by snowmelt and rain. The caves grew until their roofs collapsed and formed sink holes, which eventually joined together to form linear depressions. At cliff faces, the rock between the collapsed caves fell as talus and left the sculptured columns that form a cliff-face habitat. Where cliffs eroded and their talus decomposed into soil, the summit habitat was gradually transformed into meadows.

The most intriguing plant at the summit is *Selaginella densa*. Like all plants there, it grows slowly and hugs the ground. Over the 12,000 or so years since the last glaciers left the area, it has probably been the main plant responsible for the development of the soil profile. Its remains help bind together a very fibrous alpine peat which makes up the top 3 to 6 inches/8 to 15 cm of the established summit soils. This peat layer does three things for the plants: it holds some of the moisture from the brief summer showers; it prevents frost-heaving because of its open fibrous structure; and it insulates roots from high temperature while warming the crowns as its dark surface absorbs heat.

The moisture held by the peat is of prime importance here. In winter, winds blow most of the snow off the summits. What little remains sublimates from solid to vapor in the intense sun and rarefied air of 9000 to 10,000 feet/2700 to 3100 meters. The plants have adapted to this cold-desert environment. The nailwort *Paronychia sessiliflora* forms nearly perfect cushions. A chickweed, *Cerastium berringianum*, has developed woolly leaves and exquisite large flowers to attract the few pollinating insects that fly at these altitudes. Although many cerastiums become rank in gardens, their habit in this alpine environment is far more orderly. Woolliness (protection from desiccating winds) is probably most highly developed in the alpine forget-me-not, *Eritrichium nanum*. *Douglasia montana* protects itself against desiccation with fleshy leaves. The survival technique of *Aquilegia jonesii* (Plate 73) employs waxy, tightly clustered leaflets. *Oxytropis parryi* grows in the lee of rocks, while *Astragalus minor* clutches the ground, a single plant forming a carpet only 1 inch/2.5 cm high but as much as 2 feet/60 cm square. Each of its pods contains but a single seed, yet it is one of the few summit perennials I have seen actively colonizing disturbed mineral soil.

The insulating value of alpine peat is important in the short growing season. Measurements of soil temperature showed that at 6 inches/15 cm below the surface in July, the soil was about 69°F/21°C, but at 2 inches/5 cm below a clump of *Silene acaulis*, the temperature was 75°F/24°C, and at the soil surface in the sun it was nearer 80°F/27°C. Perhaps it is this kind of temperature differential that allows plants common in the arctic to grow happily here. *Dryas octopetala* covers acres of some of these mountaintops, but it grows best on north slopes and where sinkholes provide basins for snow to collect and give more moisture.

——————————————— Meadows ———————————————

Where the slopes are less steep, more snow collects, and the habitat is that of meadows. The lusher growth here crowds out most of the cushion plants. Frost-heaving is more noticeable and produces patches of open soil. Burrowing rodents are active, too, tilling the soil and providing more opportunities for seeds to germinate.

Sheep graze these meadows, tended by herders who live in recreational vehicles or trailers (formerly in covered wagons) parked on the ridges, from which the shepherd on horseback watches across miles of meadow. Sedges and a few grass species, heavily grazed, give this turf a carpetlike aspect. The most spectacular plant here is the alpine sunflower, *Rydbergia grandiflora* (syn. *Hymenoxys grandiflora*, Plate 70). I had expected these plants to be perennials, but mature plants showed no evidence of new crowns or of dormant buds. Instead, young plants of varying size grew in the areas of soil disturbed by frost or rodents. Such monocarpic plants can grow slowly over several seasons from a seedling to a rosette with enough energy reserve to spurt into bloom, set seed, and then die. Monocarpic plants include *Townsendia parryi*, which produces magnificent blooms that show off to advantage against the weathered limestone. *Ipomopsis globularis* produces lovely snowballs of bloom from its silky rosettes. The green gentian, *Frasera speciosa*, can grow as a rosette for more than a decade before it blooms. When it does, its square flowers are both unusual and beautiful.

Most of the meadow plants, however, are true perennials. Some, such as *Senecio werneriifolius*, form new rosettes each summer at the end of short stolons. These bloom the next year and in their turn produce another set of stolons. The pearly everlasting, *Anaphalis margaritacea*, is another successful stolon-former.

Rhizomes are modified stems that grow along the ground or work their way just beneath the soil surface. *Polygonum bistortoides* grows on slender stalks that rise from such rhizomes. In mountain meadows it sometimes coats the whole landscape in a dancing white mist.

Other perennials in the alpine meadows survive by producing clusters of rosettes from a single crown. *Penstemon procerus* forms crown clusters fully 1 foot/30 cm in diameter, covered with 19-inch/48-cm stalks of blue blossoms tiered like the roofs of a slender pagoda. In the cool, moister areas of alpine peat, the sky pilot (*Polemonium viscosum*) uses short stolons to produce next year's crop of bloom. Its flower is generally deep blue to purple, but the occasional albino forms are crystalline gems. Prairie smoke (*Geum triflorum*), a common plant of the subalpine meadow community, is another example. Its blooms never open wide; they require insects, probably bumblebees, to wriggle through the petals to get at the nectar and pollen.

Bumblebee pollination is mandatory for most *Pedicularis* species.

Pedicularis crenulata forms large patches in meadows, growing as a semi-parasite on grasses and sedges. The heads have a rhythmic spiral arrangement. One can cut open the flower to see how the anthers hold the pollen in the head, where it can be dumped on the back of vigorously foraging bees. *Delphinium nuttallianum* is another bumblebee plant. The form here grows only about 1 foot/30 cm tall and does best in disturbed areas near a snowmelt seep where it receives plentiful moisture in a cool spring. It can dry out completely in the summer, however, because it overwinters as a small dormant tuber.

The beautiful and delicate *Lithophragma glabrum* is another tuber-former. It appears to come easily from seed; in disturbed areas dense clumps form where seed capsules have fallen. The entire plant is only about 4 inches/10 cm tall. Spring beauty (*Claytonia lanceolata*, Plate 69) is a corm-forming plant that can cover the meadow in its season, but it quickly withers to pass the dry summer underground. It blooms just after the snow melts and as the gopher "eskers" emerge. These elongated mounds are a major mechanism for the production of disturbed soil habitat in alpine meadows. The common shooting stars (*Dodecatheon* spp.) grow from fleshy roots that join at a dormant bud only an inch or so beneath the surface. The most frequent here is *D. meadia* subsp. *meadia* (formerly *D. pauciflorum*), which occurs in red and occasional white or pink forms.

Geranium viscosissimum survives from year to year in the form of buds on a woody crown. It is a late-bloomer producing magnificent dark red blossoms with a two-day sexual cycle. The first day they open, and their anthers shed pollen to passing insects. By the next day the anthers have dropped and the stigma opens to receive pollen from another flower.

Taprooted plants are common in the drier meadows. I have seen an arenaria root that burrowed more than 4 feet/120 cm into the ground. The balsamroots (*Balsamorhiza*) are a beautiful group of taprooted composites of the drier meadows. *Balsamorhiza incana* is, in my estimation, the finest garden prospect of this genus. In the meadow sods, dandelions are also common, competing with the native false dandelion, *Agoseris glauca*.

The yellow *Viola nuttallii* grows in disturbed areas near snowbanks where frost-heaving is severe. Its underground stem is densely lined with dormant buds that continue the plant's growth even if the main leaves are removed by grazing or frost-heaving. The sugar-bowl clematis, *Clematis hirsutissima*, develops clusters of stems from similar underground buds. It produces urn-shaped blooms with dark sepals. As the seed matures, the enclosing sepals dry and the silky styles elongate into seedheads called "old man's beard."

The meadows are a delicately balanced community. Legumes, members of the pea family, are very important in this balance. In addition to providing beautiful masses of color and form, their roots host nitrogen-fixing bacteria. Nitrogen fertilizer cannot be derived from rocks; it must come from the air, either fixed by lightning and deposited by rain, or fixed in the soil and freed by the slow decomposition of vegetation. The legumes and their associated bacteria are responsible for much of the biologically fixed nitrogen. Lupines are the most prominent legume here, ranging from 2 to 3 feet/60 to 90 cm tall in the more fertile areas, to the dwarf *Lupinus caespitosus* in disturbed soils. This lupine is particularly well adapted for drought because of its long taproot and the dense hairiness of its crown. In addition to size variations, there are variants in flower color. Pink lupines occur occasionally, and rarely a gleaming white will stand out in an alpine meadow.

The point vetches (*Oxytropis* spp.) have keel petals that come to a point. These plants generally grow as multiple crowns from a single taproot. They are beautiful in flower, leaf, and habit. *Oxytropis sericea* is also particularly fragrant, lending the air over acres of mountainside the perfume of honey fresh from the comb. Its relative *O. saximontana* thrives in disturbed soil and loose sod nearly to the summit; where it seeds freely, it tends to produce color variation. In acidic granite areas near Cloud Peak the common legumes are dwarf clover (*Trifolium nanum*) and the larger and laxer *T. parryi*.

Talus and Scree

Talus and scree slopes are essentially extensions of the meadow environment onto steeper, less stable slopes at the foot of cliffs. The steepest slopes have a mineral soil mixed with rock debris which is in slow, continual downhill motion. The steepest moving slopes support few plants. *Physaria vitulifera* (Plate 72) is a spectacular exception; its inflated seedpods give it the name "bladderpod." The species has adapted to this environment by growing a new crown each year a little farther downhill, so that its top "walks" with the moving slope while its feeder roots remain fixed several feet uphill. Should the crown be sheared off, another can be produced from dormant buds farther back toward the roots.

On more stable slopes, *Phlox pulvinata* (Plate 104) develops into attractive mats. Although it is common in open meadows, it seems to seed most freely in disturbed areas, where color variations can occasionally be found.

Clematis columbiana var. *columbiana* (Plate 37) is a vine that runs just beneath the surface of peat pockets or through the stone mulch of talus areas. Here it forms beautiful, compact leaf clusters with nodding recurved blooms. The graceful arch of the petaloid sepals encloses the long feathery styles. The death camas, *Zigadenus elegans*, finds these habitats to its liking too. It has a very fibrous coat over its bulb, protecting it from desiccation in summer, and seedpods that glow like burnished gold in the autumn sun. Here, too, we find the wild onions *Allium brevistylum*—with individually small but graceful flowerheads—and *A. cernuum*, common on dry, consolidated talus slopes.

Shrubs and wind-dwarfed trees grow between the boulders. Currants such as *Ribes oxyacanthoides* subsp. *setosum* are attractive and common, but their thorns are a hazard to hikers. In cracks in the boulders, *Corydalis aurea* is comfortably at home as its roots wander in search of moisture and nutrients.

Cliff Faces

Even the austere setting of alpine limestone cliffs supports a specialized group of plants. In some areas the meltwater from snowbanks above seeps into the porous rock and waters ledges and the contact stone where the talus begins. Over the years these special areas have built up layers of humus from a few inches to several feet deep. These constantly watered, shady, humusy ledges are a habitat of *Primula parryi* (Plate 61). Large clumps of this plant in bloom are a glorious sight. In eastern gardens it is difficult to grow, perhaps because of high soil temperatures; in the mountains when it is in full bloom, the soil temperature is no more than 50°F / 10°C. Low soil temperature can also mean low growth rates for fungi and bacteria, which attack the plant in the warmer soils of eastern American gardens.

In cracks on the cliffs grows the lushest plant of this community, *Telesonix jamesii*. It is almost never found in the talus soil, yet on the cliffs even the smallest solution pocket in the rock will have a plant struggling to survive. Ledges provide a better foothold for plants than crevices. Here the alp lily, *Lloydia serotina* (Plate 40), thrives and looks more striking than in the summit community where it is more common.

Lower plants give some cliffs great character and begin the process of soil formation. One lichen forms a brilliant orange crust as it slowly dissolves the rock particles and eventually produces a film of humus where mosses can grow. Some mosses prefer granite boulders; others are more at home in cracks in limestone. Ferns can take root on the soil prepared by the lichens and mosses. Flowering plants such as *Antennaria* often succeed the ferns.

There are three shrubs of the rose family found in these mountains—*Petrophytum*, *Kelseya*, and the more familiar *Dryas*. *Petrophytum* and *Kelseya* are often found in the most severe cliff-face habitats. *Kelseya uniflora* (Plate 64) grows at the higher elevations and very slowly forms cushions in this severely dry and alternately cold and hot habitat, 8000 to 9000 feet / 2400 to 2700 meters in elevation. Somewhat lower and much more prolific is *Petrophytum caespitosum*, which carpets boulders in the

185

talus slopes of the great canyons draining the Big Horns. Its relation to the rose family can be seen in its spiraea-like blooms.

Snowbank Community

In sheltered areas, often at the foot of cliffs or in sinkholes, snow collects in winter and lingers long into summer. These areas produce a distinctive wet habitat. As the snow begins to melt, pink algae, mainly *Chlamydomonas nivalis*, begin to grow on its surface. At the edge of the receding snow, a little *Ranunculus* is the first flowering plant to appear. The pasqueflower (*Pulsatilla*) is not far behind; it has already begun to spread its feathery seeds to the wind by the time the snowbank has melted away. These moist areas also provide habitat for *Mertensia alpina*, a very lovely short-tubed species.

Solifluction Terraces

When snow pockets form on a slope, they push down on the soil with their accumulated weight during winter. As they melt, water saturates the soil beneath, and the clay base slips slightly downhill. This forms a bowl-shaped basin for the snow and a container for its meltwater. As this water seeps downhill, it is under pressure from the water above. When the pressure is great enough, water separates the soil particles and breaks through the sod of the meadow, and a small glacier of soil and sod begins its journey toward the basin below. These solifluction areas are major sources of disturbed soil habitat in these mountains.

Plants that struggle against competition in other habitats have an easier life here. The wallflower, *Erysimum asperum*, can take root, along with *Lesquerella montana*—both beautiful and garden-worthy plants. *Eritrichium nanum* also grows here, along with a form distinguished by some authors as *E. longissimum*; the two species are said to differ mainly in the length of their flowering stems, about 2 inches/5 cm in the former and 4 to 6 inches/10 to 15 cm in the latter. The larger alpine forget-me-not, *Myosotis alpestris*, can also be found on these terraces. The open soil is a seedbed for winter annuals, such as a minute member of the phlox family, *Gymnosteris parvula*, the entire plant only 1.5 inches/4 cm tall.

Springs and Seeps

At the level where limestone meets the impervious granite, the water from melting snow emerges as springs, seeps, and streams. In open areas these springs sport the white marsh marigold, *Caltha leptosepala*. This is one of the earliest plants to bloom, and the first flies of the season carry its pollen from flower to flower. At the drier edges of the wet area is the globe flower, *Trollius laxus* var. *albiflorus*.

Often seeps are associated with clumps of trees, and at the edges of these shady areas the elephant's head, *Pedicularis groenlandica*, can be found. Its twisted blooms are curved in such a way that bumblebees can pollinate them. Near the pedicularis, *Mitella stauropetala* sparkles in the grass, and the brilliant *Castilleja rhexifolia* provides a splash of contrasting color. In some seeps *Platanthera dilatata* waves its green candles of bloom in the breeze; in others, the very fragrant *P. hyperborea* may be found. At the edges of wooded seeps, the shrubs *Ledum glandulosum* and *Ribes lacustre* form dense thickets. The western twisted-stalk (*Streptopus amplexifolius*) is at home in the shade.

In the acid spongy humus of the forest floor are the two orchids *Listera cordata* and *L. auriculata*. The smaller of these twin-leafed orchids grows so thickly that there is no place to step around them. Rarely, *Calypso bulbosa* can be seen blooming in the black humus. The small *Platanthera obtusata* lives in the mossy banks; the little bishop's-cap, *Mitella pentandra*, shares this habitat. Shaded banks display the gem of the pyrola family, *Moneses uniflora*, its pure white blooms sparkling beside the streams that keep the soil temperature evenly at 50°F/10°C in mid-July. Others that like cool, moist seeps and streambanks include the pink *Pyrola asarifolia*, with glistening blooms held 1 foot/30 cm above its evergreen rosette; *P. secunda* (now *Orthilia secunda*), with its style like an elephant's trunk; and *Pyrola minor*, a small circumboreal plant with a short style reminiscent of that of *Moneses uniflora*. The western grass-of-Parnassus (*Parnassia fimbriata*) opens its gleaming blossoms here well after the pyrolas have gone to seed. The twinflower (*Linnaea borealis*) can make a fairy carpet on the forest floor. *Geranium richardsonii* enjoys the drier edges of this habitat.

Granite Areas

Where decomposing granite forms the major rock outcrop, as it does in the Cloud Peak area, the soil is generally acid. Ericaceous plants, found only in some acid bogs in the limestone country, thrive here. *Kalmia polifolia* (Plate 12) is a beautiful shrub, its blossoms bright-pink versions of those of its relative, the eastern mountain laurel (*K. latifolia*). The bearberry (*Arctostaphylos uva-ursi*) grows on cliffs here and produces clusters of delicately colored flowers. The arctic gentian (*Gentiana algida*) favors more open areas near the summits. *Aster foliaceus* var. *apricus* is a very neat plant which tucks itself against summit rock.

Where snowmelt accumulates on granitic basement rock it forms mountain tarns that drain into the valleys as splashing brooks. These streams are the habitat for the taller mertensias, including *Mertensia ciliata*. The stream edges also host the alpine blue violet (*Viola adunca*) and the little yellow monkeyflower (*Mimulus guttatus*). The streams and the lakes they feed also contain fine specimens of Rocky Mountain trout, more elusive than their flowers.

Lower Slopes

The slopes of the Big Horns drop quickly from about 8000 feet/2400 meters to the basins at about 3000 feet/900 meters. This produces sharp altitudinal zones with a tier of plant communities from alpine to semi-desert and prairie. In the talus as one begins to descend, racemes of sweet vetch (*Hedysarum sulphurescens*) grow gracefully on shrubby plants.

In the forest zone, the parrot's-beak pedicularis (*Pedicularis racemosa*) is parasitic on tree roots. In some areas *Vaccinium scoparium* is a ground-cover on the forest floor. The berries are good wildlife food and, if one is patient enough, they can be a camper's dessert. The coral-root orchid (*Corallorhiza maculata*) is saprophytic on decomposing wood, while the pastel Indian paint brushes, forms of *Castilleja septentrionalis*, are semi-parasitic on grasses that grow in openings in the forest. *Penstemon subglaber* frequents disturbed soil on the edges of this zone. Occasionally it can be found in a beautiful clear pink; the internal structure of each blossom is even more graceful than the stalk itself.

Prairie species grow on the slope below the forest zone. The biennial *Chaenactis douglasii* should be an excellent garden subject. The dainty, nodding *Campanula rotundifolia* grows in a deep mulch of limestone chips. *Linum lewisii* is a favorite plant, but only for the early riser, as it drops its petals before midmorning on sunny days. The most spectacular plant here is the 7-foot/2-meter crucifer *Stanleya pinnata* var. *integrifolia* or prince's-plume. It is found beside the road, but only in a narrow area of greenish soil derived from bedrock probably high in selenium; it is said to concentrate enough of this element to be toxic to stock. The blazing star (*Mentzelia* sp.) opens in the dim light of evening when it can be pollinated by bats or night-flying moths. It is a member of the Loasaceae, a largely tropical family, and is unusual because its seeds form only on the sides of its capsules. The brilliant *Oxytropis lambertii* thrives on the slopes with *Penstemon laricifolius*.

Some plants span almost the complete altitudinal range of these mountains, resulting in a long season of bloom. A fine mariposa lily, *Calochortus gunnisonii*, blooms early in the grasses of the lower slopes and later is found as high as the subalpine meadows. Dwarf goldenrod (*Solidago* sp.) also spans the altitude range, growing 8 inches/20 cm tall in the warm, dry sand near the basin, but only 2 inches/5 cm tall at the limestone summit. Asters and erigerons share this broad range—often scraggly plants, but their blossoms are lovely, and their flower structure is a striking study in color and texture.

Along larger watercourses, clematis climbs over the branches of streamside trees. Occasionally the wild hollyhock (*Iliamna rivularis*) grows in the gravel of their floodplains. Here in fall a twin-flowered honeysuckle (*Lonicera* sp.) ripens, and the seedpods of the western false Solomon's seal (*Smilacina racemosa*) glow like Christmas candy.

Beyond lies the semidesert prairie, where *Gaura coccinea* is an occasional inhabitant and gaillardias form natural rock gardens on granite boulders. Rabbit brush (*Chrysothamnus viscidiflorus*) can be a cloud of gold in its season. A closer look shows the flowerheads filled with golden trumpets typical of this branch of the composite family. A red castilleja shares these dry slopes.

The tansy aster (*Aster tanacetifolius*, syn. *Machaeranthera tanacetifolia*), an annual, sometimes covers the semidesert soil of the Big Horn Basin. This great geologic bowl between the Big Horns and Yellowstone holds steep canyons, deposits of dinosaur bones, bentonite mines, oil, and rich farmland irrigated by water from Cody Reservoir to the west. As travelers move west across this basin they leave behind the Big Horn Mountains, but with local variation the pattern of their rocks and plants and animals is repeated in range after range. The patterns I have seen on the friendly slopes of the northern Big Horns have helped me appreciate the native plants that grow there. If you should venture into their range, I hope this will add to your enjoyment of the story they have to tell.

Originally published in the Bulletin of the American Rock Garden Society, *vol. 44, no. 3, pp. 105–119 (1986). A version of this article appeared in the* Bulletin of the Alpine Garden Society (England), *vol. 45, no. 1 (1977), and the present publication appears by kind permission of the Editor, The Alpine Garden Society of Great Britain.*

Don't Discount Arizona

SONIA LOWZOW COLLINS

Much of Arizona, contrary to its popular image, is not desert. Indeed, it is a state of enormous topographical and altitudinal contrasts, with equally great climatic differences. Elevations range from about 100 feet/30 meters above sea level in the southwestern desert to almost 12,600 feet/3800 meters on the San Francisco peaks. The mountains in northern and central Arizona are considered a southern extension of the Rockies, and about 25 percent of the 3000 species of flowering plants native here are endemic either to the Rocky Mountain region generally, or to the mountains of New Mexico and Arizona alone. Another 13 percent are North American plants found only at high elevations in the Southwest, and about 3 percent are circumpolar species. This results in a total of approximately 1200 alpine and subalpine species. These include three or four dozen arctic-alpine chamaephytic plants found at elevations of from 11,000 to 12,500 feet/3400 to 3800 meters; thus the truly alpine vegetation is essentially confined to the summits of three peaks—Mount Humphrey, Mount Agassiz, and Mount Baldy. There are, however, many subalpine communities on other mountain ranges, particularly in southern Arizona.

The lowest recorded temperature in Arizona is –33°F/–36°C (at a mountain weather station), and total annual precipitation at some sites has reached almost 60 inches/150 cm. Nonetheless, the relative humidity is usually low, even in the wettest areas.

Fjellgarden, my "mountain garden," is in the White Mountains just north of the Mogollon Escarpment (the so-called Tonto Rim), at an elevation of 7200 feet/2200 meters. In my backyard—literally—grow phloxes, lupines, calochortus, townsendias, and many other genera.

Within a radius of 30 to 40 miles / 50 to 60 km one can find such moisture-loving plants as *Calypso bulbosa* and other terrestrial orchids, *Saxifraga rhomboidea*, *Dodecatheon alpinum*, *Sisyrinchium demissum*, *Viola nephrophylla*, and several gentians—certainly not the flora of a hot, arid desert.

Let us explore a few of the alpine and subalpine plants of Arizona.

Lewisia pygmaea (Plate 26) grows at elevations from 8000 to 9000 feet / 2400 to 2700 meters. One of its heaviest concentrations is in the White Mountains, where it grows on a sloping peninsula jutting out from a lakeshore, in company with *Commelina dianthifolia* and *Sedum stelliforme*. The Arizona form of *Lewisia pygmaea* is a very attractive small plant, 1 inch / 2.5 cm tall by 3 inches / 8 cm wide. The color of its flowers ranges from pale to very deep pink. It is found on very rocky, shallow scree soil overlying heavy clay; during its blooming period (June to August), it is subjected to frequent summer rainstorms. In cultivation at Fjellgarden, it pops out of the ground in May and is in full bloom by June 1, flowering intermittently until mid-autumn and dying down only after there have been frosts at night. I grow it in a moist scree—about equal parts of loam, sand, and cinder—on a south exposure.

Lewisia brachycalyx, by contrast, is found in a much greater elevational range, blooming as early as March at 5000 feet / 1500 meters, and in late May to early June at 8000 feet / 2400 meters. Its range is primarily in the areas of sandy soil extending eastward from the White Mountains. Many of the plants grow in pure sand, moist from snowmelt. The color range of the flowers in any population is considerable, including almost pure white, white veined with pink, and nearly solid pink; flower form ranges from narrow to almost overlapping petals. In full sun the leaves are nearly red, shading to white at the base. The plants are approximately 2 inches / 5 cm tall and 5 inches / 13 cm wide. In the wild they bloom and set seeds in a period of a few weeks, then quickly die down as if they had never existed. In cultivation *L. brachycalyx* retains its foliage for a considerably longer period if not allowed to go dry. The plants at Fjellgarden are in sandy scree, kept somewhat drier than *L. pygmaea*, and in full sun.

Now let us travel up to the moist mountain meadows at 9000 feet / 2700 meters, where we can find *Dodecatheon alpinum* (Plate 29). This little shooting star has thick, almost waxy leaves in a basal rosette, and flowers with a deep magenta-pink corolla. It grows in full sun in moist, heavy, acid soil; its companions are *Sisyrinchium demissum*, *Iris missouriensis* (Plate 4), *Linanthus nuttallii*, *Potentilla thurberi*, and *Potentilla fruticosa* (syn. *Pentaphylloides floribunda*), with occasional patches of *Mimulus primuloides* and *Oxalis decaphylla*. In bloom it is about 8 to 10 inches / 20 to 25 cm tall. Its range includes lower elevations in the White Mountains, as low as 6500 feet / 2000 meters at Lakeside. At these altitudes it seems to be confined to lakeshores and creek banks, where it flowers as early as June. In my garden it is grown in a semishaded woodland bed in a moist compost of woods soil, sand, and peat, becoming a moderate-sized clump. It starts to bloom in early June and continues until August, dying down in early autumn.

We now return to the more habitable elevation of 7200 feet / 2200 meters, and my own backyard. On the hillsides, along the roadsides, along the edge of the forest, and in the meadow south of the house, *Phlox speciosa* subsp. *woodhousei* explodes into a symphony of pinks each May and June. Superficially this little phlox is reminiscent of *P. nana*, although it is woodier and usually has notched corolla lobes. Within a population of wild plants there is considerable variation: colors range from pure white to deep pink; corolla lobes are notched deeply, or not at all; and the distinctive phlox "eye" may be sharply defined or almost absent. The range of the species is considerable, from 3500 to 8000 feet / 1100 to 2400 meters, and its habitat may vary from pure sand to thick heavy clay that bakes to a concretelike consistency in June (in clay soils, the plants are always found on a slope). It is equally unfussy in cultivation, accepting conditions from ordinary soil and sun to almost full shade. Unfortunately, it is not easy to propagate (again like *P. nana*). Cuttings have been impossible so far, and it is regrettable that so many phloxes set so little seed.

Phlox speciosa subsp. *woodhousei* has a long, easily damaged taproot, suggesting the possibility of root cuttings, which I have not yet attempted. The plant grows 3 to 4 inches / 8 to 10 cm tall in lean scree in full sun, although it is quite a bit leggier in partial shade. It is altogether attractive and much less demanding than some other phloxes. It is almost evergreen at this elevation. If kept moist in summer, it will often bloom again in early autumn.

After the phlox season is over here, *Penstemon linarioides* takes center stage, blooming in June to August. Its flowers are a medium blue-lavender, not showy but borne in profusion over a long period. The plant is almost shrubby, although some stems of young plants die down in winter. From a woody base, arching upright stems rise 6 to 8 inches / 15 to 20 cm, clothed in small, fresh green linear leaves. Its greatest attraction is its tolerance of difficult conditions. In the wild it often grows on calcareous soils; here it flourishes on heavy acid clay and accepts heavy scree in sun or partial shade with equal equanimity. It will tolerate considerable dryness as well as our daily monsoon through July and August and our freeze-and-thaw winters, which would be the undoing of so many of the other small penstemons unless perfect drainage were provided.

Arizona is probably the succulent capital of the nation, but the genus *Sedum* contributes little to that distinction, as there are only five native species. Oddly, none of the tender sedums so common south of the border are found within Arizona. Instead, all the natives are alpine or broadly subalpine plants, with an elevational range from 3500 to 12,000 feet / 1100 to 3700 meters.

The little *Sedum stelliforme* of the White Mountains has captivated me ever since my first glimpse of it on a rocky hillside above Big Lake.

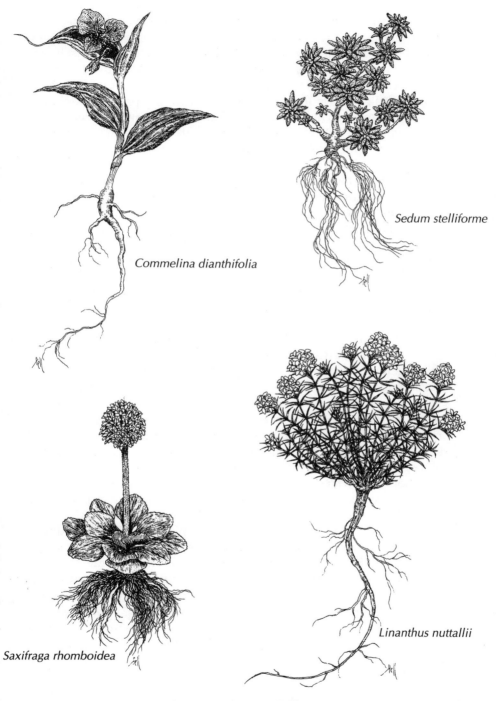

Commelina dianthifolia

Sedum stelliforme

Saxifraga rhomboidea

Linanthus nuttallii

(Drawings by Janet Fell)

193

This is an exciting subalpine plant, small and controlled in habit and unexpectedly attractive in bloom. It grows in profusion on the same rocky peninsula that is the prime habitat of *Lewisia pygmaea*, and it is found elsewhere at altitudes up to 9500 feet/2900 meters. It plasters itself onto lichened rocks and fills tiny crevices between them. Most plants are only 2 to 3 inches/5 to 8 cm in diameter and an inch or so tall. One 3-year-old plant at Fjellgarden is about 4 inches/10 cm across, spreading to about 6 inches/15 cm when in bloom. This sedum has little, twiggy, decumbent stems with 0.25- to 1-inch/6- to 25 mm rosettes of tiny lanceolate leaves at the apices and at the stem nodes. The bloom is a froth of miniature pink and white stars, completely covering the plant, in midsummer. The choicest characteristic of *Sedum stelliforme* for the rock gardener, however, is its lack of rampancy. The leaves do not detach easily, as do those of so many sedums, nor does it seed about with abandon.

On that same peninsula, at 9200 feet/2800 meters, grow a few other praiseworthy species. In addition to the *Lewisia* and *Sedum* mentioned above, there are many low, tight plants of *Commelina dianthifolia* and *Saxifraga rhomboidea*, and an occasional, much-reduced clump of *Arenaria fendleri*, but I have found no other species there. The peninsula slopes down toward the lakeshore and is a jumbled mass of rocks, large and small. The subsoil is a heavy clay, but the surface is essentially stable scree. The entire area is in full sun throughout the day.

I am particularly intrigued with the form of *Commelina dianthifolia* in this site. It grows only 3 or 4 inches/8 to 10 cm in height, and the leaves are exceptionally short and broad. The flowers are rich cobalt-blue. This species is often described as "half-hardy," but the temperature can descend to $-30°F/-35°C$ at that elevation. The plants at Fjellgarden have retained the dwarf aspect and deep blue color in rich, moist scree in full sun. They have proven completely hardy here, where there are many more freeze-and-thaw cycles during the winter than in their native habitat. I hope that wider dissemination of seedlings from these plants will determine whether their greater hardiness is a consistent characteristic, particularly in the northeastern and north-central states. If so, *C. dianthifolia* may yet be recognized as the hardy rock plant that I find it to be here; this would be a real blessing, for what else blooms with such a lovely clear blue in late summer, before the fall gentians have set their buds?

Saxifrages are, unfortunately, not very plentiful in this country. Arizona has only six native species, most of which grow on the alpine heights of Mount Baldy and the San Francisco peaks. *Saxifraga rhomboidea* shares my rocky peninsula, but I have found it elsewhere in very different habitats, usually moist shaded or semishaded sites in humus-rich soil. It is a small and not terribly exciting plant, but I love it for the oddity of its inflorescence, which gives it a charm akin to that of a monstrose or caudiciform succulent. The flat rosettes of slightly fleshy, glaucous leaves are about 2 inches/5 cm across. The bloom cluster is a multitude of tiny white blossoms in a dense ball atop a chunky stem 4 to 5 inches / 10 to 13 cm tall in earliest spring. I grow this plant in a trough, where its strange bloom is enormously effective at close range. It appreciates a pocket of rich soil and can take considerable moisture.

At the same elevational range, but in richer, meadowlike soil, grows the lovely *Linanthus nuttallii*, a beautiful member of the phlox family. From a heavy rootstock rise arching stems of fresh green, whorled leaves divided into multiple linear segments. A mature plant in bloom is 8 to 10 inches / 20 to 25 cm tall and as much across. It forms a rounded dome smothered in clusters of half-inch / 13-mm white, phlox-like blossoms, centered with yellow eyes and sweetly aromatic. The heaviest flowering is in early summer, with scattered blooms after that almost until frost. Until last year I had treasured my few plants as the rarities I thought they were, because I had previously seen only one or two plants in each of a few scattered locations. In early August 1983, however, I was collecting seed in an area west of the White Mountains along the Mogollon Rim, where I discovered an excellent new habitat of *Linanthus*. There, in deep sandy soil, they grow by the dozens (perhaps by the hundreds). Until now I have grown my plants in moderately rich scree in full sun, but I intend to try a few seedlings in a deep sandy loam. Perhaps this will more nearly approach their preferred cultural conditions, and perhaps it will also stimulate seed production, which has been poor in the garden but is copious in the wild.

Houstonia wrightii is another subalpine plant that deserves to be better known. It ranges from western Texas into New Mexico and Arizona and is a real sun-lover. The *Arizona Flora* indicates an altitudinal limit of 8000 feet / 2400 meters, but I have found plants growing in vast numbers at 8500 feet / 2600 meters. It usually grows in rocky, heavy soil or sandy loam. The plants are small—2 inches / 5 cm tall and 4 to 5 inches / 10 to 13 cm wide—and loosely caespitose, flowering very heavily in summer. The color ranges from pale lavender to a fairly deep pink. The plants bloom in full sun to part shade, but the color is more intense and the plants more compact in sun. They are very resentful of lifting and transplanting and must be heavily sheared when moved, then watered copiously to stimulate new stem growth from the base. The botanists have recently revised this genus, and little *Houstonia wrightii* is now to be known as *Hedyotis pygmaea*. Perhaps the different affinity may explain the difficulty of propagating this plant from stem cuttings, which almost refuse to form roots; however, fresh seed will germinate easily.

The presence of native orchids proves the existence of really moist areas in Arizona's mountains. In a few locations, at about 9000 to 10,000 feet / 2700 to 3100 meters, grow small colonies of the incomparably lovely *Calypso bulbosa*. Here it grows in a rich, deep, moist duff composed mainly of the partially rotted cones of fir and spruce, its ramifying fleshy white roots wandering through the surface layer and sending up its soli-

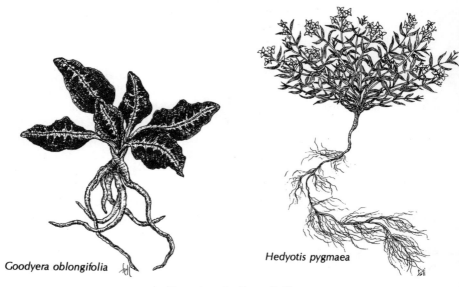

Goodyera oblongifolia

Hedyotis pygmaea

(Drawings by Janet Fell)

tary leaves and, in spring, its single 6- to 8-inch / 15- to 20-cm stems, each holding one perfect orchid. I was an orchid grower long before I became a rock gardener, and I am as charmed by the little fairy slipper as I ever was by the exotic tropical epiphytic species. It has a grace and loveliness that the blowsier greenhouse orchids just can't match. My little colony, planted in deep shade and in duff collected in its native habitat, has increased slowly but steadily and blooms here, predictably, about the first of May each year. How glad I am that *Calypso* ranges just far enough south to reach Arizona.

Another orchid that is quite common in the spruce-fir belt is *Goodyera oblongifolia*. Its flowers are not impressive, but for patterned foliage effect it has few equals. *Goodyera* is considerably easier to grow than is *Calypso*, forming good wide clumps in moist woods duff and lighting up the shady areas with its white-striped leaves.

I also like another small Arizona orchid for foliage effect: *Malaxis ehrenbergii*, which forms clumps of single-leaved plants crowded closely together, almost resembling a smaller-leaved *Maianthemum*. The blossoms are so tiny that they are utterly insignificant, but the overall pattern is quiet and effective, particularly if this orchid is planted at the base of a large shrub in the shade garden.

Originally published in the Bulletin of the American Rock Garden Society, *vol. 41, no. 4, pp. 185–188 (1983); vol. 43, no. 1, pp. 27–31 (1985).*

Cacti: America's Foremost Rock Plants

ALLAN R. TAYLOR AND PANAYOTI KELAIDIS

Cacti are an integral part of the natural rock gardens of North America, and our home rock gardens are poorer without them. This statement may strike the alpine-gardening purist as unorthodox at best and heretical at worst, but we hope to demonstrate its truth.

If cacti are exotic to European eyes, they are rather commonplace in this hemisphere. The family extends to practically every state and province of the Americas, from the southern Andes to the prairies of Alberta and Saskatchewan. No family of American plants is more widespread or characteristic of a broad range of saxatile habitats. Cacti are most at home among rocks: a few species are restricted to sandy habitats or grassy plains, but the overwhelming majority prefer to grow on well-drained rocky sites. One can travel through countless miles in the heartland of cactus country and scarcely encounter a single one on the endless flats—but climb onto the first rocky ridge, and numerous species will appear.

The cactus family is not without alpine developments. Especially in the Southern Hemisphere there are dozens of porcupines and hedgehogs in sheep's wool that haunt the highest screes. Even in the United States many cacti climb to the tops of the higher desert ranges. An intensely spiny form of *Opuntia erinacea*, for instance, hobnobs with the oldest bristlecone pines at 11,500 feet / 3500 meters on the dolomitic summits of California's White Mountains. Dozens of other species are restricted to the high, dry steppes, plateaus, and foothills of Utah, northern Arizona, New Mexico, Colorado, and Oklahoma, where subzero temperatures are a yearly phenomenon. Literally hundreds of distinct forms of cactus might be selected from among these, as well as from Chihuahuan, Sonoran, and Mojavean endemics that stray beyond their subtropical range into chill desert valleys.

Despite this diversity of range and form, and their relative ease of cultivation, rock gardeners speak furtively about this glorious family of American wildflowers. Evidently there is something *wrong* with cacti, though it is difficult to imagine what. Is the cactus plant that much more succulent than a sempervivum? Is its flower any showier than that of a lewisia? Its spines are not much more painful than those of a host of choice rock garden brooms, thistles, and buns. Cacti are really no more unfriendly than a good number of accepted alpines; indeed, they are much friendlier than the aretian androsaces or eritrichiums that shun our gardens.

The ambivalence and condescension of alpine gardeners toward cacti has resulted in an ironic twist. Nowhere in America is rock gardening practiced more extensively or with more striking effect than in the desert Southwest, with its hundreds of naturalistic plantings featuring cacti artistically placed among rocks, accompanied by interesting desert wildflowers and shrubs. The dryness and subtropical climate in most of this region preclude the use of many conventional rock plants in gardens here, but neither rocks nor good garden plants are limited to tundra. (Neither, in fact, are the plants that most of us grow in our rock gardens.) And cacti are by no means limited to the southwestern desert.

No one is better suited than the alpine gardener for the ordeal of coaxing a hardy cactus from seed to maturity. Growers can make a real contribution by selecting superior clones and compiling and disseminating information on the culture of hardy cacti in cold-climate gardens.

The dryland rock garden is an ideal setting for cacti. Here they can mingle with lewisias, manzanitas, penstemons, composites, and bulbs, just as they do in nature. The individual cactus is far more interesting when viewed in such a setting than in a pot or the collection of a specialist. Crowded with their own kind, a cactus planting may end up resembling a rock concert more than a rock garden. Few botanical sights can impress a hiker more than the sudden appearance of a solitary mound of cactus in full bloom; if you can contrive this effect in the rock garden, you can probably charge admission.

It is impossible to recreate a desert on a city lot, but it is possible to capture some of the spirit of this fascinating natural complex. The balance of this article is a description of the plant material suitable for this undertaking.

Which species of cacti are hardy, and how can they be grown? If we limit our scope solely to the members of the family that grow north of the Mogollon Rim in Arizona, east of the Sierra Nevada as far as the Great Plains, and in the colder parts of the Chihuahuan desert, the number of species is still impressive. For taxonomic confusion, cactus nomenclature rivals *Potentilla*, *Salix*, and *Astragalus*. Species names in particular are a bloody battlefield for botanists, now that a clearer conception of generic affinities has antiquated the clutter of microforms that once confounded amateurs. Without worrying too much about specific names, it is fairly easy to delineate the broad outlines of certain groups, or complexes, of cacti that can be used in the rock garden.

Size is a good criterion to use in dealing with the more interesting hardy cacti. Since our art is more concerned with the habit of plants than with their genetic relationships, it is convenient to deal with cacti on this basis. We will begin with the "ball cacti"—comprising several genera—and then discuss the cylindric "hedgehogs" (*Echinocereus*); we conclude with the much-maligned prickly pears (*Opuntia*). Since nature is the supreme gardener, we will stress the natural settings where cacti grow. This can provide hints on how to grow them in the garden.

The Ball Cacti

No cactus can begin this account better than the mountain ball cactus, *Pediocactus simpsonii* (Plate 48). It is largely restricted to mountainous terrain at higher altitudes (despite the fact that its genus name means "plains cactus") in almost every state west of the Great Plains. It is the most widespread example of a group of cacti that almost never descend below 5000 feet/1500 meters in the southern part of their range. They require a rather mesic, temperate climate. In the dry intermountain ranges of the West, this cactus can be found above 10,000 feet/3100 meters. A temperature of −52°F/−47°C was recorded in a mountain valley west of Denver where *P. simpsonii* is especially abundant. Perhaps nowhere over its range does it grow so profusely as on the top of a 9000-foot/2700-meter plateau in western Colorado, where for miles the exposed sandstone bedrock between islands of ponderosa pine and Gambel's oak is a sea of *Pediocactus* tangled with *Ericopsis* penstemons, phloxes, bright purple *Allium acuminatum, Townsendia glabella*, and selaginellas. This species (as often with cacti) actually comprises a variable complex of forms, all densely armed with centimeter-long spines concealing the body of the cactus. Most forms grow singly, but some form clumps. The spiny spheres can grow from 3 inches/8 cm in diameter in the type variety into monsters 8 inches/20 cm or more across. The loveliest form is undoubtedly the "snowball cactus," common in some localities, in which the normally amber spines are pure white.

The flowers of *Pediocactus simpsonii* are quite variable. The best forms have 1-inch/2.5-cm fragrant rose chalices which open widely. Cream, yellow, flesh-colored, and greenish tints predominate in the more westerly populations. This is the first hardy cactus to bloom in the garden, often opening its buds in March in Boulder, Colorado. Typically it occurs among rocks and scant grass in the ponderosa pine belt of the montane zone. It will descend onto plains and valleys only in moister regions where alkalis have been leached from the soil. In one valley in southern Wyoming, granite outcrops are studded with *Pediocactus* at 8000 feet/ 2400 meters elevation. The bitterroots (*Lewisia rediviva*) are just opening their first buds as the mountain ball finishes, while directly opposite, on the north-facing slope, the lodgepole pine forest is dotted with *Calypso bulbosa*.

Pediocactus simpsonii var. *robustior* is the most distinctive race of the mountain ball. It forms giant multiheaded clumps in restricted portions of the dry prairies in the northern Great Basin. The spines are blackish. The impact of a cluster of several 6-inch/15-cm in diameter heads is striking all year, even if the flowers are less brightly colored than those of its southern relatives.

A half-dozen more taxa of *Pediocactus* have been described from restricted ranges in the deserts of the southern Great Basin and Navajoan desert. This austere landscape has been so overgrazed and degraded by damming, power plants, and mining that these rare cacti are in real danger of extinction. Most are adapted to extreme desert conditions or else occur in special habitats difficult to duplicate in gardens. Until these threatened forms are available as seedling stock from responsible growers, it would be unethical to advocate their use in gardens.

Coryphantha vivipara (syn. *Escobaria vivipara*; Plate 75) is even more widespread and variable over most of the West than *Pediocactus* species, and it extends farther south than any of them. Budding cactophiles sometimes confuse it with the mountain ball cactus, but the two are quite different in both shape and spination. Although the flowers in both are produced at the apex of the stem (*Coryphantha* means "flowering at the apex"), those of *Coryphantha* are usually twice the size of the *Pediocactus* bloom, which they follow by as much as a month in the garden. *Coryphantha* may have more than 30 narrow petal-like segments in each flower, while in *Pediocactus* the segments are blunt, much shorter, and fewer in number. The flowers of the former are generally much brighter, varying from pink to virulent magenta and vibrant purple. Although they are produced on low plants, often half-hidden in dense stands of buffalo grass, they can make quite a show. *Coryphantha* generally prefers more alkaline conditions on open prairie at lower elevations, but it can climb well over 6000 feet/1800 meters even in the northern reaches of its range. It often blooms after the first rush of spring flowers, joining in a spectacular canvas of eriogonums, *Calochortus nuttallii*, *Lithospermum incisum*, *Sphaeralcea coccinea*, and the ubiquitous western rabble of castillejas, astragalus, and oxytropis. Cattle have trampled millions of these plants out of existence in the past century; in pastureland they can often be found only in pitiful rows under fence wires.

The variation in the complex is almost ridiculous. The name *Coryphantha vivipara* has been used to lump varieties with dense, interlocking white spines (variety *neomexicanus*) that occur in the southern portions of the species' range; single, barrel-like plants that can attain 9 inches/23 cm in the upper Mojave, with pale-pink flowers and variably colored spines (varieties *deserti* and *rosea*); and the thickly caespitose plants that produce dozens of offsets (hence the name *vivipara*) and abound in the high parks and on the Great Plains.

These forms and others intergrade so that accurate identification is difficult. Growing any of these from seed is a slow and tricky process, as the seed germinates unevenly and matures slowly. Unlike *Pediocactus*, which sheds its seeds from dry capsules promptly after ripening, *Coryphantha* produces a juicy, sour fruit that ripens late in the summer and usually persists through the winter, so seed is easy to collect.

Occurring over much the same range as *Coryphantha vivipara* is the similar *Neobesseya missouriensis* (syn. *Escobaria missouriensis*). This little mammillary cactus is more prominently tubercled than *Coryphantha* and has therefore sometimes been called the "nipple cactus." It too prefers the buffalo-grass prairie to mountainous terrain, but it is easily distinguished

Echinocereus pectinatus var. *neomexicanus* (Drawing by Panayoti Kelaidis)

from associated coryphanthas by its flattened rather than conical body and by the bright-red fruits that persist even longer than the greenish or russet capsules of *Coryphantha*. The brownish or straw-yellow blossoms, with a darker central stripe on each narrow segment, are quite different. Very rare pink-flowered colonies have also been reported in Montana and Oklahoma. The nipple cactus rarely grows in such dense stands as the other ball cacti. One can easily overlook a plant in full bloom, and one usually finds a small colony by noticing the bright-red fruits contrasting with the deep-green body of a plant buried in a clump of grass.

The plants are small, usually only 3 inches / 8 cm across. Patriarchs 6 inches / 15 cm across can be found where growing conditions are optimal. It makes offsets sparingly in its northern forms, which also tend to be smaller. The southern forms have sometimes been segregated under the name of *Neobesseya similis* (now *Escobaria missouriensis* var. *similis*). This robust development occurs from Oklahoma southward and appears to be almost as hardy in cultivation as the northern form. The flowers are produced in amazing profusion over a much longer period in early summer. It makes offsets more readily and is unquestionably a superior garden plant.

The Hedgehog Cacti

Echinocereus viridiflorus serves as a bridge between the ball cacti and its own "hedgehog" relatives. In the north, the green-flowered hedgehog rarely develops into the columnar form of the other hedgehog cacti; instead, it forms low, rounded clumps like the ball cacti it often accompanies in the wild from Wyoming southward. It too is a grassland species but seems to prefer somewhat less alkaline conditions than *Coryphantha* (*Escobaria*), typically occurring on gravelly benches and steep slopes in the shortgrass prairie, where it can form dense colonies among *Mertensia lanceolata*, *Leucocrinum montanum*, *Lithospermum multiflorum*, *Calochortus gunnisonii*, and *Pulsatilla patens*. When the disheveled seedheads of the pasqueflower begin to mature, hikers are apt to walk past hundreds of green-flowered hedgehogs without noticing them, for this is one of the least conspicuous cacti in the West.

It is impossible to confuse this cactus with any other when you find it in bloom. The flowers, though diminutive, are quite variable in hue, from lemon-yellow through the chartreuse range. They are always produced along the lower part of the stem, usually near ground level, and never from the top part of the stem as in the other ball cacti or in the *Echinocereus* species that share its range. It is usually floriferous, each crown encircled with a ring of 1-inch / 2.5-cm chalices for a week or more in early June. The more southerly forms produce stout columns 6 inches / 15 cm or more tall, but the typical northern plants are generally less than

3 inches/8 cm tall, often producing several heads. The radial spines are slender and comblike. Any colony may include individuals whose spine color varies from dark red to white; most lack central spines, but some may have centrals over 1 inch/2.5 cm long. This sort of variation may sound slight, but it can result in plants that look quite distinct. Most of the Colorado habitat of this lovely cactus is now under cultivation, over-grazed, or bulldozed to make way for the virulently spreading cities of the Eastern Slope of the Rocky Mountains. How many fascinating variations in this cactus have been lost because of this?

The other *Echinocereus* species of the southwestern uplands are much showier than the green-flowered hedgehog. It is hard to miss a single blooming plant of these, even from a bus! Few plants can rival the hedge-hogs in size and sumptuousness of blossom. These include some of the most popular cacti grown in pots; few people realize that their compla-cent pot plant is in reality a native of a cold climate, yearning to join its fellow wildflowers in the rock garden beyond the storm windows. Given the fascinating variety of spination in this group, the magnificent mounds they form in time, and their ease of cultivation and hardiness, it is scandalous that so little attention has been paid to them in gardening literature. And then the flowers—almost an embarrassment of riches, sometimes 5 inches/13 cm across, with 50 or more silky, iridescent seg-ments that range from white and yellow through orange, scarlet, ver-milion, magenta, purple, and pink.

If their color, size, and texture strike us as excessive in the (often gaudy) rock garden, what should we make of the spectacle that hordes of hedgehogs present on the mountains and the deserts of the West? Their magnificence should not be held against them. Over much of the West, the blooming of the hedgehog cacti is a climax of the year. After the long droughts of summer and the dry and windy autumn and winter, the brief flowering in late spring comes as a triumph of delicate beauty over the austerity of the seasons.

No fewer than five broadly defined species clusters of *Echinocereus* abound over much of the Southwest, where their tolerance of subzero temperatures is beyond question. All five groups are comprised of plants that form columns of greater or lesser height, with more or less of a tend-ency to clump. They all produce their flowers above the areoles that line the ribs, usually budding on the younger, higher portion of the stem. The spiny, spherical, or ovoid fruits are often brilliant burgundy in color, fleshy and juicy, filled with many tiny black seeds. Here the resem-blances end.

In bloom, the claret cup cacti (*Echinocereus* spp.) are the most easily distinguishable of the hedgehogs. The variation in stem size, shape, growth habit, spination, and choice of habitat within this group is be-wildering, but the perfectly formed badminton birdie of a flower is instantly recognizable. Except for a few tender relatives and some probable hybrids, the flower is at the scarlet end of the red spectrum, ranging from orange to tangerine to brilliant crimson. The iridescent green style typical of *Echinocereus* contrasts strikingly with its background; only in red castillejas are these colors combined so effectively. The individual flower remains fresh longer than any other hardy cactus blossom, usually for several days even in hot weather. The flowers of its magenta- and yellow-flowered hedgehog relatives, by contrast, commonly wilt after a single hot day, invariably closing in the evenings. Offsets in the claret cup, when they are produced, literally pop fully formed out of the strongly ribbed sides of mature stems. Many botanists have despaired of pigeonholing the endless permutations and intergradations of this complex; they usually give up and lump them all into *E. triglochidiatus* (Plate 60). [Subsequent interpretation assigns specific status to some of the plants treated as varieties in the first publication of this article, as noted hereafter.—*Ed.*]

This mouth-filling name includes plants that grow into solitary, corpulent barrels that can attain 20 inches/50 cm in height, as well as tiny pincushions that increase over time by offsetting to produce mounds a yard/meter or more across with hundreds of 1-inch/2.5-cm crowns. The fuzzy areoles along the ribs can have two, or twelve or more spines that can be fine as a hair, barely a centimeter long in *Echinocereus polyacanthus* (formerly variety *polyacanthus*); coarse and bristly, almost bony excrescences in *E. triglochidiatus* itself; wildly tousled in variety *mojavensis*; heavy and thick in the plant formerly called variety *gonacanthus*, not now distinguished taxonomically; or altogether absent in *E. inermis* (formerly variety *inermis*). These and others occupy a wide variety of ecological niches.

One sort thrives on alkaline flats in the southern Great Basin. Others appear on limestone outcrops and gypsum barrens in central and southern New Mexico. In Saguache County, Colorado, the claret cup grows in the tiny crevices of volcanic dikes, entangled with the zigzag cloak fern. Although distributed more to the south than any other cacti so far discussed, the claret cups are nonetheless mountain cacti. The finest clumps invariably grow on rocky ground, often on sheer rock faces—even hanging on the concave underfaces of sandstone cliffs. On the crags below the Box Canyon near Ouray, Colorado, large mounds of *Echinocereus coccineus* (formerly *E. triglochidiatus* var. *melanocanthus*) cling to a vertical cliff, emerging from dense mats of moss and perennials that stud the granitic chasm below the falls. This mesic mountain valley, over 8000 feet/2400 meters in altitude, is the last place one would expect to find a cactus.

Three large-flowered magenta hedgehogs occur over much of the same range as the claret cup and offer almost as much variation in stem, spine and flower. *Echinocereus engelmannii* is prevalent in western Arizona and desert California; *E. fendleri* predominates in the central parts of the Southwest; and the many forms of *E. reichenbachii* prevail in eastern

New Mexico, southeastern Colorado, and upland Oklahoma and Texas. There is no question that the last is the best hedgehog for the northern rock garden. *Echinocereus reichenbachii*, popularly known as the "lace cactus," must be one of the frontrunners for designation as the loveliest North American wildflower.

If you were to tell a rock gardener that there exists a plant that produces a wealth of flowers 4 inches / 10 cm in diameter, of the purest satiny texture, in pink, rose, or deep purple; that, furthermore, this plant is neither a weed nor a mimp; that it grows compactly in a neat mound with a unique habit, never exceeding 8 inches / 20 cm in breadth and rarely more in height; that it is long-lived, bone-hardy, and available for nickels at almost any neighborhood grocery store, you would likely be pronounced insane, especially when you informed your skeptical friend that this wonder is a cactus.

Typical specimens of the type variety *reichenbachii* are usually single-stemmed, producing offsets and branches as they age. The stem is rarely more than 8 inches / 20 cm tall (except in venerable specimens), and fluted with many shallow parallel ribs. These ribs are closely set with areoles that sprout minuscule radial spines, so symmetrically placed that each plant does appear to be dressed in lace. This semblance is enhanced in the plants with pure white spines, the prevalent form over most of the eastern and southern range of the species, abounding on limestone prairies in Oklahoma and northern Texas.

Echinocereus reichenbachii var. *baileyi* is often separated from the typical lace cactus as a distinct species on the basis of many minor but consistent characters. For the gardener it is undeniably different and worth growing in the smallest collection of cacti. Although young plants of this form are generally single-stemmed, older ones produce many offsets, each attaining about 10 inches / 25 cm in height. Variety *baileyi* varies tremendously in the color of the long, shaggy spines that completely conceal the body of the plant, which range from deep rusty reds and browns to off-white tints. These spines emerge at unequal angles from the areoles, rather than in the neat comblike arrangement of the typical lace cactus, and the spines interlock. The effect of a typical colony of this plant, which grows in dense stands on its native granite hills, is of a pack of unkempt extraterrestrials.

The flowers are no less otherworldly, both gigantic and profuse. They are often 4 inches / 10 cm across and more vase-shaped than in other members of this complex. An established garden plant of the Witchita Mountain hedgehog produces repeated flushes of flowers from late May until frost. In late July 1978, when the cactus season was ostensibly past, it opened 14 flowers simultaneously on just four heads.

This taxon occurs in a restricted area only a few miles square in the Witchita Mountains Wildlife Preserve of southwestern Oklahoma. Here the cactus has prospered no less than the free-ranging bison and long-

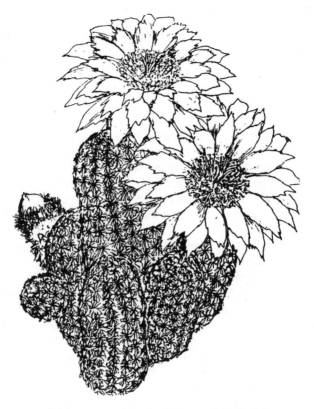

Echinocereus reichenbachii var. *reichenbachii*
(Drawing by Panayoti Kelaidis)

horn cattle that share its habitat and thrill visiting cactophiles. In the
rocky clearings of the preserve, between the open forests of post and
blackjack oaks, these cacti occur in masses embedded in thick mats of
clubmosses, *Pellaea ternifolia* var. *wrightiana,* and a wealth of southern
Great Plains wildflowers.

The form of *Echinocereus reichenbachii* var. *baileyi* formerly called variety *albispinus* is another rare plant found in Oklahoma. The spines are
less concise than in the lace cactus but even whiter. This variety is one of
the most caespitose of the hedgehogs: a single crown can sprout a dozen
or so offsets in a few years. The flowers, produced several weeks ahead
of the other varieties of *E. reichenbachii,* are bright pink with a peculiar
satiny sheen. Their segments reflex more than other forms in this complex, often obscuring the stems from sight. So far this seems to be less
prone to reblooming than other forms of the species, but the neat mound
of glistening white heads barely 4 inches/10 cm tall would warrant a
place in the garden even if it did not produce such magical flowers.

Echinocereus reichenbachii var. *perbellus* is the only other lace cactus frequently encountered. It predominates along the northern and western extensions of the overall range of the species. It generally has only single crowns, rarely more than 4 inches/10 cm in height. The flowers are similar to the type variety in their open shape, if perhaps a little smaller. Since it grows in the rather dry plains of Colorado, New Mexico, and western Oklahoma, this form is less tolerant of excessive moisture than the others; otherwise, its diminutive stature would recommend it even more to the rock garden.

Where cities or agriculture have not supplanted them, one or another of these varieties still occurs in some abundance. These cacti are native to regions characterized by considerable summer rainfall and severe winters with repeated, sudden thaws. Thus they are ideal subjects for cold-climate gardens in wetter regions. Development has already restricted the range of these remarkable plants sufficiently that conservation of wild populations should be a priority. Happily, there is no need for anyone to collect these in the wild, for no cacti have been more intensively or successfully propagated than the lace cactus. Because it can be grown rather quickly in greenhouses to a saleable height, it has become a favorite with nurseries who provide grocery-store flower departments with tiny succulents. Assuming that children have not been busy switching labels while their parents are shopping, one can be reasonably certain that any cactus labeled *Echinocereus reichenbachii* will prove true to name. If it is, it is certain to be as hardy as the phloxes and penstemons it accompanies in the wild. How happy is such a plant to be rescued by a rock gardener! Otherwise it would probably spend a miserable decade languishing in a dish garden in some dark and smoky parlor before death released it.

Alternatively, it can be raised from seed, which germinates rather well for a cactus. Seedlings grow slowly in their first year, but with careful fertilization a flowering plant can be produced in 3 years.

The New Mexico hedgehog (*Echinocereus fendleri*) is just as beautiful in its own fashion. The flowers are as large and showy, in much the same pink-magenta range, but the spines of the hardier forms are generally fewer in number (usually fewer than ten, often fewer than five) and much stouter and longer. The species has the same habit of producing a single column—occasionally three or more in a clump—that rarely exceeds 5 inches/13 cm in height in the type variety. It occurs just to the west of *E. reichenbachii* in the drier reaches of New Mexico and eastern Arizona, extending a short distance into Colorado and Utah. It is more of a desert plant than the lace cactus, as the rainfall over much of this region is less than 10 inches/25 cm annually. It demands perfect drainage and heat to grow at all in the garden, where it is a showpiece if successful. Seedlings grow more slowly and reluctantly than those of its eastern cousin. Although thousands of mature plants lie in the path of such rapidly growing cities as Albuquerque, collecting the New Mexico hedgehog is often futile. It is worth the effort to propagate plants from seed, which adapt more readily to garden conditions than hoary clumps from the desert.

There are a number of other varieties of this complex that are found in the subtropical parts of the Chihuahuan and Sonoran deserts. Some have been segregated into a separate species complex, *Echinocereus fasciculatus*, by some taxonomists. These striking hedgehogs tantalize visitors to Tucson and Phoenix in the spring, but even if garden strains were available from populations in the highest part of their range along the Mogollon Rim, it is doubtful that they would ever prove durable in cold climates. They are quintessentially desert plants that yearn for 9 months of extreme dry heat to thrive, even if they tolerate a few degrees of frost.

The purple torch cactus (*Echinocereus engelmannii*) offers greater hope on this score. It too is a desert cactus, found in the hottest and driest part of the Mojave and western Sonoran deserts. Several forms extend far north of *E. fasciculatus* in the wild. Seedlings from seed collected from these northern stations have weathered several seasons in Boulder, although more years will be needed to assess their durability in cold climates. The purple torch is the westernmost of the *Echinocereus* cacti and generally the largest. Some forms approach 2 feet / 60 cm in height, producing correspondingly large and showy flowers. This species is often featured in southwestern gardens and highway beautification plantings. The plant produces massive white or yellow spines, coarse and long, with prominent centrals. A hardy race would furnish a breathtaking centerpiece for a dryland rock garden.

The rugged terrain of the American Southwest has done more than frustrate ranchers and highway planners. As plants have shuffled back and forth through this vast region over the eons, colonies of many have been stranded here and there, far beyond their later distributional ranges. In time, these may evolve into completely new species (thus the notable endemism in this region), or they may at least develop resistance to the rigors of their changing microenvironments. *Echinocereus pectinatus* var. *dasyacanthus* is a case in point. This yellow-flowered "New Mexico rainbow cactus" is typically a plant of barren limestone slopes in the Chihuahuan desert, where conditions in summer are so intensely hot and winters sufficiently mild that no rock gardener would attempt it in a bitter climate. A botanist of our acquaintance was surprised to find this cactus growing at a high elevation more than 200 miles / 320 km north of its normal range. Although this distance may not seem great, the new-found colony represented a form that had adapted to radically different conditions. There is no question that its habitat is far colder over a much longer period in winter, and summer temperatures far milder than in southern habitat; thus it promises to provide a hardy strain of an otherwise somewhat tender cactus.

Similar colonies of *Mammillaria heyderi, Echinocactus horizontalonius,
E. texensis, Epithelantha micromeris,* and other usually tender cacti have
been found by adventurous searchers, who are beginning to disseminate
them among hardy-cactus enthusiasts. When these dozens of botanical
species are compounded by selected horticultural forms based on variations of plant shape, spination, or flower color, it is no wonder that some
northern gardeners are tempted to specialize in cacti.

The Prickly Pears

One could indeed specialize in the genus *Opuntia* alone, although
we do not advocate it. It includes a vast number of bone-hardy species
and varieties exhibiting a wide range of variation. The flat-padded
opuntia is the archetypal cactus, the one that would emerge if the non-
enthusiast were asked to draw a picture of a cactus (assuming the artist
forgot about saguaros).

The variation among prickly pears beggars description. Flower color
varies almost infinitely: straw-yellow to deep lemon and gold-flushed
hues, green, white, orange, copper, bicolors, rose, purple, and even deep
red occur. The spines can be several inches long, produced thickly
enough to hide the pad, or they may be tiny and concise or completely
lacking, as in most forms of *O. basilaris.* This variation is almost as extreme within the larger specific groups as within the genus, for the
prickly pears are still in an active state of evolution. Not only are opuntias
remarkably plastic genetically, but the entire genus is quite responsive to
environmental influence. Because most members of the genus grow
quickly, they are very much affected by the vagaries of weather, soil, and
climate. Cuttings from the same plant can assume entirely different
shapes if subjected to different conditions of moisture, soil, or exposure.

From the sand dunes of the southeastern states, north to Canada and
across to the Olympic Peninsula of Washington, and everywhere to the
south, the prickly pears have plagued livestock and careless hikers for
years. Lewis and Clark marveled at expanses carpeted with *Opuntia polyacantha* along their route, and visitors ever since have been intimidated
by the omnipresent *Opuntia* clan that dominates so much of the American landscape. Nonetheless, every one of the dozens of fuzzily delim-
ited species can yield garden plants of exceptional interest. Many are
decorative in all their forms, among them *O. clavata, O. basilaris,* and *O.
pulchella.*

Although many opuntias manifest as floppy, bug-eaten, endlessly
ramifying swarms in the wild, this does not mean the genus is hopeless
in the garden. The trick to growing opuntias lies in selecting the right
form for the right spot. They should be placed where the gradually growing mound will not be smothered by neighbors, where the pads can ripen

sufficiently in the sun to remain sturdy through variable winter weather, and where the roots will not be subject to winter rot. Although in the wild a prickly pear is just as likely to be found on alkaline flats, short-grass prairie, sand dunes, or even periodically flooded river benches, all members of this genus look and thrive especially well when elevated in the garden, placed among rocks for the swelling mound to embrace and cascade over. Properly situated in a somewhat fertile and *porous* soil, a plant of almost any species of *Opuntia* will assume unsuspected grace and remain healthy for many years. In early summer, when it produces a wealth of showy bloom, the genus comes into its own, for the flowers of most prickly pears are of fine size and brilliance.

Ball cacti or hedgehogs are usually grown massed in formidable battalions that detract from the intricate patterning of the individual plant. Opuntias, on the other hand, are never allowed more than a token appearance in the garden, usually relegated to the dingiest and most unwholesome spot. We feel that for the cold-climate dryland garden, the opuntias are supreme architectural plants that should be used much in the manner of dwarf shrubs and conifers in the alpine garden: to provide bold sculptural relief from the monotony of miniature subjects. Several contrasting opuntias—upright and procumbent, shaggy-spined and naked, rose- and yellow-flowered—planted in proximity, will eventually blend into a group that can greatly enhance the interest of a rock garden at all seasons.

Of course, their armament is the most cleverly devised among the cacti, designed to inflict maximum pain. The tiny tufts of harmless-looking glochids (barbed bristles, sometimes almost invisible) at the base of each spine are a unique feature of this genus. The cactus-grower quickly learns to respect them.

The opuntias are divided by taxonomists into two large groups: those with flat pads (*Platyopuntia*), and those whose stems consist of cylindrical segments (*Cylindropuntia*). The latter are often called by their Spanish name "cholla." There are many hardy, growable plants in both groups.

One of the most beautiful of the platyopuntias is *Opuntia polyacantha*, which occurs all over the Great Plains and into the Great Basin. Its pads are rather long and covered with spines grouped in a crow's-foot pattern. The color of the pads and spines varies considerably over the range of the species, but the generalized "hunger cactus" typically has gray pads with fine, pure-white spines. The plants are low and sprawling (they must support heavy winter snows), and a single plant can become a patch a yard/meter wide. The satiny flowers can be any color in the warm range, from pale yellow to deepest red, but are most frequently yellow or purplish rose. In some individuals the stamens are also colored: brilliant yellow-flowered specimens with dark ruby stamens are among the most beautiful in the genus.

Another opuntia famed for its beauty and hardiness is *Opuntia poly-acantha* var. *rufispina*, which has also been called *O. rutila*, or lumped with *O. fragilis*. It may be a transitional phase between these two very different plants, but it is distinctive in its own right. It is one of the most frequently encountered cacti in the Great Basin, growing at near-alpine elevations on some of the desert ranges. The spines of *O. polyacantha* var. *rufispina* are stiff and rich dark brown or purple. The typical flower is brilliant rose and often measures more than 3 inches/8 cm in diameter. The pads are quite variable in shape, although they tend to be rather small compared to other species in its range, and are sometimes almost cylindrical in form. This species is widely sought by gardeners in northern Europe, Russia, and Japan; it can withstand −20°F/−29°C without a whimper, blooming as lustily there as on the sundrenched mesas of western Colorado.

If we had to pick a favorite platyopuntia it would probably be the Mojave Desert native, *Opuntia basilaris*. Many named and unnamed forms of this striking plant are fully hardy to −10°F/−23°C. This plant tends to branch from the base, although plants with pads stacked on pads are also common. Apart from the magnificent flowers, the outstanding feature of *O. basilaris* is its complete, or nearly complete, lack of spines. The thick, smooth, purplish pads of the spineless varieties have made "beavertail" the common name for this cactus. Many varieties lack long spines but have bundles of glochids, which give the pads a tufted or quilted appearance. The flowers are large (in variety *brachyclada* they are larger than the pad), very double, and typically a scintillating rose, or an equally brilliant lemon in variety *aurea*. White flowers predominate in some populations.

Opuntia fragilis may be the least-loved prickly pear, thanks to its flimsily jointed pads, which fall apart at a touch and hitch a ride with every passing creature. (If you hate picking burrs from your socks, try pads of *O. fragilis*!) This asexual reproductive strategy has spread this species far and wide across the West, and it has also apparently selected for paucity of flower: this species rarely blooms. A southwestern Utah form of *O. fragilis*, formerly called variety *denudata*, departs in being quite floriferous. Its large pale-yellow flowers contrast beautifully with the blunt, steel-gray, spineless pads. The consistent spinelessness of variety *denudata*, along with a range that overlaps with that of *O. basilaris* var. *aurea*, suggests that this variety's peculiar characteristics derive from hybrid ancestry. This plant, which tightly fills crevices between rocks with its symmetrical gray mounds, can be compared favorably with any mimicry plant, and it is certainly one of the choicest subjects for the well-drained rock garden.

Space does not permit the description of all the hardy platyopuntias, but mention must be made of several forms and varieties of *Opuntia erinacea*. This species resembles the prickly pears so far discussed in pro-

211

ducing a dry seed capsule rather than a fleshy fruit. Its best-known variety is certainly the famed grizzly bear cactus (*O. erinacea* var. *ursina*) from Death Valley in southeastern California. Plants, which include both yellow- and rose-flowered forms, are so completely covered by long, hairlike spines up to 4 inches/10 cm in length that the pads are completely obscured. The white to gray color of these tousled spines would certainly have merited the specific name *senilis*, but the common name (invented by a nurseryman) was already well enough established to influence the choice of *ursina* when the plant was officially described. The beautiful variety *utahensis* is widespread along the eastern fringe of its overall range. It has a more procumbent habit and smaller pads. Its superseded appellation, *O. rhodantha*, described its cerise flower color. Most members of this complex are rather more upright than other flat-padded cacti. This trait has been imparted to the many hybrid swarms of prickly pears in the Southwest. *Opuntia erinacea* has also bequeathed its hybrids magnificent flowers and short, stiff white marginal bristles.

Some varieties of the *Opuntia macrocentra/O. santarita* complex (the "purple prickly pears") must also be mentioned briefly. Besides the nearly smooth, round lavender pad, some with magnificent long, dark brown or black marginal spines, these cacti are famous for their brilliant yellow, ruby-centered flowers. Cuttings taken from a roadside plant near Carlsbad, New Mexico, have proven perfectly hardy in Boulder. A problem yet to be overcome with this beautiful plant is the breakage at the joint caused by the strong winds that plague our area in winter. Since the plant is upright and retains considerable turgidity all winter, it obviously needs to be grown in the lee of a wind shield. Another clone, from deep in the Great Basin (reportedly from near Wendover, Utah, far outside its recorded range), has fared better with the wind here.

Opuntia phaeacantha, the fleshy-fruited New Mexico prickly pear, is a variable complex. This group is widely distributed throughout the southern Great Plains and far into the Southwest. Plants vary in height from 1 to 3 feet/30 to 90 cm. The pads are at least as large as a man's hand and are typically long-spined, with dark brown spines often bristling along the margins of the pad. Most forms have rather uninteresting yellowish flowers, but all have very attractive burgundy-colored fruits. Unusually attractive flowers occur in local populations of variety *phaeacantha* found in certain canyons in southwestern Colorado. Although many plants in these populations have yellow flowers, others have large dark rose flowers, while still others have flowers of brilliant scarlet. A salmon-flowered variety has also been reported from the Virgin Mountains of southern Nevada.

Much less can be said about the opuntias with cylindrical segments. There are fewer species and varieties of chollas; moreover, many of them are scarcely appropriate as rock garden subjects because of their nearly arborescent habit. For desert gardens of sufficient size for such large cacti, there are *Opuntia imbricata* from the cold northern part of the Chihuahua Desert, *O. tunicata* var. *davisii* from much the same range, and *O. echinocarpa* from the Mojave Desert. *Opuntia imbricata* is justly famous for its large purple flowers, while the others are grown mainly for their lustrous spine sheaths. In *O. tunicata* var. *davisii* these are a rich amber color, while in *O. echinocarpa* the sheaths are either straw-colored or white, yielding the common names "gold" and "silver" cholla. Properly grown, any of these can attain 6 feet / 2 meters in height. Needless to say, care should be taken in placing them in the rock garden, for a mature cholla does not take kindly to human company.

Probably the choicest of this group for the desert rock garden is *Opuntia clavata*, a mat-forming cholla which consists of short, prostrate, drumstick-shaped stems armed with wide, very stiff bone-white spines. A single plant can cover a large area in time. Although *O. clavata* rarely blooms, it is not obliged to do so: it more than justifies its keep by its fascinating appearance. This is one of the most threatened species in the genus, being restricted to a rather limited habitat near the exploding city of Albuquerque, New Mexico.

Three additional shrubby chollas are of some gardening interest, especially where heavy snowfall is not too great a threat. The most attractive is *Opuntia leptocaulis*, the pencil cholla. Although most forms of this lovely cactus are tender, some quite short-growing northern populations are found far up in the Texas panhandle, where the climate is rigorous. This fine-stemmed plant grows by preference under and among stouter plants, such as creosote bush or *Berberis trifoliata*, so that its long, slender stems find something to lean against and so remain erect. A casual glance often fails to detect the plant hidden in the center of its host, unless the cactus happens to be in fruit. The small berrylike fruits turn bright red after frost, earning it the name "desert Christmas cactus." The flowers are small and greenish and somewhat rare. We have never had any on our plants in Boulder.

Opuntia whipplei occurs widely all over northern Arizona and neighboring regions, having its center in the area of the Kaibab Plateau. Many forms of this viciously spiny plant are found, some serving as dune-catchers in the Four Corners area, others forming lovely tall candelabras on the western edge of its range. The plants are dark green, enlivened with thickly set spines that are relatively short and white-sheathed. The taller forms are very vulnerable to damage by heavy snow, which crushes the slender stalks. One of the more interesting forms of this cactus in our garden is a nearly spineless dwarf that forms a creeping mat of tiny erect rat-tails. This was found among typical plants in the Four Corners area. The flowers of *O. whipplei* are small and greenish, of little consequence.

The third shrubby cholla that grows well in cold climates is *Opuntia kleiniae*. It too suffers from slender stems that break under heavy snows. If it is to be attempted—and its purple flowers are worth the effort—it must be provided with stout support. The most naturalistic supports for these weaker chollas are the sturdy canes of their robust relative, *O. imbricata*, which can bear a heavy load of snow. A mixed planting of chollas is the stratagem we have resorted to in order to beat the problem of the heavy late-spring snows of Colorado.

One thoroughly charming opuntia remains to be mentioned—*Opuntia pulchella*. This plant is so different from other members of its genus that one taxonomist has set up a special section for it. A native of the western Great Basin, it has tiny cholla-like stems atop a tuberous root that looks like a large radish. In its native habitat, the neck of the rhizome often protrudes from the soil, hosting green and orange lichens. Even the tuber is covered below ground with a dense coat of painful glochids. The spines are long, black, and flexible. The purple flowers are very large in comparison with the plant. This plant is very difficult to grow. Collected rhizomes are almost impossible to reestablish; cuttings are relatively easy to root but take a long time to produce a noticeable specimen. A gardener who manages to grow *O. pulchella* in the garden is lucky indeed, for it is certainly one of the most fascinating cacti.

The treatment given here to the opuntias has been scandalously brief, and our friends who know this genus will note that many worthy species and cultivars have not been mentioned. We beg their indulgence and forgiveness. Few who come to the West with unjaundiced eyes would question the assertion that it would take a garden as untrammeled as the western skyline and as glorious as the canyonlands to do justice to these undeservedly neglected plants.

At this point (if you have stayed with us this long) you may yet be unpersuaded. Having progressed with us from the tiny huddled ball cacti through the magnificence of the hedgehogs, around the thickets of prickly pears, you may still agree with Reginald Farrer's sentiments about these "flattened little columns of hate." If so, we can only regret your loss. But for rock gardeners like ourselves, born and bred among the mesas and canyons of the West, the perfectly adapted cactus remains the finest symbol of the drama and beauty of our landscape. It is an indispensable ingredient in that part of it we weed and call a garden.

Acknowledgments

The authors would like to acknowledge the inspiration that laid the groundwork for this article: above all to Sam and Maryann Heacock of Denver, whose generosity with both cuttings and information encouraged us to pursue the study of cacti. Without seeing the immense variety of cacti in the Heacock's wonderful garden, we would never have believed that such a wealth existed in the family for colder climates. Allan Taylor derived much information from visits to Claude Barr's Prairie Gem Nursery, where so many fine cacti have been propagated and distributed for many years. Panayoti Kelaidis would like to express his gratitude for the many opportunities he has enjoyed to visit out-of-the-way corners in the West with T. Paul Maslin, whose knowledge of the plants and backroads of the West is surpassed only by his talent for growing them. His rock garden hovers behind several descriptions in the article. We also express our gratitude to Horst Kuenzler of Belen, New Mexico, whose consummate skill at propagating cacti may save some of the rarer ones from further decimation if not extinction.

Originally published in the Bulletin of the American Rock Garden Society, *vol. 37, no. 4, pp. 157–164 (1979); vol. 38, no. 1, pp. 1–10, and no. 2, pp. 59–66 (1980).*

Symposium on Eritrichium *in America*

B. LEROY DAVIDSON

Reginald Farrer (1930) wrote of *Eritrichium* that it was "quite content to sit up there from age to age, working out its own destiny."

With reports that a plant is difficult or impossible to cultivate inevitably come challenges from gardeners who will not agree until they have tried, and tried, and tried. In the horticultural literature eritrichiums are rated the classic example of the difficult plant, and much has been written and spoken in explanation, advice, or promise. Suggestions range from "fooling it into thinking it is winter with a blanket of cotton-wool" to a method of growing seedlings (should one be so fortunate as to have seed) "in a flat of slates arranged to resemble a crevice formation" (Royal Horticultural Society 1936).

To appreciate this lovely subject, as well as to try to fathom its nature, several expeditions have set forth into the northern Rocky Mountains and some related eastern ranges. Claude Barr made the pilgrimage and was duly impressed by the profusion and great beauty of *Eritrichium howardii* carpeting the plains at the eastern base of the limestone backbone of Montana, as recorded in an article he published in the ARGS *Bulletin* in 1968. Some further observations, experiences, opinions, and warnings may promote a better understanding of these plants, and a succession of generations grown in gardens might produce a strain that is a bit easier to grow.

———————— Taxonomy within the Genus ————————

Any taxonomic discussion of local scope should for clarity consider related subjects and other regions. *Eritrichium* is one of the much-confused genera of the subfamily Boraginoideae, an assemblage that has often been reinterpreted and revised. The synonymy for the North American members alone indicates that species once included in this genus are currently to be found disposed among no less than nine genera: *Anchusa, Brunnera, Cryptantha, Cynoglossum, Hackelia, Krynitzkia, Myosotis, Omphalodes,* and *Plagiobothrys.* This interpretation leaves as the "true" eritrichiums only the most beautiful and desirable species, and the most nearly impossible. Some plants still represented in nursery lists as eritrichiums have now been banished to one or the other of the above genera; they may nonetheless be desirable plants in themselves.

Even following such a strict delimitation, we are confronted with an extensive number of species, all of densely pulvinate, caespitose habit, all clad in furry garb, and all of arctic-alpine distribution. As is usual within this subfamily, great taxonomic importance has been attached to their fruits; the nutlets are sometimes barbed and sometimes smooth. William Wight (1902) recognized six species in North America, these being, in addition to *Eritrichium howardii* (which all workers agree is the most distinct), *E. elongatum, E. splendens, E. argenteum, E. aretioides,* and *E. chamissonis.* In his treatment the nutlets are figured, clearly showing their diversity; some are only ridged and quite smooth, others have short spines surmounting the apical ridge, which become, in still others, branched and compoundly barbed. Nicholas Polunin (1959) treated four species of the northlands (his study did not encompass the range of *E. howardii*), including the exclusively American *E. aretioides* (Plate 58), "variable in leaf and flower and loosely matted to closely pulvinate" from mountainous areas, and three others: *E. chamissonis* "from situations similar to those of *aretioides*," ranging "from Arctic Asia to Alaska and the Yukon"; *E. villosum,* Eurasian, "of sandy seashores, coarser and taller"; and *E. czekanowskii,* Siberian, of which he remarked, "may belong in an allied genus."

C. Leo Hitchcock (1955–1969) wrote of *Eritrichium,* "About four closely related species of Eurasia and western North America when strictly limited." He recognized two American species, including all except *E. howardii* within *E. nanum,* the type of which is European. His discussion stated that plants of the United States constitute the "rather weak" variety *elongatum,* and differ from the European type in being more densely pubescent; the less hairy ones, "notably those of the Wallowa Mountains," differed scarcely, if at all, from their European counterparts. He discounted the importance of seed characters, drawing attention to similar polymorphism within the plants of Europe.

Further names encountered in the literature include *Eritrichium jankae*, presumed to be an eastern European variant of *E. nanum*; *E. lati-folium* and *E. sericeum*, both said to be Himalayan; and *E. rupestre*, recorded as found in the Gobian Altai of Mongolia by Vladimir Vasak (1968). Farrer would rest well knowing that the deplored name *ter-gloviense* for his beloved plant of the Col de Clapier, Angstbord Pass, and the ridge of Padon, has fallen into disuse in favor of the prior *E. nanum*. *Eritrichium nipponicum* is probably a *Cynoglossum* species.

There seems little reason for the horticulturally inclined to continue to split hairs in the case of *Eritrichium*. The reports of greater compactness in some wild forms are often contradicted by other observers working in the same areas, and the nomenclature that attempts to resolve confusion only compounds it, in that the defined taxa cannot be plotted to form continuous distributions. Workers are at odds as to what to call the plants of Alaska, for instance; and Hitchcock has been the one to con-clude that *E. nanum* is polymorphic and widespread. Farrer said that every northern mountain range had "its own eritrichium," alluding to this polymorphism and the tendency of botanists observing it to name all the variations. The qualities of compactness, floriferousness, and (to some extent) pubescence can be affected by local conditions; only *E. howardii* stands as consistently distinct in morphology and habitat.

———— *Eritrichium howardii*: Exclusively American ————

Claude Barr (1968) gave us his impression of the plains of Montana carpeted as far as the eye could see with this bluest of prairie wildflow-ers. Farrer (1930) said of it, "A beautiful dense tuft of narrow, spoon-shaped leaves clothed in short silver hair and with larger brilliant blos-soms"—praise indeed, as he was comparing it to his beloved "King of the Alps," *Eritrichium nanum*, and Farrer could scarcely admit admira-tion for any American plant. Although this species is sometimes found on mountaintops, it is at its best as Barr saw it, down on the basal moraines at the feet of the mountains. Where it is best suited it forms a solid mass of individual tufts, numbering hundreds of thousands, al-most to the exclusion of any other flowering plant, so unique is its adap-tation to the situation: a deep formation of limestone and clay that is greasy when wet, hard and densely compacted when dry.

Those who have attempted to grow *Eritrichium howardii* in gardens suggest, but have not yet demonstrated, greater possibility of success with this species than with *E. nanum*. Charles Thurman of Spokane, Washington, has attempted it in his garden, also on a glacial deposit, though granite-derived. Gardeners who have tried it in Missoula, Mon-tana, have not been successful. Margaret Williams of Reno, Nevada, dug plants in bloom and planted them in containers in their native soil, but they died on the way home in the heat of summer. "From two sites, both quite rocky, these apparently suffered too much disturbance and the myriad of fine root hairs suffered too much damage," she writes. Rae Selling Berry of Portland, Oregon, despaired of ever succeeding with "the Trickies," as she affectionately termed them: "They strive to succeed but just plain pine away, even in the frame or cold house." A similar report came from the late Ted Greig of Vancouver, British Columbia; both the last-named gardens are in the moist Pacific Northwest.

The greatest degree of success with this species so far appears to have been that of Robert Putnam of Kirkland, Washington, also in the rain belt, with a plant dug in October. Although Thurman has speculated that these plants should only be moved when the roots are in active growth, fall collecting has proven just as favorable. This plant was removed from the shoulder of the road where it had barely escaped road repairs, and was over 1 foot/30 cm in diameter. It would ordinarily never have been considered as a subject for transplantation, but it was surely doomed as soon as spring brought the workmen back. It was put into a 12-inch/30-cm clay pot in its native soil, and this was set inside a larger pot and kept dry in the cold house through the winter. The plant appeared quite lifeless, but with the spring came little sage-green new leaves on every terminal branch, and water was accordingly given. In May, it flowered and some seed was set; at this writing it has gone through its first summer's aestivation in cultivation, appearing lifeless again, but it is living. No other plant from this collection survived; they were treated in various ways, in various soil mixtures, some overwintered in a ventilated frame, some put directly into the scree and topdressed heavily with basalt chips. It might be of interest to note here that no white individuals of this species appear to have been found, although they are not unusual within *Eritrichium nanum*.

These plains of divine, sky-blue *Eritrichium howardii* lie at altitudes around 4000 feet/1200 meters. The winters are cold, with snow coming in late October at higher elevations and tempering the air. By December the plants are buried in drifts that do not melt until late May. Thus the plant is dry and dormant for about 6 months. The soil is full of water during the brief period of growth and flowering; by mid-June it is dry, the excess having drained away and evaporated. With the ripening of the seed, the plant aestivates and does not make any above-ground growth until the following spring. Thus its life cycle is like that of true desert plants, and its tenacity is doubtless due to its ability to cling to life through the summer by its roots' being able to extract the most minute amounts of moisture.

Forms of *Eritrichium nanum*

Herbarium material of the complex of plants relating to the European species *Eritrichium nanum* includes extremes of variation in the congestion of the stems and leaves; some plants in flower are scarcely an inch, with apparently stemless flowers, while others, according to information noted from the same area in another season, are loose tufts with elongated stems. The latter form dilutes the blue effect, though they may display the "fiddlehead" character typical of the borage family, which is not apparent in the few-flowered inflorescences of the tiniest ones. Margaret Williams says that her English friends have advised her that *E. nanum* in the Alps is an extremely variable plant, much more compact and desirable in one place than another, even in regard to the richness of its color. Thurman has written, "Of one thing I am sure from observations both on Beartooth and in the Wallowas, these are consistently more compact than those seen in the Montana stations, the Big Snowy and Little Belt ranges and on Old Hollowtop."

Robert Woodward and James McPhail, of Vancouver, British Columbia, also went to Beartooth, as did Margaret Williams. The latter writes that here on this flat-topped plateau *Eritrichium nanum* grows on level sites, with what appears to be poor drainage in heavy soil, and that the plants were far easier to dig than *E. howardii*, the roots coming out in a nice ball, "undoubtedly the reason I succeeded with it (for a while)." She kept one plant in a scree bed of fine pumice and leafmold for two seasons; it flowered well and then died. This plant had been collected in a very loose, sandy soil. McPhail writes,

> Our plants were collected in July on Beartooth (10,940 feet / 3340 meters) where they grew in the company of polemoniums, myosotis, mertensias, drabas, mat-forming lupines, etc., in meadows whose soil is not at all as expected; although it contains a lot of humus, it is also full of a great deal of fine clay, so that when rubbed through the fingers it has a slippery feel. The root systems are quite compact and easily collected with a good ball of wet earth. There is little about the plant or its association to suggest it can be so ornery in captivity. Plants were put into pots of one of four composts on our arrival home: (1) their native soil alone; (2) this with equal portion of granite chip; (3) our normal scree mix, equal parts loam, leafmold and course sand with three parts granite chips; and (4) a tufa mix, like the last but with tufa passed through a quarter-inch screen for the granite. All pots were top-dressed with granite or tufa tucked well under the collars and were plunged into the sand on the alpine house staging in its sunniest part; what moisture they received was absorbed through the pots; some were double-potted with space between pots filled with sand.

By the middle of our wet and clammy October, just as we were beginning to gloat over our success, the casualties began. By spring half were dead and only two were strong enough to flower, both beautifully, both in tufa mix. As the local bees took no interest, they were hand-pollinated and one set seed. By the following spring the plants had diminished to those same two; once a plant starts sliding downhill, it deteriorates quickly in spite of anything to be done. By the following summer they were reduced to a lone one, having been unfortunately left on the ledge of the alpine house where they got rained on, and that one looks as if it would never forgive such absent-mindedness.

Bob Putnam had a similar experience. Plants from the Little Belt Mountains, treated the same as those of *Eritrichium howardii* in the same cold house, came to flowering and set some seed but passed away in summer. Thurman thinks they are naturally short-lived; he observes, "Many dead plants were to be seen in the wild among the living and this was also true with *E. howardii*, though not to such extent."

Plants of my own collecting, *Eritrichium howardii* from western Pondera County, Montana, and *E. nanum* from Old Baldy's lower reaches in the Little Belt Range, were treated experimentally in several ways similar to those described; those surviving to flower were put out into the north-facing scree in a garden in arid eastern Washington, with a climate similar to that of Thurman's, but an unusual summer of heavy rains finished them off. None planted in my garden near Seattle have survived the wetness of winter, even against a rock and with a glass shelter overhead.

Scamman (1940) wrote of this plant (in the form he called *Eritrichium aretioides*) in Alaska that it was "a charming little fuzzy plant of high mountains, with a rosette of hairy leaves covering the base . . . flowers in a capitate head, blue with a yellow eye and very fragrant." (No one else has reported fragrance.) Ruth Nelson (1953) wrote, "One of the most charming of the high alpine cushion plants; anyone who sees its patches of brilliant blue among the gray rocks of those bleak heights will never forget the thrill caused by their beauty."

Eritrichium nanum in its many forms is confined to the arctic-alpine life zone and, in the New World, from Alaska's mountains to the Yukon and down the ridges of the Rocky Mountains as far as central Colorado. It also occurs, as do many other Rocky Mountain elements, in the Wallowa Mountains of northeastern Oregon, many miles disjunct. The soils in places where these plants are found are highly mineral-derived, in many instances showing only the slightest traces of organic material. This would indicate that nitrogen is not essential to the success of this species and might even be poison. Although the roots do not penetrate deeply, such soils at such altitudes probably do not heat up in summer, and the dew is probably also a contributing factor, although it is probably absent where

E. howardii is found. It is therefore essential to keep *E. nanum* in a state of aestivation through the heat and drought of summer, without the cooling effect of water. It would be well to give shelter and coolness to the root-run by burying a sizable, porous, mossy rock on the sunny side of the plant. In the wild, plants are under snow for 8 to 10 months annually.

"I would advise a north exposure with a crevice for protection from winter rain, but *Eritrichium howardii* will appreciate a full exposure," writes Thurman. He adds, "A very limy soil is necessary for it, with at least partial drying in summer, and perfect underdrainage."

"Drainage is what was lacking with those lost here," Putnam writes, adding, "Another time I would replant in a more loose soil."

The many molds and mildews so prevalent in gardens are not bothersome at alpine altitudes. MacPhail writes,

> It is my understanding the main cultural difficulty is due to a fungus attacking the collar of the plant just above the soil level; plants examined after demise were found to have the roots still in good condition right up to the collar, which had turned soft and pulpy. For this reason it is necessary to keep the collar as dry as is possible, and they should never be watered from overhead.

Although *Eritrichium howardii* is usually found forming exclusive colonies, it does occur with such things as douglasias, drabas, and smelowskias. "It is a little puzzling trying to understand their associations in the wild," says Margaret Williams. "Why is *Douglasia montana* easy for me to grow in the garden when I cannot keep the eritrichium? The drabas have seeded and the smelowskias have become almost a pest!" *Eritrichium nanum* is very choosy about its companions, but not so much so as to disdain association with *Aquilegia jonesii* or *Synthyris pinnatifida*—on limestone with the former and on granite with the latter. These communities are seen on Hollowtop in the Tobacco-Root (Pony) Mountains, where the great summit ridges are acres of choice alpines in scree conditions, including such plants as *Arenaria sajanensis, Eriogonum ovalifolium, Penstemon procerus* (a miniature development), *Silene acaulis, Douglasia montana, Phlox hoodii* and *P. muscoides, Androsace lehmanniana,* and *Collomia debilis,* with smelowskia also, as well as dollar-size drabas and the four-bit ones, too.

Eritrichium from Seed

Henry Correvon (1939) advised growing seedlings in a flat of slates arranged to form crevices, on which the seed was planted in granite sand, peat, and slate-dust in the 0.25 inch/6 mm crevices; the flat was put out in the snow until spring, or some other arrangement made to allow alternate freezing and thawing.

Lawrence Hills (1950) advised a method similar to that used by MacPhail, who planted the seed on tufa submerged in a loose soil: "They germinated well but damped off shortly. As Hills advises setting the seedpot right out on the open ground for better ventilation and protection from overhead moisture by a glass supported with a wire framework, I'd follow this advice next time," MacPhail advises.

Thurman planted in his sandy scree soil and added ground agricultural limestone at the rate of 100 pounds to a cubic yard / meter, and left them out in the rigors of winter until the driving winds of spring, when they were sheltered in the alpine house. In summer they went into the lath house (this area normally has a prolonged summer drought).

> The *nanum* sorts will not take full sun at this elevation, but *Eritrichium howardii* seems to want it, along with dryness. They must have a high lime content to the soil and by my tests, a pH of around 8.0, and would best have a glass cover in winter, I am sure. I find a plant the size of a quarter can be grown in a single year with bloom the second year; the third year they are as large as any plant seen in the wild, and with me their demise comes in the third and fourth year. I did have one plant through four years, though not under ideal conditions. Anyone keeping a plant over four years should have a gold star!

He does not think longevity is inherent and considers 5 to 10 years in the wild to be their normal span.

Conclusion

If anything new is to be learned from the opinions and observations of those who have gone to the remote places where these tiny blue alpine forget-me-nots are found, it is probably that they can be grown, though with exacting care and patience; and that is not new! Correvon's description of his success in sphagnum beds (Farrer's "moraine") should be an inspiration. Certainly the plants should be grown in a place filled with light, though not heat, and well ventilated, whether in the open garden or under cover. The Correvon flat of vertical slates, converted to a trough garden, might prove the medium in which success will come.

It is not going to be easy to duplicate their ecological needs in the garden; what we must do through experimentation is discover under what conditions they will succeed, if any, and through a succession of seedling generations attempt natural selection of a strain more amenable to cultivation. Certainly the effect of too much water is one cause of early death. Some thoughts on the "critical factors of the quality and temperature of the snow water combined with the quality and effect of the sun's rays at great altitudes" have been heard from Bulley (in Royal Horticultural Society 1936), who deplored that "difficulty with such plants seems to be permanent."

Bibliography

Barr, Claude A. 1968. "Low Altitude Eritrichium." *Bulletin of the American Rock Garden Society* 26.2.

Correvon, Henry. 1939. *Rock Garden and Alpine Plants*. New York: Macmillan.

Farrer, Reginald. 1930. *The English Rock Garden*. 2d ed. Jack.

Hills, Lawrence D. 1950. *The Propagation of Alpines*. London: Faber & Faber.

Hitchcock, C. Leo, Arthur Cronquist, Marion Ownbey, and J. W. Thompson. 1955–1969. *Vascular Plants of the Pacific Northwest*. 5 vols. Seattle: University of Washington Press.

Nelson, Ruth A. 1953. *Plants of Rocky Mountain National Park*. Washington, D.C.: Government Printing Office.

Polunin, Nicholas. 1959. *Circumpolar Arctic Flora*. Oxford: Oxford University Press.

Royal Horticultural Society. 1936. *Rock Gardens and Rock Plants*. London: Royal Horticultural Society, Rock Garden Conference Report of 1936.

Scamman, E. A. 1940. "A List of Plants from Interior Alaska." *Rhodora* 42, 309–349.

Vasak, Ing. Vladimir. 1968. "Plant Hunting in Mongholia." *Bulletin of the American Rock Garden Society* 26.2.

Wight, William. 1902. "Eritrichium in North America." *Bulletin of the Torrey Botanical Club*.

PLATE 60. *Echinocereus triglochidiatus* (Josef Halda)

PLATE 61. *Primula parryi*
(Loraine Yeatts)

PLATE 62. *Haplopappus (Stenotis) acaulis*
(Margaret Mulligan)

PLATE 63. *Lepidium nanum* (David Hale)

PLATE 64. *Kelseya uniflora*
(Margaret Mulligan)

PLATE 64. *Kelseya uniflora*
(Margaret Mulligan)

PLATE 65. *Phlox hoodii*
(Shan Cunningham)

PLATE 66. *Physaria newberryi* (Panayoti Kelaidis)

PLATE 67. *Townsendia incana* (Shan Cunningham)

PLATE 68. *Townsendia glabella* (Panayoti Kelaidis)

PLATE 69. *Claytonia lanceolata* (Jay Lunn)

PLATE 70. *Hymenoxys (Rydbergia) grandiflora* (Jay Lunn)

PLATE 71. *Astragalus spatulatus* (Panayoti Kelaidis)

PLATE 72. *Physaria vitulifera*
(Loraine Yeatts)

PLATE 73. *Aquilegia jonesii* (Jerry De Santo)

PLATE 74. *Oxytropis sericea* (Claude Barr, NARGS Archives)

PLATE 75. *Coryphantha vivipara* (Josef Halda)

PLATE 76. *Physaria bellii*
(Bill Whelan)

PLATE 77. *Physaria alpina*
(Panayoti Kelaidis)

PLATE 78. *Penstemon eriantherus*
(Panayoti Kelaidis)

PLATE 79. *Phlox mesoleuca*
(Ted Kipping)

PLATE 80. *Phlox purpurea* (T. Paul Maslin)

PLATE 81. *Primula nevadensis* (Loraine Yeatts)

PLATE 82. *Primula angustifolia* (Loraine Yeatts)

PLATE 83. *Primula cusickiana* (Jay Lunn)

PLATE 84. *Dodecatheon pulchellum* (James Locklear)

TE 85. *Erigeron ochroleucus* (James Locklear) PLATE 86. *Arctostaphylos alpina* (Dick Redfield)

PLATE 87. *Phyllodoce coerulea*
(Todd Boland)

PLATE 88. *Sarracenia purpurea*
(Lawrence Mellichamp)

PLATE 89. *Helonias bullata*
(Lawrence Mellichamp)

PLATE 90. *Pogonia ophioglossoides*
(Frederick Case, Jr.)

PLATE 91. *Xerophyllum asphodeloides*
(Rick Darke)

PLATE 92. *Platanthera blephariglottis*
(Rick Darke)

PLATE 93. *Narthecium americanum* (Rick Darke)

PLATE 94. *Hudsonia ericoides* (Rick Darke)

PLATE 95. *Epigaea repens* (Lawrence Mellichamp)

PLATE 96. *Iris verna* (Lawrence Mellichamp)

PLATE 97. *Shortia galacifolia*
(Phil Pearson)

PLATE 98. *Iris cristata* 'Alba'
(Lawrence Mellichamp)

PLATE 99. *Trillium erectum* (Frederick Case, Jr.)

PLATE 100. *Trillium grandiflorum* (Frederick Case, Jr.)

PLATE 101. *Pulsatilla patens* (Shan Cunningham)

PLATE 102. *Phlox multiflora* (Shan Cunningham)

PLATE 103. *Phlox caespitosa* (Panayoti Kelaidis)

PLATE 104. *Phlox pulvinata* (Panayoti Kelaidis)

PLATE 105. *Asplenium trichomanes* (NARGS Archives)

Physarias: April's Garden Gold

PANAYOTI KELAIDIS

Some plants endear themselves to you the first time you see them. I'll never forget my first close encounter with the golden suns of *Adonis amurensis* one blustery January day in Paul and Mary Maslin's garden, or the spidery starfish of *Asplenium trichomanes* on a tiny cliff near Ithaca, New York. I've managed to capture the epiphany experienced with many lovely plants by obtaining seed or cuttings and growing them in my garden to refresh myself year after year with their beauty.

Physarias (sometimes commonly known as "twinpods" or "bladderpods") have never burst dramatically onto my consciousness. These universal plants of the Rocky Mountains and intermountain West might have struck me if they had a slightly more glamorous passport—the Balkans or the Hindu Kush—or the decency to be rare. Instead, they light up screes and roadsides by the acre, gradually transforming their neat little rosettes with grapelike clusters of outlandishly swollen fruit.

One comes to appreciate physarias over the course of time. As I cultivated more and more species, I noticed that their rosettes are not nearly as uniform as they appear to those hiking quickly past them in the hills. Some are large and lax, while others have very congested, overlapping leaves. Some are powdery white, and others flannelly gray. The leaf margins can be smooth or deeply toothed and indented. Physarias bloom over a very long season, and their flower color varies from a deep egg-yolk yellow verging on orange, through various primrose shades to near-white. They can start blooming as early as February in some years, with one species extending well into May, and many species are known to re-bloom in the fall.

As often happens with rock gardeners, I have become possessed by the collecting bug that won't let me rest until I have obtained a full complement of the species of a given genus. When that genus occurs over a large range and is virtually unheard-of in seed catalogs or nurseries, the task is formidable. Fortunately, Colorado lies near the epicenter of the genus *Physaria*, and I have come across most of its species in my travels. In the following account, I discuss only species that I have grown or seen in habitat; there are several species and numerous varieties I have yet to know and grow.

Botanists distinguish species in this genus by characters of their seeds and microscopic hairs. However, there are many distinctive characteristics of leaves and flowers that can help the gardener tell one species from another.

The first that many of us encounter is *Physaria vitulifera* (Plate 72), the common species of the Colorado Front Range. It occurs in vast numbers from the base of the mountains near Denver up through the foothills to subalpine elevations near the Continental Divide. It can be found on virtually any steep, hot, south-facing slope among ponderosa pines and sparse grasses from 5000 to 9000 feet / 1500 to 2700 meters across the east face of the Rockies. This typically forms single rosettes with sinuous indentations on the leaves. The medium-sized clusters of pale yellow flowers appear in April on the plains and extend to the end of June at the highest elevations. Like all the other twinpods, its bladderlike seed capsules are as interesting as the flowers. In this species they are rounded and have a bluish cast.

The only other species that occurs near Denver is *Physaria bellii* (Plate 76), which differs to the eyes of rock gardeners in its rounder leaves, more profuse flowers, and showy fruits often stained with red and purple. It is restricted to the black shales and gray limestone of the Niobrara formation along the base of the Front Range from near Denver to the Wyoming border. Although it has been proposed for endangered species status, it has taken so enthusiastically to growing on roadcuts in its narrow range that one could argue that highway engineers have been its salvation.

The most widespread species, *Physaria didymocarpa*, occurs in a number of varieties throughout most of the northern intermountain region—Wyoming, Montana, and southern Canada. Any plant with this large a range is sure to display great variability. The only form I have grown comes from central Montana and is one of the showiest physarias. It forms a compact rosette barely 5 inches / 13 cm across, with only a few yellow flowers on each stem. These blooms can be more than 0.5 inch / 13 mm across, among the largest in the genus. The form I have grown is a beautiful pale lemon-yellow, softer in tone than any other species. Its northern and montane origin suggests a greater tolerance for garden conditions than is found in other physarias.

In the late 1900s a number of physarias have been described from the vast stretches of Wyoming's deserts. Possibly the showiest is *Physaria condensata*, which occurs on barren badlands in southwestern Wyoming. It forms compact rosettes with narrow, smooth-margined leaves that somehow suggest a miniature *Saxifraga longifolia*. The flowers are small but are produced with such abandon in early spring that they create a vibrant spot of color for more than a month. The gray-blue capsules are also smaller than in other species, although they form in great numbers. This has been a long-lived and fine addition to troughs and small rock gardens, although one must be careful to provide excellent drainage, since it is a desert plant in nature.

Closely allied to *Physaria condensata*, the slightly larger *P. saximontana* occurs a short distance to the north and east of it. It also has small, congested rosettes powdered with white but is a bit more lax, with larger, soft yellow flowers. The leaves also lack teeth, and the capsules are tinged with blue-purple. It often grows on reddish limestone, making a vivid contrast in foliage and bloom. It frequently grows with *Astragalus aretioides*, an aristocratic companion plant.

It is hard to believe that any plant as distinctive, showy, and abundant as *Physaria alpina* (Plate 77) could have been first described (by Reed Rollins) as late as 1981. This species is restricted to alpine screes in the Mosquito and Collegiate ranges of central Colorado. Here it forms neat, narrow-leaved rosettes from 3 to 5 inches / 8 to 13 cm across. The flowers are large for the genus and rich yellow, deepening to orange in some individuals. On Mount Bross it paints astonishing canvases of orange mingling with the deep purple of *Oxytropis podocarpa* under the ancient bristlecone pines. On Weston Pass it grows and blooms with *Eritrichium nanum*. Either combination would be the envy of any gardener.

Largely restricted to the steep pink limestone of the Wasatch formation in southwestern Utah and Nevada, *Physaria newberryi* (Plate 66) has highly variable foliage and the typical mid-yellow flowers of the genus. In this species, the seedpods assume star status. They are among the largest in the genus and develop a remarkable prismatic shape that suggests a cubist painting. These pods are stained a deep blue-purple when approaching maturity.

Physaria acutifolia (syn. *P. australis*) is an abundant species occurring over much of Utah, Wyoming, and Colorado. It forms a beautiful rosette, reminiscent of a rosulate succulent such as *Echeveria*. The rosette can be as much as 8 inches / 20 cm across and is completely obscured in early spring by vivid, lemon-yellow flowers. There are numerous varieties of this species delineated in Welsh's *Utah Flora*, including *Physaria acutifolia* var. *purpurea*, which is tantalizingly described as having "flowers yellow or purple externally."

Rather similar to the previous species, *Physaria chambersii* occurs to the south over the complicated terrain of Utah's and Nevada's canyonlands. There are several subspecies that vary in subtle characters of their

227

seeds and geographic distribution. Typically, *P. chambersii* has smooth, round rosettes and ascending stems with pale yellow flowers. This species finds abundant scree habitat in the steep canyon country where it occurs, although plants may sometimes be found in stable soils under pinyon pines.

The most distinctive foliage plant of the genus, *Physaria floribunda*, is restricted to higher elevations in western Colorado. Its leaves are deeply cut and incised, making an almost lacy pattern on the ground. The flowers and seedpods are not remarkable in themselves, but the evergreen rosettes with filigree margins are particularly attractive.

The very distinctive *Physaria eburniflora* is restricted to the Ferris Mountains of central Wyoming. Out of bloom it superficially resembles a number of other miniature species endemic to Wyoming, but its ivory-colored flowers distinguish it from any other. In cultivation, the rosettes can reach 4 inches / 10 cm in width on a rich scree, but in a trough it stays 2 or 3 inches / 5 to 8 cm across, blooming in March and early April.

This by no means exhausts the theme of physarias in the West. In the Black Hills of South Dakota and Wyoming one of the largest species occurs: *Physaria brassicoides* makes large, lax rosettes that are unique in the genus. I have yet to grow this one in the garden, but I have no doubt that it would be amenable and distinctive. *Physaria dornii* is also large, with slightly irregular rosettes and a very restricted range in nature. Perhaps the most intriguing prospect in the genus is another very local plant from central Idaho, *P. geyeri* var. *purpurea*. The name summons up images of a red-flowered physaria, but several accounts suggest that "purpurea" alludes rather to the sepals and backs of the petals. Nonetheless, the prospect of a purple physaria is simply too appealing to dismiss out of hand.

I have just obtained seed of *Physaria alpestris* from Washington. This is the most northwesterly species and a true alpine to boot. The most recently described species as of 1990, *P. obcordata*, was discovered in the Piceance Basin of northwestern Colorado. This is a strange plant indeed, blooming on semierect stems weeks after other species are already in seed. Who knows what strange permutations of color and foliage might still exist, unknown and ungrown, in the vast corrugations of the Colorado Plateau and Great Basin?

Western American alpines and steppe plants have attracted lively debate in the late 1900s. There is no question that most western Americans require as much sun, air circulation, rain protection, and drainage as possible in most gardens. Physarias are no exception. Few plants germinate more promptly or grow more quickly than these rosulate mustards. If they are given the quick drainage of scree, crevice, or trough, you can expect most to bloom the second year. If the spot is warm enough, plants can persist for several years. Self-sown seedlings seem to live even longer.

Many gardeners would probably be content with one or two varia-tions on the theme of physaria. For lovers of rosettes, this genus promises to be a fine new contribution to sunny scree and trough gardens. Al-though the foliage is almost always a powdery white, the genus runs the gamut of shape and outline possible within the rosette form. The starfish symmetry of physarias is never more attractive than during warm spells in winter, when they are as fresh and appealing as in the summer months.

Although an individual plant lives no more than 4 or 5 years, they are so easily raised from seed, even self-sowing when happy, that there is no excuse for neglecting this distinctive genus of North American rock plants.

Originally published in the Bulletin of the American Rock Garden Society, *vol. 48, no. 2, pp. 111–116 (1990).*

The Rediscovery of Phlox lutea and Phlox purpurea

T. PAUL MASLIN

In 1887 Cyrus Guernsey Pringle visited Mexico for the seventh time, with the intention of exploring the Sierra Madre west of Chihuahua. On 5 September he and his assistant left Cusihuiriachic, locally referred to simply as "Cusi," driving their wagon and team of mules westward up a steep and muddy canyon for about 2.5 miles/4 km to the high plain across which Highway 16 now runs from Cuauhtemoc to Guerrero. Where they emerged, the altitude registered 6700 feet/2000 meters. According to Pringle's account (Davis 1936:41), they proceeded out onto the plain for a short distance and collected a few species of plants, including *Phlox nana*, and then went on to Santiago. The next morning they passed Rosario and continued northwest to Guerrero, arriving there at noon. After spending two nights at Guerrero they moved south about 2 miles/3 km, camped for a few days, then apparently moved to higher ground to the west and set up a permanent camp, presumably among oaks and pines. It was here on 14 September that Pringle collected *P. nana* again.

Later, Brand (1907) named these forms in his monograph of the Polemoniaceae. He recognized three subspecies of *Phlox nana*: subspecies *eu-nana*, *ensifolia*, and *glabella*, with three varieties of subspecies *eu-nana* and two of subspecies *glabella*. The three varieties of *eu-nana* were *albo-rosea*, *lutea*, and *purpurea*, all names proposed by Brand in this monograph. Subsequently, Wherry (1944) recognized *P. nana* var. *eu-nana* forma *purpurea* as an intermediate form between *P. nana* and *P. mexicana*, but he discussed no others of this group. In 1955, however, Wherry considered varieties *lutea* and *purpurea* to be forms of *P. mesoleuca*, and variety *albo-rosea* to be a synonym of *P. nana*.

I discovered that a yellow phlox might exist while I was preparing an article (1978) on *Phlox nana*. Foster's comment (1970) that "yellow flowers have been reported in two of the three taxa (*mesoleuca, nana* and *triovulata*) and would constitute a completely new colour in the cultivated perennial phloxes, if they could be located and introduced" stirred me to think seriously of looking for variety *lutea*. At first I thought that Brand had proposed the name on the basis of a peculiarly yellow, faded specimen from an old herbarium sheet. At Kew, however, I saw a type sheet of variety *lutea* and was impressed with the depth of yellow in this specimen. It was not difficult to persuade my wife to join me in a search for the mythical yellow phlox so close to home. (The plants now known as *P. purpurea* and *P. mesoleuca* are illustrated in Plates 79 and 80.)

In September 1978 we started out toward the type locality 1000 miles/1600 km away, where the plants should be in bloom. We made our headquarters in Ciudad Cuauhtemoc, some 60 miles/96 km west of Ciudad Chihuahua, and began our search. The area is much as Pringle described it: very large open plains of rich alluvium surrounded and interrupted by low hills rising several hundred feet above the plains, lightly covered with scrubby oaks, junipers, and several species of small pines. The plains are now completely planted, primarily to cereals and corn. The steeper slopes are often used for apple orchards, and the remaining land is fenced and devoted to grazing. This intensive use leaves little land undisturbed. The rainfall of the region is of the monsoon type, beginning in late July or early August and increasing in intensity through September and October, then slowly decreasing over the next 2 months. Spring and early summer are hot and dry, with no verdure to speak of.

From my experience with *Phlox nana* and *P. mesoleuca* var. *ensifolia* from farther north, both members of Wherry's (1955) subsection Nanae, I began looking for phloxes in the hilly areas, which are quite reminiscent of the pinyon-juniper forests near Santa Fe, New Mexico. Despite heavy grazing, these areas were full of flowers, only a few of which I could recognize. *Milla biflora* was nearly as abundant as when Pringle (Davis 1936:46) collected 2500 bulbs in 12 hours in 1887. But there were no phloxes. After three fruitless days of searching around Cusi, Guerrero, and the hilly areas between, we were ready to retreat, defeated.

By now both my wife and I had contracted what in this area should be called Cuauhtemoc's revenge, and on the way out to a hilly area west of our headquarters we pulled off the road crossing the plain for a medicine break, 3 miles/5 km west of town (kilometer 107 on Highway 16, 7200 feet/2200 meters elevation). There in the borrow ditch was a patch of incredibly brilliant vermilion-red phlox. Each flower had a bright yellow eye surrounded by a star composed of short, dark red streaks, two to a petal. No stalk had more than three flowers open at a time, but a cluster of closely grouped plants gave an impression of abundance. In this patch of intense red a single yellow flower stood out conspicuously. Here was our yellow phlox! This single flower seemed a little larger than the reds and had quite a blush of red on the edges of some of the petals. This strongly suggested either that there were two species of phlox in the vicinity which hybridized here, or that these were two color phases of a single species intergrading at this site. Also present were two orange-colored flowers, rather old and insect-ravaged, which strengthened the idea that this patch represented a hybrid swarm.

There had been no rain at this spot for some time and the ground was hard to dig, but a fair number of plants were collected along with a very small number of mature seeds. We then looked for more stands, driving slowly west for 5 miles/8 km along the wagon tracks in the borrow ditch. We spotted one more very small patch of red phlox and two or three isolated specimens along the way. The following morning more specimens were dug and additional photographs made. A few more seed capsules were also found. We then returned home to Boulder, Colorado, with the intention of returning a month later to harvest more seed and to look for more yellow specimens.

My wife was unable to join me on the second trip, but fortunately my good friend and collecting colleague, Panayoti Kelaidis, was able to go. On 22 October we set off in a snowstorm to revisit the area. This time we went directly south of Cuauhtemoc to search the plains in the vicinity of the point where Pringle emerged from the canyon on his way up from Cusi. By now flowers were scarce and the grain nearly ripe. There had been some very heavy rains, and the ground was saturated. It had snowed or rained almost continuously since we had left Boulder, but the weather, now chilly, was clear.

As we inched our way south along a vile road, it struck us that we might ask some local resident if they knew where our flowers could be found. The first persons we stopped were a young man, Raul Romero, with his wife and child, driving a wagon and mule team in the same direction we were going. I handed him the color photos of the red and yellow phlox, which he examined at great length. He seemed puzzled by the red phlox but said he knew of a patch close by which might be the yellow one we wanted. Then he suggested we accompany him to a small village, Ejido Mimbres, about 0.6 mile/960 meters farther south, where he said an old woman interested in flowers might know more. We followed him and met the woman, a fine and gracious lady. She didn't recognize the flowers from our slides but went out to pick a red flower which might be it. The flower turned out to be a 4-inch/10-cm purplish mallow—new to me, but not a phlox. Raul agreed then and there to accompany us to the spot he knew.

The area half surrounded a small lake lying in the midst of wheat fields and was partially fenced. The area around the lake had been neither grazed nor plowed. As I walked along beside a fence I suddenly saw in a small rock outcrop a beautiful pure yellow phlox! This flower had no hint of red except for the vermilion star surrounding the yellow eye. We soon found more and realized there was considerable variation in the color of the streaks forming the star, the size of the flowers, and the shape of the petals. One plant had long, narrow petals and brownish streaks almost forming Vs around the eye. It also became apparent that this patch was very extensive, but only a few flowers were in bloom and most of these were damaged by insects and weather. Furthermore, most of the capsules had shed their seed, leaving the characteristic star-shaped calyx with its reflexed sepals staring apologetically up at us. After a long search we found only 27 capsules bearing seed on the thousands of plants we examined.

The ground here was loam-covered, with a large array of grasses and numerous flowering plants, including *Calochortus barbatus* and a small sisyrinchium in seed. Against small rock outcrops there were several ferns—*Bommeria hispida*, *Cheilanthes wrightii*, *Notholaena aurea*, and *Pellaea ternifolia*. The loam, rich and dark, was also rocky, especially near the lake. The phloxes seemed to be more luxuriant and vigorous when they were growing well above the shoreline of the lake mingled with the taller clumps of grasses; however, many plants were found more or less in the open, along with small plants of various species. The phloxes were not evenly distributed over this area of several acres but occurred in patches. These patches could be extremely dense, with several hundred shoots growing in an area of perhaps 1 square yard / meter.

Both the red and yellow varieties vary tremendously in size, apparently depending on moisture and soil compaction. Plants that look superficially like seedlings might be only 4 inches / 10 cm or less tall, while others interspersed with taller grasses and growing in loose, humus-rich soil could be over 10 inches / 25 cm.

We dug up sample plants here as well as at the red phlox site west of Cuauhtemoc. The root structure of the two forms is virtually identical. Below ground the stems of both forms are noded, fleshy, and brittle. They run more or less straight down. At almost any depth from 4 inches / 10 cm to about 10 inches / 25 cm, branches usually occurred. These emerged from the soil to form leafy stalks bearing flowers or traces of them. At deeper levels transverse rhizomes were frequently found. These were slender and brittle, making it difficult to follow them, but they appeared to run 4 to 6 inches / 10 to 15 cm toward other caudices (vertical rhizomes), which in turn would branch as they rose upward. Frequently, in wet soil, caudices developed a complicated tuft of roots 5 to 10 mm below the surface. These thin horizontal roots would run out 2 to 2.75 inches / 5 to 7 cm and are undoubtedly deciduous, shriveling during the dry season only to develop again with the onset of the rains.

The stems of both the yellow and red phlox are glandular-pubescent but not densely so. The glands are minute and the hairs less than .5 mm in length. The linear leaves are distinctly different from those of *Phlox mesoleuca*, to which presumably these phlox are closely related. The longest leaves of an average stem 10 to 12 inches / 25 to 30 cm tall are found at the third, fourth, and fifth internodes above the ground, and the distances between these nodes range from 13 to 16 mm. Above the fifth node the leaves, which are opposite, rapidly become shorter, as do the internodes, until the stem is virtually hidden by these almost imbricate leaves. The leaves themselves are thick and sturdy and show little tendency to arch away from the stem. They appear surprisingly slender; but the percentage of width to length in a few of the leaves measured in the yellow phlox is 5.4 percent, that of the red is 7.2 percent, and that of *P. mesoleuca* is 8.5 percent. The length of the leaves varies according to the size of the plant. The leaves at the third, fourth, and fifth nodes of two stalks of the red phlox, for instance, averaged 57 mm and 44 mm respectively, in contrast to the short leaves of a type specimen of *P. mesoleuca* which averaged only 27 mm in length. The leaves of the yellow phlox seem shorter than those of the red, but this may be more apparent than real. A distinctive feature of these leaves is that the upper surface is glabrous while the lower surface is densely glandular-pubescent.

The calyx of both the yellow and red phloxes is about seven-eighths the length of the corolla tube. The subulate sepals are fused for about half their length; the intersepalate membranes are smooth. The bases of the calyces are densely glandular-pubescent, but the tips are much less so. As the fruit matures, the tips of the sepals roll back to expose the plump, pointed capsules; after the capsules and seeds are shed, these outwardly curled sepals dry up and persist as a star-shaped structure for a long time.

The corolla tube is about 15 mm long but varies with the size of the flower. It is glandular-pubescent throughout its length, but far less so than the sepals. The petal blades are basically suborbiculate, but there is considerable variation in their shape. They are, however, never notched nor apiculate. The flowers are large: in some the limb measures as much as 32 mm across, but the scape is extremely variable in length, varying from a few millimeters to more than 40 mm.

The seed of these phloxes was difficult to collect in both September and October. Twelve capsules of the red phlox were harvested in September, but only four of these contained 10 in all—and three were shriveled or so small that it was unlikely that they would be fertile. In October two lots of seed were collected of the yellow phlox; 2 capsules contained a total of 19 small seeds, while 25 capsules collected over a large area contained 68 seeds. In this second lot the number of seeds per capsule averaged 2.7. More than half of the seeds were asymmetrical, as though two seeds had developed within a single locule, pressing against each other during growth so that a normally symmetrical seed became truncated. The symmetrical seeds look like three equal segments of a sphere, suggesting a single seed per locule with the typical tricarpelate phlox arrangement. The medial faces of each seed make up a dihedral angle with a short groove at the center of the crest of the angle. The outer face is curved, conforming to the elongate outer wall of the locules. Around the periphery of this face the seed coat is a thin, translucent phlange about 0.1 millimeter thick. Similar phlanges also occur wherever sharp angles exist in irregularly truncated seeds. The entire seed appears wrinkled. In 10 symmetrical seeds from yellow-flowered plants, the seed averaged 3.7 mm in length, 2.0 mm in width, and about .5 mm thick. Only 4 of the 10 seeds of the red-flowered plants were symmetrical; these averaged 3.3 mm in length and 1.9 mm in width.

Morphologically the red and yellow phloxes we found in the vicinity of Cuauhtemoc seem indistinguishable. What differences there are seem to be too variable to be diagnostic. The only real difference seems to be the color of the flowers.

Brand never saw the living plants of the forms he named, nor did any other botanist, so far as I am aware, until 27 July 1977, when Robert Bye, an ethnobotanist from the Department of Biology at the University of Colorado, noted four specimens of *Phlox purpurea* along Highway 16 at about kilometer 122, on a north-facing hillside forested with oaks and pines. He also noted similar phloxes south of La Junta where the plains give way to a cut-over pine forest area. These sites are similar to the one about 10 miles/16 km southwest of Guerrero near Tonachie where Pringle found the phlox Brand later called *P. purpurea*. Bye's notes, on University of Colorado Herbarium sheet no. 310040, state that the flowers were red-pink. Bye's site is some 45 miles/70 km southeast of the type locality, but the plants undoubtedly represent the same taxon. The Pringle Herbarium at the University of Vermont kindly loaned me their type sheet of *P. nana* (Pringle no. 1334), the form Brand later called *P. eunana purpurea*. The larger of the two plants on the sheet is huge, with some leaves measuring as much as 3.5 inches/9 cm in length, the internodes near the tips of the flower shoots much longer, clearly visible and not ensheathed by the leaves. Basically, however, the plant is very similar to those collected by Bye. Bye's specimens also are virtually identical, except in color, to the forms we found.

The yellow phlox was not found again until we rediscovered it on 25 October 1978. It now appears that the red phloxes occurring at the site 3 miles/5 km west of Cuauhtemoc must represent hybrids, as does the yellow phlox, red-tinted on the petal tips, found at the same locality. In this swarm we also found two flowers of an orange color. The question arises as to how to treat these forms from a nomenclatural point of view.

While they are clearly Protophloxes (Section A of Wherry), and members of Subsection 3, Nanae, they are distinctly different from all other members of the group. I believe a reasonable procedure would be to retain Brand's names but to raise their status from variety to species.

For the moment Wherry's key (1955:31) can be modified to read as follows:

A. Duration annual; pubescence coarse, glandless; sepal-blade broad, somewhat exceeding the corolla tube; leaves opposite and oblanceolate below, passing to alternate and elliptic above. 3:5 *Phlox roemeriana.*

A'. Duration perennial; pubescence fine; sepal-blade narrow, shorter than or subequal to the corolla tube: B, B',.

B. Total style-length 6 to 8 mm; nodes numerous, with subopposite linear leaves; calyx-membranes subcarinate; corolla tube glabrous. 3:4 *Phlox mexicana.*

B'. Total style-length (1.5) 2 to 3 (4) mm: C, C'.

C. Pubescence glandless (or nearly so); calyx-membranes subcarinate; corolla tube glabrous. 3:3 *Phlox triovulata.*

C'. Pubescence glandular, at least on the inflorescence; calyx-membranes flat or wrinkly: D, D'.

D. Nodes few, not conspicuously crowded toward the tips of the shoots; corolla tube pubescent or glabrous; leaves widely spreading or recurved, linear, short (less than 35 mm long); root system rhizomatous, fairly shallowly disposed (10 or 15 mm deep): E, E'.

D'. Nodes numerous, crowded towards the tip of the shoots; corolla tube glandular pubescent, leaves linear, nearly straight, not recurving: F, F'.

E. Corolla tube pubescent. *Phlox mesoleuca mesoleuca.*

E'. Corolla tube glabrous. *Phlox mesoleuca ensifolia.*

F. Roots consisting of true roots, that is without nodes, upper leaves and stems heavily glandular pubescent both above and below, sticky, most upper leaves alternate. Corolla tube twice as long as sepals. *Phlox nana.*

F'. Roots rhizomatous, leaves and stems moderately to slightly glandular-pubescent, no pubescence on upper surface of leaves, only extreme upper leaves alternate, corolla tube as long as or lightly longer than sepals: G, G'.

G. Roots rhizomatous, relatively shallow (100–150 mm deep) flowers red-pink; eye pink or pinkish-white: *Phlox purpurea* (Brand) Maslin, based upon *P. nana* var. *purpurea* Brand, in *Pflanz.* 4:250:76. 1907, *comb. nov. Phlox lutea* (Brand) Maslin, based upon *P. nana* var. *lutea* Brand, in *Pflanz.* 4:250:76. 1907, *comb. nov.* (A close examination of the dry specimens collected by Bye shows that the eye is pale and shows no evidence of the strong yellow pigment found in *P. lutea* or the red hybrids collected west of Cuauhtemoc.)

G'. Roots vertically rhizomatous with deeply located transverse rhizomes, flower color yellow, eye yellow. *Phlox lutea*

Acknowledgments

I wish to acknowledge the assistance given me by my wife who helped drive and collect on my first expedition; Dr. William A. Weber, who permitted me access to the University of Colorado Herbarium and library; Panayoti Kelaidis, who attended me on the second expedition and worked indefatigably, collecting and driving under the most difficult conditions; and Dr. Robert Bye, who provided me with information regarding the morphology and ecology of *Phlox purpurea*.

Bibliography

Brand, A. 1907. In A. Engler, *Das Pflanzenreich, Polemoniaceae*, vol. 4, no. 250, pp. 76–77.

Davis, H. B. 1936. *The Life and Work of Cyrus Guernsey Pringle*. Burlington: University of Vermont Press.

Foster, H. Lincoln. 1970. "The Genus *Phlox*." *Quarterly Bulletin of the Alpine Garden Society* 38, 66–90.

Maslin, T. Paul. 1978. "*Phlox nana* Nuttall." *Quarterly Bulletin of the Alpine Garden Society* 46, 163–167.

Wherry, Edgar T. 1944. "New Phloxes from the Rocky Mountains and Neighboring Regions." Academy of Natural Sciences, Philadelphia. *Natulae Naturae* 146, 1–11.

Wherry, Edgar T. 1955. *The Genus Phlox*. University of Pennsylvania, Morris Arboretum monograph 3. Philadelphia: Associates of the Morris Arboretum.

Originally published in the Bulletin of the American Rock Garden Society, *vol. 37, no. 2, pp. 62–69 (1979).*

Native Primulas of
Western America

JAY G. LUNN

There are 14 recognized primula species found in the contiguous United States between the Rocky Mountains and the Pacific Ocean. Although they present wonderful displays in the wild, few are well known to gardeners. This unfamiliarity can be attributed largely to two factors: they are not commonly available from nurseries in the form of seed or plant material; and many are difficult to satisfy in cultivation.

All members of the section Parryi of the genus are found exclusively in western North America. This section is comprised of the species *Primula angustifolia, P. capillaris, P. cusickiana, P. domensis, P. ellisiae, P. maguirei, P. nevadensis, P. parryi,* and *P. rusbyi.*

Primula parryi (Plate 61) is the largest primula of this region, although individual plants vary considerably in size. This species was first collected by C. C. Parry in Colorado and described by Asa Gray as a new species in 1862. It is the most widely distributed primula of this area, occurring from Montana, eastern Idaho, Wyoming, eastern Nevada, Utah, and Colorado to northern Arizona and New Mexico. Although it has an offensive odor, it was once considered the most magnificent of the American species; with subsequent discoveries of other members of this section, it has lost some prestige. *Primula parryi* is a plant of alpine and subalpine meadows, talus slopes, streambanks, and lake margins at elevations from 8500 to 13,000 feet/2600 to 4000 meters. The scape of larger plants, which may reach a height of almost 2 feet/60 cm, bears an umbel of 3 to 20 reddish-purple flowers with yellow centers surrounded by a dark halo. The leaves are spatulate to oblanceolate, 4 to 20 inches/10 to

50 cm in length, and roughly one-sixth as wide. When I saw this plant in Great Basin National Park in eastern Nevada, its brilliant rose color initially made me think it was *Mimulus lewisii*, but upon approaching it I realized it was a primula. It was growing along both sides of a small stream that cascaded over limestone rock. Although *Primula parryi* can easily be grown from seed, it does not seem to be as floriferous in cultivation as in its native habitat; in addition, it is not long-lived in cultivation, and the flower buds are caviar for slugs.

Primula cusickiana, *P. domensis*, *P. maguirei*, and *P. nevadensis* belong to what has been referred to as the *P. cusickiana* complex. All are quite small and somewhat similar in form, stature, and flower. *Primula cusickiana* (Plate 83), the namesake of the group and the only primula native to Oregon, is distributed from the Wallowa Mountains of eastern Oregon to the high plateau region of central Idaho. Asa Gray published a description of it under a varietal name in 1886 from a collection made by William C. Cusick in Union County, Oregon, in 1881. In the western portion of its range, it grows at elevations of 4000 to 6000 feet/1200 to 1800 meters on south-facing, subalpine rocky slopes that are moist in the spring but become very dry in the summer. I have seen it in bloom with water from melting snow running past the base of the plants and an *Allium* species as its companion, but this is not its typical habitat. Farther east into Idaho, this species assumes a more diminutive form and grows among sagebrush (*Artemisia* spp.) near 5000 feet/1500 meters, and in the alpine zone at approximately 10,000 feet/3100 meters. The soil at these sites is slightly to moderately acid. *Primula cusickiana* proudly displays an umbel of one to four bluish-violet to purple flowers, darkening toward a yellow, star-shaped eye. The flowers are held above rather thick, fleshy, oblong to oblanceolate or spatulate leaves 1 to 2.5 inches/2.5 to 6 cm in length, with margins entire to denticulate. It rarely reaches a height of more than 4 inches/10 cm. Rae Selling Berry, a world-renowned Portland, Oregon, gardener and plantsperson, claimed to have smelled the fragrance of "Cookie," as she called it, before she saw the plants. I consider it to have a slight violet-like fragrance, but I would never depend on my sense of smell to find this somewhat elusive plant. Few people see it at its best in its native habitat, because it blooms in late March to early May in much of its range, when access to the mountains can be difficult. Even fewer could find *P. cusickiana* after it is dormant. There have been published reports of the successful cultivation of this difficult plant. These successes were undoubtedly wild-collected plants that bloomed sparingly the first season after collection, then steadily declined in vigor each succeeding year, until they finally failed to reappear from dormancy. Seeds from this species germinate poorly, and seedlings tend not to survive to maturity.

Primula maguirei is endemic to one purportedly rattlesnake-infested canyon of the Wasatch Mountains in northern Utah. It grows on ledges and in crevices of limestone boulders on the steep, north-facing walls.

The lowest-elevation plants are found scarcely 100 feet/30 meters above the nearby valley floor; the species occurs from 4500 to 5500 feet/1400 to 1700 meters. From a specimen collected by Celia K. Maguire and Bassett Maguire in 1932, Louis O. Williams published a diagnosis for this species in 1936. *Primula maguirei* is similar to *P. cusickiana*, except that its umbels have no more than three flowers, and the corolla is rose to lavender, with a dark ring surrounding a yellow eye. The corolla tube is twice as long as the calyx, whereas it is nearly as long as the calyx in *P. cusickiana*. With its pedicel, calyx, and corolla tube dusted with a white farina, *P. maguirei* must be considered one of the most beautiful of our native primulas. One can only wonder how the roots penetrate the crevices of the steep, rocky slopes to which the plants cling. How did the plants manage to become established there in the first place?

In the Grant and Snake ranges of east-central Nevada, *Primula nevadensis* (Plate 81) grows in limestone outcrops and nearby gravel slopes at elevations between 11,000 and 11,600 feet/3400 and 3500 meters. This plant was first described by Noel H. Holmgren in 1967. Although he, James L. Reveal, and Charles LaFrance collected the holotype for this species, Rogers McVaugh had made an earlier collection in the summer of 1945. The scape is usually overtopped by erect, oblanceolate to linear-oblanceolate leaves 1 to 4 inches/2.5 to 10 cm in length, with coarsely toothed margins. The umbels commonly contain two or three flowers, and the corolla is purple in bud and violet in full bloom, with a dark purple ring around a yellow throat. It normally blooms from the latter part of June to mid-July.

An undescribed primula was collected in the House Range of western Utah in 1981. Although it was similar to *Primula nevadensis*, which occurs 50 miles/80 km to the west in Nevada, it was given species status by Ronald J. Kass and Stanley L. Welsh in 1985. This House Range endemic was named *P. domensis*, the epithet being taken from the word "house"— *domus* in Latin. The species differs from *P. nevadensis* in that the inflorescence overtops the foliage, and the leaves are spatulate to oblanceolate. It produces umbels with up to five flowers. The corolla is purple in bud, rose to lavender when open. It is a plant primarily of the subalpine zone, growing among limestone rocks and under trees on east-facing slopes at elevations of 8200 to 9000 feet/2500 to 2700 meters. The plants grow next to rocks, logs, or trees, where they gain some relief from the hot summer sun. They bloom from the middle of May to early June.

Although an unnamed species had been collected in the Ruby Mountains of northeastern Nevada as early as 1942, no account of it had been published until Margaret Williams described it in her presentation to the Fourth International Rock Garden Conference in 1971. The report of this conference was the first published use of the tentative name *Primula capillaris*, which was adopted by Noel H. Holmgren and Arthur H. Holmgren when they published their diagnosis in 1974 for this, the smallest primula in the region. It is endemic to a very small area in the alpine zone of one canyon in the Ruby Mountains at an elevation of 10,000 feet/3100 meters. It blooms in July, bearing one or rarely two flowers on a leafless flower stalk less than 2 inches/5 cm in length. Its corolla is bluish-purple, aging to violet, with a yellow eye. The leaves are linear, or somewhat wider, 0.5 to 1.5 inches/13 to 40 mm in length. It grows on a gentle north-facing slope in slightly acid, humusy soil containing pieces of small to moderate-sized granite. Although some plants are growing in an area where there is little competition from other plants, many will be overtopped by their companions shortly after they bloom. When I visited its little corner of the world, I was amazed to find *P. capillaris* growing beside *Lewisia nevadensis* and *Marchantia polymorphea* (liverwort). One must get close and use reading glasses to enjoy this little charmer.

Farther to the east is the related *Primula angustifolia* (Plate 82) of rocky slopes and meadows in the Rocky Mountains of Colorado and northern New Mexico. This species is confined mostly to elevations from 10,000 to 14,000 feet/3100 to 4300 meters, where it blooms from late June through July. It was described by John Torrey in 1823 from a collection made in 1820 by Edwin James, the first botanist in Colorado. It was the first species of the section Parryi to be described. Although its leaves are almost twice as large as those of *P. capillaris*, it is nevertheless a dwarf plant. They usually bear only one flower on each scape, but plants with multiple crowns produce several 1- to 1.5-inch/25- to 40-mm wide, funnel-shaped flowers held just above the leaves. The corolla is bright rose-pink to purple-pink, with a yellow eye surrounded by a white ring. Plants can be grown from seed, which occasionally appears on seed lists.

The remaining members of the section Parryi are *Primula rusbyi* and *P. ellisiae*, two very similar species. They can be distinguished by the size of the calyx and the length of the corolla tube, the shape and margin of the leaves, the color of the corolla, and the time of blooming. I have grown seed obtained under both names, but the resulting plants all appear to be *P. ellisiae*. Most of my seedlings have been planted under the eaves of the northeast side of the house west of Portland, Oregon. There they receive morning sun and irrigation in summer, but little rain reaches them when they are dormant in winter. They have grown in that site for several years, blooming profusely and developing multiple crowns.

Henry H. Rusby is credited with the discovery of *Primula rusbyi*, which he collected in August 1881 from the Mogollon Mountains of New Mexico. Edward L. Greene published a description of it in November 1881 and honored Rusby by naming it after him. A slightly earlier collection may have been made by Cyrus G. Pringle in the Santa Rita Mountains of Arizona of a plant now considered to be this species. It was described by John K. Small in 1898 as *P. serra*. Included in Greene's description was the following comment:

Since the discovery of Primula Parryi of the Colorado Mountains that superb species has held an unquestioned title to the first rank, in point of beauty, among American species of this elegant genus. In P. Rusbyi it has a formidable rival.

Primula rusbyi occurs in the mountains of southwestern New Mexico and southeastern Arizona, growing on shaded hillsides, damp cliff ledges, and in moist rock crevices at elevations of 8000 to 11,000 feet/ 2400 to 3400 meters. It has been found as far south as the state of Zacatecas in central Mexico and has been reported even farther south, in Guatemala. Surprisingly, it appears to be quite hardy. *Primula rusbyi* has thin, oblanceolate to spatulate, 2- to 6-inch/5- to 15-cm leaves with denticulate margins. Its scape reaches about 8 inches/20 cm in height. The umbel has four to ten rose-red, magenta, or purple flowers with a yellow eye surrounded by a crimson ring.

Primula ellisiae was described by Charles L. Pollard and Theodore D. A. Cockerell as a distinct species in 1902. The name commemorates a Miss C. Ellis, who collected the plant about 1901 in the Sandia Mountains of New Mexico. Its distribution is limited to central and south-central New Mexico, where it grows at sites and elevations similar to those of *P. rusbyi*. It is a somewhat larger plant, with more upright leaves. The flowers are rose-violet to rose-magenta, darkening toward a yellow eye. The larger calyx of *P. ellisiae* is almost as long as the corolla tube, while the smaller calyx of *P. rusbyi* is much shorter than the corolla tube. The plants in my Pacific Northwest garden have survived without artificial protection or snow cover during prolonged periods when daytime temperatures remained below freezing and dipped as low as 6°F/−14°C at night.

There are three members of the section Aleuritia, subsection Aleuritia in the region—*Primula alcalina, P. incana*, and *P. specuicola*. This section was once known as the section Farinosa, a name descriptive of the farina or meal coating various surfaces in many of the species. *Primula incana* was given specific status in 1895 when Marcus E. Jones published a description of this plant, formerly considered a variety of *P. farinosa*, based on material he had collected in Utah. Although this species is distributed as far north as Alaska, where it may grow close to sea level, it also occurs in Montana, Wyoming, North Dakota, Utah, and Colorado, where it grows along streambanks, in wet meadows, and in calcareous bogs at 6000 to 9000 feet/1800 to 2700 meters. Plants have a rosette of leaves 1 to 3 inches/2.5 to 8 cm long, oblanceolate to spatulate, the lower surface of which is covered with white meal. Out of the rosette rises a 4- to 14-inch/ 10- to 35-cm flower stalk holding an umbel of 2 to 15 lilac flowers that fade toward the center and have a yellow eye. The meal, or farina, is also present on the flower stalk and the flower clusters. If the form of this plant appeals to you, it can be grown from seed, but it is not often available.

Primula alcalina was described by Anita F. Cholewa and Douglass M. Henderson in 1984 from collections made in east-central Idaho. Its distribution is limited to that area; it was formerly found also in southwestern Montana, but that population has apparently been destroyed by highway construction. The plants at these sites were once considered to be *P. incana*, which they closely resemble. *Primula alcalina* is distinguished from the latter by its smaller flowers, white instead of lilac. It also has a much lower chromosome number. It grows in moist, highly alkaline soils at 6000 to 7000 feet/1800 to 2100 meters.

The type material of *Primula specuicola*, which was described by Per A. Rydberg in 1913, was collected by him in 1911 near the community of Bluff in southeastern Utah. Alice Eastwood made collections of this species in the same locality in 1895, but she considered it to be *P. farinosa*. It is an endemic of the canyons of the Colorado River in southeastern Utah and northern Arizona at 3700 to 5500 feet/1100 to 1700 meters. It blooms in April and early May. One reference indicates that the specific name for this plant means "watchtower dweller." It grows on moist sandstone cliffs and alcoves, near streams, and under bluffs in loose soil consisting mostly of disintegrating sandstone. Some of these plants cling to strata lines in the sandstone cliffs, where there is almost no humus to provide nourishment, except for that carried by water trickling from above. The plants are 3 to 11 inches/8 to 28 cm tall, with 1- to 8-inch/2.5- to 20-cm long, spatulate to oblanceolate leaves, with margins crenate-serrate and crinkled. The leaves have white meal on the lower surface. The umbels consist of 5 to 40 flowers. In a single population the flower color may be lavender to rose, pink, or white with a yellow eye. The flower stalks and tan, papery leaves of the prior season's growth persist during the growing season, and the meal is conspicuous on the dried leaves. This species has been cultivated at the Denver Botanic Garden, but a source of seed may be difficult to find.

Primula egaliksensis, of the section Armerina, is the only member of this section in the region. Morten Wormskjöld described it in 1816. Although its main distribution is farther to the north, there are two disjunct locations in the contiguous states, one in Wyoming and another in Colorado. Like *P. incana*, it grows near sea level farther north, but in the southernmost part of its range it occurs at 6500 to 8000 feet/2000 to 2400 meters in wet meadows and along streambanks. This slender efarinose (devoid of farina) plant is 1.5 to 5 inches/4 to 13 cm tall; it has elliptical leaves from 0.75 to 2 inches/2 to 5 cm in length and umbels of one to three relatively small, usually white flowers with yellow centers. Its flowers do not exhibit the pin-eye/thrum-eye dimorphism of the style and anther that is so common in members of the genus *Primula*. This plant will never be the belle of the garden but might make an attractive trough plant.

The most unusual primula in the region is *Primula suffrutescens* of the section Cuneifolia. It is the only primula found in California, and its range is entirely within that state. It occurs primarily in the Sierra Nevada in the east-central part of the state, from as far south as Mount Whitney to near Lake Tahoe in the north. It is also found farther to the northwest in the Trinity Alps. This plant is scattered through its range at elevations of 8000 to 13,000 feet/2400 to 4000 meters, where it grows in rocky ground and beds of disintegrating granite near or above timberline. Asa Gray described it in 1868 from specimens, some of which were collected by William H. Brewer between 1860 and 1862; however, this primula may have been discovered by other collectors as early as 1856. It grows long, branching, rhizomatous stems that bear leaf rosettes near the tips. The leaves are thick and fleshy, cuneate to spatulate, with the upper half of the blade being crenate-dentate or serrate. The 1- to 4-inch/ 2.5- to 10-cm scape is crowned by an umbel of two to seven large rose-pink to red flowers with a yellow eye. Although it can be grown from seed, it can easily be propagated from cuttings taken in late July and placed in sharp sand. This plant is best grown in a pot and protected from excess moisture in areas that experience winter rains. In cultivation it flowers sparingly over an extended period, never producing the magnificent flush of bloom that it exhibits in the wild.

If you have the opportunity to grow any of these charming plants, you should be conscious of their plight. Some of these species have been recommended for inclusion in the List of Endangered and Threatened Plants under the Endangered Species Act of 1973. As of 1990, *Primula maguirei* had been listed as threatened, and *P. alcalina*, *P. capillaris*, *P. domensis*, *P. hunnewellii*, and *P. nevadensis* are designated Category 2 candidates; for the latter, "there is some evidence of vulnerability, but . . . not enough data to support listing proposals at this time." (*Primula hunnewellii* is generally considered to be the same as *P. specuicola*, and that rationale has been followed in this article.) In addition, the state of New Mexico has categorized *P. ellisiae* as a "sensitive" species. Although growing these primulas may be a challenge, I encourage you to try those that are not in jeopardy.

Originally published in the Bulletin of the American Rock Garden Society, *vol. 49, no. 2, pp. 125–131 (1991).*

PART THREE:
PLAINS STATES

In and About the Black Hills

JAMES H. LOCKLEAR

No one has done more to open the eyes of gardeners to the horticultural potential of the Great Plains flora than did Claude Barr. On his ranch near the Black Hills in South Dakota he started one of the first native-plant nurseries in the United States, from which he distributed plants of the Great Plains to gardens throughout this country and overseas. His writings, including many articles for the *Bulletin of the American Rock Garden Society*, brought well-deserved attention to the little-known plants of this region. His most lasting contribution, however, was his book *Jewels of the Plains*, through which we gain access to his more than 70 years of experience with this flora.

Although Barr roamed from Canada to Texas in his search for garden-worthy plants, some of his best finds came from his own backyard: the Black Hills, the Badlands, and the surrounding Dakota prairie. This region is host to a great assortment of beautiful hardy plants, many of rock garden stature.

Viewed from the air, the Black Hills region appears as an oval dome rising out of the surrounding plains. When these ancient mountains were uplifted, rock strata to the outside were pushed up and tilted on edge to varying degrees. Barr wrote with fondness of two areas of limestone that were exposed by this process: the Greenhorn limestone rings the outer perimeter of the Hills, and the Minnekahta limestone lies closer to the interior. Interesting wildflowers can be found throughout the Black Hills, but there are concentrations of special plants wherever these two limestone formations are exposed.

Barr's ranch south of the Black Hills was nearer to exposures of the Greenhorn limestone. From a distance, the escarpments and hills formed by these outcrops, which lie between the forested Black Hills and the surrounding mixed-grass prairie, appear barren and devoid of interesting plant growth. On the crests in gravelly soil, however, are a number of attractive rock plants.

Musineon tenuifolium is one of the finer ones, with flat-topped clusters of bright yellow flowers held above low tufts of foliage in the spring. The dark green leaves are finely divided, almost fernlike, making this an attractive plant even after it is finished blooming. The distribution of this member of the parsley family (Apiaceae) is centered in the Nebraska panhandle and adjacent Colorado, South Dakota, and Wyoming.

Another special plant found on the Greenhorn is little *Erigeron ochroleucus* var. *scribneri* (Plate 85). Barr enthusiastically declared this as the "crown jewel" of the plains daisies. Not exceeding 4 inches/10 cm in height and only about 6 inches/15 cm wide, this diminutive plant bears numerous gold-centered daisies with white ray florets during its spring blooming period. Variety *scribneri* is a dwarf phase of the species that occurs in rocky areas throughout much of the northwestern Great Plains.

One of the most striking plants of the region is the leather flower (*Clematis hirsutissima* var. *scottii*, formerly known as *C. scottii*). This beautiful nonvining clematis, which is sometimes associated with the Greenhorn, produces dark blue, bonnet-shaped flowers on gracefully arching stems in the spring. Barr discovered a pink-flowered form that apparently has been lost to cultivation. This species is not unlike *C. fremontii*, which occurs on the limestone-underlain prairies of north-central Kansas, except that its foliage is pinnately compound. Like many other plants in this region, the populations of this species in the Black Hills represent eastern outliers of a mainly Rocky Mountain–centered distribution.

Of all the plants found on the Greenhorn limestone, none makes a more impressive show than *Phlox alyssifolia*. This mat-forming phlox is covered with fragrant flowers over a long period in spring and early summer. While it has a rather large area of distribution in the northwestern Great Plains, *P. alyssifolia* displays its greatest range of colors on the limestone areas associated with the Black Hills. Lavender is the most common color, but various pinks can also be found, as well as whites and near-blues. The flowers may be star-shaped with rather narrow petals, or full-faced with wide petals. The flowers of *P. alyssifolia* are larger here than anywhere else in its range—1 inch/2.5 cm or slightly more across. Edgar Wherry recognized this large-flowered Black Hills phase as a subspecies, *P. alyssifolia* subsp. *abdita*, and listed it among those members of the genus "deserving wider horticultural use" in his book *The Genus Phlox*.

Two other phloxes, *Phlox andicola* and *P. hoodii*, also occur in the region. Both have white flowers and a creeping habit and are smaller than *P. alyssifolia*. A joint research project involving the Dyck Arboretum of the Plains in Kansas and the University of Nebraska Department of Horticulture has evaluated the horticultural potential of these three species.

Supported by a grant from the Perennial Plant Association, collections were made of superior wild-growing individuals of each species, to be grown in field comparison trials along with three cultivars of the popular garden plant *P. subulata*.

It is fitting that some of these trials were to be conducted at the University's research station in North Platte, Nebraska, where Glenn Viehmeyer, an acquaintance of Barr and fellow explorer of the Great Plains flora, did his pioneering work in the selection and breeding of penstemons. This work, along with other interesting projects involving Great Plains natives, has been carried on at North Platte by Dr. Dale Lindgren.

The Minnekahta limestone outcrops closer to the interior of the Black Hills, in areas typically vegetated with open stands of ponderosa pine. This pinkish-gray rock is itself quite attractive. It occurs at a number of places around the Hills and is exposed at the south entrance of Wind Cave National Park.

Weathered outcrops of this limestone are another good place to find the large-flowered form of *Phlox alyssifolia*, which appears even more attractive against the pink backdrop. Blooming with it in the spring are nice patches of *Mertensia lanceolata*, with drooping clusters of sunset-colored rose and blue flowers. *Senecio canus* is here as well, its bright yellow daisies contrasting beautifully with its silvery foliage. In crevices in the limestone the little rock fern *Cheilanthes feei* can also be found.

Potentilla concinna, a herbaceous cinquefoil of dwarf stature, also occurs on the Minnekahta limestone. While only sporting its bright yellow flowers in early spring, its neatly divided foliage, silvery beneath and green to gray on top, makes it a beautiful subject throughout the growing season. Another early spring bloomer, *Pulsatilla patens* (Plate 101), grows in thin soil over the limestone. Known to many as the pasqueflower, it is the state flower of South Dakota. The emblem of the American Rock Garden Society occurs here as well, in the form of the species *Dodecatheon pulchellum* (Plate 84). All this in just one corner of Wind Cave National Park! A checklist of the park's flora is available at the headquarters.

Although Barr found many treasures in the Black Hills, his perceptive eye was also cast upon the surrounding grasslands. In May and June the beautiful expanses of mixed-grass prairie that roll away from the Black Hills are the setting for numerous attractive wildflowers. Many of rock garden stature grow in spaces between the prairie grasses, including *Viola nuttallii*, the yellow-flowered violet of the high plains. *Nothocalais cuspidata* (formerly *Microseris cuspidata*) also manages to find a place in the prairie turf, its dandelion-like flowers held aloft on stiff stems above a basal tuft of wavy-margined leaves.

In *Jewels of the Plains* Barr spoke of the challenges of gardening in the tight, sticky clay soil that supports the prairie grasses of this region. He specifically mentioned the tendency of this soil, known locally as "gumbo," to cling to anything when slightly wet, particularly digging tools. I can attest to this, having personally experienced how gumbo can stick to vehicle tires when wet, turning them into oversized glazed donuts incapable of any sort of traction.

One plains wildflower that seems to flourish in this difficult soil is *Oenothera caespitosa* (Plate 39), known appropriately as the gumbo lily. It is one of the few plants that can grow in the raw clay soils of the Badlands formations scattered throughout southwest South Dakota. The large white flowers of this evening primrose open around sunset and begin to wither the next morning. On cloudy mornings they remain open longer.

Another species that takes gumbo in stride is *Penstemon eriantherus* (Plate 78). It can be found in barren Badlands soils as well as among the grasses of the prairie. Reaching 8 to 12 inches/20 to 30 cm in height, it bears dense, elongate clusters of lavender flowers in the spring. Each flower has a spreading lower lip which displays a dense growth of gold-colored hairs.

Some of the best displays of wildflowers in Claude Barr country are found on the tops of the rocky hills and buttes that rise here and there above the prairie. Almost any of these has *Astragalus spatulatus* (Plate 71) present, floating dozens of purple blossoms above little mounds of foliage. *Paronychia depressa*, a more lax-growing relative of the cushion-forming *P. sessiliflora*, is also common. *Lesquerella alpina* is equally abundant in rocky habitats in the region, producing numerous bright yellow flowers over low mounds of silvery, spoon-shaped leaves.

Found only occasionally in South Dakota, *Cryptantha cana* is rather common to the south in the Nebraska panhandle and adjacent parts of Colorado and Wyoming. With attractive silvery foliage and sparkling white, gold-centered flowers, this low-growing plant is one of the most beautiful wildflowers in the region. Barr called it "the gem of its genus."

One May morning in the 1940s, Barr found what must have been his most treasured discovery. At an isolated rise called Limestone Butte, not far from his ranch in Fall River County, he came across a little cushion-forming milkvetch he had not encountered before. With silvery, three-parted leaves and rose-colored blossoms, it resembled *Astragalus tridactylicus*, a species of the Rocky Mountain foothills in northeastern Colorado and southeastern Wyoming. Barr was able to propagate this plant and later offered it through his mail-order nursery, Prairie Gem Ranch.

Eventually some of these plants were obtained by Rupert Barneby of the New York Botanical Garden, an expert on the genus *Astragalus*. Barneby, who was familiar with *A. tridactylicus*, had some question about the identity of Barr's plants and requested that Barr supply him with pressed specimens. Barneby was then able to determine that, indeed, these plants were not *A. tridactylicus* but a species new to science. Thanks to Barneby's discernment, Barr now had a new name to list in his nursery catalog: *A. barrii*.

In Barneby's technical description of *Astragalus barrii*, published in a scientific journal in 1956, is a warmly written tribute to Claude Barr:

It is a pleasure to associate this delightful little *Astragalus* with the name of Claude A. Barr, keen observer and successful cultivator of the prairie and Badlands floras, who through the medium of his nursery at Prairie Gem Ranch near Smithwick has done much to introduce to gardeners here and abroad the beauties of the native vegetation.

Today Barr's milkvetch is known to occur in southwestern South Dakota, northeastern Wyoming, and southeastern Montana. Its restricted distribution makes it one of a small number of species that are truly endemic to the Great Plains. Most of the populations of this attractive little plant occur in the Powder River Basin country of Wyoming, but even there it is not very common. In South Dakota it is known from only a handful of locations; I am glad that one of these is Limestone Butte, and that Claude Barr was there exploring one spring day. It is fitting that one of the most beautiful species in the flora of the Great Plains should be discovered by and named for the man who so loved this region and its plants.

Originally published in the Bulletin of the American Rock Garden Society, *vol. 49, no. 4, pp. 297–300 (1991).*

251

Cushion Astragalus *Species*

CLAUDE A. BARR

The cushion or "bun" plants of the Great Plains and western mountain regions are apparently evolutionary developments in response to characteristic climates, elevations, and soils. These tight, low pads or mounds show a surprising uniformity of structure, though occurring in many diverse genera. In the genus *Astragalus*, about five species have been grouped by the botanist P. A. Rydberg under section *Orophaca*. Three or perhaps four of them are rock garden prospects of outstanding charm.

What a surprise it is to wander out along an almost barren Badlands ridge in late May, walking toward a vague patch of color, and to come upon a colony of *Astragalus tridactylicus* glowing in pink-purple or lavender-rose, the buns edged with the soft silvery green of the tiny, sharp-tipped tripartite leaves. In addition to the perfection of its form, its color, and its harmonious setting on light gray clay mulched with lighter limestone rubble, there is the novelty of beauty in isolation. Its companion plants, if any, are a few stunted weeds, with now and then a tuft of unthrifty grass. Very old specimens may appear to be raised on little eminences, partly because the surrounding soil has weathered away, and partly because these plants gather and hold soil that blows or washes in.

The gardener will ask what this rooting medium is that seems so well adapted to the one species, and how it might be imitated in the garden. Extremely malleable and slimy when wet, though with much apparent grit, it is very tough and hard when dry, and there is sometimes a close-textured hard shale a few inches below the surface. But knowing *Astragalus tridactylicus* for some time, you will discover that the most important factor in its native environment is freedom from competition. When taken small, it transplants with fair ease and thrives—even self-sows occasionally—on the plains, in one-third sand, one-third clay loam, and one-third gravel (including limestone). In the East it has been found to do well in one part sand, two parts loam, and two parts peat.

This species is actually found more often growing where it has some competition, and also some modification of the soil, but it does not there attain very large proportions. The spread of the crown is usually 5 to 6 inches/13 to 15 cm. Under rare optimum conditions, it may reach 16 inches/40 cm.

Astragalus gilviflorus is a plant of very similar habit and appearance in leaf, a bit looser-textured, with larger, white blossoms borne singly and almost sessile, whereas those of *A. tridactylicus* are borne one to three on a brief stem. If *A. gilviflorus* is advanced rapidly by a favorable season, the erect banners of flower will completely hide the leaves in April and May. When after unfavorable weather they come later, sometimes lasting into the season of *A. tridactylicus*, the leaves may somewhat hide the flowers, a different and hardly less attractive picture.

At times found along the margins of *Astragalus tridactylicus* colonies, *A. gilviflorus* seems to have no firm restrictions as to soil type; it may be expected in almost any gritty or gravelly clay or shaley spot. Cushions 8 to 10 inches/20 to 25 cm wide are frequent, but every individual, down to babies of an inch or so, flowers freely.

The third lovely member of this quintet is *Astragalus sericoleucus*. The plant has a distinct individuality, smooth and silky, and though it starts out as a very modest, flat bun of tiny tripartite leaves, its somewhat sinuous branching stems continually enlarge the mat, extending to 16 inches/40 cm or so. At no season do the leaves stand up; they remain very low, so that the whole plant is about 1 inch/2.5 cm tall, even when covered with the hundreds of tiny round, bannerlike flowers of royal purple, varying to lighter in some plants. Very abundant in its chosen places, it may be found on a nearly flat limestone gravel-mulched ridge top, in open sunlight, or on somewhat less stony terrain on steeper slopes. Its main flowering time is June.

In the garden *Astragalus sericoleucus* has been a puzzle to grow. It transplants readily enough as a small seedling, but a midsummer or fall drought, a dry open winter, or a hesitant, dry or wet spring may spur its departure. One plant, after many trials, is now carrying a thrifty mat of foliage into its third winter, and it has flowered well. A portion of its accustomed powdery sand, with limestone, on a slight slope 2 inches/5 cm above a path, with a bit of rock drainage and high lath shade, does the trick—so far.

Astragalus argophyllus, a rare species, is a close-textured, neat cushion or bun to 8 or 9 inches/20 to 23 cm wide, with a silvery-blue cast. In the garden its sojourn has been brief and its blossoming frustrating. The flowers are narrow-bannered, sparsely borne, and a mere nothing in color–pale lavender-straw.

Astragalus tridactylicus
Tuft about natural size; insets × 3. (Drawn from photograph by
Claude A. Barr)

By contrast, *Astragalus aretioides* is reported as cluster-flowered, purple, and in size of blossom and length of stem intermediate between *A. tridactylicus* and *A. sericeus*. One imagines it an attractive plant. Still another species of garden value grows in southeastern Montana, with flowers that are said to be definitely blue. From the appearance of plants received—and with intense regret lost before blooming—it may be a form of *A. tridactylicus*.

These fascinating bun plants, with the possible exception of *Astragalus aretioides*, are inhabitants of the high plains. *Astragalus gilviflorus* is found from Saskatchewan to Kansas, while the others are credited to extreme western Nebraska and South Dakota, Wyoming, and portions of Montana and Colorado. In conditions of light rainfall and, usually, sharp drainage, their rather barren footing provides some reserve of moisture.

Originally published in the Bulletin of the American Rock Garden Society, *vol. 9, no. 1, pp. 2–4 (1949).*

The Purple Loco and Other Oxytropis

CLAUDE A. BARR

Plants that seem styled purely for decoration are the finer species of *Oxytropis*—many members of a large genus, well represented in North America on the western plains and mountains. In simplest terms, an oxytropis plant is composed of a rosette or group of rosettes of pinnate leaves, more or less silky, often silvery. The rosettes are connected by stems so short and prostrate that the plant appears stemless. From each section arises in season a scape or leafless flowering stem, usually quite upright, bearing a spike or plume of showy pea blossoms at a fairly low height. The mat of attractive leafage adorns itself with a veritable bouquet of bloom.

At its first flowering a plant produces only one or two racemes, bearing more with age. Six to 12 spikes make a lovely show, and old plants may send up 20 to 30. The blooming period extends over three or four weeks. After this, many slender pods line the stems, turning light brown with ripening and becoming rather decorative, while the foliage retains its pleasing appearance all season.

Oxytropis lambertii has a wide range, inhabiting sandhills, gravelly plains, and mountainsides; if one comes on an extensive field of purple-red blossom, it is most likely to be this species. Wyoming and neighboring states comprise its principal area of distribution, but it is also known from Canada to Texas. The common name is purple loco, or locoweed. "Loco" is a Spanish word meaning crazy, referring to the effect the plant has on cattle, which under poor pasture conditions acquire a taste for it, becoming poisoned after eating considerable amounts for some time.

Its preference for sandhills, gravelly ridges, and limestone or gypsum, usually in dry places, suggests likely places to look for it. Now and then an extensive colony can be seen, but in the garden seed may come sparingly, providing fewer plants than might be desired.

The usual reference to the color of *Oxytropis lambertii* may be inexact. The word "purple" is more poetic than accurate; "dark purple" or "dark blue-purple" more correctly describes the dried herbarium specimen. An occasional plant displays a reddish color as fine as that of the 'American Beauty' rose. Predominantly purplish-red, it varies to lighter or darker, or rarely to purple or bluish, or white. Its flowering time is mainly June.

Oxytropis sericea (Plate 74), with its broader, more silvery leaflets, presents a denser foliage effect. Its very free and lovely flower clusters are put forth in May. Its finest color is a rich pink, which occurs in very limey sandstone. In different areas it varies to light pink, cloudy light blue, oyster-white, and dark rose. Like *O. lambertii*, it carries its flowers usually at 6 to 10 inches/15 to 25 cm, or rarely to 12 inches/30 cm.

From seed from Calgary I once grew a plant very similar to *Oxytropis sericea* but with blossoms of rich cream. Unfortunately my two plants passed on after flowering once, whether from unendurable tree-root competition or insufficient lime is uncertain. This was probably *O. sericea* var. *spicata* (formerly *O. macounii*), and it should be avidly sought.

Oxytropis sericea var. *sericea* (formerly *O. pinetorum*) grows on high north slopes in Fall River Canyon in the Black Hills, and from Montana to Oklahoma and New Mexico. In the Black Hills habitat the terrain is dry enough at times but quite shady. Against a dark background, this variety's plumes of white, faintly tinged green, show up well. Three or four spires seem to be its limit. It has now been brought to my prairie environment for testing.

I have not seen a yellow-flowered *Oxytropis*, although one sees that color mentioned now and again. *Oxytropis monticola* (formerly *O. villosa*) is a beautiful creamy color, lighter than that of *O. sericea* var. *spicata*. It dwells in a narrow area in the Black Hills, frequent there but not plentiful, and large plants have not been noted. It is highly desirable though possibly short-lived.

The form of *Oxytropis monticola* formerly known as *O. gracilis* is blue-silvery with adpressed hairs. It is long-lived, forms ample mats, and sends up many plumes of light yellow strongly tinted green—*non grata* in my garden.

On the bluffs of the Platte River in Nebraska late in June, when *Oxytropis lambertii* there was just finishing blooming, there appeared numbers of a small loco bearing one to five scapes, 4 to 5 inches/10 to 13 cm tall, with racemes of five to nine florets each. It would hardly have been distinguishable from the intermingled *O. lambertii* except for the uniformity of the short inflorescences, the freshness of the florets which

257

seemed to celebrate that particular day, and a certain brightness in its light rose-red color. This pretty little plant had to be *O. plattensis*; I saw no larger plants. [This species is no longer recognized; the plant in question was probably an unusual form of *O. lambertii.—Ed.*]

Quite different was my discovery of *Oxytropis nana* var. *besseyi* on the bluffs of the Belle Fourche River in Wyoming one mid-June day of another year. The sun of late afternoon was shining through the masses of full-blown, closely clustered plumes on ledge after ledge. The road ran closer to the bluff, and a larger colony appeared. Clearly there was a difference in this loco. I scrambled up to the level of the flowers. The florets in the great clusters were the oddest of pea blossoms, with ample banners, extra-wide wings, and keel petals so tiny the lower part of the blossom seemed to be cut away. The color, a light rose with an infusion of buff or terra-cotta, was distinctly deeper at the petal bases. Here the plumes were more than 12 inches/30 cm tall; a height of 6 to 10 inches/15 to 25 cm is more usual. There was the usual gray pinnate foliage.

Oxytropis nana var. *besseyi* grows in a mixture of gritty disintegrated sandstone and clay shale, firm to loose, or in crevices of the stone. I have not mastered the cultivation of this one in rather limited trials. My impression is that this, as well as any other oxytropis that makes large crowns, is long-lived. It is worthy of a place in any garden.

A northern species, *Oxytropis splendens*, is at home along both sides of the border between North Dakota and Montana and Canada. It is described as "striking because of additional rows of leaflets, verticillately arranged, and blue flowers contrasting with gray leaves." Most parts are conspicuously hairy. This one, though sought over many years, seems hard to come by. Twice I have obtained a tiny pinch of seed, from which came a few plantlets that met with too much drought and did not gain size enough to survive the winter.

My limited acquaintance with *Oxytropis* inclines me to accord any member of the clan close consideration. *Oxytropis lambertii* and *O. sericea* are easy to grow here. Others may be growable with a bit of luck and attention to their obvious needs for drainage and alkalinity, in most kinds. One writer mentions *O. albiflorus*, white or lavender with a purple spot on the keel, as especially neat and growing in large fields. [This species is not recognized now; it was probably only a white form.—*Ed.*] There must be other kinds worth hunting out.

There is at least one species fashioned to order for the most exacting rock gardener: *Oxytropis multiceps*, credited to Wyoming, Colorado, and Nebraska. It has the enticing quality of being a close cushion of tiny leaves with fairly large flowers of reddish-purple on very short scapes (5 mm or so).

Probably a collector can move an oxytropis plant successfully when it is in flower, but it must be a very young plant, preferably at first flowering. After a couple of years, the roots will be woody, unadaptive, and interminable in depth, destined to remain in their chosen places of solitude and to be seen and admired untouched. Seeds, however, are plentiful in season. They are ready for gathering when the long, upright, pitcherlike capsules begin to open at the throat; even after weeks of shaking and rattling by the wind, some treasure is still likely to be found in the depths of the vessels. Do not pass them up: almost any species is worthy of trial.

Originally published in the Bulletin of the American Rock Garden Society, *vol. 18, no. 3, pp. 65–67 (1960).*

Dwarf Western Asters

CLAUDE A. BARR

In the course of my horticultural education, someone advised me that all the world loves a daisy. How wise the world is, I reflected, and drew warm comfort from the assurance of so much good company. Though worldly wisdom now has taught me that the dictum is as little generalizable as the one that gentlemen prefer blondes, at the time I accepted it; and neither sophistication nor social pressure has jarred me from that original love of flowers on the daisy pattern.

Let us grant it good that all the world of flowers is not made up on the composite pattern; but let us then consider in detail some western asters. Color, stature, habit, and blooming season qualify a number of them for the attention of the discriminating rock gardener.

A dwarf among dwarfs is *Ionactis alpina* (formerly *Aster scopulorum*) of the mountains of Montana and Wyoming, ranging west to Nevada and Oregon. It is a tiny bushlet, single-stemmed at the ground, with many diminutive branches from the base that strive to produce at about the same level (between 4 and 8 inches/10 and 20 cm) flowerheads 1 inch/2.5 cm or more wide, of vivid violet-purple with small golden centers. Its crowded little leaves are dark green, and the plant is inconspicuous after the June flowering, but it repeats its lovely show year after year and does not soon become decrepit. My plants are now about 6 years old and show no signs of failure.

Aster ptarmicoides (syn. *Unamia alba*, recently renamed *Solidago ptarmicoides*) comes into flower in July, and its fine white rays radiating from creamy white disks may still be in evidence in September. Individual inflorescences last for a month. The plant requires some space to itself for good performance, and much shade and a moderate diet seem effective in restricting its height to 10 inches/25 cm. In a more stimulating setting it easily goes to 16 inches/40 cm, with no improvement in the flower crop. The heads tend to be borne at a single level in broad corymbs. One to eight stems rise from a basal tuft of light green, linear to lanceolate, somewhat ribbed leaves. The large crowns may be divided, and seedlings are very easily grown. In the wild the plant is found from Colorado and Saskatchewan eastward.

Provided with a mechanism for spreading (but not unduly), *Aster sibiricus* var. *meritus* is at its loveliest when, grown to a 2- to 3-foot/60- to 90-cm pillow, it spreads an uninterrupted blanket of gold-accented pinkish-violet. It grows 5 to 10 inches/13 to 25 cm tall (according to report, to 16 inches/40 cm in some forms). It sometimes flowers in late June, but mainly in July. At other times the very broad, somewhat toothed leaves of rich dark green are not unattractive, and the reddish-brown pappus tufts of the seedheads and the later, paler "florets" of dry, spread-out bracts carry pleasant notes to the end of the season. Moderate richness, plenty of light (though some shade is appreciated), and freedom from competition are needed for the best response. The native range of this species is from South Dakota to British Columbia and northern Alberta.

Aster oblongifolius (formerly *A. kumleinii*) rarely shows bloom until September. So wonderful are its gold and lavender that the daisy pattern is either irrelevant or a positive asset. Certainly its flower brings joy, whether as a solitary gem amid the prairie grasses, or starring a rocky slope, or in dense sheets under cultivation. The heads, with a nice balance of ray and disk, are from 1 to 1.5 inches/2.5 to 4 cm, flat or faintly up-tipped at the margin, and light-reflecting. The leaves are small, elongated-oblong, stiff and rough with short stiff hairs—not unattractive and obviously of dry-climate type. The stems are slender, stiff, and capable, when grown in too much shade, of stretching up to twice the 10 inches/25 cm of the choicest forms. Although the plant spreads by short stolons, it takes a number of years to attain a 3-foot/90-cm clump. The ray color sometimes varies to pretty shades of clear rose pink, light blue, and so on. [A clone selected by Claude Barr, 'Dream of Beauty', is still available in commerce.—*Ed.*]

I have in my garden a plant from eastern Kansas and another from Texas that have been identified for me as *Aster oblongifolius,* and subsequently I have had the selection known as 'Campbell's Pink'. These plants are leafier than the plant known as *A. kumleinii*, and the leaves sightly larger and deeper green; the stems come more thickly from the crown and are more erect and less branched. They often reach to 14 to 18 inches/35 to 45 cm in full sun. Their effect is rather plain, to my eye. Blooming time is about the same, with the exception that the blue-purple Texas visitor holds to a schedule of its own, opening regularly a full month later than the others. In a late fall it has come into bloom in November, by which time the cautious northern Great Plains plants are set for winter. The botanist P. A. Rydberg defines the native range of *A. oblongifolius* as prairies from Pennsylvania to Minnesota, to Tennessee and Texas, while his *A. kumleinii* occurs in the plains states and eastward to Missouri and Wisconsin. [As noted above, the two have now been lumped under the former name.—*Ed.*]

A distinct and delightful species of the central and southern plains is *Aster fendleri*, which sometimes flowers at 4 inches/10 cm in the hard, stony situations it frequents, and at its tallest hardly exceeds 12 inches/30 cm. The stems are apt to be quite erect, but in young or newly divided plants they branch freely. There is ample leafage, reminiscent of that of *A. ericoides*; the leaves are about 1 inch/2.5 cm long, stiff, sharp-tipped, and with a sparse fringe of tiny bristles. Much of the individuality of the plant's effect derives from the blossom heads—small golden centers and rays of medium blue-lavender, bright and pleasing. The uniquely modeled rays, tapering from midway to a sharp tip, are widely spread and daintily cupped. *Aster fendleri* is free-blooming in early September or later, although it does not produce a mass of color as do some others. It has no traveling roots, and the dense crowns it makes when not restrained by rocky footing suggest frequent division.

Aster × batesii is well-behaved; in 8 or 10 years my plants have widened their crowns less than 1 inch/2.5 cm a year. Hardly distinguishable from *A. ericoides* out of flower, with more or less the same habit and small linear leaves, it bears ray flowers in tiny crowded heads, sky-blue, blue-lavender, pale lavender, or more frequently a slaty mauve, as deadly and distasteful as a flower color can be. If all lavender- or mauve-flowered plants of this general type belong to *A. × batesii*, I have seen some charming pillows of blossom at 8 inches/20 cm. My garden plants, from southern Nebraska, make no pillows but send up divergent rods of bloom to 18 or 20 inches/45 or 50 cm, if not sheared.

With so much variation in color and habit, any aster is worthy of scrutiny. I have admitted *Aster × batesii* to this list because I found in northern Kansas, the past September, growing in a roadside ditch with its roots half exposed, a 10-inch/25-cm cluster of blossoms of thrilling light blue. During the remaining autumn days two or three divisions of this find seemed safe in my garden, and I hope they will thrive and multiply.

The choice of white asters of good character and stature would seem to be *Aster porterii*, which I have not seen. The adjectives free-flowering, fine, and delicate have been applied to it, and pictures show an open paniculate habit and flowers of fine form; there is no indication of spreading rootstocks. One author gives the height at 6 to 10 inches/15 to 25 cm, another agrees that it is low, and Rydberg's technical description defines its stature as 8 to 16 inches/20 to 40 cm. It grows on sunny open slopes in Colorado, from plains levels to 10,000 feet/3100 meters, and blooms, depending on altitude, from July to October.

Reported also from mountains from Colorado to Alaska, and from Eurasia as well, is *Aster alpinus,* with more or less solitary broad heads of violet and gold, 10 inches/25 cm tall. *Aster foliaceus* var. *apricus* is an alpine dwarf of the Rocky and Cascade mountains, with usually solitary heads of "brilliant rose-purple or violet," and *A. griseolus* is a Coloradoan of the heights, 4 to 6 inches/10 to 15 cm tall, with broad heads of purple, as many as four in a corymb. [*Aster griseolus* is not currently recognized.—*Ed.*]

Other asters with intriguing descriptions include *Aster adscendens, A. armeriaefolius, A. foliaceus* var. *canbyi, A.* × *cordalenus, A. ericoides* var. *prostratus, A. occidentalis* var. *fremontii, A. integrifolius, A. sibiricus* var. *giganteus* (formerly *A. richardsonii,* related to *A. meritus*), and *A. underwoodii.* [*Aster underwoodii* is not currently recognized.—*Ed.*] And what of a Colorado aster of rock garden dimension, that is "really red"? Such is claimed to be in existence, so there is treasure to be prospected for among the western asters.

Originally published in the Bulletin of the American Rock Garden Society, *vol. 5, no. 4, pp. 65–63 (1947).*

Rock Garden Plants of Kansas

JAMES H. LOCKLEAR

It is no secret that Kansas suffers an image problem. In the minds of many, no place is closer to the middle of nowhere than Kansas. Even the slogan of the state's department of tourism, "Linger longer in Kansas," implies that Kansas is a place people pass through to get somewhere else.

Writing about the uninviting nature of Great Basin landscapes, Panayoti Kelaidis once suggested that plantspeople should take such apparent emptiness as a signal that great riches are to be found there. It should therefore come as no surprise that there are many gems to be discovered in the flora of the Sunflower State, if one takes the time and knows where to look.

Kansas is famous for its wheat fields, and a good portion of its western half is devoted to this crop. There are, however, excellent stretches of native grassland in the hillier parts of the state that possess a wide array of wildflowers.

Some of the largest and finest tracts of tallgrass prairie in the United States are found in the unique Flint Hills of eastern Kansas. Wildflowers abound in this region; many, such as prairie violet (*Viola pedatifida*), white-eyed grass (*Sisyrinchium campestre*), and prairie iris (*Nemastylis geminiflora*), are of rock garden stature.

Farther west, mixed-grass and then shortgrass prairie dominates the landscape. It is in this part of Kansas that the finest rock plants are found. Here, particularly on rocky hilltops, river bluffs, mesas, and buttes, natural rock gardens of unexpected beauty occur.

In the mixed-grass prairie region of north-central Kansas there are two ranges of rolling hills. The eastern range, the Smoky Hills, is underlain principally by Dakota sandstone. In the western range, the Blue Hills, limestones predominate. The Blue Hills are also referred to as Post

Rock Country; a familiar sight here are miles of limestone fenceposts, quarried by the early settlers of this essentially treeless country and still standing today.

Some of the state's most distinctive wildflowers are found in the Blue Hills. Many gardeners are familiar with the Missouri evening primrose (*Oenothera macrocarpa* subsp. *macrocarpa*), which occurs here on rocky hillsides and roadcuts. A little-known local relative is Fremont's evening primrose (*O. macrocarpa* subsp. *fremontii*), once considered a distinct species: imagine a smaller-scale Missouri primrose with narrow, silvery leaves, pale yellow flowers, and a more tufted growth habit.

Another rock plant found here is resinous skullcap (*Scutellaria resinosa*)—an unfortunate name for a beautiful wildflower. Semishrubby in habit, this member of the mint family has boxwood-like foliage and bears numerous purple flowers over a long period from May into July. A shell-pink form has been found. Claude Barr, in his book *Jewels of the Plains* (1893), describes this as a species "of great charm and perfect garden behavior."

The real eye-catcher of the Blue Hills is *Clematis fremontii*. A nonvining type, this clematis sends up robust clusters of 6- to 12-inch/15- to 30-cm stems bearing large, thick, leathery leaves. The bonnet-shaped flowers, produced from April into June, look almost like porcelain. A perennial with three-season interest, *C. fremontii* bears large, attractive clusters of seed through summer and fall, and the leathery foliage, dried and brown, persists into the winter. This is a species of rocky limestone prairie.

At the opposite border of the state in south-central Kansas are the Red Hills, an area of buttes, mesas, canyons, and mixed-grass prairie, named for the brick-red color of the local soils. The scenery here is magnificent and the flora distinctive. A number of plants from the southwestern United States reach their northeastern limits in the Red Hills.

One of the very special plants of this region is *Phlox oklahomensis*. Known only from Kansas, Oklahoma, and one county in Texas, this is a low, somewhat sprawling species with narrow, rather stiff leaves. The flowers are borne in loose clusters from late March into May and are quite fragrant. Whites, blues, and pinks can be found. Edgar Wherry noted its horticultural potential in *The Genus Phlox* (1955).

There are several golden composites in the Great Plains. *Heterotheca stenophylla* (formerly *Chrysopsis*) is an especially attractive one, flowering over a long period in the summer, primarily in July. The gray-green foliage, soft to the touch from a covering of silky hairs, contrasts well with the pale gold daisies. Growing to about 12 inches/30 cm in height, it is a resident of upland sites in the Red Hills.

Another relative of the Missouri evening primrose occurs in the Red Hills. The hoary evening primrose (*Oenothera macrocarpa* subsp. *incana*) is similar in most ways to the Missouri evening primrose except for its silvery leaves. It blooms over a relatively long time in early summer, and, as a bonus, its silvery foliage makes it an attractive plant even when not in flower. It is particularly striking against the red soil of this special part of Kansas.

As the Smoky Hill River makes its way from Colorado across western Kansas, it passes through a region of badlands in Trego, Gove, and Logan counties. One of the ironies of the plains is that the most delicate wildflowers often occur in the harshest habitats, and such is the case in these badlands.

One of the finest plants found in this region is the needle-leaf gilia (*Gilia rigidula*). Its overall habit resembles that of a creeping phlox, except for its bright blue flowers with yellow throats. Blooming in April and May, this species could be a good substitute for *Phlox subulata* in drier gardens.

The oval-leaf bladderpod (*Lesquerella ovalifolia*) makes its home on the rocky knolls and barren clay soils of this region. This is the most attractive of all the Great Plains lesquerellas, forming relatively large mounds of round, silvery leaves. The flowers are a nice yellow and are produced from April into June.

"The prime rock aster of the Plains," wrote Claude Barr of Fendler's aster (*Aster fendleri*). Growing only 10 to 12 inches/25 to 30 cm tall, this fall-bloomer occurs in rocky areas throughout much of western Kansas. The composite flowers have lavender-blue ray florets and yellow centers. On harsh soils in the badlands this plant assumes a domed shape.

Probably the part of Kansas that people find least interesting is the high plains. A vast stretch of nearly level land, this is shortgrass prairie country. Scattered here and there throughout this region, however, are areas of rocky hills, and these are the places to search out the finest wildflowers.

In the southwestern corner of the state, north of Elkhart, the historic Santa Fe Trail passes a prominent landmark called "Point of Rocks." On these rocky bluffs overlooking the Cimarron River, a wide array of rock plants can be found.

Two dwarf prairie clovers occur here, *Dalea jamesii* and *D. tenuifolia*. The latter is a refined, decumbent version of the larger purple prairie clover (*D. purpurea*, syn. *Petalostemon purpureum*); it lights up the scene with its clusters of bright, rose-purple flowers. *Dalea jamesii* is a tufted plant with silvery, tripartite leaves and orange-yellow blossoms. The plumelike teeth of the calyx add to the attractiveness of the plant as it finishes flowering in early summer.

Two daisies of southwestern origin also thrive in this semiarid habitat. The blackfoot daisy (*Melampodium leucanthum*) bears white flowers with yellow centers. It grows to 10 inches/25 cm tall and flowers over a long season beginning in June and lasting into September. Barr referred to it as "a veritable rock garden jewel." The Rocky Mountain zinnia (*Zin-*

nia grandiflora) is a shorter, mounded plant, producing golden-yellow daisies over a similarly extended period.

A markedly different assemblage of plants is found in the rocky habitats of northwestern Kansas. Here, a person acquainted with the flora of Wyoming's plains and basins would find familiar species. On bluffs above the Arikaree River north of St. Francis a number of these can be found, including *Arenaria hookeri, Astragalus hyalinus, A. spatulatus, Lesquerella alpina,* and *Paronychia depressa.* The silky orophaca (*Astragalus sericoleucus*), common in southeastern Wyoming and the Nebraska panhandle, occurs on eroding hillsides in three northwestern Kansas counties.

A number of other desirable rock plants are more widely distributed over the high plains of western Kansas. The Easter daisy (*Townsendia exscapa*) starts blooming in March and is setting seed by the time May arrives. A low, tufted plant, its flowering is assurance that spring is coming soon.

Another dwarf composite, the babywhite aster (*Chaetopappa ericoides,* syn. *Leucelene ericoides*), has a very different growth habit. It grows in colonies of slender stems, generally under 6 inches/15 cm in height. Its foliage is heath-like and the daisies, produced in early summer, are only 0.5 inch/13 mm across. The effect is pleasing, though, and this plant may have potential as a groundcover.

As the name implies, the lavender-leaf evening primrose (*Calylophus lavandulifolius,* syn. *Oenothera lavandulifolia*) has gray-green foliage reminiscent of garden lavender. This matted, almost shrubby rock plant produces a daily yield of afternoon-opening flowers from May through June. The deep yellow petals are somewhat angular, giving a square look to the flowers. Barr called this plant, found throughout western Kansas, "a gem of the first water."

Narrowleaf bluets (*Hedyotis nigricans*) occur throughout Kansas, but more compact forms can be found in the western part of the state. This attractive, semishrubby plant has dark green linear leaves and blooms over a long period beginning in May. The small, waxy flowers are produced in crowded panicles. White is the typical color, but pinks are sometimes found.

Blooming from May into July, *Evolvulus nuttallianus* is another small semishrub of the prairies and plains. The foliage is linear-oblong and very silvery. In the axils of the leaves are morning-glory flowers 0.5 inch/13 mm wide, of pinkish-lavender.

Many other rock plants from western Kansas could be listed, but I hope those described provide a glimpse of the wealth of the state's flora. Others that should be mentioned include *Minuartia michauxii* var. *texana* (formerly *Arenaria*), *Hedeoma drummondii,* numerous *Astragalus* species, *Tetraneuris scaposa* var. *scaposa* (formerly *Hymenoxys*), *Paronychia jamesii,* several species of *Penstemon,* and *Polygala alba.* Descriptions of these can be found in Barr's *Jewels of the Plains.*

267

For those who want to explore the flora of Kansas while traveling through the state, the first rule is to keep off Interstate 70. There are many fine two-lane highways that will take you through more scenic areas. To see the Blue Hills, follow Highway 18 or Highway 24 through north-central Kansas. To take in the Red Hills, travel Highway 160 between Medicine Lodge and Meade. Highway 83 south of Oakley (on Interstate 70) will take you close to the Smoky Hill River badlands.

Let me also extend a warm invitation to rock gardeners to visit the Dyck Arboretum of the Plains in Hesston, Kansas. Situated about 35 miles/55 km north of Wichita, this is a young, developing institution emphasizing in its collections plants native to the state. Most of the species described in this article can be found in the Prairie Demonstration Garden. Perhaps you will want to linger awhile in Kansas.

Bibliography

Barr, Claude A. 1983. *Jewels of the Plains*. Minneapolis: University of Minnesota Press.

Wherry, Edgar T. 1955. *The Genus Phlox*. University of Pennsylvania, Morris Arboretum monograph 3. Philadelphia: Associates of the Morris Arboretum.

Originally published in the Bulletin of the American Rock Garden Society, *vol. 48, no. 3, pp. 181–185 (1990).*

Some Texas Plants in the Rock Garden

DONALD W. HUMPHREY

Mention the Hindu Kush, the Atlas, the Pyrenees, the Big Horns, or the Siskiyous, and rock gardeners conjure up entrancing visions of alpine meadows sprinkled with choice, rare, and therefore painfully desirable alpines. Mention Texas, and one is more likely to think of prickly pear cactus than alpines. But first impressions are not always trustworthy, and in a big country one must be patient enough to look far and wide for good things.

Texas has one of the largest flora in the United States, with nearly 5000 species of higher plants, of which 379 are endemic to Texas. This diverse flora includes subtropical species in the lower Rio Grande valley; coastal plain species along the Gulf; familiar eastern wildflowers in the forested eastern margin of the state; plants of the high plains in the northern panhandle; scattered outliers of Rocky Mountain flora in Guadalupe Mountain and Big Bend national parks; and the fascinating flora of the Chihuahuan desert in West Texas.

Texas has 10 reasonably well-defined plant zones: the pinewoods of eastern Texas; the Gulf prairies and marshes; the post oak savannah and blackland prairies intermingling west of the first two zones; the cross timbers and prairies in the north-central part of the state; the southern Texas plains of the lower Rio Grande; the Edwards Plateau, a distinctive limestone upland of south-central Texas; the rolling plains and the high plains in the northern panhandle; and the arid Trans Pecos mountains and basins. Elevations vary from sea level along the Gulf coast to 8751 feet/2669 meters at Guadalupe Peak in the Trans Pecos. Rainfall ranges from more than 50 inches/125 cm in eastern Texas to less than 1 foot/30 cm annually in the western part. Soils vary from acid in the east to basic and locally alkaline in the west.

Only a few species of alpine or subalpine plants are found in the Chisos and Guadalupe mountains, but the state has many fine plants for the rock garden and wild garden. My experiences may interest particularly that ever-increasing group of gardeners who live in the southern part of the United States; although many Texas plants are completely hardy, some are of questionable hardiness in USDA Zone 7, and others are apparently frost-tender.

My first experience with Texas plants came from the 1968 seed list of the American Horticultural Society, which included wildflowers from Bexar County, Texas, where San Antonio is situated. San Antonio is farther south than New Orleans as well as large portions of northern Mexico, and I should have expected little success in my Virginia garden, but I ordered seed of fourteen species, three of them shrubs. Only eight species came up, six survived, five bloomed, and two are with me still. My comments are confined to the six survivors.

Lygodesmia texana belongs to the chicory (*Cichoria*) group of the Asteraceae. The genus is known as "skeleton plant" because its leaves are reduced to bracts. The plant is a fleshy-rooted perennial to 1.5 feet/45 cm tall, freely branched and truly skeleton-like. Its flowers are lavender and rather showy. My plant never got above 10 inches/25 cm, bloomed the first year, and expired. It is not showy or elegant, but I would be glad to have it back. The genus is widespread in the West and northern Mexico. Probably the best chicory is *L. grandiflora*, a species under 1 foot/30 cm tall with threadlike leaves and large pale purple flowers, found from Idaho to Arizona.

Alophia drummondii (formerly *Eustylis purpurea*), called "purple pleatleaf," belongs to a genus of the Iridaceae largely confined to South America. I think of it as a small purple *Tigridia* with its ephemeral flowers held vertically rather than horizontally. I still have it. It is bulbous, with a few pleated leaves and a zigzag stem. With me it is generally about 1 foot/30 cm tall and blooms for a few weeks in midsummer. It becomes dormant in fall. It needs full sun and an average garden soil. Seeds received from Mrs. Bettina Blackmar of Luling, Texas, about whom more later, produced plants superior to the Bexar County seeds.

Menodora heterophylla is of a curious genus of the Oleaceae ranging from southern Colorado to southern California and deep into Mexico. It is perennial from the deep root, but some species of the genus are shrubs or subshrubs. The seeds are large and encased in a spongy covering. In my garden *M. heterophylla* formed a decumbent plant with several stems to 7 inches/18 cm long, blooming the first year. It is sometimes called "redbud" in Texas, not to be confused with *Cercis*. The buds are red, but on opening they fade to yellow. The species does not bloom profusely but has a long season, and the flowers are eye-catchers. I lost my plant, but if I could get seed again I would try it in a sandy soil in a protected spot. All members of this genus would seem worthy of a trial in southern rock gardens.

Lesquerella recurvata is a member of a large American genus that might be thought of as the New World's answer to the Old World's *Alyssum*. This one is an annual with several branching stems set with bright yellow mustard flowers. It bloomed and departed, but it is one of the small annuals that I believe have a place in the rock garden. Six of the 18 Texas species of this genus are perennial. I have grown *L. ovalifolia*, a very nice rock garden plant, though not long-lived with me. It is a high plains species found from northwest Texas northward.

Berberis trifoliata (formerly *Mahonia trifoliata*) is a first-rate shrub with silvery, patterned leaves. Its flowers are reputedly saffron-scented and the red fruits edible, hence the name "currant-of-Texas." My three plants have survived five Virginia winters and are attractive if somewhat sprawling; they have yet to bloom. In its native habitat the species attains 6 feet/2 meters in height.

Gilia incisa is a dowd. Authorities cannot agree whether it is annual, perennial, or biennial. It does not matter; I mention only it so you may be on guard against it. Its small, pinched, lavender-blue flowers make no show on the weedy plant.

I have grown *Allium drummondii* from seed and had it in bloom the second year. It is an attractive if not showy *Allium*, a plains species found from Nebraska to northern Mexico. The scape is usually under 1 foot/30 cm, with white to pink flowers about 0.25 inch/6 mm across, produced in spring. The leaves are narrow, rather flat, and channeled on the underside.

My second brush with Texas plants came about fortuitously. I received a letter from an ARGS member, Mrs. Bettina Blackmar of Luling, Texas, a rural town northeast of San Antonio. She was interested in receiving seeds of *Marshallia obovata* var. *scaposa* which I had offered in the 1970 seed list. Her letter contained a packet of *M. caespitosa* seeds. Thus began a correspondence of several years, with exchanges of seeds and plants. Many of the following plants or seeds came to my garden from Mrs. Blackmar.

The genus *Tradescantia* contains some 60 New World species, from diminutive annuals to large perennials up to 3 feet/1 meter tall. Many are overlarge or too vigorous for the rock garden. Last spring Mrs. Blackmar sent me another that merits a place in the choicest rock garden— *T. reverchonii*. The prostrate leaves are 6 inches/15 cm or more in length in my garden, 1 inch/2.5 cm broad, rather gray, and set with bristly hairs at nearly right angles to the leaf blade. The three-petaled flowers are a pure, bright blue, and more than 1 inch/2.5 cm across. Each lasts only a day, but the blooming period is fairly long. Another species that sounds equally good is *T. tharpii,* ranging north to Kansas, Oklahoma, and Missouri. Its large, three-petaled flowers may be purple, pink, or blue.

Androstephium coeruleum, a cormous plant of the Liliaceae, has been known as *A. violaceum, Milla coerulea,* and *Brodiaea coerulea.* Mrs. Blackmar sent me three corms, and I still have them after 5 years. Walter Carlton, a fine Texas naturalist and photographer, later brought me about 20 more. Nearly all my plants have three to five linear leaves. They begin emerging by late February, but the flower buds do not appear until mid- to late March, when the leaves are 2 to 4 inches/5 to 10 cm long. The flowers remind me of a violet-purple daffodil, with a funnel-shaped corolla about 1 inch/2.5 cm long. The plant needs a sunny site where it will not be overpowered or lost during its dormant period in summer and fall. The bulbs have not increased here.

Hesperaloe parviflora is the "red-flowered yucca" of prairies and mesquite thickets of central Texas. I have two plants sent me by Mrs. Blackmar. The larger is planted on a south slope in a bed of gravel, rock, and sand some 24 inches/60 cm deep. My plant has only a few leaves, and seeing the 5-foot/1.5-meter stems with their inflorescences of rosy or salmon flowers is an idle hope for me.

In the spring of 1973 I received several young plants from Mrs. Blackmar labeled *Nolina macrocarpum;* I suspect they are really *N. texana,* a species with numerous narrow leaves with stringy margins. [*Nolina macrocarpum* is not recognized, but a species *N. microcarpa* is listed.—*Ed.*] The flowering stems are very short for the genus, seldom longer than 18 inches/45 cm. The numerous small white flowers are borne in a dense compound cluster. The plants survived the winter in good shape.

The genus *Cooperia* belongs to the Amaryllidaceae and is closely related to *Zephyranthes,* having been at times included in that genus. Five species are listed from Texas. Through the kindness of Mrs. Blackmar I have *Cooperia pedunculata, C. drummondii,* and *C. smallii.* The first two are white-flowered, and the last is lemon-yellow. These plants are bulbous with a few linear leaves. The flowering scapes are from 6 to 12 inches/15 to 30 cm tall, bearing salver-form flowers. Their blooming period is quite protracted—from early spring to late summer—and their tendency to bloom following rain has given them the local name of "rain lilies." *Cooperia smallii* produced two flowers this past summer. The 2-inch/5-cm, erect yellow lily-like flowers are attractive but rather short-lived.

More floriferous is *Habranthus tubispathus* (formerly *H. texana*), a Texas endemic belonging to a genus otherwise found mainly in South America. Its flowers are orange-yellow and are shaped much like those of *Cooperia* but held horizontally rather than upright.

Manfreda (formerly *Polianthes*) *maculosa,* sent to me last spring, has successfully wintered without protection in an exposed site in sandy soil. It has six to ten glaucous basal leaves blotched with darker green or brown spots. It is nearly deciduous in winter, but not so much as *M. vir-*

ginica. The flowering stem is as much as 2 feet/60 cm tall, and the purplish or greenish-white flowers are 2 inches/5 cm long. I do not know whether they emit the strong evening perfume characteristic of *M. virginica*.

Alophia, a genus of bulbous irids, is sometimes included in *Herbertia*. Only one species is found in Texas, *Alophia drummondii*, endemic to the southern Texas grasslands. The pleated leaves are up to 1 foot/30 cm long and sheathed at the base. The 2-inch/5-cm flower is borne on 1-foot/30-cm stalk. The flower is composed of three large outer perianth segments and three short, pointed inner ones; the color is pale to dark lavender, white at the base. Seeds germinated readily, and plants with two or three leaves grew 5 inches/13 cm tall the first summer. The leaves appear to be evergreen, which may be a limiting factor in growing them in the north. Plants in the garden have survived temperatures at least as low as 17°F/−8°C.

Plants of the genus *Commelina* may be invasive in warmer gardens, but *C. dianthifolia* is worth a try where it is hardy. It is a tuberous-rooted perennial 6 inches/15 cm or so in height. Its brilliant blue flowers are produced sporadically during summer. My plant fell victim to its neighbors; in its native Trans Pecos country, it probably has little competition.

Plants of *Ranunculus macranthus* came to me from Mrs. Blackmar. The cluster of short, rather tuberous roots took hold rapidly in the garden. The common name, "large buttercup," is apt both for the flower and for the plant. The flowers are bright yellow, up to 1.5 inches/4 cm across, and have eight to eighteen petals. The plant begins blooming in April on short stems, which elongate as the plant goes to seed, reaching 18 inches/45 cm. It looks unkempt for a while, then turns brown and dies back, to reappear as a loose rosette of leaves in the fall, staying green all winter. It seeds around modestly. I think it a very fine plant, if a little large for the rock garden. It is native to the southwestern United States and Mexico.

In the same consignment I received plants of *Oenothera speciosa*, looking particularly peaked. I planted their stringy roots in a part of the rock garden needing rehabilitation; the rhizomes raced across it, sending up an abundance of 1-foot/30-cm stems topped by many lovely 3-inch/8-cm pink flowers with pale yellow centers. I wouldn't be without it, but don't plant it near anything choice. It has been in cultivation for a long time; in the coal fields of the Appalachian plateau of Tennessee I found it one of the most common flowers in the yards of the mountain people. Its Spanish name, *amapola del campo* ("poppy of the field"), seems particularly apt.

One oenothera-like plant sent to me has remained a mystery. I think it is *Calylophus lavandulifolius*. It is a woody-based, decumbent, nearly caespitose plant with short linear leaves. Its yellow flowers are more than 1 inch/2.5 cm across and have the ephemeral texture common to *Cistus* and *Papaver*. One plant in a dry sunny spot bloomed profusely over a long period and then died. Another in half shade, competing with fescue, has survived several years, but it does not look healthy nor does it bloom abundantly. The species ranges north to South Dakota, so it should be perfectly hardy. If well grown it is a real charmer and merits front rank in the rock garden. Cuttings have failed to root, and I am resigned to losing it.

Other Texas *Oenothera* species I have grown are *O. brachycarpa* and *O. triloba*. These are nearly stemless rosette plants resembling dandelions, with bright yellow flowers opening predictably at dusk, so quickly you can watch them expand. *Oenothera brachycarpa* is the more western species, with flowers nearly twice as large as those of *O. triloba*. The former is described as a perennial, the latter as a winter annual or biennial; however, neither is long-lived. After the plants die they leave a rosette of woody seed capsules at ground level, which when wet can be pried open and the contents spread around.

Oenothera macrocarpa subsp. *macrocarpa* (formerly *O. missouriensis*) is too well known to need a description, and *O. drummondii* turned out to be a weedy species whose yellow flowers appeared so late that I never saw them except as withered rags the following morning. I may have had a poor form.

Texas boasts 12 species of *Phlox*, including several midwestern and eastern species. However, the only phlox of Texas provenance I have grown is the wild form of the annual *P. drummondii*. It seeds around mildly and puts on a brilliant display of red during summer, when color is welcome in the rock garden. Its various color forms run the gamut through red, purple, lavender, pink, and white, with eyed forms not uncommon.

There are 23 species of *Penstemon* in Texas, but most are rather large for the small rock garden. Five are endemic, and of these I have grown only *P. triflorus* from the Edwards Plateau. It is reminiscent of *P. cobaea* but more refined, with maroon flowers lined with lighter color within. It has not been permanent with me, but its hybrid with *P. cobaea* has lasted well. *Penstemon cobaea* is well known, growing from Texas to Nebraska; in its better color forms in its native range it is a truly superb plant.

Penstemon murrayanus is definitely not a rock garden plant but it is so unusual that it deserves mention. It forms a few large cabbagy, glaucous leaves from which springs a 3- to 4-foot/120-cm stem with perfoliate leaves, looking as though the stem had grown through them. The stem is topped by bright red flowers more than 1 inch/2.5 cm long, over a long period in early summer. The plant requires staking in my garden. In a sandy soil it is not difficult to grow, but the evergreen leaves should probably be given protection in the north. It comes from the sandy regions of Texas, Louisiana, Arkansas, and Oklahoma.

Eustoma russellianum (formerly *E. grandiflorum*) is the pride of Texas. A well-grown plant with many 2-foot/60-cm stems bearing large, purple, tulip-like flowers is a breathtaking sight. A member of the Gentianaceae, it is found on the southern plains from Nebraska to Texas. It is a short-lived perennial with a white, carroty root that will not survive our northern Virginia winters without a thick but loose mulch. However, if I lift the roots and place them in sand in a cutting frame, they winter safely and will bloom when set out in the garden. Growing the plant from the small, abundant seeds is the surest means of increase, although the seedlings stay tiny for an inordinate time. Its spectacular beauty should guarantee it a place in warmer gardens.

Ipomopsis rubra is an eastern representative of a western genus, found in the southeastern states from North Carolina to Texas. It is a biennial or annual, forming an attractive rosette of much-divided filiform leaves. In summer it sends up a single stem topped with numerous tubular red flowers, spotted within. It is much like *I. aggregata*, often seen in abundance on the lower mountain slopes of the western states. Among low-growing lilies or other spiky plants, it is an excellent filler and accent. It does best in a light, well-drained soil in full sun. It does not require staking.

Admittedly, many of the plants described in this article are rather large for the smaller rock garden, but no larger than many plants regularly recommended in the literature. Most are plants of eastern Texas, but the Edwards Plateau, the northern panhandle, and the Trans Pecos have many other perennials, annuals and subshrubs that could and should find a place in our rock gardens.

Who has grown *Centaurium beyrichii*, the beautiful mountain pink of rocky limestone hillsides? How many gardens are graced by *Nicolettia edwardsii*, a lovely annual daisy of the Edwards Plateau? Is yellow-flowered *Allium coryi* hardy in northern gardens? Is *Talinum aurantiacum*, with its inch-/2.5-cm orange flowers, in cultivation—or indeed any of the other seven Texas *Talinum* species, apart from *T. parviflorum*? Have any of our members ever seen low-growing, scarlet-flowered *Silene plankii* from the Franklin Mountains? These questions conjure up that most tantalizing desire of rock gardeners, to bring new plants in from the wilds to be enjoyed and acclimatized in our gardens and shared with others.

Originally published in the Bulletin of the American Rock Garden Society, *vol. 36, no. 2, pp. 100–106 (1978).*

PART FOUR: NORTHEAST

On Eastern Cliffs

JAMES E. MITCHELL

[This is a condensation from a series of articles the author prepared for a planned book, never published. Because the status of some lands mentioned and the access routes to some of the trails have changed, reference to these matters has been deleted in this version. The reader wishing to visit these sites should consult with relevant state and federal land management agencies. Also deleted were many remarks on Mitchell's collection of the plants mentioned for his garden and wildflower nursery.—*Ed.*]

———— Camel's Hump and Mount Mansfield ————

Camel's Hump Mountain, situated about 10 miles/16 km from Waterbury, Vermont, has an altitude of 4083 feet/1245 meters, only 310 feet/95 meters lower than Mount Mansfield. From places where both mountains can be seen at once, Camel's Hump actually seems to be the higher of the two. [The author described an approach via a trail beginning at the base of the mountain, 3 miles/5 km from the small town of North Duxbury.—*Ed.*]

For a quarter-mile/400 meters along our trail the trees have been showing the effect of high altitude in their dwarfer and more contorted form, until few are more than 10 feet/3 meters tall; the spruces and firs, many a half-century or more old, are no more than 6 feet/2 meters tall. Peeping around under the dwarf trees, we suddenly see in the dense shade a fine sheet of *Empetrum nigrum* that has made a mat about 3 feet/1 meter in diameter, falling gently over a bare rock. Its fine evergreen foliage makes it beautiful, and it is covered with oval blue-black fruit, an alpine worth trying in gardens. This plant, so plentiful in the White Mountains, on Mount Katahdin, and in spots in eastern Maine, is rare in the Green Mountains.

This difficult plant does not need the mountain air: it grows at sea level along the Gaspé North Shore in eastern Quebec, and a colony has been found on the eastern tip of Long Island, New York. It should be taken up with a good quantity of the mountain soil clinging to its roots, to preserve those mysterious elements whose presence in the soil is necessary for the growth of this and many other difficult American alpines. Plant this mass of roots and black mountain grit in a soil composed of three parts ground acid peat and one part pure sand and give the plants shade from the noonday sun; a northern exposure and a wet moraine are preferable.

A little farther up the trail, the conifers suddenly cease; here there are no dwarf spruce or fir mats a few inches high, clinging to the rocks, as seen on Mount Washington. When the conifers have decreased to about 2 feet/60 cm in height, they suddenly give way to masses of *Vaccinium angustifolium* and its variety *laevifolium*, mixed together with a real alpine, *V. uliginosum*. An occasional clump of *V. vitis-idaea* subsp. *minus* can also be found above the tree line. We have scarcely passed the last stunted firs when *Minuartia* (formerly *Arenaria*) *groenlandica* shows its cheerful flowers everywhere in sun and partial shade. All along the trail grows Labrador tea (*Ledum groenlandicum*), here in a good dwarf form.

The south side of the Hump is an abrupt perpendicular face several hundred feet straight down; however, a good mountain-climber will have no trouble finding a way along the face. One day in July, while working along the face of this cliff, I found a very dwarf form of *Solidago multiradiata* var. *arctica* (formerly *S. cutleri*) and, clinging to the cliffs, the only *Salix uva-ursi* ever found on this mountain. The foliage of this willow was very different from that of *S. uva-ursi* as found on Mount Washington, but botanists have pronounced it the same species.

Unlike Camel's Hump, which is a sharp isolated peak, Mount Mansfield is a long high ridge; from many distant parts of the state, the whole ridge has the appearance of a human face, with a very long space between the nose and chin, looking straight up to the sky. The forehead is on the south end of the ridge; the nose is sharp and distinct, and the chin at the north end is the highest part. [The author took a route designated the "Barnes Camp Trail" about 3 miles/5 km to Taft Lodge, then climbed to the base of the chin on a steeper trail.—Ed.]

If we take half an hour to explore the Adam's apple we shall find most of the plants which we shall later find on the chin. However, today we are climbing the chin, and this is our first real climbing, where we shall have to use our hands to assist our feet. A half mile/800 meters of this, and we stand on the chin, Vermont's highest peak.

All over the chin above the tree line, the prevailing shrubs are the three alpine blueberries, *Vaccinium caespitosum, V. uliginosum,* and *V. angustifolium,* all good dwarf shrubs for the acid-soil rock garden. Here, on the highest point among the alpine grasses, are several mats of *Diapensia lapponica.* This is its only station in the Green Mountains.

Minuartia groenlandica and *Potentilla tridentata* (recently renamed *Sibbaldiopsis tridentata*) are everywhere, and a little searching will locate *Solidago multiradiata* var. *arctica,* but it is not common here, nor is *Salix uva-ursi.* The very rare fern *Dryopteris fragrans* formerly grew on this mountain, but botanists have uprooted the last known plants here and "conserved" them by placing them in their hay cabinets, which they euphoniously call herbariums.

On the lip, the long narrow part of the crest between the nose and the chin, are several large tracts of the lovely *Vaccinium vitis-idaea,* in as good form as the best White Mountain one, and far better than the form I found on the knife-edge in Smuggler's Notch, only about a half-mile/800 meters away in a straight line.

_____ Smuggler's Notch _____

Smuggler's Notch is probably the most celebrated scenic attraction in the Green Mountains of Vermont, mountains noted for their beauty and visited by thousands of tourists every summer. Of more direct concern to us, the cliffs in this Notch are the habitat of one of the most interesting plant communities in New England.

The scenery through the Notch is of great beauty and grandeur. The points of interest to the average visitor are the Big Spring, the Elephant's Head, and Hunter and His Dog, all on the east side of the highway, and the caves on the west side. The cliffs on both sides are from 300 feet/ 90 meters to a quarter-mile/400 meters back from the road; on them and in their fissures grow remarkable plants of great interest to rock gardeners.

Although both sides of the Notch abound in rare alpines, there are more species, and more plants of each species, at the base of the tallest cliffs on the west side than in any other spot of equal size elsewhere in the area. One clear, hot July morning, I led a small group of amateur botanists on a collecting trip there. We drove our cars to the highest point of the highway and parked where the road began to descend to the north. We walked back a little, and facing the cliffs to the west, we could see several places where great sections of the cliffs had broken away and huge masses of rocks had tumbled down the mountainside. To the largest of these debris falls we made our way.

The base of the cliffs and top of the debris were about a quarter-mile/ 400 meters ahead, hard climbing through thick brush over boulders and through gullies and ravines with no marked trail. It took 45 minutes of the hardest kind of work to negotiate that quarter-mile. On leaving the road we were at once arrested by the profusion of ferns of all the more common varieties, and we soon found the beautiful holly fern *Polystichum braunii*; indeed, it was in the Notch that Frederick Pursh, the German botanist, first found it. Another good rock garden fern, the rock polypody (*Polypodium virginianum*), grows in masses on shaded boulders all through the Notch, very abundant near the highway but not plentiful on the high cliffs; it is easy to grow in dense shade. The rocks over and around which we scrambled were covered with large healthy plants of *Saxifraga virginiensis* in full bloom. This common saxifrage is an excellent plant for our rock gardens if given a moist position in light shade.

As we laboriously proceeded through a dense tangle of shrubs, we began to see the mountain form of the fancy fern, *Dryopteris expansa*, a most beautiful species which improved in width and laciness as we went higher. A half-dozen species of violets, including *Viola canadensis* in full bloom, appeared on every hand.

Bearing slightly to the left, to keep directly opposite the Elephant's Head, after about 40 minutes we emerged from the taller growth and saw, about 50 yards/meters ahead, the rock debris that was our goal. The instant we left the shade of the tall trees, we were alert for the first mountain saxifrages. As the trees gave way to low shrubs, off to the right we noticed a wet ledge rising just above the brush. There we saw our first Scotch bluebell (*Campanula rotundifolia*) waving its first bells of the season on long, graceful stems. About the easiest of the campanulas, it encircles the globe in the Northern Hemisphere, and while it varies much in its wide range, it is always a fine alpine.

Approaching the ledge, we discovered that sterling little rock fern, the rusty woodsia (*Woodsia ilvensis*), a 5-inch/13-cm gem that should be in every garden. Suddenly one of my young companions called out. She had just passed me and was kneeling among the shrubs, gazing at a plant—rare indeed—among the rocks. It was *Castilleja pallida*; like all the castillejas, it has the taint of parasitism, and I doubt that any of the genus is worthy of a gardener's attention.

The shrubs had decreased; there were more broken rocks. As we looked toward the cliffs, we gazed over a river of boulders and small disintegrating stones hurled from 1000 feet/300 meters above by the action of frost and ice. This stone river is about 200 yards/meters long, up to the base of the cliffs, with the largest pieces lowest down. Nearer the cliffs, the stone disintegrates and in part turns to soil, with the solid bedrock showing through here and there. Under and through this rocky debris, throughout the growing season, there filters a steady flow of water from the drip of the cliffs above, creating a natural moraine. The lower part contains few plants, as the fresh flow of rock over it every spring kills any that may try to get a foothold here; on the sides and under the shelter of projecting ledges, however, there are many alpines. Looking toward the cliffs, we saw off to the right a wide space covered with vegetation and abloom with color. There the conformation of the ledges had turned the spring flow to the side; a gravelly soil up to 1 foot/30 cm deep had formed. This, with the steady drip of water filtering through, furnished the ideal moraine for plant treasures, and it teaches better than any book how to make a moraine in the rock garden.

While still in the thin shrubbery just below the open moraine, we found on a damp ledge the fine white-flowered alpine *Draba arabisans*, which gets its specific name from the similarity in shape of its foliage to that of an arabis. In the wild it is a thin, straggling plant, but in cultivation in full sun it is a close tuft of foliage covered in spring with white arabis-like flowers; unlike the arabis, however, it never becomes straggly nor crowds out other plants. I first brought it into cultivation as an experiment, but it is now recognized as one of the best white-flowered drabas.

We had scarcely begun to climb the open moraine and were still among the large boulders when we found, growing out between them, two very rare and almost unknown alpines—*Hedysarum boreale* and *Astragalus robbinsii* var. *minor* (formerly *A. blakei*), very closely related members of the great pea family, and very much alike. The principal distinction between the two genera is found in the seedpods: that of *Hedysarum*, by constriction of the pod, is divided crosswise into two to eight sections, each containing one seed; that of *Astragalus* has no cross sections, but in some species may be divided into two chambers lengthwise by the intrusion of the dorsal or ventral sutures (front or back seams). These two species, found also at Lake Willoughby, Vermont, are of about equal size, from 12 to 18 inches/30 to 45 cm tall in the wild. The flowers are pea-shaped, bright red in the *Hedysarum* and varying from white to blue in the *Astragalus*. The upper surfaces of the leaves of both are glossy green, but the lower surfaces are quite distinct and give a means of identification when there are no flowers or seeds. The underside of the leaf of *Hedysarum boreale* is glossy and is a slightly different shade of green from the upper side, while the underside of the leaf of *Astragalus robbinsii* var. *minor* is gray. We found some mature seed of the *Hedysarum*, but the *Astragalus* seed was not ripe. The seed should be planted outdoors immediately, as the action of frost seems a necessity for germination.

By this time our party was scattered along the rocky moraine, and one of them found, out in the open sun, a small plant of the rare *Saxifraga aizoides*. As we ascended the cliffs, on dripping wet portions we found lovely sheets of this saxifrage, sometimes 2 feet/60 cm across, just beginning to bloom. Its foliage is quite mosslike, very dark green, and never more than 1 inch/2.5 cm tall. The flowers, on 1-inch/2.5-cm stems, are a nice clear yellow with orange or red stamens, which give the flowers a deep orange appearance. This saxifrage is seldom seen in cultivation in

America, but it can be successfully grown in a wet moraine shaded from hot sun.

All over the moraine, and on the cliffs where not too dry, we found the sterling *Saxifraga oppositifolia* creeping over the rocks, with foliage not over 0.5 inch/13 mm tall; it too can be found here in large green mats 1 foot/30 cm or more wide. In mid-July its blooms had long faded; but if you come here in the middle of May, you will find it in full bloom, great red to purple blooms on 2- to 4-inch/5- to 10-cm stems. Then you would also find snow in the shaded spots here. One May day I had the pleasure of seeing a fine sheet of this saxifrage in full bloom, hanging from a rock shelf within a foot/30 cm of a 15-inch/38-cm icicle. This is not a difficult plant on a moraine in shade, or in a moist spot facing north. We meet it again at Lake Willoughby, Vermont, but nowhere else until we reach the shores of the Gulf of St. Lawrence; the White Mountains of New Hampshire and the Adirondacks of New York do not know it.

Here too we found an *Arenaria* species, mistaken by some for *Minuartia groenlandica*, but I identified it as *Arenaria verna* var. *propinqua* (now *Minuartia rubella*), a much smaller plant and a true perennial. *Minuartia groenlandica* is an acid-soil plant plentiful on Mount Mansfield, but I have never seen it in Smuggler's Notch. By this time someone in the party had found the silver-encrusted saxifrage, *Saxifraga paniculata* (formerly *S. aizoon*), in full bloom, its airy spray of cream-colored flowers rising 6 to 10 inches/15 to 25 cm above the beautiful rosettes. It grows singly and in bunches well up under the shade of overhanging shrubs, its rosettes forming silvery sheets several feet across. It is one of the easiest and best saxifrages for the rock garden. The great English writer Reginald Farrer says that it is a sun-lover, and that in the Alps the finest plants are on acid granitic formations, while the plants on limestone are much inferior. This is not true in America, where it is never found on granitic formations, but always on lime-bearing rocks, and the finest plants are always in some shade.

Here and there on the sides of the moraine, and higher up on the part protected from the spring rockslides, we found that splendid rock garden shrub *Potentilla fruticosa* (syn. *Pentaphylloides floribunda*). It is gray-leaved, with yellow roses from 1 to 1.5 inches/2.5 to 4 cm across, and it blooms all summer. Plants grown from European seed, and native plants from farm pastures in western Vermont, may reach 3 or 4 feet/1 meter in height, but this mountain strain grows from 12 to 18 inches/30 to 45 cm high; plants brought down into my garden have stayed dwarf. I regard this strain, which I call 'Montana', as one of the best and easiest of rock garden shrubs, which will grow anywhere if a little lime is scattered about its roots.

The botanist's paradise is directly opposite the Elephant's Head, an enormous mass of projecting rock. I had botanized those cliffs, and as the group sat eating our lunch, I explained that the flora on those opposite cliffs was much the same as on our side, but that I had found there one species that had never been found elsewhere in the Notch. On a high knife-edge just south of the Elephant's Head, I had discovered a large patch of *Vaccinium vitis-idaea* subsp. *minus*. This acid-soil plant seemed out of place on that limestone cliff, but to this high edge of solid rock no lime-charged water could rise from below, so that all the water came from the sky and was absorbed by the foot-/30-cm-thick covering of humus built up by thousands of generations of plants. This layer of humus was highly acid even though it rested on a limestone foundation, so it was a fine home for the vaccinium.

As we ate our lunch, we could see growing in the solid mountain wall, only a few feet away, a neat little plant with two oval-shaped leaves about 1 inch/2.5 cm long, from which rose a 2- to 3-inch/5- to 8-cm stem bearing a single purple flower much like an inverted violet. This is *Pinguicula vulgaris*, very rare in New England but occurring on the Gaspé Peninsula. It dies down in the fall to a little bulblike root, not 0.25 inch/ 6 mm in diameter, which is considered a great delicacy by field mice in my rock garden. Perhaps not as showy as *P. grandiflora*, a native of Ireland, it is a good and interesting alpine.

After lunch, we tried the right side of the moraine, which is protected from rockslides and is covered with vegetation. Here one member found, among a tangle of *Potentilla fruticosa*, a few plants of *Gentianella amarella*, a very rare species of much interest to the strictly botanical members of the party, but—being an annual—of little interest to the rock gardener.

All, however, were greatly interested in a little fern we found here, tucked back into the rock crevices completely away from the sun's rays: that dainty gem, the green spleenwort (*Asplenium trichomanes* var. *ramosum*, formerly *A. viride*), said by Asa Gray to be widely distributed but rare. It is the most difficult fern I have yet tried to grow. It is scarcely 3 inches/8 cm tall and always grows on lime-containing rocks, generally in fissures and always in deep shade. One of the party found another, even smaller alpine fern, the dainty *Woodsia alpina*. Off among the large boulders we found the rock-inhabiting *Clematis occidentalis* (formerly *C. verticillaris*), with large blue flowers. This beautiful plant grows in small numbers over many of the lime-containing ledges in Vermont. It varies greatly in color, in shades of pink, blue, and purple. It grows slowly in cultivation and makes a good rock garden plant.

Near the base of the high cliffs just north of the botanist's paradise, we discovered a real fernery. Here in about 100 feet/30 meters of cliff we found green spleenwort, rusty woodsia, alpine woodsia, and hundreds of maidenhair spleenwort—the last none too common on these cliffs. *Asplenium trichomanes* (Plate 105) has no superior as a rock garden fern. It is graceful and pretty and easy to grow in light shade. It has much the same appearance as a large green spleenwort, but the stipe (leaf-stem) is black, while that of the green spleenwort is green. Maidenhair spleenwort is one of the easiest ferns to grow, while green spleenwort is one of the most difficult, and of course much rarer.

Scattered all over were thousands of plants of the rare *Erigeron hyssopifolius*, a 6-inch/15-cm daisy with grassy foliage and light pink to lavender flowers. It is inclined to be straggly here in the mountains, but when brought down to our gardens it becomes a dense tuft of foliage and blooms much more profusely. While not showy, it is better than many of the European rock plants and will apparently grow anywhere.

When all these plants had been collected, and we had searched in vain for *Draba cana* (formerly *D. stylaris*), a white-flowered species the great botanist Cyrus G. Pringle had found here half a century before, tired but happy we began our descent. As we began the homeward drive, the setting sun was disappearing behind the mountain ridges and someone said, "It is the end of a perfect day."

The White Mountains

Situated in northern New Hampshire and extending into western Maine is the group of granitic mountains known collectively as the White Mountains. For many years considered the highest peaks east of the Mississippi River, they are now known to be about 400 feet/120 meters lower than the Mount Mitchell Range in North Carolina, and they probably are also surpassed by one or more peaks of the Torngat Mountains in northern Labrador. They are a range of many peaks, yet they cover an area only about 35 miles/90 km square. They are quite distinct from the backbone of the main Appalachian system, which is represented in New England by the Green Mountains of Vermont.

The White Mountains are divided into several distinct subranges by deep depressions that cut through them in a generally north-south direction. The largest and most important subrange is known as the Presidential Range, from the fact that its highest peaks were named after our early presidents. Mount Washington, the highest, towers almost 1.25 miles/2 km above sea level (6284 feet/1917 meters, to be exact). Its crest can be reached by several different trails and, more easily yet, by the celebrated Cogwheel Railroad, which climbs the western side of the mountain, while the equally famous Toll Road furnishes excellent access for automobiles up its eastern slope.

For many years botanists have known that a unique plant community grows on these mountains, quite unlike the flora of the surrounding country, and with few exceptions not met again until 160 miles/260 km northeast on Mount Katahdin; then skipping 200 miles/320 km, it turns up in the Shickshock Mountains of the Gaspé Peninsula, and also in Newfoundland, the coast of Labrador, and western Greenland.

There are many places in these mountains famous for the abundance of alpine plants. The Alpine Garden, Tuckerman Ravine, and King Ravine are just three of the scores of places where many rare plants can be found; yet many people get to the top of Mount Washington, look around, and see nothing but *Minuartia groenlandica*. This is a pretty plant, but it is short-lived in our gardens. I have heard several persons say that there are few flowers on Mount Washington, yet I know of spots containing several acres where it is scarcely possible to take three steps without treading on some rare mountain gem. I gathered one little clump about 6 inches/40 cm square which contained plants of *Diapensia lapponica*, *Loiseleuria procumbens*, *Salix uva-ursi*, and *Potentilla (Sibbaldiopsis) tridentata*, all mingled together. There is, of course, little chance for vegetation other than lichens on the tops of the higher White Mountain peaks: the uppermost sections are composed of great heaps of enormous angular boulders with practically no soil.

Up the Toll Road

The Mount Washington Toll Road is a remarkable piece of engineering, rising a mile/1600 meters in 8 miles/13 km. On an August day, my son Earl, A. F. Emberley of Ayers Cliff, Quebec, and I, all experienced plant-hunters, did not go to the top, because we were after real botanical finds seldom found on wind-swept peaks. Shortly after passing the Half-Way House we began to see plants of *Vaccinium vitis-idaea* subsp. *minus* and a dwarf form of *Ledum groenlandicum*. Above the Half-Way House some of the mileposts had disappeared, but we proceeded about 1.5 miles/2 km farther, until we parked at the spot where the Nelson Crag Trail comes out onto the Toll Road. On the opposite side of the road was a water tub fed from a never-failing mountain spring with ice-cold water, clear and sparkling. This spot proved to be the center of a real alpine garden not marked on the maps; although nearly 2.5 miles/4 km before the summit, it is one of the best alpine plant stations in the White Mountains.

Our contour map showed us to be at approximately 5000 feet/1500 meters altitude, between 1200 and 1300 feet/370 and 400 meters below the summit, which we could see clearly from this point. The mountain flattened out; here was a spot of about 5 acres/2 hectares that, while not level in comparison with the Great Gulf below and Nelson Crag above, appeared like a great undulating mountain park. From it the north slope descended rapidly into the Great Gulf, one of the largest glacial cirques in the White Mountains.

The east and west boundaries of our natural rock garden were the winding Toll Road; on the west it terminated in a narrow swale, and across the swale was a patch of low shrubs. In these 5 acres/2 hectares or so there were hundreds of thousands of low-arctic plants. Here we found *Loiseleuria procumbens* and *Diapensia lapponica* in masses, along with great

287

patches of the dwarf arctic willow *Salix uva-ursi* creeping along over the rocks, never more than 4 inches/10 cm high. This is an easy plant to grow almost everywhere in rock gardens. *Loiseleuria* is also a tiny shrub, never over 2 inches/5 cm high; large plants may cover a square foot, but most have scarcely a quarter of that expanse. The plant has beautiful pink flowers in July and is known in Europe, where it is also native, as "mountain azalea," although it is not an azalea at all. You must give this and other plants found here a highly acid soil. When you dig one of these plants you notice at once the jet-black soil, plainly composed of nothing but the disintegrating granitic rock and the humus from the decay of untold generations of plants.

About 25 feet/8 meters from where we parked was a low perpendicular ledge, not over 6 feet/2 meters high, draped with great mats of *Empetrum nigrum* loaded with oblong black fruits fully 1 inch/2.5 cm long and 0.5 inch/13 mm in diameter—the largest and finest fruit I have ever seen on this species. This ledge faced north so that the crowberry received little direct sunlight; where this plant is found at lower elevations, as in the Green Mountains, it is invariably in some shade. When we bring it down to our gardens, we must give it rather heavy shade; it is a difficult plant in cultivation, but it can be grown.

Here too we found thousands of *Rhododendron lapponicum* in mats from 1 inch/6 cm square to a fine one that Emberley gathered, which was practically circular and fully 2 feet/60 cm across. He found this in a depression where there was plenty of soil and was able to get it with a big ball of earth on its roots. I told him that he probably could not make such a big plant live, but I saw it in full bloom in his garden the following spring. This is the true *R. lapponicum* and has been made the type species of a section of the genus found in all boreal regions of the Northern Hemisphere. From all accounts, our representative is the poorest species in the section and the most difficult to grow.

Scattered all over this mountain garden, which we named Nelson Crag Garden, were thousands of clumps of *Minuartia groenlandica* of a somewhat different type from those in the Green Mountains. We saw plenty of *Vaccinium vitis-idaea* subsp. *minus* in its best form, covered with berries just turning bright red. The low, dense growth makes the White Mountain form the best I have found anywhere. With its beautiful glossy, dark green foliage, lovely pink flowers in late June, and bright red berries in fall and early winter, this can be considered one of our finest native alpines. Take up the plant with plenty of soil and set it out in a soil stuffed with peat, and you should have no trouble with it. Another vaccinium that grows all over these mountains is *V. uliginosum*, a dwarf blueberry with blue-green foliage and tasty fruits. This too does well in a soil full of acid peat.

On the west side of our garden the mountain had been hollowed out, and the wash from the rocks above had deposited a clayey soil. Fed from below by hidden mountain springs, it formed a damp swale 12 to 20 feet/4 to 6 meters wide and 100 feet/30 meters long. Here grew thousands of *Kalmia polifolia* (Plate 12), the pale laurel, about 1 foot/30 cm high, with many of the plants still covered with relatively large, deep pink blooms. This beautiful mountain form is a great improvement over that growing in the lowland swamps of the north.

On the edge of this swale we found many clumps of the endemic *Geum peckii* in full bloom, some in the clay of the swale and others in the black mountain soil. The plant grows about 6 inches/15 cm tall and has golden flowers 1 inch/2.5 cm or more across. It is a fine plant here in the mountains but must be planted in rich damp soil in partial shade in our gardens, for if planted in full sun it grows very slowly.

The next day we tried the left side of the road. Exploration of both sides of the trail below the Toll Road showed that for nearly 0.25 mile/ 400 meters below the road, the trail led by easy grades through a fine alpine-plant region covering many acres.

Loiseleuria procumbens, Rhododendron lapponicum, Diapensia lapponica, Potentilla (Sibbaldiopsis) tridentata, and arenarias were found in thousands, and here too we noticed that some of the *Empetrum* appeared to have red berries. Our first impression was that the berries were not mature and had not reached the black or ripe stage, but a little close observation showed that the berries were not so long and that the foliage was somewhat different. I placed it as *E. eamesii* subsp. *atropurpureum* (formerly *E. nigrum* var. *purpureum*), which is considered to be a distinct species by some botanists and is named *E. purpureum*; it is much rarer than *E. nigrum*.

Here too, within 20 feet/6 meters of the trail, we found the rare alpine *Arctostaphylos alpina* (Plate 86), which has little resemblance to the common bearberry, *A. uva-ursi*. Its leaves are much broader than those of the bearberry, of an entirely different shade of green, and so wrinkled by the prominent veins as to appear corrugated; the ripe fruit is jet-black. Unlike the common bearberry, this species is not evergreen but sheds its leaves in October. It is not a difficult plant in gardens. Although we found plenty of it here, it is distinctly a local plant; there are probably more than a hundred stations of it in the White Mountains, but the stations are not large, so few plant-hunters have found them.

We also found several plants of the dwarf birch *Betula nana* (formerly *B. glandulosa*) creeping over the rocks. I thought this a nice dwarf shrub until later in the day, when I had climbed up over Nelson Crag and had come out on the Toll House Road near the spot where the Six Husbands Trail crosses it, about a mile/1600 meters above where our truck was parked. Close to this trail I found a score or more *B. nana* plants much smaller than usual; their round leaves, not over 0.5 inch/13 mm across, and their creeping habit gave them much the appearance of the partridgeberry (*Mitchella repens*).

All over this section of the mountain, in more or less shady places, we found the clubmoss *Huperzia* (formerly *Lycopodium*) *selago*. This is a true alpine, found above the treeline on most of our northern mountains. It grows in little tufts about 3 inches/8 cm tall and is the only clubmoss that I would think of bringing into my garden. I find it easy to grow in shade.

Huntington Ravine is one of the large glacial cirques so numerous in the White Mountains; while not as large as the Great Gulf or Oakes Gulf nor as deep as Tuckerman's Ravine, it is indeed a great trough cut into the side of Mount Washington. Like all these, it has a small stream formed from the dripping cliffs above and flowing over its floor, and its wet cliffs and rocky floor support an interesting flora.

While my two companions went down to the floor of the ravine, I went down about halfway and then began traversing. This kept me among the dripping rocks, but it necessitated many a retreat and advance. I kept moving along, however, and was soon rewarded by finding, in a damp, densely shaded spot, several hundred plants of *Phyllodoce coerulea* (Plate 87), of all sizes from little 1-inch/2.5-cm seedlings to old plants 6 inches/15 cm tall. Many of the older plants were in full bloom, the flowers resembling little light-blue tubs, relatively large for such small plants. *Phyllodoce coerulea* is closely related to the European heaths and might well be called "American blue heather." It is a fine plant for moist, shaded spots in rock gardens. It is not really a rare plant on the Presidential Range but may be found on the damp headlands of all the gulfs and ravines; however, nobody except the real plant-hunter ever sees it.

I was to have one disappointment, however: I could not find anywhere on these damp cliffs even a single plant of another heath, *Harrimanella* (formerly *Cassiope*) *hypnoides*. I did find it later on the damp walls of King Ravine, 10 miles/16 km northwest of Huntington Ravine.

My two companions had found the floor of the ravine very interesting. Their best find consisted of several plants of *Arnica mollis* in full bloom. The plants were about 10 inches/25 cm tall, with the stems surmounted by yellow daisies about 2 inches/5 cm across. This has been considered a difficult plant, but if it is planted in full sun on a wet moraine, no trouble will be experienced.

By the time my companions below had finished examining the floor, I had worked around to the head of the ravine and signaled to them that I was going up over the headwall to the top. On arriving at the top, I found myself close to the Six Husbands Trail. I spent some time examining wet ledges on both sides of this trail and found stations of *Phyllodoce coerulea* on each side, but no *Harrimanella*.

The Six Husbands Trail goes straight south to the Alpine Garden, situated southeast of the summit. This section of the mountain is comparatively level and covered mostly with alpine grasses and sedges. Here and there are spots, sometimes 50 feet/15 meters across, in which there are few grasses, but where *Diapensia*, *Rhododendron lapponicum*, and *Salix uva-ursi* abound. In this area there was no *Loiseleuria*, so plentiful below the base of Nelson Crag.

In one of the open spots near this trail, mixed with the rhododendron and *Salix uva-ursi*, I found several mounds about 1 foot/30 cm across that at first glance appeared to be *Diapensia*. Noticing a difference, I examined them closely and found that I had discovered *Silene acaulis* var. *exscapa*. The ordinary *S. acaulis* is easy anywhere in full sun. Its variety *exscapa* has been found in many parts of the Presidential Range but only in small clusters, and it may be called rare.

_____ Mount Albert in the Shickshock Mountains _____

Mount Albert, the second-highest mountain on the Gaspé Peninsula (3775 feet/1150 meters) lies directly west of the center of Tabletop Mountain, with the Sainte Anne River between them. It is in many ways a remarkable mountain. Its rock is a soft serpentine, essentially a hydrated magnesium silicate, with magnesium present in sufficient quantity to be deadly to many kinds of plants. Like Tabletop, it is a great high tableland covered mostly with gray lichens and mosses. Everyone who has visited Mount Albert agrees that this drear, dead appearance is its most outstanding characteristic; nonetheless, it supports on its seemingly naked slopes, in its moist hollows, in its many crevices, and among its decomposing boulders a unique vascular flora of probably more than 100 species.

I spent two days on its north edge, going up on the top for a short time each day, and then put in a third day among the wild crags of Devil's Gulch on the east side, also reaching the top on its eastern end. Our trail for three days ran along the base of the mountain parallel with its north side, generally about 0.5 mile/800 meters from the cliffs. Along this steep escarpment are a dozen little wild brooks fed by the snowbanks on the slopes; in many damp places near these brooks there is very luxuriant vegetation, but between them everything looks lifeless. Conifers such as black and white spruce (*Picea mariana* and *P. glauca*) and balsam fir (*Abies balsamifera*), growing on the slopes and on top, were stunted and withered, showing the deleterious effect of excessive magnesium.

The most outstanding botanical feature here is the immense area covered by *Adiantum aleuticum*, rare in eastern North America. Other rare ferns here include *Cystopteris montana*, a very dwarf relative of the bulblet bladder fern, growing in the tight rock crevices beside the brooks that leap down the north edge, as well as among the rocks on the flat mountaintop. On the walls of Devil's Gulch I found a relative of the

Christmas fern, *Polystichum scopulinum*, with very rigid broad but short evergreen fronds. Known from only a few other stations, all in California and the Rocky Mountains, this fern is worth trying to grow in rock gardens. Another rare fern found on the dry walls of Devil's Gulch is *Aspidotis densa*, a little 4- to 6-inch/10- to 15-cm fern. It has wiry, triangular fronds and is a true alpine.

Along the north side and on top were most of the alpines of granitic mountains—*Empetrum nigrum*, *Loiseleuria procumbens*, all the White Mountain vacciniums, *Harrimanella*, *Phyllodoce*, and *Rhododendron lapponicum*—but they all had an unhealthy and stunted appearance. By contrast, the rarest plants—those found in the east only here—nearly all looked healthy and rugged, showing that through the centuries they had adapted to the serpentine soil.

Growing along crevices in the rocks and on the serpentine detritus were thousands of dense cushions of a very pretty plant, *Armeria maritima* subsp. *sibirica* (formerly *A. labradorica*), with lilac-colored hemispherical heads, often 1 inch/2.5 cm across, on 2- to 10-inch/5- to 25-cm stems. Most armerias are easy in the garden. Late in the season only a few blooms could be found, but there were thousands of seeds.

One notable feature of the Shickshock Range is the large number of willow species, and at least half a dozen of them might well be brought into cultivation. One, *Salix fuscescens*, is an attractive little creeper. Another beautiful little willow with soft, silky white foliage has been variously called *S. desertorum* or *S. brachycarpa*. It grows from 1 to 2 feet/30 to 60 cm tall and was plentiful on Mount Albert's tableland.

There are probably a half-dozen species of *Arenaria* and *Minuartia* on Mount Albert. One, *Minuartia marcescens*, I readily identified from M. L. Fernald's description. First found on Mount Albert, it was later discovered on serpentine rocks in Newfoundland. The specific name refers to the leaves: marcescent leaves are those that die in the fall but remain in a withered state on the stem. The plant forms close little tufts with small persistent branches. The leaves are narrow, bright green, and leathery. The blooms, at least 0.75 inch/2 cm across, are either white or blue-tinted with a yellow center, and the height is not over 6 inches/15 cm.

Among the good alpines of Mount Albert is a creeping goldenrod, *Solidago simplex* var. *nana* (formerly *S. decumbens*). Here too I found *Viola palustris*, a small light mauve violet with creeping stems. There are not many violets in Gaspé, but this one is apt to be confused with another mauve-flowered species, *V. selkirkii*; they are readily distinguished by the creeping stolons of *V. palustris*, which are absent from *V. selkirkii*. On the north edge I found several stations of *Anemone parviflora* with seedheads still retained, and near one snowbank a few blooms about 1 inch/2.5 cm across, pure white until examined closely, when the base of each petal proved to be light blue.

Among the other plants that have been found on Mount Albert, either on the tableland or on its steep sides, are *Arabis alpina, Arnica mollis, Rubus arcticus, Parnassia parviflora, Ranunculus allenii, R. pygmaeus, Armeria maritima* subsp. *sibirica, Achillea millefolium* var. *borealis,* and *Aster foliaceus.* It is a vast area with great possibilities, and probably not more than a quarter of it has been explored by botanists.

_____ Katahdin: The North Basin _____

As we entered the mouth of the North Basin of Mount Katahdin, at 5267 feet/1606 meters the highest point in Maine, the trail turned west and began a gradual rise, and the forest thinned out to a stand of thin shrubs, among which small mountain ash were conspicuous. Across the basin extends an enormous terminal moraine of all sizes of boulders, many of them 15 to 20 feet/5 to 6 meters in diameter. This, the terminal moraine of the local glacier coming out of North Basin in the Ice Age, must have taken thousands of years to accumulate. It is 0.75 mile/1200 meters wide and extends back into the basin at least 0.5 mile/800 meters; the layer of loose rock is hundreds of feet thick.

We were soon on top of the center of this mass of boulders, whence we could see the whole of the North Basin. Despite the name, this is not on the north side of the mountain; it is a craterlike depression scooped out of the middle of the eastern slope. North Peaks (4734 feet/1444 meters) are small elevations rising a little above the top plain at near the center of the mountain, just behind the center of the basin's headwall. From the mouth of the basin to its headwall is about 1 mile/1600 meters. The floor of the basin, while generally level, is very irregular, with an average altitude of 3000 feet/900 meters.

The north and west walls of the basin rise abruptly from 1200 to 1500 feet/370 to 500 meters above the floor. The south side is a very steep slope covered with talus. The east side is the mouth of the basin with its giant terminal moraine. Two little ponds, only a few meters across, are near the center of the basin.

There is ample soil among the boulders all over the terminal moraine, and here we found lovely sheets of *Vaccinium vitis-idaea* subsp. *minus* of the finest earth-hugging form. Here too was *V. angustifolium,* and, quite remarkable at this altitude, the common Canadian blueberry, *V. canadense.* In company with the vacciniums was the crowberry (*Empetrum nigrum*), as well as an abundance of bunchberry (*Cornus canadensis,* syn. *Chamaepericlymenum canadense*). We found a lovely little unknown goldenrod (*Solidago* sp.) with large flat yellow heads on 10-inch/25-cm stems; it is not *S. multiradiata* var. *arctica,* which we might expect to find here. Like that species, it blooms very early.

On the floor, not far from one of the little ponds, I found a very dwarf form of *Kalmia angustifolia* with extraordinarily bright pink flowers. Lower down, the color is usually a rather poor, faint pink. This is a good rock garden plant, doing well anywhere in neutral or acid soil in full sun.

A remarkable shrub grew here on the floor of the basin—a prostrate form of the tamarack, *Larix laricina*, sometimes called "American larch." This tree attains a height of 60 feet/18 meters in the lowlands, and the creeping form, 12 to 18 inches/30 to 45 cm tall, looked truly odd to me. I do not think that it has any garden value.

I also found *Loiseleuria procumbens* on the basin floor. This little beauty is not as plentiful on the parts of Katahdin that I visited as it is on the Presidential Range.

On some of the broader shelves I found clumps of *Juniperus communis* var. *montana* (formerly variety *nana*) only 6 inches/15 cm tall. Not only is it very dwarf, but the foliage is much finer and softer than that of the common juniper. I had never seen it before in the United States, but I found it very plentiful on the Ile du Massacre in Bic Harbor, Quebec.

The part of the north wall nearest the mouth of the basin was the driest and therefore the poorest botanizing ground, but we had not gone more than a third of the way to the basin's head when I began to find things. About halfway I ran into a moist, interesting spot where the vegetation made me exclaim, "Lime!"

Here were magnificent plants of *Campanula rotundifolia* with extra-large bells—the kind we find on lime soils. Of course this plant grows occasionally on acid soils, but these acid-soil plants are never plentiful and cannot compare with those growing on lime. In the same area were dozens of fine dwarf specimens of *Potentilla fruticosa* (*Pentaphylloides floribunda*) in full bloom, a mass of golden flowers 1.5 inches/4 cm across. There were hundreds of clumps of *Castilleja pallida*, the best I had seen south of Gaspé.

In this moist spot I found scores of the lovely orchid *Platanthera dilatata* with extra-long spikes and extra-large flowers, the best I have ever seen. They are one of the easy hardy orchids in moist soil, but I hardly expect these plants to hold their size in my garden.

Well up on the north wall as I was approaching the west headwall, I found some lovely clumps of the rare *Viola selkirkii*. These little clumps in full sun were a mass of bloom. About an hour later I found two or three clumps of *V. conspersa*. The boreal *V. palustris* has also been found on these walls. In one spot I saw quite a quantity of the two eastern heaths, *Harrimanella hypnoides* and *Phyllodoce coerulea*.

Shortly after noon I reached the headwall that forms the west side of the basin. Knowing that the botanist Fernald had found a very dwarf form of the rare *Andromeda polifolia* at about 4200 feet/1300 meters on this headwall, I went up high and soon found a shelf with plants of this rare species, only 3 inches/8 cm high. I also found a dwarf galium with cream-colored flowers which proved to be *Galium kamtschaticum*. It was low and rather scraggly, but I thought it might be good in cultivation. *Arnica mollis*, a rare plant on Katahdin but plentiful in some spots on the Presidential Range of New Hampshire, has been found on both the north and west walls of this basin, but I was not fortunate enough to meet it there.

Originally published in the Bulletin of the American Rock Garden Society, *vol. 17, no. 2, pp. 41–56 (1959); vol. 18, no. 1, pp. 24–25 (1960); and vol. 20, no. 2, pp. 82–85 (1962). Two additional sections, not excerpted here, appeared in vol. 19.*

Unsolved Mysteries of the Pine Barrens

G. G. NEARING

Pine barrens stretch along the Atlantic coast intermittently from Cape Cod to the Gulf of Mexico, with those of New Jersey receiving the lion's share of botanical attention—partly because they occupy perhaps the largest uninterrupted area of typical barren conditions, and partly because they are easily reached from centers of population, but even more because of the many rarities concentrated there. Pine barrens are not all alike, but they have certain characteristics in common, and largely similar plant communities.

For centuries rivers have been carrying into the sea a vast volume of soil eroded from the Appalachian Mountains, and the waves have been tossing back a portion of it, chiefly sand. Thus extensive sand flats are built out from the eastern edge of the continent, shaped by ocean currents and by the gradual rising or sinking of stretches of the coast.

There is relatively little fertility in sand, and relatively few eastern American plant species consent to so lean a diet. Over time, these few have covered the sand gradually with dead plant material, until the accumulated humus offered conditions favorable for species of the more fertile soils farther inland. However, the pitch pines that have always dominated the barrens are highly inflammable, and fires, often human-set, have been frequent. With what little humus accumulates periodically burned away, the barrens remain barren.

The pines and scrub oaks are so stunted that little timber of value is produced, and there is no longer much demand for them as fuel. An extreme of this stunting may be seen in a section called the Plains, ironically perhaps, because it includes the highest elevations in that part of New Jersey, a ridge of what seem to be ancient dunes. Here the trees, even those centuries old, average in some places only 3 feet/1 meter tall, a condition surprisingly like that seen on mountains at timberline, even though the highest elevation in the Plains is 149 feet/45 meters. The cause of this phenomenon is much debated, but fire and starvation undoubtedly are the chief factors. Among these miniature pines and oaks grow dwarf shrubs appropriate to the rock garden—although the only actual rocks in the vicinity are a few small pebbles.

Most noteworthy, though not the showiest, is *Corema conradii*, the broom crowberry, much like the true crowberry of the far north, *Empetrum nigrum*; the black berry, however, is replaced by a tiny dry fruit. The male plant shows a fluff of brown and purple stamens in early spring, but the chief attraction is the dark green heath-like foliage of the tufted shrublet, ranging in height from 6 inches/15 cm to 2 feet/60 cm. *Corema conradii*, though abundant in the pygmy forest, is very rare elsewhere in the barrens and northward along the coast. It is surprising to find it again plentiful on Gertrude's Nose, a 2000-foot/600-meter ridge in the Shawangunks 150 miles/240 km to the north. This formation consists of great cliffs of hard white metamorphosed sandstone, on whose very summit, in white sand mixed with a little upland peat, *Corema* thrives, thrusting its roots into crevices of the stone. These two situations, the pine barren and the mountain summit, have in common their white sand, apparent drought, and thin shade from dwarfed trees. Both sites also have frequent fog. Thus we may expect *Corema* to respond well to rock garden conditions.

Another heath-like shrub of the barrens is *Hudsonia ericoides* (Plate 94), which grows inland, with its close relative *H. tomentosa* nearer the shore. Its gray-green clumps, seldom higher than 6 inches/15 cm, are crowned with showy bright yellow flowers in late spring and early summer, but when out of bloom, the dull foliage is not particularly ornamental. It follows the coast far to the north, and there it too appears unexpectedly on bare summits. Unlike *Corema*, it transplants with difficulty; only very young specimens can be moved with any hope of success.

Common and typical of the barrens is the 1-inch/2.5-cm-tall creeping shrub *Pyxidanthera barbulata*. Although it does not follow *Corema* and *Hudsonia* to the summits, its near relative *Diapensia lapponica* is arctic and alpine, seldom venturing below timberline in temperate latitudes, and too temperamental for our rockeries.

Arctostaphylos uva-ursi, the bearberry, is a third plant with distribution on rockless barren and rocky summit. Carpeting large areas between the pines with its black-green foliage, under which the pearly flowers and dark red berries are mostly concealed, it appears again on northeastern mountains and in the north—an excellent though aggressive groundcover for sterile soils. Sometimes difficult to establish, it compensates by growing eventually with too much vigor, better for an unused bank than for the rock garden.

Leiophyllum buxifolium, the sand myrtle, deserves special appreciation for its adaptability in any light acid soil. In the barrens its stems may straggle to a height of 2 feet/60 cm or more, retaining too few of the tiny, boxwood-like leaves. The form better suited for rock gardening occurs on the bare mountain summits of the Carolinas, where, as a variety once known to botanists as *hugeri* and in horticulture as *prostratum,* it grows dwarf and compact. Nonetheless, there are dwarf forms in the barrens too, and because the color of the abundant flowers varies from white to shades of pink, the best should be searched for. Cuttings root rather easily.

Everywhere the dry sands in early summer are ornamented with profusely flowering tufts of *Minuartia caroliniana,* a pretty thing but not the best sandwort for cultivation. I was amused to see it compete in a damp lakeside sand garden with *M. groenlandica* from Sams Point, the highest summit of the Shawangunks—both spreading like weeds.

Grasslike tufts of evergreen, grayish, wiry leaves rise in foot-high fountains here and there among the sheep laurel. So unusual a plant suggests a surprise at blooming time, when it produces a stalk up to 3 feet/1 meter high, not unlike a miniature yucca, with numerous small flowers clustered in a 6-inch/15-cm-wide head the shape of an inverted top. This is the turkey's-beard, *Xerophyllum asphodeloides* (Plate 91).

In the driest and sandiest places are occasional colonies of the prickly pear cactus *Opuntia humifusa.* Its linked green pancakes sprawl over the parched banks, giving little hint of the large, glorious flowers that sit flat upon them in early summer. Found also on rocky hilltops and ledges, this cactus suits the rock garden well, and of all northeastern native plants it is perhaps the easiest to establish.

As you drive through the sparse pines, a palisade of deep green looms ahead: white cedars (*Chamaecyparis thyoides*) standing so close together that you can hardly walk between them. In fact, you do not walk there—you must wade. The barrens are intersected by bogs and winding, sluggish streams, covering areas almost as wide as the sands, with a plant community even more fascinating. Here are plants restricted in cultivation to the bog garden.

The transition from dry to wet may follow the sharp line of some long-disintegrated dune. More often there is an intermediate grassy region where moisture lies a few inches beneath the sandy surface. In fact, most of the barrens are not really dry at all, but full of moisture at a depth of a few feet, easily accessible to plant roots. The lush thicket-growth in the bogs testifies to fertility derived from fallen leaves, which soak and rot there instead of being burnt as they are on the sands.

The bog and ditch thicket, often almost impenetrable, consists of various shrubs, some of which extend into the barrens. The mountain laurel

(*Kalmia latifolia*), abundant in woods not actually wet, intermingles with the sheep laurel (*K. angustifolia*), which endures more water here, as it does in the mountains. Its smaller red flower clusters are less showy than those of *K. latifolia* because they nod beneath the foliage crown, but because *K. angustifolia* grows only 2 to 3 feet/60 to 90 cm high, it deserves a little space in the garden.

Appreciated because its lily-of-the-valley racemes open in March and stay in flower through many frosts, the water-edge evergreen *Chamaedaphne calyculata* makes dense stands to 2 feet/60 cm high. Perhaps among its millions of plants there may be one a little dwarfer, with greener leaves and larger flowers.

If the flowers of *Lyonia mariana*, the staggerbush, which has very sparse foliage, could be superimposed on *Chamaedaphne*, what a marvelous plant we should have! These bells of white, some tinged with rose, are like giant blueberry flowers nodding in clusters from yard-high stems, followed by an intricate brown-and-white capsule. In spite of the thinness of its deciduous leaves and its stiff stems, the staggerbush is worth growing, if only for the winter arrangement of the capsules, but its flowers would grace any low shrub border. All these shrubs are ericaceous, requiring a peaty soil and mulching.

Everywhere in the swamp, thickets glisten with the dark green domes of the inkberry (*Ilex glabra*), with small white flowers and black berries close to the twig. Some individuals hold more winter leaves than others, and some are more inclined to sucker, but I have seen selected specimens in cultivation with almost the ornamental value of boxwood, and certainly superior hardiness.

Among the innumerable sweet pepperbushes (*Clethra alnifolia*) with their upright spikes of white flowers are a few dwarf shrubs with spikes that nod. These are the sweetspire or Virginia willows (*Itea virginica*), rather rare so far north.

Conspicuous everywhere in the wetlands is *Magnolia virginiana*, holding its shiny tropical-looking leaves well into winter and all summer offering up its pale gold, fragrant chalices one by one. Unlike the southern, fully evergreen *M. grandiflora*, this swamp magnolia is entirely hardy as a shrub or suckering tree considerably north of New York city.

Sometimes the dark blotch in the distant bog is not magnolia but *Smilax laurifolia*, draping the treetops with the heavy, black-green foliage popular for use by florists. It is a rare vine in the north.

I will mention only a few of the rarest and most ornamental plants of these wet soils. The pine barrens gentian (*Gentiana autumnalis*) is one of the most ornamental gentians, rather easily grown from seed, and there is a splendid white variety, truly rare—as even the blue one is coming to be, with collectors always on its trail.

Also to be found here is a strange, brown-flowered pedicularis relative, *Schwalbea americana*, a little-known and decidedly local habitant of grassy, dampish places, growing with colicroot (*Aletris farinosa*), whose little spires look confusingly like the later-flowering lady's tresses (*Spiranthes*), a commonly found white orchid of swamps.

In and out of the bogs and ditches appear the charming bog orchids (*Calopogon tuberosus*), as well as the quainter and less showy *Pogonia ophioglossoides* (Plate 90), and the white-fringed orchid (*Platanthera blephariglottis*, Plate 92). For those who know its secret hideouts, *Arethusa bulbosa* is in these bogs too. All the bog orchids succeed in a well-made sphagnum bog.

The swamp pink (*Helonias bullata*, Plate 89) chooses the shadier recesses in wet sphagnum, under the white cedars and magnolias. Its dense heads of shimmering purplish-pink thrust up a foot/30 cm or more from the lax crown of evergreen leaves. Rather desirable, it is also one of the rarer species, although it spreads south along the coast and into the bogs of the southern mountains.

Rarer still is *Narthecium americanum* (Plate 93), the bog asphodel, a liliaceous plant suggesting a small yellow loosestrife, known only in a few acres of sunny mud, where its narrow spikes rise a foot/30 cm or so high from grasslike leaf rosettes. Of about the same dimensions or a little smaller is the related *Tofieldia racemosa*, a white-flowered bog plant more common to the south. Both would make attractive subjects for the bog garden if they could be made to grow and thrive, but since they will not, they should be left unmolested.

One of the most conspicuous plants, though small in size, is the yellow milkwort (*Polygala lutea*), which has blazing orange-yellow, cloverlike heads on stiff stalks. It grows and seeds itself freely in any sphagnum bog, blooming with all the liberality of an annual, although it seems to be biennial, with attractive little rosettes of smooth leaves the first season.

No account of the bogs could skip the pitcher plant (*Sarracenia purpurea*, Plate 88), with its water-filled leaves set to trap unwary insects, while red flags wave above from the drumlike flowers. More curious than beautiful, it grows well in any sphagnum bog. So too will the little sundews (*Drosera* spp.), spreading their sticky fingers with similar carnivorous intent, but flowering prettily like a tiny white forget-me-not. The most common here is *D. rotundifolia*; if the leaves happen to be a little out of round, we are looking at *D. intermedia*. Very different, larger, and much more ornamental is *D. filiformis*, with rushlike leaves bristling all over with purplish, glistening glands on which dead insects dangle; its showy flowers are purplish or pink.

The edible cranberry (*Vaccinium macrocarpon*) is cultivated in vast prepared bogs, where the more beautiful plants enumerated here may occur as weeds. Yet the flower of the cranberry is not to be despised, with its intriguing dark dart of united stamens poised before the curled-back pink corolla as though to strike at some intruder on the moss. The narrow creeper it springs from soon outwears its welcome in a garden by forking interminably through and over the choicer things, pushing its big red blobs of berries into the wrong places.

Sabatia difformis, a gentian relative once known as *S. lanceolata*, is a true bog plant with good white flowers; the pink *S. stellaris* belongs rather to the salt marshes, where it tints hundreds of acres with soft rose over a long season.

Two last species must close this brief account. First is the curly grass fern (*Schizaea pusilla*), so small that the eye must be trained to find it; yet botanists spend more time on this than on all the other pine barrens rarities. It will not grow for you, and if it would, you would hardly enjoy looking at a tiny tuft of spiral-leaved grass, emitting fertile stems 2 to 3 inches/5 to 8 cm high, surmounted by a structure resembling the paw of a mouse.

The climbing fern (*Lygodium palmatum*) twines its handsome evergreen leaves in a few swampy thickets known to pine barrens enthusiasts, whither it has been driven by the relentless persecution of its admirers. Once sought out for Christmas decorations, it has vanished from most of its original range but survives here and on certain mountains.

Originally published in the Bulletin of the American Rock Garden Society, *vol. 11, no. 1, pp. 7–13 (1953).*

301

The New Jersey Pine Barrens

RICK DARKE

New Jersey's reputation for crowded conditions and an abundance of asphalt would seem to make it an unlikely place for a botanical outing. Most travelers on the New Jersey turnpike are probably unaware that to the east lies a near-wilderness area the size of Grand Canyon National Park. The New Jersey pine barrens occupy more than 1 million acres/400,000 hectares in this 4-million-acre/1.6-million-hectare state. The area is truly a national treasure, and if you have only one chance to see it, mid-June should be the time.

The coastal plain of New Jersey forms a low dome, with a belt of hills separating the inner and outer sections. The pine barrens occupy an area that corresponds roughly with the outer coastal plain. The word *barrens* was applied to it by mid-seventeenth-century European settlers, whose viewpoint was agricultural: the coarse sandy soils are largely infertile and unsuited to farming.

In the heart of the barrens, the outlook from a spot such as the Apple Pie Hill fire tower reveals an apparently endless expanse of pines. Radiating from the base of the tower are a few sandy roads, part of a confusing network of local trails, stagecoach roads, and fire roads that crisscross the barrens. The roads are maddeningly alike and can pose formidable navigation problems for the uninitiated.

It is undoubtedly a monotonous landscape. Seldom exceeding 30 feet/9 meters high, scrubby and irregularly branched, the pitch pine (*Pinus rigida*) is the characteristic forest tree. This three-needle pine ranges from New Brunswick, Canada, to Georgia, but nowhere except in the pine barrens of New Jersey does it dominate such extensive acreage.

To travelers bound for the New Jersey beaches from Philadelphia, the miles of pine-lined roads that must be traveled are perhaps boring, but for the connoisseur of unusual landscapes the pitch pine imparts a stark beauty to the barrens. On a moonlit night, light shines through the open canopy of the pines to brighten the sand beneath your feet, and you can walk these woods without the aid of a lantern. But there is much more to the pine barrens than the pines.

The region is famous in the botanical community for its many rare and unusual species. Fourteen northern species reach the southern limit of their coastal plain distribution in the pine barrens.

One is the tiny curly grass fern *Schizaea pusilla*, whose common name derives from the grasslike appearance of its narrow fronds. *Schizaea* can be frequently found growing on raised "hummocks" in boggy areas in the pine barrens but has not been found further south. Its northern distribution is disjunct, possibly because of past glaciation and the sinking coastline. After a limited occurrence on Long Island, it is not seen again until Nova Scotia and Newfoundland.

More than a hundred southern species reach their northern limit in the pine barrens, including turkey-beard (*Xerophyllum asphodeloides*, Plate 91). Closely related to the western beargrass (*X. tenax*), turkey-beard flowers in late May or early June from a basal tuft of grasslike leaves.

There are surprisingly few true endemics here. Pine barrens sand myrtle (*Leiophyllum buxifolium*) and pickerel morning glory (*Stylisma pickeringii*) occur very rarely outside the New Jersey pine barrens. However, the exciting nature of the barrens' flora has less to do with exclusivity and more with unique communities and the local abundance of otherwise rare species.

The existence of the pine barrens and the origins of its unusual floral composition pose many questions. Fossil records show that many modern genera, including pines and oaks, grew in the area as long as 70 million years ago. Yet it is almost certain that their occurrence has not been continuous, in view of dramatic changes in geology and climate since then. During the last major glaciation, southern movement of the ice sheet stopped 30 miles/50 km short of the edge of the present pine barrens, and the close proximity of the glacier probably created near-arctic conditions on the coastal plain. Many of the temperate species that make up the present barrens flora probably moved in after the glacier subsided about 10,000 years ago.

One factor certain to have had a major influence on the nature of the vegetation is the long-term high incidence of fire. The coastal plain is made up largely of unconsolidated coarse sands and gravel deposited by ancient seas. The dry soils, high winds, and abundant fuel supply contribute to frequent and wide-ranging fires, both naturally occurring and human-set. It is likely that not a single acre of the barrens has escaped burning during the past century alone. The pine barrens forests represent a "fire climax," and if fires were artificially prevented for a long enough period, the species composition would be dramatically altered.

Most species that successfully inhabit the region today are highly flammable yet quite resistant to fatal damage by fire. For example, among pines, the pitch pine has the unusual ability to sprout from dormant buds both basally and along the trunk and branches. This sprouting in response to fire injury contributes to its irregular form. Many other pine barrens trees, shrubs, and herbs can be burned to the ground repeatedly, only to resprout from underground rootstocks. Nowhere is this more apparent than in the approximately 12,000 acres/4800 hectares known as the "plains" or "pygmy forest." Here the pitch pines rarely top 9 feet/3 meters, and there seems to have been selective pressure toward a serotinous race whose cone scales open only after firing. The pines are accompanied by similarly dwarfed oaks and various ericaceous shrubs, and the plains forest is almost impenetrable on foot. The origin of the plains is still open to conjecture; however, fire frequency in the area has historically been twice that of the surrounding barrens and appears to have been a major factor.

Despite this importance of fire, water is considered to be the region's most abundant and valuable natural resource. The ultimate source of all water in the pine barrens is the 45 inches/112 cm of rain that falls each year. Most of this filters rapidly through the porous soils, filling an immense reservoir, the Cohansey aquifer, that underlies the barrens. The aquifer is estimated to contain more than 17 trillion gallons/64 trillion liters of water.

All the streams and rivers that flow in the pine barrens originate there. The surface water is usually tea-colored, not because of pollution but from the leaching of harmless organic materials. Especially by modern standards, the water is exceptionally pure. Captains of sailing ships once filled their barrels with "cedar water" from the barrens, valuing its quality of remaining potable much longer than ordinary river water.

The high acidity of the pine barrens environment has been a strong selective agent in regard to both plants and animals. The soil in general ranges from pH 3.5 to 5.0, and the waters are equally acidic. Although there are certain notable animal species, such as the endangered pine barrens tree frog, there is not the diversity found among the plants, because the young of many animal species cannot tolerate such high acidity. Not surprisingly, most pine barrens plants are acid-tolerant, and the heath family (Ericaceae) is particularly well represented.

Although the pine barrens comprise many plant communities, perhaps the single most easily observable factor influencing species distribution within the barrens is the availability of moisture. The surface soils hold little rainfall, and in the uplands growing conditions are quite dry. The whole of the barrens is at or below 200 feet/60 meters above sea level, however, and the difference between upland and lowland often seems a matter of a few meters. The aquifer is seldom more than 20 feet/6 meters down, and in lowlands the water table is frequently at or near the surface, creating numerous lakes, swamps, and bogs.

The drier upland areas are characterized by pitch pine forests. *Pinus rigida* is the dominant tree, accompanied by various oaks, including blackjack oak (*Quercus marilandica*), post oak (*Q. stellata*), chestnut oak (*Q. prinus*), and black oak (*Q. velutina*). The evergreen inkberry holly (*Ilex glabra*) is common in the shrub layer, as are huckleberries, including *Gaylussacia baccata*, and blueberries, including *Vaccinium vacillans* and *V. corymbosum*. Mountain laurel (*Kalmia latifolia*) puts on a spectacular show in sunny openings in early June; forms with pink flowers and deep red buds can be found. Herbaceous species in the drier woods are relatively few, but they include the ubiquitous bracken fern (*Pteridium aquilinum*) and cow-wheat (*Melampyrum lineare*), whose small, yellow, snapdragon-like flowers last from early summer until fall.

There is a wealth of color and interest to be found in dry sunny sites. Occurring in small patches and occasional huge drifts, golden heather (*Hudsonia ericoides*, Plate 94) covers itself with bright yellow flowers in late May. *Hudsonia* is not a true heather but a member of the rock-rose family (Cistaceae). *Leiophyllum buxifolium*, another May-bloomer, often creates dramatic sweeps of white. It is frequent in the plains areas, which also have a greater occurrence of such unusual pine barrens species as pyxie-moss (*Pyxidanthera barbulata*) and broom crowberry (*Corema conradii*). The banks of the roads leading through the plains shimmer with sunlight reflected off the glossy leaves of bearberry (*Arctostaphylos uva-ursi*). In addition to turkey-beard, sun-loving perennials in dry areas include June-blooming pine barrens sandwort (*Arenaria caroliniana*), goat's rue (*Tephrosia virginiana*), and the fall-blooming *Liatris graminifolia* and *Aster linarifolius*.

Owing to past logging there are no longer vast stands of white cedar (*Chamaecyparis thyoides*); however, this stately evergreen is still invariably found along streams, rivers, swamps, and bogs throughout the barrens. It is in these wetland habitats that the vegetation exhibits its greatest color and diversity. Trees growing in association with the cedars include trident red maple (*Acer rubrum* var. *trilobum*), black gum (*Nyssa sylvatica*), and sweetbay (*Magnolia virginiana*). Ericaceous shrubs include swamp azalea (*Rhododendron viscosum*), fetterbush (*Leucothoe racemosa*), leatherleaf (*Chamaedaphne calyculata*), staggerbush (*Lyonia mariana*), and sheep laurel (*Kalmia angustifolia*), the last equally at home in dry conditions. Spaghnum mosses blanket the bases of trees in the cedar swamps, as well as much of the surface in between. The sphagnum species vary in color from bright green to wine-red, creating a colorful mosaic.

The herbaceous members of the bog flora begin a glorious display of color in late April with the flowering of golden club (*Orontium aquaticum*). Bright yellow spikes of this aroid rise above blue-green foliage like jacks without pulpits. May brings thousands of pitcher plants (*Sarracenia purpurea*, Plate 88) into bloom; before the month is over, *Arethusa bulbosa*, one of the rarest of the pink pine barrens orchids, will be flowering on the hummocks. Two more pink orchids, the rose pogonia (*Pogonia ophioglossoides*, Plate 90) and the grass pink (*Calopogon tuberosus*), open in June, along with various bladderworts (*Utricularia* spp.), both yellow and purple. Three sundews—*Drosera rotundifolia, D. intermedia*, and *D. filiformis*—are common in the sphagnum carpet. The rare bog asphodel (*Narthecium americanum*, Plate 93) adds its yellow spikes, and by late June the surface of the bog has become a golden haze dotted with pink. Pink-flowered milkworts (*Polygala cruciata, P. brevifolia*) and orange-flowered *P. lutea* begin in June, frequently accompanied by white-fringed orchis (*Platanthera blephariglottis*, Plate 92) in August. In damp soil, the exquisitely blue *Gentiana autumnalis* is at its spectacular peak in late September.

In the 1600s the pine barrens could be dismissed by settlers as worthless, but today population pressures and dwindling resources elsewhere are having their impact. The region has not been undisturbed in the past. A once-flourishing iron industry was responsible for the lumbering of huge tracts. In the nineteenth century Joseph Wharton, a Philadelphia entrepreneur, amassed large holdings in the barrens with the intent of exporting water to his city. The New Jersey legislature passed laws forbidding such export, and the state later purchased Wharton's holdings to create the Wharton State Forest.

Protection of this unique natural area solely through land acquisition is impractical, however: this area is simply too vast. In 1978, recognizing the national significance of the pine barrens, Congress established the Pinelands National Reserve, offering increased federal environmental protection to the area. New Jersey followed with the Pinelands Protection Act in 1979, which includes some of the strongest land-use legislation in the country. The Pinelands Commission oversees implementation of a comprehensive management plan designed to preserve and protect the area's natural resources. The future of the pine barrens looks bright.

Bibliography

Forman, Richard, ed. 1979. *Pine Barrens: Ecosystem and Landscape*. New York: Academic Press.

Hand, Louis B., et al. 1979. *Plant Life of Wharton State Forest*. Trenton: New Jersey Division of Parks and Forestry.

Harshberger, J. W. 1916. *The Vegetation of the New Jersey Pine Barrens*. Philadelphia: Christopher Sower.

McCormick, Jack. 1970. *The Pine Barrens: A Preliminary Ecological Survey*. Trenton: New Jersey State Museum.

Originally published in the Bulletin of the American Rock Garden Society, *vol. 47, no. 1, pp. 21–26 (1989).*

Trailing Arbutus

IDA A. THOMAS

Any gardener who has ever seen or smelled trailing arbutus (*Epigaea repens*, Plate 95) in early spring has wished to possess it in the garden. Not knowing, however, that it is primarily a matter of selecting the right location and providing the right kind of soil, that gardener has failed to have it grow when plants were brought in from the wild or purchased from a nursery. Few of our "vanishing Americans" have been wasted to the extent that arbutus has been in digging it from the wild, only to have it slowly die in the garden, although for some weeks it may appear alive.

Having known the charm of trailing arbutus from early childhood, I determined to establish it when I came to live where I could enjoy a garden. Several times, I obtained plants or large sods from extensive plantings on properties of friends in New Jersey, Pennsylvania, and Maine, as well as from various nurseries in the south or north. The plants all eventually died, until I learned how to prepare the soil properly.

Now I have one large patch, about 3 by 4 feet/90 by 120 cm, 8 years old, and several smaller patches. They are between the north side of a garage and a path, with good light and early morning and late afternoon sun. The slightly sloping soil, providing proper drainage, was acid to begin with, but not of the right composition. I added lime-free sand and a quantity of peat moss, and three or four bags of shredded oak leafmold from a section of New Jersey where kalmia and arbutus thrive. The last is a most important factor.

A healthy specimen of trailing arbutus has a large mass of very fine fibrous roots that are well supplied with a mycorrhizal fungus. The mycelium, or underground vegetative part of the fungus, envelops the roots of the other plant and functions like hair roots, absorbing from the soil and giving to the plant substances necessary for the latter's nutrition. Certain other plants of the heath family depend on such associations.

I prepared the soil close to a small established plant of arbutus, brought from Maine and planted a couple of years before, without disturbing it, and then I worked some of the soil in all around it. This plant soon began to show its appreciation of this treatment and has spread over a large area, blooming each spring. Unfortunately, it is almost white, not pink.

By bringing in soil from a site where arbutus grows, you are likely to get the necessary mycelium to start the plants in a new site. Then the plants take care of themselves as they increase in size. The first year it is necessary to supply water at all times, but arbutus does not like a soil that remains too wet. If you are using city water, it is advisable to collect rainwater for it.

In the interest of conservation, you should not gather plants from the wild; however, if a tract is being built on or cut over, removing shade and resulting in the death of the groundcover plants, it is true conservation to collect what you can and plant it in a properly prepared plot. If there are many plants to choose from, the best are the smaller ones. Be careful to dig deep and 1 foot/30 cm from the plant all around it, to not disturb the mycorrhiza on the roots.

A year and a half ago, I was given some arbutus seed in late June. I found this to be the easiest, though not the quickest, way to get plants. In the bottom of a pan, I placed a layer of drainage material and 1 inch/2.5 cm of peat moss, well packed down. On that I placed a mixture of one part each of sharp sand and peat moss and two parts of crushed oak leafmold. I watered this thoroughly after tamping it well, having inserted a 2-inch/5-cm clay pot with a cork in the bottom in the middle of the mixture—the top just below the top of the larger pan. This small pot I kept filled with water all the time. Over this soil mixture I scattered the fine seed very sparsely and gave it a gentle spray of water to settle it; then I covered the pan with a sheet of glass and newspaper and placed it against the north side of the garage, in a box of peat moss to further prevent drying out.

Within a month, green fuzz appeared all over the surface; after a few weeks more, I could distinguish arbutus foliage. The tiny plants were not permitted to dry out, although the glass cover was raised a little to give air; with the peat moss around the pot and the water in the center, this was not too difficult. In October, before really cold weather, I took the seed pot into the greenhouse. In early December, I transplanted some of the little plants, from 0.25 to 0.5 inch/6 to 13 mm across, into small pots, using the same soil mixture. Although the plants were tiny, the roots were 1 to 2 inches/2.5 to 5 cm long; it is very important not to break these roots.

The plants were kept very cool all winter. In early spring, I put the pots into a box with peat moss well packed about them and set the box on the north side of a row of shrubs. A tub of rainwater was close at hand, so that I could water the plants whenever they needed it. This was practically every day, for they must not be allowed to dry out.

Last fall some of the plants were 1 inch/2.5 cm across. All the pots were buried to their tops in a frame filled with sand and covered with a layer of pine needles and sash, which had been raised a bit all winter. Now early in February, they look fine and will be ready to plant in the garden in spring. A few little plants set out along the garage look just as healthy.

If you have choice plants of a good pink color, they can be increased from cuttings, soon after the plants have bloomed or in early fall. Take tips 3 to 5 inches/8 to 13 cm long; if they have started to layer themselves, so much the better. Dig the roots carefully to disturb them as little as possible, and keep the soil on them.

A mixture of one part each of clean sharp sand and rubbed peat moss is a good rooting material, but I like to add one part vermiculite, thoroughly soaking the mixture before inserting the cuttings. Here again, I put the small pot of water in the middle of the propagating pot. Only the tip of the cutting is left above the surface, which is kept moist and shaded, and nice roots are in evidence in 2 to 3 months.

If you take cuttings in early summer, keep them in the frame in shade until you pot them in early fall in the same soil mixture. If taken in the fall, they are best left undisturbed until the next spring when new growth has started. Be sure to protect them over winter in the frame with oak leaves or pine needles.

Originally published in the Bulletin of the American Rock Garden Society, *vol. 7, no. 2, pp. 44–46 (1949).*

Trollius laxus

NORMAN C. DENO

The expanse and homogeneity of the woodlands of the eastern United States ensure the survival of most of its characteristic species. There are only six endangered species listed for Pennsylvania, and one of these is *Trollius laxus*.

It may come as a surprise to discover that there is a native trollius in Pennsylvania; however, it is rare. I know of only one station in the wild, providing the phrase "in the wild" can be applied to the roadbank of a major highway in northern New Jersey. It appears to exist in this location thanks to regular mowing of the bank, as it does not stray into the acres of adjacent marsh and untilled fields. This may suggest the reason for the precariousness of its existence: it is intolerant of competition, yet it favors the neutral, moist soil that is so conducive to the growth of grasses.

One of the few stations reported for *Trollius laxus* in Pennsylvania is Centre Furnace, Centre County. The furnace itself still stands 500 feet/ 150 meters from my house, and the marsh is in sight from my window. There are springs over the low brow of the hill, and I can see streams joining below. Marsh marigolds (*Caltha palustris*) and marsh violets (*Viola cucullata*) still grow down below, but it was more than a century ago that *Trollius laxus* was last seen at Centre Furnace.

Any discussion of *Trollius laxus* must first face a problem of nomenclature. There is a common Rocky Mountain species also known as *T. laxus*. The western form may be doubtfully distinct botanically, but from the horticultural viewpoint, the two forms are different, the eastern form being much the more attractive. The western form, as I have seen it on Beartooth Plateau in Wyoming and on Washington Pass in the North Cascades, has greenish-white or cream-colored flowers, smaller than those of the eastern form and often on taller and more upright stems. Many flowers seem to be misshapen. The leaves are smaller and are also on more upright stems. The western form has sometimes been treated as a separate species, *T. albiflorus*, but is presently named *T. laxus* subsp. *albiflorus*.

The eastern form has more distinctly yellow flowers, although there is a hint of brown in the yellow, and it is far from a true buttercup yellow. The flowers are a bit larger, and those here are invariably perfectly formed. As the flowers nestle in their ruff of sumptuous deep green foliage, they make that perfect bouquet that so delights the rock gardener. Young plants will open full-sized flowers only 1 to 2 inches/2.5 to 5 cm above ground level. At this stage they are particularly charming because the foliage is a rich deep green with some bronze shading.

The western form is portrayed in Harold W. Rickett's *The North-western States* (1971) and in his *Central Mountain and Plains States* (1973). Fortunately, different photographs were used, and both clearly depict the rather poor flower color. The *Northeastern States* volume depicts a single flower of the eastern form and discusses its haunting off-yellow color. Rickett treats both eastern and western forms as *Trollius laxus*, although he comments on the potential validity of the name *T. albiflorus*. One would expect the two forms to have different cultural requirements, because the eastern form is found in neutral soil at low altitudes, and the western form typically grows at 8000 to 10,000 feet/2400 to 3100 meters in open bogs, in the company of *Kalmia*, *Phyllodoce*, and other acid-loving plants.

I initially grew plants of the eastern form in an artificial wet-sand bog, constructed by excavating an area 1 yard/meter square to a depth of 1 foot/30 cm. The depression was lined with a single watertight sheet of black polyethylene and filled with sand. No fertilizer, humus, soil, or any form of nutrient was added. The addition of very much of any of these would soon have rendered the tiny bog anaerobic, a condition that would have killed *Trollius laxus*. Sufficient nutrient seems to sift in from dust and rains, judging by the good growth obtained.

Seed is set naturally here. The seeds are black and shiny, as is characteristic of so many of the Ranunculaceae. Equally characteristic is the way they take their time about germinating; they require continuously moist conditions while they debate when and if they will sprout. Once germinated, they grow slowly and steadily in typical buttercup fashion. Their slowness is balanced to some extent by their freedom from insect pests and rabbit damage, no doubt because of the toxins also typical of the Ranunculaceae. It takes some time to acquire a sizable number of flowering plants, and *Trollius laxus* is not apt to be seen on any bargain counters.

Much to my surprise, seedlings slowly began appearing outside the wet-sand bed. These plants may be somewhat less luxuriant, but they grow, flower, and are fully as beautiful as those in wet sand. This development has proved that *Trollius laxus* will succeed in limestone woodland, provided some sunlight is present and some moisture is available throughout the summer. As it spreads, I begin to dream of naturalizing it in the marsh below, so that it can again be listed as found at Centre Furnace, Centre Country. Perhaps once again it will contribute its part to the floral beauty of April in central Pennsylvania.

Originally published in the Bulletin of the American Rock Garden Society, *vol. 35, no. 2, pp. 71–74 (1977).*

PART FIVE: SOUTHEAST

Rock Plants of the Middle Atlantic States

EDGAR T. WHERRY

This article covers some 35 species, little known but worthy of use in rock gardens, native chiefly to the southern half of the area covered in the eighth edition of Asa Gray's *Manual of Botany*. Habitats and ranges are added to suggest cultural practices. Many of these species are winter-hardy well north of their natural haunts, especially if planted in heat-absorbing dark soil; and those from cool mountain heights can often withstand lowland summers if light-colored, heat-reflecting mulch is furnished.

Cymophyllus fraserianus has rosettes of evergreen, inch-wide, strap-shaped leaves, and in spring long-stalked knobs of pearly florets, tipped by a mop of stamens. Its habitat is subacid humus in partial shade, in the high mountains of South Carolina to Pennsylvania.

Callisia graminea (formerly *Tradescantia rosea* var. *graminea*), unlike the coarse, floppy garden spiderworts, is a well-behaved little gem. Every morning through the summer its neat tufts of grassy foliage are decked with tiny three-segmented flowers of bright rose. It grows in subacid gravel in sunny spots, from northern Florida to Virginia.

Allium stellatum produces globes of lavender stars late in the growing season. This species does not become weedy, unlike its relative *A. cernuum*. It is found in sunny prairie loam, from Texas to Saskatchewan—a wide range of climatic conditions.

Clintonia umbellata has rather coarse leaves but bears in spring attractive umbels of speckled white, six-pointed stars followed by decorative black berries. It grows in subacid humus, in partial shade, in the mountains from Georgia to western New York.

315

Streptopus roseus or rosy-bells has a habit similar to Solomon's-seal (*Polygonatum*), but its flowers are charming pink. The Appalachian variety, differing from the New England one in having glabrous flower-stalks, can stand warmer summers. It is found in acid humus in partial shade, in mountains from Georgia to Pennsylvania.

Trillium nivale is a cute little dwarf. Its snowy flowers open before the winter snows have fully melted. It favors dry neutral gravel and partial shade, ranging from Kentucky to Minnesota.

Hexastylis shuttleworthii (the mottled wild ginger, formerly considered an *Asarum*) has heart-shaped, glossy leaves, in selected clones beautifully colored. It grows in subacid humus in partial shade, in mountains from Georgia to West Virginia.

Eriogonum allenii, the Appalachian sulfur-flower, is the one northeastern member of the buckwheat family deserving a place in the rock garden. It is a rather massive plant, with oblong leaves dark green above and brown-woolly beneath, producing for a long period in late summer profuse light yellow flowers. It occurs in dry gravel and full sun, in the shale-barrens of Virginia and West Virginia.

Paronychia argyrocoma or silverling makes cute little mats of silky leaves, with negligible flowers in bracts of pure silver. It can be seen in acid humus pockets in granite or sandstone, in full sun, in mountains from Georgia to West Virginia. The related though dissimilar shale starling, *P. virginica*, has needlelike leaves and pale yellow stars from late summer to frost.

Stellaria pubera, a native chickweed with dark green leaves setting off the white, ten-pointed stars in late spring, is sometimes a bit too rampant. It grows in slightly acid humus and partial shade, from northern Florida to New Jersey and Illinois.

Anemone caroliniana is a showy spring flower with numerous sepals of white, pink, or lavender-blue. It is usually seen in subacid soil in full sun, from northern Florida to North Carolina and out over the prairies.

Delphinium tricorne, the spring larkspur, has pinkish to violet-blue flowers in 6- to 12-inch/15- to 30-cm racemes early in the season. It habitat is neutral loam of alluvial woods or shaded limestone ledges, from Georgia to western Pennsylvania, and west to Oklahoma and Minnesota.

Stylophorum diphyllum, the celandine poppy, is a must for every shady rock garden, though a bit tall and inclined to seed too freely. It has pale green, strikingly cut leaves and 2-inch/5-cm golden poppies all through spring. It grows in neutral loam and partial shade, from southwestern Virginia to Missouri and up to the Great Lakes.

Cardamine douglassii, the lavender bittercress, has charming, delicate-hued flowers in earliest spring. It is found in neutral loam and partial shade, from Virginia to Missouri and up to southernmost Canada.

Draba ramosissima, the rock twist, is not showy but curious. It makes festoons of intertwining stems with profuse tiny white cress flowers in spring, followed by spiral seedpods. It grows on limestone ledges in full sun, from Tennessee to Maryland.

Sedum telephioides, the Appalachian stonecrop, is related to the garden live-forever. It differs in its glaucous, bronze-margined leaves and pinkish flowers in late summer. It occurs in acid or rarely in neutral gravel, in mountains from Georgia to western New York.

Heuchera pubescens and *H. longiflora*, the alumroots, have flowers of no consequence, but the leaves are strikingly mottled gray-green and bronze, especially colorful in winter. They are found on limestone ledges and neutral loam in partial shade; the showiest clones are from western Virginia and North Carolina.

Heuchera villosa has rather coarse but attractively lobed leaves, green or bronzy, and the plant is notable for the profusion of tiny white flowers in late summer. It frequents subacid humus in the mountains from Georgia to West Virginia.

Spirea betulifolia var. *corymbosa*, a dwarf shrub, has flat-topped clusters of pinkish flowers in summer. It occurs in subacid gravel and partial shade, in mountains from Georgia to Pennsylvania.

Pachysandra procumbens is related to but more attractive than the Japanese *P. terminalis* so widely used as a groundcover. The American species spreads only slowly, so it is safe in a rock garden; the leaves, at least in clones from the northern part of its range, are evergreen and bronze-mottled in winter, and the flowers arising from the rootstocks in earliest spring are a delicate pink. It grows in neutral loam and considerable shade, from northern Florida to Kentucky.

Rock gardeners try various native violets, and often kill acid-requiring ones like *Viola pedata* by planting them in limy soil. A newly discovered violet from the mountains of West Virginia and southwestern Pennsylvania, *V. appalachiensis*, is the tiniest of the genus in our region, only a couple of inches high, and spreads by runners into neat little mats. It thrives in subacid loam, in partial shade.

Erigenia bulbosa, a diminutive member of the Apiaceae, derives its common name, pepper-and-salt, from the way the blackish-red anthers speckle the tiny white petals. Another common name is harbinger-of-spring, which indicates why it is recommended for the rock garden: it comes up very early, often while snow is still on the ground. Its habitat is neutral loam and partial shade, from Alabama to New York and Minnesota.

Dodecatheon amethystinum is a veritable rock garden jewel, dwarfer and earlier-blooming than the well-known shooting-star *D. meadia*. Its petal color is deeper, as indicated by the species epithet. After the seed is ripe the foliage withers away, so care must be taken not to dig up the dormant root. It grows on limestone ledges in partial shade, from Pennsylvania to Missouri and Wisconsin.

Amsonia ciliata is a well-behaved member of the Apocynaceae, with

317

grasslike foliage and lovely pale blue stars in late spring. It is found in subacid gravel in full sun, from Georgia and North Carolina to Texas and Missouri.

Lithospermum canescens, the eastern puccoon, produces spiral stems of lustrous yellow trumpets in spring, so attractive that one wonders why it is so little grown in our rock gardens. A relative, *L. caroliniense,* is said to have larger and more deeply flowers, but it seems to be rare and hard to come by. Its habitat is neutral gravel in partial shade, from Georgia to Texas and southern Canada.

Monarda russeliana, unlike most members of the mint family, does not spread too rapidly to be safely planted in the small rock garden. This monarda—called "beebalm" or "horse-mint"—is dwarf for the genus, scarcely 2 feet/60 cm tall, and has the merit of producing its purple-dotted lavender flowers in spring. It grows in neutral or somewhat acid gravel in partial shade, from Alabama to Texas and southern Illinois.

The rare shrublet *Conradina verticillata,* glade-mint or Cumberland rosemary, has attractive lavender flowers in spring. It occurs in limestone glades in partial shade, in Kentucky and Tennessee.

Cunila origanoides, rock-mint or American dittany, is herbaceous but bushy. It has neat foliage and a profusion of minute purplish flowers in autumn. On frosty mornings following early winter rains, it produces striking ice-ribbons from the old stems. It occurs in subacid gravel in partial shade, from Florida to Texas and southern New York.

Campanula divaricata, a fairy bluebell, will please rock gardeners partial to diminutive flowers (though on rather tall plants). Its cute little bells with projecting clappers are produced over a long period in summer. It is from subacid gravel in open sun, in mountains from Georgia to Maryland and Kentucky.

Chrysopsis mariana, like all the golden asters, is worthy of a place in the rock garden, since it does not spread like so many composites. This one has flowerheads 1 inch/2.5 cm across and is easy to grow in acid gravel or loam, and full sun. Its native range is from Florida to Texas and southeastern New York.

Chrysogonum virginianum or green-and-gold has 1.5-inch/4-cm heads with only five rays. It is a low-growing woodland plant, spreading into mats by runners. There are many clones, some remaining only a few inches high, others reaching 1 foot/30 cm; some bloom only in spring, but many continue through the growing season. It grows in neutral to moderately acid humus-rich loam in partial shade, from Florida to Louisiana and southern Pennsylvania.

Aster oblongifolius, like a number of other native asters, is suitable for the rock garden but too little known. It forms large bushy clumps or festoons and produces an extraordinary profusion of blue-rayed heads comparatively late in autumn. Its habitat is neutral gravel in open sun, from Alabama to central Pennsylvania and far out over the prairies.

The rock garden merits of *Coreopsis auriculata* have been praised by several writers. It has the advantage of blooming late in spring, after much early spring bloom is past. It favors slightly acid loam in partial shade, from the Gulf states to Virginia.

Marshallia grandiflora or Barbara's-buttons is one of the rayless composites, but its copious long disk-florets make lovely pink heads in early summer, borne on long stems above the basal leaf rosettes. It is found in damp, moderately acid gravel, in the open, in mountains of North Carolina and Pennsylvania.

Although several native species of *Senecio* are used to some extent in the rock garden, the southern *S. millefolium* deserves to be better known. Its leaves are dissected in a delicate lacy pattern, and the flowers are cute little yellow daisies. Its habitat is full sun, in acid humus pockets in granite ledges, in mountains from South Carolina to Virginia.

Originally published in the Bulletin of the American Rock Garden Society, *vol. 17, no. 2, pp. 57–60 (1959).*

The Virginia Shale Barrens

DONALD W. HUMPHREY

[Two responses to this article are reprinted following it. As they originally appeared, these commentaries also contained discussions of nomenclature; for this edition nomenclature has been brought into conformity with current usage, so that material has been deleted here, with only useful descriptive and cultural remarks retained.—*Ed.*]

The area around Clifton Forge, Virginia, in Bath, Botetort, Craig, and Allegheny counties, is part of the Valley and Ridge physiographic province, which extends from New York to Alabama. Except for some very rare occurrences of basalt, the rocks are folded sedimentary strata composed of limestone, sandstone, quartzite, and shale. The limestone is found mostly in the valleys and underlies the best agricultural land, so the natural vegetation of these areas has been altered and largely replaced. The higher ridges are formed by white and red sandstones or by quartzites. Shales are found mainly in valleys, on low hills, and on the intermediate slopes of the higher ridges.

Because of the characteristic erosional pattern on the shales, they are easy to recognize even from a distance. The slopes are steep, and the drainage pattern is branched and intricate. Because of the steepness of the slopes and the loose, unconsolidated nature of the shale soils, these areas are commonly referred to as "shale barrens." To the botanist, they are remarkable for their characteristic flora, including a number of endemic species.

Clifton Forge lies in the valley of the Jackson River in a spectacular mountain setting. On a trip to the shale barrens, we headed south along Highway 220, following the Jackson River to where it joins the Cowpasture River to form the James, one of Virginia's largest rivers. We followed the general course of the James to the white sandstone cliffs of Eagle Rock. Here we turned northwest along Craig Creek and encountered our first shale barren. Four conspicuous plants there were shale barren endemics: *Clematis coactilis, C. albicoma, Eriogonum allenii,* and *Senecio antennariifolius.*

Both clematises form neat, erect clumps about 1 foot/30 cm tall and 1 foot or more across. The opposite leaves are simple in *Clematis albicoma,* and in *C. coactilis* they are considerably more hirsute. The latter's small, thick-sepaled, nodding flowers, which look like upside-down vases, are greenish-yellow, whereas those of the former tend toward lavender-purple.

Eriogonum allenii is an eastern representative of a largely western genus, some species of which are choice rock garden plants. The same can hardly be said of *E. allenii,* however, for it is a large, coarse plant growing to 2 feet/60 cm tall. Its basal leaves are large and oblong, smooth above and densely hairy below.

Senecio antennariifolius is an excellent rock garden foliage plant. The ovate leaves form a compact basal clump up to 8 inches/20 cm across and densely white-hairy, especially on the underside. In May, the plant bears typical yellow composite flowers on stems about 1 foot/30 cm high.

One of the plants I collected from this barren (I saw it at no other site) was *Commelina erecta* or its variety *angustifolia.* As one who has often pulled the weedy annual *C. communis* from the garden, I am skeptical of any of them. These perennial plants were, however, less than 4 inches/10 cm tall in dense clumps. I planted them in both a moist and a dry site. Those in the moist site bloomed abundantly for three weeks; their clear blue flowers, over 1 inch/2.5 cm across, had an ephemeral loveliness until the noon sun shriveled them. Those in the sunny, dry spot stayed low and bloomed sparsely. This species is widely distributed in the eastern United States but is considered a characteristic shale barren plant.

An annual phacelia, probably *Phacelia dubia,* had already bloomed and died on this steep, south slope. I tried to collect seeds, but most of the capsules had already burst. This plant hazes the spring barrens with a delicate blue. Here, too, I collected a plant of *Ruellia purshiana,* which grew to some 10 inches/25 cm tall and proceeded to produce large numbers of cleistogamous flowers.

Our second stop was above the barrens of Craig Creek, where we found a different flora in the acid woodland of oak and other deciduous trees. We found *Iris verna* (Plate 96) in relative abundance, the largest form we encountered on the trip, with leaves more than 1 foot/30 cm long and 1 inch/2.5 cm wide. Two days later on Bald Knob in Bath County at an elevation of over 4000 feet/1200 meters, I collected a diminutive *I. verna* from peaty soil in the rocky quartzite talus. This iris is quite variable in its flowers, not only in size but in general form, depth of color, and size of the orange blotch on the falls.

At this stop we also found several clumps of *Galax urceolata* (formerly *G. aphylla*, *G. rotundifolia*), a marvelous plant for the shady wild garden. It is much more common southward. The real find here, however, was *Polygala polygama*. Listed as a biennial, mine is nonetheless acting as a perennial. It is a delicate rock garden plant with several wandlike stems to 6 inches/15 cm tall, set along the upper inch or two with a number of small pink flowers. This plant also sets cleistogamous flowers from stems at or just below the surface of the soil. Not uncommon throughout this region is the well-known *P. paucifolia*, a lovely plant that is unfortunately difficult to grow well.

Later, in a moist, shady section along Craig Creek, we came upon our first stand of *Phlox latifolia* (formerly *P. ovata*) in full bloom. This is an excellent phlox for either rock garden or border. The specific name describes the basal, evergreen leaves, 2 to 5 inches/5 to 13 cm long, on somewhat woody stems. The flowering stems are 15 inches/38 cm or more long, and the inflorescence is generally flat-topped in the form of a corymb, carrying dark pink flowers 1 inch/2.5 cm or more across. It blooms for well over a month in the garden.

Without in any way deprecating the value of *Phlox latifolia*, we were actually looking for a much rarer, locally endemic plant, *P. buckleyi*. This unique phlox has flowers of much the same color and height as *P. latifolia*, but its 4-inch/10-cm evergreen basal leaves are narrow and grasslike. Its cauline leaves are narrowly lance-shaped. For another 15 miles/24 km as we ascended Craig Creek we saw *P. latifolia*, but no *P. buckleyi*.

After arriving at Newcastle, Virginia, we started back to Clifton Forge on a forest road parallel to Craig Creek but about 5 miles/8 km north of it. It was here that we found *Phlox buckleyi* in a large colony along the road, growing in a sandy soil derived from decomposed sandstone. Here too, Russell Kirk, one of the wider-ranging members of our group, came across a colony of *Chamaelirium luteum* in full bloom. The day was getting late and we were all tired, so we headed back to Clifton Forge through some of the most charming jumbled mountain scenery imaginable.

The next day we went west along the Jackson River to the Covington; then we turned northeast on Highway 220, climbing rapidly by a series of switchbacks affording superb views of the Jackson River valley and some tantalizing but apparently inaccessible shale barrens along the west side of the river.

After visiting Falling Springs, a scenic waterfall, we dropped down into the Jackson River valley again and followed it upstream awhile, leaving it on the Bath County line. Our next stop was a shale barren where we were looking in particular for another endemic, *Trifolium virginicum*, a rare clover with nearly white flower heads, suitable for the rock garden. We did not find it, but we did find *Allium oxyphilum*, a shale barren endemic considered by some to be a variety of *A. cernuum*. I have both in my garden, and *A. oxyphilum* differs from *A. cernuum* in having yellow-green foliage rather than the bright green of the latter. Its flowers are pure white without any pink, and the tepals open wider, making the flowers appear larger and more deeply cut.

Another plant common throughout the barrens but not strictly endemic is *Draba ramosissima*, a small perennial with neat rosettes of dark green, toothed leaves, bearing small white flowers on stems a few inches high. In the loose shale the main stem becomes prostrate and largely covered with sliding rock. It is consequently difficult to find the roots, and it does not transplant well. We also found a good colony of *Phlox buckleyi* at this site.

We pressed on to Blowing Springs recreation area for a picnic lunch. En route we left the dry shales and passed through rich deciduous forest, seeing many fine azaleas (*Rhododendron calendulaceum*) in bloom, varying from pale yellow to red-orange.

Following lunch, we retraced our route for a few miles, then drove through the old spa towns of Warm Springs and Hot Springs in the lovely, domestic Warm Springs valley. Development has obliterated many acres of *Rhododendron catawbiense* and the beautiful pink azalea *R. prinophyllum* (formerly *R. roseum*). This sweet-smelling azalea was in full bloom, but except for a few plants, *R. catawbiense* was a week away from flowering. Along this linear crestline we found the small *Iris verna* previously mentioned, as well as other typical "bald" plants, including *Clintonia umbellulata* and *Menziesia pilosa*.

Leaving the ridge, our route now lay down a narrow paved road in a series of switchbacks offering superb views of the forested country to the east. This road, Route 606, leads to Clifton Forge. On the cutbanks bordering the road were great numbers of bird's-foot violets (*Viola pedata*). A month before, passing along this same road when the flowers were in bloom, we had noted the predominance of the bicolored form over the solid-colored. In a number of these the two upper petals were distinctly reddish rather than purple. And here my wife spotted, and we collected, a plant with pure albino flowers.

On the next day we worked northward. Along the road north of Douthat State Park we found *Oenothera fruticosa* subsp. *glauca* (formerly *O. tetragona*) in bloom, its fresh, clear yellow blooms brightening the road shoulders. Collected plants have larger, hairy foliage unlike that of the nearly glabrous form I grow as *O. fruticosa*, but these plants are small, the flowering stems rising hardly 1 foot/30 cm above the basal rosettes. This may be due partly to a dry southern exposure in well-drained, sandy soil, but it seems to be a distinct form.

A little farther on we found *Chrysogonum virginianum* blooming. The few ray flowers of this composite give it an appearance quite unlike most of its relatives. Its neat, spreading growth makes it desirable for the wild or rock garden.

We were now following a northward-flowing stream tributary to the Cowpasture River. Eventually shale outcrops began to appear along the road shoulders, and here we found *Asclepias quadrifolia* in bloom. This pale-pink-flowered milkweed is deliciously scented, and although it grows at least 1.5 feet/45 cm tall, the sparse-leafed single stem would seem to allow it a place in the rock garden, particularly where low-growing or prostrate plants could carpet the ground beneath it. Nearby, in a meadow, we found *Hypoxis hirsuta* blooming abundantly, the yellow flowers starring the grasslike foliage.

Where the stream we were following began to cut steeply to the lower elevation of the Cowpasture River, we found a marvelous shale barren. Here on a steep slope, almost a cliff, we found *Clematis albicoma* still in bloom. The pure white funnel flowers of *Convolvulus spithamaea* subsp. *purshianus* made an attractive display on 1-foot/30-cm, upright stems covered with simple, gray-hairy leaves. *Senecio antennariifolius* was abundant, as was *Eriogonum allenii*. *Sedum glaucophyllum* clothed rocky outcrops, and numerous other plants common to the shale barrens made the spot an interesting natural rock garden.

One species common here was *Oenothera argillicola*. This remarkable biennial is a shale barren endemic. Its growth form is low and bushy, spreading to 2 feet/60 cm or more. Its bright yellow flowers are as much as 4 inches/10 cm across, though on some plants they may be only 1 inch/2.5 cm or so. It is a charming and worthwhile garden plant, which if started early from seed indoors may be grown as an annual. Two plants in my dry wall began blooming in late August, continuing through September.

We were to have stopped at a 100-foot/30-meter shale cliff called Ratcliffe Hill along the Cowpasture River, but we made a wrong turn and missed it. Since the homing instinct was getting strong, we did not go back. The interesting feature of this outcrop is the presence of *Dicentra eximia* growing among typical shale barren plants. This species is often common at higher elevations of the Appalachians, but its occurrence in the shale barrens is unusual. A month earlier I had collected one of these plants, placing it at the upper edge of my rock garden where to date it is still smaller and more compact than other plants of the species in my garden.

Along the upper reaches of the Cowpasture we stopped to visit a large colony of *Phlox stolonifera*. Blooming was past, but the bright-green rosettes were scattered widely among the grass and other low-growing plants. The plants were compact and sparse in full sun, but larger and more luxuriant in half-shade. *Phlox stolonifera* is one of five species of phlox common in this part of Virginia: *P. latifolia* and *P. buckleyi* have already been mentioned; *P. divaricata* may be found in large colonies in rich alluvial soil, sheeting the ground with blue.

Undoubtedly the most common phlox throughout the shale barrens is *Phlox subulata*. For miles and miles along Great North Mountain in Highland County, this plant is uniformly a very pale bluish-white varying to almost white. This is probably the plant referred to as subspecies *brittonii*. Along the Cowpasture River various shades of pink predominate.

Our last stop was to view a colony of *Opuntia humifusa* subsp. *humifusa* (formerly *O. compressa*). This prickly pear is the only cactus commonly found in the southeastern United States, occurring on sterile soils of pine and shale barrens and rocky places. The greenish-yellow flowers are attractive but do not last long. The trip was then officially disbanded and we headed into the streams of traffic with new plants for the rock garden and the hope that we could soon introduce them through the seed exchange to other members of the American Rock Garden Society.

More on the Virginia Shale Barrens

LEONARD J. UTTAL

I live just a few miles from the southern limits of the strange ecological niche known as the Virginia shale barrens. I have been up and down nearly all the stations Mr. Humphrey wrote of so accurately, so I feel I know their little-realized potential.

The genus *Clematis*, in particular the upright herbaceous sorts, are distinctive plants of this region. The best is *C. coactilis*. A common name for this species could be "ghost leather-flower," because the plants are covered with whitish fuzz. The fuzzy, urn-shaped, suspended flowers later stand erect in seed, with typical plumy tails, also ghostly white.

Clematis viticaulis is the rarest of our endemic leather-flowers, found only at a few stations in two counties. It has given up the genus's usual habit of sprawling far and wide and confines itself to neat clumps. To me, it is the best of the lot, for it flowers throughout the growing season.

Ruellia pedunculata is essentially a plant of the Ozarks, and *R. purshiana* one of the Appalachians. They are quite different in appearance: *R. pedunculata* bears its flowers on wiry peduncles, while *R. purshiana* bears them on short peduncles from the lower axils. The Ozark species is much better in the garden. *Ruellia purshiana* tends to deteriorate to strict cleistogamy (the production of non-opening fertile flowers) under the oversolicitous regimen of garden life. It is not limited to the shale barrens.

Eriogonum allenii, to be sure, is coarse compared to the jaunty little eriogonums of the West, but I would not fault it as an accent plant in the garden, because it has a large truss of sulfurous flowers—if it can be transplanted. I have only succeeded in moving small, young plants, and none of them have yet come to flower.

Allium oxyphilum, the white nodding onion of the shale barrens, is now regarded as just one of the minor varieties of a wide-ranging continental species, *A. cernuum*. In the garden, they cross freely, resulting in hybrids of a washed-out color—and I warn you, they can take over.

The showy bindweed of the shale barrens, *Convolvulus spithamaea* subsp. *purshiana*, has a consistent felty pubescence. This is another attractive species you will regret putting in a garden, because it extends its stolons everywhere when once established.

Endemism in the shale barrens is significant. In addition, it is the disjunct eastern home of some plants not found again until the western mountains. Some other plants are closely related not to eastern species but to western ones. For example, the very desirable *Senecio antennariifolius* is the eastern analogue of the widespread western *S. canus*. I like the eastern plant better because it is less leafy-stemmed.

Many plants of the shale barrens look different from those growing in different habitats nearby, but are really no different genetically. Thus some continental plants, particularly composites, take on a different appearance (usually more succulent and glabrous) when they grow near the sea. So many of the "different lookers" have received names in time past that the synonymy is massive.

———— Further Notes on the Virginia Shale Barrens ————

EDGAR T. WHERRY

Having been one of the earlier explorers of the shale barrens and their flora, I was glad to see this remarkable assemblage of American rock plants written up. A few corrections and comments seem to be in order, however.

The eastern member of the buckwheat family, *Eriogonum allenii*, is admittedly outsized for many rock gardens, yet its profuse yellow flowers borne in late summer when little else is in bloom suggest its desirability. It is quite satisfactory on the large-scale rock slope at the Henry Foundation at Gladwyne, Pennsylvania.

Senecio antennariifolius would indeed be desirable if a long-lived strain could be found, but the common form seems monocarpic, dying out after blooming.

A word of warning is in order in regard to the attractive *Convolvulus spithamaeus* subsp. *purshianus*: this plant spreads rampantly by rhizomes, and if one once puts it in a small rock garden, it will crowd out all diminutive treasures.

Originally published in the Bulletin of the American Rock Garden Society, *vol. 28, no. 1, pp. 47–52 (1970); vol. 28, no. 3, pp. 130–131; vol. 28, no. 3, p. 143.*

Granitic Flat-Rocks: Natural Rock Gardens of the Southeast

JOHN J. WURDACK AND MARIE WURDACK

The granitic flat-rocks of southeastern United States are scenic natural rock gardens with an unusual community of plants. This distinctive flora is centered in northern Georgia, with extensions northward as far as southernmost Virginia and westward into Alabama. The total area of exposed rock is an estimated 8000 acres/3200 hectares, about three-quarters of which is in Georgia.

The flat-rocks were known to the early plant explorers William Bartram, André Michaux, Thomas Nuttall, and Lewis Schweinitz. Their botanical history was admirably summarized by Rogers McVaugh in 1943; subsequent studies, especially at Emory University and Duke University, have further refined that ecological knowledge.

The best known of the flat-rocks is Stone Mountain near Atlanta, Georgia. Some of the more common distinctive plants can still be seen there, as well as at Echols' Mill in Oglethorpe County, Georgia, and along Old Flat Rock Road in Kershaw County, South Carolina; however, the flora on these outcrops has been much disturbed by park development and quarrying. Essentially undisturbed are most of the rock areas at Mount Panola and Mount Arabia, both in DeKalb County, Georgia, and now public property; Heggie's Rock in Columbia County, Georgia; and Forty Acre Rock in Lancaster County, South Carolina. Most of the floristically rich flat-rocks are not prominently elevated above the surrounding piedmont; Stone Mountain is atypical.

Many of the flat-rock plants are also found elsewhere, but some are nearly or entirely restricted to these outcrops. *Diamorpha* is mostly confined to flat-rocks, and *Amphianthus* entirely so; both are monotypic genera. *Amphianthus pusillus, Draba aprica, Isoetes melanospora,* and *Sedum pusillum* are listed among Georgia's protected plants. *Isoetes piedmontana, Portulaca smallii, Minuartia* (formerly *Arenaria*) *uniflora,* and *Sedum pusillum* have been cited among North Carolina's "primary concern" plants.

The habitats on the outcrops include bare rock, rock crevices, shallow depressions or weather pits (often seasonally water-filled), vegetation mats or islands, and seepage zones, as well as the forested margins. The most common trees at the outcrop edges or in larger island groves on the rocks include red cedar (*Juniperus virginiana*), lollolly pine (*Pinus taeda*), black oak (*Quercus nigra*), and, on some outcrops, *Q. georgiana.* Attractive shrubs include *Chionanthus virginica,* the fringe tree, and *Aesculus sylvatica* as well as its hybrid with *A. pavia*—both dwarf buckeyes. Three ornamental vines are also found on some flat-rocks: *Gelsemium sempervirens,* the yellow jessamine, ranging north to southeastern Virginia and barely hardy in protected places near Washington, D.C.; *Lonicera sempervirens,* the coral honeysuckle; and *Bignonia* (formerly *Anisostichus*) *capreolata,* the cross vine, ranging north to eastern Maryland and Illinois.

The outcrops themselves, apart from the moisture-accumulating areas and vegetation islands, often have a dense and attractive growth of lichens (particularly *Cladonia* spp.) and mosses. In the shallow depressions, depending on the depth and persistence of the water, are seasonal miniature rock gardens, with spring or fall annuals or deciduous perennials such as *Amphianthus,* several species of *Arenaria* and *Minuartia, Diamorpha, Isoetes,* and *Senecio.* Around the more developed vegetation islands or in seepage areas is a larger flora with fewer endemics, including *Coreopsis grandiflora* var. *saxicola, Houstonia, Lindernia, Opuntia, Phacelia, Rhexia, Xyris, Yucca,* and several species of *Hypericum, Oenothera, Selaginella,* and *Tradescantia.*

The natural rock gardens are at their best in early April. Then the marginal areas show peak flowering of shrubs and vines. The larger tree islands and seepages have patches of *Sedum pusillum, Phacelia dubia* var. *georgiana, Amsonia ciliata,* and *Tradescantia hirsuticaulis;* the weather pits are zoned pink, white, and yellow with *Diamorpha smallii, Minuartia uniflora, Nothoscordum bivalve, Schoenolirion croceum,* and *Senecio tomentosus.* By summer most of the spring plants have vanished into seed or belowground dormancy, and the summer flora does not compare in showiness with the vernal display. However, there are minor flashes, with *Hypericum frondosum, H. prolificum,* and *H. lloydii, Oenothera fruticosa* (sometimes identified as variety *subglobosa*), *O. linifolia* (sometimes identified as variety *glandulosa*), *Talinum teretifolium, Polygala curtisii, Liatris microcephala, Rhexia mariana, Callisia* (formerly *Tradescantia*) *rosea,* and *Coreopsis grandiflora* subsp. *saxicola.* In autumn the desiccated lichens and mosses freshen; the confederate daisy (*Helianthus,* formerly *Viguiera, porterii*) gilds the Georgia and Alabama outcrops; and *Agalinis* and *Carphe-*

phorus make pink-purple splashes on or near the rocks. The coralberry (*Symphoricarpos orbiculatus*) bears its long-lasting fruits, *Spiranthes cernua* flowers, and the winter annuals again sprout to prepare for another spring floral climax.

Many of the flat-rock plants are suitable for rock gardens. Most are hardy at least as far north as the Potomac Valley; however, not all those listed below have yet been grown in our garden at Beltsville, Maryland.

Amsonia ciliata is a long-lived perennial with very narrow leaves and blue flowers in spring, more pleasant in a rock garden than the commoner *A. tabernaemontana*.

Minuartia uniflora, a winter annual a few inches tall, whitens the flat-rock depressions in spring. It is probably easy if one can fuss with gathering the seeds for resowing in the fall. *Minuartia* (formerly *Arenaria*) *alabamensis* is now included in *M. uniflora*. This and *M. glabra*, also annual, are related to the widespread perennial *M. groenlandica*, which occurs at higher elevations in the south.

Carphephorus bellidifolius is a pleasant-looking low composite, fall-flowering and thus doubly desirable. It is actually a species of sandy woodlands bordering flat-rocks, at least in South Carolina.

Coreopsis grandiflora var. *saxicola*, a perennial, flowers for 4 months in summer and fall in Maryland. Although rather large and sprawling for a small rock garden, it grows much trimmer on the flat-rocks.

Diamorpha smallii is a winter annual, the early spring glory of the flat-rocks, with masses of plants 1 to 3 inches/2.5 to 8 cm tall turning the weather pits pink. It should be cosseted like *Minuartia uniflora*.

Houstonia pusilla is an annual, even smaller and just as desirable as the well-known bluets. Its flowers are lavender with a reddish eye.

Hypericum frondosum, a shrub to 4 feet/120 cm tall with large yellow flowers, is quite hardy in Maryland. It is common only on Stone Mountain in Georgia but widespread in the Tennessee cedar glades.

Hypericum lloydii, a heath-like shrub usually 6 to 12 inches/15 to 30 cm tall, is common on Forty Acre Rock and hardy in Maryland. The flowers are rather small but a good yellow over a long period in summer and fall.

Liatris microcephala, a very trim species, occurs at Echols' Mill. It is attractive in flower, tending to sprawl in a well-watered garden.

Nothoscordum bivalve, an onion with odorless foliage, often produces its white flowers in both spring and fall, remaining dormant in summer's heat. It is quite hardy, rather inconspicuous but pleasant.

Phacelia dubia var. *georgiana*, another winter annual, has rather pale purple-blue flowers, dainty and desirable like the widespread typical variety.

Rhexia mariana, a perennial happy in dryish places, begins flowering later than *R. virginica* and lasts until frost. The petals are white to pale (rarely rich) pink. All 13 species of *Rhexia* have been tried at one time or another in Maryland, and only *R. mariana*, *R. nashii*, and *R. virginica* have survived more than a few winters.

Schoenolirion croceum is a modestly pleasing liliaceous perennial widespread in the Southeast. Its grasslike leaves and bright yellow flowers appear in early spring. It is dormant in summer, with the leaves reappearing in fall. It has been hardy and long-lived in Maryland.

Selaginella tortipila is common only at Heggie's Rock but there forms large low mats. This and the sandhill species *S. arenicola* are very desirable for rock gardens, but perhaps not reliably hardy northward.

Senecio tomentosus, an attractive species with a woody base, has woolly leaves which die down in summer and reappear in fall, and yellow flowers. It grows in large colonies on the flat-rocks and is widespread in southeastern United States and hardy in the north.

Talinum teretifolium is the most widespread of the eastern species. Although similar to the others, it is desirable for the flowers that open late on summer afternoons. Another species, *T. mengesii*, has also been recorded from a few flat-rocks. All the southeastern fameflowers (including *T. parviflorum*, formerly *T. appalachianum*, and *T. calcaricum*) are hardy in Maryland.

Tradescantia hirsuticaulis, a low-growing and very desirable perennial from the South, is especially common on the Georgia flat-rocks. It flowers in April, the leaves dying back in summer and reappearing in late fall. Our Maryland colony of the common blue-flowered form has persisted for 10 years, but a plant with pink petals died out after a few seasons.

Callisia rosea (formerly *Tradescantia rosea*, *Cuthbertia rosea*) occurs on the Georgia flat-rocks only in the typical form of this most desirable but rather short-lived perennial. Even more attractive and commoner, at least on the coastal plain, is the narrow-leaved variety *graminea*.

Helianthus porterii (formerly *Viguiera porterii*) is a showy and very late-flowering (September through November in Maryland) annual composite, usually 12 to 18 inches/30 to 45 cm tall on the flat-rocks but more robust in gardens. The species is named for a Pennsylvania clergyman-botanist who was the first naturalist (in 1846) to visit Stone Mountain.

Originally published in the Bulletin of the American Rock Garden Society, *vol. 36, no. 1, pp. 53–56 (1978).*

A Few Plants of the Carolinas

ERNEST H. YELTON

The Carolinas have been a mecca for botanists over the past three centuries, so it is not surprising that the American Rock Garden Society turned to this area for its fiftieth-anniversary meeting in 1984. One hundred eighty plant families, 951 genera, and 3360 plant taxa make their home in the Carolinas. B. W. Wells, in his book *The Natural Gardens of North Carolina*, lists 10 main plant associations in our state: seaside dunes and live oak and salt marshes; inland marshes; swamp forests; aquatic vegetation; evergreen shrub-bogs; savannahs or grass-sedge bogs; wire grass sandhills; old fields in transition and regrowth; the great forest; and the Christmas-tree lands of the boreal forest of the mountains.

In each of these areas one can find good subjects for the rock garden, adaptable to a wide array of habitats. In fact, North Carolina and South Carolina are the *only* home of several fine rock garden plants; in some instances, one must go to the Japanese highlands or Chinese woodlands to find similar species—an intriguing pattern of disjunct species distribution that has never been fully explained.

That "unsinkable Molly Brown" of plantdom, Lester Rowntree, author of *Hardy Californians*, visited Chimney Rock, North Carolina, in 1940 and stated, "it reminds me of the Sierras, the flora reminds me of the redwoods." Other observers have commented on the pear-shaped sandhill lakes and their similarity to the lakes seen from the air on the Alaskan tundra of the Yukon delta. The dwarf forests of the New Jersey pine barrens share the same plants as the turkey oak forests of the sand-dunes country near Pinehurst. The deep, dark spruce woods of the Smoky Mountains are quite similar to those of the Gaspé Peninsula or Acadia National Park in Maine. Forty Acre Rock and other granitic outcrops are very similar to Mount Monadnock, with huge blocks of exfoliated stone and xerophytes growing in the 1-inch/2.5-cm-deep soil along the rock seams. One can pick one's favorite plant habitat in the Carolinas.

The seasons offer a magnificent range of spectacles: the pogonias in full bloom in Green Swamp; the rhododendrons atop Roan Mountain in late June; the sand-myrtle cliffs of Linville Gorge in early May; the magnolias and wild azaleas of the Smokies and Wayah Bald; the magnificent foliage from the Blue Ridge Parkway toward Looking Glass Mountain—all have indelibly etched themselves in my memory.

Of the plethora of potential rock garden plants available in this diversified state, I can mention only a very few of my favorites. It is difficult to choose.

In the sandy swamplands of the southeastern corner of the state grows the Venus fly-trap, *Dionaea muscipula*, an insectivorous plant capable of quite fast leaf movement to catch flies and other bugs. The process of digestion of the imprisoned insects and means by which the closure of the steel-trap-shaped leaflets is triggered was studied intensively by Charles Darwin. The fly-trap is fairly low-growing (2 to 3 inches/5 to 8 cm tall) and does best on a bog or moraine. In its native setting, the plant responds to frequent burning of the surrounding grasslands by blooming more profusely and spreading into the burned areas. It blooms in May with a white, five-petaled, 0.5-inch/13-mm in diameter flower on a stalk about 1 foot/30 cm tall; this plant's chief attraction, however, is the foliage. You will find it difficult to establish fly-traps purchased in the gift shops and nurseries, where they are grown on damp sphagnum. These plants have a long taproot, which in their native setting goes down at least 18 inches/45 cm to find subterranean water during the dry, hot summers, and this root is necessary for their survival outdoors.

Within the same general zone may be found the rose pogonia, *Pogonia ophioglossoides* (Plate 90). Green Swamp, a Nature Conservancy reserve, is the best place to see masses of these lovely, fragrant rose orchids blooming in May. The half-size cattleya-type blooms are displayed on 1-foot/30-cm scapes with as many as three blossoms per stem; they look quite out of place in the acidic black muck surrounding open ponds. This orchid is difficult to transplant and grow in the garden. I recommend that you view it in its natural setting. North Carolina has 59 species of orchids, several of which are to be found in Green Swamp preserve. A plant similar in appearance to the rose pogonia, but much rarer, is *Cleistes divaricata*, which grows in mountain areas in sphagnum bogs.

Another beauty of the inland marshes is *Orontium aquaticum* or golden-club, a member of the arum family. This plant may be found sporadically throughout the East Coast states. It reminds me of a calla lily without the white scape or hood. The white spadix is about 4 inches/10 cm long, with a bright golden tip. The leaves are beautifully veined and make a nice rosette. The whole plant looks rather startling, rising so neat and clean out of the black muck around Eastertime. It is fairly easy to grow in proper bog conditions.

Another plant of the coastal plain, this one from the Amaryllidaceae, is the atamasco lily (*Zephyranthes atamasco*), which is more common in South Carolina. Exceptional use of this small pale pink, bulbous plant is made at Cypress Gardens, an old converted rice plantation lake near Monck's Corner, South Carolina. The kurume and indica azaleas blooming on islands surrounded by the deep black water of the pond are fringed along the shore by atamasco lilies at Eastertime (but do not go on Easter Sunday if you like a little peace and quiet with your flowers.) This plant is easily raised in any moist location.

One of the oddities of the plant world, found in coastal ponds and roadside ditches filled with water, is the bladderwort *Utricularia purpurea*. It is a small raft of rootlets kept afloat by small air-filled bladders, from which arise in midsummer tiny, soft purple, spurred flowers on threadlike stems. Green Swamp is an ideal site to see this insectivorous plant, also investigated by Darwin. The little bladders trap small plankton swimming in the water. This plant is a member of the same family as the butterworts (*Pinguicula* spp.), which catch insects on the sticky surfaces of the leaves. For the lazy rock gardener, all that is needed for its culture is a pool of water.

Continuing to the pine barrens and acidic loams of the lower Piedmont, we find pyxie moss (*Pyxidanthera barbulata* var. *brevifolia*), with foliage much more mossy than the typical *P. barbulata*, which grows in the pine barrens of New Jersey as well as in Virginia and the Carolinas. This is one of the most beautiful members of that famous rock garden family, the Diapensiaceae; two other representatives in the southern Appalachians are *Shortia galacifolia* (Plate 97) and *Galax urceolata*. Pyxie moss is quite a spectacle in late March when the solid mass of soft green foliage is sprinkled with white, five-petaled stars. Rotten pine needles and just a bit of moisture in semishade are required for this rather stubborn plant. It is best to use the acidic sandy soil so common to the xerophytic woods of the sandhills rather than making up an artificial soil, because there seems to be some sort of mycorrhizal symbiosis necessary for absorption of essential nitrogen and other nutrients.

Found in close proximity to the pyxie moss is the box sand myrtle (*Leiophyllum buxifolium*). The eastern forms are much taller than those found on the high rock outcrops of Linville Gorge and Grandfather Mountain at 6000 feet/1800 meters; the latter, formerly called variety *prostratum* but now regarded as an environmental variation, is much more desirable for its compactness and density of bloom heads. Many state that this form, when grown from seed, reverts to the regular form, but I have found that seedlings do retain much of their dwarfness. Seeds are the best way to propagate this shrub, because rooting it is quite difficult. The dwarf variety makes a shrublet of shiny, dark green elliptic leaves about 0.25 inch/6 mm long; some forms have a soft pink cast to the flowers, which are borne in tiny corymbs of 15 to 20 florets, each about 0.2 in/5 mm wide, in April and May. This plant is seen at its best on Grandfather Mountain at the overlook and swinging bridge. Interestingly, this plant has been considered for placement in the Diapensiaceae rather than the Ericaceae. It probably needs mycorrhizal association in cultivation. The leggier eastern forms are much easier to grow than the dwarf forms, but not so desirable.

Another member of the Ericaceae from the sandhills near Southern Pines is *Vaccinium crassifolium*, the creeping blueberry. This has much the same foliage as *Leiophyllum*, but it is a creeper and sends out fairly long runners up to 1 foot/30 cm in length. The bloom is bell-shaped and reminds one of lily-of-the-valley. An extra bonus are the nice blueberries in the late summer. This blueberry can be grown easily in moist sandy acid loam.

The pine barrens gentian, *Gentiana autumnalis*, also grows in our sandhills. I believe that our forms have larger blooms and deeper color than the New Jersey forms. For gentian-lovers, it would be worth the trip to Green Swamp in early October to see this one; it is better than many of the European or Asiatic species. Unfortunately, it is rather difficult to grow, and seeds are not easy to come by in most years. It seems to prefer a "pocosin" or savannah acidic soil with semishade and moisture. The trumpets are deep blue with white or soft green throats and often occur up to three on a stem. This is one of my favorite wildflowers.

The grassy-leaved spiderwort, *Callisia graminea* (formerly *Tradescantia rosea* var. *graminea*) is also a native of the sandhill country. The foliage is less than 0.13 inch/3 mm wide and slender, up to 8 inches/20 cm in length. This spiderwort grows in a dense clump, usually in sandy loam in open woods. This form is much preferred to *Callisia rosea*, which is coarser in foliage and flower. The flower cymes of *C. graminea* bear as many as 15 soft rose blossoms on drooping stems atop a slender stalk extending just above the grassy foliage. The best flowering time is in May, although they continue to bloom well into July. Ants dote on these clumps for their nests, so I would recommend treatment with chlordane if ants are noted, because they can do much damage.

In the upper coastal plain near the fall line is found *Hypericum lloydii*, one of the finest members of this large genus. It occurs chiefly in xerophytic areas and on rock outcrops, notably at Forty Acre Rock, where it grows in the acid humus accumulated in the crevices of the weathered granite. The plant is easy and grows well in full sun, bearing a great summer-long profusion of soft feathery golden flowers on a compact bush dressed heavily with fine linear leaves of light green. It can be propagated readily from cuttings or seeds.

Another plant from generally the same locale is *Talinum teretifolium* of the Portulacaceae. This resembles the well-known *T. okanoganense* in plant habit and foliage—succulent and admirably equipped to survive the hottest spot on the hottest rock in the garden. The blooms begin in early June and continue throughout the summer to frost. They arise from the foliage clumps on long 18-inch/45-cm stalks on which float beautiful lavender-pink stars, which open fully in the afternoon and close at night. This plant seeds freely over the whole garden but is so shallow-rooted that the small, fleshy, awl-shaped rhizomes are easily removed. A good place to find it in the wild is on Rocky Face Mountain in Alexander County, North Carolina, where it grows on rocky outcrops in granite pockets.

My favorite member of the phlox tribe is *Phlox stolonifera*, one of the parents of *P. × procumbens*. Mr. and Mrs. Tom Shinn, learned amateur plantspeople and pillars of the North Carolina Wildflower Preservation Society, have found and cultivated a beautiful pure white form named 'Shinn's White', which has proven an exemplary garden plant, growing in sun or semishade equally well. A slightly moist location seems to be the ideal spot, especially along a creekbank or in woods mold. This plant blends well with the April rush of bloom, when it is good to have a flower that goes with any color. It does not exceed 10 inches/25 cm in height, so it will not overpower its neighbors, and it is easily propagated from cuttings or divisions.

In the mountain counties of North Carolina may be found several members of the genus *Phacelia*, the best being *P. fimbriata*. This annual resows itself once established, but not obtrusively so. The 12-inch/30-cm plants have pinnately lobed leaves, with a crowning inflorescence of as many as 15 florets of finely fimbriated cups, creating a soft fluffy mound of white in May. The species is most effective as a groundcover under shrubs, such as rhododendrons, or along streambanks. This should be sown where it is to grow because the plant resents moving. Another equally effective member of this family is *P. bipinnatifida*, with larger, soft blue flowers, but coarser in habit and foliage.

The queen of the mountain coves is *Shortia galacifolia* (Plate 97) or Oconee bells. The foliage resembles almost exactly that of its larger cousin *Galax urceolata*, being bright and shiny owing to a layer of cutin on the surface. *Shortia* makes an excellent groundcover in semishade and moist conditions. Its height does not exceed 8 inches/20 cm, and the white, fringed bells in early spring are a bonus to the beautiful foliage. This plant slowly spreads on short runners, which root easily, or the fresh seeds may be sown promptly with some success on sphagnum. Ants love the seeds and will beat you to them unless a close watch is kept; the seeds ripen quite early in summer.

Another woodland cove plant from our mountain counties is *Polygala paucifolia* or gaywings. These resemble pink, fringed dragonflies on a 5-inch/13-cm creeper in April. This is the equal of the European *P. calcarea* or *P. chamaebuxus* in plant habit and bloom. It is not as easy in cultivation, however, and seems to need a mycorrhizal companion for good results.

Polygala paucifolia
(Drawing by Laura Louise Foster)

Mountain bogs offer *Sarracenia rubra*, the sweet pitcher plant, a diminutive member of the insectivorous pitcher-plant family (Sarraceniaceae), growing to 16 inches/40 cm tall and bearing nicely scented flowers with rose-colored hoods. This is to be preferred over *S. purpurea* because of the bonus of fragrance. *Sarracenia flava* is too tall for the average rock garden. Sarracenias may be found in abundance in the Green Swamp area, although the sweet pitcher plant is confined mostly to our mountain counties.

The Shinns have made a special effort to raise sarracenias and have beautiful examples of them in their bog garden. The blossoms of *Sarracenia rubra* are maroon on the outer surface and greenish within, and droop on the scape above the leaves in April and May. They are quite easily cultivated and thrive in any boggy seep.

Another plant of the mountain bogs and seeps is *Helonias bullata*, the marsh pink, a member of the Liliaceae. This forms a low rosette of evergreen leaves from which rise a 1-foot/30-cm spike carrying a thick swarm of tiny pink flowers, each with six petals. Its seeds are of very low fertility, unfortunately, and one must use division of the rhizomes for certain reproduction.

From the highest peaks comes the roan lily, *Lilium grayi*. This plant is smaller than *L. superbum*, a handsomer plant that grows too large for most rock gardens. The roan lily has a hanging bell-shaped flower, with as many as nine florets per stem, of a lovely orange-red heavily dotted with black. Its average height is 2 to 3 feet/60 to 90 cm, but it may reach 6 feet/180 cm in the wild. It blooms in midsummer and loves a fair amount of cool moisture, which precludes its cultivation in the hotter Piedmont. Its seeds are borne prolifically, and one must break dormancy by stratification to germinate them well.

The rich mountain woodlands are the home of *Delphinium tricorne*, which may be found sparingly as far north as West Virginia and Kentucky. These plants may reach 18 inches/45 cm tall, bearing the deep purple, spurred florets in April. The foliage is densely cut and unobtrusive in the semishaded rockery. Seeds are the best means of propagation.

Along the Blue Ridge Parkway on cliffs where water seeps out of the rock may be found *Hypericum buckleyi*, another of the 30 species of *Hypericum* found in North Carolina. This forms a dense shrublet up to 18 inches/45 cm tall, covering itself with golden stars in July; it is not easily overlooked by the gardener. This plant must have a moraine to give its best, but the foliage has a distressing habit of shedding soon after flowering if the soil gets too moist, and dieback becomes a major problem, so very sharp drainage seems to be necessary. Seedlings grow well, and acid leafmold with plenty of sand makes a good potting mix for them.

From a few of our western counties, along high rocky ridges above 4000 feet/1200 meters elevation and at bases of cliffs with a northeasterly exposure, comes *Rhododendron vaseyi*, the pinkshell azalea. Why should I include a shrub that can reach 15 feet/5 meters in the wild in a list of rock plants? Usually the pinkshell azalea does not exceed 3 or 4 feet/1 meter, and it bears the loveliest soft pink flowers imaginable; some forms are white but just as lovely. The plant is well behaved, and the foliage has a glaucous sheen during the summer. In the fall the leaves turn a beautiful scarlet. This plant is interesting botanically because it represents an intergrade between the rhododendrons, which have ten stamens, and the azaleas, which have only five; *R. vaseyi* has five to seven stamens. This azalea is becoming quite rare in the wild, but fortunately it is easily cultivated and widely grown around the world.

One could make an interesting rock garden from this list alone, but these are only my favorites. Why not come to Carolina and select yours out of our many hundreds of garden-worthy plants?

Originally published in the Bulletin of the American Rock Garden Society, *vol. 41, no. 4, pp. 179–184 (1983).*

Some Small Eastern American Irises

B. LEROY DAVIDSON

The two small crested irises of eastern North America are frequently confused in gardens, for the good reason that—except for size—they appear much alike. There are, however, significant details by which they may be distinguished.

These little woodland irises belong to a large group of irises shared between eastern Asia and eastern North America, with one in western North America (*Iris tenuis*, a narrow endemic of northwestern Oregon). This group is now classified as section Lophiris, but for many years they were called "Evansia irises" in honor of the man who first introduced the Asiatic species to Western horticulture.

Iris lacustris has been established as a species in its own right by its distinct chromosome number, but we still need to learn to distinguish it on sight. Separating *I. lacustris* and *I. cristata* on the basis of the shape of the flower segments is misleading. It is very likely that many of the plants grown under the misapprehension that they are the true "blue iris of the lakes" are in reality only poor, small, pale forms of *I. cristata*.

Iris cristata (Plate 98) is larger in all its parts, averaging about twice the size of *I. lacustris*. It is also the more variable of the two. It has two centers of distribution—the Appalachians and the Ozarks—and its flower color varies from white and near-white through pastel tints of orchid, lilac, lavender, and blue to deep purple and violet. Except in white forms, there is always a characteristic marking on the falls; a "squared-off" border of pigment surrounds a little white apronlike patch, on which there are one to three small, raised comblike crests, as well as some gold penciling. Plants of the Ozarks are not markedly different, except for a tendency to be smaller and paler.

Iris lacustris is found on limestone rocks and gravels in association with the northern coniferous forest community around the upper Great Lakes. It is almost nonvariable. It is usually a pretty azure, but occasionally white. All except the white forms bear a pattern similar to that of *I. cristata* on the falls, with similar crests and gold marking.

The unmistakable botanical distinction between the two is based on the length of the perianth tube, quite a reliable criterion. In *Iris cristata* the distance between the top of the rhizome and the ovary is far less than the length of the perianth tube, which separates the ovary from the floral lobes above. In *I. lacustris* the opposite is true; its seed capsule rests atop a short stalk and on a true stem, whereas that of *I. cristata* sits almost on the rhizome at ground level. These proportions are frequently misinterpreted, probably because of the overall size difference between the species.

The seeds of the two are very much alike, having a peculiar development of the raphe, which appears as a sort of gelatinous little spring. This seems to assist in the dehiscence of the capsule and dispersal of the seeds from it. On exposure to air the raphe dries and shrivels.

It is often said that these two irises cannot easily be grown in the same garden. This probably stems from the fact that the native soils supporting *Iris cristata* are slightly acid (pH 6 to 6.9) while those on which *I. lacustris* is found are nearly neutral (pH 7.1 to 9). Both species, however, are about equally tolerant of a variety of soils as long as they are cool and loose with humus, well drained but always moist and never boggy. *Iris cristata* can survive some drying in shady positions. The soft leaves of both species are favored by slugs and snails. In dappled shade sheltered from afternoon sun they will romp away on short, slender stolons, which root down to form broadly spreading colonies.

A hybrid between the two was reported to have been made in British Columbia and shown in England in 1955. This is not impossible, although we know now that the different chromosome numbers of the two should prevent their being interfertile. There is also a record of a cross of *Iris lacustris* with the related Japanese *I. gracilipes*, shown in England in 1965. Some years ago a plant was distributed as 'Oliver Twist', purported to be a hybrid of *I. cristata* with *I. tectorum*, the roof iris. It is probable, however, that at least some of the plants under this name were only a poor form of *I. tectorum*.

Both blue and white specimens of *Iris lacustris* are occasionally found in cultivation. Of the variable *I. cristata* there are a number of selected clones, most found as wild plants. There is at least one good vigorous white form among the number of albinos recorded; 'White Pearl' was one, although it may have had a blue tint. 'Crested Ivory' is well described by its name. 'McDonald', a seedling from an Oregon nursery, has the faint typical pattern, and 'Millard' seems to have been similar, as was 'Whisper'. 'Skylands' was apparently a shade darker. 'Crested Fairy' was described as bicolored, and 'Gold Crest' a mid-lavender with more yellow lines. 'Abbey's Violet' seems to be the darkest of all. Many other good forms are probably grown without being named—for example, a good "pink" and a clear azure, both found in eastern Tennessee and possibly still in some gardens.

Originally published in the Bulletin of the American Rock Garden Society, *vol. 40, no. 4, pp. 166–170 (1982).*

The Elusive Shortia

H. LINCOLN FOSTER

In the winter of 1968, my wife, Timmy, and I heard that a large portion of the type site for Oconee bells (*Shortia galacifolia*, Plate 97) in Pickens and Oconee counties of South Carolina was soon to be flooded by dams already under construction by the Duke Power Company, and so we determined to make an excursion there at blooming season. Frederick Case supplied us with the name of Charles Moore of Brevard, North Carolina, an employee of the power company who could guide us.

In January 1969 I wrote to Mr. Moore of my interest in this beautiful plant, asking about its distribution, rarity, and possible color variations, and hinting that I hoped sometime to visit shortia country at flowering season. Mr. Moore promptly rose to my bait, writing, "Why don't you come down to North Carolina and let me give you a conducted tour. The middle of March is a sure time to see the display." He also referred me to a series of journal articles about *Shortia galacifolia* by Dr. P. A. Davies of the University of Louisville. Mr. Moore had provided much information and assistance to Dr. Davies, based on his many years of amateur plant-hunting, collecting, and observation in the Blue Ridge and Smoky mountains.

In preparation for our foray, I followed up these references and others turned up in the course of my reading. I found a considerable and fascinating history of this single American species.

Shortia galacifolia was first collected by the French botanist André Michaux, who during the latter part of the eighteenth century had spent 11 years in North America seeking plants to grace the gardens of France. Shortia, however, was not dispatched by Michaux as living plant material, perhaps because he did not see the plant in bloom and recognize its charm. The material he gathered for his herbarium was placed in his cabinets in Paris. Among a group labeled "Plantae incognitae" ("Unknown plants") was a sheet with a single shoot with five mature leaves, three juvenile leaves, a portion of the rhizome with a few hair-shoots, and two flowering stems without petals. These stems showed the five sepals and small leafy bracts beneath, and a remaining pistil with elongated curved style. The label read, "Hautes montagnes de Caroline. Un pyrola spec. Un genus novum?"

There is still some question as to just where and when Michaux collected the particular specimens that became part of his herbarium. What we are sure of is that Asa Gray, on a trip to Europe in 1838–1839 to study American plants at various herbaria, found this specimen. Piqued, I suspect, by the suggestion that it might represent a new genus, he determined after careful investigation and consultation to christen the plant.

On April 8, 1839, Gray wrote to a friend and fellow American botanist, John Torrey, as follows:

> But I have something better than all this to tell you. I have a discovered a new genus in Michaux's herbarium—at the end, among *plantae incognitae*. It is from the great unknown region, the high mountains of North Carolina. We have the fruit, with persistent calyx and style, but no flowers, and a guess that I have made about its affinities has been amply borne out on examination by Decaisne and myself. It is allied to Galax, but it is "un très distinct genus," having axillary one-flowered scapes (the flower large and a style that of a Pyrola, long and declined). Indeed I hope it will settle the riddle about the family of *Galax* and prove Richard to be right when he says *Ordo Ericarum*. I claim the right of a discoverer to affix the name.
>
> So I say, as this is a good No. American genus and comes from near Kentucky, it shall be christened *Shortia*, to which we shall stand as godfathers. So *S. galacifolia*, Torr. & Gr., it shall be. I beg you to inform Dr. Short, and to say that we will lay upon him no greater penalty than this necessary thing—that he make a pilgrimage to the mountains of Carolina this coming summer and procure the flowers.

Dr. Charles Wilkins Short of Kentucky, trained in medicine but active as a botanist and professor of science, was known to Gray only as a correspondent. Though he collected widely in the southern states, it is doubtful that Short ever saw the plant that bore his name, since he died 14 years before its rediscovery.

Despite his obvious excitement about the plant, Gray himself did not make the rediscovery, but not for lack of hunting. Following a clue on the herbarium sheet—"Hautes montagnes de Caroline"—and with knowledge from Michaux's journal that the Frenchman had visited the high country, Gray made a journey in late June 1841 with two friends, John Cary and James Constable. From headquarters in Ashe County,

North Carolina, they visited most of the high country above 5000 feet/ 1500 meters. Gray reported on the trip in a letter to Sir William J. Hooker of England, which was published in 1842 in both the *American Journal of Science* and the *London Journal of Botany*. There Gray wrote:

> We were unsuccessful in our search for a remarkable undescribed plant with a habit of *Pyrola* and the foliage of *Galax*, which was observed [originally] in the high mountains of Carolina. The only specimen extant is among the "Plantae Incognitae" of the Michauxian herbarium, in fruit only: and we were anxious to obtain flowering specimens, that we might complete its history; as I have long wished to dedicate the plant to Professor Short of Kentucky.

A footnote to this passage contains the first published description of the new genus *Shortia*, assigning it to the family Diapensiaceae.

In summer 1843, in the company of another botanical friend, William S. Sullivant, Gray again explored for plants in the mountains from Maryland to Georgia, always with an eye peeled for the elusive shortia. Again the plant eluded him. In fact, its very existence became the subject of skeptical doubts among Gray's botanical friends, and there may even have been a few with unspoken questions about the authenticity of the herbarium specimen in the cabinet in Paris.

Before his two excursions to hunt for what he must himself have begun to think as rare a chance of discovery as Bartram's Franklinia Tree, never again to be found in the wild, Gray consulted Michaux's journal for further clues. He passed over what has since, in the light of its eventual rediscovery, been interpreted as very clear directions for finding *Shortia*. On pages 45 and 46 of the French text, published in the *Proceedings of the American Philosophical Society* in 1889, is this passage:

> The roads became more difficult as we approached the headwaters of the Kiwi [now the Keowee] on the 8th of December, 1788. . . . There was in this place a little cabin inhabited by a family of Cherokee Indians. We stopped there to camp and I ran off to make some investigations. I gathered a new low woody plant with saw-toothed leaves creeping on the mountain at a short distance from the river. [Michaux camped there for three days. On December 11 he made a 3-mile/5-km foray into the hills.]
>
> . . .
>
> I came back to camp with my guide at the head of the Kiwi and gathered a large quantity of the low woody plants with the saw-toothed leaves that I found the day I arrived. I did not see it on any other mountain. The Indians of the place told me that the leaves had a good taste when chewed and the odor was agreeable when they were crushed, which I found to be the case.

For some time after the rediscovery of *Shortia*, botanists considered this to be the passage in Michaux's journal that pointed to the type site, and shortia is in fact abundant at the headwaters of the Keowee. However, it is likely that they were misled in thinking that this passage referred to shortia, as Gray himself probably realized when he read it.

The key word is "woody": shortia is not a woody plant in the strict sense, even though its growth habit is quite similar to those of *Epigaea repens* and *Gaultheria procumbens*, both classed as creeping shrubs. Even a large quantity of shortia would have provided Michaux with nothing but herbaceous material. Moreover, he could hardly have thought that shortia leaves have a good taste and an agreeable odor. He must actually have been describing wintergreen (*G. procumbens*), although it seems surprising for him to refer to it as a "new" plant—or was it to him?

We can be almost certain, at any rate, that it was not on this December 1788 trip that Michaux found the herbarium sample of shortia that Gray located later, because by December every remnant of the flower parts would have disappeared. The persistent style on the herbarium specimen suggests that it must have been collected not later than June or possibly early July.

Michaux had been in the same general area the preceding year, arriving there on June 14. He records, "We remained there more than two hours to rest our horses and to eat strawberries which were there in abundance." There is no mention of his collecting the plant he later labeled "Un pyrola spec. Un genus novum?" but it may have been that this was when he collected the specimen, not immediately identifiable, and that it became part of the general collection of plants he made later in his eventual destination to the West—hence "Hautes montagnes de Caroline."

The first rediscovery of living *Shortia galacifolia* did not fall to the lot of any of the botanists engaged in its pursuit, but to 17-year-old George McQ. Hyams of Statesville, North Carolina, in May 1877—who was, however, unaware of the significance of his find. The occasion was later described by George's father in a letter to Asa Gray:

> We were passing along the road and my attention was called to an elevated hillside that I could not ascend as being at that time rather exhausted, being 60 years old, requested him to ascend and bring whatever was in flower. I have forgotten the locality, but he is fully known to it as he lived within two miles [three kilometers] of the place for several years.

The elder Hyams was a purchasing agent and collector of medical plants for a Baltimore drug company and managed the root and herb warehouse for Wallace Brothers in Statesville. Although he was familiar with plants of the region from years of collecting herbs, this particular plant was new to him, despite its resemblance to the common *Galax*, which he frequently gathered. It was not until more than a year later that he dispatched a sample of the plant for identification to a friend, Joseph W. Congdon.

Congdon had his ear to the ground in the botanical world. He wrote to Gray, announcing that he thought he had in his possession a flowering plant of *Shortia galacifolia*. Gray hastily replied, "Do send the plant."

Gray, by this time the leading American botanical authority, leaves us in no doubt how he felt when at last he had on his work table a flowering specimen of the plant that nearly 40 years ago had stirred him in Paris. Immediately he wrote to William M. Canby, a botanical friend who had occasionally taunted Gray with sly remarks about the mythical shortia:

> No other botanist has the news. If you can come here I can show you what will delight your eyes and cure you effectively of the skeptical spirit you used to have about *Shortia galacifolia*. It is here before me with corolla and all from North Carolina! Think of that! My long faith rewarded at last.

To emphasize the strength of his feelings, he confessed that the rediscovery of Michaux's shortia gave him a hundred times the satisfaction that his recent election to the Académie des Sciences of the Institute de France had done, though that was one of the highest honors for a professional botanist.

Within the week Gray sent off a letter to the elder Hyams, warm in his praise of the discovery, and lamenting that he had not sooner sent the specimen so that the immortality of his son might have been assured by inclusion in the edition of Gray's *Flora*, which had recently gone to press. But he promised an early recognition by way of an article in *Silliman's Journal*. He concluded by warning Mr. Hyams that he and his friend Mr. Canby would descend on them the following May.

George Hyams's name appears as collector on the herbarium sheet which Dr. Gray made of the first flowering specimen of *Shortia galacifolia*, now in the Gray Herbarium at Harvard. Young Hyams must have felt considerable pride in June 1879, when he guided an illustrious group of botanists to the station of his find, though too late in the season for blossom.

In that group, besides Gray and his family, were William M. Canby, Charles S. Sargent, and J. H. Redfield. Both Gray and Redfield published accounts of the trip, Gray in the *American Journal of Science* and Redfield in the *Bulletin of the Torrey Botanical Club*. Redfield's account records the occasion with some added information about the trade in native plants for the drug market:

> Being now in McDowell County, the *Shortia* locality was visited under the guidance of Mr. George M. Hyams, the actual discoverer. In the secluded and well-protected station, well overshadowed by

345

Rhododendrons and Magnolias, was seen the little colony of the plant, so long sought and by many so long doubted. Its companions were *Mitchella repens, Asarum virginicum,* and *Galax aphylla.* The space over which the plant extended was perhaps 10 feet by 30 feet [3 meters by 9 meters] and in all there may have been 50 to 100 plants. As the plant multiplies by stolons it is remarkable that its area should be so restricted and since in the struggle for life of two allied plants the weaker "must go," Dr. Gray suggested the possibility that its stronger cousin, the *Galax,* had crowded out the *Shortia.* And here, indeed, in what may be the last foothold of the rarity, *Galax* appeared to be actually doing so. Yet the plants, though comparatively few, were vigorous and healthy. Other stations may be looked for; but they must be hard to find. When we consider the long search which has been made for this plant, how all the mountain region of the Carolinas and Tennessee has been examined by the sharp optics of Buckley, Rugel, M. A. Curtis, Dr. Gray, Canby, LeRoy and Ruger, the Vaseys, elder and younger, Chickering and others, it is very certain that if there be other localities they must be few and far between.

It is rather curious that *Shortia galacifolia* was first discovered in North Carolina in the Catawba River headwaters, where it is much rarer than in its major center of distribution in Pickens and Oconee counties of South Carolina. It was in the latter area that Dr. Sargent found it in 1886, while searching for the *Magnolia cordata* mentioned in Michaux's journal. In his party were the young Boynton brothers, natives of the area. For the next few years they continued the search for other possible sites of the elusive shortia. In 1889 Frank E. Boynton published in *Garden and Forest* an account of the trip he and his brother Charles had made in the spring of the year:

We camped the first night at the White Water Falls, which alone are worth a considerable journey to see. The Jocassee Valley, our destination, is at the mouth of White Water Creek, or rather at the junction of White Water and Devil Fork. I wished to see if *Shortia* was growing as high up in the mountains as these Falls, which are at least 1000 feet [300 meters] above the Jocassee. No *Shortia* was found, however, until we reached the valley, which has an altitude of about 1200 feet [370 meters] and here it grows by the acre. Every little brooklet is lined with it. Most of these little water courses are in deep narrow gorges where the sun hardly penetrates, except during the middle of the day. All these steep banks are literally covered with *Shortia.* What is comforting to the botanist is that it can hardly be exterminated. It is on land too steep to be cultivated and there is such an abundance no amount of collecting can ever affect it strenuously. Our party took away bushels of it, and no one could tell that a plant had been disturbed, so thickly is it growing. No idea of the beauty of this plant can be formed until it has been seen in its native home. The mass of glossy green and white, once seen, can never be forgotten.

The home of *Shortia* is a strange mixture of North and South. As a rule it grows under the shade of rhododendrons and tall kalmias. ... To see *Shortia* in blossom and in its glory one must get there about the 20th of March, not later than March 25th.

The spring of 1969, when Timmy and I were guided into shortia country by Charles Moore, was cold and late. Even in the final week of March, to which we had delayed our visit on Mr. Moore's advice, few blossoms were open. We were therefore unable to hunt for the color forms that had been hinted at in one of P. A. Davies's papers on pollination of shortia: "Corollas are normally white but color variants are frequent. Using the Ridgway Color Standards (1912), the colors varied from light rosolane purple to pale forget-me-not blue."

We did see great sheets of shortia foliage on the shores of the Horsepasture and White Water rivers; and along one small side stream on exposed rather sandy, high banks we found swarms of young seedling plants, which Mr. Moore encouraged us to collect because it was within the area to be flooded by the Jocassee Dam. All these rescued plants traveled successfully back to our garden, Millstream, and are still thriving here. A few have a slight pink tinge to the corolla. Seedlings from these plants have self-sowed along the woodland paths where they are established. Perhaps one day there may be a blue-flowered seedling.

I cannot resist the temptation to speculate a bit about the evolutionary history of shortia. There is some fossil evidence that it was fairly widespread in the mesophytic forests during the Tertiary, at least in eastern Asia and North America. During the ice ages much of it was eradicated in the northern part of its range, and the remnants found refuge in the mountain valleys south of the ice. In addition to the remnant population of *Shortia galacifolia* in the never-glaciated southern Appalachians, there are five other species of this genus in Asia. In the Japanese uplands is *S. uniflora*, admittedly more beautiful than our native. Almost identical in leaf pattern and growth habit, though not as widely stoloniferous, it has somewhat larger bells, more deeply fringed, of a pale but definite shell-pink. Also from Japan is *S. soldanelloides*, formerly known as *Schizocodon soldanelloides*, which is of a more clumping growth habit, though the leaves are quite similar to those of *Shortia galacifolia* and *S. uniflora*. The flowers are smaller than those of the other two but of a rich old rose, somewhat paler at the deeply fringed edges of the bell and shot with reddish streaks and scintillations within. There is a rare and exquisitely lovely white-flowered form as well. These bells are carried in campaniles of up to six at the summit of the 4- to 6-inch/10- to 15-cm scape above the mound of polished deep green leaves, which frequently retain their glowing red-bronze winter coloring through flowering season, which is about a month later than that of *S. galacifolia* and *S. uniflora*. Their seed also ripens later, usually not until fall. There are a number of varieties of *S. soldanelloides* based on leaf form: variety *ilicifolia* (holly-leaved), and variety *macrophylla*, with leaves nearly twice the normal size with more prominent toothing, are best known. There is also a diminished alpine form, smaller in all its parts. Other species come from the Taiwanese mountains and the Himalayas; these were discussed by B. LeRoy Davidson in the *Bulletin* volume 37, pages 188–192.

It is somewhat puzzling that during the 10,000 years or so since the retreat of the last ice sheet *Shortia galacifolia* has not spread north again from its refuge in the southern Appalachians. It certainly is adapted to growing far north of its present range. When transported to Connecticut and Massachusetts it will thrive if given proper conditions. It can endure the cold of a snowless winter and the heat and even the occasional droughts of our New England summers, and it will self-sow in suitable sites. Why then has it not slowly self-sown northward? One likely explanation lies in the combination of its site preference and the brief viability of its seeds.

By experiment it has been established that only very fresh seeds germinate. Seed ripens in our area about the middle of June and, if sown immediately, germinates within two weeks. Following germination, the seedlings, of very tiny size and slow development, do not persist unless they are kept moist; a brief period of drought annihilates them.

In the Blue Ridge, *Shortia* blooms in late March and early April and ripens its seed in May. The seed is very light and could easily be blown up out of the moist draws and streamsides where it grows under *Kalmia* and *Rhododendron maximum* or on the steep eroded slopes along tributary creeks. Some of the thousands of seeds produced annually must reach sites where the substrate and moisture are suitable for germination, but following germination, the minute seedlings that sprouted in the well-drained uplands would be at the mercy of the high temperatures and droughts of midsummer.

Young plants, if they can be brought through the critical period of infancy, may have a tiny rosette of four leaves by fall, still only 0.5 inch/13 mm across. During the second year, if conditions are favorable—and by now it has become more tolerant as the feeding roots strike more deeply—the plant will make appreciable growth of new foliage, larger in the leaf blade and in the petiole. By the third season it may even develop a flower bud in the center of the new husky rosette. From then on the plant will make offsets by extending underground stolons until it forms a sizeable carpet.

At the end of each runner is an overlapping arrangement of leaves, a few long-petioled and up to 3 inches/8 cm long in the blade, and at the center many smaller leaves. In autumn among these smaller leaves are produced pointed buds from which arise the flowers and new stolons.

The flowers are very rapid to develop in the first warm days of spring, and though delicate in appearance they are remarkably resistent to frost or even late snow. These blossoms, up to three from a bud, are carried singly on a naked reddish scape with two or three small, colored bracts just below the five-parted calyx. The five sharply pointed sepals are a glowing pink, a color strong enough to show through the petals. The five petals, generally pure white but occasionally pale pink or, by report, pale blue, are slightly fringed at the flaring tips and united below to form an open bell. The five golden stamens, alternate to the petals and attached to the lower rim of the corolla, surround the three-lobed stigma on an elongated style, all forming a most elegant design of pink, white and gold.

These handsome flowers are not as transient as their elegance might suggest. Because there are few insects flying when shortia flaunts its inviting flowers, fertilization is frequently delayed for many days. Though I can find no references to the actual agents of fertilization, I suspect that it is carried out by small flies, or in desperation by self-pollination. I do know that every flower that opens sets seed. When fertilized, by whatever means, the united corolla falls away, carrying with it the attached stamens, to leave the still beautiful cluster of pink sepals and bracts around the swelling, pear-shaped capsule with long pistil persistent. The green-white capsule rapidly enlarges and takes on rich tones of reddish-brown before, in June, it begins to split longitudinally into three segments, exposing a myriad of small, yellow-brown granules adherent to the ovary. That is the moment to collect seeds and to sow them immediately. It is possible that their fertility might be prolonged if they were refrigerated.

For quick, easy propagation, a clump may be lifted after flowering and divided into as many parts as there are offsets at the ends of the runners. Each runner will have sent down many fine feeding roots as it advanced the previous season. It is wise to treat these separated runners as recently rooted cuttings. Pot them up and keep them moist and shaded, or coddle them until well established if planted out in a permanent site. Large divisions with plenty of roots establish fairly readily in acid, leafmold soil in shade.

Shortia endures and flowers in quite dense shade, or it succeeds in a fairly open site on a north slope, where in fall it colors more brilliantly than in deep shade. The coloring of the foliage does not, however, appear to be entirely related to amount of light; it may be affected by soil factors, or it may be genetically controlled.

Because a considerable portion of the small natural homeland of *Shortia galacifolia* has now been cleared of vegetation and is within hydroelectric impoundments, it is fortunate for gardeners that this rare plant has been introduced into horticulture and has proved amenable to cultivation. Special credit should be given to Charles Moore, who has long been a student of the distribution of the species in the wild. When he learned of the plans to flood large segments of the plants' native home, he alerted gardeners and botanical gardens and guided many aficionados into the remote area to rescue the plants, and established large clumps in his own fascinating garden of wildflowers.

Originally published in the Bulletin of the American Rock Garden Society, *vol. 42, no. 1, pp. 1–10 (1984).*

Eastern American Trilliums

FREDERICK W. CASE, JR.

Trilliums are among the most familiar and beloved early spring flowers of the eastern United States. Some enjoy great popularity for their quiet beauty and grace; others, especially among the sessile types, cannot be called beautiful. Rather, they possess curious, gnomelike, fantastic, or even amusing characteristics. The folk-names of many species indicate the place they hold in the lore of the region: wood lily, mayflower, stinking benjamin, wet-dog trillium, bloody noses, and wake robin.

As a genus (or a distinct family, as some botanists believe), trilliums range widely across North America and Asia. By far the greatest number of taxa occur in the mountains, upper piedmont, and foothills of the southeastern United States, from the Carolinas to Alabama, and on the Cumberland Plateau and surrounding areas of Kentucky and Tennessee. Additional species range northward along the Appalachians into Canada and Newfoundland, and westward to the edges of the prairies in Minnesota, Nebraska, and Iowa. Farther south, a few species occur in Missouri, Arkansas, Mississippi and Louisiana. One or two species reach Texas.

In the western United States there are at least two pedunculate and four or five sessile trilliums, mainly near the Pacific coast. Trillium species occur in Asia as well, ranging from Russia and the Himalayas to Japan and Kamchatka.

A relative of *Trillium*, *Paris*, occurs in Europe and Asia. Vegetatively, it somewhat resembles the bunchberry (*Cornus canadensis*, syn. *Chamaepericlymenum canadense*), and its greenish flowers are fascinating but certainly not showy. The Indian cucumber-root (*Medeola virginica*) is another relative, unshowy yet interesting and widespread in acid woodlands of the eastern United States.

Taxonomy

Taxonomically, the genus *Trillium* has been poorly understood in the past. The literature, both botanical and horticultural, is a morass of misnomers, incorrect distributions, and general misinformation. Few can be absolutely certain that they refer to a given taxon as its author intended. The confusion results from many factors. The species often display minute structural differences which tend to be obliterated or obscured in dried herbarium material. Trillium seedlings often flower while they are much smaller than typical plants of their species. Several species seem to mutate frequently and have produced a variety of color forms. A few closely related species hybridize freely when they occur together. Some of the hybrids, especially when one of the parents is a color mutant, may mimic color patterns of other species.

Fortunately, studies are under way in American and Japanese universities that may erase much of the confusion. Tools of modern taxonomic analysis utilize refined chromosomal and biochemical techniques that can throw much light on relationships.

A fine revision of the sessile trilliums by John Freeman (1975) is the most definitive and helpful paper on that group yet to appear. I will generally follow his treatment. [Subsequent revisions are noted parenthetically in the text.—Ed.]

It is not my purpose, in any sense, to write a taxonomic paper; rather, I intend to discuss the eastern species of trillium from the point of view of my own field experience and from growing them in the garden.

The genus *Trillium* consists of two subgenera: subgenus *Phyllantherum*, the sessile trilliums, in which the flower is borne directly on the bracts (leaves); and subgenus *Trillium*, the pedunculate trilliums, in which the flower is borne on a short stalk, the peduncle, above the leaves.

The Pedunculate Trilliums

The pedunculate trilliums are particularly useful and showy in the garden, especially the woodland and wild garden. I will discuss those species that I believe to be fairly distinctive wild populations, if not taxonomically discrete species, from the point of view of occurrence, culture, and ecology.

Trillium catesbaei Ell.

Catesby's trillium occurs in the southern Appalachians and Great Smoky Mountains, from the upper piedmont of Alabama and Georgia, along the mountains into Tennessee and North Carolina. It is one of the so-called nodding trilliums, in which the peduncle recurves below the foliage. Fortunately, the leaves are relatively narrow in this species so that the flower is well displayed.

Trillium catesbaei usually grows about 12 to 15 inches/30 to 38 cm tall, with the leaves held upward well above the flower. The leaves frequently fold somewhat over the midrib into a boatlike shape, with the veins well engraved into the surface. The leaves are dark maroonish-green when young. The relatively large flowers, up to 2 inches/5 cm across, have strongly reflexed petals, either narrow or wide, which range in color from white to deep, rich rose-purple. The very large stamens are bright yellow and strongly recurved, and the ovary six-angled. In the wild the plants seldom form clumps; instead, they grow singly or in loose, open associations of a few plants.

Catesby's trillium grows most frequently in rather open, well-lit woodlands of a fairly dry nature, often where the soil is strongly acid. It is frequent in "laurel slicks," those junglelike entanglements of *Rhododendron maximum* and *Kalmia latifolia* on steep hillsides in the Appalachians. In deep shade it often fails to bloom. The finest forms I have seen, from the gardener's standpoint, occur in mountain valleys on the North Carolina/South Carolina border. Here, on flats along small mountain streams, occur truly lovely deep-rose forms with broad petals.

For me *Trillium catesbaei* grows readily. I grow it in my Saginaw, Michigan garden in neutral to acid sandy soil, moist in spring but rather dry in late summer. It receives considerable light for at least several hours a day. Seedlings of the white forms appear in bare spots in my garden, but the deep-rose form has not appeared here yet from seed.

Small enough for a background spot in the rock garden and ideal for the acid woodland or rhododendron bed, this early to midseason species merits a place in all well-maintained natural gardens. Appalachian wildflower nurseries sell it.

Trillium cernuum L.

The nodding trillium is ill understood. There appear to be at least two entities masquerading under the name *Trillium cernuum*. In the north, the plant usually known as *T. cernuum* var. *macranthum* Wieg. (the varietal name is no longer recognized as valid) is a fairly distinctive plant. It is tall (up to 24 inches/60 cm, though averaging 15 to 18 inches/ 38 to 45 cm), with rhombic leaves forming a nearly closed umbrella over the stem. The flower nods on a peduncle which deflexes at its base so that the flower hangs below the leaves. The peduncle, however, is fairly straight for most of its length. The leaves obscure the flower. The petals are thin-textured, narrow, strongly recurved. The delicately built, lavender-purple stamens divide about equally into filament and anther sac. The ripened ovary, a large, six-angled pyramidal red berry, is showy, juicy, and fruitily aromatic. Because the leaves elevate during the ripening period, the fruit is better displayed than the flower.

Nodding trillium prefers cool moist soils. It often grows in alder thickets along streams, on the borders of cedar swamps, or in low damp spots in forests of beech and maple. It seldom abounds in any location, yet it is not particularly rare within its range.

As a garden plant it is not easy, nor is it showy or distinctive horticulturally. It is difficult in warm soils; some forms are too tall for the rock garden, and in most forms the flowers are inconspicuous because they are obscured by the large leaves. For those whose passions run to collections of species, it is worth having, but its tallness, miffiness, and lack of showy flowers relegate it to third class among garden trilliums.

This form of *Trillium cernuum* occurs from Newfoundland to Manitoba across the north, then southward into Illinois and Indiana. South along the Appalachians its range is less clear, perhaps because of the confusion of this with other species or forms.

In the Blue Ridge and Great Smoky mountains the plant called *Trillium cernuum* by botanists, gardeners, and growers differs considerably from the northern plant. It has been called *T. rugelii* by earlier botanists, and acceptance of this taxon as a valid species seems to be coming back into favor. Along the Black Warrior River in Alabama and in the Appalachian foothills in Georgia, however, I have seen plants that seem nearly identical with the form known as *macranthum*.

Trillium rugelii Rendel

Rugel's trillium, included by some within *Trillium cernuum*, differs from northern *T. cernuum* in its much shorter, more reflexed peduncle, heavier-textured, creamy-white broad petals, and larger, thicker, and very dark maroon anthers. The fruit is considerably smaller and darker red when ripe than that of *T. cernuum* in Michigan.

Trillium rugelii is a vigorous plant in most forms, with large, rhombic leaves on a 15- to 24-inch/38- to 60-cm plant. Its flowers last long compared to those of *T. cernuum*. It occurs from northern Georgia through Smoky Mountain National Park and in the Blue Ridge Mountains of North Carolina. Johnson (1969) reported it also from Tennessee and Alabama.

Where I have observed it, it grew in very rich woods on slightly acid to neutral soils, either along flats of small streams or on steep, rich slopes just above the floodplain soils. It is easy of cultivation, but the short, curved peduncle carries the flowers well hidden below the leaves, which limits its usefulness in the garden.

In several locations where we found the plant growing with *Trillium vaseyi*, hybrid swarms occurred. Color forms varied greatly, with dark maroon, pink, rose, and rose-and-white-flecked types present. Unfortunately, these hybrids produce their lovely flowers so obscured on their short recurved peduncles that they are rendered almost useless as garden subjects.

Current studies will undoubtedly throw new light on the nature of *Trillium rugelii*. I consider it a valid species. Plants listed as *T. cernuum* by Appalachian wildflower dealers will probably prove to be a mixed bag and include plants of *T. rugelii*.

Trillium erectum L.

This species (Plate 99), perhaps the most widely distributed of the eastern pedunculate trilliums, is my unabashed favorite. Not that it is the showiest species—in Michigan, no plant ever gave me a greater chase when I was a kid trying to locate it. None has ever given me greater pleasure, either, as it has with its early flowering, its rich coloring, its fetid yet nostalgically pleasant faint stench, and its penchant for mutating to produce showy and desirable color forms.

The wake robin occurs from the Appalachians of Georgia to Maine and Quebec. In the acid-soil regions along the entire Appalachian chain and in the woodlands of glaciated New England and eastern Ontario, it often abounds. Westward in Michigan and Ohio, where acidic rocks and soils are less abundant, the plant is relatively local or rare. Although it has been reported from Minnesota, Wisconsin, and Illinois, the only authenticated stations there suggest that the plants have escaped from gardens or arboreta.

Trillium erectum is often confused with the closely related red hybrid segregate of *T. flexipes* formerly designated forma *walpolei*.

Typically, *Trillium erectum* is a medium-tall plant, from 12 to 20 inches/30 to 50 cm, but not so tall in relation to leaf size as *T. cernuum*. The leaves are very large, broadly rhombic, and rich apple-green. The flowers may be borne stiffly erect on their peduncles, or more often leaning to one side, sometimes almost declined. Obviously large, colorful, erect forms are the most desirable horticulturally. Local races vary. Petals—in the typical forms a dark red-maroon—fade with age to a more purple color. They are longer than broad, sharply pointed, and slightly cupped forward. Forms with ovate, broad petals occur, as do very flat flowers. Although some of these types have been given subspecies names, many grow in mixed populations with *T. flexipes*. I am convinced that these forms represent hybrids and hybrid swarms, as they are duplicated in lower Michigan where the two species intermingle. We have also produced some of the same kinds of color and structure forms from controlled crosses in our garden.

More than one gene appears to control the color of what is to the eye a solid, dark maroon-red petal in *Trillium erectum*. Consequently, mutations occur involving deletions of certain but not all color genes. The result may be a petal with a dark base and lighter distal portions, or the re-

355

verse, a white base and darker extremities. Multiple deletion mutations produce white petals or pale-yellow or green ones.

When these color forms hybridize, beautiful, bizarre, and surprising color patterns result, nearly all desirable horticulturally. These forms should not be confused with the entirely dissimilar variegated and monstrous forms produced in *Trillium grandiflorum* by mycoplasma pathogens.

Besides the mutant color forms that can occur in any population of *Trillium erectum*, certain color races seem to dominate in certain districts. In some higher parts of the southern Blue Ridge Mountains, a form with narrow white to greenish petals abounds; the maroon-black ovary contrasts showily. This form is otherwise typical *T. erectum* in petal shape, plant aspect, and odor.

Trillium erectum flowers may last for two weeks in cool weather. When fresh, they emit the fetid odor of wet dog, but mercifully, the odor cannot be detected more than a few inches from the blossom. The fruit of the typical *T. erectum* is distinctive: the ripe berry is quite spherical, with six shallow ridges, crowned with the three short stigma tips, and the entire structure is a shiny dark maroon or blackish color. Compared to the ripe fruits of *T. cernuum* or *T. flexipes*, the berry is quite small.

Red trillium grows in both evergreen and deciduous woods on light humus soils, or in the rich, drier peaty soil of old cedar-hemlock swamps (at least in Michigan). Soil reactions are mildly acid, and the soil is generally cool in summer.

As a garden plant, it is easy except in poorly drained clays. It is large for the rock garden but ideal for woodland settings or near shrubs. In my garden it seeds and hybridizes abundantly.

Trillium erectum var. *blandum*

On the west side of Great Smoky National Park, in the general vicinity of Gatlinburg, Tennessee, grows a plant I once interpreted as *Trillium simile*; I was informed by a student of the group that it should be called *T. erectum* var. *blandum*. It has since been raised to specific status as *T. flexipes*. This taxon, present as the lower-elevation representative of the *T. erectum* complex, is truly a fine horticultural subject. Its general aspect suggests *T. erectum*. The plant produces very large, oval-petaled, heavy-textured creamy-white flowers, each with a maroon-black ovary. The faintly musty-scented flowers stand strongly erect and are nearly as showy as those of *T. grandiflorum*. Petals remain in good condition for two weeks.

The plant differs from the ordinary white-flowered forms of *Trillium erectum* in being vastly superior in size, color, and texture. It has proven a good garden plant in cold central Michigan, even though our climate is far more severe than that of Tennessee. Bloom size increases as plants become established and strong clumps develop. I regard this plant as one of the best of the larger pedunculate trilliums for garden use.

Trillium flexipes is one of those poorly understood entities that has been much confused with others in the past, and on which there is much current study. Regardless of the outcome of taxonomic research, the form is superb. It forms very large colonies where it occurs, often cascading down a wet roadside outcrop and nearby talus by the hundreds.

Trillium vaseyi Harbison

Some botanists consider *Trillium vaseyi* only a variety of *T. erectum*. I disagree with them on the basis of both taxonomic characters and field ecology, although I acknowledge that the two species are very closely related. The plant is certainly distinct horticulturally.

Trillium vaseyi is a very large, late-blooming plant. It stands from 14 to more than 24 inches/35 to 60 cm tall and has flowers that can be easily the largest of any eastern trillium. The deep maroon-red, faintly and pleasantly scented blossoms appear after most other species have finished flowering. They reflex on the peduncle so as to be partially hidden beneath the leaves. The blossom, often over 4 inches/10 cm in diameter, opens flat with recurved petal lips. Compared to many forms of *T. erectum*, the flowers last longer and open later. The umbrella of leaves sometimes measures more than 15 inches/38 cm across. The plant is impressive to see and makes an excellent accent in the garden.

In the wild its preferred habitat is in the "coves"—small side-valley amphitheaters eroded by small tributary streams—mainly in the south and southeastern edges of the Smoky Mountains and Blue Ridge Mountains. Rocky ledges and platforms near trickles in humus-rich, mucky, damp soils suit it best.

In our severe climate, this is not an easy plant. Although it does not perish in winter, it is difficult for me to provide the wind protection and moisture it prefers as it develops in spring. Yet it always blooms, even if the leaves and flowers show a little damage. Under more favorable conditions it is a superb garden subject, although it seems rarely to be cultivated outside its native areas. According to the literature, white forms and hose-in-hose double forms occur, but I have not seen them.

Trillium simile

From current works I have been unable to ascertain to what plant this name correctly applies. Plants I have found or been shown by other fieldworkers have proven to be *Trillium flexipes*, *T. rugelii*, or *T. erectum* f. *blandum*. Robert C. Johnson (1969), in his Ph.D. dissertation, considered it to be the albino form of *T. vaseyi*. If the name is valid, its use awaits a clearer scientific delineation of the taxon to which it should apply.

Trillium flexipes Raf.

Also known as *Trillium declinatum* and *T. gleasonii*, this much-mis-understood plant is really quite distinctive and, in its best forms, a useful horticultural subject. The plant is large—up to 30 inches/75 cm tall when growing in rich soil. The flowers, borne on 3- to 5-inch/8- to 13-cm peduncles, may be stiffly erect or declined at various angles below the large, rhombic leaves. Petal texture is usually quite leathery, making the blooms of the best forms long-lasting. The 3-inch/8-cm flower may be quite flat with rather broad, ovate petals, or the petals may be narrow and reflex strongly, with curled margins on a récurved peduncle. The finest garden forms I have seen came from the limestone country near Louisville, Kentucky, where the species is abundant.

Flowers of good forms last three weeks or more in cool weather, making it the longest-lasting pedunculate trillium in the garden. The pyramidal fruits, as large as crabapples, are rich pink-rose in color and strongly six-angled, emitting a fruity fragrance.

Trillium flexipes, as currently understood, ranges in the American midlands from northern Alabama to Wisconsin and Minnesota, thence eastward into New York and Maryland. In the driftless areas of Wisconsin and Minnesota I have seen plants which appeared to be intergrades with *T. cernuum*.

Where the range of this species overlaps that of the red-flowered *Trillium erectum*, and where acid and limestone soils occur in proximity, extensive hybridization occurs between these species. Some of the hybrid patterns occur so frequently that they were at first considered distinct forms and were named *T. flexipes* f. *walpolei* and *T. flexipes* f. *billingtonii* Farwell, no longer accepted names.

Where suitable conditions occur, in Michigan, Ohio, and Kentucky, large hybrid swarms and their backcrosses produce a delightful array of plants. Flowers in a variety of maroon, rose, speckled, spotted, and shaded colors abound. Because there are multiple genes influencing the various parts of the petals, hybrids appear which are white basally and red distally, or the reverse, mimicking the painted trillium. In my garden, wholly new color variations have appeared. Through controlled pollination, my wife and I have produced garden hybrids identical in color patterns with some of the wild forms. When we crossed the large, heavy-textured, erect-flowered types of *Trillium flexipes* from Kentucky with *T. erectum*, superior, erect-flowered forms with excellent carriage and color resulted. Even picotee forms—cream, margined with purple flecks—have appeared. We are trying to find ways to propagate these desirable types more rapidly.

Trillium grandiflorum (Michx.) Salisb.

This magnificent species (Plate 100) is the best-known and best-loved of the trilliums and a favorite spring flower of all outdoor-lovers in the Northeast. In cultivation it can be as large as any species and is always very showy. Great masses of this plant fill the woodlands of the Great Lakes region, Ontario, and parts of New England in the spring. It ranges southward in upland regions of the Cumberland Plateau and Appalachians to North Carolina and Tennessee, but becomes local southward. The species occurs in all but the waterlogged soils of bogs and floodplains but thrives best on sandy or loamy hillsides.

Standing from 8 to more than 20 inches/20 to 50 cm tall, with leaves up to 8 inches/20 cm long and less rhombic than in the *erectum* complex, the plant bears a relatively large flower on a 3-inch/8-cm peduncle. The flowers are more deeply cupped than in many pedunculate species, almost funnelform at their bases but widely spreading at their distal ends. The petals, each up to 3 inches/8 cm long and half as broad, are thin-textured but very white, with deep and conspicuous veins. In spite of the thin texture, the petals last long and gradually turn from white to pink to deep rose with age. The fruit is six-angled, green, and inconspicuous.

Trillium grandiflorum is larger and in every way showier than the commonly grown forms of its western counterpart *T. ovatum*. It has also the advantage of being far more winter-hardy.

In European gardens the plant is grown with considerable light and fertilizer; with such treatment very large plants develop. There is no doubt that this is the best species for massing and landscape effect in the woodland garden. It is a long-lived, clump-forming plant.

Like other species, it has various forms. Various hose-in-hose double types occur, and rock gardeners know of the magnificent form with about 30 petals. Double forms have appeared many times in the wild, and both highly symmetrical, lovely forms and rather ragged doubles exist.

There is a coveted form in which the backs of the petals are pink, even in bud. I have been fortunate not only in obtaining such forms in commerce, but also in finding my own very good pink-backed form in southern Michigan. Seedlings of these are appearing in my woodland garden, with better color than in the wild forms. I have not, however, found a form in which the face of the petal opens a good pink. That would be a real find!

In recent years a vogue has developed in rock gardening and other horticultural circles for local forms of *Trillium grandiflorum* which occur with green-striped petals, blotches, or other aberrations, including alteration of the plant body form itself: clusters of leaves replacing the flower, or a knot of petals, white-and-green-streaked, without leaves, or very commonly, long, narrow, petiolate leaves—sometimes several sets of them—and very distorted flowers. I have seen one in which there were long-petioled leaves at ground level and a long stalk bearing a much variegated and distorted flower, with miniature three-petaled but distorted blooms emerging from the stamen tips. Earlier botanists considered these strange plants mutations or teratological forms. Some gardeners have spent a goodly sum trying to obtain as many of these as possible. Although some are beautiful, they result from a disease. Dr. Gary Hooper, Michigan State University, and I have demonstrated that the condition originates not from mutation but from the presence in the tissues of mycoplasma organisms (Hooper, Case et al., 1971). These organisms, larger than viruses, seem capable of producing on developing tissues an influence similar to that of genes. The infection spreads slowly in wild populations until entire colonies show the disease symptoms. Infected plants turn maroon-red months early and die down. Weakened plants generally disappear from wild colonies.

This mycoplasma disease can spread to other species: we have seen it in *Trillium erectum* and *T. undulatum*. However unfortunate it may be that gardeners have invested considerable sums in these showy but diseased plants, no sensible gardener ought to harbor them. Certainly, diseased clones ought not to be spread around the world under the guise of horticultural forms.

Trillium persistans Duncan

In 1971 Duncan described a new trillium from the mountains of northeastern Georgia. Known thus far only from a 4-mile/10-km square area in which the plant is rare, local, and difficult of access even where it is present (because of dam development), this plant has been given federal endangered status.

A distinctive, small trillium, *Trillium persistans* has lanceolate, somewhat drooping leaves with three conspicuous large, light-colored veins per leaflet. The flower somewhat resembles a depauperate first-blooming seedling of *T. grandiflorum* or *T. catesbaei*; it is distinguished by the failure of the petals to spread very widely at first. The blossom diameter is about 1 to 1.5 inches/2.5 to 4 cm; the petals individually are quite narrow and somewhat undulate. The small flattened ovary is strongly six-ribbed. As the flower ages, the distal portion gradually deepens to dark rose-purple. The proximal area near its attachment retains its white coloration in the form of an inverted V. This color pattern of the aging flower is diagnostic for this species.

Plants as rare as this should not be collected by amateur botanists or gardeners. Since there will always be avid collectors and plantsmen who "must have the plant at any cost," it is my view that seedlings of this and other extremely rare species should be raised by botanical gardens or university gardens, and that cultivated material ought to be introduced into the horticultural trade at the earliest possible moment. This would provide a source of plants for the specialist-collector-grower but would not put pressure on the wild populations through illicit collecting.

The specific epithet *persistans* refers to the long-lasting nature of the plant, which remains healthy and green until late autumn. Persistent trillium is also one of the earliest trilliums to appear, blooming in February and March (into early April) in its wild haunts. Through a quirk of fate I collected three plants of this species with *Trillium catesbaei* near the type locality some years before the plant was even described. They are fully hardy at Saginaw, Michigan, but their seeds have not germinated.

As a garden subject, I would rate the species second-class, although in size it is a good plant for the rock garden. *Trillium persistans* was honored with a painting on the U.S. endangered species postage-stamp series.

Trillium nivale Riddell

If I could choose only one pedunculate trillium for the rock garden, I would not hesitate to select the snow trillium. First, one of its preferred habitats is on limestone outcrops and the talus slopes below, so it is a true rock plant. Second, it is tiny, like many of the best rock plants, but has large and conspicuous flowers for its size. Third, it is the very first wildflower to bloom in our region, often ahead of the skunk cabbage.

Trillium nivale grows mainly on limestone soils and outcrops, or secondarily on rich, limey riverbank soils, in a narrow band from western Pennsylvania through Ohio and Indiana to Iowa and southern Minnesota. It is rare and local over much of its range but is said to be abundant in parts of its western distribution, even persisting in fencerows after the forests have been lumbered.

At first only 2 to 3 inches/5 to 8 cm tall, the plant enlarges in bloom (as does the painted trillium); vigorous plants may attain 6 inches/15 cm. Flowers, surprisingly large and showy for the size of the plant, are usually clean white with conspicuous yellow stamens, up to 2 inches/5 cm in diameter. The ovary, six-angled in most trilliums of this group, is instead obtusely triangular in cross section. The 2- to 3-inch/5- to 8-cm ovate leaves are glaucous and distinctly petiolate. The peduncle, erect in flower, reflexes strongly as the flower ages and is strongly reflexed before the petals deteriorate.

Because the snow trillium blooms from early March into April, it frequently is subjected to very cold night temperatures. The plant often freezes solid in bloom night after night without apparent harm.

The snow trillium requires a site free of competition. It inhabits eroding limestone ledges, ravine summits where continued erosion keeps sunny areas free of grass, or loamy floodplain soils where periodic flooding prevents development of dense woodland vegetation. For it to be permanent in the garden, one must simulate the competition factors of the wild. Give it a slightly open, flat area, mulched with lime chips, a crevice in a limestone boulder, or a spot free of plants at the boulder's base. Under these conditions the snow trillium can be one of the best American rock plants, long-lived and freely seeding about.

We had the pleasure this year, after a 40-year search, to be part of the rediscovery of *Trillium nivale* in abundance in Michigan. The plant had been considered extinct here.

Trillium pusillum Michaux

In the Coastal Plain, piedmont, and southern Cumberland Plateau forest lands, from Maryland and Virginia to Alabama and Kentucky, grow several charming dwarf trilliums that are all very rare, local, and largely unknown to gardeners. Many of these populations may now or soon have legal protection as threatened or endangered species owing to their discontinuous or very local occurrence. I hope, however, that these taxa can be brought into cultivation and made available commercially, for they have traits that make them ideal subjects for the rock garden.

Trillium pusillum grows more stiffly erect than *T. nivale*, averaging just slightly larger, from 4 to 8 inches/10 to 20 cm tall. The somewhat drooping, narrowly oval, blunt-tipped leaves are green to bluish or maroon-flushed. The flower is quite large for the plant, upfacing, either white or white on the face with a rose reverse. The blossoms are 2 inches/5 cm or more across, spreading widely, with very undulate petals.

Races of *Trillium pusillum* bloom just after *T. nivale*, early in the season and well ahead of most other trillium species, filling a gap in the garden schedule. The flowers persist a long time. Since, like *T. grandiflorum*, they gradually turn rose, they also provide a touch of color before they fade.

Trillium pusillum grows in generally acid-soil swamps and stream bottomlands, in soggy soils at the upper limits of the floodwater level, and occasionally in upland swamps. Where colonies occur, plants are generally abundant.

In my garden, the species grows and blooms well without the moisture of its native habitat. So far it has been completely winter-hardy. The purist would not find it a rock plant, but in size and charm it is perfectly suited for a featured spot in a rockery. It grows well in a neutral to slightly acid pocket of not-too-fertile soil.

The discontinuous distribution of *Trillium pusillum* with lack of geneflow between populations for a long time has led to structural differences among colonies. Most of these are minor, but plants from the northern part of its range in northern North Carolina, Virginia, and Maryland have been given varietal status as *T. pusillum* var. *virginianum* Fernald.

In this variety, the flower peduncle is either vestigial or absent, and the flowers sessile or subsessile. These blooms face stiffly upward, giving the plant a different aspect from any other pedunculate trillium. This, coupled with the usually rose reverse of the petals and the smaller size of the plant, make it completely charming and horticulturally desirable. It is, however, a very rare and local plant.

Trillium pusillum var. ozarkanum

Botanists have variously considered the Ozark trillium either a species or a variety of *Trillium pusillum*. It differs from typical *T. pusillum* in being taller, up to 10 inches/25 cm or so tall, with more ovate pointed leaves, which generally have five prominent veins instead of three as in typical *T. pusillum*. Early in the bloom period the leaves also tend to have a deep maroon undertone absent from typical *T. pusillum*. The flowers, on strong peduncles, average larger than those of the type, with distinctly wavy-undulate margins and very conspicuous recurved yellow stamens. Bloom time in my garden is just reaching its peak as typical *T. pusillum* varieties fade.

Trillium pusillum var. *ozarkanum* grows on rocky hillsides, in open fields, in open oak and mixed deciduous forest-pine woods, or in shaley, rocky, dry streambeds. It occurs in the Ozark Mountains of Arkansas and Missouri, and in Kentucky, often in association with mountain laurel, arbutus, sourwood trees, and other acid-soil plants. Plant collectors and wildflower nurseries of the Ozark region occasionally offer it. Its size and manner make it highly desirable for the rock garden.

The Ozark trillium grows well for me and is one of my favorite plants. It is completely winter-hardy. It has not seeded about here as have many other plants.

Trillium texanum

The Texas trillium was also formerly united with *Trillium pusillum* by most botanists and is clearly a close relative. It is the only eastern trillium I have not seen in the wild, although I have seen the plant in John Lambert's Mountain Fork River Arboretum at Mena, Arkansas. In general aspect it resembles *T. pusillum* but is narrower in all respects. The almost linear petals are undulate, clear white, and spreading. The narrowly linear leaves, blunt-tipped and green, spread rather than droop as in *T. pusillum*, and tend to fold or reflex across the upper surface, giving the leaves a slight "boat" shape.

Native to the wetter coastal plain regions of eastern Texas, this trillium grows in acid woods and boggy ground, often in company with osmunda ferns. Like other relatives of *Trillium pusillum*, it represents local, disjunct variants of a once uniform and widespread species. If it proves winter-hardy here, it will be a worthy garden subject as a variation on a theme.

Trillium undulatum Willd.

The painted trillium can be the beauty of the genus, or it can be disappointing. This apparent paradox stems from its manner of development. The plants emerge relatively late in the season and develop rapidly. Buds open when the plant is scarcely 4 inches/10 cm tall. Growth and expansion continue for several more days until the plant reaches its full height of 15 to 24 inches/38 to 60 cm. At this time, the full-blown flower may be 3 inches/8 cm across, with thin-textured white petals beautifully blotched and penciled with deep red at the base. If plant development has proceeded like this, the plant is a great beauty; but if the flowers are pollinated before expansion is complete, a hormone reaction occurs, the petals turn watery and translucent, the colors fade rapidly, and the petals wither and fall. A prematurely pollinated plant disappoints, to say the least.

Wide-ranging, the painted trillium occurs from Quebec and central Ontario southward in acid-soil regions to the mountaintops of the Great Smoky Mountains and the Blue Ridge of the Carolinas and Georgia. It requires cool soils, hence its restriction to higher elevations southward. In New England, it is widespread at most elevations in suitable acid soils. Westward the species reaches into the "thumb" of lower Michigan, where it is a very rare, protected plant. Reports from north and west of these Michigan stations lack specimen documentation, and at least some of them result from misidentifications of the *Trillium erectum* × *T. flexipes* hybrid segregates with basally red-blotched petals (see *T. flexipes* f. *billingtonii* Farwell, discussion in Case and Burrows, 1962).

Growing this demanding species can be difficult outside its natural areas of occurrence. Not only must it have suitable cool temperatures and pH, but it nearly always grows in deep brown, peaty forest duff.

Although the painted trillium is not native in my immediate area, I have grown it for years in the deep shade under beeches and oaks by excavating a large area to a depth of about 10 inches/25 cm. On the bottom of the excavation I place about 3 inches/8 cm of washed silica sand (sandblaster's sand). On this sand I place the trillium rhizomes, for in the wild, in Michigan and in North Carolina, they invariably grow with the rhizome in contact with mineral soil but deeply covered with acid duff. Over the rhizomes I place a mixture of sand, Canadian peat, and oak and pine duff, bringing the mix up to the level of the surrounding soil. This shaded bed is then mulched with oak leaves and pine needles.

Wildflower dealers offer this species. It is worth a try, but I am uncertain as to how it will perform in the hotter American midlands.

-------------------- The Sessile Trilliums --------------------

The sessile trilliums, subgenus *Phyllantherum*, comprise a large and confusing group of American trilliums. Most are less showy of flower than those of the pedunculate group, but all hold interest for the gardener. In this group, the "leaves," really enlarged bracts on the flower scape, possess, in eastern species, varying degrees of green-and-bronze mottling. Even without the flowers, they are worthy of cultivation as accent plants. The flowers differ from those of the pedunculate group in that the petals and sepals stand directly upon the leaf-bracts (i.e., they are sessile). Except in one species, the petals are erect and somewhat connivent (closed), rather than spreading to reveal the reproductive organs within. Petal colors are mostly maroon or bronzy reds intermixed with varying degrees of green and brown. Yellow- and green-flowered species occur, and albino, partial albino, and pallid color forms abound. Sessile species occur only in the continental United States and adjacent Canada.

The latest taxonomic treatment (and in my opinion the most useful and accurate by far) is that by John D. Freeman (1975). Serious students and gardeners must consult Freeman's work to gain insights into the nature of the "species" in this section, for all previous works badly confuse populations and forms. (Some species in this subgenus appear less distinct from one another than do species in subgenus *Trillium*.) Freeman divided subgenus *Phyllantherum* into three somewhat informal "species groups" which he feels show affinities among themselves, though they do not represent taxonomic sections in the usual sense. Freeman's classification appears in Table 1; my discussion follows this outline.

Table 1. Eastern Sessile Trilliums

Group I, the *Trillium recurvatum* group.

T. recurvatum	*T. lancifolium*

Group II, the *Trillium sessile* group.

T. sessile	*T. reliquum*
T. decumbens	*T. discolor*
T. underwoodii	*T. stamineum*
T. decipiens	

Group III, the *Trillium maculatum* group.

T. maculatum	*T. ludovicianum*
T. foetidissimum	*T. gracile*
T. cuneatum	*T. viride*
T. luteum	*T. viridescens*

Trillium recurvatum Beck.

The aspect of this species is tall and lanky, but the plant varies considerably depending on its vigor, the local race, and the type of soil on which it grows. The species ranges from northern Alabama to extreme southwestern Michigan, and from Ohio and Kentucky west into Iowa, Illinois, and Missouri, and to northern Louisiana. It can be locally abundant or very rare. Its common names include prairie trillium, toad trillium, and perhaps most imaginative of all, "bloody noses," a folk-name in parts of Missouri.

Structurally one of the most distinctive of the sessile species, *Trillium recurvatum* is tall, with strongly petiolate leaves up to 6 inches/15 cm long and heavily to rather obscurely mottled. The sepals recurve to become adpressed to the scape below the leaves, a feature found (to a lesser degree) in only one other sessile trillium. The petals, usually rather ovate-lanceolate, are acute at the tips, condensed into an almost stalk-like claw at the base, and are about 1 to 1.5 inches/2.5 to 4 cm long. Their color is dark red-maroon to purple, fading to brownish-red with age and varying in color forms to greenish brown or even pure yellow. The clearest colors make particularly desirable subjects for garden use. The rhizomes are rather narrow, elongated, and brittle and must be handled with care. The plant is completely winter-hardy.

In most of its habitats it grows in clay or lime soil. Riverbank or low woodlands constitute favored situations northward. In my garden it tends to form small offsets which, in my sandy soil, are slow to mature.

The open growth habit and darkly mottled leaves make this an interesting if not terribly showy plant. It is common enough over most parts of its range that reasonable collections for horticulture ought not to injure wild populations. Wildflower dealers from Indiana westward to the Great Plains may occasionally offer this species.

Trillium lancifolium Raf.

Trillium lancifolium appears to be poorly known, but its narrow segments, its almost wire-thin petals, and its rather delicate proportions make it a desirable contrast plant in the wild garden.

The lance-leaved trillium ranges from 8 to 18 inches/20 to 45 cm tall, with somewhat drooping, sessile, narrowly lanceolate-elliptic mottled leaves. With narrowly linear, crepe-paper-textured, crinkled, purplish-green petals 1 to 2 inches/2.5 to 5 cm long, the plant is one of the most distinctive of all sessile trilliums. Its entire aspect—scape, leaves, and petals—is one of narrowness.

Found from South Carolina to Alabama, especially in areas adjacent to the Cumberland Plateau in Alabama and Georgia, it seems not to have a generally distributed population, occurring instead in local areas with wide gaps between colonies. Besides the localities bordering the Piedmont, it occurs in the vicinity of Lookout Mountain, Tennessee, and much farther south in Georgia and Florida in areas bordering the Chattahoochee River. The colonies I have seen grew on clay floodplains and adjacent streambank soils in mature woods which, in that area, are somewhat brushy and rank. The plant is both local and unobtrusive where it occurs; until one is experienced, locating it in the wild is not easy.

The narrow, linear white rhizomes grow just below the surface of the heavy soil and break easily. Pieces of broken rhizome soon produce small plants. The generally delicate aspect of this species seems to imply that it might lack hardiness. This seems not to be so, for it has survived seven winters, some of them very open and bitter, in central Michigan.

Trillium lancifolium seems to be unknown to most gardeners, at least in the north. This is a pity, for it is quite unlike any other species. I prize it highly and am trying to find a ready means to propagate my plants for distribution.

Trillium sessile L.

Trillium sessile, the toad trillium, inhabits a wide range from western Virginia westward to around the Indiana/Illinois state lines; it is largely absent from Illinois but abundant again in Missouri and northern Arkansas. Northward it reaches to southwestern Michigan, where it is very rare, to all of Ohio, and eastward into southwestern Pennsylvania and barely into southern New York. Southward, it ranges into central Kentucky and Tennessee, with a few outlying stations in Alabama and North Carolina. It grows in a great variety of woods, thickets, and even fencerows and hog pastures, preferring a rich, fairly heavy limestone soil.

Horticulturally a much misunderstood species, most plants illustrated in magazines as *Trillium sessile* do not represent the species, but rather either *T. cuneatum* or one of the superficially similar western species. True *T. sessile* is a plant of low stature, rarely more than 10 inches/25 cm tall, with relatively broad, obscurely mottled, broadly sessile leaves. The sepals spread but do not reflex. The 1-inch/2.5-cm petals, widest at the middle and tapering without a claw to their base, range in color from rich maroon-purple to dingy liver-brown or greenish-yellow.

One of the most tolerant of trilliums, its chief horticultural value lies in its adaptability to most climates and soils, and in its early blooming. It deserves a place in the garden even though it is not as showy as some. Plants offered as *Trillium sessile* by many dealers may prove to be other species.

In Kentucky, west of Louisville, *Trillium sessile* intergrades with *T. recurvatum*. Intergrades possess narrower leaves than *T. sessile*, with varying degrees of the petiolate condition. Their petals, too, vary between those typical in either species.

Trillium decumbens Harbison

If I had to choose just one sessile trillium for the garden, it would be this species. Truly decumbent, its great, strikingly mottled leaves spread flat on the forest litter and rocks among which it grows. The first time we found it in the wild, we were amazed; the plants resembled ancient oil lamps, with the 4-inch/10-cm petals the red, glowing flames. The fact that this species often grows in large patches accentuates its striking manner of growth.

Trillium decumbens rises from a stout, deeply buried rhizome. The 5- to 8-inch/13- to 20-cm scape bends and lies along the ground. The sessile leaf cluster, up to 10 inches/25 cm in diameter on robust plants, bears at its center relatively short green sepals, but very erect, slightly twisted, lanceolate, 3- to 4-inch/8- to 10-cm, dark red-maroon petals. When sunlight strikes these large petals, the "ancient lamp" effect is stunning.

The species appears very early in the season but blooms from mid- to late season. Long before the buds open, the highly colored leaves draw attention in the garden. As fruits develop, the stem elongates somewhat but remains decumbent. The leaves are short-lived and soon dry up or rot away, leaving the scape and fruit to mature over the summer.

A natural rock plant, the decumbent trillium is found in sloping rocky woods, talus below shaley ledges, and at the bases of massively weathered tufalike limestone boulders. Typically it forms colonies of hundreds, neatly spaced so that the leaf tips just touch. We have seen it growing in fully mature woods where dense shade develops early, as well as in open second-growth woods of oak and maple, where there is sufficient light to allow some grasses to grow.

Trillium decumbens occurs in a narrow band from northwestern Georgia to Tuscaloosa, Alabama, mainly in foothills of the Cumberland Plateau and the Ridge and Valley provinces. It is not present in every available habitat within its range as some species of trillium are: rather, large colonies occur sporadically.

Rock gardeners ought to make every effort to get this species into cultivation, for it is truly an outstanding plant. Although it can be locally abundant (Freeman, 1975), its range is limited. Alabama conservationists have expressed special concern that it might be collected excessively. It should be propagated, not collected from the wild (Freeman et al., 1979).

Planted in a well-drained, slightly acid loam, this species has not only wintered well for me but has self-sown. Its manner of snuggling up to the contours of garden ledges or against a rock is unlike that of any other species. Those who have seen it, desire it.

Trillium underwoodii Small

I have found Underwood's trillium in the wild only once. Of medium stature, it stands from 5 to 10 inches/13 to 25 cm tall, with sessile, lanceolate leaves. The leaves bear conspicuous mottling in light and dark greens; according to Freeman (1975), the mottling varied from colony to colony. The sepals, lanceolate to ovate and 1 to 2 inches/2.5 to 5 cm long, diverge or spread. The oblanceolate to narrowly elliptic petals are 1.5 to 3 inches/4 to 8 cm long. Flower color varies from dark purple or maroon to brownish-purple, or greenish-yellow. This variation is influenced both by the genetics of the individual plant and the age of the flower; most sessile species lose their rich reddish tones with age and develop a liver-brown, less attractive color. Plants we observed in John Lambert's arboretum collection in Mena, Arkansas, were particularly fine in both leaf and flower coloring.

In *Trillium underwoodii* the stamens bear very short filaments and lateral pollen sacs on a connective which extends a millimeter or two beyond the pollen sacs. The stigmas are very short and recurved upon the ovary.

Although the species is very closely related to *Trillium decipiens* and like it in many respects, Freeman (1975) asserted that they can usually be distinguished readily in the field. *Trillium underwoodii* apparently does not grow in mixed populations with its closest kin. Its short, erect scape permits the drooping leaves (at flowering) to touch the substrate, a trait not seen in the taller *T. decipiens*.

Trillium underwoodii blooms in the wild from mid-February to April. It occurs from Mobile, Alabama, across north Florida to western Georgia, extending northward into the Piedmont, especially in Alabama. We found it growing along the base of ravine slopes near a small stream, in beech and oak woods. The soil was slightly sandy and very rich in humus. Plant companions at this station were acid-soil species.

Trillium decipiens Freeman

The epithet *decipiens* means "deceiving" and refers to the similarity between this species and *Trillium underwoodii*. A much taller plant, with stiffly spreading leaves, the former's scapes attain heights up to 1 foot/30 cm. The broadly lanceolate petals range from greenish-brown to maroon, the maroon tones fading to liver-brown with age. The strongly mottled lanceolate leaves often have a light band of pale green along the midrib and almost maroon tones below the greens; this would render the plant striking in the garden even if it never bloomed. The flowers are large in proportion to the leaves, making them quite conspicuous for this type of trillium.

We have seen a very robust form growing in acid woodlands in Alabama, and on limestone soils in woods and along streambanks near Mariana, Florida. It grows in much the same habitats as the sessile and prairie trilliums farther north, preferring the lower slopes of wooded bluffs along streams.

369

A few of the Florida plants have survived one severe, open winter here at Saginaw. This past spring we collected a few rhizomes from plants farther inland in Alabama which may prove to be even hardier. Our experience with widely ranging Coastal Plain and Piedmont plants, from the Mobile Bay area eastward into the Carolinas, has been that populations from Alabama tended to be more winter-hardy than those from farther east.

In Florida, we found a whitish fungus destroying the leaves and fruits of many plants of some populations. Persons collecting this species from the wild ought to take great care not to introduce this disease to their gardens or to new areas where it might spread to other species.

Trillium reliquum Freeman

This very rare trillium has a peculiar distribution. It grows along the Savannah River near Augusta, Georgia, and in adjacent South Carolina, and also disjunctly in southwestern Georgia near the Chattahoochee River. In both localities it grows among mature oaks and beeches on bluff summits and slopes to the floodplain.

This species, like *Trillium decumbens*, has scapes which can be semi-decumbent, although, in my experience, not as strikingly as the description of the species by Freeman implies. The scapes, with a slight S-shaped bend, stand no more than 8 to 10 inches/20 to 25 cm tall. The sessile, blunt-tipped leaves show beautiful mottling of light and dark greens underlain with maroon tones. The flowers are rather nondescript, with lanceolate-ovate, maroon-purple petals about 1 to 1.5 inches/2.5 to 4 cm long. Yellow-petaled forms occur.

Trillium reliquum blooms from mid-March to late April in the wild. In my garden it blooms in mid to late May, one of the later species here. Although the Augusta form is winter-hardy, it does not grow well or flower well for me. A deep forest species, its leaves are extremely sensitive to windburn, so it not desirable horticulturally. As the rarest of the sessile trilliums in the East, it deserves designation as an endangered or threatened species and should be left in the wild.

Trillium discolor Wray ex Hooker

After *Trillium decumbens*, this species would be my choice as the best sessile trillium for the rock garden. It is a small plant, with leaves held close to the ground, rarely growing 6 inches/15 cm tall in cultivation, but occasionally achieving 8 to 10 inches/20 to 25 cm in the wild.

The sessile leaves, richly blotched in dark green over a softly mottled background and broadly ovate-elliptic, appear very early in spring. In its native haunts the plant blooms early, but in my northern latitude the leaves and buds appear, followed by several weeks of waiting. Finally, when most of the other trilliums begin to fade, the delightful lime- to lemon-colored flowers appear. The short, wide, tapered petals have greenish veins and are distinctly apiculate. The flowers last long but slowly fade to a light straw color. Fresh blooms are spicily fragrant.

This trillium is restricted almost entirely to the upper tributaries of the Savannah River system in the Piedmont of Georgia and South Carolina and the Blue Ridge Mountain valleys of North Carolina. Although it grows in a variety of woods, it prefers small flats along mountain streams where thickets of *Leucothoe*, *Kalmia*, and *Rhododendron* occur. Here the most vigorous plants grow in bright, open areas under tall trees.

The small size, late blooming, distinctive lemon coloring, hardiness, and attractive leaves all season make this a truly outstanding plant for the rock garden. It is, however, a very local species. If it is not yet designated for protection under the Endangered Species Act, it probably will be, for a large part of its limited range has been destroyed through the building of power dams and impoundments. I have grown this plant in Michigan for almost 20 years; it is beginning to seed around the parent colony, and I will attempt to make seed available.

Trillium stamineum Harbison

A large and distinctive species, *Trillium stamineum* is practically unknown to gardeners outside its range. It is the only trillium with spreading, corkscrew-twisted petals borne directly atop the obscurely mottled leaves. It is like no other trillium.

Scapes stand 12 to 20 inches/30 to 50 cm tall, with leaves variably lanceolate to ovate-elliptic, usually fairly broad for their length and weakly mottled to plain green. The petals are short, 1 to 1.5 inches/2.5 to 4 cm long, twisted, and dark maroon in most forms, although I have a form with pale yellow petals overlain with pink. Clear yellow forms have been reported. In this species, as in *Trillium discolor*, the petals are apiculate. The stamens are massive, erect, clustered into a conspicuous ring, almost more apparent than the petals to a visiting insect.

Trillium stamineum is too tall for the usual rockery; nevertheless, one should grow it for its distinctive flower. A place at the back of the rock garden or in a woodland setting would be best. It is completely winter-hardy in central Michigan.

This species grows natively in a north-south band from northern Alabama and Mississippi into Tennessee. Within this area it is locally abundant in rich woods, on ledges, and on slopes above and descending onto floodplains. We have found it growing with *Trillium recurvatum* but have seen no evidence that they hybridize.

Trillium maculatum Raf.

This large and very showy trillium ranges across the middle and outer Piedmont and Coastal Plain of South Carolina, Georgia, and Alabama, and locally south into the panhandle of Florida.

Plants range in height from 1 to 2 feet/30 to 60 cm tall, with sessile, elliptic to broadly elliptic leaves. The leaves may be obscurely to strongly mottled. In the best forms we have seen (near Augusta, Georgia) the leaf markings were especially prominent, with light, medium, and dark bronze-green blotches, some underlain with a deep maroon-red. The petals, distinctly spatulate, broadest beyond the middle, and stiffly divergent-erect, are rich maroon-red to dark garnet. The color does not fade to the dull liver tones of so many of the sessile trilliums. The spotted trillium is thus a colorful and particularly desirable garden plant. Bicolored yellow-and-purple and pure-yellow-flowered forms occur, but we have not seen them. In leaf and flower color, this species is almost more desirable as a garden plant than the larger and more vigorous *Trillium cuneatum*, which is of similar aspect.

Trillium maculatum blooms very early, both in the wild and in the garden. It grows in a variety of rich woodlands of both upland and floodplain. We have seen it on both acidic and limestone soils.

This trillium has been much confused by botanists with other Coastal Plain and Piedmont species. Much of the literature prior to Freeman's treatment (1975) may refer to other entities and should be used with caution.

Despite its Deep South distribution, plants from near Augusta, Georgia, have proven completely hardy here for many years. A few plants were obtained from western Florida. These were relatively taller, with smaller leaves and flowers than those from Augusta. It remains to be seen how they will prosper.

Trillium foetidissimum Freeman

The fetid trillium strongly suggests *Trillium sessile* in general size and habit. Its leaves, however, are far more strongly mottled and are carried at a slightly different angle. One gets the impression, in the field, that the leaves are carried at a precise right angle to the stem and droop less at the tips than do those of *T. sessile*. The ranges of these two species do not overlap, but specimens of either from horticultural sources could easily be mistaken for the other.

In *Trillium foetidissimum* the leaves are more conspicuously mottled with more varied tones; the ovary is not distinctly six-winged; and the stigmas are usually not as long as the ovary at flowering. The scent of the flowers in *T. sessile* is spicy if unpleasant, while those of *T. foetidissimum* have, according to Freeman, a "strong, nearly stifling, carrion odor."

Trillium sessile occurs in midland states, mostly north of Tennessee and Arkansas; *T. foetidissimum* occurs east of the Mississippi River in southern Mississippi and that portion of Louisiana east of the Mississippi River.

We found it growing in low woods along a small river in rather trashy thickets, and also in more attractive cover on lower ravine slopes near the headwaters of small rills. It grew on open forest floors in leaf-mold, and occasionally on low rocky outcroppings. Plants were mostly scattered, with little tendency to form clumps. Freeman (1975) said that *Trillium foetidissimum* inhabits floodplains, river-bluff forests, and ravine slopes under beech, magnolia, and pine.

This is an attractive plant, particularly in leaf. If it proves sufficiently winter-hardy for northern gardeners, it will be very useful in the rockery. Otherwise, it is sufficiently like *Trillium sessile* that it will not be badly missed.

Trillium cuneatum Raf.

Trillium cuneatum, also widely known as *T. hugeri*, is one of the plants frequently illustrated as "*T. sessile*," especially in European publications. A large trillium, it is worthy of a featured spot in the wildflower garden.

Plants stand 1 to 2 feet/30 to 60 cm tall and bear large cordate-ovate, acuminate leaves strongly mottled in light and dark green with some maroon undertones. These leaf markings fade and blur somewhat during the season, but it remains a good accent plant until it dies down at season's end. In the best garden forms, 2- to 3-inch/5- to 8-cm, cuneate, heavy-textured, 1-inch/2.5-cm maroon-purple to bronze-purple petals stand upon the leaves. The petal bases are not narrowed or thickened into a claw in this species. The narrower sepals may be green or maroon to purple on the upper surfaces.

An early emerger and bloomer, *Trillium cuneatum* remains in bloom for weeks. When fresh, the flowers have a faint, pleasant scent. Older blooms lack odor and fade to the usual liver-brown, detracting somewhat from the plant's beauty.

Last spring we found plants in Tennessee that developed undertones of orange as the flowers aged. Some of these now grow in my garden, where we will observe them. If they still show promise, we will attempt to self-pollinate them and work toward producing orange trilliums.

Trillium cuneatum grows natively on Ordovician limestone soils in southern Kentucky, Tennessee, western North and South Carolina, Georgia, Alabama, and northern Mississippi, occurring farther south into the Piedmont and Coastal Plain as one moves toward the Mississippi River. It grows in a variety of woods and thickets, from very mature beech and oak forests to dry scrubby oak. Plants from Georgia and Alabama that we have observed have smaller, narrower petals of darker purple-maroon than those from Tennessee and Kentucky. The largest plants we have ever seen grew near Huntsville, Alabama, in a mature beech woods. They stood fully 2 feet/60 cm tall, with immense leaves and 4-inch/10-cm petals.

As with most of the maroon-purple sessile-flowered species, forms occur with brown, liver, greenish-yellow, or lemon-yellow petals, as well as bicolors with dark bases and green or yellow extremities. We grow a beautiful, clear light green form from the hills of northern Georgia—not very large, but very attractive.

Despite being rather closely associated with specific limestone soils in the wild, the plant is extremely easy to cultivate in almost any garden soil. Even in my unsuitable sandy acid soil seedlings appear regularly. Appalachian wildflower nurseries offer it (often as *Trillium sessile*), and it is well worth growing.

Trillium luteum (Muhl.) Harbison

Except for flower color and petal shape, the general description of *Trillium cuneatum* might serve also for *T. luteum*. In *T. luteum*, the somewhat narrower, lanceolate petals range in color from pale lemon-yellow to a strong, clear, darker yellow in wild plants. However, some of these darker yellow forms, transplanted to my garden, consistently yield paler, greener tones. The flowers emit a pleasant lemon scent.

An excellent garden plant, it occurs naturally in western North Carolina, and more abundantly in eastern Tennessee, where it is the only sessile trillium in Great Smoky Mountain National Park (Freeman, 1975); northward and westward it occurs into south-central Kentucky. In the vicinity of Gatlinburg, Tennessee, the blooming plants literally light up the forests and roadsides with a soft yellow glow.

It prefers to grow in rich, moist, rocky woods and lower hillsides, often on lower slopes above a small streambed. Unlike some sessile species, however, it is not confined to river-drainage situations. In southern Kentucky, *Trillium luteum* and *T. cuneatum* occur in the same woodlots, a situation seldom seen elsewhere. In such stations obvious hybrids and intergrades abound.

Authors prior to Freeman frequently lumped *Trillium luteum* with *T. viride* Beck, or with various pallid color forms of other species. Consequently, the confusion in the literature about its range and characteristics is considerable. Freeman's treatment (1975) seems to me best to reflect the situation which exits in nature.

Trillium ludovicianum Harbison

The Louisiana trillium stands about 6 to 12 inches/15 to 30 cm tall. The bracts or leaves are sessile, lanceolate to broadly ovate, and from 3 to

5 inches/8 to 13 cm long. The leaves are mottled distinctly, but not so strongly as in *Trillium decipiens* or *T. underwoodii*. Petals are linear-oblanceolate, 1.25 to 2.25 inches/3 to 5.5 cm long, and somewhat divergently erect. In color they are green, merging into purplish at the base so that the flowers appear distinctly bicolored. The ovary is six-angled.

This species, according to Freeman (1975), is somewhat intermediate between the species found in Missouri, Arkansas, and the Texas-Louisiana border country, and the sessile species found farther east.

We have not seen it in flower yet, but we have seen the plant and collected it in the wild in central Louisiana. We were able to visit only one small station. Here, under beeches, magnolias, and a scattering of pines, on small ravine bluffs along a stream, the Louisiana trillium grew in heavy leafmold at the bases of trees and around old rotten logs. In this woods, which had recently been grazed, the plants were not common. Freeman (1975), however, averred that it is locally abundant in central Louisiana. He gave its range as "Upper Coastal Plain of Louisiana (west of the Mississippi River) and eastward into Mississippi." It is very local in Mississippi and is said to intergrade there with *Trillium cuneatum*.

Since we have just obtained this species this past summer (1980), we cannot yet comment on whether or not it will prove hardy. Except for the avid collector, this species, like several others from the Gulf Coast region, is not essential to gardeners, for its horticultural differences from other, thoroughly hardy and readily obtainable species are minimal.

Trillium gracile Freeman

Trillium gracile is another sessile species with which I am only slightly acquainted. We found it growing abundantly on floodplain alluvium of tributary streams to the Sabine River system in extreme western Louisiana. The plants we found had been completely inundated, and although covered with dry mud, they were in full bloom.

Scapes of this species stand 8 to 12 inches/20 to 30 cm or more tall. The sessile, elliptic or elliptic-ovate leaves (bracts) are only 2.5 to 3.5 inches/6 to 9 cm long; the apices of those we saw were bluntly rounded. The leaf color was a dull blue-green with some darker spotting, but lacking the dramatic coloration of some of the more southern sessile trilliums found farther east. The petals are linear-elliptic, fairly short, 1 to 1.5 inches/2.5 to 4 cm long, their tips acute or rounded. Freeman gave the color as either dark purple or yellow. Those we saw were exclusively dark purple. Because of the flooding, the plants we observed were deteriorating; we noted no characteristic odor. Freeman likened the odor to that of the morel mushroom (*Morchella*).

Trillium gracile grows in open to dense pine and hardwood forests on slopes, streambanks, and alluvium. While Freeman said that the soils where it grows are usually sandy, where we collected our plants the soil was distinctly clayey. The species ranges from extreme southeastern Texas eastward into Louisiana, where it occurs primarily on the upper coastal plain of counties bordering on Texas.

We have yet to see how it winters in central Michigan. Like *Trillium ludovicianum* and *T. foetidissimum*, if it fails to survive here, it is not sufficiently distinctive horticulturally to be deeply mourned. If it is hardy, then from the collector's viewpoint, hurrah!

Trillium viride Beck

In northeastern Missouri and southern Illinois, in counties close to the Mississippi River, grows a trillium which has been much confused with *Trillium luteum*. This plant, *T. viride*, the green trillium, seems to be quite distinct.

A moderate plant, *Trillium viride* stands 10 to 18 inches/25 to 45 cm tall, with elliptic leaves either dark green or very faintly mottled. The leaves are somewhat blunt-tipped and exhibit numerous stomata on their upper surface (Freeman, 1975:44), a feature generally not found in other sessile species. The petals are narrow, spatulate to linear, up to 2 inches/5 cm long, and somewhat clawed (narrowed basally). The petal color is frequently dark purple at the base, becoming green to yellowish-green distally. All-purple and all-green forms occur. In my plants there is a tendency for the petals to be divergently spreading and somewhat twisted.

Trillium viride grows in rich woodlands, rocky but damp hillsides, and slopes above river flats, often on limestone soils. We were surprised to find it at its best in very thin, open sites, often quite brushy and grassy, with a minimum of tree cover.

Plants from Missouri have proved difficult to grow and even more difficult to flower here. This may be because of the sandy, dry, acidic nature of my soils, but in any case it is unfortunate, for the dark leaves and green flowers make this a desirable garden plant.

Trillium viridescens Nutt.

This Ouachita-Ozarkian mountain species bears a close relationship and physical similarity to *Trillium viride*. It grows somewhat taller, to over 18 inches/45 cm, with broader leaves with acuminate tips. Mottling of the leaves may be absent or obscure. The leaves tend to be carried at right angles to the scape. The narrowly linear to spatulate petals stand erect with a graceful single twist. The petal color is clear green above a dark maroon base; yellowish-, green, and all-purple forms appear.

Trillium viridescens occurs in southwestern Missouri, all of western and northwestern Arkansas, and eastern Oklahoma, with a few stations known from extreme Kansas and northeastern Texas. Its habitat is rich soil on slopes, bluffs, talus, and river alluvium under mature trees. Magnificent native colonies grow in John Lambert's Mountain Fork River Arboretum near Mena, Arkansas, often in surprisingly heavy floodplain soils among canebrake.

A handsome species, well worth cultivation, *Trillium viridescens* has proved difficult for me. It is prone to a leaf dieback here so early in the season as to interfere with food manufacture; consequently plants linger but do not flower well. Perhaps my soil is the problem.

Afterword

From the standpoint of the collector, there is no such thing as a "bad" trillium species. All evoke uncommon interest; many present a real challenge to those who search for them; and some possess great grace and beauty. Surely they are among the loveliest of American wildflowers and a noble contribution to the world's forests and gardens.

In this day of concern for endangered species, I am sure that some readers will feel that one ought not to discuss or encourage the growing of any "rare" species. True, some trilliums are rare and local, but within their ranges, all but two or three species are really quite common. Wise collection, coupled with propagation and nursery availability, is quite feasible, and should in my opinion be undertaken. It will not endanger any species if approached properly.

I sit on the Technical Advisory Committee on Endangered Plants for the Michigan Department of Natural Resources. It is our function to review, recommend, and establish the rarity status of our native Michigan plants. I also speak before many garden clubs and conservation organizations and have heard all kinds of statements and arguments relating to our native plants. Many are irrationally overzealous and some, such as the frequent statement that picking trilliums kills the plant, are simply untrue.

Endangered species laws seek to protect rare wild plant populations or to prohibit commercial exploitation of wild plants. The purpose of such laws is not to prohibit entirely the growing of these species or the sale of nursery-propagated stock.

I believe that a worthy function of plant societies, arboreta, and botanical gardens is to obtain, propagate, and disseminate stock of even rare or endangered species to gardens and nurseries. Such organizations, working closely with conservation departments, can monitor and grow with continuity from generation to generation many desirable rare plants. By introducing selected horticultural forms, these institutions and organizations can help to satisfy the demands of collectors and gardeners, thus removing from wild populations the pressure of illicit collecting and black-market trading, which unfortunately will exist so long as no other source of plants is available to the inveterate collector.

_____ A Note on Propagation _____

From seed, or from rhizome divisions and offsets, trillium propagation is quite easily accomplished. In my opinion, wise and carefully monitored collection and dissemination should be undertaken.

Both trillium seeds and rhizomes have built-in dormancy factors which must be considered in propagation. Trillium seeds have a double dormancy. A first period of low temperatures stimulates the emergence of a root from the seed. A second period of shoot or stem dormancy is necessary, which in nature usually involves a second winter before the shoot dormancy is broken. Trillium seeds thus usually take at least 2 years to appear above ground. Maturation from that point requires from 3 to 7 years, depending on species, soil fertility, and other cultural factors.

Trillium rhizomes also have a bud dormancy. New growth is not initiated until the buds have been cooled sufficiently following a given period of growth. If the top of the plant is removed, the plant will make no further growth above ground that season. It will, however, appear again the following season after the required low temperatures break the bud dormancy.

Unless one is prepared to care for seeds in a frame or pot for several years, I believe it is more practical for gardeners to sow the seeds in a suitable spot in the wild garden and let development take its own course.

Trillium rhizomes may be scarified or partially girdled to produce a ring of buds which will ultimately develop into offset rhizomes. Once formed on the girdled rhizome, however, these offset buds must undergo the required dormancy-breaking temperatures before any growth appears above ground.

Propagation is not difficult, but it does take time. Someone with the proper facilities ought to undertake a program of tissue culture and experimental dormancy-breaking to speed the propagation process.

Bibliography

Case, Frederick W., Jr., and George L. Burrows IV. 1962. "The Genus *Trillium* in Michigan: Some Problems of Distribution and Taxonomy." *Papers of the Michigan Academy of Sciences* 47, 189–200.

Duncan, Wilber H., J. Garst, and G. Neese. 1971. "*Trillium persistens* (Liliaceae), a New Pedicellate-Flowered Species for Northeastern Georgia and Adjacent North Carolina." *Rhodora* 73, 244–248.

Freeman, John D. 1975. "Revision of *Trillium* subgenus *Phyllantherum* (Liliaceae)." *Brittonia* 27, 1–62.

Freeman, J. D., A. S. Causey, J. W. Short, and R. R. Haynes. 1979. *Endangered, Threatened and Special Concern Plants of Alabama*. Department of Botany and Microbiology, Agricultural Experiment Station, Auburn University, Series No. 3. Auburn, Alabama.

Gates, R. R. 1917. "A Systematic Study of the North American Genus *Tril-*

lium, Its Variability and Its Relation to *Paris* and *Medeola*." *Annals of the Missouri Botanical Garden* 4, 43–92.

Hooper, G. R., F. W. Case, Jr., and R. Myers. 1971. "Mycoplasma-like Bodies Associated with a Flower Greening Disorder of a Wild Flower, *Trillium grandiflorum*." *Plant Disease Reporter* 55, 1108–1110.

Johnson, R. G. 1969. *A Taxonomic and Floristic Study of the Liliaceae and Allied Families in the Southeastern United States*. Unpublished Ph.D. dissertation, West Virginia University, Morgantown.

Originally published in the Bulletin of the American Rock Garden Society, *vol. 39, no. 2, pp. 53–67; no. 3, pp. 108–122 (1981).*

Viola pedata:
The Bird's-foot Violet

 Introduction

EDWARD J. ALEXANDER

To see the bird's-foot violet, *Viola pedata*, in its native habitat is to desire it for the garden: it is the most beautiful American violet, whether in its rare bicolored form or in the more common bright lilac one. Even though it is not a rock plant, it is a great adornment to any rock garden in which one can persuade it to become permanently established. So rarely is this the case, however, and so numerous are the gardeners who desire it, that all too frequent raids are made on the diminishing number of extensive wild stands. This deplorable practice could be remedied by a proper examination of the plant's natural growing conditions, applying what is learned to grow it well and in commercial quantities.

The largest colonies and finest plants occur in the wild in open, sunny areas, where the soil is remarkably poor, usually clay or sand or a mixture of the two with some gravel. They are not in woodlands or in rich loam. In fact, the largest and most floriferous plants are in the loose sandy clay of railroad and highway cuts and embankments, where there is little competition. Therefore, if one wishes to make a successful and permanent establishment of this plant, these soil conditions should be duplicated.

Viola pedata is unrelated to any other American violet in flower form, and in that it bears no cleistogamous (non-opening, fertile) flowers and no stolons or "runners." It reproduces only by seed from petaliferous flowers, and by fission of the short, upright rootstock. There are also remarkable physiological differences. In fact, *V. pedata* has no close relatives among all the violets of the world; *V. pinnata* of Northern Europe and Asia approaches nearest but differs in flower structure.

This, then, is a truly American plant, with a natural range from Maine to Minnesota, south to eastern Texas and northern Florida, with great variation in color, size, form of flower, petal shape, and leaf design. The bicolored variety has its area of most frequent occurrence in an east-west belt across the middle of this range.

Viola pedata is one of the oldest known American violets, having been first described by John Banister in 1688 and first pictured by Plukenet in 1691. Its first appearance in European gardens was in 1759, when the plant was listed by Philip Miller as growing in the Chelsea Physick Garden. This was the bicolored variety, apparently the only one known to the writers mentioned. Since Linnaeus in 1753 knew no other variety, it is the historical type of the species. Not until 1789 did the concolorous variety become known to botanists. In that year William Curtis published its picture as plate 89 in the *Botanical Magazine,* calling it *V. pedata* and indicating that it was the same variety known to previous writers. This error was the cause of much subsequent bickering over the name, all of which could have been avoided by looking in de Candolle's *Prodromus* (1824), where the two varieties were clearly first named. There the concolorous plant was called *V. pedata* var. *lineariloba* and the bicolored one *V. pedata* var. *atropurpurea.* In this same article the name *V. pedata* var. *bicolor* made its first appearance, but only in synonymy, so it is invalid. Frederick Pursh, to whom it is accredited, never used the word *bicolor;* "*V. atropurpurea* Rafinesque" was also published only as a synonym in de Candolle's work.

Since *Viola pedata* contains such a complex of variations in both color and cutting of the leaf, it is necessary to have varietal names to designate the stable ones. Under the rules of nomenclature these are as follows:

> *Viola pedata* var. *atropurpurea* for the bicolor variety.
> *Viola pedata* var. *lineariloba* for the concolored variety.
> *Viola pedata* var. *lineariloba* f. *alba* for the albino form.

[These plants are no longer given varietal status; only *V. pedata* is a recognized taxon.—*Ed.*]

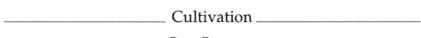

Cultivation

BURR BRONSON

Viola pedata has been of interest to me for many years, ever since I found it on the shores of Walden Pond of Thoreau fame. Here plants grew by hundreds in full sun in a soil of sand and pine humus. There were none of the bicolored variety here; I first saw those on the sunny side of a country road in Missouri, where for several miles the roadside was blue with both varieties growing together. I received permission from the road commissioner to dig a few to take back to my garden. He said he would be glad if I took them all as they were a pest, and in a few weeks the road scraper would scrape them off in an effort to get rid of them. Little did he know that in cutting off the tops he actually was propagating them, as every root would soon produce a new top, and where one grew before, a half dozen would replace it.

Three years ago my interest was furthered after reading, in Reginald Hills's *Propagation of Alpines*, that the many color breaks and leaf forms should be propagated and made available. I found that there were all shades of blue, lilac, pink, and even dark red, as well as white, cream, and blue-white. Division was the method advised, but I could not find any cleavage for division in the carrot-like rootstock or caudex.

A few weeks later, in an article by Will C. Curtis of Garden in the Woods, I found the answer to dividing *Viola pedata*. Curtis wrote, "Stored plants brought into the greenhouse in late winter, and forced for two weeks, can be divided almost indefinitely. Every leaf with a small cap of basal tissue and a root will grow and produce another plant." This I found to be true, but I also found that the smaller the division, the longer it took to produce a new plant of blooming size. Having no greenhouse, I waited until growth started in April, and then, with a single-edged razor blade, sliced the carrot-like root lengthwise, first in half, then in quarters, then eighths, depending on the thickness of the carrot. After dusting each cut side to protect against root rot, I planted each section in a pot of soil consisting of one-half sand, one-quarter peat, and one-quarter compost and pine duff. The pots were placed in a shaded coldframe until new growth started and then gradually given increasing amounts of sunlight. The new plants bloomed the following May.

Since my first attempt, I have learned many things about growing this plant. It does not like dampness around the crown, which will result from too deep planting. To avoid this I leave 0.25 inch/6 mm of the caudex out of the ground and place a ring of granite grit or coarse sand around the collar. I have also found that division can be done any time from April to August, even with the plant in full bloom, and the new plants will bloom the following year.

Given acid, sandy soil in full sun, the violets will not only bloom in May but will start blooming again in August and every month until heavy frost. I now have many colors, including the rare white, and as they require the same conditions as my dwarf heathers, I grow them in the heather garden.

The introductory segment was originally published in the Bulletin of the American Rock Garden Society, *vol. 4, no. 3, pp. 105–106 (1946); the segment here titled "Cultivation" appeared in vol. 23, no. 3, pp. 135–137 (1965).*

PART SIX: THROUGHOUT NORTH AMERICA

Anemones in the West

PANAYOTI KELAIDIS

What group of hardy plants is more adaptable or varied in nature and in the garden than anemones? Species of the genus *Anemone* can be found from the permafrost of the Arctic to the littorals of the Mediterranean. In North America, *A. tuberosa* thrives in the desert Southwest among cacti and agaves. *Anemone caroliniana* is still common along the eastern fringes of the Great Plains. For many rock gardeners, the most frequently cultivated anemones are woodland groundcovers that thrive best in light shade; the common European wood anemone, *A. nemorosa*, is typical of this group.

American Woodland Anemones

Several species of *Anemone* growing in North America superficially resemble the European wood anemone. The best known is the eastern wood anemone, *A. quinquefolia*, which occurs sporadically in the rich soils of deciduous forests throughout the eastern United States and Canada. It is somewhat more delicate than its European relative and seems less vigorous in cultivation. It differs in having leaflets divided into five rather than three segments.

Anemone oregana, *A. deltoidea*, and *A. lyallii* are three rhizomatous anemones found widely west of the Cascade Mountains in cool woodland. The first also occurs on the drier eastern Cascade and Blue mountains of Washington and Oregon; there are even records of some anemones quite like these far to the east in the Uinta Mountains of Utah. Although most western wood anemones in cultivation closely resemble the European species in general effect, they lack its adaptability to cultivation.

One wood anemone largely restricted to the interior ranges of the West is *Anemone piperi*, a narrow endemic of the wet mountain ranges bordering the Idaho panhandle. It is much larger and more vigorous than other western wood anemones and would be interesting to attempt in cultivation, although I know of no one who has managed to grow it.

Mountain Anemones

The anemones most commonly encountered at higher elevations in the Rocky Mountains are clump-forming meadow plants with deeply divided hairy foliage and comparatively small flowers. These are the "thimbleweeds," noticeable for neat spherical, cottony seedheads that are irresistible to seed-collectors. This group, though relatively unattractive, appears frequently on seed lists.

The tall thimbleweed (12 to 18 inches/30 to 45 cm in some forms) with deep red flowers that occurs through the Rockies is *Anemone multifida* (syn. *A. globosa*; Plate 7). It has proven a little too easy in cultivation and quickly spreads by self-sown seeds in any open or partly shaded situation. A tiny form found in the higher mountains of the Great Basin and western Rockies has been segregated by some authors into a different species, *A. tetonensis*. It looks exactly like the cultivated *A.* × *lesseri*, and I suspect that this putative hybrid may trace its ancestry to the Rockies.

The loveliest representative of this section is unquestionably *Anemone drummondii* (Plate 50), which occurs in a variety of forms throughout the western and northern portions of the Rockies, the Cascades, and the Sierra Nevada. It is usually intensely hairy and quite compact. The flowers vary from white to quite deep blue and are much larger than those of the thimbleweeds. It has been compared to the European *A. baldensis* as well as to a refined dwarf pulsatilla. Unfortunately, it does not seem very easy to keep or flower in the garden.

Alpine Anemones

Two anemones that occur sporadically throughout the Rockies are usually found near timberline, but often far higher. *Anemone narcissiflora* (Plate 57) is by far the better known. It is abundant in high mountains over much of Eurasia, and several subspecies have been described in Alaska. It is absent in most of the Rockies, but in central Colorado it suddenly becomes a common plant in large willow thickets at lower alpine levels around South Park and Trail Ridge in the northern and eastern parts of the Front Range.

Anemone narcissiflora forms low mounds of dark green, deeply divided foliage crowned with clusters of large, brilliantly white flowers, two to five on a stem, each filled with a boss of yellow stamens. From a distance they resemble tazetta narcissi. The Colorado form is so much larger in flower and smaller in stature that it has been described as a separate species by "splitting" botanists; however, modern botanists usually recognize the former *A. zephyra* only as *A. narcissiflora* subsp. *zephyra*. The seeds of this anemone are flat, ovoid, purple flakes that quickly lose viability in storage. It is imperative to sow them shortly after ripening to obtain any germination at all; as a result, few have managed to grow this lovely plant in their gardens.

Anemone parviflora is widespread in the tundra of Alaska and northern Canada and occurs sporadically throughout the Rockies down to Colorado. It forms tiny mats of deep green leaves, which are cuneate and quite distinct from those of any other anemone. It is so small and blooms so early in the season that it is easily overlooked. When first open, the flowers are nearly stemless and resemble a few-sepaled *Dryas*. As the season progresses, the stems elongate to 5 inches/13 cm or more, ending in a spherical seedhead that eventually explodes into a cottony mass. Since *Anemone parviflora* usually grows near lingering snowbanks and along icy rivulets, it is no surprise that it is difficult in cultivation.

The Pasqueflowers

Over the past century botanists have batted the pasqueflowers back and forth relentlessly between the genera *Anemone* and *Pulsatilla*; at present they seem to have settled in the latter. There is no question that this group has many distinct characteristics.

Some westerners confuse the issue hopelessly by calling them all "wild crocus" because they are among the earliest flowers to bloom in the prairies and mountains throughout their range. *Pulsatilla patens* (Plate 101) is certainly one of the most widespread wildflowers in the West, occurring from the Great Plains and pinyon-juniper woodlands up to subalpine forests and climbing above 12,000 feet/3700 meters in parts of the Saguache Range of central Colorado. It is possible to find pasqueflowers blooming from late March to early July in most years.

Typically, the common pasqueflower is a pale lavender muted by many hairs on both the sepals and the foliage. It is obviously closely allied to the common European pasqueflower, *Pulsatilla vulgaris*, which is usually a much richer violet. The native species appears to be rather more difficult to grow than the European—probably a recommendation to most gardeners, since *P. vulgaris* can quickly become a nuisance by self-sowing.

If it is possible to tame the pasqueflower, the "old man of the mountain" remains a holy grail to most gardeners. Surely no western plant speaks more eloquently of alpine heights than *Pulsatilla occidentalis*. Rarely found much below timberline, it seems to grow best on exposed ridges far above the trees. It is common throughout the Olympics, Cascades, and Sierra Nevada as well as in the Rockies from Alberta to Montana, and south and west to the Wallowas.

Superficially *Pulsatilla occidentalis* resembles the large white-flowered phase of the European *P. alpina*, common in the granitic portions of the Alps. Its foliage, however, is much more finely divided into a deep green filigree resembling some strange rattlesnake fern (*Cheilanthes*). The flowers are that virginal white reserved for alpines and tropical orchids. They are rounder and more open than the flowers of *Pulsatilla patens*. The ripening seedheads do not form the hysterical starry mop typical of pasqueflowers, but look far shaggier and more substantial and constitute even more of a spectacle than the flowers.

Occurring in much wetter mountains, *Pulsatilla occidentalis* often does not flower until deep snowbanks melt in July or even August. Thus it is more familiar to summer tourists than is its widespread cousin.

Other Anemones

Quite a few other anemones occur in America; some, like *Anemone cylindrica*, are simply giant thimbleweeds with tiny flowers, suitable only for gardeners with unquenchable curiosity. *Anemone canadensis* is often sold in wildflower nurseries. This tall, slender plant is quite lovely, forming white constellations of flower in meadows and open woodland in the central United States and southern Canada; however, it can be a pest in gardens.

Anemone tuberosa is North America's only anemone largely restricted to desert regions. It has a low mound of foliage springing up very early in the season and a tall stem with pale pink or orange blossoms. It is widespread in rocky habitats in the chaparral of the southwestern United States. Most of the regions where it grows rarely experience prolonged frost, and it has not proven hardy in Colorado.

Anemone caroliniana, like certain Mediterranean anemones or *A. keiskeiana* from Japan, has the peculiarity of producing its mounds of foliage in midwinter. In early spring it covers itself with aster-like, many-sepaled blossoms of bright blue, pink, or white. It is quite common in some parts of the southern Great Plains where farming has not entirely supplanted the native vegetation. It appears to be difficult in cultivation.

The American anemones may not compare in variety to those in Eurasia; nevertheless, like our native primulas and gentians, they display novel features that cannot be found in their Eurasian cousins. We should get to know them better.

Originally published in the Bulletin of the American Rock Garden Society, *vol. 44, no. 1, pp. 7–11 (1986).*

Dodecatheon

EDITED BY LAURA LOUISE FOSTER

The genus *Dodecatheon* provides the floral emblem of the North American Rock Garden Society. To explain the derivation of the name of this genus I can do no better than to quote Roy Elliott in his book *Alpine Gardening*:

> The name *Dodecatheon* (*dodeka*, "twelve," and *theoi*, "gods") goes back to very ancient times, when Pliny is supposed to have bestowed the name on a flower which he considered to display the majesty of all six gods and six goddesses. And if you wonder how on earth the worthy Pliny came to discover a plant which ranges from Maine to Texas, the answer is the obvious one that he didn't. Many of our plant names, such as Iris and Narcissus, are of great antiquity, going back to earliest recorded times. When Linnaeus came to gather together all known names in his *Genera Plantarum* (1736), there were many names, needless to say, for which no record of the particular plant existed. Rather than waste these names, Linnaeus, much to the subsequent horror of botanists, used up the old names on new genera for which names had to be found. This is a possible explanation of Pliny's apparent visit to America.

According to John Ingram (1963), Phillip Miller, author of the eighteenth-century *Gardener's Dictionary*, claimed to have seen the shooting star in an English garden in 1709, although it disappeared from cultivation shortly thereafter and was not reintroduced until 30 years later. Before Linnaeus published the generic name *Dodecatheon* for this plant in 1754, it had been illustrated by Plukenet and Mark Catesby; the latter had dubbed the plant *Meadia* in honor of Dr. Richard Mead, an English physician and patron of science. It was under this name that Miller described it in 1752. According to Miller, Linnaeus was unwilling to accept the generic name *Meadia* because Dr. Mead was not a great botanist, but was willing to commemorate him in the name of the original species, *Dodecatheon meadia*. Despite Linnaeus, Miller continued to use *Meadia* in the eighth edition of his *Dictionary* (1768); as late as 1891, Otto Kuntze still championed that name, following the doctrine of absolute priority, beginning with the first edition of Linnaeus's *Systema Naturae* (1735), in which this plant is not mentioned under any name.

At present, the name *Dodecatheon* is the accepted one. The next question is how it should be pronounced. The usual rule for English speakers is that in botanical names they place stress, whenever possible, on the antepenult or third syllable from the end. Thus most of us probably say "do-de-KAY-the-on." However, some prefer to stay a bit closer to the continental vowels (as in Spanish, for instance), giving the also popular pronunciation "do-de-KA-the-on" ("ka" as in "cat"). Another suggestion is to ignore the English stress rule and give one stressed syllable to each of the two roots forming the compound: DO-deka-THE-on.

In assigning the correct specific name to each plant, unfortunately, we run into a real puzzle. We all know a dodecatheon when we see one, but how do you tell them apart?

Most members of the genus more or less resemble one another. They are all perennial plants growing from a short underground caudex furnished with long fleshy roots and a cluster of basal leaves, which generally wither away, frequently along with the roots, in the heat and drought of summer. As the old posterior portion of the caudex dies, new growing points form on the tip. New plants are produced vegetatively from the base of the thick fleshy roots or from rice-grain bulblets (characteristic of a few species) clustered around the caudex. Flowering stems may range in height from a 4 to 18 inches/10 to 45 cm, and they can bear from one to as many as 125 nodding, inside-out flowers hung from the tips of gracefully bending pedicels in a loose umbel. The four or five upturned lobes of the corolla vary in color from white through shades of rose to deep red. From the base of these sharply reflexed petals, the corolla tube with protruding stamens (their number equal to the number of lobes) and the single pistil form a down-stabbing "beak" variously marked with bands of maroon, yellow, black, and white. Once the flower has been fertilized, the corolla and stamens shrivel and fall away, and the pedicels straighten to hold the seed capsules upright. At maturity, the summit of the capsule opens: either the tip breaks off (operculate), or it splits down the seams for a short distance (valvate). In the latter case, the open capsule has distinct acute points at the tip.

Dodecatheons are fairly widespread, with one or more species native to all states of the United States except Hawaii and the New England states. Because they usually grow in specialized habitats—from mountains, to dry short-grass prairies, to lush swampy lowland meadows—there is considerable variation in the genus and even within individual species. Taxonomists have been busy lumping and splitting the genus into species, subspecies, varieties, and forms, creating new species with new names or reducing former species to subspecies or varieties, or even mere synonyms. Local floras are more likely to give specific status to plants considered only variations or subspecies by taxonomists studying a wider geographical range.

H. J. Thompson's comprehensive study (1953) of the genus reduced to 14 species (with 21 subspecies) more than 170 combinations of names that had been used. In general, Ingram (1963) followed Thompson's nomenclature. I have no intention of venturing onto the miry ground of nomenclature and suggest you get Thompson's or Ingram's monograph, or both, and decide for yourselves. In the meantime, I offer below a selection of comments about dodecatheons that have appeared in previous *Bulletins*.

[In the first volume of the *Bulletin* (1943), Edgar T. Wherry discussed *Dodecatheon amethystinum*:]

When it comes to distinguishing species, considerable difficulty arises. The characters used in the diagnostic keys in our floras and manuals are not easy to check, and when one tries to apply them to the plants in the field, in the western United States where the majority of the 20 or so species occur, these keys often fail to work.

In the midland and eastern states there is no such problem, for there are only two well-marked species in this region, and they are decidedly different in aspect. The commoner, more widespread one is *Dodecatheon meadia*. It was discovered in Virginia by Rev. John Banister about 1675, and named by Linnaeus in 1753. It attains its greatest abundance, however, in the prairie states, where it attracted the attention of the early explorers and was mentioned in their journals. Its flowers range from pure white to pink or purplish, and although not unattractive, it is a bit heavy for the small rock garden.

The second midland-eastern species had to wait a long time for recognition. Regarded by the early botanists who saw it as a mere variant of the common one, it was named as a variety of that by Norman C. Fassett in 1929. Two years later he raised it to the rank of a species, and as such it is made the subject of the present study. Discovered in western Wisconsin, it has been found to grow also in Minnesota, Iowa, Missouri, and central Pennsylvania.

Dodecatheon amethystinum is well named the jewel shooting star, for it is a veritable jewel among plants both in its native haunts and in the rock garden. It is more delicate than *D. meadia*, and the petals are of a deeper hue, a lovely amethystine violet. It blooms in early May, a week or two earlier than the other. The capsules develop soon after the flowers have faded, and the seed may be collected in a few weeks. The foliage then withers away, but vitality remains in the bulbous crown, and new leaves appear with the first touch of the following spring.

In deciding how to plant it in the rock garden, one should bear in mind that it is a northern species. It can withstand severe winter conditions but is rather intolerant of summer heat. In the wild it grows on moist, mossy, north-facing cliffs, where the soil is cool throughout the growing season. It should be planted, then, in a lean soil in a sheltered part of the garden, where the summer sunlight does not fall directly on the ground.

Dodecatheon amethystinum is an herbaceous perennial with a basal rosette of rather large elliptic-oblong leaves. In early spring it sends up, to a height of 5 to 10 or rarely 15 inches/13 to 25 or rarely 38 cm, a slender stem bearing a few-flowered umbel. The pedicels at first curve so the flowers assume a nodding position, but they become erect as the capsules mature. The five strongly reflexed corolla lobes are of a brilliant amethystine hue. They hide the calyx, but when this is looked for, it is found to bear five short lobes which are tipped, as are also the bracts at the base of the umbel, with tiny red points. The golden cone of anthers projects out for about 0.25 inch/6 mm. The straw-colored cylindrical capsules are thin-walled and produce numerous small brownish seeds.

It can be told from *Dodecatheon meadia* by the latter being coarser and taller (when fully developed 15 to 25 inches/38 to 63 cm high), the numerous flowers being paler in hue and the longer calyx lobes not red-tipped, the anther cone 0.33 inch/8 mm long, the bright brown ovoid capsules thick-walled, and the seeds brown.

[Ten years after Dr. Wherry wrote this article, H. J. Thompson reduced *Dodecatheon amethystinum* to a synonym of *D. pulchellum*, a very widespread and variable species, mostly western in distribution. Dr. Wherry had this to say on the subject in the August 1973 issue of the *Connecticut Plantsman*:]

[This] treatment was well-nigh incredible; although it is a typical temperate-climate lowland riverside plant, it got taxonomically tossed into subjective synonymy with *Dodecatheon pulchellum*, an arctic alpine which ranges from Alaska at increasingly high altitudes down to southern Mexico. Such disregard of plant geographic relationships seems unworthy of acceptance.

[In volume 22 (1964), Frank H. Rose of Missoula, Montana, wrote an article on the dodecatheons of his state. Though not much of a gardener, he was a plant and seed-collector of considerable note and widespread knowledge of the flora of Montana. He had been a member of the ARGS for many years, and many of his collected plants and seeds had found their way into the gardens of members of the society.]

Hitchcock et al. (1955–1969) gave Montana three species—*Dodecatheon jeffreyi*, *D. conjugens*, and *D. pauciflorum*, of one, two, and four varieties respectively. This is a great simplification from the 30 or more names previously used. No sooner was Hitchcock in print, however, than Ingram (1963) raised one of Hitchcock's varieties to a full species and changed the name of the species under which the other three varieties are left.

Ingram said that *Dodecatheon pauciflorum* is a synonym of *D. meadia*. *Dodecatheon radicatum* seems to be a synonym [for *D. pulchellum*] recognized by both authors. Ingram raised *D. cusickii* to a full species. I like that because it is here in Montana, and I am already acquainted with it. Better carry a magnifier to the field with you, though, to be sure of the thickened capsule walls and the pointed valve tips that separate it from *D. conjugens* subsp. *viscidum*, which is equally or more glandular-pubescent, but usually shows clearly the operculate capsule (flat-tipped points on the capsule valves), or if only the [unopened] pods are available, the style thickened at the base.

Size, leaf shape, number of flowers, color, pubescence, and most other characteristics vary greatly, especially in *Dodecatheon meadia*, on different sites, and I still have a lot of plants to look at before I can always be sure.

Dodecatheon jeffreyi gives me no trouble. It grows where you would expect *Primula parryi* to grow, in a wet place, but sometimes on up the slope where the ground dries quite hard in late summer. Its yellowish-white, thickened, brittle roots, tending downward instead of horizontally, are quite characteristic, although unmentioned by botanists. Like *D. meadia*, when favorably grown it is too big for the small rock garden. Its pale flowers open only inches out of the soil, but seed may ripen a yard/meter higher up. Like all dodecatheons, it may be dug when the seed ripens and can be kept out of the soil until the following spring, and still grow. It is better with this one not to let it dry to brittleness, as some others may, but to keep it damp, as under a tarp on the cellar floor.

Dodecatheon conjugens grows all purple in some areas, and half white-flowered in other localities. To identify it, however, you need only note the wavy ring, the yellow to purple filaments and roughened connectives, its lanceolate to spatulate leaves, glandular or lacking pubescence; finally, note the operculate capsule with square-tipped valves when open, indicated by the thickened style base in immature plants. All I have seen grow in well-drained sites and may become quite dry in late summer, with roots so brittle they can only be dug in moist weather. The root crown is all that is needed. Either full sun or the shade of a western yellow pine seems equally satisfactory. They mingle and probably hybridize with *D. cusickii* and possibly *D. meadia*. Our plant is chiefly the subspecies *viscidum*.

Dodecatheon meadia subsp. *meadia* (formerly *D. pauciflorum*) grows here in sunny wet meadows, timber-shaded bogs, under western yellow pine, as scattered clumps in grassland, and in other habitats. It usually has smooth, tapered leaves, but these also vary. Its size may vary depending on the site, but its capsules should open with valves that come to a sharp point.

Dodecatheon pulchellum (formerly *D. pauciflorum* var. *watsonii*; Plate 84) is a tiny alpine plant with a single large flower. As in many alpines, the flower seems out of proportion to the plant and is brightly colored. It grades into larger and multiflowered varieties at lower elevations, and perhaps would do this in the garden.

[Laura E. Jezik of Seattle, Washington, wrote an article entitled "Two Unusual Dodecatheon Species," which appeared in volume 24 (1966). Once again the problems of dodecatheon nomenclature turn up:]

Dodecatheon patulum is not often mentioned in the literature. Farrer and Clay were both aware of it, as was Correvon. Munz (1959) listed it as a subspecies of *D. clevelandii*.

This Californian, from hot adobe land in the northern Sacramento Valley, is a good creamy white or light yellow, with a prominent red-black central zone. It is about 3 inches/8 cm tall. It is a colonizer, locally covering acres so thickly that it is difficult to avoid plants while walking. It is said to favor slightly alkaline areas. I found it growing with 2-inch/5-cm *Orthocarpus erianthus*, an annual, which gilds acres with its tiny calceolaria-like pouches at the tips of its stems; *Baeria chrysostoma*, another annual, 3 inches/8 cm high of bright daisy; *Brodiaea capitata*, ever-present and ever-lovely; and several other bulbous and annual plants, as well as perennial lupines. *Dodecatheon patulum* keeps its feet out of the water and climbs every rise, if only slight. It grows among volcanic rocks, and without them both in full sun and under deciduous oaks. It is sometimes subject to slight frosts as late as mid-March.

Occasionally, genetic memories of family redness dominate and there is a small colony of pink-flowered plants. These are fewer-flowered than the type and more delicate. The central zone is redder than black; next to this is a golden stripe, then a short white one; and the outer two-thirds of each corolla lobe is a good true pink.

Like many other plants from the valleys of California, it has a short period of active growth. It breaks dormancy at about the end of February, is in full bloom by mid-March, and has spent its seed and disappeared by the first of April.

In the garden, in my maritime climate, this plant requires a hot scree with perhaps some attention to its liking for alkaline soil. Gardens that can provide the unbearable heat of its summer home could grow this in clay, but water would have to be carefully managed.

Dodecatheon glastifolium Greene has now been included in the variable species *D. conjugens*. It differs a bit in being very long-pediceled, and it has distinct leaves—wavy, waxy, nearly succulent, and deep green. I have this in colors ranging from a good red to a hot pink, a mauve, a pale pink, and a white good enough to be named.

Though it is listed from Modoc County, in the extreme northeastern corner of California, I found quantities of it west of the mountains in Shasta County, growing in the foothill community with small deciduous and evergreen oaks, redbud, ceanothus, and others. It prefers a soil with more vegetable matter than does *Dodecatheon patulum*, and full sun in mild climates.

The habit of early dormancy in dodecatheons adapts them to positions in full sun. With the exception of the two wet-growing species *Dodecatheon dentatum* and *D. jeffreyi*, most western dodecatheons are better in sunny screes than in shade. All of them will be found growing in full sun; some of them are always there; and a few, like *D. hendersonii*, will grow in open glades in sunny woodlands.

Of the more than 15 species I grow, all except the wet-growers have been found more often in clays than in any other type of soil. These native clays are prairie and hot-land clays, not packed and compacted as garden clays are, and they are not often saturated. In the garden the same conditions can be obtained by using a loose soil with nourishment, both mineral and vegetable, but with perfect drainage.

[In volume 34 (1976), there is a note on colonizing *Dodecatheon meadia* in an Illinois woodland, by Mrs. Ralph Cannon of Chicago:]

One of our encroachments on the indigenous wild flowers that cover our Illinois woodland garden was to plant some *Dodecatheon meadia*. My neighbor had many of these growing in his woodland where his cattle grazed and offered us all we wanted. We moved about 50 rosettes and tried to plant them in the moist dappled shade of the trees, an environment similar to that from which they were taken; however, they were not happy. The next spring saw poor bloom, short stems, and few colors. As the rosettes began to disappear, we moved all the plants to other shady spots among the many trees. A year passed with no signs of improvement. We hated to lose these beautiful native flowers and so decided to move the plants again to an entirely different environment, a sunny meadow.

The sunny areas in our woodland and orchard are planted with thousands of daffodils that grow in the unmowed grass. Here all the shooting stars from the shady locations were moved, to grow or be abandoned. The following April, they came up briskly as beautiful, healthy plants flourishing in the grass. There were hundreds of blooms, the tall stems carrying umbels of glistening white, lavender, or rose flowers.

We allowed the seeds dropped by these healthy parent plants to grow in a natural pattern cast by the wind and rain. The colonization has produced hundreds of new plants. I think we have made a garden within a garden. They have far exceeded our expectations and have made a major contribution to our woodland.

[Edith Hardin English, a noted botanist and plantswoman from Seattle, Washington, mentioned two species and one variety of dodecatheon in her article "Western Water Dabblers," which appeared in volume 6 (1948):]

The primrose family offers us several water-loving plants in the genus *Dodecatheon*. It is pleasing to see *D. dentatum*, a dainty, fairylike little shooting star, growing along a mountain brook, its ethereal blossoms reflected in the quiet pools. As the name suggests, its leaves are noticeably toothed, and its flowers are pure white—normally, rather than by the albinism that is common in this genus. In cultivation, *D. dentatum* thrives and produces an abundance of flowers if given shade and plenty of moisture.

Should we desire color, it may be found in the robust, violet-rose blossoms of *Dodecatheon jeffreyi*. A number of strains of this species occur within our region; however, for use along a rock garden stream, it is wisest to select those with short, stout stems.

Such true water-loving plants should not be confused with the arid-land species of dodecatheon that we find on the prairies and on the hills of eastern Washington. These are suitable for drier parts of the rock garden, but they would not display any degree of contentment if planted with their feet in water.

[Ray Williams of Watsonville, California, whose articles on dryland gardening appeared from time to time in the pages of the *Bulletin*, wrote a brief paragraph about *Dodecatheon hendersonii*, which appeared in volume 17 (1959):]

Dodecatheon hendersonii is one of our most attractive spring flowers and is quite common in the Gabilans and the Santa Cruz Mountains of California. It grows best in light chalky soil, often with solid rock only a few inches underneath. From the flat rosette of grayish-green leaves the flower stems, sometimes 10 inches/25 cm tall, rise to bear three to six (sometimes more) shooting stars in a range of colors from white to purple, always with the black stamen circle which gives them their other common name, "mosquito bills." It is not happy with summer moisture.

[A brief note in volume 16 (1958) by an anonymous author warns the reader:]

Dodecatheons germinate easily from early spring sowings, but in a few weeks the leaves usually turn yellow and disappear. Do not throw out the seed pots, for the plants are behaving normally and will show new growth very early the next spring.

Bibliography

Hitchcock, C. Leo, Arthur Cronquist, Marion Ownbey, and J. W. Thompson. 1955–1969. *Vascular Plants of the Pacific Northwest*. 5 vols. Seattle: University of Washington Press.

Ingram, John. 1963. "Notes on the Cultivated Primulaceae, 2: *Dodecatheon*." *Baileya* 11, 69–90.

Munz, Philip A., and David D. Keck. 1959. *A California Flora*. Berkeley: University of California Press.

Thompson, H. J. 1953. "The Biosystemics of *Dodecatheon*." *Contributions from the Dudley Herbarium of Stanford University* 4, 73–154.

Originally published in the Bulletin of the American Rock Garden Society, *vol. 42, no. 2, pp. 53–62 (1984).*

Drabas for an Alpine Spring

JEANIE VESALL

While many native Minnesotans revel in the length and severity of our winters, we gardeners stoically suffer, contenting ourselves with seed lists and study weekends. An unseasonal February thaw finds many of us roaming the edges of our snowy gardens attempting to alleviate a raging case of "cabin fever." For Minnesota gardeners, spring's arrival will always be a miracle.

My husband David and I first shared our interest in alpine wildflowers on our honeymoon, backpacking in Glacier National Park. Exquisite flowers were everywhere on the heels of the retreating snow. No Minnesota spring was ever like this. Years later, we learned that a few gardeners had tamed some of these plants, and we made our decision: we would be rock gardeners.

We planted our first rock garden with the colorful, predictable phloxes and dianthus, but touring the gardens of local experts, we were fascinated by the tightly fitted limestone crevice beds crowded with miniature cushions. Plants such as lewisias, saxifrages, and drabas were new to us, and they were the ones we wanted to grow.

Pleasing alpines among the boulders of our garden proved a challenge. The scale was wrong and the soil too fat. In our early enthusiasm, we carefully collected plant souvenirs from the mountains, only to have them succumb immediately. One did survive, though—a small, white-flowered draba from the Big Horn Mountains. We decided to try more species of this genus. Now in late March or early April the tiny, crowded buds on the draba cushions bring the first hint of spring. As the bright yellow and white blooms open, bees from our hive visit often.

In the wild, drabas are an evolutionarily successful genus of more than 250 species, mostly found in the mountains and boreal regions of the Northern Hemisphere. Particularly well represented in western North America, Europe, and Turkey, drabas favor rocky and gravelly areas without a lot of competition from other plants. While some gardeners, such as Will Ingwersen, may dismiss many drabas as of "only botanical interest," we enjoy the subtle differences in foliage and flower. Unlike so many rock plants, the genus has a purity unadulterated by the meddling of horticulturists; even natural hybrids are uncommon.

These small, brilliantly flowered buns are easy to grow and are able to survive a wide variety of conditions, making them a good choice for a beginning rock gardener. Unlike some other high-alpine plants, many drabas display the same beautiful form and flower in the garden as they do in their natural habitat. The best place to showcase these tiny plants is a trough, raised bed, or rocky crevice. Most draba species develop a deep taproot and appreciate the protected root run of a crevice. The cushions are supported by the surrounding rock and thick gravel mulch and quickly assume tight alpine habits.

For the same reason, some drabas do well in our tufa bed. Our raised bed constructed of close-fitting Mississippi River limestone is equally successful. This bed is built up over a mound of limestone gravels of several sizes, coarse sand, peat moss, and assorted rocks. As the tiny plants are positioned in the crevices, we remove some of the basic soil mixture and refill around the plant with an unmeasured concoction—mostly limestone and granitic grit—and much smaller proportions of our sugar-fine acid sand, oak leafmold, and a dash of bonemeal. The bonemeal, which we used most consistently last year, seemed to improve flowering provided it was at the very bottom of the planting hole, out of reach of our resident raccoons. The raised bed faces south but receives some midday shade.

We water the raised bed thoroughly once a week and more often if the weather is hot and windy. During the hottest part of the summer, we mist the garden in the morning in addition to regular watering. Sharp drainage assures the plants a longer, healthier life, and the cushions assume a characteristic mounded form. In our large, boulder-strewn scree bed, planting in pockets of soil with a good dose of grit in the individually prepared holes also encourages condensed growth.

Most of the drabas remain disease-free with any of these growing conditions. Weekly fungicide spraying during the heat and humidity of our midwestern summer keeps the tightest, fuzziest plants healthy. As in the wild, drabas like their own space in the garden; we have had some losses when the foliage of other plants touched the cushions. Ants tunneling below the cushions need to be dealt with quickly.

The genus is highly variable in the wild, and species overlap and intergrade. Thus gardeners should try the same species from several different sources and select the seedlings with the best characteristics.

Drabas are not difficult from seed. Germination, even of older seed, is rapid, with no cold treatment needed. David starts the seeds in our basement under lights. He transplants them when very tiny to a gritty mix. Because I have an abundance of seedlings, I can plant drabas throughout the crevice bed, giving it the look of an alpine bunnery. Garden-grown drabas occasionally set much seed, and collecting it is good insurance against the loss of the shorter-lived species. Self-sown seedlings occur, too. Even sowing seed directly into a crevice or piece of tufa will often produce plants.

Cuttings are also an effective method of propagation. I have rooted cuttings taken in late summer in clay pots filled with coarse sand and protected with a plastic cup in the coldframe. In midsummer last year, I succeeded by placing the whole pot of cuttings in a sealed, zip-lock bag under the basement lights, a much cooler place than outdoors.

Catalog and seedlist writers, having exhausted all the possible variations of yellow, fuzzy cushions, leave the beginner confused as to which drabas to choose. Taxonomy does not make the choice any easier; the tiny size of the plants and the numerous similarities between species can lead to questionable identification, or none at all. Thus one of our favorites from the Wallowas, a choice cushion of woolly-gray rosettes, is still known to us simply as *Draba* sp. By trying many species we have, however, discovered that there are drabas for every gardener. Some are easy and good-looking, others difficult to grow and extremely choice.

Though perhaps not the best of the North American drabas, *Draba incerta* is easy and one of our favorites. Our plants came from seed gathered during a memorable trek to Mount Townsend on the Olympic Peninsula with Phil Pearson, Steve Doonan, and Ned and Betty Lowry. The gray-green cushions are looser and more open than some, but the large, light yellow flowers are produced in abundance. *Draba paysonii* var. *treleasei* (Plate 53), from the same trip, after two summers in the crevice bed, is a minute fuzzball of 12 rosettes. Tom Vanderpoel, another aficionado of the genus, rates it the finest North American draba. He saw it in perfection on Clay Butte in the Beartooth Mountains of Wyoming, the ancient 4-inch/10-cm cushion covered with huge, fragrant yellow flowers. Why is it that the gem of any alpine genus is so rarely vigorous?

Draba oligosperma occurs throughout the West, from the Cascades to the Sierra Nevada and the Rockies. It is common but extremely variable in form. Often likened to *D. incerta*, the best specimens of *D. oligosperma* have smaller, more rigid leaves gathered into ball-like clusters. This draba expands into a firm mat given lean soil and sun. The flowers are typically a rich, brassy yellow, but some sources mention white-flowered forms. Definitely easier than *D. paysonii*, and needing no microscope to be admired, this is a premier North American draba.

Draba ventosa occurs at high altitudes in the Rockies and a few locations farther west. It is supposed to have large yellow flowers peeking out from a cluster of rounded leaves cloaked in silver down. A plant we purchased under that name last year has green, bristle-covered, pointed leaves, leaving us to wonder about its authenticity.

Cavorting with *Kelseya uniflora* on the limestone cliffs of Idaho, *Draba oreibata* is a promising white-flowered species that has recently shown up on seed lists. Another little white draba from the Big Horns, which piqued our interest from the first time we saw it, remains our special pet despite our continuing failure to identify it. Last year this draba set enough seed to share a few with the experts.

A common plant of the West, *Draba densifolia* is one of a large group of drabas whose leaves are edged, rather than covered, with stiff hairs or bristles. This feature allows the green of the foliage to show through and contrast pleasingly with the color of the flowers. The narrow, lanceolate foliage is a bright grass-green and is whorled into dense rosettes. Planted in a crevice, this draba slowly forms a rounded, prickly bun. (This species name has often been given erroneously as *D. densiflora*, an invalid misspelling.)

Drabas will reward any gardener with their bright flowers and superb foliage cushions, and will give beginning rock gardeners a chance of success with high alpine plants. Happily at home in our gardens, they will always remind us of springtime in the mountains.

Originally published in the Bulletin of the American Rock Garden Society, *vol. 48, no. 2, pp. 84–88 (1990). A section of the article dealing with Old World drabas has been omitted here.*

Dryas in the Wild

MITCH BLANTON

The value of dryas in the garden is widely recognized. Their attributes include a pleasing growth form, intricately patterned leaves, lovely rosaceous bloom, persistent feathery styles in fruit, and an unusually long life. What is not so generally realized is that dryas is an extremely important, constructive member of many alpine and arctic ecosystems.

The geographic distribution of the genus *Dryas* is immense. It is found at the northernmost reaches of land throughout the arctic region, in most mountain ranges of the Northern Hemisphere, and even in open boreal woodlands. The most important species are *D. octopetala, D. integrifolia,* and *D. drummondii.* As many as 20 distinct forms have been identified, but their exact taxonomic placement is uncertain. For example, Porsild (1947) thinks that there are eight or nine intersterile species in North America, whereas Hultén (1968) and Hitchcock et al. (1961) contend that at least several of these are interfertile races of a single species, *D. octopetala.*

Numerous field studies have revealed a number of interesting ecological roles played by dryas. In Alaska it has been found to be an important pioneer in recolonizing land at sites of recent deglaciation. Where glacial retreat has exposed denuded, nitrogen-poor soils of sand, gravel, and glacial till, the first plants to appear are legumes and dryas, the seeds of which are adapted to wind dispersal. Remarkably, it was found that roots of dryas form nodules containing organisms capable of nitrogen fixation, and that these organisms are similar to those found in other non-leguminous nitrogen-fixers such as *Alnus* and *Myrica.* The presence of the pioneers is brief. In the course of about 100 years they reach a zenith, decline, and are suppressed by plant successors that benefit from the soil nitrogen and humus provided by the pioneers.

These findings are especially significant for those who seek to determine the sequence of events that might have occurred in the establishment of a flora following the retreat of the continental ice sheets some 10,000 years ago. Dryas leaves are conspicuous in fossil formations from those times; this, together with its present-day geographical distribution and ecological role, indicates that dryas probably played a similar pioneering role in the vegetative reinvasion of the area covered by the Pleistocene ice.

The constructiveness of dryas is also evident in alpine plant communities of Europe and North America, where it may occur in a successional regime, as a sort of climax community, or in a cyclical situation. In the first instance, where calcareous material is found, a unique type of succession may occur. Lime-tolerant pioneers, particularly dryas, create and trap humus, which provides an ideal seedbed for grasses. The grasses form thick tufts, which in turn eventually suppress the pioneers. Succession continues, and the accumulation of organic matter lowers the pH until eventually, acidophilous species come to dominate. In the second instance, on ridges and in fellfields where wind velocities are extreme, dryas may be part of what might be considered a climax community. Third, in areas where frost-heaving and solifluction create an unstable soil condition, dryas stands may form islands of refuge for other plant species. The combined forces of needle ice and soil creep kill the vegetation at the edges of these dryas colonies, but within the mats a stable microsite is created in which other species can survive. The repeatedly bared soil is available for recolonization, so that a stable stand of vegetation is never attained, yet the plant community present at any one time does not appear to vary in appearance or abundance.

Finally, the habitats occupied by dryas in alpine regions are replicated to a great extent in the high arctic. There dryas (especially *Dryas integrifolia*) is a dominant member of polar semideserts, fellfields, and gravelly river flats and fans; it also occurs, though to a much lesser extent, in dwarf shrub/heath and lichen/moss/heath communities. The ubiquity of this genus in the rock desert landscape of boreal ecosystems has led to these areas being named "dryas barrens." It is clear, when all the available information is considered, that dryas was and is instrumental in the establishment and maintenance of the tundra as we know it today.

Bibliography

Bambert, S., and J. Major. 1968. "Ecology of the Vegetation and Soils Associated with Calcareous Parent Materials in Three Alpine Regions of Montana." *Ecological Monographs* 38, 127–167.

Bliss, L. C., ed. 1977. *Truelove Lowland, Devon Island, Canada.* Calgary: University of Alberta Press.

Braun-Blanquet, J. 1932. *Plant Sociology.* New York: McGraw-Hill.

Hitchcock, C. Leo, Arthur Cronquist, Marion Ownbey, and J. W. Thompson.

1955–1969. *Vascular Plants of the Pacific Northwest*. 5 vols. Seattle: University of Washington Press.

Hultén, Eric. 1968. *Flora of Alaska and Neighboring Territories*. Stanford, California: Stanford University Press.

Lawrence, D. D., et al. 1967. "The Role of *Dryas drummondii* in Vegetation Development Following Ice Recession at Glacier Bay, Alaska." *Journal of Ecology* 55, 793–813.

Polunin, Nicholas. 1959. *Circumpolar Arctic Flora*. Oxford: Oxford University Press.

Porsild, A. E. 1947. "The Genus *Dryas* in North America." *Canadian Field Naturalist* 6, 175–189.

Viereck, L. A. 1966. "Plant Succession and Soil Development on Gravel Outwash of the Muldrow Glacier, Alaska." *Ecological Monographs* 36, 181–199.

Originally published in the Bulletin of the American Rock Garden Society, *vol. 41, no. 3, pp. 158–160 (1983).*

Rock Garden Phloxes

EDGAR T. WHERRY

"Incomparably the most important that America has yet evolved for the benefit of the rock garden," was Reginald Farrer's characterization of the genus *Phlox*. He was not satisfied, however, with the relatively few sorts he had been able to obtain: "That we should sit contented with even 'Vivid' and 'G. F. Wilson' among the phloxes makes one ashamed, as one goes through the long list of exquisite and longed-for alpines that are still vainly offering themselves to us on the desert mountains of America." When he tried to ascertain what species there were, he had at hand only August Brand's 1907 monograph. This German author never visited America and knew few of the species in living condition, so he misinterpreted a good many of them.

For some years I have been carrying on a technical study of the genus. There prove to be more than 60 species, and a dozen of these are of prime importance to the rock gardener. Farrer's "longed-for alpines," however, turn out to be largely mythical.

It will be noticed that *Phlox douglasii* does not appear in the present list. For some mysterious reason, whenever the identity of any western needle-leaved phlox has been in doubt, it has generally been called "*douglasii*." Study of the type material and a visit to the type region in northeastern Oregon has shown that this epithet belongs to a narrow-leaved cushion plant with abundant sticky glands, growing in dry sandy land at moderate altitudes. Dwarf phases of it bear the name *rigida*, while subspecies *hendersonii* is a compact high-alpine derivative. A relative with longer and broader leaves, endemic in western Montana, had been named *missoulensis*. This series of phloxes has apparently not proved satisfactory for the eastern rock garden. [*Phlox douglasii* is no longer recognized as a species; *P. rigida* and *P. hendersonii* now have species rank.—*Ed.*]

I also omit other species, for one or another reason. *Phlox amabilis,* the lovely Arizona desert-star phlox, can scarcely be expected to thrive in cultivation. *Phlox kelseyi,* another often-misinterpreted taxon, is a denizen of alkaline lands. *Phlox longifolia,* the most widespread western species, is a plant of sagebrush country with little horticultural promise. Bush phlox (*P. speciosa*), a shrub from Idaho and adjoining states, has stunning pink, notched flowers and has not yet been successfully cultivated far from its native home. *Phlox stansburyi,* a name that has been mistakenly applied to several different western species, is actually only a long-flowered variety of *P. longifolia* found in southern sagebrush communities.

Phlox andicola

As one travels west across the prairies in spring, the climate becomes less and less moist, and the eastern phloxes disappear from the floral landscape one by one. The most drought-resistant, *Phlox pilosa* subsp. *fulgida,* makes a brilliant show in strips of unbroken prairie left between highway and railway here and there, but it gives out around longitude 96°. For 300 miles/480 km there are no phloxes at all, but around longitude 102° the genus again becomes evident; the first species encountered is *P. andicola.* This specific epithet is a misnomer, for the plant's habitat is not in the least andean; it should be called the "plains phlox," because it grows on gentle rocky slopes and sandy flats from northwesternmost Kansas and eastern Colorado to west-central North Dakota. The needle-leaved shoots, pushing up through the sand, suggest fairy Christmas trees: the flowers are pearly white or pinkish, and selection yields desirable broad-lobed forms.

Being the easternmost of the western species, *Phlox andicola* might be expected to thrive in eastern rock gardens, and it is said to have proved satisfactory in some of them. It prefers a sandy loam with a high proportion of sand, good drainage, and full sun. In the wild, a sparse accumulation of grass litter often protects the soil surface around it. When its needs are met, the crowns will send out slender rootstocks which turn up at the tip to produce new shoots.

The phloxes known as *Phlox canescens, P. hoodii* (Plate 65), and *P. muscoides* are only subspecies, progressively diminishing in size, and are short-leaved derivatives of *P. andicola.* They, and their cunning little square-shoot relative *P. bryoides,* resist all coddling and usually die out rapidly in the eastern lowland rock garden. [In his later work, Wherry recognized *P. hoodii* as a species, and reduced *P. canescens* and *P. muscoides* to subspecies of *P. hoodii. Phlox bryoides* is now included in *P. hoodii* subsp. *muscoides.—Ed.*]

Phlox alyssifolia

Although it is best developed on the bare, rocky slopes of buttes and hills in the high plains country from northwestern Nebraska and adjacent Wyoming to southern Saskatchewan and western Montana, the alyssum-leaf phlox ascends to considerable altitudes in the Black Hills of South Dakota. An especially good form abounds on a small hill rising near the railroad station at Lusk, Wyoming. One clone from this locality has been assigned the epithet 'Sevorsa', but most of the clumps are typical of the species. It is a low-growing plant with thick, white-margined, hairy oblong leaves. It varies from place to place; one can readily select from its colonies individuals with flowers of good size and petal-form, and glowing pink hues. A large and striking variant has been designated subspecies _abdita_. The nearest relative of _Phlox alyssifolia_ among widespread species is _P. caespitosa_ (Plate 103), which has smaller and thinner leaves; the epithet _kelseyi_, sometimes applied to it, belongs to a quite different plant.

In eastern lowland rock gardens _Phlox alyssifolia_ is reported to be not at all easy. Coming from regions of sparse rainfall and low humidity, it seems to resent the greater amount of moisture to which it is subjected here. It may be expected to grow, if at all, in a sandy loam mixed with plenty of limestone chips, on a sunny, well-drained slope where snow does not accumulate deeply. In its native haunts the soil is sometimes thinly covered with pine needles and other litter, so a mulch of such materials may benefit it.

Ira Gabrielson mentions the related _Phlox albomarginata_ and a plant I consider a subspecies of it, _P. albomarginata_ subsp. _diapensoides_. These are diminutive alpine derivatives of _P. alyssifolia_ endemic in a limited area in western Montana and adjacent Idaho, and they are no doubt even more difficult to grow in humid lowland regions.

Phlox adsurgens

This remarkable species is a native of the coastal mountains and western slopes of the Sierra Nevada and Cascade Mountains in California and Oregon between latitudes 39° and 45°. Its only close relative is the Appalachian _Phlox stolonifera_, native nearly 2500 miles/4000 km away. Before the last glacial period their mutual ancestor evidently grew in what is now north-central Canada. This phlox is not, as sometimes supposed, an alpine, but grows at moderate elevations on wooded slopes, under coniferous trees. It seems to bloom best when peeping out from beneath a thicket, receiving sunlight part of the day. The stems, creeping over the leaf-litter, are set with lustrous, ovate, subevergreen leaves; in spring they send up flowering shoots a few inches tall, bearing large flowers. Some variants have perhaps the most entrancing coloring in the genus: the corolla lobes are deep salmon-pink at the tip, grading to pinkish-white at the base, with an intense rose stripe down the paler portion, as in some lewisias.

In his book *Western American Alpines*, Ira Gabrielson remarked, "This phlox is a most delectable thing, and so comparatively easy to grow that it will doubtless be in general cultivation within a few years." Alas, in the eastern American lowlands, this prediction has not worked out. The plant fails to thrive, blooms sparsely if at all, and soon dies. In a garden where the soil is kept cool all summer by trickling spring water, it did well for a time, but it was nearly smothered by accumulations of soggy oak leaves. It will be worth trying elsewhere, in acid humus-rich soil, sheltered from midday and early afternoon sun, and on such a steep slope that most tree leaves blow away. Perhaps someday a strain adaptable to general rock garden cultivation may be developed.

Phlox bifida

The sand phlox is a midland species, ranging from central Tennessee to eastern Kansas, north to southern Michigan and eastern Iowa. While especially frequent on sand hills—notably in Sand Dunes Park in northern Indiana—it also grows on rocky slopes and cliffs of both sandstone and limestone. Its sprawling stems, clothed with narrow leaves up to 2.5 inches/6 cm long, form attractive open tufts and festoons, starred in spring with lovely flowers. The petals are often so deeply notched that there seem to be ten rather than five of them; their hue varies from white to delicate lavender or, less commonly, lilac. During winter the clumps may look nearly dead, but new growth appears in early spring and soon develops the lax flower clusters. As no two plants are ever exactly alike, a group of seedlings will present an interesting study in variation. *Phlox bifida* is distantly related to the eastern *P. subulata* and to a Rocky Mountain rarity, *P. multiflora* subsp. *patula* (Plate 102); their corolla lobes are less deeply notched.

In rock gardens this phlox is not as widely used as it deserves to be. It is not especially difficult, asking only a well-drained soil and full sun; it will even form its festoons on a wall garden. Certain of its variants and relatives are noteworthy. The form once called *Phlox stellaria*, properly *P. bifida* subsp. *stellaria*, differs in the pubescence being sparser and the notches in the corolla lobes shallower. A rare relative from northern Oklahoma has been named *P. oklahomensis*; its flowers are more deeply colored, and it deserves rock garden trial. Farrer's favorite, 'G. F. Wilson', appears to be a hybrid between *P. bifida* and *P. subulata*. The hybrid between *P. bifida* and *P. nivalis*, which appeared spontaneously in the garden of Mrs. J. Norman Henry near Gladwyne, Pennsylvania, has large flowers of bright pink; it circulated under the (invalid) name *P. henryae*.

Phlox diffusa

Perhaps the phlox to which the epithet *douglasii* is most often mis-applied is the western mountain plant named *Phlox diffusa* by Bentham in 1849. This is the western analogue of *P. subulata* of the east: a mat-forming plant with sparsely hairy, needlelike leaves and abundant flowers. It grows over a vast territory from the Coast Range to the western Rockies, California to British Columbia, with one subspecies in South Dakota, climbing from forested foothills to alpine heights, and thus it is decidedly variable. Its stems always tend to sprawl, and its hairs are always pointed; however, there is no gradation toward a tufted, glandular-haired form. The flowers vary in details of lobe outline and hue—from pure white to clear pink and deep lavender—and often hide the foliage. The Black Hills representative, known as subspecies *scleranthifolia*, tends to form festoons and has especially delicate leaves and flowers. In drier, low-altitude valleys the herbage may become more hairy, grading into *P. hoodii* subsp. *canescens*.

One of the few western phloxes which grow reasonably well in eastern rock gardens, this species, as Gabrielson remarked, "will undoubtedly be the first of the [western] needle-leaved phloxes to become generally cultivated." For low-level gardens, stock should be obtained from other than alpine occurrences, and even then it had best be planted where its soil will not be strongly heated by the summer sun. In the wild it grows most abundantly in gravel derived from siliceous igneous rocks and sandstone, although locally it may enter limestone barrens.

In the more arid regions this phlox grades through its subspecies *subcarinata* into *Phlox austromontana*, which has stiffer and sharper leaves, and often larger flowers. Whether this denizen of the desert hills can ever be successfully cultivated in humid climates remains to be seen.

Phlox divaricata

Although it is often called "blue phlox", the corollas of this species are never really blue, normally ranging from lavender to lilac. The name I prefer, "woodland phlox," refers to the fact that it thrives best in mature woods. It grows from longitude 96° to the Appalachians, and locally down stream valleys to the eastern seaboard. It was one of the earlier members of the genus to be introduced into European horticulture, having been sent by John Bartram to Peter Collinson about 1739. The latter referred to it as "a very pretty lychnis, with pale blue flowers and sweet smell." In the original Linnaean type specimen, the corolla lobes were deeply notched; this is the form that has been called variety *canadensis*, but it is no longer so distinguished. Plants native to the Mississippi Valley have mostly notchless lobes and have been designated variety

409

laphamii. Both these varieties (or subspecies) spread by stolons as well as by seeds, to form ravishing drifts of lavender lasting well through spring. They have various color forms, including albinos.

A shade-loving plant like this cannot be expected to thrive in the dry, sunny rock garden; its place is in an adjacent bit of woodland or among shrubbery, where it receives only dappled sunshine and the soil remains somewhat moist.

From the colonies of *Phlox divaricata* var. *laphamii* in western Florida Mrs. J. Norman Henry has selected a striking color form in which the lobes are deep lavender and the eye intense red-purple; this has been named 'Chattahoochee', after the river valley where it is native. In spite of its southern origin, it seems entirely hardy at least as far north as latitude 41°.

A hybrid of *Phlox divaricata* with *P. paniculata*, known as *P. × arendsii*, has large pink flowers; blooming for a long period in summer, it deserves a place in the rock garden.

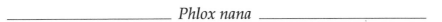

Phlox nana

In 1848 Nuttall applied this epithet to a phlox collected by his friend Dr. Gambel at Santa Fe, New Mexico. It still flourishes there, its large purple-pink flowers beautifying the rocky slopes and open pine woods; it is now known to extend southward through that state and western Texas some distance into Mexico. Species characters include a terminally constricted corolla tube and a very short style. Many variants have been named in subsequent years, and the nomenclatorial tangle is rather complex. Suffice it to state that the original representative of the species has short leaves well covered with sticky glands. In 1905 Greene proposed for a long-leaved, less viscid variant the epithet *mesoleuca*; in 1907 the German monographer Brand named much the same plant subspecies *ensifolia*. As the leaf difference is too trivial to justify species separation, Brand's classification is the only acceptable one. [Subspecies *ensifolia* is no longer a recognized taxon. *Phlox mesoleuca* is a recognized species.—*Ed.*] A glandless extreme, once known as subspecies *glabella*, now has specific rank as *P. triovulata*.

Because it grows in dry conditions, the Santa Fe phlox would not have been expected to thrive in moist-climate rock gardens. However, several years ago some collector sent to England, allegedly from western Texas, a clump of *Phlox nana* under the misspelled name "mesaleuca"; this not only grew, it prospered so well that it received awards of merit and other commendations. Perhaps the clone suited to English conditions would not thrive in eastern North America, but there may be others that would. If any of our members have occasion to visit Santa Fe or the mountains to the south or southwest—including the Davis Mountains of Texas—it is to be hoped that they will bring back some roots and experiment. The species is so showy and blooms over such a long period—in spring and often again in summer and fall—that it deserves repeated trial.

Phlox nivalis

There has been so much confusion as to the relationships of this phlox that a discussion of its history is in order. It was one of the species sent to England in early colonial times and was figured by Plukenet in 1691. Linnaeus intended to name it *Phlox subulata*, but he cited in connection with that epithet a specimen subsequently collected by Kalm in New Jersey, where *P. nivalis* does not grow. It was first brought permanently into horticulture in 1788, when it was collected by John Fraser in South Carolina. When publishing a color plate of one of the Fraser plants—a fine upstanding pink-flowered form—in 1798, Curtis mistakenly called it *P. setacea*. In the early 1820s, a Dr. Wray sent a white-flowered variant from Augusta, Georgia, to the firm of C. Loddiges in England, and they issued a color plate of it under the name *P. nivalis* ("snowy") in 1823. Under the rules of nomenclature this publication was insufficient, but the epithet was validated by Sweet in 1827. Since pink and purple represent mere color forms, the name has to cover them also.

Asa Gray refused to distinguish *Phlox nivalis* from *P. subulata* and thereby led Charles Darwin to become so confused as to their pollen relations as to exclaim that these phloxes are "perplexing in the highest degree." They are actually similar only in foliage.

Some horticulturists use the epithet "nivalis" for white color forms of *Phlox subulata*, but the crowning case of confusion has been the reintroduction of the form of *P. nivalis* figured by Curtis in 1798 as *"Phlox camla,"* purported to be a hybrid between scarcely related species. [This form is still in commerce as *P. nivalis* 'Camla'.—*Ed.*]

Besides the originally named white form, there are many lovely colors. In comparison with *Phlox subulata*, *P. nivalis* is less compact, and its coloring is on the whole more brilliant, with less tendency toward magenta.

Phlox latifolia and Its Relatives

The first reference to this phlox was made by Plukenet in 1700; the species epithet *ovata* was assigned to it by Linnaeus. Confused by the fact that the early plant had produced but a solitary flower, Michaux renamed it *Phlox latifolia* 50 years later. [The name *P. latifolia* has been reassumed under the latest revision as of this publication.—*Ed.*] It has frequently been confused with *P. carolina*, named by Linnaeus in 1762, but the two are really quite distinct. The name "mountain phlox" has been applied to the present species because of its abundant occurrence in the Appalachian Mountains from northern Georgia to east-central Pennsylvania. The forms most frequently met have flowers of a rather dingy magenta hue, but locally there are attractive purple and pink variants.

In May 1929, I was driving through the hills of Walker County, Alabama, on the lookout for interesting native plants, when I discovered near the village of Oakman a spectacular relative of *Phlox latifolia*. This bears abundant large, soft pink flowers and was duly named *P. ovata* var. *pulchra* ("beautiful"), later raised to specific rank as *P. pulchra*; it has thrived in a few rock gardens.

Phlox carolina, another Linnaean species, is distinctly different from *P. latifolia*, and their epithets should never be combined, as has sometimes been done in horticultural literature. This species differs in having longer sterile shoots, more numerous stem nodes, and small flower parts. It is exceedingly variable from one locality to another, and the nomenclature of its variants is rather confused. In an article in *Bartonia* I have endeavored to straighten this out, recognizing several more or less distinct subspecies. Mrs. J. Norman Henry discovered a stunning form near Warm Springs, Georgia. This makes a conspicuous evergreen rosette, from which arise, all through summer and autumn, shoots bearing huge inflorescences, with flowers of a most striking clear bright pink. It is to be known as *P. carolina* 'Gloriosa'.

Phlox pilosa and Its Relatives

Besides two mossy phloxes, Plukenet's 1691 plate included a drawing of the species subsequently named by Linnaeus *Phlox pilosa*. The original representative of the species had narrow leaves and rather small white flowers; subsequently, pink and purple forms were introduced, but their horticultural value is slight. An especially vigorous race from northeastern Illinois, with silvery lavender flowers, was invalidly dubbed *P. argillacea*, and when cultivated in England under that name it received awards of merit; in the eastern United States it seems to grow only indifferently. The prairie representative of the species, known as variety *fulgida*, produces brilliant splashes of color in what remains of that formerly vast grassland, but it fails to thrive in cultivation. There is, however, a form of more southern range with considerable horticultural promise. This has relatively broad leaves and showy flowers of excellent pink to white hues; abounding in the Ozarks, it has been called *P. pilosa* subsp. *ozarkana*.

The related *Phlox floridana* differs from *P. pilosa* in the way the glabrous oblong leaves gradually shorten at many nodes up the stem.

Its more frequent forms have raucous purple flowers, and moreover these have failed to prove amenable to cultivation. However, Mrs. Henry has found near the Gulf of Mexico a variant remarkable in several respects, which was named variety *bella*, although this is not now an accepted taxon. This form remains dwarf, has fine glossy foliage, and produces good clusters of soft pink flowers nearly throughout the growing season. Fortunately, too, when planted in dryish sandy soil and protected from bleak northwest winds, it has proved winter-hardy as far north as latitude 41°.

Another related species, *Phlox amoena*, has several attractive color forms. The "*P. amoena*" of the trade is, however, an utterly different hybrid.

Originally published in the Bulletin of the American Rock Garden Society, *vol. 4, no. 2, pp. 17–27 (1946).*

Fabulous Phloxes

PANAYOTI KELAIDIS

Late April and May are synonymous with phloxes in the rock gar-den. These are often hybrids of *Phlox subulata*, the commonest mat-form-ing species growing wild along the eastern seaboard. Discriminating rock gardeners have sought cultivars with more vivid flower color or special qualities of form and habit, but it is surprising how few of these are available from more than a handful of specialist nurseries; even ex-tensive rock garden collections sometimes lack the better forms. If we were to judge from most rock gardens in America, we would conclude that the numerous species and endless variations of creeping phloxes found west of the Mississippi were largely figments of the late Dr. Wherry's imagination.

Eastern Creeping Phloxes

The first phloxes to be introduced to cultivation were naturally the species that grew wild where North America was first settled. Reginald Farrer wrote, "The day that saw the introduction, more than a century since, of *Phlox subulata*, ought indeed to be kept as a horticultural festi-val." Most garden centers sell these like peonies and irises, by color. The cultivars seen there are usually the Emerald series—'Emerald Pink', 'Emerald Blue', and so on—mediocre selections of this highly variable plant. Anyone who has seen the dazzling cultivars available from rare-plant nurseries (or even ordinary garden centers, in Europe) will have nothing to do with these emerald mediocrities. A few of the better culti-vars include the following.

Phlox subulata 'Scarlet Flame,' fast-spreading and large, has flowers of a vivid, deep rosy red that is the closest thing to scarlet seen in a creeper until the Mexican phloxes came on the scene. 'Red Admiral' and 'Crackerjack' are both miniature red-pinks with rather small flowers that smother the cushions. The plants rarely exceed 1 foot/30 cm in width after several years. 'Crackerjack' is slightly more vivid as they grow in Colorado—one of the brightest of miniature phloxes.

'Ellie B.' is usually listed as a *Phlox subulata* cultivar; it has the shallowly cleft flowers characteristic of *P. subulata* subsp. *brittonii*. It is a miniature white. There may be some confusion in the trade between this tiny plant and the somewhat larger 'Sneewichen', which has slightly coarser, lighter-colored leaves.

'Ronsdorf Beauty', a cultivar selected in Europe, forms compact cushions studded with rosy pink flowers with dark purple eyes, quite a dramatic departure. The petals are rounded and give the flower a pleasingly softened form.

'Laura' has delicate, pale pink flowers of a luminous shade with no eye markings whatsoever. 'Coral Eye' is utterly distinct with near-white petals set off by a deep pink eye.

There are three other wild creeping phloxes that occur east of the Mississippi. *Phlox subulata* subsp. *brittonii* has tiny needlelike leaves that form wide cushions resembling the common creeping phlox, but its flowers have slightly cleft petals. It is mostly commonly cultivated in a form called 'Rosea', often listed as a botanical variety. The cleft petals are taken to great lengths in the midwestern *P. bifida*, so that its flowers may appear to have ten narrow petals rather than five wide ones. The foliage of this phlox is much longer than in any other creeping phlox, and the plants do not root as they creep but arise from a central tuft. In nature *P. bifida* is usually found on very sandy soils, and it can become a pest by self-sowing on the scree in the rock garden. It produces seedlings abundantly on the fellfield section of the Denver Botanic Gardens, varying from pale platinum-blue shades to quite dark stars. The darkest purple-lavender form I have ever seen was growing among countless hundreds in the rock garden of Betty Blake in southern Michigan: it has flowers a trifle smaller than other forms, and the plant stays rather compact as well. It was distinct in enough characters that I believe it deserved to be recognized with a cultivar name, and it is now sold as 'Betty Blake'. Mina Colvin, a well-known plantswoman from Indiana, first introduced the tiny-flowered cultivar 'Starbrite' with its clouds of tricolored flowers. She is commemorated in 'Colvin's White', the best-known albino *P. bifida* currently in the trade.

There are two showy hybrids with vivid lavender-blue flowers that suggest some *Phlox bifida* ancestry. 'Millstream Jupiter' occurred at the Fosters' famous Connecticut garden; it has strong lavender flowers with dark markings near the eyes, and only shallow toothing. It roots slightly along the stems and has shorter leaves than ordinary *P. bifida*. 'Boothman's Variety' was presumably named for Stuart Boothman, a famous English nurseryman active earlier in the twentieth century. It has good blue flowers with very dark eyes that make quite an impression. It has the rapidly spreading, deep green leafy stems typical of *P. subulata*. This is occasionally offered as a form of *P. douglasii*, surely an example of British humor. The real Douglas phlox, now known as *P. caespitosa* (Plate 103), is restricted to the mountains of the Pacific Northwest and bears little resemblance to this or virtually any other plants bearing its name in European nurseries.

The last commonly grown eastern creeping phlox is *Phlox nivalis*. This grows wild farther south than other creeping phloxes. Most of the year it looks rather similar to the common subulata-type creepers, but at flowering time it produces a stem 3 to 4 inches/8 to 10 cm tall (rather like *P. stolonifera*) with a handsome cluster of flowers that are usually over 1 inch/2.5 cm in diameter. For years, the only form of this phlox in cultivation was a British selection called 'Camla', but practically anything under the name *P. nivalis* is sure to produce showy bright pink flowers. This is the only eastern phlox I find a trifle tender in Denver. Many shoots show tip damage every winter and look unsightly until bloom time, when new growth usually covers up the browned-off leaves. It would be well worth selecting plants of this phlox for greater sun and cold tolerance.

Western Creeping Phloxes

European gardeners are mystified and often annoyed that so few species of western phloxes are grown in their gardens. When they finally come to America and see that much of the western landscape is made up of a vast, continuous mat of tiny cushion phloxes, they are dumbfounded. How could plants so common in nature be virtually absent from gardens? I wonder too.

Of course, many western microphloxes are dryland plants that may not grow well in wet climates. This should certainly not be a problem in gardens throughout the continental parts of the United States, yet one rarely finds native phloxes here either. Our native creeping phloxes sometimes occur by the million; most of Wyoming, Utah, Nevada, and Idaho are actually held together with an uninterrupted mat of *Phlox hoodii* (Plate 65). This species would be an ideal subject for gardeners to seek out in bloom and take short cuttings or even rooted pieces of superior forms, so that it could assume its proper place in gardens as harbinger of spring. *Phlox hoodii* is the first to bloom in nature or the garden, usually peaking in March. The commonest forms are pure white, although blush-pinks and even lavenders occur in Idaho and other lucky states. The flowers are quite variable in size and shape as well, although the plant is always diminutive. It occasionally forms very tight cushions that are magnificent in troughs, but it can spread several inches a year from subterranean rhizomes.

Phlox andicola is found to the east of *P. hoodii* on sandy areas in the Great Plains. This is the one western phlox I would nominate as a potential hazard: it forms a dense tangle of underground rhizomes that can spread up to 1 foot/30 cm a year on sandy soil or scree, quickly inundating a bed. The flowers are invariably pure white stars with clearly visible yellow stamens that glow in contrast. It can be found as far south on the Great Plains as the Pawnee Buttes north of Denver, although it is much commoner in the Nebraska Panhandle northward over the Great Plains.

Phlox alyssifolia is another sand-loving phlox, with a similar range in nature, that adapts easily to the dryland garden. It has short, broad, deep-green leaves and very full, round white blossoms. When established, it too can spread widely from underground rhizomes. Both this and the previous species were first widely distributed by Claude Barr, and at least one famous Pennsylvania garden still has thriving colonies of these ramping through its sand beds.

Phlox multiflora (Plate 102) is especially common in the foothills around Denver, although this Front Range form seems to be disappointing in the garden. The plants form rather lax cushions, and the pink flowers are just too sparse. Farther west, in North and Middle Parks, this species is a dominant ground cover in the sagebrush meadows. Here it forms flat pancakes with heavily blooming mounds of white or pink that are deliciously fragrant. Has anyone tried growing these? When tamed, they will be among the showiest rock garden flowers.

Eight years ago Paul Maslin and I took cuttings of good lavender forms of *Phlox pulvinata* (Plate 104) in the Snowy Mountains of Wyoming. We returned with these to Colorado, rooted them, and grew them in the Denver Botanic Garden for several years. Placed in too hot a spot, one by one they gradually dwindled and would have been lost if Andrew Pierce had not taken a piece to his home in Evergreen. Andrew's specimen is quite famous now, and many of us have admired this giant mat that seems to cover itself with bright lavender flowers several times during the growing season—notably when Andrew's garden is open to a tour. He has shared cuttings of this plant far and wide, and we are once again growing this vigorous form of our showy and deliciously scented alpine phlox.

Phlox missoulensis is closely related, with longer, hairier leaves and icy-blue flowers for a long season in the spring. This has proven permanent and easily grown in sunny scree soils. The Missoula phlox is sometimes listed as a subspecies of *P. kelseyi*, a very widespread phlox with coarse blunt leaves that specializes in growing among grass and sedges

417

in inhospitable, alkaline cattle wallows throughout the intermountain west. Jeanne Anderson has succeeded in taming Kelsey's phlox in her Idaho Falls garden.

Phlox condensata is the commonest alpine phlox in Colorado. On Hoosier Pass this can form rock-hard cushions with dark-eyed white blossoms. Who will finally grow this majestic native alpine—or introduce the dark rose-pink forms of *P. austromontana* and *P. jonesii* common in parts of southern Utah and northern Arizona? There are a dozen or so desirable species, and countless variations.

Let us dream that one day soon we may find named forms of this or that western phlox in local garden centers alongside the brightest and best easterners. Our western natives possess two sterling qualities to recommend them: most are quite drought- and heat-tolerant, and most will put up with any native soil you might have in your garden. Moreover, all the western native phloxes seem to have a rich, heady fragrance somewhere between jasmine and heaven.

Originally published in the Bulletin of the American Rock Garden Society, *vol. 47, no. 1, pp. 13–16 (1989).*

A Garden of Catchflies

ARTHUR R. KRUCKEBERG

A vast and unwieldy genus is *Silene*, liberally stocked with worthless perennials of lank habit and minuscule flowers, not to mention multitudes of drab annuals. But here and there in this botanical wasteland are gems that give *Silene* status in the rock garden. Thus I dare to paraphrase Reginald Farrer, and justifiably. Farrer would pontificate about this or that species until his worshipful readers were left with a dozen or so species that they might dare to use in the English rock garden.

When you go soft on a clan, as I have, it is much harder to be critical, to relegate to the compost heap the less-than-perfect plant. For the past 10 years I have been collecting silenes and their kin, such as *Lychnis*, *Melandrium*, *Petrocoptis*, and *Heliosperma*. At first I took no thought as to the garden value of my motley assemblage; I was simply trying to poke away at the problem of how the many patterns in *Silene* evolved and how the species might be related. Collections of living plants—first from North America, then from abroad—were subjected to the kinds of research uses that keep a botanist happily engaged for years. I counted chromosomes, made hybrids, and asked the hybrids whether they were fertile. The answers they gave have at times been cryptic, but by now I know something of the family relationships of most species in the United States.

This kind of cloistered study would tell a plantsperson little about what were best among the American silenes for rock gardens. Nonetheless, amassing a botanical collection of natives has been far from irrelevant to gardening. My wife, whose critical eye would permit only the most tasteful combinations of plant textures and habits in our garden, has suffered to see silenes brought home for trial, only to flunk the test of esthetic appeal.

Recently, however, I have been able to please her more often with the cast-offs from my research greenhouse. Of the western silenes, she will take all the *Silene californica*, *S. hookeri*, and *S. petersonii* I can bring home. We are particularly fond of the soft red form of *S. californica* from the Trinity River country in northern California. The low mounds of gray foliage that cushion the masses of shell-pink flowers of *S. hookeri*—especially forms from Jackson and Josephine counties in Oregon—are tantalizing. Would that we could make them last in our garden!

Our greatest gardening successes have been with the eastern United States species and some of the hybrids they have produced in response to my ministrations. Clearly the *Silene caroliniana* alliance is outstanding, and usually available in seed exchanges. Typical *S. caroliniana* is a tight-rosetted plant with long strap-shaped leaves and a glandular inflorescence, bearing many soft pale pink to white flowers. It is rather common in the sandy soils of the coastal plains and piedmont of the Carolinas and northern Georgia. It flowers like mad for us in the wet Northwest from April to June. Other named forms of *S. caroliniana* are comparable in stature and flowering habits. *Silene caroliniana* subsp. *pensylvanica* is simply a nonglandular form of the typical plant. It frequents dry sunny habitats from upper North Carolina and southern Virginia all the way to New Hampshire, and west to Tennessee. The third variation on the *S. caroliniana* theme is subspecies *wherryi*, the westernmost outlier of the group. With somewhat broader leaves and fine pink flowers, *S. caroliniana* subsp. *wherryi* presents the boldest face of the three. It has long been a favorite among rock gardeners. My deep pink-flowered plants came from Harold Epstein, and a paler pink from Mrs. J. N. Henry.

Red silenes of North America are few in number, and even fewer pass the size-texture-shape test for the rock garden. Most of them are tall, rank things that do best scrambling through dry shrubbery for support. Here we place the rampant *Silene laciniata*, at home elbowing its way up through the twigs of chaparral in cismontane southern California. But its inland counterpart, currently called subspecies *greggii*, has an entirely different ecology, preferring the rock outcrops and grassy openings in the pine forests of the southwest, from Arizona to Texas and south into the Valley of Mexico. I would have high hopes for subspecies *greggii* in the more arid rock garden; there it should hold to a conservative stature and still yield its lovely fringed and laciniated firecracker-red flowers. The specific epithet, *laciniata*, describes its petals, each one "pinked" out uniquely by divine shears.

Nature erred when she put the big red stars of *Silene regia* and *S. subciliata* on bean poles! Both are rare enough to be collectors' items and real novelties for the wild garden; but they would need support for their heavy trusses of big crimson flowers waving atop 3-foot/1-meter stems. *Silene regia* occurs in a vanishing habitat—the prairie and open woodland—from the central states of Missouri and Illinois, southeast to northern Georgia. Only one or two of the collectors I have induced to look for regal *S. regia* have found it. Glen Winterringer, botanist of the Illinois State Museum at Springfield, sent me seed, and his account of getting the seed tells a much too frequent story of vanishing Americans. He writes:

> As you know this species of *Silene* is one of the rare ones in Illinois. The plant from which these seeds came grew in Lawrenceville, Lawrence County, Illinois. It was transplanted from a roadside station about 5 miles/8 km northeast of town to a garden. When we visited the original locality of the plants there was no sign and the roadside had just been mowed.

If *Silene regia* is rare, its Gulf Coast counterpart, *S. subciliata*, has all but vanished. I owe my only collection of this tall but elegantly flowered fire pink to Caroline Dorman of Saline, Louisiana. In 1957 she assured me of a share in this treasure, accompanying her offer with these comments,

> Yes, I have grown *Silene subciliata* for years, but the rabbits have almost destroyed them. Happily, however, this past August, I rediscovered it in the same locality where I first found it, and the *only* place I have ever seen it. It is in the western edge of Louisiana. I must hurry back and get seeds before they dehisce.

A month later two plants arrived:

> I am sparing you two roots of my *Silene subciliata*, for I have not been able to get back to the collecting site. I want you to have it, for it has the most spectacular flowers of any species I have seen—the purest red. When it puts up in spring, pinch back, so you will get more flowering stems. Its only fault is it is too tall and slender.

The tall stature stays with any interspecific hybrid I have made, and as they are sterile, further selection for low stature is out.

The real fire pink is *Silene virginica*. That a westerner should attempt to eulogize the long-time favorite of eastern gardeners may be a little presumptuous. It is larger in every way than any of the *S. caroliniana* clan, but for that superb red, you must tolerate a little more herbage. It may grow to 15 inches/38 cm or slightly higher. Here in Seattle we have seen it flower in a deep loamy sand where a charred stump acts as its foil.

If redness and middling-low stature is kinship, then *Silene rotundifolia* must, as Sampson Clay avers, join *S. virginica* in a family portrait. Breeding tests contradict this notion. The hybrids between the two, made both ways, are sterile "mules." *Silene rotundifolia*, a viscid, weak-stemmed, almost trailing version of the fire pink, is nearly as elusive to the collector as are *S. regia* and *S. subciliata*. It occurs sparingly along the Appalachian plateau on rocky banks and open cliffs. My sole collection came from the Chimneys, a gorge of Pocket Creek in the Whitwell Pocket area of southern Tennessee. If one can overlook the rather loose and floppy herbage, then the large, soft red petals radiating from the fuzzy-glandular, gray-green calyx will cast their own charm.

I have a weakness for two white catchflies of eastern North America. True, they are tall and wandlike, but their masses of starry blooms are compensation enough for me. One of the two, *Silene stellata*, is the only silene I know with whorls of four leaves at a node. It is fairly common from Texas east to the Atlantic seaboard and northward to New York. *Silene ovata*, on the other hand, must be classed as one of the real "elusives." Ben Smith of Raleigh, North Carolina, followed all the leads at his disposal before he found it, and then only one plant. It is doing beautifully in our research greenhouse, has set copious seed, and its progeny are on the increase. Its white stars exsert their stamens eccentrically, so that they are massed at one edge of the corolla—just so some nocturnal insect can easily bedaub itself with pollen. The large ovate leaves of this rare southeasterner are in pairs, sparingly disposed along the long wiry stems. Both *S. stellata* and *S. ovata* are much too large for the rockery, but do not overlook their value in the wild garden or the perennial border. They would surely give demure charm to a summer's floral display.

One might ask why I have not mentioned *Silene polypetala*, once known as *S. baldwinii*. I am saving the best for last. Close to *S. caroliniana* in its prostrate habit, it surpasses them all in flower. Huge rose-pink blooms that almost mask the small spoon-shaped leaves would be distinction enough, but their showiness is grandly enhanced by the intricate fringing at the tips of the broadly wedge-shaped petals. The botanist would describe this remarkable filigree work in such terms as these: "Blade flabellate, conspicuously fimbriate, margins ciliate." The total effect in looking down on a mass of its flowers is that of a symmetrical mosaic of pink stars, each ray sculpted into an intricate lacework. I found that Fred C. Galle of the Ida Cason Gardens in Chipley, Georgia, was nearly the only living soul growing this species, and was also successfully propagating it, so I begged him for plants. He generously provided them and wrote as follows about the source:

> According to Dr. Wilbur Dundan, of the Botany Department of the University of Georgia, *Silene polypetala* had only been found in one location in the state. From his old herbarium notes, I started a search for the plant. The plants were located in Talbot County on a steep, wooded hillside overlooking the Flint River, north of the county bridge about 75 yards/meters. I only found one colony but was led to believe that the plant was fairly abundant in this area.

This species may well become another vanishing American, at least in the wild. It propagates readily by shoot cutting and by seed.

I want to turn now to some of the unusual hybrids that have been borne of my meddling into the private lives of silenes over the years. Of the thousands of crosses made (mostly of academic interest only), I can compile a list of two dozen or so that can be bragged about. Limiting myself to hybrids of eastern United States species only, I come up with the following tally shown in Table 1.

Table 1. *Silene* hybrids produced by the author.

Hybrid	Habit	Flowers
S. polypetala × *S. caroliniana*	Compact	Pale pink to white-tinged pink; fringed petals
S. polypetala × *S. caroliniana* subsp. *wherryi*	Compact	Pink; fringed
S. polypetala × *S. rotundifolia*	Spreading	Pale red; fringed
S. polypetala × *S. virginica*	Low, erect	Pale red; fringed
S. caroliniana × *S. caroliniana* subsp. *wherryi*	Compact	Pink
S. caroliniana × *S. rotundifolia*	Spreading	Pink to pale red
S. caroliniana × *S. virginica*	Low, erect	Shades of red to pink
S. caroliniana subsp. *wherryi* × *S. virginica*	Low, erect	Shades of red to pink
S. rotundifolia × *S. virginica*	Spreading	Soft, pale red

All but one group of these hybrid combinations are sterile. The sterile hybrids can be perpetuated readily by vegetative means. The fertile exception, the *Silene caroliniana* group crossed with *S. virginica*, has been produced in the past, both spontaneously and with intent. When I wrote the Rex Pearce Seed Company in New Jersey for details on the source of their *wherryi-virginica* hybrids known as "Avalon hybrids", the terse postcard reply was, "Bees!" With later selfed and backcross progeny, I have recovered in some degree various combinations of parental flower color and habit.

Objectivity compels me to admit that some of these hybrids are curiosities that do not achieve the merit of their parents. They do add variety to the array of silenes in the specialist's collection. But, not being wholly subject to modesty, I must sing the praises of the crosses of *Silene polypetala* with *S. caroliniana* and with the two red species, *S. rotundifolia* and *S. virginica*. Of the Polypetala hybrids, Caroline Dorman says,

> It is unbelievable! They are the *toughest* silenes I have ever tried. In our hot climate, all of them have a strong tendency to damp off, even *S. virginica*. I had a broken hip and was away from home three months, and September of that time was very dry. I lost only one

plant, and that was because a mole ran under and aerated it. This winter we have had snow, and freeze after freeze, but those silenes did not even flinch. I made a few cuttings when they came, and even those poorly rooted plants came through. You simply must introduce these wonderful rock garden plants to horticulture.

Later she writes,

They are the most beautiful rock garden plants I have seen. And most adaptable. Remember, you sent mine with flowers and buds, yet they lived through our hot summer with almost no care. Mine are growing among rocks, in gritty soil, but with humus too. They get morning sun—until about one o'clock. But in the north, I presume they would like full sun. I know that rock gardeners will welcome these lovely things. Last year I had blooms on *S. polypetala* × *S. caroliniana*, and they were white or delicate pink. Now there are blooms on *S. polypetala* × *S. virginica*, and they are a beautiful coral rose. Other plants are full of buds, and I can scarcely wait for them to open.

Originally published in the Bulletin of the American Rock Garden Society, *vol. 19, no. 1, pp. 1–8 (1961).*

Rock Garden Ferns

JAMES R. BAGGETT

———————————— *Asplenium trichomanes* ————————————

The genus *Asplenium* is one of nature's richest gifts to rock gardeners, containing at least a dozen desirable species. Not all of these are easy subjects in the garden; in fact, one or two might be considered nearly impossible, and others fairly difficult in many environments. Borderline winter-hardiness limits the garden possibilities of some, and others are poorly adapted to heat and other factors associated with lowland areas. However, *A. trichomanes* (Plate 105), the maidenhair spleenwort, combines beauty, grace, and small size with an easy temperament in the rock garden.

Before discussing this one species further, it may be of interest to summarize some of the general characteristics of the genus, particularly as they apply to nontropical species. The hardy aspleniums are small, varying generally from about 2 inches/5 cm to 1 foot/30 cm in height, with most of the better ones reaching only 4 to 8 inches/10 to 20 cm under garden conditions. All are evergreen or nearly so, and they are closely tufted with rhizomes described as ascending or shortly creeping, spreading gradually by multiplication of the crown or rhizome clump. The leaves vary in form from simple or pinnatifid to tripinnate with finely lobed or incised segments, but there are examples of dichotomous branching. Most are once-pinnate with the leaflets incised, lobed, or toothed to some degree. The new leaves are extended by uncoiling, or in fern terminology, they have "circinate venation." The sori are oblong, usually straight, short, and are at an angle to the midrib. There is an indusium which opens on the edge nearest the midrib.

In the usual broad classification, *Asplenium* is placed in the family

Polypodiaceae, along with all typical ferns. At the other extreme, a modern treatment, Tutin et al. (1964), placed this genus in a narrow family Aspleniaceae, along with two others of interest to rock gardeners—*Phyllitis* and *Ceterach*—and a fourth genus, *Pleurosorus*. Since that time, *Phyllitis* and *Ceterach* have been sunk in *Asplenium*. The closely related *Camptosorus* (the walking fern) would no doubt be in this family also, since it is included in *Asplenium* by some botanists. Among the aspleniums the hardy ones are very much in the minority; there are probably at least 100 tropical or subtropical species with a tremendous variety of size and form to be enjoyed in greenhouses. In older books, some large ferns such as the lady fern were included in this genus, but they have been rightfully removed.

The maidenhair spleenwort has a remarkable distribution, which should give some indication of its adaptability. Though frequently described as being widely distributed in the temperate areas of the Northern Hemisphere, it is found also in the Southern Hemisphere and on high mountains in the tropics. For example, it grows in Australia, New Zealand, and on mountains of 5000 feet/1500 meters or higher in the Hawaiian Islands. I could not obtain specific botanical references, but Britten (1879) listed its occurrence in Peru, and in Guatemala at 10,000 feet/3100 meters. In North America it is found from Nova Scotia and Alaska to as far south as Georgia, Arizona, and Mexico. It is very uniform in appearance throughout the world, although races differing in chromosome number have been recognized. In some areas it is described as being very abundant, for example, on old walls in England. It is, however, quite rare in the western states, perhaps because the summers in much of that area are typically very dry. It is always found on rocks, and usually in moist, mossy situations. Although it is often said to favor limestone, it is also found on sandstone, and in Oregon it occurs in the Cascade Mountains on basalt.

This fern is medium-sized, small enough to fit in the rockwork among small rock garden plants but large enough to be decorative. In shady, moist, rich conditions it may reach 12 inches/30 cm, but 5 to 8 inches/13 to 20 cm is a typical size range, and in exposed, dry sites it may be as small as 3 to 4 inches/8 to 10 cm. The once-pinnate leaves are narrow, curving, and graceful. The largest leaflets on a 6-inch/15-cm leaf are only 0.25 inch/6 mm long, usually with the undersides bulging with sori all the way to the top of the leaf. The rachis is smooth, shiny, dark brown, and persistent for several years after the leaflets drop. Because this fern is nicely evergreen and has a dense tuft of leaves, it may be just as well to leave it in its natural, unpruned state most of the time, with old leaves and bare, wiry leafstalks accumulating. Most ferns would be too messy to tolerate in a well-kept garden without grooming.

I grow the typical form and two horticultural varieties—one with incised leaflets, known as 'Incisum', and another with a somewhat open terminal crest, known as 'Cristatum'. Both varieties are of unknown original source, and both are fertile forms. The varieties do not seem to differ from the normal type in cultural characteristics, but both may tend to be smaller, and the incised variety is less upright. Even though the differences in leaflet form seem to be minor, the plants differ considerably in general appearance. Since 'Incisum' is fully fertile, it is obviously not one of the sterile plumose forms described by Reginald Kaye (1968) and James Britten (1879). It resembles a variety pictured as *Asplenium trichomanes incisum* Moule in Kaye's book; however, that form is said to show its leaflet character in the second year, while the variety I have can be recognized earlier. A form called 'Incisum' was found in 1899 in Tennessee, according to Jesse M. Shaver (1954), whose figure shows more irregular division of the leaflet. Kaye also described a form 'Cristatum' which also may differ from the plant I have been growing. Because the mutations which produce aberrant forms occur independently and in plants with different genetic backgrounds, it is not surprising that such differences occur.

The universal occurrence of this fern in moist, rocky habitats makes some of its basic cultural requirements apparent; however, although good drainage and adequate soil moisture are required, a vertical, shady cliff is not a necessity. Planted in a peaty, gritty mix containing some nourishment, and with irrigation as needed, it grows in various sites in the rock garden. I have them in east-facing rocks with full sun until noon, north-facing rocks with some full sun in the afternoon, in full shade in a planter near a building, and between low stones used to separate paths from raised beds. The amount of sun tolerated would obviously depend on the severity of the summer climate.

I ignore the question of limestone preference, growing most of my ferns in pockets among basaltic rocks and not adding lime to the soil mix. I supply gypsum in generous quantity to all my soil mixes, but I have never had any proof that there is a benefit. Some authors recommend a mixture of humus and limestone chips as a growing medium. If young plants are yellow, poor in growth, and having difficulty in getting established, feed them lightly and cautiously with ordinary all-purpose fertilizer dissolved in water, or with whatever type of nutrients you prefer to use, until growth is satisfactory.

Propagation may be by division of large specimens, but like collected plants, the new sections can be difficult to establish. Strong young plants grown from spores are the best planting stock, and by using this method we will spare the dwindling natural populations. *Asplenium trichomanes* and its fertile varieties are among the easiest of ferns to raise from spores. The spores are produced in abundance and are available on the leaves all fall and winter. Like their mothers, the young ferns are untemperamental, as ferns go, and they should grow up to be adaptable and pleasing rock garden plants.

———— *Cheilanthes lanosa,* C. *fendleri,* and C. *eatonii* ————

Of the many species of *Cheilanthes* encountered in the literature, and perhaps on rocky mountainsides, several stand out as interesting, beautiful, and easy to grow. For this article I have selected *C. lanosa, C. fendleri* and *C. eatonii.* In including the last I am ignoring its marginal hardiness because of its generally good disposition and good looks.

The members of the genus *Cheilanthes* are typically small ferns which have woolly or mealy leaves and live in exposed rock habitats. Most are densely tufted, growing from short and compact rootstocks, but there are some that form fairly open colonies. The fronds are persistent, tending to stay green during the winter, with brown to purplish stipes which are scaly, at least when young. The blades are from one- to four-pinnate and may be finely divided into beadlike segments. One of the most important points for recognition of the genus is the arrangement of the sori. These are placed around the margins of the leaf segments, tending to merge into a continuous line. The margin of the leaf is rolled in, forming an indusium or cover for the sori, but as the sporangia mature, they mostly become exposed.

Because the genus *Cheilanthes* is very closely related to *Notholaena,* a few species have been moved by botanists from one to the other. In some manuals the descriptions of the fruiting bodies are the same; in one, it is reported that in *Notholaena* the revolute leaf edge does not cover the sori, but this difference cannot be very great. *Notholaena* species usually have farina on the underside of the leaf, and the members of this genus I have seen have less finely divided fronds.

There are between 100 and 125 species of *Cheilanthes,* widely distributed throughout the world, mostly in arid subtropical and tropical regions. Only a few of them are hardy enough to be generally grown in North American gardens. There are about 25 species in the United States, mostly distributed from southern California to Texas.

Cheilanthes lanosa forms a dense but rapidly enlarging clump, with fronds about 7 or 8 inches/18 or 20 cm tall. The fronds are bipinnate with a very dark reddish-brown stipe, lightly covered with small hairs and narrow scales. Both leaf surfaces have hairs, but not enough to affect the color, which is yellowish-green. The undersides of the maturing leaves become shiny brown from the densely crowded sporangia, which contribute greatly to the general appearance of the plant.

Cheilanthes lanosa is the easternmost member of the genus in the United States, ranging from Connecticut to Minnesota and south to Georgia and Texas. Its habitat is on rocky outcrops, ledges, and talus slopes, especially in limestone or shale. It may be the hardiest of the species under discussion and is perhaps the most widely adapted of all *Cheilanthes* species for rock garden culture. Unfortunately, it is not among the prettiest, but it is still to be recommended.

Cheilanthes fendleri is a prettier fern and somewhat smaller, spreading into more open colonies, typically around 6 inches/15 cm tall. In a sunny exposure and lean soil it may stay half that size, a real pygmy spreading slowly among the rocks. The fronds are more finely divided, being tripinnate and with much smaller segments, which are beadlike because the indusia or rolled leaf edges cover most of the underside. The color is less yellow than that of *C. lanosa,* and the characteristic appearance of the leaf reverse comes not from sporangia but from a profusion of long, broad papery scales which become reddish-brown as they mature. The stipe is covered with light-colored, narrower scales. The sporangia are well hidden from view.

Cheilanthes fendleri ranges from western Texas to Colorado and Arizona. In Texas it grows at altitudes up to 8000 feet/2400 meters, and in Arizona up to 9500 feet/2900 meters. In Colorado it is listed as ranging from Montrose and Los Animas counties in the south, to Larimer County which borders on Wyoming, at altitudes up to 7500 feet/2300 meters. This suggests considerable hardiness, and I have had no problem from winter kill in western Oregon. My knowledge of its use by gardeners in other areas is limited, however, so it would be speculative to suggest a range of garden adaptation. My original plant came from a nursery as *C. tomentosa* and has been growing happily in my garden for about 5 years. The same clone has apparently been rather widely distributed, and because of this, *C. tomentosa* may have gained an undeserved reputation for hardiness. In fact, *C. tomentosa* can be readily identified by its really heavy coating of woolly hairs; it is known as the woolly lip fern and is usually not considered hardy enough to be grown north of its northern limits in Tennessee to West Virginia. I have not grown the real *C. tomentosa.*

Cheilanthes eatonii leads this group for appearance, mostly because of its gray-green color. A thin coating of wool on the upper leaf surface and a mat of it covering the lower surface add a touch of silver. With maturity the wool underneath turns somewhat yellow, and the sori emerge as a ring of dark beads around the segment margins. An additional point of identity is a covering of long, straw-colored scales on the stipe and the rachis of the leaf segments. Although the leaf is classed as tripinnate, only the basal segments of the primary pinnae are again subdivided, so that the leaf closely resembles that of the bipinnate *C. lanosa. Cheilanthes eatonii* is about the same size as *C. lanosa* and forms a tighter clump. Because of its color, it is especially interesting among black or red rocks.

The natural range of *Cheilanthes eatonii* is very similar to that of *C. fendleri,* but it does not get so far north. In Colorado it grows only in the southeastern quarter at altitudes of 3500 to 6500 feet/1100 to 2000 meters. In Texas and Arizona it reaches 8000 feet/2400 meters, nearly the same as *C. fendleri,* but I have little doubt that it is more tender. Several of my plants were eliminated by a ten-day period of 10°F/−12°C weather without snow in January of 1972. However, a few days of similar temperatures without cover, and −10°F/−23°C with snow in December 1972, failed to damage the remaining six plants. *Cheilanthes lanosa* and *C. fend-leri* have not been damaged by these winter conditions.

These ferns are remarkably tolerant of sun. In Oregon they can easily be grown in full exposure, and they should have such conditions for at least half the day so they will remain compact. In hotter climates light afternoon shade will be beneficial, but if drought is not severe they should not need much protection. In cool, wet climates, such as northwestern Washington, they should be given full sun and good ventilation as well. It helps to place the more tender species in a sheltered spot away from the cold winter winds that are so destructive in some areas. Several of the less hardy ferns I am trying are planted in a small rock garden close to the south-facing front of the house. Here, where there is protection from north winds and some heat from the house, grow the only survivors of several species of *Cheilanthes* and *Pellaea*, which perished elsewhere during the cold winter of 1972–1973. This space is not wasted on *C. fendleri* and *C. lanosa*, because they do not need it; however, there are two plants of *C. eatonii* growing there as insurance.

None of these three ferns seems to be particular about soil type, though good drainage should be provided, as for all rock ferns. They respond to good fertility by rapidly making a dense and vigorous clump, but after they are established, they seem to require less nourishment than some, such as the aspleniums, to maintain a good plant and survive. *Cheilanthes eatonii* has needed some feeding to recover from winter and make new growth, but *C. fendleri* and *C. lanosa* are best with the combination of minimal fertility and much exposure to make interesting dwarf plants.

Propagation by division in spring is easy with the open colonies of *Cheilanthes lanosa* and *C. fendleri*, but less so with the tight clump of *C. eatonii*, which I have propagated only by spores. Sporelings of most *Cheilanthes* are not difficult, except that they are intolerant of long residence in tight, moist containers. They also survive poorly when kept in pots for extended periods, so they should be planted in the garden as soon as they are large enough to survive. Even though they are tolerant of sun, they appreciate shading with a shingle until they become established.

Cheilanthes are free from pests; I do not remember seeing aphids on them, or slug damage. Such advantages, and their natural and charming appearance growing in rocks, should make these ferns worth a try in anyone's garden.

_____ *Woodsia scopulina*, *W. ilvensis*, and *W. obtusa* _____

Among the smaller ferns useful for the rock garden, the genus *Woodsia* is perhaps less favored than *Cheilanthes* or *Asplenium*. This is probably because these ferns lack the firmly evergreen leaves of the other two genera, and the silvery appearance often given by the scales or hairs of *Cheilanthes*. They are nonetheless easy, interesting, and beautiful ferns that belong in every rock garden. Although all the woodsias may be worthy of culture, only three will be discussed here.

The genus *Woodsia* is comprised generally of small to medium-sized, densely tufted ferns which grow in rocky habitats. The number of species in the genus is a matter of great disagreement, ranging from 21 to 40 depending on the botanical author consulted. They are ferns of cooler areas, either northern or high-altitude, and many are very hardy (four are found in Alaska and two of these, *W. alpina* and *W. glabella*, range to near the arctic coastline). Woodsias are found around the Northern Hemisphere and in South America, and one species in Africa. Eight species are found in the continental United States: *W. alpina*, *W. ilvensis*, *W. glabella*, *W. mexicana*, *W. obtusa*, *W. oregana*, *W. plummerae*, and *W. scopulina*. In addition, there are *W. appalachiana* (or *W. scopulina* var. *appalachiana*) and *W. cathcartiana* (or *W. oregana* subsp. *cathcartiana*).

Among the genera of small rock ferns, *Cystopteris* is the nearest relative of woodsias. Woodsias somewhat resemble *C. fragilis* in size and general appearance, but woodsia foliage has more substance and is more persistent through the season. The key character distinguishing *Woodsia* from *Cystopteris* and other ferns is the inferior indusium, or covering of the sorus. In *Cystopteris* the indusium is a simple hoodlike structure which attaches to one side and partially under the sporangia. The sporangia of *Woodsia* are formed on the indusium, which resembles a saucer or bowl, except that it is usually split into many scalelike segments. The form of the indusium, along with the presence and characteristics of hairs or scales, is important in differentiation of *Woodsia* species. The leaves are pinnate to bipinnate, with considerable similarity among the common species.

The Rocky Mountain *Woodsia scopulina* is medium in size among the species, commonly reaching 5 to 7 inches/13 to 18 cm in height. The leaves are essentially bipinnate, with the pinnae well spaced. The sori are borne in profusion, giving the undersides of the leaves a brown and thickened appearance. The most important identifying character is the presence of hyaline, jointed hairs with glandular tips on the rachis and leaf undersides, with a few on the upper leaf surface. The indusium is readily visible and could be described as moderately dissected with uneven or ragged segment tips.

Woodsia scopulina is primarily a fern of western North America from Alaska and Saskatchewan to California, New Mexico, and Arizona, also ranging sparsely into Quebec, Ontario, and northern Wisconsin. It grows in rock crevices and talus slopes. Some botanists claim it prefers calcareous soils and others, noncalcareous, so I suspect it is mostly indifferent. In central Oregon it is common in rugged lava flows at about 4000 feet/

1200 meters elevation, where its roots penetrate the spaces between rough pieces of basalt. The summers are dry, but there is adequate moisture the rest of the year. The soil around the roots consists of a little pumice dust and decaying organic material. In the garden this woodsia gets along well in rock crevices and ledges filled with the usual organic-gritty soil mix and some nourishment to get it started. It is tolerant of normal irrigation and winter rains, provided there is good drainage, and it is fairly drought-tolerant when established. In my garden it is dependable and pleasing, requiring no special care. It does best in afternoon or partial shade; although it will grow in full sun, the foliage browns in midsummer under such conditions. With some shade the leaves will often stay green and attractive through August, but they characteristically become brown toward the end of summer. New growth sometimes occurs in the cool moist weather of fall. At the end of the season or during winter, the leaves should be removed completely.

The rusty woodsia, *Woodsia ilvensis*, is slightly smaller, though not the smallest of the genus, commonly growing to 4 or 5 inches/10 or 13 cm. Although it can closely resemble *W. scopulina*, the pinnae are usually less reflexed and less deeply incised and have fewer divisions. The two species can be differentiated readily with a lens: *W. ilvensis* has scales mixed with long slender hairs which are usually present in profusion, becoming matted over the sori. The indusium in *W. ilvensis* is split into many more and thinner segments, but these are difficult to see and differentiate from the foliage hairs when only under magnification.

Woodsia ilvensis is widely distributed around the entire Northern Hemisphere but is limited to northern or mountainous regions. It ranges as far south as about 35° latitude in Japan and the United States. In North America its range includes Alaska, much of Canada, the north-central and northeastern states, and isolated locations in eastern mountains as far south as North Carolina. It is absent from the Pacific Northwest. Its habitat is the usual rocky situation, but generally not on limestone.

Aside from its possible aversion to limestone soils and rocks, the culture of *Woodsia ilvensis* is the same as that of *W. scopulina*, and I find them equally easy to grow.

The blunt-lobed woodsia, *Woodsia obtusa*, is the largest woodsia found in North America and perhaps in the world. It can reach about 20 inches/50 cm in height, with an open, rangy, and sometimes untidy appearance. Although the common name suggests blunt lobes, this seems to describe only the sterile leaves, because the fertile leaves could easily pass for giant versions of *W. scopulina*. Besides its size, this fern can be recognized by the short, stiff, glandular bristles which occur thickly on the stipe and rachis, and by the indusium. This is comprised of five or six broad segments and looks like a star with ragged points. The stipe and rachis are sparsely adorned with scales.

The range of *Woodsia obtusa* is much more southerly than the pre-

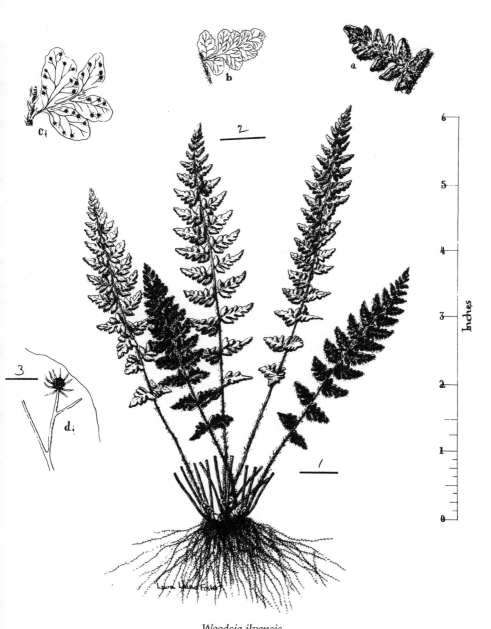

Woodsia ilvensis
(Drawing by Laura Louise Foster. Courtesy of Hunt Institute for Botanical
Documentation, Carnegie Mellon University, Pittsburgh, Pennsylvania.)

433

ceding species, including the southern states to western Texas, north to Minnesota, and east to Ontario. It is missing from the western states. Its habitat is more diverse, including well-drained banks and shallow soil over rocks as well as truly rocky situations. In many areas it is very abundant, earning the name of "common woodsia."

Woodsia obtusa is easy to grow, and though not so small, compact, or desirable in many rock gardens as other species, it has its place. There is a certain pleasure in ferns that plant themselves around the garden by spores, and this one does it almost to the point of being a weed. It is easy to pull out, however, and I have found it necessary to eliminate very few of them. More than the other woodsias, *W. obtusa* tends to produce new leaves continually, making it possible, by trimming out the older ones, to have green presentable foliage nearly all year. In spite of its southerly range, it appears to be adequately hardy, and along with the other two species should thrive in gardens over much of North America.

Bibliography

Britten, James. 1879. *European Ferns*. London: Cassell, Peter, Galpin, and Co.

Kaye, Reginald. 1968. *Hardy Ferns*. London: Faber and Faber.

Shaver, Jesse M. 1954. *Ferns of Tennessee*. Nashville, Tennessee: George Peabody College for Teaching.

Tutin, T. G., et al. 1964. *Flora Europaea*. Cambridge: Cambridge University Press.

Originally published in the Bulletin of the American Rock Garden Society, *vol. 30, no. 4, pp. 129–133 (1972); vol. 32, no. 4, pp. 124–128 (1974); vol. 33, no. 4, pp. 175–178 (1975).*

Notes on Contributors

Contributors who did not supply biographical information, and deceased contributors for whom published information could not be found, are omitted from these notes.

Claude A. Barr (1887–1982) of Smithwick, South Dakota, issued the first catalog of his Great Plains wildflower nursery, Prairie Gem Ranch, in 1932, and eventually introduced more than 80 species to cultivation. His book *Jewels of the Plains* appeared in 1983. He received the NARGS Award of Merit in 1965 and the Edgar T. Wherry Award in 1973.

Marvin E. Black of Seattle, Washington, was the city arborist for 16 years, taught urban forestry, and served as an officer of several forestry and arboriculture societies. He coordinated 15 study weekends and conferences for the NARGS and the Hardy Plant Society. He was an active hiker, seed collector, writer, lecturer, and practitioner of ikebana. He received the NARGS Award of Merit in 1984.

Rick Darke is curator of plants for Longwood Gardens in Pennsylvania, which holds more than 10,000 species and varieties. His specialties include grasses (the subject of his *For Your Garden: Ornamental Grasses*, 1994), Mediterranean-climate plants, magnolias, and eastern North American plants. In addition to acquiring and curating these holdings, he teaches at the Garden and lectures extensively. He is active in many professional and conservation organizations. His photographs of plants and landscapes have appeared in many books and magazines. His large home garden in the piedmont of Landenberg, Pennsylvania, features native plants and ornamental grasses.

B. LeRoy Davidson of Seattle, Washington, holds a degree in ornamental horticulture and landscape design and worked in that field until his retirement. He authored 65 contributions to the *Bulletin* over the years. He has been very active in support of the Northwest Chapter of the NARGS, especially in organizing study weekends and field trips. He has conducted extensive studies of *Lewisia*, *Penstemon*, and *Iris*, and is writing a monograph on the first. He received the Marcel LePiniec Award in 1972 and the Marvin Black Award in 1992.

Dr. Norman C. Deno is professor of chemistry at Pennsylvania State University. He has created a large and complex garden in central Pennsylvania and conducts ongoing research on seed germination, described in his invaluable manual *Seed Germination Theory and Practice* (1994). He has been a NARGS member since 1960 and has received both the NARGS Award of Merit and the Carlton R. Worth Award.

Edith L. Dusek began gardening at age 10 with woodland wildflowers in Illinois and has had three gardens in the Puget Sound area of Washington over the past 40 years. Her father was a botanical artist, and she, her husband, and their son are nursery growers. Her articles have appeared in publications in the United States, Canada, Japan, Britain, Czechoslovakia, and New Zealand, often illustrated with her photographs. Her special interests include woodland and bog plants, trilliums, lewisias, orchids, and ferns.

Margery Edgren of Woodside, California, formerly gardened in Pennsylvania, where she was a frequent exhibitor in the Philadelphia Flower Show, winning numerous awards in the rock garden classes, including the Edith Scott Wilder Award for best entry in the show for a miniature rock garden. She now coordinates volunteer propagation of California native plants at the Strybing Arboretum in San Francisco. Her articles, particularly on growing plants under artificial light, have appeared in various journals, and she has lectured at winter study weekends and at meetings of other societies.

H. Lincoln Foster (1906–1989) was a stalwart of the NARGS, serving as director (1949–1955) and president (1964–1968) and establishing many of the society's policies. He and his wife, Laura Louise Foster, created a famous garden, Millstream, near Falls Village, Connecticut, where Mr. Foster developed many plant selections and hybrids, particularly phloxes and saxifrages, while pursuing a career as a high school teacher and textbook author. His book *Rock Gardening* (1982) is a basic work, and many of his and Mrs. Foster's articles are collected in *Cuttings from a Rock Garden* (1990). He lectured internationally and was active in natural history and conservation societies. His many honors include recognition by the Alpine Garden Society, Garden Clubs of America, and Massachusetts Horticultural Society, as well as all three of the major NARGS awards. A memorial symposium for him appears in the NARGS *Bulletin* 47(3), pp. 149–155 (Summer 1989).

Laura Louise Foster (1918–1988) was active in the NARGS from

1943, serving as the *Bulletin* editor from 1978 to 1984. She was a noted botanical illustrator whose drawings appear in Mr. Foster's *Rock Gardening* and in many issues of the *Bulletin*. She is the author of *Keeping the Plants You Pick* (1970) and coauthor of *Cuttings from a Rock Garden* (1990). She received the NARGS Award of Merit (1979) and Edgar T. Wherry Award (1988).

John F. Gyer, a retired chemical engineer, combines woodland gardening with bean farming in Clarksboro, New Jersey. He and his wife, Janet, have been NARGS members since 1972 and are active in the Delaware Chapter of the NARGS and also in the Philadelphia Botanical Club and other regional plant groups. He is also a volunteer at the Winterthur Garden, where he is carrying on a study of trillium biology.

Sean Hogan, formerly horticulturist at the Botanic Garden of the University of California, Berkeley, has gardened in both the Bay Area and in the extreme desert habitat of Christmas Valley, Oregon. He conducts many classes, lectures, and field trips, and is president of the Western Chapter of the NARGS. His specialties include western American plants, especially the Portulacaceae and Cactaceae, and desert and rock ferns. He has published numerous articles and described several new species; he wrote the entry on *Lewisia* for the new *Flora of North America* being prepared at the Missouri Botanical Garden in St. Louis.

Donald W. Humphrey is manager of Green Spring Gardens Park in Fairfax County, Virginia. An NARGS member since 1964, he pursues a wide range of activities from plant geography and ecology to propagation and hybridizing. He has introduced species new to cultivation in the garden.

Panayoti Kelaidis is curator of the Rock Alpine Garden at the Denver Botanic Gardens, Colorado, where he also maintains a notable home garden with his wife, Gwen Kelaidis, editor of the NARGS *Bulletin*. He is the author of many articles and a Renaissance Travel Guide, *A Guide to Locating Rocky Mountain Wildflowers*. He has lectured around the world, collecting seed on his travels and introducing a great variety of plants to cultivation, particularly western American drylanders and those from similar climates worldwide. He is a leading member of the NARGS and was an organizer of the Second International Rock Plant Conference (1986). He has received the Award of Merit, the Edgar T. Wherry Award, and the Marcel LePiniec Award, as well as the Florence de Bevoise Award of the Garden Clubs of America, and the ASLA Merit Award for the design of the Rock Alpine Garden.

Boyd C. Kline, well known to gardeners as cofounder of the Siskiyou Rare Plant Nursery, is now retired from the postal service and still gardens at the original site of the nursery in Medford, southern Oregon. His growing specialties include lilies, calochortus, silenes, clematis, and rare alpine and bulbous plants. He is a leading authority on the flora of the Siskiyou Mountains and has provided seed to growers worldwide for many years. An NARGS member since 1953, he received the Marcel LePiniec Award in 1964.

Dr. Arthur R. Kruckeberg is professor emeritus of botany at the University of Washington in Seattle, where he headed that department from 1971 to 1977. His research concentrated on plant ecology and genetics. He is an avid gardener and maintains a 4-acre arboretum at his home, growing many rock garden species along with the woody plants that have been his longtime specialty. In addition to many research and popular articles, he has written two books, *Gardening with Native Plants of the Pacific Northwest: An Illustrated Guide* (1982) and *Natural History of Puget Sound County* (1991). He is a founder and past president of the Washington Native Plant Society and has been active in other conservation causes. An NARGS member since 1960, he is a recipient of the Edgar T. Wherry Award.

James H. Locklear is director of the Nebraska Statewide Arboretum. His special research interests include the ecology and horticultural potential of Great Plains plants, conservation of rare and threatened species, and the cushion and mat plant communities of the Plains. An NARGS member since 1980, he has also gardened in Kansas before moving to Nebraska. His articles have appeared in *American Horticulturist*, *Horticulture*, and several regional publications.

Sonia Lowzow Collins (d. 1994) was a skilled grower of alpines who operated a small nursery, Fjellgarden, in Arizona, trading plants and seeds worldwide. She was active in NARGS affairs and published several articles in the *Bulletin*.

Jay G. Lunn, now retired from the U.S. Forest Service, gardens with his wife, Ann, just west of Portland, Oregon, with special interests in primulas, rhododendrons, lewisias, and Northwest native plants. He travels extensively in search of rare species to photograph, and a number of his photos illustrate this volume. The Lunns have been NARGS members since 1978. They are also very active in the American Primrose Society, which honored them in 1993 with the Dorothy Stredicke Dickinson Award for outstanding service.

James MacPhail, retired curator of the Alpine Garden at the University of British Columbia Botanical Garden in Vancouver, gardens at home in West Vancouver. He has made many field expeditions, often introducing seed of species new to cultivation. *Pacific Horticulture* has published several of his articles. An NARGS member since the 1960s, he is a recipient of the Award of Merit.

Dr. T. Paul Maslin was professor of zoology at the University of Colorado and curator of the zoological collections there. He was also an expert on the flora of the American Southwest and introduced many species and selections through his garden in Boulder and the Denver Botanic Gardens, among them the Chihuahuan phloxes. He received the Marcel LePiniec Award in 1982.

James E. Mitchell (d. 1963) was a botanist and native-plant nurseryman who frequently led field trips to the mountains of New England during the 1930s and 1940s.

Dr. G. G. Nearing of Ramsey, New Jersey, was a well-known hybridizer of rhododendrons and other woody plants, and inventor of the propagation system known as the "Nearing frame." He edited the NARGS *Bulletin* from 1951 to 1954.

Wayne Roderick has gardened since early childhood in central coastal California. He worked at the Botanic Garden of the University of California, Berkeley, for 16 years, where he headed the California section, going on to become director of the East Bay Regional Parks Botanic Garden. Now retired, he is a very active gardener, lecturer, and guide to California native plants in the wild, especially famed for his expertise on bulbous genera. He has made dozens of field trips throughout the world. An NARGS member since 1950, he received the Marcel LePiniec Award in 1981; he has also been honored with awards from the University of California, California Garden Clubs, California Horticulture Society, and California Native Plant Society, and he is the first American to receive the Alpine Garden Society's Lyttel Trophy.

Dr. Ronald J. Taylor, professor of botany at Western Washington State University in Bellingham, specializes in the study of native Northwestern plants, especially those of alpine and desert areas, and conducts field-oriented workshops and lectures. He is the author of a series of color field guides including *Sagebrush Country*, *Northwest Weeds*, *Mountain Plants of the Pacific Northwest*, and *Rocky Mountain Wildflowers*.

Jeanie Vesall has an academic background in biology with graduate study in ecology and ornithology. She gardens in Bear Lake, Minnesota. An NARGS member for the past 10 years, she has traveled widely in pursuit of interests in natural history, especially birds. Her Zone 4 garden, well suited to alpines with its dependable winter snow cover, is on the Minnesota Horticultural Society's Distinctive Garden Register and hosts educational tours.

Dr. Edgar T. Wherry (1885–1982), initially active as a soil chemist, was professor of botany and ecology at the University of Pennsylvania and a mainstay of the Morris Arboretum there. He conducted many field studies on the flora of the eastern and midwestern United States, resulting in such books as *The Fern Guide: Northeastern and Midland States* (1941), *Southern Fern Guide* (1964), *Wildflower Guide: Northeastern and Midland States* (1948), and *The Genus Phlox* (1955). He helped to establish several preserves in Pennsylvania and was active in the American Fern Society and National Wildflower Preservation Society as well as the NARGS. He edited the NARGS *Bulletin* (1943–1948) and received the Award of Merit (1965). The Edgar T. Wherry Award commemorates him. A symposium in his memory appeared in the *Bulletin* 40(4), pp. 159–162 (Fall 1982).

Robert Woodward of West Vancouver, British Columbia, is a retired teacher whose plant-related activities, in addition to gardening and field trips, include photography and lecturing. His articles have appeared in publications of the NARGS, Alpine Garden Society, Scottish Rock Garden Club, and Alpine Garden Club of British Columbia. An NARGS member since the 1960s, he is a recipient of the Award of Merit.

Dr. John J. Wurdack is a retired plant taxonomist who has worked in taxonomy, field botany, and herbarium management for the New York Botanical Garden and the Smithsonian Institution. He spent more than 5 years in the field in South America as well as collecting and distributing seed from the southeastern United States. In addition to several monographs on genera in the tropical family Melastomataceae, he contributed sections on that group to the floras of Brazil, Venezuela, Ecuador, and the Guianas. He has gardened in Beltsville, Maryland, since 1961, where his special interests include *Arisaema, Asarum, Trillium,* and other plants of the southeastern United States. and eastern Asia. He received the NARGS Award of Merit in 1991.

Ernest Yelton, a retired physician, gardens in Rutherfordton, North Carolina. He is interested in many aspects of gardening and joined the NARGS around 1960. He has been awarded the Silver Medal of the American Rhododendron Society.

Index

NOTE: Common names of plants do not appear in the Index. Geographical names are cited only when the text deals specifically with places.

441